AMERICAN PASSAGES

VOLUME I: TO 1877

BRIEF FOURTH EDITION

Edward L. Ayers
University of Richmond

Lewis L. Gould
University of Texas at Austin, Emeritus

David M. Oshinsky
University of Texas at Austin

Jean R. Soderlund
Lehigh University

WADSWORTH
CENGAGE Learning™

Australia • Brazil • Japan • Korea • Mexico • Singapore • Spain • United Kingdom • United States

WADSWORTH
CENGAGE Learning

American Passages, Volume I: To 1877,
Brief Fourth Edition
Edward L. Ayers, Lewis L. Gould, David M. Oshinsky, Jean R. Soderlund

Senior Publisher: Suzanne Jeans

Senior Sponsoring Editor: Ann West

Development Editor: Colleen Kyle

Assistant Editor: Megan Chrisman

Editorial Assistant: Patrick Roach

Senior Marketing Manager: Katherine Bates

Marketing Coordinator: Lorreen Pelletier

Marketing Communications Manager: Caitlin Green

Senior Content Project Manager: Jane Lee

Senior Art Director: Cate Rickard Barr

Senior Print Buyer: Sandra Milewski

Senior Rights Acquisition Specialist: Katie Huha

Production Service: S4Carlisle Publishing Services

Text Designer: Diane Beasley

Senior Photo Manager: Jennifer Meyer Dare

Cover Image: George Caleb Bingham, 1811–1879, *Fur Traders Descending the Missouri*, 1845. Oil on canvas, 29 x 36½ in. Credit : Image copyright © The Metropolitan Museum of Art/Art Resource, NY.

Compositor: S4Carlisle Publishing Services

Library of Congress Control Number: 2010929826

Student Edition:
ISBN-13: 978-0-495-91520-1
ISBN-10: 0-495-91520-3

Wadsworth
20 Channel Center Street
Boston, MA 02210
USA

Cengage Learning is a leading provider of customized learning solutions with office locations around the globe, including Singapore, the United Kingdom, Australia, Mexico, Brazil, and Japan. Locate your local office at **international.cengage.com/region**

Cengage Learning products are represented in Canada by Nelson Education, Ltd.

For your course and learning solutions, visit **www.cengage.com**

Purchase any of our products at your local college store or at our preferred online store **www.cengagebrain.com.**

Printed in the United States of America
1 2 3 4 5 6 7 14 13 12 11 10

BRIEF CONTENTS

CONTENTS

SPECIAL FEATURES

Doing History

MAPS

PREFACE

Like other teachers of history, we have seen our students intrigued by the powerful stories of this nation's past. But textbooks often bear little resemblance to our favorite works of history or to the best kinds of teaching. Textbooks tend to replace the concrete with the abstract, the individual with the aggregate, the story with the summary. They can remove entire regions and ethnic groups from the flow of American history and relegate them to separate chapters, isolated and frozen in time. They can give away the end of the story too easily, squandering drama.

We believed that we could write a book that captured what we love most and what explains the most about history. We decided to write the first U. S. history text in which time stood front and center. Time is what makes history *History* rather than sociology, anthropology, or economics. Time—and the dramatic pace of events—is what most textbooks have sacrificed in the name of convenience and false clarity. In short, we set out to write a more *historical* history text.

Now in its fourth brief edition, *American Passages* is unique in its insistence, in every part of every chapter, that time, with the characteristics of sequence, simultaneity, and contingency, is the *defining nature* of history. Sequence shows how events grow from other events, personalities, and broad changes. Political, social, and cultural history naturally intertwine, and simultaneity shows how apparently disconnected events were situated in larger shared contexts. Contingency shows how history suddenly pivots, how it often changes course in a moment.

The focus on time is easily apparent in the table of contents, in the Passages sections, in the timelines, in the Doing History features, and in the narrative analytical history that is the core of the book. Every chapter covers a specific time period and integrates the themes and events of that period as they cannot be integrated in a more distended account. Our account of the post–Civil War era, for example, deals with integrated periods rather than abstractions such as "urbanization" and "industrialization."

❖ Organization and Pedagogy

American Passages is written to convey the excitement and uncertainty of this nation's past—to see it whole. To balance the chronological approach—to help students see long-term developments and processes—eight "Passages" essays and chronologies help students see long-term developments and processes.

Each chapter in the text contains a wealth of review material to help students keep track of major events, important people, and larger movements. They begin with chapter outlines, chronologies, and "Making Connections" questions that review earlier material in context. "Identification" terms appear in boldface throughout the chapters, are defined on the page where they first appear, and are listed at the end of the chapter for easy review. At the end of every chapter, chapter summaries review key points, and "Making Connections" sections guide students forward to place the current chapter's content in perspective.

❖ Features

The features for the Brief Fourth Edition have been streamlined while maintaining *American Passages*' chronological emphasis.

Doing History

In each chapter, "Doing History" boxes feature two to four brief excerpts from primary sources on related topics, presenting varying perspectives and providing students with manageable opportunities to "do history." Brief commentary by the authors guides students, and assignable "Questions for Reflection" encourage critical thinking or can be used to spark class discussion.

Doing History Online

To give students additional exposure to primary source material, "Doing History Online" notes in the text margins connect students to an array of online resources that permit them to explore history in a deeper and more systematic way. Links to these sources may be found on the student CourseMate website for *American Passages*.

Making Connections

To emphasize recurring themes and trends and spark critical analysis, we have included a section at the beginning of every chapter (except for the first chapter) that highlights key points of the previous chapter and a section at the end of every chapter (except for the last chapter) that previews the content to come. "Making Connections: Looking Back" and "Making Connections:

Looking Ahead" will help remind students of the importance of relating events from one period to another—and will help to keep the narrative a seamless stream in spite of chapter-by-chapter assignments.

❖ Changes to the Brief Fourth Edition

Offering a streamlined narrative and features program, the Brief Fourth Edition has been revised to highlight *American Passages*' strengths while providing a more flexible, briefer text. Unique to the Brief Fourth Edition, the overall chapter count has been reduced from 32 to 30 chapters. Two chapters on the Civil War, 1861–1865, have been combined into one, and two chapters on the Progressive Era have also been combined and streamlined into one. The final two chapters of the text have been restructured: Chapter 29 now covers the presidencies of Ronald Reagan, George H. W. Bush, and Bill Clinton. Chapter 30, "A Conservative Nation in a Globalizing World," covers the period from 2000 to 2010, including updated coverage on the 2008 election, the "Great Recession," and the recent historic passage of health care legislation.

Throughout the text, details have been carefully pruned, enhancing narrative coherence and providing flexibility for instructors who wish to assign additional materials. At the same time, the narrative is still animated by excellent political history coverage, modern scholarship, and vivid quotes and examples. The overall narrative has been reduced by 25 percent.

The pedagogy supporting each chapter has been augmented with detailed chapter outlines and "Looking Back" questions at the beginning of each chapter, glossary definitions, and streamlined end-of-chapter materials that make it easier for students to find what they need. Doing History feature boxes emphasize primary source analysis skills and offer students competing perspectives on key issues.

The colorful new maps in this brief edition include helpful locator and topographical features that make them easier to read and richer as learning tools. Many of the images are new and also larger so that students can better see important details.

In addition to the changes in formatting and appearance, we have carefully reviewed each chapter for clarity and new scholarship and incorporated revisions and updates throughout. We are grateful to the reviewers who provided many helpful suggestions as well. Specific revisions include the following.

Revisions to Chapters 1 through 8 include new Doing History features on the Deerfield Raid of 1704 and the gradual abolition of slavery in the North. Special attention was given to tightening up the end of Chapter 8 ("The New Republic Faces a New Century, 1800–1815") to allow for a smoother transition into Chapter 9, which covers the period following the War of 1812.

Chapters 14 and 15 have been combined to cover the entirety of the Civil War, and Chapter 16 has been reworked to cover Reconstruction only. In addition, there is a new Doing History feature on Religion and Reform.

In Chapters 17 through 23, the two chapters on Progressivism have been combined into one Chapter 19, titled "Progressivism: Agendas for Change, 1901–1914." New Doing History features include McKinley and the start of the Philippine insurrection in 1899 as well as the torture issue.

In Chapters 24 through 30, most changes relate to popular culture, science, and medicine. There is a longer and more detailed section on the growth and impact of television and sports and a section on how wonder drugs and other discoveries have increased our life span. There is new material relating to the story behind the Iwo Jima flag raising, the impact of Soviet spying, the Cuban Missile Crisis, the importance of Cesar Chavez, and the legacy of Watergate (including the self-identification of Deep Throat). Chapter 30 takes the story up to 2010, with coverage of President Obama's first term, the economic downturn, the debate over the definition of marriage, and deepening debates over climate change.

❖ Learning and Teaching Aids

The *American Passages Brief* program includes a great variety of learning and teaching aids—many linked to specific text features. The instructor supplements are aimed at providing instructors with useful course management and presentation options. The student supplements are designed to expand learning opportunities—and to provide students with a solid source of review material to ensure their success in the course.

Instructor Resources

The *Instructor Website* (**www.cengage.com/login**) contains a wealth of teaching resources for instructors using American Passages, 4e. An **Instructor's Resource Manual** written by James Mills of the University of Texas at Brownsville and Texas Southmost College is available at the website and includes chapter-by-chapter lecture outlines and teaching tips as well as suggestions for class discussion and essay assignments. Also available on the Instructor Website are **PowerPoint® lecture** and **personal response system** slides, access to general teaching resources, and a link to HistoryFinder (see description below), which instructors can use to create their own primary source–based student assignments or lecture presentations.

eInstructor's Resource Manual Prepared by James Mills of the University of Texas at Brownsville and Texas Southmost College, this manual has many features, including instructional objectives, topics for discussion, class starters, writing assignments, chapter outlines, and suggested readings and resources. It is available on the instructor's companion website.

PowerLecture CD-ROM with ExamView® and JoinIn® This dual platform, all-in-one multimedia resource includes the Instructor's Resource Manual; a test bank written by D. Antonio Cantù of Bradley University; Microsoft® PowerPoint® slides of both lecture outlines and images and maps from the text that can be used as offered, or customized by importing personal lecture slides or other material; and *JoinIn®* PowerPoint® slides with clicker content. Also included is ExamView, an easy-to-use assessment and tutorial system that allows instructors to create, deliver, and customize tests in minutes. Instructors can build tests with as many as 250 questions using up to 12 question types, and using ExamView's complete word-processing capabilities, they can enter an unlimited number of new questions or edit existing ones.

HistoryFinder This searchable online database allows instructors to quickly and easily download thousands of assets, including art, photographs, maps, primary sources, and audio/video clips. Each asset downloads directly into a Microsoft® PowerPoint® slide, allowing instructors to easily create exciting PowerPoint® presentations for their classrooms.

WebTutor™ for BlackBoard or WebCT® With WebTutor's text-specific, preformatted content and total flexibility, instructors can easily create and manage their own custom course website. WebTutor's course management tool gives instructors the ability to provide virtual office hours, post syllabi, set up threaded discussions, track student progress with the quizzing material, and much more. For students, WebTutor offers real-time access to a full array of study tools, including animations and videos that bring the book's topics to life, plus chapter outlines, summaries, learning objectives, glossary flash cards (with audio), practice quizzes, and weblinks.

CourseMate *History CourseMate* Cengage Learning's History CourseMate brings course concepts to life with interactive learning, study, and exam preparation tools that support the printed textbook. Watch student comprehension soar as your class works with the printed textbook and the CourseMate content developed for the *American Passages* Brief Fourth Edition. History CourseMate goes beyond the book to deliver what you need! History CourseMate includes an integrated eBook, interactive teaching and learning tools including quizzes developed by Thomas Born of Blinn College, flash cards, videos, and more. It also includes EngagementTracker, a first-of-its-kind tool that monitors student engagement in the course. Go to login.cengage.com to access these resources and look for this icon which denotes a resource available within CourseMate.

Student Resources

CourseMate *History CourseMate* For students, CourseMate provides an additional source of interactive learning, study, and exam preparation outside the classroom. Students will find outlines and objectives, focus questions, flash cards, quizzes, primary source links, and video clips. In addition, CourseMate includes an integrated ***American Passages Brief*** **eBook**. Students taking quizzes will be linked directly to relevant sections in the ebook for additional information. The ebook is fully searchable and students can even take notes and save them for later review. The ebook links to rich media assets such as video and MP3 chapter summaries, primary source documents with critical thinking questions, and interactive (zoomable) maps. Students can use the ebook as their primary text or as a companion multimedia support. Go to login.cengagebrain.com to access these resources, and look for this icon to find resources related to your text in CourseMate.

Wadsworth American History Resource Center gives students access to a "virtual reader" with hundreds of primary sources including speeches, letters, legal documents and transcripts, poems, maps, simulations, timelines, and additional images that bring history to life, along with interactive assignable exercises. A map feature including Google Earth™ coordinates and exercises will aid in student comprehension of geography and use of maps. Students can compare the traditional textbook map with an aerial view of the location today. It's an ideal resource for study, review, and research. In addition to this map feature, the resource center also provides blank maps for student review and testing. Ask your sales representative for more information on how to bundle access to the HRC with your text.

cengagebrain.com Save your students time and money. Direct them to www.cengagebrain.com for a choice of formats and savings and a better chance to succeed in class. Students have the freedom to purchase à la carte exactly what they need when they need it. There, students can purchase a downloadable ebook or electronic access to the American History Resource Center, the *American Passages Brief* premium study tools and interactive ebook in CourseMate, or eAudio modules from *The History Handbook* (see below). Students can save 50 percent on the electronic textbook, and can pay as little as $1.99 for an individual eChapter.

Reader Program. Cengage Learning publishes a number of readers, some containing exclusively primary sources, others a combination of primary and secondary sources, and some designed to guide students through the process of historical inquiry. Contact your sales rep or go to Cengage.com to browse through the many options.

Rand McNally Atlas of American History, 2e This comprehensive atlas features more than 80 maps, with new content covering global perspectives, including events in the Middle East from 1945 to 2005, as well as population trends in the United States and around the world. Additional maps document voyages of discovery; the settling of the colonies; major U.S. military engagements, including the American Revolution and World Wars I and II; and sources of immigrations, ethnic populations, and patterns of economic change.

Custom Options

Cengage Learning offers custom solutions for your course—whether it's making a small modification to *American Passages* to match your syllabus or combining multiple sources to create something truly unique. You can pick and choose chapters, include your own material, and add additional map exercises along with the Rand McNally Atlas to create a text that fits the way you teach. Ensure that your students get the most out of their textbook dollar by giving them exactly what they need. Contact your Cengage Learning representative to explore custom solutions for your course.

❖ Acknowledgments

I am grateful to my husband, Rudolf Soderlund, and my family for their support throughout this project. Many colleagues in the colonial and early national periods shared their ideas orally and through their publications. I have appreciated the feedback from instructors and students on earlier editions. As always, I am indebted to my co-authors Edward Ayers, Lewis Gould, and David Oshinsky for their collegiality and commitment to making this a great U.S. history text.

Jean R. Soderlund

I would like to thank Amanda Mushal for her imagination, hard work, and good advice in the revision of this edition. Finally, I am very appreciative of my co-authors, who have been engaged scholars, thoughtful critics, devoted teachers, and good friends throughout the years it took us to write *American Passages*.

Edward L. Ayers

I would like to acknowledge the help of the following former students who contributed in constructive ways to the completion of this textbook: Martin Ansell, the late Christie Bourgeois, Thomas Clarkin, Stacy Cordery, Debbie Cottrell, Scott Harris, Byron Hulsey, Jonathan Lee, John Leffler, and Nancy Beck Young. Karen Gould gave indispensable support and encouragement throughout the writing of the text. At Cengage Learning, I benefited from the guidance, patience, and understanding of Jane Lee, Charlotte Miller, Amy Pastan, Henry Rachlin, Jennifer Sutherland, and Ann West. I am grateful as well to all of the readers of my chapters who made so many useful and timely criticisms.

Lewis L. Gould

I would like to thank my colleagues and students at the University of Texas for allowing me to test out an endless stream of ideas and issues relating to modern American history, and also for their thoughts on how a good college textbook should "read" and what it should contain. As always, the support and love of my family—Matt, Efrem, Ari, and Jane—was unshakable. Above all, I must commend my co-authors and my editors for their remarkable patience and professionalism during this long collaborative process.

David M. Oshinsky

Reviewers

The authors wish to thank the following reviewers, who provided essential advice for the preparation of the fourth edition:

Charles Cox, *Bridgewater State University*
Brian Daugherity, *Virginia Commonwealth University*
David Fitzpatrick, *Washtenaw Community College*
Yolanda Harding, *University of Central Florida*
Scott Holzer, *Jefferson College*
Marc Horger, *Ohio State University*
Timothy Kelly, *West Valley College*
Paul Kelton, *University of Kansas*
Patricia Knol, *Triton College*
Arnold Krammer, *Texas A&M University*
Timothy Lehman, *Rocky Mountain College*
Peter Mathison, *St. John's Prep*
Richard McMillan, *Los Angeles Pierce College*
Michael Namorato, *University of Mississippi*
Phillip Papas, *Union County College*
Gail Parsons, *Gordon College*
Keith Pomakoy, *Adirondack Community College*
David Rayson, *Normandale Community College*
Horacio Salinas, *Laredo Community College*
James Sefton, *California State University, Northridge*
Howard Segal, *University of Maine, Orono*
David Snead, *Liberty University*
Timothy Wood, *Southern Baptist University*
Steven Woodsum, *Brunswick High School*

ABOUT THE AUTHORS

EDWARD L. AYERS is President and Professor of History of the University of Richmond. Named National Professor of the Year in 2003, Ayers has written and edited ten books. *The Promise of the New South: Life After Reconstruction* (1992) was a finalist for both the National Book Award and the Pulitzer Prize. *In the Presence of Mine Enemies, Civil War in the Heart of America* (2003) won the Bancroft Prize for distinguished writing in American history and the Beveridge Prize for the best book in English on the history of the Americas since 1492. Ayers created *The Valley of the Shadow: Two Communities in the American Civil War,* a website that has attracted millions of visitors.

LEWIS L. GOULD is the Eugene C. Barker Centennial Professor in American History *emeritus* at the University of Texas, where he won awards for both undergraduate and graduate teaching. He is currently the editor of the Modern First Ladies series with the University Press of Kansas and the general editor of the Documentary History of the John F. Kennedy Presidency with LexisNexis. His recent books include *The Modern American Presidency* (2003); *Grand Old Party: A History of the Republicans* (2003); *The Most Exclusive Club: A History of the Modern United States Senate* (2005); and *Four Hats in the Ring: The 1912 Election and the Birth of Modern American Politics* (2008).

JEAN R. SODERLUND is Professor of History and Deputy Provost for Faculty Affairs at Lehigh University. Her book *Quakers and Slavery: A Divided Spirit* won the Alfred E. Driscoll Publication Prize of the New Jersey Historical Commission. Soderlund was an editor of three volumes of the *Papers of William Penn* (1981–1983) and co-authored *Freedom by Degrees: Emancipation in Pennsylvania and Its Aftermath* (1991). She has written articles and chapters in books on the history of women, African Americans, Native Americans, Quakers, and the development of abolition in the British North American colonies and early United States. She is currently working on a book-length study titled, *Violence and Peace on the Delaware: The Evolution of Liberal Society in Colonial New Jersey and Pennsylvania*.

DAVID M. OSHINSKY is the Jack S. Blanton Chair in History at the University of Texas at Austin and a Distinguished Scholar in Residence at New York University. Among his publications are *"A Conspiracy So Immense": The World of Joe McCarthy* (1983), which was voted one of the year's "notable books" by the *New York Times,* and won the Hardeman Prize for the best work about the history of the U.S. Congress; and *Worse Than Slavery* (1996), which won both the Robert F. Kennedy Book Award for the year's most distinguished contribution to human rights, and the American Bar Association's Scribes Award for distinguished legal writing. His most recent publication, *Polio: An American Story* (2005), won both the Pulitzer Prize for History and the Hoover Presidential Book Award.

AMERICAN PASSAGES

PASSAGES Prehistory to 1763

And so we journeyed for seventeen days, at the end of which we crossed the river [Rio Grande] and traveled for seventeen more. At sunset, on plains between some very tall mountains, we found some people who eat nothing but powdered straw for a third of the year. Since it was that season of the year, we had to eat it too. At the end of our journey we found a permanent settlement where there was abundant corn. The people gave us a large quantity of it and of cornmeal, squash, beans and cotton blankets. . . . From here we traveled [to where people] gave me five emeralds made into arrowheads. . . . Since they seemed very fine to me, I asked them where they had gotten them. They told me that they brought them from some very high mountains to the North.*

Cabeza de Vaca, 1542

From 1534 to 1536, the Spanish explorer Álvar Núñez Cabeza de Vaca and three other people traveled through what today are Texas and northern Mexico, trying to reach Mexico City. They had been part of an expedition to Florida that ran afoul of Apalachee Indians, escaped across the Gulf of Mexico in makeshift boats, then were enslaved in Texas by Karankawa Indians. In his *Relación*, Cabeza de Vaca described their adventures, including the harrowing passage across the gulf, long journeys without food, and sojourns among Texas Indians.

Warpaths, ocean voyages, hunting trails, trade routes, death, communication, and exchange among people: creating societies in America embodied passages of every kind. Asians migrated across the Bering land bridge and along the Pacific coast more than ten thousand years ago, settling throughout North and South America. They created distinct cultures in every part of the hemisphere, from the Aztecs of Mexico to the Iroquois of eastern North America. Over thousands of years, American civilizations rose and fell as empires built pyramids and temple mounds, developed cities and cultures, and competed for territory and trade.

*Martin A. Farata and José B. Fernandez, *The Account: Álvar Núñez Cabeza de Vaca's Relación* (Houston, TX: Arte Público Press, 1993), 103.

In the fifteenth century A.D., Western Europeans came to America to fish, trade, and establish colonies, bringing new technology, lust for wealth, and destructive microbes that spelled death for millions of Native Americans. The Europeans adapted their traditions and goals to exploit the abundant, yet often unfamiliar, resources of the Western Hemisphere. The Spanish struck it rich with the Potosí and Zacatecas silver mines that financed their religious wars in Europe and became the envy of other nations. Privateers from France, England, and the Netherlands attacked the Spanish silver fleets, while their explorers searched unsuccessfully for mines in North America. They did find treasures, but in furs, sugar, tobacco, and rice.

To reap fortunes from the earth, the colonizers first exploited Native Americans, who died in such numbers from disease and harsh treatment that Europeans turned to another continent, Africa, for laborers. Portugal developed the Atlantic slave trade during the fifteenth century, initially buying slaves to toil on sugar islands near Africa. With the development of sugar, and later tobacco, rice, and indigo in America, the Portuguese and other Europeans purchased millions of people from African merchants for transport across the Atlantic. For more than 350 years, the cultures, sweat, and blood of

Natives Harpooning Whales. An illustration from the Flemish engraver Theodor de Bry's *America* (1590) of Native Americans pulling harpooned whales to shore as Europeans look on.

enslaved Africans enriched the new and evolving societies.

From the sixteenth century on, Europeans battled for North America with Native Americans and among themselves. The French settled Canada and the Mississippi Valley, primarily for furs. Spain held Florida, Texas, and New Mexico as outposts to protect its silver mines and fleets. The English founded colonies in New England, the Chesapeake, and the Carolinas for economic opportunity and religious freedom. In 1664, they pushed the Dutch out of New Netherland, thus connecting their chain of colonies along the Atlantic. Throughout the Americas, Europeans hoped for a new chance in what they considered the New World.

The thirteen mainland British colonies had various beginnings, charters, provincial governments, economic bases, peoples, and religions. Yet they all had ties with England in terms of their language, imperial government and laws, culture, and commerce. During the eighteenth century, the colonies forged closer bonds with the English—with greater participation in imperial wars, increased trade, and better communication. At the same time, the British provinces also became more distinctly American, as people from Africa, Ireland, and the European continent diversified the population and its culture. With natural population growth and swelling immigration, the British colonies expanded westward.

Native Americans responded to depopulation, defeat, and white expansion by creating new worlds of their own. Despite some military successes, they ultimately reshaped their communities and cultures as disease worked its tragic course and European American societies grew. The surviving members of Indian nations often merged to forge new ethnic identities, or lived together in multi-ethnic communities, often with whites and escaped slaves. Some retained remnants of their land within white settlements, while the majority moved to the frontier for political autonomy.

Three centuries passed from the time Western European fishermen first camped on North American shores until Great Britain and its colonies expelled France from the continent with the Seven Years' War. By 1763, the land and people of America had permanently changed.

CHRONOLOGY	38,000 B.C.	A.D. 1500	1600
POLITICS AND DIPLOMACY	**38,000–12,000 B.C.:** Ancient hunters migrate to America **A.D. 300–1600:** Ghana, Mali, and Songhai empires in West Africa **A.D. 700–1450:** Cahokia and other Mississippian centers in North America **A.D. c. 1000:** Leif Eriksson's colony on Newfoundland **1420:** Prince Henry of Portugal begins exploration **1492:** Christopher Columbus crosses Atlantic Ocean	**1513:** Juan Ponce de León explores Florida for Spain **1519:** Magellan's expedition to circumnavigate world **1521:** Hernán Cortés defeats Aztecs **1528:** Cabeza de Vaca to Florida and Texas **1540:** Coronado explores American Southwest **c. 1550:** Iroquois form confederacy **1565:** Spanish found St. Augustine, Florida **1585:** English colony at Roanoke Island **1599:** Spanish destroy Ácoma	**1607:** English colony at Jamestown **1608:** French establish Quebec **1620:** Separatists found Plymouth **1630:** Puritans establish Massachusetts Bay colony **1634:** The *Ark* and the *Dove* arrive in Maryland **1642:** English Civil War begins **1643:** New England Confederation **1663:** Carolina proprietors receive character **1664:** English forces conquer New Netherland
SOCIETY AND CULTURE	**1324:** Gonga-Mussa's pilgrimage to Mecca	**1507:** Martin Waldseemüller names New World after Amerigo Vespucci **1517:** Martin Luther challenges the Church of Rome **1534:** English Act of Supremacy **1536:** John Calvin's *Institutes of the Christian Religion* **1542:** Bartolomé de las Casas's *A Short Account of the Destruction of the Indies* **1585:** John White's drawings of Roanoke **1590:** Theodor de Bry's *America*	**1636:** Harvard College established; Roger Williams's exile to Rhode Island **1637:** Anne Hutchinson tried for heresy **1638:** First printing press in the English colonies **1639:** French establish first hospital in North America **1647:** Massachusetts requires town schools **1649:** Maryland's act for religious toleration **1650:** Anne Bradstreet's *The Tenth Muse Lately Sprung Up in America* **c. 1661:** Henri Couturier's portrait of Peter Stuyvesant **1662:** Halfway Covenant **1663:** John Eliot's Bible in Massachusetts Indian language
ECONOMICS AND TECHNOLOGY	**pre-2500 B.C.:** Corn developed as staple crop in central Mexico **c. 1200 B.C.:** Corn produced in American Southwest **1440s:** Portuguese mariners take Africans as slaves **c. 1450:** European fishermen at Grand Banks off Newfoundland **c. 1452:** Portugal begins sugar production on Madeira **c. 1460:** European improvements in navigation and ships **1478:** Abraham Zacuto calculates latitude using sun	**1502:** Enslaved Africans imported in Spanish America **1503:** Spanish Casa de Contratación to supervise trade **1540s:** Silver mines at Zacatecas and Potosí **1562:** John Hawkins interlopes in slave trade **c. 1585:** Growth of Amsterdam as mercantile center	**1602:** Dutch East India Company **1617:** Tobacco successful staple crop in Virginia **c. 1619:** Africans arrive in Virginia **1621:** Dutch West India Company **1640s:** Sugar production in English West Indies **1642:** French found Montreal for fur trade **1651:** First English Navigation Act **1672:** Royal African Company **1673:** Regular postal route between Boston and New York **1670s:** Shift to slaves in Chesapeake

1675	1700	1750
1675: King Philip's War; Bacon's Rebellion **1680:** Pueblo Revolt **1681:** William Penn receives Pennsylvania charter **1688:** Glorious Revolution in England **1689:** Massachusetts, New York, and Maryland revolutions **1691:** Salem witchcraft hysteria **1699:** French establish Louisiana	**1712:** Slave revolt in New York City **1732:** Founding of Georgia **1739:** Stono Uprising in South Carolina	**1754:** Albany Congress **1756–1763:** Seven Years' War **1763:** Pan-Indian War in Ohio Valley and Great Lakes region
c. 1674: *Mrs. Freake with Baby Mary* by unknown artist **1682:** Publication of *The Narrative of the Captivity and Restoration of Mrs. Mary Rowlandson* **1687:** Isaac Newton's *Principia Mathematica* **1688:** Germantown, Pennsylvania, Quakers issue antislavery protest **1690:** John Locke's *Essay Concerning Human Understanding* **1693:** College of William and Mary founded **1695:** Jews worship openly in New York	**1704:** First regular newspaper in Anglo-America, *The Boston News-Letter* **1716:** Theater built in Williamsburg, Virginia **1720:** Theodore Jacob Frelinghuysen's revivals in New Jersey **1721:** Smallpox inoculation in Boston **1731:** Benjamin Franklin's circulating library in Philadelphia **1739:** George Whitefield tours northern colonies	**1751:** Benjamin Franklin's reports on electricity **1752:** Adoption of Gregorian Calendar in Anglo-America **1761:** John Winthrop observes the transit of Venus **1763:** Rise of Delaware prophet Neolin
1698: Royal African Company loses slave trade monopoly **1699:** Woolen Act	**1700s:** Adoption of rice in South Carolina **1720s:** Expansion of German and Scots-Irish immigration **1732:** Hat Act **1733:** Molasses Act **1740s:** Eliza Pinckney cultivates indigo in South Carolina **1740s:** "Consumer revolution" in British colonies	**1750:** Iron Act, Georgia legalizes slavery **1750s:** British colonial trade expands with Southern Europe **Early 1760s:** Economic slump in British colonies

1

Contact, Conflict, and Exchange in the Atlantic World

Prehistory to 1590

Christopher sighted the Carribean island of San Salvador on 10/12/1492. He discovered 2 more continents that where unknown to the Europens. Native Americans, Africans, and Europeans created New traditions and Societies.

When the Italian navigator Christopher Columbus sighted the Caribbean island of San Salvador on October 12, 1492, he initiated the conquest of two continents whose vast extent and wealth were previously unknown to Europeans. For Native Americans living in cities and villages throughout the Americas, these white men and their sailing ships spelled demographic catastrophe. For Africans, European colonization sparked the transatlantic slave trade. Yet together, Native Americans, Africans, and Europeans created new traditions and societies. Although the Europeans won the contest for power, the American colonies were shaped by the exchange of knowledge, culture, and work among all participants.

❖ The First Americans

Estimates of the number of Native Americans in 1492 vary widely, from 8 million to more than 100 million. They possessed widely divergent cultures. The Aztecs of central Mexico and the Incas of the Peruvian Andes lived in state-level agricultural societies, whereas the Hopi and Zuñi Indians of the Southwest were pueblo dwellers, and the Iroquois and Algonquians inhabited the eastern woodlands. Cultures diverged with adaptation to the many different habitats of the Americas.

Native American Societies Before Contact

Archaeological evidence supports a theory that the first Americans migrated by boat from Asia or crossed the Bering land bridge from Siberia to Alaska more than 10,000 years ago. As glaciers from the last Ice Age receded, groups migrated throughout the hemisphere, adapting to the widely varied environments. Initially they hunted game, fished, and collected berries, seeds, and nuts. Later, ancient Americans began cultivating crops and developing settled societies in Mesoamerica—present-day Mexico and northern Central America—and in Peru. Of greatest importance was the development of maize, or Indian corn. Mesoamericans also domesticated beans, squash, chili peppers, and avocado. Higher yields spurred population growth, a greater division of labor, and the emergence of cities.

Between 1200 B.C. and Columbus's arrival, a series of great civilizations emerged in Mesoamerica and the central Andes. Ancient Americans built cities and extensive trade networks and developed systems of religion and knowledge, art, architecture, and hierarchical social classes. The people of the Valley of Mexico built the city of Teotihuacán, with its grand pyramids, east of Lake Texcoco. Its population of about two hundred thousand depended on intensive farming of nearby irrigated lands. The **Maya**, at their height from 300 to 900 A.D., built cities of stone pyramids, temples, and palaces, with populations ranging to more than sixty thousand.

Maya Inhabitants of the Yucatan Peninsula whose civilization was at its height from 300 to 900 A.D. Their civilization included a unique system of writing, mathematics, architecture, sculpture, and astronomy.

Maya kings, considered divine, extended their empire to more than fifty states and maintained trade with distant peoples. The Maya had a numeral system based on units of twenty, hieroglyphics, knowledge of astronomy, and several calendars.

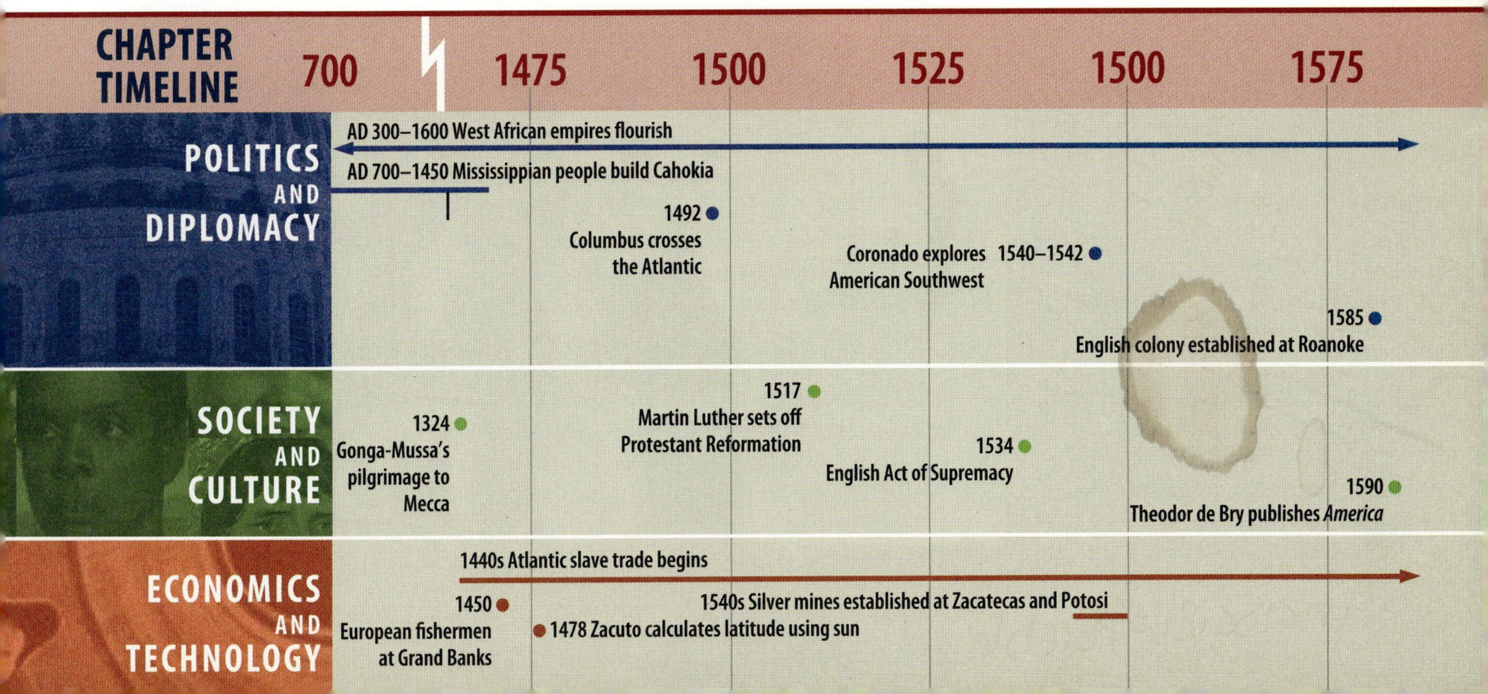

Aztecs Inhabitants of the Valley of Mexico who founded their capital, Tenochtitlán, in the early fourteenth century. Prior to the arrival of the Spanish, the Aztecs built a large empire in which they dominated many neighboring peoples. Their civilization included engineering, mathematics, art, and music.

The **Aztecs** settled in the Valley of Mexico around 1200 and built a militaristic state. Their capital, Tenochtitlán, founded in 1325, was built on two islands in Lake Texcoco, which they connected to the shore by causeways. By the time the Spanish arrived in 1519, the Aztecs controlled territory from the Pacific to the Gulf Coast. The Aztecs required tribute from the people they conquered: gold, turquoise, cotton, and human beings for sacrifice.

Native Peoples of North America

The Hohokam ~~made~~ grew their own food which feed thousands of people in their villages

(George H. H. Huey/CORBIS)

Hohokam Vessel, 900–1100 A.D. A fine example of Hohokam pottery from present-day Arizona, this Sacaton red-on-buff jar dates from a period in Hohokam history when crafts flourished in jewelry, sculpture, textiles, and pottery.

To the north of the Valley of Mexico, the first mainly agricultural societies developed in the deserts of the present-day American Southwest. The Hohokam cultivated Indian corn, cotton, squash, and beans in Arizona, building irrigation canals to draw water from nearby rivers. In what is now northern Arizona and New Mexico, Colorado, and Utah, Anasazi farmers relied on rain and floods to water their crops. One of their settlements was Pueblo Bonito in Chaco Canyon, which housed perhaps a thousand people. Descendants of the Anasazi were called Pueblo (meaning "village" or "people") Indians by the Spanish for the adobe villages in which they lived.

Farther east, in a large area drained by the Mississippi River, by 1000 B.C. early Americans developed civilizations characterized by large earthen burial mounds, some sixty feet high. These mounds entombed the dead and such grave goods as copper spoons and beads made from seashells. The Adena-Hopewell people, who built the Great Serpent Mound located in southern Ohio, lived in small villages along rivers, hunted game, fished, farmed, and maintained a trading network extending from the Gulf Coast to Lake Superior. By 800 A.D., people in the Mississippi Valley had constructed large towns, including Cahokia, near present-day St. Louis, Missouri. By 1450, the region's population had declined, perhaps as a result of illness spread by urban crowding.

The Great Serpent Mound, more than one-quarter mile long from the triangular tip to the tail, demonstrates the knowledge of astronomy of these ancient people. According to anthropologist William F. Romain in *Mysteries of the Hopewell* (2000), the mound is oriented to true astronomical north, and its measurements

(Jim Wark/Peter Arnold Images/Photolibrary)

Cahokia: Monk's Mound. This prehistoric site, located in southern Illinois near St. Louis, Missouri, was the center of a flourishing Mississippian culture and was built around 900 A.D. Nearly 100 feet high, it was the largest pre-historic structure in the New World.

Anasazi = Pueblo = village/people

MAP 1.1

North American Peoples Before Columbus's Arrival

This map shows the approximate locations of some Native American groups in North America in 1492. Because disease often preceded French, Dutch, and English colonization, many native people had moved from earlier settlements by the time of European contact.

conform to the standard Hopewell 1,053-foot unit of length. The large oval and serpent's head almost precisely face the setting sun on June 21, the summer solstice; the serpent's body is aligned to the rising and setting moon.

Along the Atlantic seaboard and extending inland to the Appalachian Mountains lived Native Americans of two major language groups: the Algonquian and the Iroquois (see Map 1.1). In most areas of the eastern woodlands, fertile soil and moderate rainfall and temperatures supported agriculture, hunting, and gathering. Algonquian-speaking people along the Atlantic coast included the Micmacs and Algonquin in Canada, the Pequots in New England, the Lenapes of the middle Atlantic region, and members of the Powhatan confederacy in what became Virginia. Many of the Iroquois lived in central New York State and belonged to five tribes—the Mohawks, Oneidas, Onondagas, Cayugas, and Senecas—who banded together in the Iroquois confederacy.

Doing History Online

Native American Oral Traditions

Go to the CourseMate website for this chapter and link to Primary Sources. Read documents 1 to 3 and consider: What are some of the advantages and disadvantages to relying on written transcriptions of oral traditions?

www.cengagebrain.com

The various Indian peoples of the eastern woodlands had much in common. They held land cooperatively, not as individuals or families, and most Indians had a mixed economy of agriculture, gathering, fishing, and hunting. Women were responsible for raising corn, squash, beans, and, in the Chesapeake region especially, tobacco. They also gathered nuts and fruit, built houses, made clothing, took care of the children, and prepared meals, while men cleared land, hunted, fished, and protected the village from enemies. The combination of corn, squash, and beans enriched the soil, providing high yields from small plots of land; eaten together, these foods were high in protein. Eastern woodlands people used nets and weirs to catch fish, and to ensure good hunting, they periodically burned forest underbrush, stimulating the growth of lush grass and promoting the growth of berries.

Indian religions were diverse in many ways yet incorporated a common worldview. The peoples of the eastern woodlands believed that the earth and sky formed a spiritual realm of which they were a part, but not the masters. Spirits inhabited the earth and could be found in plants, animals, rocks, or clouds. These Native Americans also believed in a Master Spirit or Creator who was all-powerful and all-knowing, but whose presence was rarely felt. Religious leaders called *shamans*—usually men, but sometimes women—performed rituals to influence the weather, cure illness, interpret dreams, bring good weather, and predict the future.

The kinship group, or extended family, formed the basis of Native American society. The heads of kinship groups chose the band's chief leaders, called *sachems*, who assigned fields for planting, decided where and when to hunt, managed trade and diplomacy, and judged whether to go to war. Among Algonquian-speaking natives, most heads of extended families were men, but in Iroquois culture, women served as clan leaders and therefore had a share of political power. Iroquois society was matrilineal, with family membership passing from mother to children, and matrilocal, as the husband left his native family to live with his wife's.

Thus, in 1492, highly complex and differentiated societies existed in North and South America. Dense populations inhabited parts of South, Central, and North America. Throughout the hemisphere, Indian people had distinctive cultures influenced by their environments. Despite this wide diversity, most Europeans adopted the single name that Columbus mistakenly employed: Indians. An alternative the colonists used was "savages." The view of many Europeans that Native Americans had uncivilized societies was used to justify forcible conquest.

❖ Beginning of European Overseas Expansion

Like the peoples of the Americas, Europeans spent most of their energy producing food. They farmed wheat, rye, and other crops; raised livestock; and gathered nuts and berries. In contrast to Native Americans, Europeans could own land individually and thus enjoyed property rights. European societies were patriarchal: men were the heads of their families, and political power was nearly always in the hands of men. Although women occasionally inherited the throne, as did Isabella of Spain and Elizabeth I of England, men controlled government, the church, and the military. Married women were considered subordinate to their husbands.

In the fifteenth century, the pope headed a united Catholic Church in western and central Europe. At the same time, monarchs were consolidating national power in Portugal, Spain, France, and England, providing financial support and a greater sense of national identity to fuel European expansion. In turn, wealth from distant empires and trade funded wars among these emerging nations.

Trade with the East

In the fifteenth century, eastern trade was a chief source of riches for affluent Europeans, who desired spices such as black pepper, cinnamon, and cloves, as well as silk, cotton cloth, and jewels from India, the East Indies, and other parts of East Asia. Before 1500, Arabs controlled eastern trading centers, and Italian merchants then distributed the spices and other goods throughout Europe by pack trains and coastal shipping. European cities, including Venice, Genoa, Paris, Amsterdam, Barcelona, and Lisbon, became centers of trade and banking. Their growth accompanied the development of unified political states. In Portugal, Spain, France, and England, commercial interests supported the development of small feudal states into nations to promote social order, commercial monopolies, and standardized codes of law.

Portugal Explores the West African Coast, 1424–1450

Early in the fifteenth century, **Prince Henry of Portugal (1394–1460)**, called "the Navigator," decided to challenge the Arab and Italian hold on commerce with the East. He also hoped to increase Portugal's power by adding territorial possessions, promoting trade with Africa, and spreading Christianity.

Prince Henry of Portugal (1394–1460) Henry "the Navigator" established a school for navigators and geographers. He sought to increase the power of Portugal by promoting exploration of trade routes to the East by way of Africa.

In 1420, cartographers knew a great deal about the Mediterranean Sea and had produced highly accurate charts of its shorelines and harbors. But European sailors knew nothing of the West African coast south of Cape Bojador. Seamen had heard that monsters and perhaps even Satan dwelled in the area's waters. Prince Henry challenged current wisdom by sending ships down Africa's coast to find a route to the East. Advances in navigational technology, including the use of the compass, astrolabe, and quadrant, and improved ship design made such voyages possible. The Portuguese developed the small but sturdy *caravel* for their ocean voyages, and adopted lateen (triangular) sails for agility. The Portuguese mounted artillery on the caravels and by 1500 had introduced the practice of broadside fire, sinking enemy vessels with gunfire instead of boarding them with foot soldiers.

Portuguese ships were cramped and uncomfortable places to live on a voyage that might last months or even years. Only the senior officers had regular sleeping quarters; the rest of the seamen slept on deck, or below in bad weather. Their shipmates included rats and cockroaches. The sailors ate hard bread, beans, salt pork, and beef, and drank mostly wine, since their casked water quickly became foul.

❖ Africa and the Atlantic Slave Trade

The Portuguese explorers ventured farther down the West African coast, finally sailing past Cape Bojador in 1434. Within a few years the Portuguese established a lucrative coastal trade in slaves, gold, and pepper in the Senegal region and farther south and east to the Gold Coast and Benin (see Map 1.2). Between the 1440s and 1505, Portuguese traders transported forty thousand Africans to perform domestic labor in Portugal and Spain and to work on the sugar plantations of the Azores, Madeira, and Canary Islands.

West African Cultures

From before 300 A.D. to 1600, a succession of empires—Ghana, Mali, and Songhai—dominated western Africa. These empires had large armies, collected tribute over vast distances, and traded with Europeans and Arabs. West Africans were

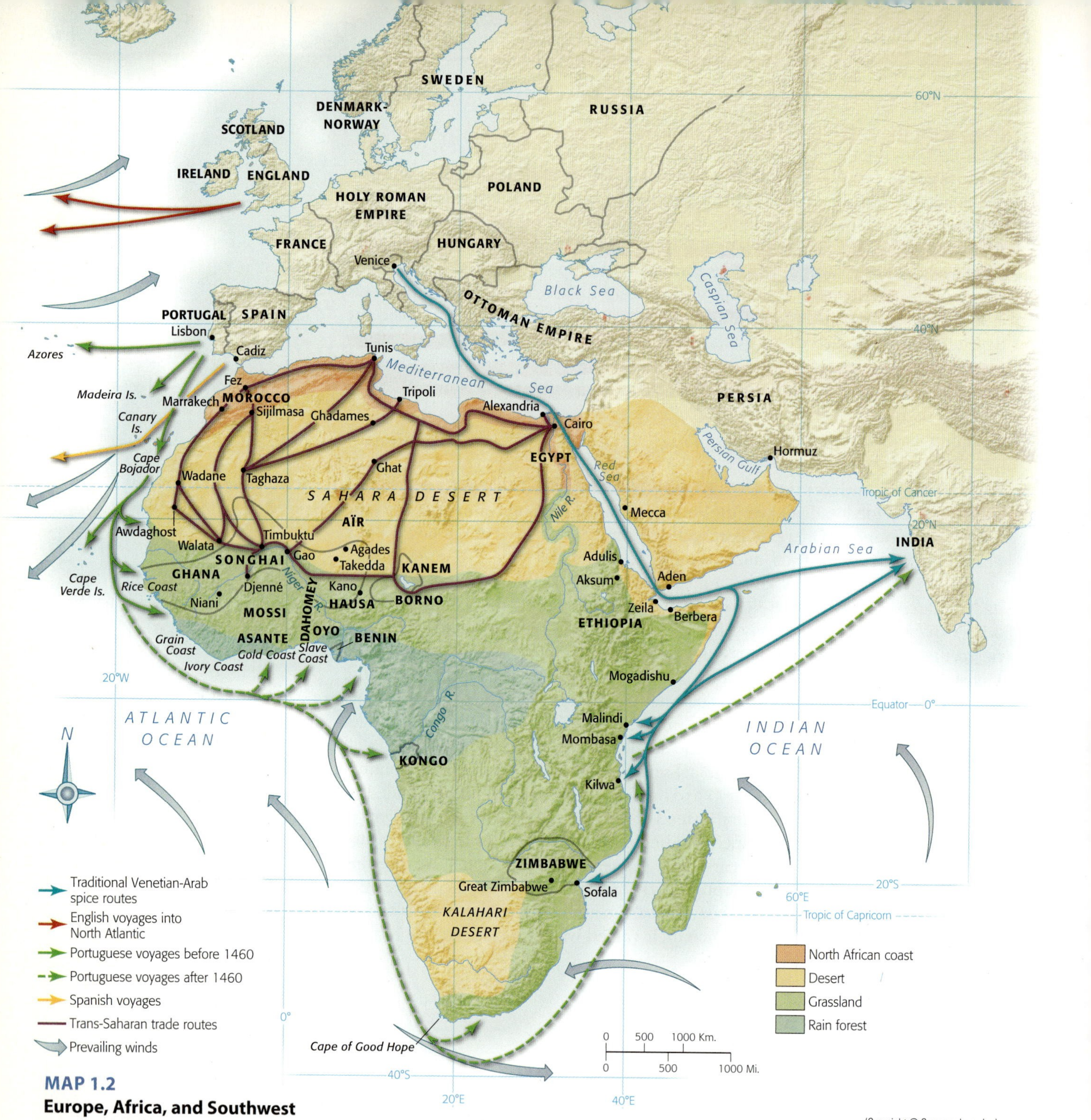

MAP 1.2

Europe, Africa, and Southwest Asia, c. 1500

Exploration of North and South America was an outgrowth of trade in the Eastern Hemisphere. Europeans delivered cloth and other manufactures to northern Africa; then camels carried the cargo across the Sahara to cities such as Timbuktu, Gao, and Djenné. There they loaded gold, ivory, and kola nuts for return to the Mediterranean. Africans also traded with Asia to obtain cloth, porcelain, and spices.

predominantly agricultural people. By 1100, Ghana had declined as a result of droughts that dried up several rivers. Mali then took control, as its monarchs regulated the all-important gold trade. The Mali kings were followers of Islam: one of the most famous, Mansa Kankan Mussa, made a pilgrimage to Mecca in 1324 to fulfill his religious duty as a Muslim. His caravan is said to have included more than sixty thousand people and eighty camels carrying gold.

Mali provided stable government over a wide area until the fifteenth century, when **Songhai** successfully challenged its dominance. Songhai was centered at Gao. Under Sonni Ali, who ruled from 1468 to 1492, Songhai captured Timbuktu, an important trading and cultural center of Mali. Askia Mohammed, who ruled from 1493 to 1528, expanded the empire even farther, strengthening ties with other Muslims and reforming government, banking, and education. After his reign, however, Songhai declined, and Moroccans conquered Timbuktu in 1593. Beyond these empires, along the West African coast lay smaller states with highly developed cultures. Although influenced by Islam, they retained much of their traditional religions: like Native Americans and Europeans, the people of Africa kept religion central to their lives and endowed their leaders with both political and religious authority.

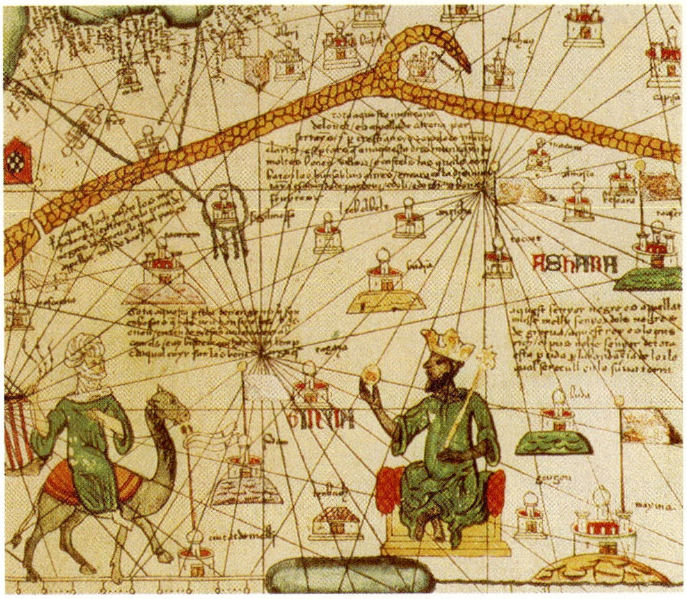

(The Granger Collection, New York)

European Map of Northwest Africa. This 1375 European map of northwest Africa shows an Arab trader approaching Mansu Musa of Mali, who is holding a large nugget of gold.

Most important in traditional African religions was a single all-powerful God, the Creator. Beneath the Creator were lesser gods, including gods of rain, animals, trees, and hills. These gods could be benevolent or harmful, so people sought positive relationships through rituals, sacrifice, and prayer. Africans also believed that their ancestors watched over the extended family. When the eldest father, or patriarch, of a kinship group died, his spirit became a god. Before his death, the patriarch acted as the extended family's priest; he communicated with the family's ancestors through prayer and the sacrifice of animals. The patriarch also served as political leader. Thus, in many African societies, the state, religion, and family united under a single hierarchical structure.

Kinship in West Africa varied from one culture to another; extended families could be either patrilineal or matrilineal. In all cases, however, a child belonged to only one kin group. In patrilineal societies, descent flowed from father to child. In matrilineal groups, descent proceeded from mother to child. Polygyny, or having more than one wife, was generally reserved to men of high status. The extended family held land in common and assigned plots to individual families. Women and men worked in fields growing crops such as rice, cassava, wheat, millet, cotton, fruits, and vegetables. They kept livestock and produced food for their own use and for the market, where women were the primary traders. Artisans were skilled in textile weaving, pottery, basketry, woodwork, and metalwork. Over the years, West Africans had experienced the rise and fall of empires and developed diverse, complex cultures by the time Europeans arrived on their shores.

Songhai Dominant West African state in the fifteenth and sixteenth centuries. Askia Mohammed (ruled 1493–1528) expanded the empire; reformed government, banking, and education; and adopted Islamic law.

The Atlantic Slave Trade Begins

Over the course of four centuries, beginning in the 1440s, Africa lost more than 10 million people to the **Atlantic slave trade.** Slavery had existed throughout the world for centuries before the Portuguese arrived on the West African coast. African slavery was different, however, from the institution that developed in the Americas. Most African slaves were prisoners of war; others had committed some offense that caused their kinfolk to banish them. Although trans-Saharan traders transported a few Africans for sale to wealthy Europeans, most slaves remained in West Africa, where they became members of a household, married, and had children. Enslaved Africans could be transferred from one owner to another at will, but their children could not be sold and were frequently emancipated.

Atlantic slave trade In the 1440s Portugal initiated the trans-Atlantic trade that lasted four centuries. During that time, other European nations participated in a commerce that took more than 10 million people from Africa.

The plantation slave system that became dominant in America began on the island of Madeira, off West Africa, in the mid-1400s. To supply its new sugar plantations with laborers, Portuguese merchants purchased black slaves from Muslim trans-Saharan traders and from Africans along the coast. When sugar

Doing History Three Views of European–Native American Encounters

The first document is Christopher Columbus's diary account of sighting land in the Americas. The second is from a later voyage and was recorded by Peter Martyr, who did not personally witness the speech by the Taino leader. The third was recorded generations later, a legend passed down by New Englanders about the response of the god Maushop to English settlement.

Admiral Christopher Columbus's Diary Account of Reaching America, *October 12, 1492*

At two hours after midnight the land appeared, from which they were about two leagues distant. They hauled down all the sails . . . passing time until daylight Friday, when they reached an islet of the Lucayas, which was called Guanahani in the language of the Indians. Soon they saw naked people; and the Admiral [Columbus] went ashore in the armed launch. . . . The Admiral brought out the royal banner and the captains' two flags with the green cross. . . . The Admiral [announced] . . . in the presence of all, he would take, as in fact he did take, possession of the said island for the king and for the queen his lords. . . .

I, he says, in order that they would be friendly to us—because I recognized that they were people who would be better freed [from error] and converted to our Holy Faith by love than by force—to some of them I gave red caps, and glass beads which they put on their chests, and many other things of small value, in which they took so much pleasure and became so much our friends that it was a marvel. . . .

But it seemed to me that they were a people very poor in every-thing. All of them go around as naked as their mothers bore them; and the women also, although I did not see more than one quite young girl. And all those that I saw were young people, for none did I see of more than 30 years of age. They are very well formed, with handsome bodies and good faces. . . . They should be good and intelligent servants, for I see that they say very quickly everything that is said to them; and I believe that they would become Christians very easily, for it seemed to me that they had no religion.

Source: Oliver Dunn and James E. Kelley, Jr., *The Diario of Christopher Columbus's First Voyage to America, 1492–1493* (Norman: University of Oklahoma Press, 1989), 63–69.

A Native Leader's Speech to Columbus

While the admiral [Columbus] was listening to divine service on the shore, they noticed one of their chief men; he was an octogenarian and an important man, but, for all that naked, with many in attendance on him. He stood by in wonder, his eyes and face intent, while the service was being carried out; then he presented the admiral with the gift of a basket, which he was carrying in his hand, full of his country's fruits, and sitting in the admiral's presence, with Diego Colón as interpreter, who

proved an extraordinarily profitable commodity, the Portuguese colonized the small islands in the Gulf of Guinea to create new sugar plantations. The mortality rate was high and the demand for laborers great, spurring growth of the slave trade on the Gold Coast. By the end of the fifteenth century, Portugal had developed both the plantation system and the commercial mechanism for purchasing human beings from African traders.

❖ Columbus and the Age of Exploration

Once Portugal had established trade on the West African coast, Spanish merchants tried to participate. Prince Henry appealed to the pope, who in 1455 gave Portugal sole possession of lands to the south and east toward India and, thus, a monopoly on the Atlantic slave trade. In the Treaty of Alcaçovas (1479), Spain recognized Portugal's sphere of interest in Africa, and Portugal acknowledged Spain's claim to the Canary Islands. As the Portuguese sailed south, they came to recognize the vastness of the African continent, making rapid progress sailing understood their language since they were near his home, the man made the following speech: "News has been brought us that trusting in your powerful hand you have voyaged to these lands until now unknown to you, and have brought no ordinary fear to the people living there. I warn you then to be aware that souls have two paths when they leap forth from the body: one gloomy and hideous, prepared for those who cause trouble and are the enemies of the human race; the other delightful and pleasant, appointed for those who in their lives have loved peace and quiet among nations. If therefore you remember you are mortal and that rewards will be duly assigned to each in accordance with his present actions, you will attack no one.

Source: Geoffrey Eatough, ed. and trans., *Selections from Peter Martyr,* vol. 5 (Turnhout, Belgium: Brepols, 1998), 68.

A New England Legend About the European Arrival

On the west end of Martha's Vineyard is a hill with a large cavity, which has the appearance of the crater of an extinguished volcano. . . . The Indians nearby have a tradition that a certain deity resided there before the Europeans came into America, and that his name was Maushop. He used to step out on a ledge of rocks that ran into the sea, and take up a whale, which he broiled on the coals of the volcano, and often invited the Indians to dine with him, or gave them the leftovers of his meal. Once to show their gratitude to Maushop for his great kindness to them, they offered to him all of the tobacco that grew on the island in one season. This was scarcely enough to fill his great pipe, but he received the present very graciously, smoked his pipe, and turned out the ashes of it into the sea, which formed the island of Nantucket. Upon the coming of the Europeans into America, Maushop retired in disgust, and has never since been seen.

Source: Karen Ordahl Kupperman, ed., *Major Problems in American Colonial History: Documents and Essays* (Lexington, MA: Heath, 1993), 12.

QUESTIONS for REFLECTION

1. How did the perspective of the Indians compare with that of Columbus?
2. Why is it necessary to use legends and secondhand accounts to gain knowledge about Native American perspectives?
3. What are the possible pitfalls of using each of these sources: Columbus's diary, Martyr's account, and the New England legend?

around it after 1482, when King John II of Portugal stepped up the program of discovery. In 1487 Bartholomeu Dias rounded the Cape of Good Hope. The Portuguese now knew that a sea route to India existed.

Meanwhile, the Spanish monarchs Isabella and Ferdinand decided to fund **Christopher Columbus's** search for another route to Asia. A native of Genoa, Italy, Columbus sailed on merchant voyages to Iceland, Ireland, and the West African coast. In 1484, he sought patronage from John II of Portugal for a voyage west across the Atlantic in the belief that Asia was within reach. When John turned him down, Columbus sought support from Isabella and Ferdinand, who approved his request in January 1492. In August 1492, Columbus sailed west from the Canaries, taking advantage of the favorable current and trade winds. When the ships reached San Salvador in the Bahamas in October, Columbus thought they had located the East Indies. Hoping to establish trade, Columbus sailed southward to Cuba, then touched Hispaniola, where Native Americans offered gold in return for the trade goods he brought. The Spanish lost their flagship *Santa Maria* on a coral reef and used its timbers to build a fort on Hispaniola.

Columbus, Christopher (1451–1506) Italian mariner who sailed for Spain in 1492 in search of a western route to Asia. He located San Salvador in the West Indies, opening the Americas to European exploration and colonization.

Leaving a small contingent of men at the fort, Columbus set out for home in January 1493; he encountered a violent storm and sought shelter in Portugal.

King John II, whose explorers had not yet reached India by sailing around Africa, refused to believe that Columbus had located Asia. The lands he had found, the king claimed, lay within Portugal's sphere.

Spanish and Portuguese "Spheres," 1493–1529

Isabella and Ferdinand rejected Portugal's argument for claiming lands, and they petitioned Pope Alexander VI, who was Spanish, to grant them dominion over the newly discovered lands. After negotiations with John II, the pope brokered the **Treaty of Tordesillas (1494)**, which established a line of demarcation about 1,100 miles west of the Azores. Portugal retained its rights to the Atlantic slave trade and the sea route around Africa to India. Spain received permission to explore, conquer, and Christianize all lands and people to the west (see Map 1.3). The question of where Portuguese and Spanish spheres should be divided in the Far East was left unresolved until 1529, when the Treaty of Saragossa placed most of Asia within Portugal's sphere.

Between 1493 and 1529, Portugal and Spain sent out expeditions to explore their spheres. Columbus made three more voyages to the west, while the Portuguese completed their efforts to reach India. In 1497–1498, Vasco da Gama rounded the Cape of Good Hope and sailed across the Indian Ocean, returning to Portugal with a cargo of pepper and cinnamon. In 1500, Portugal instructed Pedro Álvares Cabral to find the Cape of Good Hope by sailing west. Instead, he

MAP 1.3
European Explorations, 1492–1542
Before 1542, Spain and Portugal dominated European exploration. Generally conforming to the 1494 Line of Demarcation, Portugal's sphere of influence extended over Brazil (in eastern South America), Africa, and South Asia. Spain claimed the rest of South and Central America. France and England sent out explorers but did not establish permanent colonies in North America until the early seventeenth century.

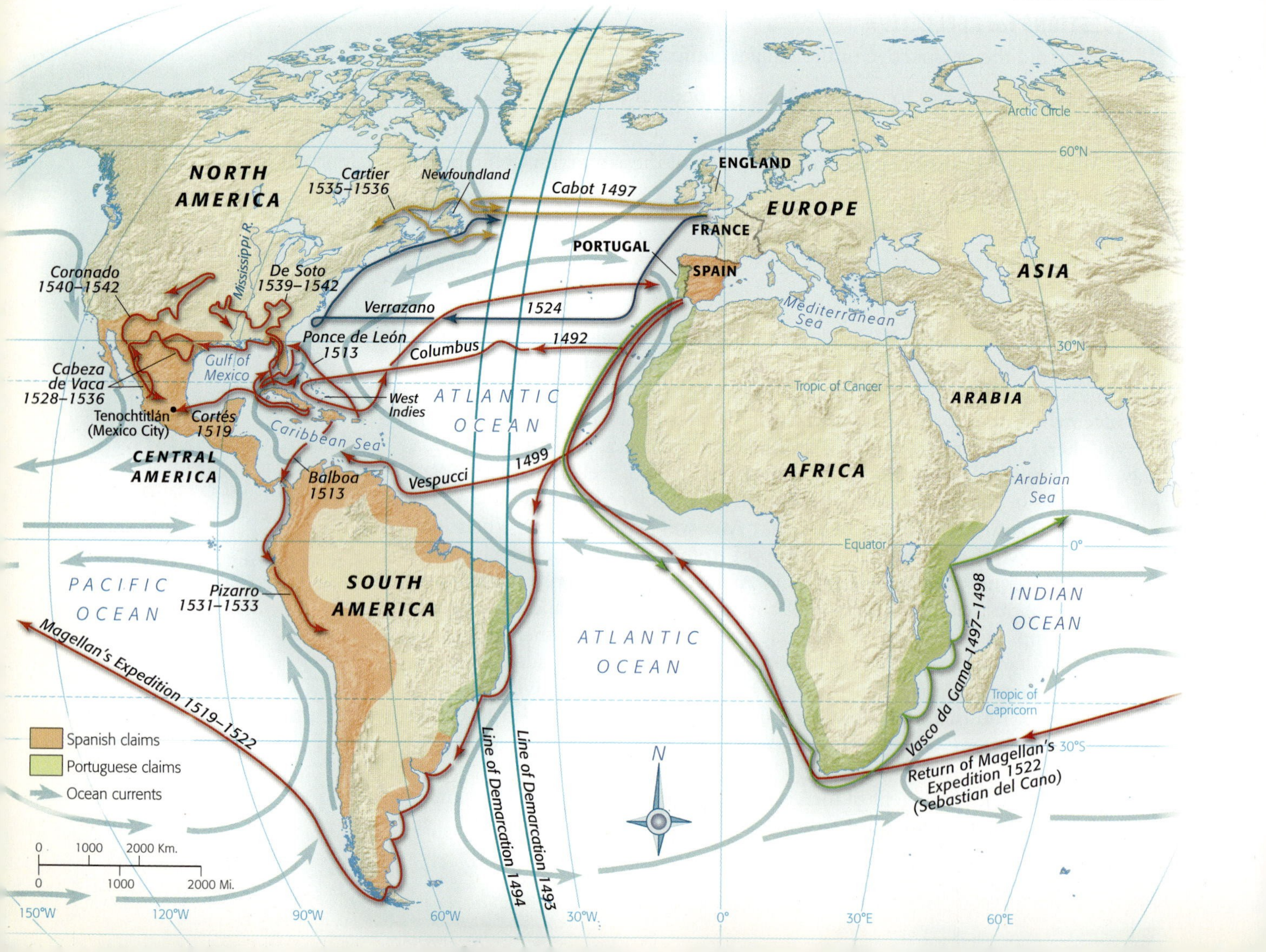

touched the coast of Brazil, and since a section of Brazil lay east of the Line of Demarcation, Portugal claimed that part of South America. The Italian captain Amerigo Vespucci made two separate voyages, in 1499 and 1501, for Spain and Portugal, respectively. His explorations revealed that South America was a huge land mass that had to be circumnavigated to reach Asia. In recognition of his insight, the German cartographer Martin Waldseemüller applied Vespucci's first name, Amerigo, not that of Columbus, to the newly "discovered" continents.

Treaty of Tordesillas (1494) Treaty between Spain and Portugal that located the Line of Demarcation 370 leagues (about 1,000 miles) west of the Azores. It expanded the principle of "spheres of influence."

An Expanding World

Europeans continued to search for a western sea route to Asia. Ferdinand Magellan convinced King Charles I of Spain that he could sail around the cape of South America and claim the Molucca Islands. With five ships, in 1519 he set out on an expedition that would take three years. The voyagers faced shipwreck, a harrowing passage through the straits subsequently named for Magellan, and starvation. The Pacific was so much wider than anticipated that the mariners had to eat ship rats and leather. When inhabitants of the Philippines killed Magellan, Sebastian del Cano took command, returning to Spain with one surviving ship, laden with cloves. Together Magellan and del Cano commanded the first circumnavigation of the globe, but demonstrated that the southwest passage was much more difficult than previously thought.

England and France ignored the pope's division of the world between Spain and Portugal and decided to seek a northerly route, the "northwest passage," to the East. During the fifteenth century, seafarers from England and France fished off the coast of Newfoundland, and some had camped ashore. King Henry VII of England sent the Italian navigator John Cabot (Giovanni Caboto) in search of a northwest passage in 1497. Cabot's expedition reached Newfoundland and possibly Nova Scotia, but when he returned the following year, most of his ships were lost, and he died at sea. Yet Cabot's efforts supported England's later claim to land in North America.

In 1524, the French King Francis I sent another Italian sea captain, Giovanni da Verrazano, to look for the elusive northern route to Asia. Landing at Cape Fear (now North Carolina), Verrazano sailed north along the Atlantic seaboard to Newfoundland, finding no evidence of a waterway through the continent. In expeditions in 1534 and 1535, Jacques Cartier hoped to find the route by way of the gulf and river of St. Lawrence. Although neither explorer found a northwest passage, they established France's claim to part of the continent.

❖ The Spanish Empire in America, 1519–1590

For several decades the Spanish had little interference from other Europeans in exploring and colonizing the New World. By 1543, Spanish settlements extended south to Chile and north through Mexico. Spanish explorers had crossed North America from present-day Florida to California. Spanish conquistadores in search of fortune advanced from island to island in the Caribbean, then moved through Mexico and Central America. The Spanish Crown had three primary goals in colonizing America: to enlarge its power among European nations, exploit the wealth of the New World, and convert Native Americans to Christianity.

Spanish Invasion and Exploration, 1519–1542

When the Spanish found little gold on Hispaniola, they enslaved its inhabitants and expropriated the land. Many natives died when forced to work on plantations, so the colonists sent slave-raiding parties to other islands and to the mainland.

Conquistadores like Juan Ponce de León, known for his fruitless search in 1513 for the legendary "fountain of youth," also sought Indian slaves. The same year Vasco Núñez de Balboa led explorers across the Isthmus of Panama; they became the first Europeans to see the Pacific Ocean.

As Spanish explorers became aware of the vastness of the Americas, they organized militarily to subdue the natives living there. Despite the small size of their armies, the Spanish prevailed thanks to their superior weaponry and the impact of European diseases such as smallpox. The most famous of the conquerors was **Hernán Cortés** who launched an expedition against the Aztecs in 1519. With an army of only six hundred, Cortés marched to Tenochtitlán without opposition and seized the emperor, Moctezuma. When Cortés outlawed human sacrifice and demanded gold, the Aztecs rebelled, killing Moctezuma and forcing the Spanish and their allies to retreat, slaying a third of Cortés's troops. By 1521, however, smallpox had ravaged the Aztec capital, Cortés returned and, after a long siege, destroyed Tenochtitlán building by building. The Spanish rebuilt the city as Mexico City, the capital of New Spain. To the south, Francisco Pizarro had defeated the Incas of Peru by 1538, aided by the smallpox that preceded him. Others expanded into Argentina and Chile.

Cortés, Hernán (1485–1547) Spanish explorer who conquered the Aztecs initially in 1519, retreated when they rebelled, then defeated them again, aided by a smallpox epidemic, in 1521.

In 1528, Pánfilo de Narváez led an expedition to Florida that opened the way to later exploration of territories that became the southern United States. Narváez and his men landed at Tampa Bay, and then marched northward through insect- and snake-infested terrain. They made the mistake of kidnapping a chief of the Apalachees, sparking an Indian attack and compelling Narváez and his men to flee by boat across the Gulf of Mexico. When storms separated the craft, most of the explorers, including Narváez, were lost at sea, and the survivors were captured by native Karankawas. Eventually one of the Spaniards, Álvar Núñez Cabeza de Vaca, who had become an Indian priest and healer, escaped with three others, including an African slave named Esteban. Hoping to reach New Spain, for several years they lived with Native American peoples, earning the Indians' friendship and respect with seemingly miraculous cures. When they finally reached Mexico City in 1536, de Vaca's report of their journey excited interest in exploring lands north of Mexico. In 1540, an army of 336 Spanish and about 1,000 Indians marched north under the command of Francisco Vásquez de Coronado, following Indian legends of golden cities (the so-called Seven Cities of Cibola). They encountered the Hopi of northeastern Arizona and buffalo-hunting Indians of the Great Plains, saw the Grand Canyon, traveled as far east as Kansas, and left descriptions of a substantial part of what became the American Southwest.

Aztecs Defending Tenochtitlán. This drawing depicts Aztecs defending the temple of Tenochtitlán, which was overthrown by the Spanish conquistador Hernán Cortés in 1519–1521. The city's main temple was the site of ritual human sacrifices.

Unknown to Coronado, an expedition led by Hernando de Soto, governor of Cuba, came within a few hundred miles of his own company at about the same time. In 1539, de Soto and about six hundred troops landed in Tampa Bay. During the next three years they trekked through the Southeast to the Tennessee River Valley, plundering towns, stealing food, enslaving Indians, and killing those who resisted. They followed the Tennessee River south into Alabama, then traveled west toward the Mississippi River. After de Soto died of a fever in 1542, the three hundred survivors of his expedition safely reached New Spain by boat.

In 1542, the initial period of Spanish expansion throughout the Americas came to a close. Without discovery of precious metals, the Spanish had little reason to push farther into North America. Instead they focused their colonizing efforts on Mexico, Peru, and Bolivia, where the richest silver deposit in the Americas was discovered in 1545.

Demographic Catastrophe and Cultural Exchange

Contact among Europeans, Native Americans, and Africans after 1492 changed societies in both hemispheres. This process, called the *Columbian exchange*, included transmission of disease, food, technology, and culture. Disease, in particular smallpox, was the chief ally of the Spanish in their drive through Central and South America. The European diseases, including influenza, measles, and bubonic plague, were particularly deadly because the microbes were new to America and the Indians lacked immunity. Native populations declined as much as 90 percent, as whole tribes were eliminated and others weakened severely. Some regions of the continent seemed uninhabited to European latecomers like the English and French because of prior contact with disease.

The Columbian exchange also included livestock and crops that diversified cultures across continents. European settlers imported horses, sheep, cattle, pigs, and chickens. Some Indians, especially on the Plains, adopted horses and became skilled riders; others raised pigs and fowl. For their part, Indians introduced the Europeans and Africans to crops that soon had a major impact on world population growth: Indian corn (or maize), tomatoes, potatoes, peppers, beans, chocolate, pumpkins, and tobacco. The white potato of South America became a major staple in Europe; the sweet potato and Indian corn were important throughout the world. While Europeans brought firearms and iron tools, Native Americans showed them how to build canoes and catch fish using weirs.

Native Americans generally resisted assimilation to Spanish culture. They retained their languages, clothing, housing, agricultural methods, and, to a considerable extent, religion. The degree to which they blocked acculturation depended largely on class. The Spanish focused their attention on local Indian leaders (*caciques*), many of whom learned to speak Spanish, converted to Christianity, and adopted Spanish-style clothing. Their sons attended schools where they learned Latin and other advanced subjects. Other Indians avoided most Spanish ways of living and accepted others. They raised and ate chickens but grew wheat primarily to pay as tribute. They abhorred cattle, but groups like the Apaches quickly accepted the horse. Natives favored their digging sticks over the European plow, which required the use of draft animals.

The Spanish System

The goal of the colonial government was to control and convert Native Americans and use their labor to exploit the wealth of the New World. The Spanish were only partly successful in imposing their rule over the Indians. The colonial government was most effective in central Mexico and the Andes, where the Spanish could substitute their rule for that of the Aztecs and Inca. But Native Americans in northern Mexico, Florida, Arizona, New Mexico, and central Chile, who had never been subject to outside control, evaded Spanish rule. Many in the fringe areas, such as the Apaches, avoided Spanish domination altogether because their bands were highly mobile and autonomous.

Following a mandate from the pope, Spanish missionaries believed that it was an act of humanity to introduce the Indians to Catholicism. At first, missionaries expected most Native Americans to accept Spanish religious practice without change, because many Indians consented to baptism and voluntarily built churches in every town. But most Indians merged the European faith with rituals and beliefs

> **Doing History Online**
>
> **Images of the New World**
>
> Go to the CourseMate website for this chapter and link to Primary Sources. Examine documents 4, 5, 10, 12, and 13. What do the images suggest about European expectations and impressions of the New World?
>
> www.cengagebrain.com

of their traditional religions, resulting in *syncretism*, the blending of two faiths. Some natives added the Christian God to their polytheistic system; others focused on the saints. The retention of native beliefs and practices disappointed many Spanish priests, who would accept nothing less than complete submission to Catholicism. Nevertheless, some priests, including **Bartolomé de las Casas**, condemned Spanish policies. In his *A Short Account of the Destruction of the Indies*, written in 1542, las Casas described atrocities in one colony after another, informing the king of "the excesses which this New World has witnessed, all of them surpassing anything that men hitherto have imagined even in their wildest dreams."

Las Casas, Bartolomé de (1474–1566) Spanish missionary who condemned Spanish colonial policies toward Native Americans. He described atrocities in his book, *A Short Account of the Destruction of the Indies* (1542).

sovereignty Supreme political power. In Spanish and English colonial America, sovereignty rested in the monarch. Under the U.S. Constitution, sovereignty rests in the people (voters).

viceroy Governor of a country, province, or colony who rules as the representative of the sovereign.

The Spanish colonial administration was hierarchical and tied closely to Spain. **Sovereignty**, or supreme political power, rested in the monarch, who ruled by divine right. Directly below the monarch was the Council of the Indies, located in Spain and composed of men who knew little about the New World. The council regulated trade, appointed officials, made laws, and determined who should be allowed to emigrate. The highest officials residing in America were the **viceroys.** In the sixteenth and seventeenth centuries, the Spanish empire consisted of two viceroyalties: New Spain, with its capital in Mexico City, and Peru, with its capital in Lima. The viceroyalties were divided into provinces, ruled by governors and *audiencias*, who advised the governors and functioned as courts. Neither Spanish colonists nor Indians had much say in making and enforcing laws. The right of subjects to appeal official decisions to the king, however, introduced flexibility into the governmental structure. In central Mexico and Peru, Spanish officials took power away from the ruling native elite, but native leaders at the local level often retained their positions. These caciques headed the Indian towns, collected tribute, and recruited forced laborers.

The Crown regulated commerce through the Casa de la Contratación, a government-controlled trading house founded in 1503 in Seville. Spain pursued the economic policy of **mercantilism**, which held that nations had monopolistic rights to trade with their colonies. Under mercantilism, the primary goal of economic activity was to achieve a favorable balance of trade and the acquisition of specie (gold and silver). Colonies were to serve as markets for goods from the home country and provide raw materials, gold, and silver to increase its wealth. All merchants desiring to send ships to Spanish America needed permission from the Casa, as did anyone wishing to emigrate. To the monarch, a crucial function of the Casa was registration of imports of precious metals, because the king received one-fifth, called the **royal fifth,** of all silver and gold. Colonists had to obtain permission to build plantations and mines. In return they paid taxes to the king and, if they found precious metals, the royal fifth.

mercantilism Economic policy of the sixteenth to eighteenth centuries. European nations claimed the monopoly to trade with their colonies, which were to serve as markets for goods from the home country and provide raw materials, gold, and silver to increase its wealth.

royal fifth A tax on silver and gold of which one-fifth of its value went to the king of Spain.

When Columbus obtained gold from the inhabitants of Hispaniola, he raised expectations of great wealth. However, the explorers at first met disappointment. Even the Aztecs failed to satisfy the Spanish thirst for gold, so most colonists turned to agriculture to make their fortunes. Then, in the 1540s, the Europeans located two immensely rich silver mines, one at Potosí in present-day Bolivia and the other at Zacatecas in Mexico. Between 1500 and 1650, about 181 tons of gold and 16,000 tons of silver officially reached Europe from the Americas. American silver and gold helped to create inflation throughout Europe, because the immense supply depressed their value and the prices of other goods increased. Merchants depended on the bullion to pay for luxuries from the East. Goods worth about one-half the value of the metals were returned to the colonies.

Forced Labor Systems

Because Spanish immigrants were few in number and had no intention of working in the mines or fields, they adopted ways to compel Native Americans to work. In 1550, the white colonists remained a small percentage of New World inhabitants, with a population of about 100,000 in New Spain alongside an estimated 2.6 million Native Americans in central Mexico alone. But if some European settlers hoped to have millions of Christianized Indian workers do their bidding, they were disappointed.

When the first explorers on Hispaniola tried to consign the native Arawaks to slavery, most of the Indians died. In 1500, the Spanish Crown ruled that only Indians captured in a "just war" could be forced into perpetual bondage. This judgment had little impact because conquistadores could define as hostile any natives who resisted capture. In 1513, the government drew up a document called the *Requerimiento* (or Requirement), which explorers read when they entered an Indian town for the first time. The Requerimiento informed the natives that they must accept the Catholic faith and Spanish rule, or the soldiers would "make war against you . . . take you and your wives and your children and . . . make slaves of them . . . and shall do to you all the harm and damage that we can."

By the time Spain outlawed most Native American slavery in 1542, the Arawaks of the West Indies had been destroyed. The Spanish had expropriated their lands for sugar plantations, replacing the Indians with enslaved Africans. On the mainland, the Spanish government established two forms of forced Indian labor. With the *encomienda* system, Indians living on specified lands had to pay tribute to individual colonists and sometimes provide labor for which they received minimal wages. At first, the system included no transfer of land to the colonists, but as the numbers of Native Americans declined and Spanish increased, the colonists took Indian property for farms and ranches. After 1600, facing a severe decline in the Indian population, the government devised the *repartimiento* system: Indians could now be forced to work in mines, agriculture, or public works for several weeks, months, or even a year. For example, natives labored for yearlong stints at the Potosí silver mines in Bolivia. At Potosí, workers assigned as carriers had to climb some six hundred feet through tunnels about as wide as a man's body with heavy loads of silver ore on their backs. As the Indian population continued to decline, the Spanish attempted to increase the length and frequency of work periods. Indians resisted these changes, sometimes successfully.

As early as 1502 on West Indies plantations, the Spanish had looked to Africa to meet their insatiable labor demands. They had already purchased Africans from Portuguese traders to work in Spain and on the sugar plantations of the Canary Islands. During the sixteenth century, ships transported approximately seventy-five thousand Africans to Spanish America, with perhaps an equal number dying en route, either in Africa or at sea. The Spanish imported Africans to work on sugar plantations in the West Indies and coastal areas of the mainland, where severe work regimes and rampant disease resulted in high death rates.

❖ Protestant Northern Europeans Challenge Catholic Spain

In the sixteenth century, French and English activity in America was confined to minor, sporadic fishing and trading expeditions. But religious and political change in Northern Europe provided the impetus to test Spain's domination of the New World. In the age of Reformation and religious wars, America became both a refuge for religious dissidents and a battlefield on which European nations fought for wealth, glory, and power.

The Protestant Reformation, 1517–1598

Luther, Martin (1483–1546) German theologian and leader of the Reformation. His opposition to the wealth and corruption of the papacy and his belief that salvation would be granted on the basis of faith alone rather than by works caused his excommunication from the Catholic Church (1521). Luther confirmed the Augsburg Confession in 1530, effectively establishing the Lutheran Church.

When the German monk **Martin Luther** launched the **Protestant Reformation** in 1517, the Catholic Church was the dominant faith in western and central Europe. Luther believed the church had become corrupt and saw the sale of indulgences, which were supposed to reduce the amount of time a deceased person spent in purgatory before moving to heaven, as an example of moral decline. Luther believed that Christians received salvation as a gift from God in return for faith ("justification by faith") rather than for good works: making pilgrimages, giving money to the church, or attending mass, for example. Luther also challenged the authority of priests, arguing that Christians should seek the word of God in the Bible, which he translated into German to make it accessible to laypeople.

Luther's teachings led to the division of Western Christianity, as common people and rulers alike adopted his beliefs. In Germany, composed of many individual states, some princes accepted Lutheranism and others remained Catholic, requiring their subjects to follow their example. Lutheranism spread through northern Germany and into Scandinavia and inspired other critics of Catholicism to offer variant Protestant doctrines. The most influential was **John Calvin** (1509–1564), a native of France, who attempted to create a model society in Geneva, Switzerland. Followers of Calvin established churches in what became known as the Reformed tradition, including the French Huguenots, English Puritans, Scottish Presbyterians, and Dutch and German Reformed. Calvin went further than Luther in arguing that humans could do nothing to save themselves. According to his concept of **predestination,** God alone determined who would be saved (the "elect"). Through communion with God, the elect learned that they were saved; they strove to live blamelessly to reflect their status. Calvinists disciplined individuals for dancing, wearing fancy clothes, and insubordination. Calvin came close to establishing a theocracy in Geneva, in which the church fathers ruled in the name of God.

Calvin, John (1509–1564) French-born Swiss Protestant theologian who broke with the Roman Catholic Church (1533) and set forth the tenets of his theology, the Reformed tradition including Puritans, Huguenots, Presbyterians, and Dutch Reformed, in *Institutes of the Christian Religion* (1536).

predestination A theory that states that God has decreed who will be saved and who will be damned.

The Reformation in England, 1534–1588

In England, opposition to the Catholic Church—its bishops, taxes, monasteries, and rituals—had surfaced years before Luther. Thus, Henry VIII found sympathy for his own break with Rome. Henry wanted to marry Anne Boleyn, whom he hoped would provide a male heir, but the pope refused to allow an annulment of his marriage to Catherine of Aragon. To solve the problem, Henry prevailed on the English Parliament to pass the Act of Supremacy (1534), mandating that the king be "taken, accepted, and reputed the only supreme head in earth of the Church of England." The Crown dissolved the monasteries and confiscated their property. But the Church of England from its inception allowed a fairly wide range of doctrine. In 1552, under Henry's son, Edward VI, the revised Anglican prayer book incorporated many Protestant beliefs. After Edward's death in 1553, however, Henry's daughter Mary I attempted to force England back to the Catholic Church. Her persecution of Protestants and marriage to the staunch Catholic Philip II of Spain inspired an English nationalism that fused loyalty to church and state. When Mary died in 1558, her half-sister, **Elizabeth I,** the daughter of Anne Boleyn, became queen. The new English monarch and a large proportion of her subjects saw Spain as a threat to their national church, now Protestant, and their independence as a nation.

Elizabeth I (1533–1603) Queen of England (1558–1603), she succeeded the Catholic Mary I and reestablished Protestantism in England. Her reign was marked by several plots to overthrow her, the execution of Mary, Queen of Scots (1587), the defeat of the Spanish Armada (1588), and domestic prosperity and literary achievement.

Under Elizabeth, the English confronted Spain on a number of fronts. England became a dominant Protestant power, supported the Dutch revolt against Philip II, and challenged Spain's claims to the New World. Although pragmatic and more interested in power than theology, Elizabeth confirmed England's break with the pope and approved earlier moderate Protestant reforms. The Act of Uniformity (1559) required adherence to the Anglican Book of Prayer. The queen suppressed resistance from both Calvinists, who wanted further reforms, and supporters of Rome. Some Catholics turned to Elizabeth's cousin, Mary, queen of Scots, a Roman Catholic and the heir to the English throne. In 1587, after several unsuccessful plots on Elizabeth's life, Mary was tried as a conspirator and beheaded.

One of the most fervent supporters of Mary, queen of Scots, was Philip II of Spain. Throughout Europe he strove to wipe out the Protestant heresy. When many of his Dutch subjects adopted Calvinism, Philip retaliated with his Inquisition, executing thousands. The Dutch rebelled. In 1581, the northern part of the Netherlands, composed of seven provinces, including Holland, declared its independence as the United Provinces. When Elizabeth sent aid to the United Provinces in 1585, she was in effect declaring war on Spain. In 1588, Philip sent his mighty armada of 130 ships and thirty thousand men to invade England. The English defeated the armada, preserving their national sovereignty and religion.

Queen Elizabeth I. Ruling from 1558–1603, Queen Elizabeth I stabilized Great Britain as a Protestant nation after decades of religious strife and defeated Spain when its Armada attempted to invade in 1588. This portrait, attributed to John Bettes the Younger, is testament to Elizabeth's enduring reputation as one of Britain's most respected monarchs.

French Huguenots and English Sea Dogs

In France, persecution led some Protestant Huguenots to look to America as a refuge. In 1555, a group of wealthy Frenchmen sent Huguenot settlers to Brazil. When disputes occurred among the colonists, some returned to France; the Portuguese, who claimed Brazil, killed or enslaved the majority who remained. In 1562, Huguenots tried again, establishing Charlesfort on the South Carolina coast, in part to attack the Spanish silver fleet as it headed home. When the Spanish moved against the small French colony in 1564, they found it already abandoned. But the Huguenots attempted another settlement that year, this one at Fort Caroline on the St. Johns River in northern Florida. The Spanish quickly destroyed it, murdering most of the settlers.

The English "sea dogs"—privateers unofficially supported by the Crown—learned a great deal about the New World from the Huguenots. With Elizabeth I's ascension to the throne in 1558, seafarers and colonizers like John Hawkins, **Francis Drake**, Humphrey Gilbert, and Walter Raleigh gained favor and support. The most famous of the English privateers was Francis Drake, who in 1572, with the help of Native Americans and runaway African slaves, intercepted the mule train carrying Potosí silver across Panama. Five years later, he set out to circumnavigate the globe. Following Magellan's route through the straits, he attacked Spanish towns along the Pacific coast, explored the North American coast for evidence of a northwest passage, and returned to England in 1580 by way of Asia and the Cape of Good Hope. Six years later, when England and Spain were formally at war, Drake attacked Spanish ports in America, including St. Augustine in Florida, which he looted and burned.

Drake, Sir Francis (1540–1596) English naval hero and explorer who was the first Englishman to circumnavigate the world (1577–1580) and was vice admiral of the fleet that destroyed the Spanish Armada (1588).

While Drake was making his fortune through piracy, other sea dogs hoped to make their mark by starting colonies. They decided to ignore Spain's claim to North America. In 1585, led by Walter Raleigh, the first group of settlers arrived at **Roanoke Island,** in what is now North Carolina. After their ships returned home leaving them with short supplies, the colonists tried to force neighboring Indians to provide food. A pattern of hostility quickly emerged between the English and Native Americans. Ultimately the settlers disappeared, and the fate of this "Lost Colony" has never been determined. The English did not colonize successfully in North America until the founding of Jamestown in 1607.

Roanoke Island England's first attempt to establish a colony in North America was at Roanoke Island in 1585.

CHAPTER REVIEW, PREHISTORY TO 1590

SUMMARY

- When Europeans made contact with Native American and West African cultures in the fifteenth century, they found many diverse, complex societies with sophisticated political and social systems and extensive trade networks.
- The arrival of Portuguese traders in West Africa triggered the development of the Atlantic slave trade, to which Africa would lose more than 10 million people over the course of four centuries.
- Seeking a trade route to Asia, Christopher Columbus landed in the Americas in 1492, opening the New World to European conquest and settlement.
- In the wake of the Spanish conquest of America, approximately 90 percent of the Native American population died as a result of disease, war, and exploitative working conditions.
- By 1590, the Spanish Empire extended from South America through the West Indies and Mexico, providing a model for later colonizers, who also sought wealth and power.
- In the mid-sixteenth century, Britain, France, and Holland began to challenge Spanish dominance in America. Like Spain, these nations sought to expand their national power, exploit native labor, establish new trade routes, and spread Christianity.

IDENTIFICATIONS

Maya
Aztecs
Prince Henry of Portugal
Songhai
Atlantic slave trade
Christopher Columbus
Treaty of Tordesillas
Hernán Cortés
Bartolomé de las Casas
sovereignty
viceroy
mercantilism
royal fifth
Martin Luther
Protestant Reformation
John Calvin
predestination
Elizabeth I
Francis Drake
Roanoke Island

MAKING CONNECTIONS: LOOKING AHEAD

Spain's empire in America and Portugal's Atlantic slave trade established models of exploitation for other European nations. In Chapter 2 we examine how England, France, and the United Provinces (Netherlands) joined the contest for American colonies.

1. What impelled the English, French, and Dutch to become colonizers?
2. What was the significance of England's defeat of the Spanish Armada in 1588?
3. Why do you think the English emulated so much of the Spanish pattern of colonization despite their religious animosity and war?

RECOMMENDED READINGS

Cook, Noble David. *Born to Die: Disease and New World Conquest, 1492–1650* (1998). Demonstrates the significance of disease in the European conquest of Native American peoples.

Davidson, Basil. *The Search for Africa: History, Culture, Politics* (1994). A readable history by a veteran historian of the continent.

Dixon, E. James. *Bones, Boats, and Bison: Archeology and the First Colonization of Western North America* (1999). Clear review of archaeological evidence of the first Americans.

Elliott, J. H. *Empires of the Atlantic World: Britain and Spain in America, 1492–1830* (2006). The first section of this book explores similarities in the settlements of New Spain and Jamestown.

Fagan, Brian M. *Ancient North America: The Archeology of a Continent*, 4th ed. (2005). Informative synthesis of the archaeology of North America, updated to include new discoveries in the Americas and Asia.

Klein, Herbert S. *The Atlantic Slave Trade* (1999). Surveys the growing literature about the international slave trade.

Klooster, Wim, and Padula, Alfred, eds. *The Atlantic World: Essays on Slavery, Migration and Imagination* (2005). Insightful essays by major historians in the field provide an accessible volume on development of the Atlantic world between 1500 and 1800.

Nash, Gary B. *Red, White, and Black: The Peoples of Early North America*, 4th ed. (2002). An excellent introduction to the meeting of cultures in the New World.

Schwartz, Stuart B. *Victors and Vanquished: Spanish and Nahua Views of the Conquest of Mexico* (2000). A very good collection of documentary sources on Mexican society and the Spanish invasion.

Weber, David J. *The Spanish Frontier in North America* (1992). The best synthesis on Spanish exploration and colonization north of Mexico.

CourseMate Go to the CourseMate website at www.cengagebrain.com for additional study tools and review materials for this chapter.

2

Colonization of North America

1590–1675

MAKING CONNECTIONS

LOOKING BACK

Chapter 1 examined the cultures of the people of North and South America, Africa, and Europe at the time Europeans began exploring and colonizing other parts of the world. The chapter considered the impetus for exploration and its initial consequences. Before starting Chapter 2, you should be able to answer the following questions:

1. In what ways were the cultures of Native Americans, Africans, and Europeans similar?
2. In what ways were their cultures different?
3. What were the positive and negative results of interactions among these three groups?
4. Why did the Portuguese and Spanish explore the globe?
5. What was the process by which the Spanish took control of Central and South America?

In 1590, the only permanent European settlement in what is now the United States was St. Augustine, the struggling Spanish town in Florida that the English privateer Francis Drake had burned four years earlier. Spain was much more concerned with its silver mines and West Indies plantations than in colonizing along the Atlantic coast, yet it wanted to prevent intrusion by other nations, for good reason. Although Spain expanded in Florida and New Mexico in the 1600s, the English defeat of the Spanish Armada and the Dutch surge in overseas trade eroded Spanish control of the New World. France, England, the Netherlands, and Sweden all established colonies in North America by 1638, prospering from the West Indies sugar boom, Canadian fur trade, and Chesapeake tobacco. In addition, New England offered a haven for Puritan dissenters. Unlike the Spanish, England's colonization proceeded with little regulation from the Crown, resulting in a variety of social, economic, and political structures.

For Native Americans from New Mexico to Canada, European colonization was a disaster. Colonial farms destroyed Indian hunting lands, altering the ecological balance of plants and animals. Although many Native Americans resisted the European invasions, disease seriously undermined their power. The fur trade also changed the cultural values of many Indians, drawing them into Atlantic commerce and weakening traditional ways.

❖ The Spanish in North America

Native Americans killed the Franciscans

To strengthen Spain's hold on North America, in 1581, the viceroy of New Spain gave **Franciscan priests** permission to establish missions among the Pueblo Indians of the Rio Grande Valley. The friars named the area San Felipe del Nuevo México. The missionaries described the Pueblos as friendly, but by the time a party arrived in 1582 to escort the Franciscans back to Mexico, the missionaries had been killed by the Native Americans.

Franciscan priests Members of the Roman Catholic order of Saint Francis of Assisi; they served as missionaries in colonial Spanish America.

Settlement of New Mexico

Despite this setback, the Spanish remained interested in the region. Conquistadores needed permission from the Crown to invade new lands, however, for the king had issued Orders for New Discoveries (1573), which more strictly regulated colonization, in part to protect Native Americans from the atrocities Bartolomé de las Casas had described decades before. In 1595, the viceroy authorized **Juan de Oñate** to undertake an expedition with his own funds. Oñate, a native of Mexico, inherited great wealth and obtained even more by marrying Isabel Tolosa Cortés Moctezuma, a descendant of both Cortés and the Aztec emperor. The expedition proved expensive as delays increased costs. Finally, in 1598, 129 soldiers, their families, servants, and slaves, ten Franciscan missionaries, and seven thousand livestock headed north. Oñate expected his investment to yield an empire that would extend from the Atlantic to the Pacific.

Oñate, Juan de (1549?–1624?) Spanish explorer and conquistador who claimed New Mexico for Spain in 1598 and served as its governor until he was removed on charges of cruelty in 1607.

Upon arrival in New Mexico, Oñate declared Spanish sovereignty over Pueblo lands. In a ritual complete with trumpets and high mass, he promised peace and prosperity to those who cooperated. The Spanish asserted that the Pueblos

CHAPTER TIMELINE 1600 1615 1630 1645 1660 1675

POLITICS AND DIPLOMACY

- 1598–1600 Spanish expedition into New Mexico
- 1605 French establish Port Royal
- 1619 Virginia assembly is formed
- 1637 Pequot War
- 1660 Charles II of England becomes king

SOCIETY AND CULTURE

- 1616–1618 Plague epidemic in New England
- 1637 Anne Hutchinson tried for heresy
- 1649 Maryland's act of toleration
- 1663 John Eliot's Bible in Massachusetts language

ECONOMICS AND TECHNOLOGY

- c. 1619 Africans arrive in Virginia
- 1621 Dutch West India Company founded
- 1651 First English Navigation Act
- 1672 Royal African Company founded

Ácoma Town located in New Mexico on a mesa west of the Rio Grande. When the Pueblos defended Ácoma in 1598, the Spanish killed many people, took the survivors prisoner, and destroyed the town.

acquiesced "of their own accord." The Franciscans founded missions in the largest pueblos and supervised construction of a church in the Tewa pueblo, Yungé, which the Spanish designated as their capital, San Gabriel. For some months, the Spanish and the Indians coexisted without serious incident. But soon the Indians tired of providing food, which they had intended as gifts but the Spanish considered tribute. The soldiers resorted to murder and rape to obtain supplies. The crisis came in December 1598 when a Spanish troop demanded provisions from the people of **Ácoma,** a pueblo high atop a mesa west of the Rio Grande. The Pueblos refused to give flour to the soldiers and killed eleven men when the soldiers attempted to take the food by force. Oñate moved swiftly, his small army laying siege to Ácoma with several cannons, as native men and women defended the town with arrows and stones. The Spanish leveled the town, killed approximately five hundred men and three hundred women and children, and took the survivors prisoner. Each man over age twenty-five had one foot cut off. The Ácomas would not rebuild their town until the late 1640s.

It would prove a temporary victory for Oñate. Another pueblo town resisted the following year, and colonists began to complain of food shortages and the governor's mismanagement; meanwhile, the Franciscans charged that Oñate's cruelty to the Indians made conversion difficult. Oñate was removed as governor, tried, and found guilty of mistreating the Native Americans and some of his settlers. He was banished from New Mexico but sailed to Spain, where he received a knighthood. After his departure, New Mexico became a royal province. Pedro de Peralta, the next governor, established a new capital at Santa Fe in 1610. As late as 1670, only twenty-eight hundred Spanish colonists inhabited the Rio Grande Valley, scattered on farms and ranches along the river.

(Jupiterimages)

Mission at Ácoma. The Mission San Estevan del Rey at the Pueblo Ácoma is an example of architecture in colonial New Mexico built by Native Americans. Constructing the mission required hauling the materials up the steep slope of the mesa, which rises nearly 400 feet above the valley.

Spanish Missions in New Mexico and Florida

The Franciscan missionaries, who assumed a major role in colonizing the Spanish borderlands, were members of the Catholic religious order that Francis Bernardone of Assisi had founded in Italy in 1209. Unlike other religious brotherhoods, which remained in seclusion, the Franciscans operated in the world among ordinary Christians. The Orders for New Discoveries of 1573 gave primary responsibility to the friars for "pacifying" the Indians of New Mexico and Florida. The friars initially offered gifts of food, metal tools, beads, and clothing. During the first part of the seventeenth century, many Pueblos seemed to accept the Franciscans' message, and agreed to build convents and churches. In New Mexico, the Spanish had started more than fifty churches by 1629; in Florida, missions extended west from St. Augustine to the Gulf Coast and north into Georgia (or Guale, as the region was called).

The Native Americans who came under Spanish control in theory could choose whether to accept Christian baptism, but they recognized that soldiers supported the priests. The Franciscans expected the natives to learn the catechism and enough of the Castilian (Spanish) language to communicate and to adopt European dress, food, and farming methods. Many Indians embraced Catholicism, but in doing so, they modified the religion, blending it with native practices. With the "Lady in Blue," they created a religious tradition that both the Indians and Spanish accepted. In the 1620s, Plains Indians reported that a nun appeared to them, telling them in their language to become Christians. Although the woman remained invisible to the missionaries, on a trip to Spain, one priest discovered that a Franciscan nun, María de Jesús de Agreda, claimed to have made flights to America with the help of angels. Her claims and the Indians' visions together created the resilient legend of the Lady in Blue.

❖ The English Invade Virginia

New Mexico and Florida remained marginal outposts in the Spanish empire. Spain's control was tenuous because its military forces were small and its cultural influence was weak. After the defeat of the Spanish Armada, Philip II's government could not keep other European nations out of North America. During the first decade of the seventeenth century, the English, French, and Dutch sent expeditions to fish, search for a northern passage to the East, trade for furs, and establish colonies.

English Context of Colonization

Seventeenth-century England was an intensely hierarchical society in which the king claimed divine right, or God-given authority, and the nobility and gentry dominated Parliament. But it was a society undergoing turmoil and change. Elizabeth I's successor was her cousin, James I, who governed from 1603 until 1625, followed by his son, Charles I. Both James and Charles had strife-torn reigns marked by power struggles with Parliament, culminating in Charles's loss of the English Civil War and his beheading in 1649.

Parliament was composed of two houses: the House of Lords, made up of nobles and high church officials, and the House of Commons, whose representatives from the counties and boroughs were elected by male landowners, an estimated 15 to 30 percent of all Englishmen. By imposing levies without Parliament's consent, James I and Charles I challenged Parliament's prerogative to approve or reject new taxes. For their part, the legislators tried to whittle away at royal powers. The fundamental issue concerning the balance of power between the king and Parliament remained unsettled until the Glorious Revolution of 1688 (see Chapter 3).

Economic developments loosened English society, giving individuals greater opportunity to change from one social class or occupation to another. As the woolen industry expanded, landowners sought to raise more sheep, sparking the **enclosure movement:** landlords ended leases for tenant farmers living on their lands, confiscating common fields that peasant communities had shared for generations. In 1500, peasants farmed 70 percent of arable land in England; by 1650, they farmed only 50 percent. Thus, many tenants were forced from the land. Some went to London, where the population expanded from 55,000 in 1520 to 475,000 in 1670. Others signed up as colonists for America.

enclosure movement Economic process in which English landlords ended leases for tenant farmers living on their lands, confiscating common fields that peasant communities had shared for grazing their livestock and raising crops.

For merchants, a developing economy spelled opportunity. Investors formed **joint-stock companies** to explore trade routes and establish new markets. The companies obtained capital by selling stocks. These investments were risky, because shareholders were liable for all company debts. The stocks could also be immensely profitable, as in the case of Francis Drake's circumnavigation of the globe, which brought a 4,600 percent profit from silver and gold captured from Spanish ships. Joint-stock companies provided capital for the first permanent English colonies in America. Unlike the Spanish monarchy, the English Crown had little role in funding, or even governing, its first New World settlements. In 1606, James I granted a charter to the **Virginia Company** with rights to settle colonies in North America. The Virginia Company had two groups—one in London and the other in Plymouth, in the west of England—that were awarded overlapping claims along the eastern coast of North America. Either could settle in the overlapping area, but initial colonies had to be at least a hundred miles apart.

joint-stock companies Formed to explore trade routes and establish new markets, the companies obtained capital by selling shares of stock.

Virginia Company In 1606 King James I chartered the Virginia Company; one group was centered in London and founded Jamestown, a second group from Plymouth in western England founded the Plymouth colony.

Jamestown and Virginia

Jamestown First permanent English settlement in America (1607), it was located on the James River in Virginia.

Powhatan (1550–1618) Algonquian leader who founded the Powhatan confederacy and maintained peaceful relations with English colonists after the marriage of his daughter Pocahontas to John Rolfe (1614).

Opechancanough (1545?–1644?) Brother of Powhatan. In the 1620s Opechancanough organized a military offensive against English settlers.

In 1607, the Virginia Company of London funded the first permanent English colony at **Jamestown.** The initial 104 settlers arrived in May 1607 after an exhausting winter crossing. The native inhabitants watched them select a site on the James River, chosen for safety from Spanish attack, but next to malarial swamps. The Native Americans called their territory Tsenacommacah, or "densely inhabited land." They were Algonquian-speaking Indians; most belonged to a confederacy that **Powhatan,** head of the Pamunkey tribe, had forged in eastern Virginia. Before the arrival of the English, the chief unifying force among the bands of the Powhatan confederacy was the threat from powerful enemies, the Manahoacs and the Monacans, who controlled lands to the west. One of Powhatan's brothers was **Opechancanough,** described as having "large Stature, noble Presence, and extraordinary Parts" and being "perfectly skill'd in the Art of Governing." Historical evidence suggests that Opechancanough had spent time in Spain and was well prepared with knowledge of Europeans when the Jamestown settlers arrived.

The English colony's first decade was a struggle. The company ran Virginia as a business enterprise, keeping control of government, land, and trade. Settlers were company employees, not landholders. To satisfy investors, the company instructed the colonists to search for gold and silver mines, find a passage to Asia, and establish industries and trade that would offer handsome returns. Among the first Jamestown settlers were many gentleman adventurers, who by definition avoided manual labor. Not one of the settlers described himself as a farmer.

Smith, John (1580–1631) English colonist, explorer, and writer. His maps and accounts of his explorations in Virginia and New England were invaluable to later explorers and colonists.

When the colonists failed to locate mines or a passage to the East, their lives became aimless. Rather than plant crops or even hunt and fish, they expected the company and neighboring Indians to provide food. When sufficient provisions failed to arrive, the settlers starved. One of the leaders, a young officer named **John Smith,** took control in 1608, stabilizing the colony briefly by making everyone work. When criticism of his strict discipline reached company officials the next year, they removed him from command. During the particularly bitter winter of 1609–1610, some of the colonists dug up graves to eat the corpses. By spring 1610, only sixty colonists remained of at least six hundred who had come to Jamestown in three years, the majority dying of starvation and disease.

In 1609, the Virginia Company hoped to salvage its investment by exploiting the land. To recruit farmers, the company offered each emigrant one share of stock and a parcel of land after seven years of service. Still, the Jamestown settlers

(Ira Block/National Geographic Image Collection)

James Fort Wall, Jamestown, Virginia. Archaeologists working to retrieve evidence from the site of the first permanent English settlement.

refused to work. When Sir Thomas Dale arrived as governor in May 1611, he found nothing but a few gardens planted and the inhabitants at "their daily and usual work, bowling in the streets." He established his Laws Divine, Morall and Martiall, which were mostly martial. For the first offense of failing to work regular hours, an idler was tied neck to heels all night. The punishment for a second offense was whipping, and for a third offense, death. Although the required hours of work were reasonable, the punishments specified in **Dale's Laws** became a scandal in England, discouraging prospective emigrants. In the words of John Smith, "No man will go from [England] to have less liberty there."

Dale's Laws (1611) Governor Thomas Dale of Jamestown in 1611 established his "Laws Divine, Morall and Martiall" to bring the colony under control. The harsh punishments became a scandal in England and discouraged emigration.

During the early years at Jamestown, the English seemed irrational in their dealings with the Native Americans. To many colonists, the natives were barbarians. Some settlers did attempt to trade for food, but others burned Indian villages and crops. In 1608–1609, Captain John Smith tried to force the sachems to provide food. The Indians had spared his life several times; nevertheless, he kidnapped two men, obligating Opechancanough to beg for their release. Next, he entered the Pamunkey village with soldiers demanding food, which the Indians refused to give, and again he humiliated the tall sachem, forcing him to comply or be killed in front of his men. Opechancanough probably never forgot this scene. Between 1609 and 1614, full-scale war existed between the Virginia colonists and the Powhatan confederacy. Eventually the English, with reinforcements from the Virginia Company, defeated Powhatan, taking control of the James River.

In contrast to Spain, the English Crown failed to take responsibility for protecting any rights of Native Americans. When colonists had sufficient power, they enslaved Indians, sending them away from their homelands to prevent escape. The English justified expropriation of native lands with the belief that the king of England, as the Christian monarch, received sovereignty over North America from God. Thus, the Virginia Company obtained rights to land from the Crown, not the Indians. Another basis for taking native territory was the legal concept of ***vacuum domicilium***, which meant that lands not occupied could be taken. Even when the English purchased land from the Indians, their contrasting concepts of ownership caused grave misunderstanding. Whereas the colonists believed in private property, the natives thought they were selling the rights to use lands for hunting, fishing, and communal farming. They expected to continue using the territory they had "sold" for these purposes.

vacuum domicilium English legal doctrine meaning that lands not occupied could be taken. It served as a basis for taking Native American territory.

Tobacco and Slave Labor

Demand for land became paramount in Virginia after 1617, when the colonists discovered tobacco as a staple crop. Though James I called smoking "a custom loathsome to the eye, hateful to the nose, harmful to the brain, dangerous to the lungs, and in the black stinking fumes thereof, nearest resembling the horrible stygian smoke of the pit that is bottomless," the habit soon consumed England. The mercantilist advantages were clear. With production in Virginia, the English could acquire tobacco from its own colony and generate an industry to process the leaves. Tobacco became the first staple crop in England's colonial mercantilist system, followed by sugar, after 1640, in the West Indies.

In 1619, the Virginia Company updated the land policy, granting "headrights" of one hundred acres of land to those who came before 1616 and fifty acres to those who came after. Virginia settlers fell into two categories: freeholders who paid for their own transportation, and servants whose way the Virginia Company or someone else financed. Recipients of headrights did not pay for the land, but owed quitrents, annual payments to the company, of one shilling per year for each fifty acres. Also in 1619, the Virginia Company relaxed its hold on the government of Virginia by establishing an assembly of elected delegates. The governor,

Doing History Online

Life in Virginia

Go to the CourseMate website for this chapter and link to Primary Sources. Examine Documents 2, 3, and 4. How do these items relate to one another? What do they reveal about life in Virginia during the first years of English settlement?

www.cengagebrain.com

who was appointed by the company, retained the right to veto all laws, and the Virginia Company adopted English common law to replace the martial law under which the colony had operated. Although these reforms gave settlers a greater stake in society, the cultivation of tobacco ensured Virginia's ultimate success. During the 1620s, tobacco drew high prices—as much as three shillings per pound. Virginia became the first North American boom town: between 1617 and 1623, approximately five thousand new immigrants arrived. Yet the Virginia Company still failed to show a profit.

Initially, English servants provided most of Virginia's labor, but the colony's planters needed as much labor as they could afford to strike it rich from tobacco, so they also purchased Africans. Though some Africans became servants with terms shorter than lifetime bondage, others probably were slaves. Little is known of their status during the early decades. In 1625, twenty-three of the twelve hundred Virginia colonists were Africans. In 1660, about nine hundred blacks and twenty-four thousand Europeans lived in the Chesapeake Bay area.

Until the 1660s, conditions for Africans were dynamic. Some Virginia blacks achieved freedom and married, and a few acquired land and enjoyed legal property rights. Even so, most Africans remained in bondage, a practice the Virginians had adopted from the Portuguese, Spanish, and Dutch. In purchasing people from slave traders, the white colonists bought into the Atlantic slave system. Early Virginia documents distinguished consistently between white servants and blacks, always with the suggestion that Africans were subordinate. In a 1627 will, Governor Yeardley bequeathed his "goode debts, chattels, servants, negars, cattle or any other thing" to his heirs. Censuses of the 1620s also point to the lower regard for Africans: English settlers were listed with full names, whereas most Africans were enumerated simply with a first name or designated as "negar" or "Negro." Virginia also excepted blacks, but not white servants, from the obligation to bear arms.

The Colony Expands

Despite the tobacco boom, Virginia faced difficulty for many years. Because mortality remained high and settlers had few children, the population grew slowly despite immigration that averaged about a thousand people per year. Young men and women who left England to become servants in Virginia gambled with their lives to obtain land that they could not gain at home. Dysentery, typhoid fever, and malaria took their toll on new settlers who suffered a period of "seasoning" after their arrival in Virginia (see *Doing History: Reports from Early Virginia*). A 1625 census provided ample evidence of high rates of mortality and family disruption: many of the married couples were childless, in part because of high infant and childhood mortality.

Although the bankrupt Virginia Company lost its charter in 1624, immigration to the colony continued. Its economic promise helped convince the English Crown to claim it as a royal colony. By 1621, Opechancanough and a prophet named Nemattanew recognized the threat of increased immigration and the permanence of English settlement. Nemattanew inspired a nativist religious revival among the Powhatans, rejecting Christianity and European customs. Opechancanough organized a military offensive to push the English back into the sea. When several whites killed Nemattanew in 1622, Opechancanough rallied his troops, slaying one-fourth of the settlers before the colony could react. A ten-year war followed in which each side tried to annihilate the other but failed, and in 1632 both sides agreed to peace. Yet desire for new tobacco lands placed constant pressure on the Powhatans, so in 1644, Opechancanough launched another attack. After two years of war, the Powhatans submitted, and Opechancanough was

Doing History Reports from Early Virginia

In 1610, the Virginia Company published a propaganda tract, written anonymously and entitled A True Declaration of the Estate of the Colonie in Virginia, with a Confutation of Such Scandalous Reports as Have Tended to the Disgrace of So Worthy an Enterprise. *As the title makes clear, the author's purpose was to rebut the accounts of disease, hunger, and death that had reached investors and potential emigrants in England. The first document quotes from this promotional piece, detailing the economic potential of the colony. Conditions in Virginia remained dreadful for immigrants in the 1620s, however, as Richard Frethorne tells his parents at home in England. A year after the 1622 massacre by the Powhatan confederacy, the Englishman reports ongoing hostilities and the settlers' constant fear of "the Enemy."*

A True Declaration of the Estate of the Colonie in Virginia, *1610*

The Councell of Virginia . . . [received a report] that the country yieldeth abundance of wood, as Oak, Wainscot, Walnut trees, Bay trees, Ash, Sassafras, live Oak, green all the year, Cedar and Fir; . . . Masts and excellent boards of forty, fifty and sixty length, and three foot breadth, when one Fir tree is able to make the main Mast of the greatest ship in England. He avouched . . . that there are divers sorts of Minerals, especially of Iron ore, lying upon the ground for ten miles circuit; (of which we have made trial at home, that it maketh as good Iron as any is in Europe:) . . . the woods do harbor exceeding store of Beavers, Foxes and Squirrels, the waters do nourish a great increase of Otters; all which are covered with precious furs; that there are in present discovered dyes and drugs of sundry qualities; that the Oranges which have been planted did prosper in the winter, which is an infallible argument, that Lemons, sugar Canes, Almonds, Rice, Aniseed, and all other commodities which we have from [the Mediterranean trade] may be supplied to us in our own country, and by our own industry: that the corn yieldeth a treble increase more than ours; and lastly, that it is one of the goodliest countries under the sun; enterveined with five main Rivers, and promising as rich entries as any Kingdom of the earth, to whom the sun is so nearer a neighbor.

Source: Peter C. Mancall, ed., *Envisioning America* (Boston: Bedford Books, 1995), 125–126.

Richard Frethorne, a Virginia Servant, Writes Home, *1623*

Loving and kind father and mother, my most humble duty remembered to you, hoping in God of your good health, as I myself am at the making hereof. This is to let you understand that I your Child am in a most heavy Case by reason of the nature of the Country, [which] is such that it causeth much sickness, as the scurvy and the bloody flux and divers other diseases, which maketh the body very poor, and weak. And when we are sick there is nothing to Comfort us; for since I came out of the ship, I never ate anything but peas, and loblollie (that is, water gruel). As for deer or venison I never saw any since I came into this land. There is indeed some fowl, but We are not allowed to go and get it, but must Work hard both early and late. . . .

[P]eople cry out day and night, Oh that they were in England. . . . For we live in fear of the Enemy every hour, yet we have had a Combat with them on the Sunday before Shrovetide, and we took two alive and make slaves of them. But it was by policy, for we are in great danger, for our Plantation is very weak by reason of the dearth, and sickness, of our company. . . .

Good Father, do not forget me, but have mercy and pity my miserable case. I know if you did but see me you would weep to see me.

Richard Frethorne,
Martin's Hundred

Source: Susan M. Kingsbury, ed., *The Records of the Virginia Company of London*, vol. 4 (Washington, DC: U.S. Government Printing Office, 1935), 58–62.

QUESTIONS for REFLECTION

1. What kinds of economic enterprises did the Virginia Company emphasize in the 1610 tract? Did these prove successful in the colony?
2. What were the main problems that Frethorne describes in his letter?
3. With such different assessments of the situation in Virginia, should we believe one account more than the other? Why?

captured and murdered by a guard. The 1646 treaty required the Native Americans to live on lands north of the York River and, to symbolize their subordination, pay an annual tribute of twenty beaver skins.

❖ Fishing, Furs, and Settlements in the North

While settlers and Native Americans struggled for Virginia, European adventurers explored and colonized the region to the north. By 1600, groups of fishermen monopolized specific waters, such as the French who caught walrus in the Gulf of St. Lawrence. The beaver furs that Europeans obtained from Native Americans became popular in Europe for making felt hats, exciting merchants in France, the Netherlands, and England to seek more permanent arrangements. All three nations claimed the northern territories as their own, ignoring the Indians' prior ownership.

Champlain, Samuel de (1567–1635) Founder of New France (now Canada), with a temporary base at Port Royal on the Bay of Fundy in 1605 and the main settlement at Quebec on the St. Lawrence River in 1608.

Dutch West India Company Chartered in 1621 by the Dutch government to establish commerce and colonies in America. It received broad powers, including the rights to make war and sign treaties.

New France

In North America, French traders focused on furs. When a French ship sent to North America in 1582 returned with a cargo of furs earning a 1,500 percent profit, merchants enthusiastically organized more voyages. In 1608, **Samuel de Champlain** established a base at Quebec, which means "the place where the river narrows" in Algonquian, an ideal location for controlling the Canadian interior (see Map 2.1).

For two decades, Champlain strengthened trading ties with the Micmac and Algonquin Indians and made new alliances with several groups: the Montagnais, who lived in the region north of the St. Lawrence River; and the Hurons, who were Iroquoian and lived north of Lake Ontario. Their location enabled the Hurons to link French outposts with the interior, the source of the most valuable furs. In 1609, to demonstrate allegiance to his allies, Champlain helped them fight a group of Iroquois from what is now New York, thus making the Five Nations enemies of New France. He also explored the watershed of the St. Lawrence River and lands as far west as Lake Huron.

(The Granger Collection, New York)

Indians of New France, 1701. A pen-and-ink drawing, c. 1701, attributed to Charles Becard de Granville.

In 1627, Quebec was still essentially a trading post with about a hundred French inhabitants, including a few women. The company received a charter for territory from the Arctic Circle to Florida and from the Atlantic to the Pacific, with a monopoly on the fur trade. The company also sent Jesuit priests, who established missions in Indian villages and learned their languages, looking for similarities between the two cultures in an effort to make the Indians part of French society. But by 1663 just three thousand French settlers lived in the colony. The Crown revoked the company's charter, making New France a royal province. From the beginning, the government refused to allow Protestants, the most likely immigrants, to settle there; it wanted to maintain control of the society through the Catholic Church. Further, New France developed under feudal land tenure, in which wealthy lords received large manors, or seigniories, along the St. Lawrence River. Ordinary settlers on these manors became tenants rather than independent farmers. Lacking the opportunity to improve their status in the New World, French peasants were reluctant to make the dangerous transatlantic voyage.

The fur trade and small population made French relations with the Native Americans different from those of New Spain and Virginia. Rather than driving trading partners from the land or exploiting their labor, the French found that the most efficient way to obtain furs was to offer desirable products from

Europe, including textiles, guns, metal tools, pots, and alcohol. One French priest reported that, at least for a while, the Montagnais thought they were getting the better deal: "I heard my [Indian] host say one day . . . showing me a beautiful knife, 'The English have no sense; they give us twenty knives like this for one Beaver skin.'" Nevertheless, the French arrival had tragic effects for the Indians of Canada, who succumbed to disease in large numbers. The demand for furs altered cultural attitudes and intensified hostility among Indian nations. In keeping with their religion, Indians had taken only what they needed from nature; with the fur trade, natives killed animals just for their furs and in numbers far greater than before. As a result, the balance of nature that the Native Americans had maintained was broken.

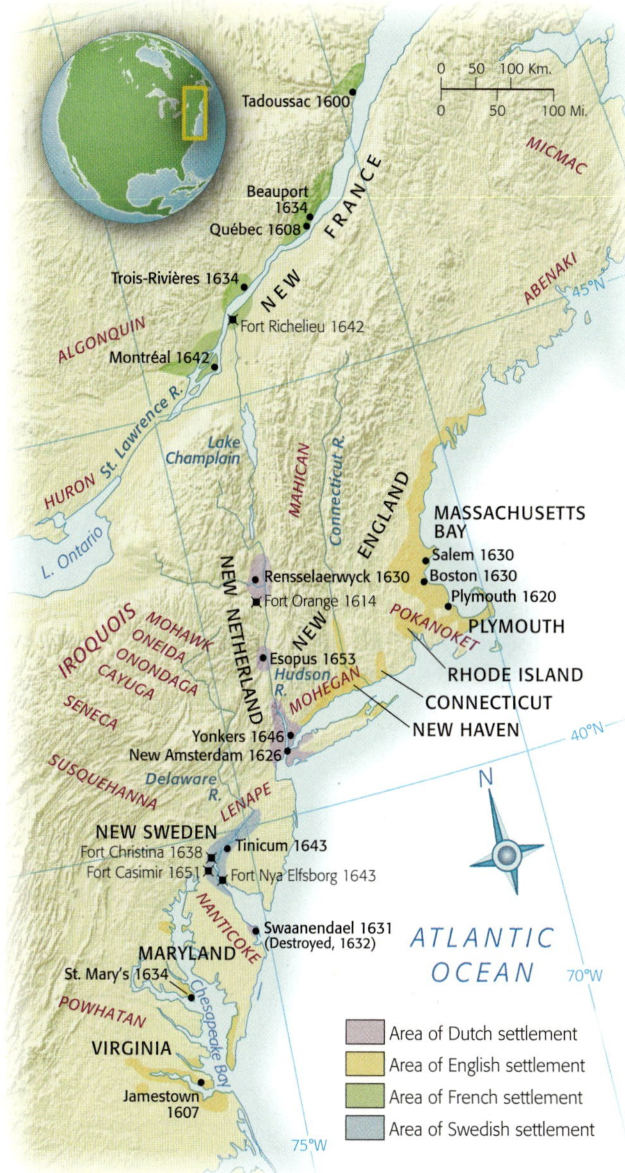

MAP 2.1

Eastern North America, 1650

By the mid-seventeenth century, northern European nations had established colonies along the Atlantic coast from French Quebec and Montreal in the St. Lawrence Valley to the English settlements on Chesapeake Bay. Although at this date all of the colonies were relatively small, New England and the Chesapeake were expanding agricultural societies, while the French, Dutch, and Swedes concentrated on trade.

New Netherland

In the first decade of the seventeenth century, the Dutch too challenged the dominance of Spain in the New World. The seven northern United Provinces had declared independence from Spain in 1581 and remained at war until 1609, when they signed a twelve-year truce. With its expiration, the war resumed and continued as part of the Thirty Years' War, which ended in 1648 with the Treaty of Münster, recognizing Dutch independence.

Despite this ongoing struggle, Dutch commerce flourished. In 1602, merchants formed the United East India Company, which six years later had 160 ships around the globe. In 1609, the company sent out Henry Hudson, an Englishman, to search for the long-sought northwest passage through North America. He sailed up the river that later bore his name, in what is now New York State, trading for furs with the Native Americans. The pelts brought a good return in Holland, so the company dispatched traders, who set up a post near the present site of Albany. In 1621, the Dutch government chartered another group, the **Dutch West India Company,** to establish commerce and colonies in America. Like the East India Company, it received broad powers, including the rights to make war and sign treaties. During the seventeenth century, the Dutch muscled their way to control a large part of international commerce, including the Atlantic slave trade and routes to Asia.

In 1624, working for the Dutch West India Company, Cornelius Jacobsen May founded New Netherland to provide a base for trade in the Hudson River region. The first colonists were mostly Protestant refugees from the Spanish Netherlands. They established their primary settlement, called New Amsterdam, on Manhattan Island, and maintained trading posts at Fort Orange (near what is now Albany) and on the Delaware and Connecticut rivers. As in Jamestown, the first settlers were employees of the company who received no land of their own. The company paid for their transportation, tools, livestock, and two years' worth of supplies, assigning them company land on which to farm. The government consisted of appointed company officers headed by a director-general, or

(New York Public Library/Art Resource, NY)

New Amsterdam in 1643. This view of New Amsterdam suggests a bustling trading port with two successful Dutch inhabitants. At the bottom behind the woman are four African laborers who reflect the growth of slavery in the city.

governor, with wide powers. The colonists could not elect an assembly or any of their officials.

With good soil, the lucrative fur trade, and lumbering, the colony prospered economically, though its population grew slowly. People of many nationalities and religions arrived to take advantage of the Dutch policy of religious freedom, but few Dutch could be convinced to emigrate. In 1629, the company attempted to spur population growth by offering huge manors, called patroonships, to any member of the company who transported fifty persons to work his land. On the Hudson River, each patroonship extended for miles along one or both banks. Similar to New France, the settlers were tenants of the manor. This arrangement actually discouraged immigration because the manors tied up large tracts that might otherwise go to small farmers.

At first, New Netherland had good relations with the Indians because the colony grew slowly and depended on the fur trade. But in the region surrounding New Amsterdam, relations began to deteriorate around 1638. As with the English, the Dutch and natives had different conceptions of landownership. Although the Indians understood that they had sold rights to share the land and intended to continue using it themselves, the Dutch believed they had bought exclusive rights. Beginning in 1640, the Dutch and Indians of the lower Hudson Valley fought a series of damaging wars that ended only in 1664, when the English took control of New Netherland and made peace with the Native Americans.

❖ Religious Exiles from England

While the colonizers of Virginia, New France, and New Netherland had primarily economic motives, the English founders of Plymouth, Massachusetts Bay, and Maryland sought places where they could practice their religion free from persecution and at the same time earn a decent living. Seventeenth-century England was rife with religious controversy. The government required attendance at Anglican worship; dissenters who refused to obey could be imprisoned and fined. Roman Catholics could also be punished if they refused to take the oath of supremacy to the king, which denied the authority of the pope. The search for freedom of worship became a major impetus for crossing the Atlantic.

By 1603, when James I took the throne, two strains of English Calvinism, or **Puritanism,** had developed. One group included the Separatists, or Pilgrims, who founded the Plymouth colony in 1620; the others, known as Puritans, established the Massachusetts Bay colony ten years later. Both groups charged that the Anglican church needed to be "purified" of its rituals, vestments, statues, and hierarchy. The Separatists started their own congregations, abandoning all hope that the church could be reformed. The Pilgrims' decision to begin a colony in America was the ultimate expression of this separatism. The Puritans hoped to reform the Church of England from within. Their purpose in founding Massachusetts Bay was to develop a moral government that they hoped the people of England would someday make their own.

Puritanism Radical strain of English Protestantism that demanded purification of the Anglican church, including elimination of rituals, vestments, statues, and bishops.

The Plymouth Colony

The Pilgrims were a small band who had originated in Scrooby, England, where they established a separate congregation. In 1607, when some were jailed as nonconformists, they decided to leave England for the Netherlands, but were unhappy there, so they made an agreement with a group of London merchants who obtained a patent for land from the Virginia Company. In exchange for funding to go to America, the Pilgrims promised to send back fish, furs, and lumber for seven years. In September 1620, the *Mayflower* departed Plymouth, England, crowded with 102 passengers, about 20 crew members, and assorted pigs, chickens, and goats. Headed for Virginia, the ship reached Cape Cod on November 9. In shallow waters, fearing shipwreck, the exhausted travelers built their colony at **Plymouth.** They were outside the jurisdiction of the Virginia Company and therefore lacked a legal basis for governing themselves or claiming land. The group avoided turmoil by drafting and signing the **Mayflower Compact,** a social compact by which they agreed to form a government and obey its laws. The London merchants eventually obtained title to the land.

The settlers' first years at Plymouth were difficult, though they found unused supplies of corn left by Indians struck down by epidemic disease and chose the site of a deserted Patuxet village with relatively clear fields. Over the first winter they built houses, but half of the colonists died of illness and exposure to the cold. In the spring of 1621, they planted corn with the help of **Squanto,** perhaps the lone surviving Patuxet, and other crops. Squanto and neighboring Pokanokets helped the Plymouth colony despite earlier problems with Englishmen. At harvest in 1621, the Indians and colonists celebrated together for three days. Soon after their feast, the ship *Fortune* arrived with thirty-five new settlers, for whom no food was available until the next year's crop. After the colonists filled the *Fortune* with furs and lumber in hopes of starting to repay their debt to the London merchants, the French captured the ship.

By 1623, though, the Plymouth colony was well established and growing as new immigrants arrived. The community solved the problem of food supply by assigning individual plots to families. In 1626 the London merchants agreed to sell the land to the colonists for a large sum, which they paid by 1645, receiving a patent of ownership. Although Plymouth's economic fortunes improved, the colony remained small and self-consciously separate from the larger group of English dissenters who streamed into New England.

Plymouth Colony established by the English Pilgrims, or Separatists, in 1620. The Separatists were Puritans who abandoned hope that the Anglican church could be reformed. Plymouth became part of Massachusetts in 1691.

Mayflower Compact (1620) When the *Mayflower* reached Cape Cod and the colonists decided to settle there, they lacked the legal basis to establish a government. Thus, the adult males of the colony signed a mutual agreement for ordering their society, later referred to as the Mayflower Compact.

Squanto (d. 1622) Patuxet Indian who helped the Plymouth colonists develop agricultural techniques and served as an interpreter between the colonists and the Wampanoags.

Massachusetts Bay

The Puritan migration to Massachusetts Bay was much larger and more tightly organized than the Plymouth settlement. During 1630, the first year, seven hundred women, men, and children arrived in eleven ships. Though at least two hundred died during the first winter, the colony grew quickly from the influx of about twelve thousand people to Massachusetts during the 1630s. From King Charles I, the Massachusetts Bay Company obtained a charter specifying its government and the colony's boundaries. When most of the company officials emigrated, taking the charter with them, they greatly strengthened the colony's independence from the Crown and the Anglican church.

Thus, the Massachusetts Bay colonists did not answer to London merchants who expected handsome profits. The Puritans themselves financed colonization; they included wealthy investors as well as many middling families who could pay their own way. As a result, the founders devoted much of their energy to creating a model society. In the words of leader John Winthrop, the colony would be "as a City upon a Hill, the Eyes of all people are uppon us . . . wee shall be made a story and a byword through the world." The Puritans believed that they had a covenant with God that bound them to create a moral community. As Calvinists, they held that individuals were saved from eternal damnation by faith rather than by good works. Men and women could seek to avoid sin and work hard throughout their lives, but unless they were among God's chosen, or the "elect," they would go to hell. They thought that if they maintained a moral society, the Lord would help it prosper.

Margaret Gibbs, 1670. Painted by an unknown artist, this portrait depicts the seven-year-old daughter of Robert and Elizabeth Gibbs. Her elaborate clothing reflected the family's wealth.

In Massachusetts, the Puritans restructured the company government to create their version of a godly commonwealth. According to the Massachusetts Bay charter, the company officials were a governor, deputy governor, and executive board of eighteen "assistants," to be elected by "freemen" (stockholders) who would meet in a general assembly called the General Court. These officers could make laws and regulations, appoint lower officials, grant lands, and punish lawbreakers. The colony's leaders changed the rules to allow all male church members (the male elect), not just stockholders in the company, to become freemen. In theory, every freeman would be a member of the General Court, or colonial legislature. But as the population grew and towns formed quickly, freemen voted in town meetings for representatives to the assembly.

With the governor and assistants, the General Court drew up a law code for the colony, which after several revisions was published as the *Laws and Liberties of Massachusetts* (1648). The code was a combination of biblical law, English common law, and statutes tailored specifically to colonial needs. It protected the liberties of individuals by upholding trial by jury and due process of law, including the rights of the accused to receive a prompt public trial and call witnesses. It also prohibited feudal tenure of lands and outlawed slavery, "unlesse it be lawfull captives, taken in just warrs, and such strangers as willingly sell themselves or are solde to us." This provision limited the possibility that whites would be enslaved but had little effect on black bondage.

The Puritans attempted to create a government operated according to God's will, as determined by the colony's leaders. The Puritan government was composed of members of the elect; ministers advised the magistrates but could not serve officially. The government required all inhabitants to attend Puritan churches. Persons who disagreed with orthodox doctrines could be expelled, whipped, fined, and even executed. The church was the center of each town, with all property owners paying taxes for its support. Unlike the Jamestown settlers, a large proportion of Puritan immigrants came in families.

Doing History Online

Plan for a Massachusetts Town, 1636

Go to the CourseMate website for this chapter and link to Primary Sources. According to Document 14, what issues were the settlers of Springfield most concerned about at the time of its founding? How do these issues compare to the concerns of the early Virginia settlers?

www.cengagebrain.com

New England Society

The Puritan notion of an ideal community defined the ways in which the Puritans acted toward one another and toward outsiders. If the model society were to succeed, everyone had to have a place in the family, church, and commonwealth. Like other English, the Puritans kept a hierarchical social order. In the family, the husband was superior to the wife, but together they ruled the children and servants. In the church, the minister and elders dominated the congregation. In the community or commonwealth, the officials led the people. Ideally this hierarchy required little coercion: people saw themselves as part of the community and worked for the common good, or "weal" (hence "commonwealth"), rather than for their own benefit. They understood that all humans were equal spiritually but accepted social inequality as the will of God.

Most Puritan women accepted a subordinate place in their society without complaint. They viewed themselves as part of a community and a family, with duties determined by their sex and age, not as individuals with rights equal to those of men. Women raised children; kept the house and garden; preserved fruits and vegetables; made beer, cider, cheese, and butter; tended livestock and poultry; spun and wove cloth; sewed clothing; cared for the sick; and supervised the training of daughters and servants. Women often conducted trade among themselves, separate from the commercial networks of their husbands. Men had responsibility for raising grain, cutting firewood, and maintaining the fences, buildings, and fields. Only men could vote in church and town meetings, serve as government officials, or become ministers. Puritans recognized women's ability in public matters, but expected them normally to confine themselves to accepted women's tasks. The role of Puritan women in the church, where they were expected to keep quiet, was indicative of their place in society. On the one hand, women were the spiritual equals of men and were held responsible for the religious education of their children. On the other hand, the Puritans emphasized the inheritance of Eve, who, they believed, had led Adam to sin in the Garden of Eden.

In this patriarchal society, children deferred to their fathers, assuming a subservient role until they were able to establish households of their own. Though some New England colonists held servants and a few owned enslaved Africans, sons and daughters were the majority of the workforce. Families on average had five children who reached adulthood; persons who survived childhood diseases often lived past age sixty or even seventy. Thus, eldest sons could be middle aged before their fathers died and willed them control of the family homestead. Younger sons, who had little hope of receiving the farm, often moved away from their parents, settling in the new towns that developed throughout New England. Parents usually attempted to give all of their children a start in life, with a farm, apprenticeship, money, or college tuition to sons and personal property or cash to daughters.

Connecticut and Rhode Island

Connecticut was an early destination of people looking for good land. The first Puritans went there to trade with Native Americans, but when news of attractive land in the Connecticut Valley arrived in Massachusetts, many settlers decided to move; a group of Puritan noblemen founded Connecticut in 1636. Lacking a charter from the king, the founders agreed on the Fundamental Orders of Connecticut, which created a General Assembly of representatives from each town. In most respects, the Connecticut government resembled that of Massachusetts, with the exception that freemen, or voters, did not have to be church members. The assembly elected a governor, who could serve only one year at a time, and a group of magistrates who functioned as the upper house of the assembly. As in Massachusetts, Puritanism was the only recognized religion and received tax support.

As white settlement expanded, relations between the Puritans and Native Americans deteriorated. Like other English, the Puritans believed that the Indians worshipped the devil and had barbarous customs. They presented a dual threat because their customs could corrupt the holy commonwealth and because they resented their loss of lands. The 1637 war against the Pequots of eastern Connecticut showed the lengths to which the New England settlers would go to eliminate the Indian threat. The Pequots, a powerful tribe, attempted to unite New England Indians against the English. In May 1637, troops from Massachusetts and Connecticut, with their Indian allies, the Narragansetts, attacked a Pequot village on the Mystic River before dawn, killing hundreds of sleeping women, children, and old men. The Pequots who escaped this massacre, mostly young men absent from the town, were later executed or enslaved. The Treaty of Hartford (1638) declared their nation dissolved.

The founding of Rhode Island resulted from another kind of emigration from Massachusetts, that of people who refused to submit to the Puritan magistrates. The first was **Roger Williams**, an independent-minded minister who had studied divinity at Cambridge University, where he became a vocal Separatist. In 1631, he immigrated to Massachusetts Bay, where he accused the government of holding fraudulent title to its territory because the king had no authority to give away Indian lands. The Puritan officials ordered him to be quiet; he refused, soon attacking the laws requiring church attendance and tax support of Puritan churches. Williams believed that government would pollute the church, not that giving legal preference to one religion was unfair. When the General Court banished Williams from Massachusetts for challenging the government in 1636, he went south to Narragansett Bay. There he purchased land from the Narragansett Indians, establishing Providence Plantation at the Great Salt River. With the sympathizers who joined him, he created a society based on religious toleration, separation of church and state, and participation in government by all male property owners.

Williams, Roger (1603–1683) English cleric in America who was expelled from Massachusetts for his criticism of Puritan policies. He founded Providence Plantation (1636), a community based on religious freedom, and obtained a charter for Rhode Island in 1644.

Another exile from Massachusetts was **Anne Hutchinson**, who in 1634 arrived in Boston with her husband, merchant William Hutchinson, and children. Hutchinson became convinced that Bostonians placed too much emphasis on good works and not enough on faith. She was a follower of one of Boston's ministers, the influential John Cotton, who stressed the importance of the individual's relationship with God over the obligation to obey laws. To the orthodox Puritan faction led by Governor John Winthrop, Hutchinson was a threat for several reasons. She emphasized individual judgment over communal authority, thus questioning the rule of colonial leaders. She told the Puritan patriarchs that God spoke to her directly, so she did not need the assistance of ministers in interpreting God's will. Furthermore, Hutchinson went outside the accepted role of women by taking a public stand on religion. In 1637, Winthrop's government put Hutchinson on trial for defaming ministers and exiled her from the colony. With her family and supporters, she founded a colony at Portsmouth on Narragansett Bay.

Hutchinson, Anne (1591–1643) English-born American colonist and religious leader who was banished from Boston (1637) for her religious beliefs, which included an emphasis on an individual's direct communication with God.

Following the settlement of Williams and Hutchinson on Narragansett Bay, several other dissenters established colonies there. The 1644 Rhode Island charter granted by Parliament united four settlements under one representative assembly, which could pass statutes consistent with the laws of England. The Rhode Island colonists based their government on Williams's principles of freedom of worship, separation of church and state, and wide participation in government.

The Proprietary Colony of Maryland

In 1632, Charles I granted a charter for Maryland to George Calvert, the first Lord Baltimore, who had served in high office until he converted to Catholicism. Although Calvert was forced to resign, he remained a royal favorite and requested a grant in America to build a haven for Catholics. He also expected to support his family by selling the land. He died before actually obtaining the charter, so his son, Cecilius Calvert, the second Lord Baltimore, became lord proprietor of Maryland. The colony was carved out of the northern part of Virginia. Calvert received ownership of the soil and was sovereign in government, subject only to the king. The proprietor planned a feudal system in which manorial lords received large tracts depending on the number of tenants they transported. For example, a person who brought five laborers to Maryland at a total cost of £20 received a manor of two thousand acres.

The colony grew slowly. Mortality was high and immigration sluggish. By 1642, Calvert had granted rights for only sixteen manors, mostly to wealthy Catholic friends. To improve his income, Calvert distributed farms to less wealthy immigrants, who had to pay annual quitrents. During the seventeenth century, rich investors acquired sixty manors, but by far most settlers were small landowners. This extension of landownership beyond Calvert's circle of loyal supporters created problems. Under the charter, Calvert was obligated to call together an assembly of freemen, or landowners, to enact laws, but they disagreed over who ought to draft laws. By 1638 a compromise was reached, and the colony finally had a legal basis for governing and punishing crime.

But the struggle for power between the proprietor and freemen continued. The ordinary planters, who formed the majority of freemen and were mostly Protestant, resented the power of the Catholic elite and had little sympathy for Calvert's vision of a society in which all Christians could worship freely. Religious and political strife became most acute in Maryland during the English Civil War and the Puritan Commonwealth, from 1642 to 1660.

The Impact of the English Civil War

Over two decades, the English Civil War transformed the political situation in England. The war resulted from a contest for power between Parliament and Charles I, who imprisoned opponents without due process and launched a crusade to force all his subjects, even those in Presbyterian Scotland and Catholic Ireland, to conform to the Anglican church. In 1642, war broke out between the "Cavaliers," or royalists, and the "Roundheads," or parliamentary forces, of whom many were Puritans. Oliver Cromwell led the Roundheads to victory in 1648; the following year they beheaded the king.

The revolutionaries attempted to rule through an elected Parliament, but conflicting factions of Puritans and radical sects undermined their plans. Some radical theorists wanted an entire restructuring of society, calling for extension of the vote to all men and redistribution of land. The gentry and wealthy merchants who had led Parliament to victory utterly rejected these ideas. In 1653 they named Cromwell the Lord Protector of the Commonwealth of England, Scotland, and Ireland. He ruled alone, backed by the army, until his death in 1658. An attempt failed to make his son Richard the successor, and two years later, the monarchy was restored. The accession of Charles II did not mean a complete reversal to the time of his father, however. The king confirmed Parliament's right to approve taxes and abolished the royal courts that had punished opponents of the Crown. But the Restoration brought the Cavaliers back into power, making the Anglican church the state religion once again.

The struggle for power during the English Civil War and its aftermath had repercussions in the colonies. Initially the rebellion of English Puritans against the king raised hopes among New Englanders that English society would be reformed. Of more practical importance to the colonies was the lack of English military protection. Plymouth, Massachusetts, Connecticut, and New Haven counted among their enemies the French, Dutch, Native Americans, and Rhode Island. In 1643, they formed the New England Confederation, agreeing to share the cost of war, provide soldiers in proportion to population, and make no treaties without each colony's consent. The New England Confederation was the only successful league of colonies in English North America before the Revolutionary War. In assuming power to conduct war and make treaties, it went beyond colonial rights. The English government, in the midst of civil war, was too preoccupied to react.

In the Chesapeake colonies of Virginia and Maryland, the English Civil War and its aftermath were more disruptive. In 1652, the English Commonwealth removed the royalist Virginia governor, William Berkeley, because he had proclaimed Charles II the king upon his father's execution. In Maryland, the parliamentary revolt weakened the position of Lord Baltimore, whose authority came directly from the king. Protestants, especially Puritans, opposed Lord Baltimore, even though he had encouraged them to migrate from Virginia, where they had suffered Governor Berkeley's persecution. Calvert had approved the Act Concerning Religion (1649), which guaranteed freedom of religion to all Christians, but he faced a political challenge from Maryland Puritans, who sought to establish a commonwealth. Calvert appealed to Oliver Cromwell, who confirmed his proprietorship, but Lord Baltimore regained control of the colony only in 1657, after a period of local civil war.

❖ English Colonization After 1660

The accession of Charles II in 1660 initiated a new phase of colonization, in which the English government paid more attention to its colonies than it had before the civil war. In 1662, the Crown granted Connecticut a charter, and the following year it confirmed the charter Rhode Island had received from Parliament. To tighten colonial administration, the king and Parliament approved a series of navigation acts that formed the basis of a mercantilist colonial policy.

Navigation Acts

The English Commonwealth, recognizing the growing economic value of the colonies, had passed the Navigation Act of 1651. The law required that goods brought to England or its colonies from Asia, Africa, or America be carried on English ships (including those of English colonies). Goods from European nations had to be transported on either English ships or those of the country of origin. The chief purposes of the act were to encourage growth of England's merchant marine and challenge Dutch trade. The Commonwealth went further between 1652 and 1654, with the first Anglo-Dutch War, by attacking Dutch vessels in the English Channel and North Sea.

The Navigation Acts of 1660, 1663, and 1673 confirmed the 1651 restrictions on transport and created a list of "enumerated articles"—major colonial products including tobacco, sugar, indigo, cotton, ginger, and dyewoods—that could be shipped only to England or another English colony. The colonists could not sell these goods directly to other nations. The "articles" first went to England, where they were taxed and reexported by English merchants, who benefited from the business. Conversely, with some exceptions, goods shipped from other nations to the English colonies had to go to England first. The colonists came to resent the charges English middlemen added to products going in both directions. The English government created a colonial administration to enforce the acts, but the results were complicated and inefficient, and smuggling continued.

The Carolinas

Charles II was penniless when he ascended the throne and owed substantial debts to his supporters. Expansion of the colonial empire permitted him to repay these creditors and at the same time advance England's commerce and national power. Carolina became the first post-Restoration colony on the North American mainland after England obtained Spain's concession of lands north of present-day Charleston with the Treaty of Madrid (1670). Anthony Ashley Cooper, Governor William Berkeley of Virginia, and John Colleton, a West Indies planter, became proprietors of Carolina, along with five other associates. They obtained a charter like Maryland's and received wide latitude in matters of religion. They drew up the Fundamental Constitutions of Carolina, creating a complicated feudal society with nobles and lords, a scheme the ordinary settlers of Carolina refused to accept.

Two colonies developed in Carolina. Small planters from Virginia built the first, which later became North Carolina. As early as 1653, people had settled on the shores of Albemarle Sound, where they raised tobacco, corn, and livestock. The Albemarle settlement, which remained poor, was a haven for pirates and difficult to govern. In 1691, the Carolina proprietors effectively established North Carolina by appointing a separate governor. In 1670, Anthony Ashley Cooper organized the second Carolina colony at Charles Town. Many of its early settlers came from the West Indies island of Barbados, which had run out of vacant land. The Barbadian planters had money to develop plantations in South Carolina and brought African slaves to do the work. The proprietors offered generous acreages to household heads for each person brought to the colony. From the colony's founding, a large proportion of South Carolinians were African slaves. They produced food, livestock, firewood, and barrel staves for Barbados.

New York and New Jersey

To control eastern North America, the English next had to seize New Netherland: they attacked in 1664 on several grounds, including John Cabot's 1497 voyage to the region and Dutch illegal trade with English colonies. James, the duke of York, Lord High Admiral of the Navy, urged his brother, Charles II, to send a fleet. The king granted James a proprietary charter for lands between the Connecticut and Delaware rivers, as well as Long Island, Nantucket, Martha's Vineyard, and part of present-day Maine. The charter gave the duke wide governmental powers, even dispensing with an assembly, and allowed James to force out the Dutch. After the second Anglo-Dutch War (1665–1667), James assumed ownership and called his colony New York, but granted the land between the

Delaware and lower Hudson rivers to John Lord Berkeley and Sir George Carteret, who named the area New Jersey.

Despite his extensive powers, James realized that he had to make New York attractive to inhabitants. He gave residents the choice of keeping their Dutch citizenship or becoming naturalized as English subjects. In 1665, he issued a legal code, called the Duke's Laws, which guaranteed freedom of religion, recognized preexisting titles to land, and allowed New Englanders on Long Island to form town governments. The New York government consisted of a governor and council appointed by the duke but no legislature.

When England and the Netherlands continued their rivalry in the third Anglo-Dutch War (1672–1674), the Dutch easily recaptured New York. After sixteen months, they returned the colony to England as part of the Treaty of Westminster (1674). Receiving a new charter, James resumed possession of New York and reconfirmed his grants to New Jersey, which had been divided into two colonies. Carteret held East New Jersey, while Berkeley sold West New Jersey to a Quaker, Edward Byllinge, who then transferred title to a group of coreligionists, including William Penn. Penn's colony would contribute to the growing diversity of English colonies in North America.

CHAPTER REVIEW, 1590–1675

SUMMARY

- British, French, and Dutch expansion ended Spanish dominance of North America during the seventeenth century. Spain retained landholdings in Central and South America and the borderland territories of New Mexico and Florida.
- The nature of interactions between white colonizers and Native Americans depended on colonizers' goals, the number of white settlers, and European attitudes toward native peoples.
- Contact between Native Americans and Europeans inevitably caused the devastating spread of epidemic disease among Native American populations.
- Many English settlers were drawn to the colonies by the prospect of economic opportunity and religious freedom. New England became a refuge for religious dissidents, in particular, the Puritans.
- Drawn to the New World primarily by economic considerations, many French and Dutch settlers became involved in the fur trade. Whereas French relations with neighboring Native Americans were relatively amicable, Dutch interactions were frequently violent.
- The 1660 restoration of Charles II to the British throne resulted in the founding of the Carolinas and a series of wars between the British and the Dutch over the territory of New Netherland.

IDENTIFICATIONS

Franciscan priests
Juan de Oñate
Ácoma
enclosure movement
joint-stock companies
Virginia Company
Jamestown
Powhatan
Opechancanough
John Smith
Dale's Laws
vacuum domicilium
Samuel de Champlain
Dutch West India Company
Puritanism
Plymouth
Mayflower Compact
Squanto
Roger Williams
Anne Hutchinson

MAKING CONNECTIONS: LOOKING AHEAD

After 1660, with restoration of the English monarchy, the government began tightening administration of the colonies. This included enforcement of the Navigation Acts, which restricted colonial trade. Chapter 3 considers internal conflicts and wars that the colonists faced as their societies matured and as they participated more fully in the expanding empire. Also significant after 1675 was the shift to enslaved African labor in the southern colonies.

1. Why did the English Crown expand the Navigation Act, which the Commonwealth initiated in 1651?
2. What changes did the English government make in colonial administration after 1675?
3. What was the importance of the African slave trade to colonial development in North America?

RECOMMENDED READINGS

Anderson, Virginia DeJohn. *Creatures of Empire: How Domestic Animals Transformed Early America* (2004). Demonstrates the significance of livestock in English settlement and conflict with Native Americans.

Armitage, David, and Braddick, Michael J., eds. *The British Atlantic World, 1500–1800* (2002). Collection of essays that support the Atlantic World model in studying the English colonization of North America.

Berlin, Ira. *Many Thousands Gone: The First Two Centuries of Slavery in North America* (1998). An important synthesis of stages in the rise of slavery in the British colonies and Louisiana.

Greene, Jack P. *Pursuits of Happiness: The Social Development of Early Modern British Colonies and the Formation of American Culture* (1988). Provides a useful framework for understanding the various ways in which British settlements evolved.

Kupperman, Karen Ordahl. *Indians and English: Facing Off in Early America* (2000). A perceptive analysis of the complexity of encounters between Native Americans and Europeans during the early seventeenth century.

Mancall, Peter C., ed. *The Atlantic World and Virginia, 1550–1624* (2007). A collection of eighteen essays that provide context for Jamestown's founding by focusing on developments in America, Africa, and Europe.

Mancall, Peter C., and Merrell, James H., eds. *American Encounters: Natives and Newcomers from European Contact to Indian Removal, 1500–1850* (2000). A collection of path-breaking articles.

Merwick, Donna. *The Shame and the Sorrow: Dutch-Amerindian Encounters in New Netherland* (2006). Examines the conflict between the Dutch settlers of Manhattan Island and their Algonquian neighbors.

Morgan, Edmund S. *American Slavery, American Freedom: The Ordeal of Colonial Virginia* (1975). A detailed, stimulating account of English settlement and the transition to slavery.

Ulrich, Laurel Thatcher. *Good Wives: Image and Reality in the Lives of Women in Northern New England, 1650–1750* (1982). A thoughtful study of the various roles of colonial women.

CourseMate Go to the CourseMate website at www.cengagebrain.com for additional study tools and review materials for this chapter.

3

Crisis and Change

1675–1720

MAKING CONNECTIONS

LOOKING BACK

Chapter 2 discussed the colonization of North America by the Spanish, French, Dutch, and English during the seventeenth century. Although the colonies varied in political organization, economic development, labor, religion, and relations with Native Americans, we can also determine common patterns. Before starting Chapter 3, you should be able to answer the following questions:

1. What were the economic goals of the adventurers who founded each of the following colonies: New Mexico, Jamestown, New France, New Netherland, and Massachusetts?
2. What was the significance of religion in the development of each of these colonies?
3. How did the settlement of Rhode Island compare with the founding of Massachusetts Bay?
4. How did the English Civil War affect the colonies?
5. Why were the relations of the English with Native Americans in Virginia different from Indian–French interactions in Canada?

In February 1676, Narragansett Indians burned Lancaster, Massachusetts, killing many of the English settlers and taking others prisoner, including Mary White Rowlandson, a minister's wife, and her three children. The Narragansetts had joined the Wampanoags and other New England Algonquians to destroy the European settlements. Their leader was the Wampanoag sachem, Metacom, called King Philip by the colonists. In her account, *The Narrative of the Captivity and Restoration of Mrs. Mary Rowlandson*, Rowlandson began her captivity with hatred toward the Indians, whom she called "Barbarous Creatures." But she came to respect some as individuals and was most impressed, she wrote, that while the Algonquians had little corn, "I did not see (all the time I was among them) one Man, or Woman, or Child, die with Hunger."

King Philip's War, as the English settlers called it, was just one of the crises that afflicted colonial America in the last quarter of the seventeenth century; others included the Pueblo Revolt in Spanish New Mexico and Bacon's Rebellion in English Virginia. An unstable English government disrupted politics in the colonies when James II, a Roman Catholic, succeeded his brother King Charles II in 1685. James's attempt to make sweeping changes in both the home and colonial governments met strong resistance. The Glorious Revolution quickly ended his reign. In Massachusetts, the impact of years of political uncertainty helped spread witchcraft hysteria from Salem to other towns. From 1689 to 1713, European wars spilled into North America, fueling hostilities in Florida and Canada among Native Americans, English, French, and Spanish. As the English colonies expanded and matured, their economies and labor systems diverged, particularly with the entrenchment of slavery. Despite revolutions and wars, southern planters built successful staple crop economies, while northerners profited from trade.

❖ Rebellions and War

The wars of 1675 to 1680 in New England, Virginia, and New Mexico resulted from pressures that had been building for decades. In Massachusetts, the spread of settlement forced Native Americans to defend their homes. In Virginia, demands of former servants for good land precipitated a civil war, and in New Mexico, severe droughts deepened opposition to forced labor, impelling the Pueblos to rid themselves of Spanish overlords. After the upheavals, elites in each settlement made changes that avoided further serious revolt.

Decline of New England Orthodoxy

By 1675, Massachusetts seemed to have lost sight of the goals of its first settlers. When the Indians attacked, Puritan ministers warned the sons and daughters of the founding generation that God was punishing them for their faithlessness and sin. In fact, Puritan church membership had declined since 1650, especially among men. One problem was that the children of nonchurch members could not be baptized. In 1662, the clergy devised an alternative to full church membership, the **Halfway Covenant,** which permitted adults who had been baptized but who were not yet saved to be "halfway" members. In congregations that accepted this innovation, people could assume partial status by showing that they understood Christian principles and would strive to obey God. As unconverted

Halfway Covenant The Puritan practice whereby parents who had been baptized but had not yet experienced conversion could bring their children before the church and have them baptized.

CHAPTER TIMELINE 1680 · 1685 · 1690 · 1695 · 1700 · 1705

POLITICS AND DIPLOMACY

- 1675–1676 King Philip's War and Bacon's Rebellion
- 1688–1689 Glorious Revolution in England
- 1691–1692 Salem witchcraft hysteria
- 1693 Spanish regain control of New Mexico
- 1701 Iroquois sign treaty of neutrality

SOCIETY AND CULTURE

- 1682 Rowlandson's *Narrative*
- 1687 Newton's *Principia Mathematica*
- 1688 Beginning of antislavery protests
- 1690 Locke's *Essay Concerning Human Understanding*

ECONOMICS AND TECHNOLOGY

- 1670s Shift to slaves in Chesapeake
- 1698 Royal African Company loses monopoly
- 1700s Rice is adopted in South Carolina

members, they were not entitled to take communion, but they could have their children baptized.

The growth of competing religions in New England also proved to Puritan ministers that their model society had failed. Believing theirs to be the only true religion, Puritans rooted out dissent. After 1650, the Quakers and Baptists threatened religious unity. The Society of Friends, or **Quakers,** was a radical Protestant sect born in the turmoil of the English Civil War. Like the Puritans, they were reformers who believed that the Church of England was corrupt and should be purified of its rituals, decorations, and hierarchy. But they also claimed that the Puritans also practiced false doctrine by paying ministers to preach, relying too much on the Bible as the word of God, and retaining the sacraments of baptism and communion. The Friends believed that God communicated directly with individuals through the "Spirit" or "Light." They worshipped by gathering in plain meetinghouses to "wait upon the Lord," sitting in silence for the Spirit to inspire one or several of the congregation to communicate God's message. Ministers, who included women as well as men, regularly received inspiration to speak.

Quakers (Society of Friends) Protestant sect originating in the English Civil War that challenged the authority of the Church of England and New England Puritans.

praying towns Established by John Eliot, praying towns were villages in which the Indians were supposed to adopt English customs and learn the fundamentals of Puritan religion.

Metacom (c. 1639–1676) Wampanoag leader who waged King Philip's War (1675–1676) with New England colonists who had encroached on Native American territory.

Appalled by these Quaker teachings, Puritan leaders tried to prevent their spread by deporting the traveling missionaries. The Friends were stubborn, however, and they repeatedly returned to Massachusetts. The Puritan magistrates arrested and whipped them, and in 1658, the General Court prescribed the death penalty for Quakers who returned after banishment. The hangings of several Quaker missionaries caused consternation on both sides of the Atlantic and caused Charles II to intervene. During the decades following 1660, Puritans realized that their policy of intolerance had failed; attendance continued to decline. The Baptists, whose objection to infant baptism was their chief disagreement with orthodox Puritans, increased in numbers after approval of the Halfway Covenant, which they vehemently opposed. They believed that a church should include only the saved—indeed that only the saved should be baptized. Despite persecution, dissenters successfully formed congregations throughout New England.

(The Granger Collection, New York)

Metacom. Metacom, the Wampanoag leader, who in 1676 tried to drive the New England settlers back "into the Sea."

King Philip's War, 1675–1676

Since the massacre of the Pequots in 1637, the Puritans and Native Americans of New England had managed an uneasy peace. The colonists traded for furs with local nations and with the Mohawks, the closest nation of Iroquois in New York. Some Puritan ministers, of whom John Eliot is best known, convinced several local tribes who were greatly diminished by disease and loss of lands to dwell in **praying towns.** In these villages, adjacent to but separate from the towns of white settlers, the Indians were supposed to adopt English customs and learn the fundamentals of Puritan religion. By 1674, Eliot had organized fourteen praying towns of Native Americans who took the first steps toward giving up their traditional ways.

The unceasing expansion of white settlers into the frontier, however, destroyed the relative peace between the Algonquians and the settlers of New England. By 1675, more than fifty thousand whites inhabited the region. These settlers occupied more and more of the hunting, fishing, and agricultural lands of the Indians. Trouble began in 1671 when the Plymouth government attempted to force the Wampanoags to surrender their firearms and obtain permission to sell land. **Metacom** (or King Philip) built a league with neighboring tribes. When John Sassamon, an Indian educated at

Harvard College, informed the Plymouth government of impending attack and was murdered, the white authorities hanged three Wampanoags for the deed.

In 1675, Metacom mobilized Algonquians throughout New England, attacking fifty-two English towns (see Map 3.1). But by the end of summer 1676, with the help of the Mohawks, the colonial governments turned back the attack, as disease, hunger, and a weapons shortage weakened Metacom's troops. The Algonquians destroyed twelve towns, killed many colonists, and took others prisoner. White frontier settlement would not return to its 1675 limits for another forty years.

For the Indians of southern New England, the war was calamitous. Thousands died, and many others were enslaved. Even bands that supported the English lost autonomy. Some Indian men later fought in the colonial militia against Metacom, but when the war was over, all Native Americans in southern New England had to live in praying towns, where they worked as servants or tenant farmers for neighboring whites. Metacom was killed, his head kept on a pole in Plymouth for twenty years; his wife and son were sold as slaves.

Bacon's Rebellion (1676) Colonial revolt led by Nathaniel Bacon, in which landless freemen attacked neighboring Indians and burned Jamestown in an attempt to gain land and greater participation in the Virginia government.

War in the Chesapeake

Virginia faced a similar crisis in **Bacon's Rebellion**, which involved civil war among the English as well as Indian–white conflict. But at its root, the chief issue

MAP 3.1

New England at the Time of King Philip's War, 1675–1676

The Indians and English destroyed and damaged each other's towns throughout Plymouth, Rhode Island, and Massachusetts. The Narragansetts, who lived in Rhode Island and had assisted the Puritan governments against the Pequots in 1637, entered King Philip's War after an English army invaded their territory.

was land: How could the competing interests of landless immigrants and dispossessed natives be resolved? By 1670, approximately forty thousand colonists lived in the Chesapeake, including native-born sons and daughters of early settlers as well as more recent arrivals. Among the new immigrants were servants who expected to obtain land on completing their terms. In the 1670s, however, many Virginians discovered that the combination of low tobacco prices and high land prices blocked their dream of obtaining plantations. They received headrights, or individual rights to land, but could find no good vacant tobacco acreage to claim.

Part of the problem, these landless freemen believed, was that the Indians held too much territory. Specifically, the 1646 treaty between the Virginia government and the Powhatans designated the area north of the York River for Native Americans. This agreement had been acceptable to whites in the 1640s, but was unsatisfactory thirty years later, when white settlement was pushing north (see Map 3.2). Many freemen also recognized that wealthy planters, powerful in government, speculated in large acreages that they left empty while others starved for land. The first flames of war occurred in July 1675, when some Doeg Indians attempted to take hogs as payment for a settler's unpaid debt. After people on both sides were killed, the Susquehannocks got involved. When they attacked frontier settlements, a thousand-man army of Virginia and Maryland colonists marched against their village on the Potomac River. Vastly outnumbered, several Susquehannock sachems agreed to negotiate, but when they left their stockade, the colonists murdered them. During the winter of 1675–1676, the Susquehannocks retaliated, raising fears that King Philip's War had spread south. Discontented and vengeful colonists responded indiscriminately, killing friendly and hostile Indians alike.

MAP 3.2
Expansion in the Chesapeake Colonies, 1650–1700
The settler population of Virginia and Maryland grew slowly until the 1640s and then increased to forty thousand by 1670. The resulting competition for land contributed to the outbreak of Bacon's Rebellion. In the wake of the uprising, settlers pushed into former Indian lands north of the York River.

The landless freemen found a leader in Nathaniel Bacon, a twenty-nine-year-old wealthy councilman who evidently saw an opportunity to challenge Governor Berkeley's leadership. Bacon and his supporters demanded more land, the displacement of Indians, and a greater voice in the Virginia government. Governor Berkeley declared Bacon a traitor and sent troops to end his forays against the Indians. He also called new elections, but these brought many Bacon supporters into the Virginia assembly (the House of Burgesses). The delegates passed measures that extended suffrage to landless freemen, taxed provincial councilors, and placed limits on the terms and fees of local officials. Despite these reforms, Bacon's army burned Jamestown and virtual civil war ensued among English colonists. Few white fatalities occurred, however; rebels vented most of their frustration by killing Indians. The rebellion finally ceased with Bacon's death, probably of dysentery, in October 1676. The war marked a serious defeat for the Indians of the Chesapeake, who lost the protection of the 1646 treaty and gradually surrendered their lands.

Bacon's Rebellion awakened the Virginia elites to the dangers of a large class of landless freemen but resulted in no substantive political change. A new assembly in 1677 reversed the reform acts of the 1676 House of Burgesses, including the law extending the vote to landless freemen. Rather than create a society in which power and wealth were distributed more evenly, in which Virginia once again would offer opportunity to poor Englishmen, the planter elite began importing more enslaved Africans. Bound for life and restricted by laws, black slaves could not demand farms or a voice in government. Immigrants opted for settlement in New Jersey, Carolina, and Pennsylvania during the 1670s and 1680s, because those areas offered better options than Virginia.

Doing History Online

Royal Description of Nathaniel Bacon, c. 1676

Go to the CourseMate website for this chapter and link to Primary Sources. Read Documents 1 through 7, on Bacon's Rebellion. How persuasive is the description of Nathaniel Bacon provided in the official report? Are there reasons to doubt its accuracy?

www.cengagebrain.com

The Pueblo Revolt, 1680–1693

Across the continent in New Mexico, another uprising disrupted colonization as the Pueblos drove out the Spanish—and kept them out for thirteen years. The Pueblos, who lived along the Rio Grande (see Map 3.3), had the advantage of a

MAP 3.3

New Mexico in the Seventeenth Century

The Spanish had established their colony in 1598 by sending soldiers, their families, and Franciscan missionaries north through the Rio Grande Valley. In 1680, at the time of the Pueblo Revolt, the Spanish population remained small and centered in the capital, Santa Fe.

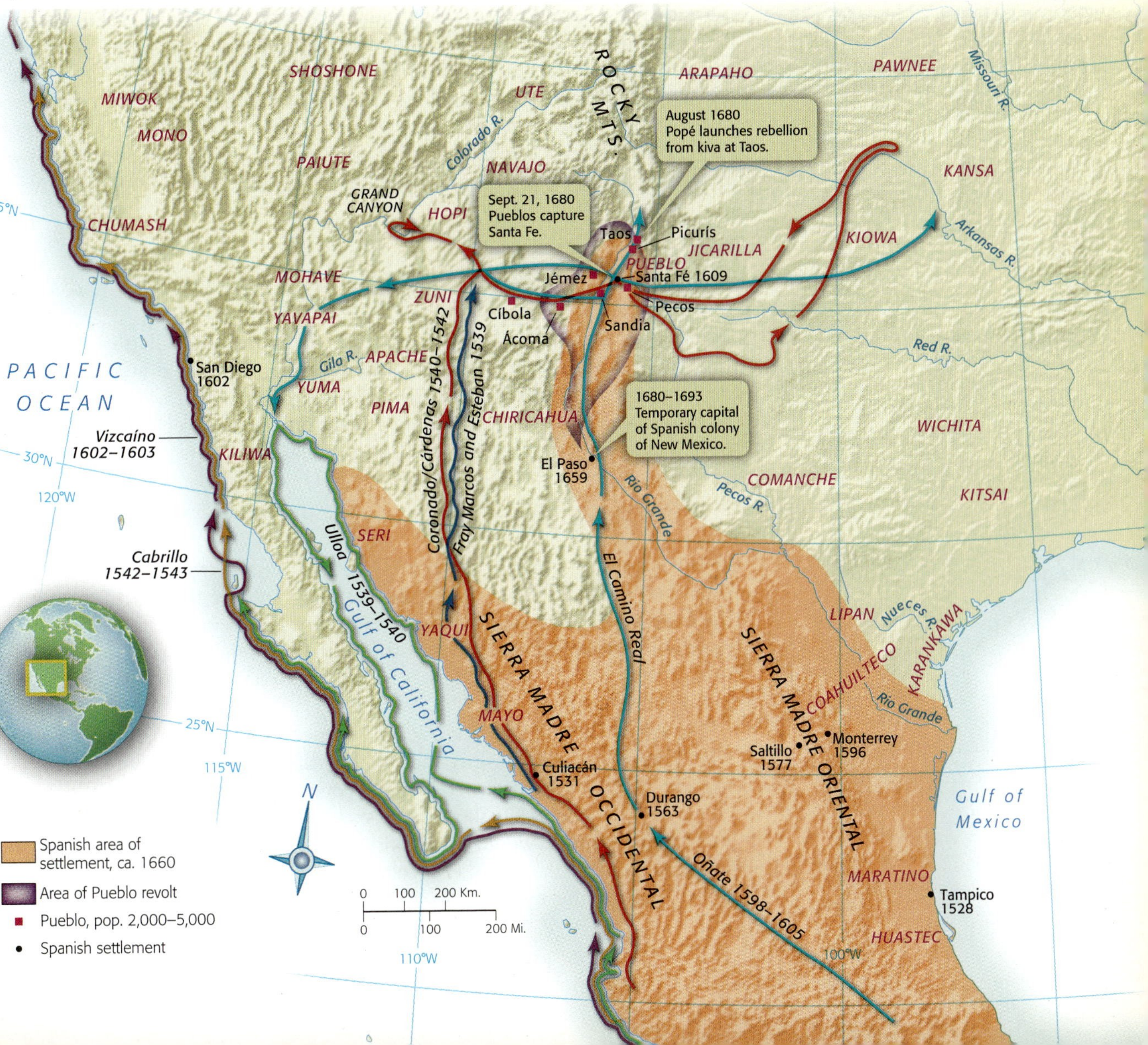

(© South West Museum, Los Angeles, CA/The Bridgeman Art Library)

Madonna. Pueblo Indian hide painting of a Christian Madonna, 1675.

Popé Leader of the successful 1680 Pueblo rebellion against Spanish colonists and priests in New Mexico.

much smaller white population in New Mexico; the Spanish hold over the missions was tenuous. Nevertheless, the Hispanic settlers and priests demanded forced labor and strict adherence to Christianity. A number of Indian towns had rebelled during the previous half-century, but the Pueblos became more distressed during the 1670s, when New Mexico endured severe drought. As famine persisted, they faced Apache and Navajo attacks and became convinced that the root of their troubles lay in their rejection of ancient gods, the katsina. To bring rain and renewed prosperity, some presented gifts to the katsina and performed dances that the Spanish had outlawed. When punished, the Indians felt even greater resentment, and they finally revolted.

The leader of the 1680 rebellion was **Popé**, a shaman of the village of San Juan, north of Santa Fe. He organized a general insurrection, sending knotted ropes to allied villages, indicating when the uprising should start. On August 10, 1680, the Pueblos launched a full-scale attack, killing four hundred colonists and twenty-one priests. When Santa Fe fell to the rebels on September 21, the whites escaped south, settling in the area of present-day Ciudad Juárez, Mexico. Some Spaniards explained the revolt as God's punishment for their sins, whereas others blamed the harsh labor and efforts to repress native religions. The Pueblos destroyed churches, broke up church bells, and burned images of Christ and the saints.

By 1692, as famine continued, the Pueblo alliance fell into disarray. The new Spanish governor of New Mexico, Don Diego de Vargas, marched north to Santa Fe with 160 troops. Though many Indians resisted, the Spanish reestablished control over the province. In December 1693, after a three-day siege, Vargas's troops took Santa Fe, killing all of the Indian men and making slaves of the women and children. The Spanish subsequently retained a foothold in New Mexico but not without further struggle; another revolt broke out in 1696. Afterwards, the Spanish and Pueblos lived together in relative peace, but only because the Hispanics eased requirements for tribute, forced labor, and adherence to Christianity.

❖ William Penn's "Holy Experiment"

Penn, William (1644–1718) English Quaker leader who obtained a charter for Pennsylvania from Charles II in exchange for a debt owed to Penn's father. Penn intended to establish a model society based on religious freedom and peaceful relations with Native Americans, in addition to benefiting financially from the sale of the land.

In England, the Quaker leader **William Penn** approached Charles II with a petition to establish a new colony in America, one that would avoid bloodshed by dealing justly with the Indians. Although the Pueblos had not yet driven out the Spanish, Penn knew of King Philip's War and Bacon's Rebellion. He was determined to do things differently in Pennsylvania.

Plans for Pennsylvania

In 1681, the king approved Penn's request for a charter for Pennsylvania. The new proprietor received the right to enact laws and impose taxes with the consent of the freemen but was required to submit all laws for approval to the home government. And to protect the status of the Church of England, the charter stipulated that twenty Anglican inhabitants could request a minister from the bishop of London.

In establishing Pennsylvania, Penn hoped to provide a haven for Quakers, who faced persecution in England because they would not pay tithes for church support or attend Anglican services. He conceived of his colony as a "holy experiment," a place where Quakers could exercise their beliefs without interference and the government would operate like a Quaker meeting, acting in unison as it followed God's will. A Quaker ideal was to live according to the doctrine that all were equal in the eyes of God; thus, they rejected certain customs, such as

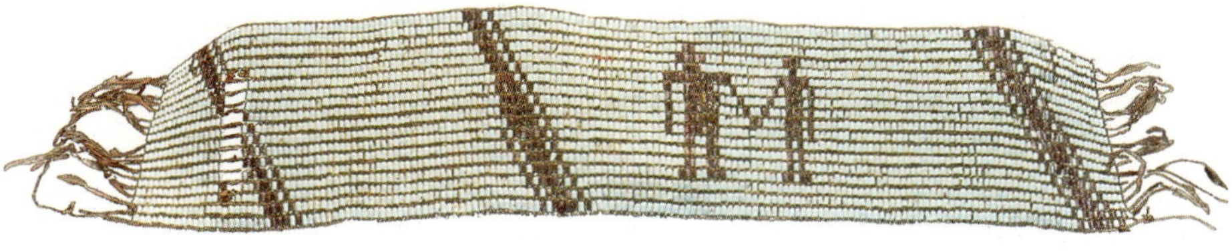

(Wampum belt, made by Lenni Lenape Indian people, Pennsylvania, American School/© Atwater Kent Museum of Philadelphia/Courtesy of Historical Society of Pennsylvania Collection/The Bridgeman Art Library)

Wampum Belt, 1682.
Wampum belt, which, according to legend, the Lenape gave to William Penn in 1682. It has become a symbol of Penn's efforts to preserve peace with the Indians of Pennsylvania.

removing one's hat in the presence of superiors. For practicing their faith, they were jailed and fined, and when they refused to pay, local English officials took their property. Following Quaker ideals, Penn also intended to pay the Lenape Indians for their land and resolve conflicts peacefully. He paid the Lenapes a much lower price than he in turn charged the settlers, however, and assumed the Indians would leave after they sold their land.

Penn intended to make a fortune from Pennsylvania, summing up his goals: "The service of God first, the honor and advantage of the king, with our own profit." He spent a great deal of time planning the colony, establishing an assembly with two houses, both elected by the freemen, defined as adult males who owned at least fifty acres of land or paid taxes on other property. During the early decades, when servants received fifty acres at the end of their term of service, nearly every man in Pennsylvania could vote. Penn did not extend that right to women or alter the common law restrictions on married women. Though female Friends took an active role in their meetings as ministers, missionaries, and supervisors of discipline, their legal status in the Quaker commonwealth was similar to that in other colonies. Penn also drew up specifications for his capital city, **Philadelphia,** conceiving the city as a large "green country town," with wide streets in a grid pattern, public parks, ample lots, and brick houses.

Philadelphia Capital of colonial Pennsylvania and Delaware River port founded by William Penn.

A Diverse Society

Penn sold land briskly: six hundred people bought seven hundred thousand acres within four years. Most of the buyers were Quaker farmers, merchants, artisans, and shopkeepers from England, though many also originated from Scotland, Ireland, Wales, Europe, the West Indies, Maryland, and New York. The settlers moved into an area inhabited by the Lenapes, who welcomed the newcomers, and by Swedes, Finns, and Dutch, who served as intermediaries with the Indians. The Lenapes, or Delawares as the colonists later called them, had conducted trade with the Dutch as early as 1610 and yielded land to the whites. By the time Penn and his thousands of colonists arrived, the Lenapes had declined significantly in size from disease. As they sold their lands, some moved to northern or western Pennsylvania, while others remained on marginal tracts in the Delaware Valley.

The European "old residents" integrated with the new arrivals, though not without friction. The Swedes, Dutch, and Finns continued to worship in their own congregations but became naturalized as English subjects; some served in the assembly and local government. The old residents made up a large part of the population in the Lower Counties (later Delaware), leading to conflict as the different interests of the Lower Counties and Pennsylvania became clear. In 1704, after two decades of wrangling, the three southern counties obtained their own separate Delaware assembly.

Pennsylvania got a boost from its late arrival on the colonial scene because its merchants could tap existing networks in the Atlantic economy. Substantial traders came from New York, the Chesapeake, and the West Indies, bringing their connections and capital to build breweries, tanneries, warehouses, wharves, and ships. Farmers found a market for wheat, livestock, and lumber in the West Indies. By 1700, Philadelphia had become a thriving port town, with seven hundred houses and more than three thousand people. But for William Penn, his colony was deeply disappointing: land sales reaped smaller profits than he had hoped, the costs of administering the colony soared, and he went seriously into debt. Although the province became prosperous and quite successful as a tolerant, diverse society, Penn reckoned it a failure.

❖ The Glorious Revolution and Its Aftermath

The founding of Pennsylvania coincided with the Crown's effort to tighten its administration of the colonies. The Privy Council at first appointed temporary committees to address colonial concerns, then in 1675 formed a permanent committee, the Lords of Trade, which met sporadically. Even after 1696, when the more formalized **Board of Trade and Plantations** was established, this lacked authority to appoint colonial officials or enforce laws. These powers belonged to a host of governmental offices, including the secretary of state, the Treasury, and the War Office.

Board of Trade and Plantations English government body established in 1696 to gather information and give advice about the colonies.

Dominion of New England

While experimenting with these committees, the Crown made other efforts to rein in the colonies, starting with the Massachusetts Bay colony. In 1678, Charles II required Massachusetts to send agents empowered to renegotiate the charter. He specifically wanted the New Englanders to comply with the Navigation Acts and apologize for having coined their own money. The colonists delayed action, though they sent regrets for having passed laws contrary to the laws of England. They offered to renounce any "except such as the repealling whereof will make us to renounce the professed cause of our first coming hither."

Impressed by neither the Puritans' arguments nor the speed of their response, the English government revoked the charter in 1684. In February 1685, before a royal governor could be appointed, Charles died, and his brother James, a Roman Catholic, became king. With the Privy Council's consent, in 1685, James combined Massachusetts, New Hampshire, and Maine under the **Dominion of New England;** he added Plymouth, Rhode Island, and Connecticut in 1686 and New York and New Jersey in 1688. Apparently James's plan for the colonies was to create two large dominions, one north of the fortieth degree of latitude (the approximate location of Philadelphia) and one to the south. These dominions would supersede colonial charters, eliminating the confusing diversity of laws and political structures. Representative government would end.

Dominion of New England In an effort to centralize the colonies and create consistent laws and political structures, James II combined Massachusetts, New Hampshire, Maine, Plymouth, Rhode Island, Connecticut, New York, and New Jersey into the Dominion of New England.

Andros, Sir Edmund (1637–1714) English colonial administrator in America whose attempt to unify the New England colonies under his governorship (1686–1689) was met by revolt.

For Massachusetts Puritans, the Dominion of New England was a disaster. James's governor-general, **Sir Edmund Andros,** made sweeping changes that undercut the Puritan notion of a covenanted community. He levied taxes without the approval of a representative assembly, restricted the power of town meetings, mandated religious toleration, and confiscated a Boston church for use by Anglicans. Andros enforced the Navigation Acts, favored his own cronies over the Puritan elite in distributing patronage, required landowners to obtain new land titles from the Crown, demanded payment of quitrents, and took control of common lands. A number of colonists who rebelled by refusing to pay taxes without a voice in their passage were jailed and fined.

Revolutions of 1689

Governor Andros managed to avoid serious revolt until the spring of 1689, when news of James's removal from the throne reached Massachusetts. The king's rule had been as heavy-handed in England as in the colonies, and Protestants feared James would make England a Catholic nation under authoritarian rule. Thus, parliamentary leaders forced him into exile in France, inviting his Protestant daughter, Mary, and her husband, William of Orange, the leader of the Dutch, to take the throne. The **Glorious Revolution**, though bloodless, had long-lasting results in England: it permanently limited the king's power by establishing parliamentary control of taxation, supremacy of law, and autonomy of the courts.

Glorious Revolution (1688) English Revolution against the authoritarian policies and Catholicism of James II. The revolution secured the dominance of Parliament over royal power.

On the morning of April 18, 1689, many of Boston's populace formed companies with the militia. Numbering more than a thousand by afternoon, the insurgents, who included several Puritan ministers and some wealthy merchants, deposed the dominion government. They interpreted the revocation of the charter and James's illegal taxation and expropriation of lands as part of a "popish plot" that Protestant New England must help destroy. With the dominion gone, Plymouth, Rhode Island, and Connecticut reactivated their charters, but Massachusetts, which had lost its charter under Charles II, had to negotiate a new one. The resulting 1691 Massachusetts charter, which annexed Plymouth to the Bay colony, established a royal province with an elected assembly and a governor appointed by the king. The charter required freedom of worship and forbade religious restrictions on voting.

Revolutions also took place in New York and Maryland in the wake of James II's loss of power. New York fell into turmoil with news of William and Mary's ascent to the throne in England and the revolt in Boston. In the city of New York, insurgents included merchants and artisans who had been denied economic privileges to trade and mill flour under James's government. In 1689, led by **Jacob Leisler**, a German-born merchant and militia captain, the insurgents forced the lieutenant governor back to England and elected a Committee of Safety to replace James's council. When Henry Sloughter, the new governor appointed by William and Mary, arrived in 1691, however, he reinstalled James's councilors and executed Leisler for treason. In Maryland, simmering resentment of Protestants against the Roman Catholic proprietor, Charles, Lord Baltimore, erupted in the summer of 1689. By July 1689, a handful of Maryland leaders, aroused by rumors that Catholics were plotting with the Indians to destroy Protestants, formed the Protestant Association. The association raised troops but defeated the proprietary government without a shot.

Leisler, Jacob (1640?–1691) German-born merchant and militia captain in New York who in 1689 led a rebellion of merchants and artisans who had been denied economic privileges to trade and mill flour under James II's government. Leisler was executed for treason when the new governor appointed by William and Mary arrived in 1691.

The three provincial revolutions of 1689, in Massachusetts, New York, and Maryland, had similarities to England's Glorious Revolution in the relative absence of bloodshed and the recurring theme of "popish plots." They failed, however, to bring about permanent change in the constitutional relationship between England and its colonies. The provincials, lacking delegates in Parliament, continued to endure taxation and mercantilist regulation without their assent. The colonial revolts of 1689 resembled Bacon's Rebellion of 1676; they too mobilized out-of-power elites against those who controlled the colonial governments.

Witchcraft in New England

When Governor William Phips arrived in Boston Harbor with the new Massachusetts charter in May 1692, he found the colony in disarray. **Witchcraft hysteria** had erupted months earlier in Salem Village, a farming community north of Boston. Since 1675, the Bay colony had faced one crisis after another: King Philip's War, loss of the charter,

Witchcraft hysteria (1691–1692) The prosecution of almost two hundred people in Salem, Massachusetts, and its environs on charges of practicing witchcraft.

(Examination of a Witch, 1853 (oil on canvas), Matteson, Tompkins Harrison (1813–84)/© Peabody Essex Museum, Salem, Massachusetts, USA/The Bridgeman Art Library)

Examination of an Accused Witch. A mid-nineteenth century painting by Tompkins Harrison Matteson depicting a physical examination of a young girl for a devil's mark, which would be considered evidence that she was a witch.

Andros's dominion, the Revolution of 1689. Accompanying this turmoil were structural changes in the society, as traditional religious authority yielded to elites whose power rested on their mercantile wealth. The Salem witch mania was a tragic holdover from a passing culture. Its fury was aggravated by the psychological reaction of traditionally minded folk to the new, more commercial, secular New England society.

Belief in witchcraft was embedded in traditional European and Anglo-American culture. The colonists believed that both God and Satan influenced everyday events. When something bad happened that they could not explain, they turned to supernatural explanations. In England, witchcraft had been a capital offense since the time of Henry VIII in the early sixteenth century; colonial governments followed suit in condemning those who gave "entertainment to Satan." During the seventeenth century, the Puritan governments charged many more men and women with witchcraft than did other English colonies: 350 New Englanders were accused between 1620 and 1725. Of these, the Salem episode accounted for almost 200.

The witchcraft cases of Salem in 1691–1692 at first resembled those in other places and times. Several girls experimented with magic, aided by a slave woman, Tituba, and her husband, John, who together baked a "witch cake" of rye meal and urine and fed it to a dog. The girls started having fits, presumably caused by witches. Apparent possession spread to other village girls, leading to the arrest of three women as witches: Tituba; a poor beggar, Sarah Good; and an ailing elderly woman, Sarah Osborne. These three alleged witches were the sort of people traditionally prosecuted for the crime. But, while the Salem craze commenced in the time-worn pattern, it soon engulfed people of all social levels. Accusations descended on prosperous church members, a minister, a wealthy shipowner, and several town officials. Hysteria spread from Salem to adjacent towns. Of those executed, fourteen women and five men were hanged on "Witches Hill" and another man was crushed to death with stones.

Governor Phips, supported by influential clergymen, had allowed the prosecutions to proceed after his arrival but put a stop to them when the accusers

Doing History Online

Salem Witchcraft

The accusations of witchcraft in Salem involved a number of social and cultural institutions for which the Massachusetts Bay colony and New England have become famous. Go to the CourseMate website for this chapter and link to Primary Sources. Read Documents 8 through 13 on the trial of Bridget Bishop. Which institutions played a role in the crisis? What role did each play?

www.cengagebrain.com

pointed to people at the highest levels of society, including his own wife, Mary. It had become clear, to many besides the governor, that the situation was out of control. After Salem, witchcraft accusations no longer assumed their earlier importance in New England society.

❖ Wars and Rivalry for North America

From 1680 to 1713, the Spanish, English, French, and many Indian nations battled for territory in North America. Despite the political and social turmoil of the 1680s and early 1690s, the English settlements were the most populous and dynamic European colonies on the continent (see Map 3.4), with more than seventy thousand settlers in New England alone. By the mid-1680s, New France had approximately ten thousand settlers, while Spanish Florida consisted of a few missions and the fortified town of St. Augustine. Despite declining populations, many Native American peoples remained powerful in eastern North America, in particular the Five Nations of the Iroquois in New York. The three primary areas of dispute on the continent were Florida and Guale (later Georgia), Louisiana and Texas, and Canada. Conflict occurred against the backdrop of two long European wars, known as King William's War and Queen Anne's War to the English colonists.

MAP 3.4
North America in 1700
Significant change had occurred in North America since the early 1600s. Along the Atlantic coast the English now had settlements from Maine (part of Massachusetts) to South Carolina. As the English population expanded, Native Americans declined, with many groups absorbed into other nations, such as the Catawbas of South Carolina.

Colonial Conflicts in the South

Beginning in 1680, the English colonists of South Carolina decided to take advantage of smoldering unrest among the mission Indians of Guale and Florida to attack the Spanish colony. The Native Americans had rebelled against forced labor and efforts to stamp out their traditional religions, killing Spanish missionaries and destroying property. The Carolinians raided Guale and Florida, capturing Native Americans to sell as slaves in the West Indies. The English also wanted to control the deerskin trade in the Southeast. By 1686, the Carolinians had thrust the missionaries out of Guale. Then in 1704, during Queen Anne's War, an army under former Carolina governor James Moore crushed the missions in Apalachee. The Carolinians obtained help from their trading partners, the Yamassees, and from many of the mission Indians. Moore's troops inflicted brutal torture, burning people alive. The surviving Apalachees dispersed, losing their identity as a nation. The Spanish retained St. Augustine and a fort they built at Pensacola in 1698, but lost control of Guale and most of Florida.

The Spanish were also threatened by French efforts to establish a colony in Louisiana. At risk, the Spanish knew, were their silver mines in Mexico and domination of the Gulf of Mexico. In 1682, René Robert Cavelier, **Sieur de La Salle**, had explored the Mississippi River from New France to the gulf, naming the territory Louisiana in honor of King Louis XIV. La Salle sailed to France, then returned to set up a colony, which quickly dissolved from disease, loss of ships, and attacks by Karankawa Indians. In 1687, La Salle's own men murdered him.

La Salle, Sieur de (1643–1687) French explorer in North America who claimed Louisiana for France (1682).

The French incursion in the Gulf of Mexico inspired the Spanish to expand their settlements in the borderlands. In 1690, they founded missions among the Caddo people of eastern Texas and western Louisiana, from whom they took the Caddo word *Tejas* or *Texas,* meaning "friends." Three years later, when the Caddos blamed the friars for bringing smallpox, the friars fled. The Spanish abandoned Texas until the French once again entered the area.

By 1700, the French and Spanish had become allies. In 1699, Pierre LeMoyne, Sieur d'Iberville, resumed the French search for the mouth of the Mississippi River, building forts at Biloxi Bay and on the Mississippi to establish French possession. Spain might have forced the French out of Louisiana with quick action, but when the grandson of French King Louis XIV took the Spanish throne, the two nations became allies against the English, Dutch, and Austrians in the War of the Spanish Succession. Although the French–Spanish alliance gave Louisiana a chance to develop without interference from New Spain, the colony grew slowly, and depended on trade with the local Natchez Indians. In 1708, about a hundred white soldiers and settlers lived in Louisiana.

Canada

Conflict developed in the north when the Iroquois confederation attacked New France to stop French fur trading in the Ohio Valley and Illinois. The Iroquois defeated New France in 1683, but war continued as the English, French, and Native Americans struggled over trade routes and territory. The outbreak of King William's War in 1689 fueled the contest, as the Five Nations attacked settlements in Canada, while the French and their Indian allies destroyed English frontier outposts from New York to Maine. Though the European belligerents agreed in the Peace of Ryswick (1697) to return to prewar status in North America, the Canadians won an important victory over the Iroquois and their English allies. The Five Nations signed a neutrality treaty in 1701. Frustrated by New York's failure to provide reinforcements, they ended their alliance with the English. New France then developed trade, religious missions, and agricultural settlements in the Great Lakes and Illinois Territory.

The renewal of hostilities between the English and French in 1702 with Queen Anne's War again brought raids on the New England frontier. In 1704, the Canadians and Native Americans attacked Deerfield, Massachusetts, burning houses and barns, killing inhabitants, and taking many captives (see *Doing History: The Deerfield Raid of 1704*). The English once again took Port Royal but called off an attack on Quebec when they lost nine hundred men in storms on the St. Lawrence River. This time, however, the peace treaty gave the victory to England (which had joined with Scotland in 1707 to form Great Britain). In North America, the **Treaty of Utrecht (1713)** ceded Nova Scotia (formerly Acadia), Newfoundland, and control of the Hudson Bay territory to the British. Yet the British had failed to oust France from North America.

Treaty of Utrecht (1713) Ending Queen Anne's War between Great Britain and France, the Treaty of Utrecht ceded control of Nova Scotia, Newfoundland, and the Hudson Bay territory to the British.

❖ The Entrenchment of Slavery in British America

Despite wars, rebellions, and witch hysteria, the most significant development in British North America during the late seventeenth and early eighteenth century was large-scale investment in enslaved Africans. Historians have long puzzled over how people who increasingly prized their own freedom deprived other human beings of liberty, and often life itself. The decisions of thousands of individual colonists to purchase men, women, and children who had been seized from their homelands in Africa left an indelible imprint on American society and culture. The slave buyers could not foretell the monumental effects of their actions. They responded to economic conditions: their need for workers, the declining availability of white servants, and the developing Atlantic slave trade.

Adopting Slavery

The English, like other Europeans, believed that hierarchies existed in human society and, indeed, all of nature. Humans were superior to animals, Christians superior to "heathens." English language and culture also differentiated sharply between white and black, with whiteness suggesting purity and goodness, whereas blackness was imbued with filth and sin. In African religion, social customs, dress, and political organization, the Europeans found serious deficiencies, just as they had found deficiencies among Native Americans. The people of sub-Saharan Africa, the English thought, were lower on the scale of humanity than they were and could justifiably be enslaved. In choosing slavery, the mainland English colonists were following the example of the Portuguese, Spanish, Dutch, and even their countrymen in the West Indies, where thousands of African slaves, outnumbering whites, toiled in sugar fields.

Colonists also viewed their investment in slaves as an economic decision. In Virginia and Maryland, planters purchased Africans because they needed large numbers of workers to grow tobacco. Chesapeake settlers had learned that Native Americans, who easily escaped enslavement and died in catastrophic numbers, would not fill their labor needs. White servants filled the gap until about 1675, when the supply of English servants began to decline in Maryland and Virginia. For example, the founding of the Carolinas, New Jersey, and Pennsylvania, where land was plentiful, gave servants a wider range of options. Chesapeake planters searching for an alternative labor supply turned to African slaves. In 1660, only nine hundred blacks resided in the Chesapeake, some of whom had come as servants and were free. By 1720, blacks composed one-fifth of the population. A similar increase occurred in the Carolinas, where 38 percent of the residents in 1720 were African slaves. The situation was different in New England, where only 2 percent of the population was enslaved, and in the middle colonies (New York, New Jersey, Pennsylvania, and Delaware), where about one resident in ten suffered perpetual bondage.

The Slave Trade

Though smugglers like John Hawkins had interloped earlier in the Spanish trade, England officially became involved in the Atlantic slave trade in 1663. Charles II granted a monopoly to supply captives to the English colonies first to the Company of Royal Adventurers, then in 1672 to the **Royal African Company.** When those two companies could not meet the demands of labor-hungry colonists, smugglers got involved, so in 1698, the Crown opened the slave trade to any English merchant who wanted to participate. As a result, the supply of Africans in the English colonies soared and slave prices declined, thus encouraging colonists to invest in even more black labor.

Royal African Company English trading company granted the monopoly from 1672 to 1698 to supply enslaved people from Africa to labor in the English colonies.

The experience of enslavement and transit across the Atlantic Ocean was dehumanizing and perilous. Probably half of those sold into slavery died while still in Africa awaiting transport or during the Atlantic passage. Approximately three-quarters of those taken to English North America came from the area of West Africa between Senegambia and the Bight of Biafra, with the remainder coming mostly from Angola. As European sea captains made successive trips to

Doing History The Deerfield Raid of 1704

During Queen Anne's War, approximately 250 Indians and French attacked Deerfield, a town on the northwestern Massachusetts frontier, killing 50 and taking 112 captives. Though it was just one of many raids in the long struggle among England, France, and Native Americans in North America, the Deerfield attack gained renown through the narratives of participants. The following are excerpts from three documents: the narrative of Stephen Williams, a ten-year-old captive of a Pennacook leader he called "master"; a report on the raid by Governor-General Philippe de Rigaud de Vaudreuil of New France; and a letter criticizing the raid by Vaudreuil's rival, Claude de Ramezay, governor of Montreal.

Stephen Williams's **Narrative,** ***c. 1707***

The French and Indians came and surprised our fort and took it. And after they had broken into our house and took us prisoners, they barbarously murdered a brother and sister of mine as they did several of our neighbors. They rifled our house and then marched away with us that were captives, and set our house and barn afire as they did the greatest part of the town. . . .

There my master took away my English shoes and gave me Indian ones in the room of them which I think were better to travel in. Then we marched 5 or 6 miles further where we took up our lodging. Then one English man ran back to Deerfield which provoked them much: they told us if any more ran away they would burn the rest. There they slew our Negro man. The next morning we traveled about 2 or 3 miles [and] then they murdered my ever-honored mother who having gone over a small river [in] which water running very swift flung her down. She being wet was not able to travel any further.

Governor-General Vaudreuil's **Report to the French Minister of the Marine,** ***April 3, 1704***

My Lord,

. . . Neutrality continues to last with the Iroquois, My Lord, and I will not be the one to break it. . . . I am making no war that could turn them against us, sparing on their behalf the inhabitants of the lands of Albany. The lands of Boston are a different story, My Lord, as I have already had the honor of informing you. The Abenakis having informed me that the English had killed some of their people the last fall and asking for my help, I sent this winter a party of 250 men, French as well and Indians, commanded by Sir De Rouville, *lieutenant reformé* who acquitted himself very

the coast, African traders had to reach farther and farther into the continent to find enough people to enslave. Some captives marched five hundred miles or more to the sea in "coffles," the term given to the files of shackled prisoners. On the coast, they were confined in enclosures and often exposed to the sun for long periods without adequate food and drink. The Europeans branded and then loaded them into ships for the voyage across the Atlantic, called the **middle passage,** which could take from three weeks to more than three months. Weather permitting, the captives spent their days on deck—the men in chains, the women and children unrestrained. At night, and around the clock in bad weather, slaves occupied spaces about the size of coffins in the hold of the ship, where temperatures could soar. Disease was often rampant. Some slaves attempted suicide by jumping overboard or refusing to eat.

middle passage Transport of slaves across the Atlantic from Africa to the Americas.

Africans also rebelled violently, attacking captains and crews and occasionally taking over ships. Because they were unfamiliar with ocean navigation, mutineers had the best hope of success when their ship was still in African waters and large numbers could carry out the revolt, escaping to shore. When rebels failed, punishment was swift and brutal. The slave trader Bosman worthily. They took 150 prisoners and did not know the number of dead. . . .

Your very humble and obedient servant,
Vaudreuil

Claude de Ramezay's Letter to the Minister of the Marine, _November 14, 1704_

My Lord,

. . . Monsieur De Vaudreuil, instead of carrying out the plan of attack that I had put together, and that I had the honor to inform you of last year of going this spring with seven or eight hundred Frenchmen and whatever Indians we could find to ravage the settlements above Boston from Salem to Piscataway, where there is reason to believe that being the masters of the countryside, we would have done much damage to the enemies of the King and we would have much glory for the nation, [and] the confidence of our mission Indians as well as the others, instead the actions he has taken which have produced exactly the opposite effect, as you will soon learn, My Lord.

Last winter Monsieur de Vaudreuil sent a detachment of forty-eight Frenchmen and about two hundred Indians who captured a small village of around forty houses, where they defeated or took prisoner about one hundred and fifty persons of all ages and of all sexes. . . . We lost in this expedition eleven French and Indians who were killed. It is impossible to imagine the cruelties carried out by the Indians on the return journey, killing about fifty-six women and children in cold blood, which discredits the French nation, seeing that it was a man named Rouville, a lieutenant reformé in our troupes, who commanded this party, to whom one can impute this cruel deed against the rights of man. They have, as we have learned, taken reprisal against Acadia, which they have practically desolated and reduced to beggary without us having made any sort of effort to help that poor fledgling colony. . . .

Your very humble, very grateful and
very obedient servant,
De Ramezay

Source: Evan Haefeli and Kevin Sweeney, eds. *Captive Histories: English, French, and Native Narratives of the 1704 Deerfield Raid* (Amherst: University of Massachusetts Press, 2006), 161–162, 80–82, 85–86.

QUESTIONS for REFLECTION

1. How did Stephen Williams describe the events at Deerfield and during his first days in captivity?
2. According to Vaudreuil, why did the French and Indians attack Deerfield?
3. What accounts for the contrasting view of de Ramezay to Vaudreuil's report on the Deerfield raid?

described an incident when a sea captain placed an extra anchor in the ship's hold. The enslaved Africans,

> unknown to any of the ship's crew, possessed themselves of a hammer, with which, in a short time they broke all their fetters in pieces upon the anchor . . . they came above deck, and fell upon our men, some of whom they grievously wounded, and would certainly have mastered the ship, if a French and English ship . . . came to our assistance with shallops and men, and drove the slaves under deck: notwithstanding which, before all was appeased, about twenty of them were killed.

Upon arrival in America, the Africans faced the ordeal of sale by auction or prearranged contract. They were stripped naked and examined for disease and physical defects. Because the greatest need was for strong field hands who would provide years of labor, plantation owners paid the highest prices for healthy young men in their prime. Buyers paid less for women, children, and older men. For both the Africans and their owners, the year following debarkation was most critical, as Africans endured serious illness and high mortality from the new disease environment.

Systems of Slavery in British North America

black codes (colonial) Laws passed by colonial assemblies to define slavery and control the black population.

As more and more Africans arrived, colonial assemblies instituted **black codes** to define slavery and control the black population. Before 1660, Maryland had officially sanctioned perpetual bondage, but Virginia moved more slowly. Enough flexibility existed in Virginia society to allow black servants to gain freedom, earn their livelihoods, and in some cases acquire land. In the 1660s, however, Virginia joined Maryland in enacting laws that recognized differences in the terms of white servants and African slaves. By law, slavery lasted a person's lifetime, descended from mother to child, and was the normal status of blacks but never whites.

In the late seventeenth and early eighteenth centuries, Virginia and Maryland created clearly articulated caste systems based on perceptions of race. Skin color denoted status: all Africans and their descendants encountered severe discrimination, whether enslaved or free. The Virginia assembly ruled that any master who killed a slave during punishment was not guilty of a felony. Conversely, no black person, slave or free, could strike a white, even in self-defense. Evolving black codes banned interracial marriage, forbade owners from releasing their slaves except in special cases, and restricted enslaved blacks from traveling without permission, marrying legally, holding property, testifying against whites, or congregating in groups. Over the course of the eighteenth century, other British colonies passed similar codes that ranged from fairly moderate New England laws to extremely harsh codes in Carolina. In the life of an African slave, these laws had force, but more direct was the power of the master over work and family. To be a slave meant that someone else possessed your body and could command your daily activities. The owner chose your job; he or she decided whether your children would stay with you or be sold.

The work Africans and native-born African Americans performed varied by region. In the Chesapeake and Carolina, most slaves spent long hours planting, weeding, and harvesting tobacco, corn, and rice. Plantation owners assigned slaves to different tasks, though most still raised the staple crop. Some men became drivers and artisans; some women served as nurses, cooks, and spinners. Both women and men performed domestic service. Agricultural production in the middle colonies and New England centered on grains and livestock, which demanded less labor than tobacco or rice, so most parts of the northern countryside had relatively few slaves. Exceptions included New York and neighboring eastern New Jersey, which had difficulty attracting European immigrants; thus, well-to-do farmers purchased large numbers of Africans to work their land. Most northern slaves lived in the port towns, where women worked as cooks and household servants and men labored at crafts, domestic service, and as shipbuilders and sailors. In New York City, blacks were about one-fifth of the population and in Boston and Philadelphia about one-tenth.

A source of comfort to slaves who had lost their African homelands and kin was to establish new families in America. Slaves achieved some autonomy from their masters by creating families and kinship networks. All knew, however, that owners could destroy loving relationships by selling away spouses, children, brothers, and sisters. The ability of blacks to form families changed over time and varied from one region to another. African American women had more children than their African mothers had, creating communities of slaves on large plantations. Whereas most of the first Africans dwelled in white households with just a few blacks, their offspring, known as "country-born" slaves, lived with parents, brothers, and sisters.

Slave Resistance and Early Abolitionists

For many slaves, family and kin helped to reduce their feelings of despair; for others, nothing relieved the pain of lifetime bondage. Many resisted their masters' power by staging slowdowns; pretending illness; destroying crops and tools;

running away; or committing violence. Before 1713, blacks in the West Indies, where their large population made success seem possible, staged seven full-scale revolts. In contrast, on mainland North America, just one slave revolt had occurred by the early 1700s, primarily because blacks were so outnumbered by whites. In New York City in 1712, about twenty slaves set fire to a building, attacking the white men who came to extinguish it. Nine whites were killed, and terror spread up and down the Atlantic coast. As in the case of later slave revolts and conspiracies, the revenge wreaked on the black community surpassed any violence the rebels had committed. In the wake of the New York revolt, thirteen slaves were hanged, three burned at the stake, one tortured, and another starved to death in chains. Six committed suicide to avoid execution.

As slavery became entrenched in North America, a few white colonists questioned its morality. They feared slave rebellions and abhorred the violence needed to enslave Africans, transport them to the colonies, and keep them in bondage. Slavery was morally repugnant, they believed, because all humans are equal in the eyes of God. Some Quakers were early opponents of the institution. According to John Hepburn of New Jersey, for example, slavery violated the Golden Rule to do unto others as you wish others to do unto you. In the context of rising importation throughout the colonies, however, the protests of Hepburn and a few other critics had little effect.

❖ Economic Development in the British Colonies

Despite differences in agriculture, labor, and commerce from one region to another, the mainland colonies were all part of the Atlantic economy, dominated by the staple crops of sugar, tobacco, and rice. The developing mercantile economies of New England and the mid-Atlantic region depended heavily on the slave system, because their chief market was providing food for the multitudes of blacks laboring on West Indies sugar plantations.

Northern Economies and Seaports

Family farms and dependence on the sea characterized New England's economy. Because agriculture failed to provide a lucrative staple crop, rural New England families raised livestock, wheat, rye, Indian corn, peas, other vegetables, and fruit. They ate most of what they produced—a fairly monotonous diet of brown bread, boiled or baked peas, boiled meat and vegetables, and dark beer or apple cider—within their families and communities.

Fishing and shipping developed as important industries during the seventeenth century. The New England fishers initially sold their catch, in return for manufactured goods such as shoes, textiles, glass, and metal products, to London merchants, who sent the fish to Spain, Portugal, and the Wine Islands, off the coast of Africa. The fishing industry spurred the growth of maritime trade, as New England merchants formed partnerships among themselves and with English merchants, encouraging a local shipbuilding industry. The New Englanders exported fish, barrels, and other wood products. They imported wine, fruit, and salt from the Wine Islands, and rum, molasses, sugar, dyes, and other goods from the Caribbean. Soon, aided by the Navigation Acts, they were the chief carriers of goods along the North American coast, exchanging enslaved Africans and rum distilled from West Indies molasses for Pennsylvania wheat and livestock, Chesapeake tobacco, North Carolina tar and turpentine, and South Carolina rice.

The economy of the middle colonies resembled New England's in a number of ways but was much more prosperous agriculturally. With plenty of good land, farmers raised wheat and livestock commercially, purchasing servants and some slaves to supplement family labor. The region had two ports: one at New York

Vue de Boston. An idealized view of Boston with laborers and British soldiers at the time of the American Revolution. Francois Xav. Habermann created such views for Europeans who were eager for information about events in North America.

City and the other at Philadelphia. Though neither city matched Boston in population or commercial importance before 1750, both quickly surpassed the Massachusetts seaport after that date. New York merchants maintained links with Amsterdam, the Dutch West Indies, and New Spain even after the English takeover in 1664. Philadelphia Quakers exploited their connections with Friends in other ports, especially in England and the West Indies.

Maritime trade encouraged the development of port cities in the British provinces, including Boston, New York, Philadelphia, and Charleston. Until 1750, merchants of Boston and other seaport towns in Massachusetts and Rhode Island dominated colonial trade. The ports thrived because they forged commercial links between farmers and external dealers, housing the markets through which imports and exports flowed. The maritime industry itself created demand for shipbuilders, suppliers of provisions, rope and sail makers, carters, dockworkers, and sailors. Sailors became an important segment of the labor force; they were a varied lot. Some went to sea only part time, to supplement the income of their farms. Others chose seafaring as a career, dividing their time between shipboard and the taverns and boardinghouses of port towns along the Atlantic coast. Some had no choice in the matter, for they were enslaved Africans whose masters purchased them to work on the ships.

Commercial growth brought social change, distinguishing an urban lifestyle from the countryside. Some merchants became fabulously wealthy from transatlantic and coastal trade. They spent their income conspicuously, building costly mansions, purchasing enslaved Africans as household servants, and wearing expensive clothes. They lived comfortably, with servants and slaves to do their menial chores. Other city dwellers were much less fortunate because they earned minimal wages or lacked employment. Seamen and artisans, dependent on overseas trade, could expect little work during the winter, when few ships sailed. City folk were also at greater risk of death than those who lived in the country: some arriving ships spread smallpox and other diseases to the dense urban populations. The towns lacked adequate sanitation facilities, so garbage and waste cluttered streets, polluting the water supply.

Sailors led a difficult and dangerous life. Crews on ordinary merchant ships were small, so seamen worked long hours loading and unloading the ship, maintaining the rigging and sails, and pumping water from the bilge, a backbreaking job. The organization of labor on board was hierarchical, with power descending from the captain, and crewmen had little hope of moving up through the ranks, for captains were generally from affluent families. When conditions on ship became insufferable, the seamen rebelled, deserted, or even turned to piracy. As pirates, they plundered merchant vessels and port towns, sharing the proceeds evenly among themselves, electing officers, and recruiting much larger crews than could be found on merchant ships. One pirate, Joseph Mansfield, admitted in 1722 that "the love of Drink and a Lazy Life" were "Stronger Motives with him than Gold."

Plantation Economies in the Chesapeake and South Carolina

From 1675 to 1720, tobacco remained king in Maryland and Virginia, and planters increasingly purchased enslaved Africans instead of white servants. The wealth of plantation owners grew with each child born to a slave mother. At the same time, the richest planters bought up the land of small farmers who found it difficult to compete with the slaveholders. The wealthiest man in early-eighteenth-century Virginia was Robert Carter of Lancaster County, called "King" Carter. A slave trader and land speculator, he parlayed his inheritance of £1,000 and a thousand acres into an estate of £10,000 in cash, three hundred thousand acres of land, and more than seven hundred slaves. Carter, with his relatives and friends, formed a tightly knit group of Chesapeake gentry.

In 1720, and throughout the rest of the century, Chesapeake society was hierarchical. At the bottom of the social structure were African and country-born slaves who owned no property and had little hope for freedom. Above them were the nonlandholding whites, perhaps 40 to 50 percent of white families, who rented land and owned a horse or two, some cows, a few pigs, tools, and some household goods, but rarely held bound servants or slaves. Often they were in debt to the local merchant-planter for needed manufactured goods, such as ammunition, fabric, shoes, and tools. Next up in the hierarchy were small landholders whose incomes allowed them to live more comfortably, with pottery, more furniture, and nicer (though still quite small) homes. In the upper 5 percent were the gentry, who owned many slaves, held large acreages, and usually acted as merchants as well. They served as intermediaries for smaller planters, selling tobacco abroad and importing manufactured goods. In this way, they became creditors of their poorer neighbors, who often owed them substantial debts. In Maryland and Virginia, the merchant-planters conducted trade without the development of port cities. Ships docked at their plantations along the many tributaries of the Chesapeake Bay to load casks of tobacco and unload imported goods. Merchant-planters and rural artisans, including slaves, provided goods and services for the community without centralizing their activities in towns. Even the two capitals, Williamsburg and Annapolis, remained small throughout the colonial period.

Situated in a semitropical climate, South Carolina developed a plantation economy that was linked to, and in many ways resembled, the West Indies. Most early settlers in South Carolina, both black and white, came from the English colony of Barbados, where land was in short supply and almost entirely devoted to sugar cultivation. White planters claimed Carolina headrights, then sold corn, salt beef, salt pork, barrel staves, firewood, and Native American slaves to the islands. South Carolinians enslaved the Indians they captured in raids throughout the American Southeast and obtained them from native traders in exchange for guns, ammunition, and cloth. Native Americans also supplied deerskins, which found a ready market in England, though they were not valued quite so highly as Canadian furs.

Despite the growth of large plantations in Virginia and Maryland between 1675 and 1720, more than one-third of white families lived in small cabins and rented rather than owned land. The men who supported Nathaniel Bacon came from this group. They rarely owned servants or slaves to help grow tobacco. They possessed some livestock and agricultural tools, but most used wooden rather than pottery dishes, and lacked bed and table linens, knives, forks, spices, and books.

Yamassees Native Americans who traded with South Carolina merchants but, after enduring fraud and other unfair practices, in 1715 with help from the Creeks waged an unsuccessful war against the colony.

As with the northern fur trade between Europeans and Indians, the Carolinians used English trade goods to establish alliances with native groups. Such major trading partners as the **Yamassees**, however, quickly discovered that white merchants used theft, violence, rum, and false weights to gain unfair advantage. In 1715, in league with the Creeks, the Yamassees attacked white settlements, nearly destroying the colony. The whites saved themselves by getting help from the Cherokees. The Yamassees and Creeks were defeated, their people killed, enslaved, or forced to migrate from the coastal area. White South Carolinians then expropriated their lands.

The settlers wanted the new territory because they had found an export that became much more lucrative than provisions, enslaved Indians, or deerskins. Planters had experimented with a variety of crops—tobacco, cotton, sugar, silk, wine grapes, and ginger—but rice proved most successful in the wet lowlands of the Carolina coast. Also significant were the skills in rice production that many Africans brought to America. Rice exports expanded rapidly in South Carolina, reaching 1.5 million pounds per year by 1710 and nearly 20 million pounds by 1730. The chief markets for rice were Europe and the West Indies. Carolinians first sent their crop directly to Portugal, but in 1705 Parliament added rice to the list of enumerated products that had to be shipped to England first, taxes paid, and then reexported to Europe. The colonists argued that in the case of southern Europe, this detour made their crop arrive too late for Lent, when much of it was consumed. In response, Parliament allowed South Carolina after 1731 to trade directly with Spain, Portugal, and Mediterranean Europe, but the larger share of the rice crop, which went to northern Europe, still required transit through Britain.

The conversion to rice transformed South Carolina society, affecting the black population with special force. Before planters adopted full-scale rice production, slaves had performed a variety of jobs in crafts, timber, livestock, and agriculture. Their workloads were moderate, especially in comparison with the West Indies. Rice monoculture changed this situation altogether, and planters imported thousands of Africans. In the coastal areas north and south of Charleston, blacks reached 70 percent of the population in the 1720s. With high importation and harsher working conditions, death rates surged. As in the Chesapeake, wealthy planters bought up neighboring farms while investing heavily in slaves. They created large rice plantations, worked by growing numbers of African slaves. Small planters moved to the periphery, where they raised grain and livestock for the rice district and the Caribbean. The rice planters found the Carolina lowlands isolated and unhealthy, so they left their plantations part of the year. However, the Carolinians supervised their plantations directly—unlike British West Indian sugar planters who fled to England, leaving management in the care of overseers.

Charleston, where the rice planters spent at least several weeks each year, was the fourth largest city in the British colonies. The port channeled the trade in provisions, deerskins, rice, slaves, and English manufactures. Charleston remained smaller than Boston, Philadelphia, and New York because British and New England shippers controlled its trade. Without a strong merchant community, the South Carolina seaport lacked the impetus for shipbuilding and associated crafts.

CHAPTER REVIEW, 1675–1720

SUMMARY

- The period between 1675 and 1720 was characterized by white expansion in North America. The French established settlements in the Great Lakes region and Louisiana, and Quaker William Penn founded the colony of Pennsylvania as a "holy experiment" in peaceful Native American–white relations.
- European expansion generated widespread Native American resistance to white encroachment and sparked armed conflicts such as King Philip's War and the Pueblo Revolt.
- The late seventeenth century was a time of great domestic turmoil; the colonies witnessed uprisings such as Bacon's Rebellion and hysteria during the Salem witch trials.
- James II's assumption of the British throne sparked resistance to royal control and, in the case of Protestant colonists, against Catholic rule.
- The institution of slavery became entrenched in colonial society as trade in enslaved people and staple crops became central to both northern and southern economies.

IDENTIFICATIONS

Halfway Covenant
Quakers (Society of Friends)
praying towns
Metacom
Bacon's Rebellion
Popé
William Penn
Philadelphia
Board of Trade and Plantations
Dominion of New England
Sir Edmund Andros
Glorious Revolution
Jacob Leisler
witchcraft hysteria
Sieur de La Salle
Treaty of Utrecht
Royal African Company
middle passage
black codes
Yamassees

MAKING CONNECTIONS: LOOKING AHEAD

Chapter 4 pursues the development of North America through the Seven Years' War, a time when the British colonies achieved greater political and economic maturity. Expansion of settlement put even greater pressure on Native Americans, and economic development entrenched slavery more firmly. Intellectual and religious trends such as the Enlightenment and Great Awakening crossed colonial boundaries, helping to create a shared American culture.

1. How did settler–Indian relations evolve after 1720?
2. How did Scots-Irish and German immigration in the eighteenth century compare with English settlement before 1700?
3. What was the impact of the Enlightenment on colonial thought and culture?

RECOMMENDED READINGS

Haefeli, Evan, and Sweeney, Kevin, eds. *Captive Histories: English, French, and Native Narratives of the 1704 Deerfield Raid* (2006). An excellent collection and introduction based on the editors' published research.

Hinderaker, Eric, and Mancall, Peter C. *At the Edge of Empire: The Backcountry in British North America* (2003). Explores the patterns of interaction among Europeans and Native Americans, with a chapter on conflicts from 1675 to 1704.

Hoffman, Ronald, et al., eds. *Through a Glass Darkly: Reflections on Personal Identity in Early America* (1997). Interesting essays relating individual biography to colonial development.

Jordan, Winthrop D. *White over Black: American Attitudes Toward the Negro, 1550–1812* (1968). Basic source on the construction of ideas about race in Anglo-America.

Lovejoy, David S. *The Glorious Revolution in America* (1972). The best introduction to the colonial revolutions of 1689.

McCusker, John J., and Menard, Russell R. *The Economy of British America*, 1607–1789, *with Supplementary Bibliography* (1991). An excellent survey of economic and demographic development.

Miller, Randall M., and Pencak, William, eds. *Pennsylvania: A History of the Commonwealth* (2002). A well-illustrated book with excellent essays on Native Americans and the colonial and Revolutionary periods.

Morgan, Jennifer L. *Laboring Women: Reproduction and Gender in New World Slavery* (2004). Explores the significance of women's reproduction in the development of slave systems in British America.

Thornton, John. *Africa and Africans in the Making of the Atlantic World, 1400–1680* (1998). An influential work demonstrating the impact of Africa and Africans on the slave trade and the development of colonial American societies.

Tomlins, Christopher L., and Mann, Bruce H., eds. *The Many Legalities of Early America* (2001). Path-breaking essays that explore relationships among early Americans through the law.

CourseMate Go to the CourseMate website at www.cengagebrain.com for additional study tools and review materials for this chapter.

4 The Expansion of Colonial British America

1720–1763

MAKING CONNECTIONS

LOOKING BACK

Chapter 3 described how the population of the English colonies expanded by approximately 400 percent between 1675 and 1720; the colonists faced challenges from Native Americans, settler unrest, and efforts by the Crown to consolidate authority. At the same time, the British provinces became full participants in the Atlantic trading system, importing thousands of enslaved Africans to work on southern plantations and in northern cities. Before starting Chapter 4, you should be able to answer the following questions:

1. Why did New England Indians wage King Philip's War?
2. Why did Virginia freemen rise up in Bacon's Rebellion?
3. Were the revolutions of 1689 in Massachusetts, New York, and Maryland related or separate events?
4. Why did the English North American colonies adopt slavery?
5. What was the impact of European wars on North America?

In 1721, smallpox hit Boston viciously, infecting about 6,000 residents and killing 844. Business stopped for several months, as almost every family battled the contagion. In many respects, this epidemic was unremarkable in the British American colonies, but this time, one Puritan minister took an unprecedented step. Cotton Mather, who thirty years earlier had helped aggravate the Salem witch hysteria, encouraged a Boston doctor, Zabdiel Boylston, to test **inoculation**. Mather had learned from Onesimus, his African slave, and from English scientific papers that inoculation was used in Africa and Turkey to prevent smallpox epidemics. Many doctors, as well as much of Boston's populace, condemned the proposal. Nevertheless, Dr. Boylston inoculated about 250 persons over the course of a year. Those who submitted to the procedure had a much lower death rate than Bostonians who contracted the disease naturally.

Mather was far ahead of his time in advancing the theory that disease was caused by an invasion of the body by viruses. Significantly, it was a minister, rather than a physician or scientist, who advanced this hypothesis. During the eighteenth century, science lacked the rigid boundaries of complexity and specialization that would later separate it from other fields of intellectual endeavor. American theologians and philosophers, as well as doctors, naturalists, and astronomers, read the latest scientific literature from England and Europe. The great divide between science and religion did not yet exist.

inoculation Medical procedure tested in 1721 by a Boston doctor, Zabdiel Boylston, to prevent smallpox epidemics. The procedure involved introducing the smallpox virus into an individual's body, thereby giving the person what was usually (but not always) a mild case of the disease.

Mather's support for inoculation has been called the greatest contribution to medicine by an American during the colonial period. Certainly it represented change. The **Enlightenment**, a new intellectual movement, was spreading from Britain to the colonies and bringing important changes. During the years 1720 to 1763, the British provinces experienced intellectual, religious, and social ferment as they continued to expand through North America. As new knowledge, beliefs, and consumer goods arrived from Europe, colonists from Maine to Georgia (founded in 1732) increasingly lived within a common cultural framework. With rising wealth, colonial elites supported colleges and purchased books and luxury goods. Immigration into the British colonies also promoted regional diversity, as the newcomers from Europe settled on the frontier from Pennsylvania to Georgia, and the numbers of enslaved Africans grew to 40 percent of the southern population. The Europeans came looking for land: when they set up farms in contested territory, they provoked conflicts with the Native Americans, French, and Spanish, resulting in a series of wars that lasted a quarter-century. When the Seven Years' War ended in 1763, the

Enlightenment Philosophical movement of the eighteenth century that emphasized the use of reason to scrutinize previously accepted doctrines and traditions and that brought about many humanitarian reforms.

CHAPTER TIMELINE

1735 | 1740 | 1745 | 1750 | 1755 | 1760

POLITICS AND DIPLOMACY

- 1732 Georgia founded
- 1739 Stono Uprising
- 1754 Albany Congress
- 1754–1763 Seven Years' War
- 1763 Paxton Boys revolt

SOCIETY AND CULTURE

- 1721–1722 Smallpox inoculation in Boston
- 1739–1740 George Whitefield tours colonies
- 1752 Gregorian Calendar adopted in Anglo-America
- 1763 Rise of Neolin

ECONOMICS AND TECHNOLOGY

- 1733 Molasses Act passes
- 1740s "Consumer revolution" expands in British colonies
- 1750 Georgia legalizes slavery
- Early 1760s Economic slump in British colonies

British colonies took a great deal of pride in their contribution to the victory, offering it as evidence of their economic and political maturity within the empire.

❖ Intellectual Trends in the Eighteenth Century

The willingness of Mather and Boylston to try inoculation reflected the growing inclination to find natural rather than supernatural causes for unexplained events. The Enlightenment blossomed first in Europe and then in America, and inspired new technology as well as new concepts of human freedom. For Americans, its greatest significance lay in the acceptance of natural rights philosophy, which paved the way for independence and republican government.

The Enlightenment and Colonial Education

Newton, Sir Isaac (1642–1727) English scientist who discovered universal laws that predictably govern the motion of planets, moons, and comets; the motion of falling bodies on earth (gravity); and the ebb and flow of tides.

Locke, John (1632–1704) English philosopher and author of *An Essay Concerning Human Understanding* (1690), which challenged the notion of innate knowledge, and *Two Treatises on Civil Government* (1690), which discussed the social contract.

In the late seventeenth century, two English theorists, **Isaac Newton** and **John Locke**, had challenged traditional notions that humans had no role in determining their fate, that they could only trust in God to rule the universe. They confronted this older view without denying the existence of God. Newton discovered universal laws that predictably govern the motion of planets, moons, and comets; the motion of falling bodies on earth (gravity); and the ebb and flow of tides. His work demonstrated that the universe operates according to fixed principles, which humans are capable of detecting and understanding. Locke built on Newton's breakthrough in his *Essay Concerning Human Understanding* (1690). Locke argued against the accepted belief in innate knowledge—that infants are born with ideas implanted by God in their minds. He contended that all knowledge is gained by experience, not preordained at birth. Humans are born with the ability to learn, to use their acquired knowledge to benefit society.

Locke, and the Enlightenment thinkers he inspired, believed in freedom and the possibility of human progress, in the right of people to improve the conditions in which they live. Science, of course, was an important means of such improvement. The English philosopher also had a major impact on eighteenth-century politics, in particular providing a theoretical basis for the American Revolution and the U.S. Constitution. In *Two Treatises on Civil Government* (1690), he argued that humans, according to natural law, had rights to life, liberty, and property. By social contract, they formed governments to guarantee those rights. If a state failed in its obligation, the people had the duty to rebel and establish a new government.

After 1720, as newspapers became more available and reprinted articles from London, provincial readers became familiar with Enlightenment thought. Many colonists learned to read, though the availability of formal schooling varied widely by region, class, and gender. Everywhere, schools emphasized moral behavior and used religious texts. Nowhere did a system of universal, free, public education exist, though New England made the greatest effort of the British colonies to educate its populace. In the 1640s, the Massachusetts legislature established petty (elementary) and Latin grammar (secondary) schools. Connecticut and Plymouth passed similar legislation. Although some towns ignored the laws, most New England children learned to read, whether from their parents, at the town school, or at dame schools, where women in their homes taught young girls and boys for a fee.

South of New England, colonial governments did not require town schools. In the middle colonies, churches and private teachers offered instruction. Affluent

Quaker and Anglican boys were most likely to obtain formal education, but in the Chesapeake, with dispersed settlement, neither Maryland nor Virginia had many schools. Upper-class boys and girls had private tutors, while middling families in some localities pooled their resources to establish schools. Large numbers of poor whites obtained no education at all. Very few slaves learned to read and write, for owners thought these skills would breed discontent and enable slaves to forge passes, facilitating escape.

New England also surpassed other regions in higher education; the Puritans established Harvard College in Massachusetts in 1636 and Yale College in Connecticut in 1701. William and Mary, founded in Virginia in 1693, was the only other college in the British colonies before the 1740s. None of the colonial colleges admitted women. Most early graduates became clergymen; others went into medicine, public service, teaching, commerce, and agriculture.

natural philosophy The study of astronomy, physics, and chemistry, which was introduced into American college curricula under the influence of the Scottish Enlightenment.

Franklin, Benjamin (1706–1790) American public official, writer, scientist, and printer. He proposed a plan for union at the Albany Congress (1754) and played a major part in the American Revolution. Franklin helped secure French support for the colonists, negotiated the Treaty of Paris (1783), and helped draft the Constitution (1787). His numerous scientific and practical innovations include the lightning rod, bifocal spectacles, and a stove.

Developments in Science and Medicine

After 1720, influenced by Scottish universities that quickly absorbed Enlightenment thinking into their curricula, American colleges expanded their course work to include French, English literature, philosophy, and science. They offered mathematics and what was then called **natural philosophy**—astronomy, physics, and chemistry. The transatlantic scholarly community that developed included academics like John Winthrop of Harvard College, as well as largely self-taught men like Benjamin Franklin and John Bartram. Scientists took from the Enlightenment a commitment to observe and experiment with natural phenomena to obtain information that would lead to human progress.

Two colonists who contributed prodigiously to the growth of science were John Winthrop and Benjamin Franklin. Winthrop was the most renowned professor of natural philosophy in British America, with research interests in such wide-ranging subjects as sunspots, mathematics, earthquakes, and the weather. In 1761, he participated in an important international scientific effort to calculate the distance between the Earth and the sun, made possible by the transit of the planet Venus across the face of the sun. Perhaps best known for his diplomacy and political leadership during the Revolutionary era, **Benjamin Franklin** has become a symbol of the American Enlightenment for his efforts to improve society through science, inventions, and civic organizations. Franklin was born in Boston, ran away at age seventeen from an apprenticeship with his older brother, and arrived in Philadelphia nearly penniless. He built a highly successful printing business, publishing a newspaper, books, and *Poor Richard's Almanack*, which gained a wide readership. Throughout his life, Franklin put the Enlightenment ideal of human progress into action. He founded a debating club to discuss politics, morals, and natural philosophy, and he helped establish the first American lending library, a hospital, and the College of Philadelphia. Franklin's experiments in electricity yielded information about its properties, including the basic concepts of "plus" and "minus." His inventions included bifocal eyeglasses, the lightning rod, and an iron stove that was more efficient than colonial fireplaces.

(The Philadelphia Museum of Art, Art Resource, NY)

Benjamin Franklin. *Portrait of Benjamin Franklin in England,* 1762, by Mason Chamberlin. At this time Franklin was serving as the Pennsylvania assembly's agent in London.

John Bartram, also of Pennsylvania, was the most energetic of American naturalists; his chief contribution to science was collecting specimens of New World plant life. His efforts greatly expanded botanical knowledge of the Western Hemisphere, for he sent specimens to such scholars as Carl Linnaeus, the Swedish author of the modern classification system. At the same time, medicine was beginning to develop as a profession. During the colonial period, men with formal medical education comprised a small proportion of the people who provided care for disease, physical injury, and childbirth. Having completed formal course work abroad—the first medical school in the British colonies, located in Philadelphia, did not open until 1766—educated physicians were at the top of their profession and charged the highest fees. Consequently, they practiced primarily in cities. Below them were men who learned their craft as apprentices; though they assumed the title of doctor in the colonies, they were actually akin to the surgeon-apothecaries of Great Britain. As surgeons, they performed emergency procedures such as setting bones, amputating limbs, and removing superficial tumors but no major surgery. As apothecaries, they prepared and prescribed drugs for a variety of illnesses.

midwives Women who traditionally attended at childbirth, treated the ill, and prescribed herbal remedies. They learned their skills through informal apprenticeships and from witnessing the childbirths of neighbors and relatives, and received payment for their services.

Female **midwives** traditionally attended at childbirth, treated the ill, and prescribed herbal remedies. Having learned their skills through informal apprenticeships and from witnessing the childbirths of neighbors and relatives, they received payment for their services. During the colonial period, childbirth was the province of women. As an expectant mother's labor began, she called together a group of women, presided over by the midwife, who assisted in the birth. If complications occurred, the midwife manipulated the infant manually but would not perform a cesarean section. In the worst cases, the midwife had to kill the child; sometimes the mother died. Without modern antibiotics, women faced the constant threat of infection during pregnancy and in the weeks following delivery. In the last half of the eighteenth century, the practice of obstetrics changed. In 1762, **Dr. William Shippen, Jr.**, returned from studying medicine in England and Scotland to give lectures in anatomy to Philadelphia midwives and doctors. Shippen established an obstetrical practice of his own, quickly attracting well-to-do patients who expected a higher level of care than they received from midwives.

Shippen, Dr. William, Jr. (1712–1801) Trained in medicine in England and Scotland, Shippen initiated his practice of obstetrics in 1762, giving lectures in anatomy to Philadelphia midwives and doctors. Soon he accepted only male students.

❖ The Great Awakening

As Enlightenment ideas gained sway, many Protestant ministers embraced Christian rationalism, a theology that stressed moral, rational behavior and the free will of individuals to lead their lives and achieve salvation. To others, however, Christian rationalism was heretical, for it rejected the Calvinist belief that salvation came from grace, as the gift of God, and that people must be saved to be full members of the church. From the 1720s to the 1760s, ministers from various denominations called for the renewal of these beliefs in a series of religious revivals known as the **Great Awakening.** Several of the most important Awakeners brought the impetus for revival from Europe and Great Britain. Religious ferment convulsed British North America, spreading from the churches to threaten social and political authority.

Great Awakening Immense religious revival during the 1720s to the 1760s that swept across the Protestant world.

Religious Diversity and Early Revivals

In 1720, the British provinces varied widely in religious and ethnic makeup. New England was the most homogeneous, for Massachusetts, New Hampshire, and Connecticut remained predominantly Puritan and of English descent. The established Puritan churches received tax support, but Anglicans, Baptists, and Quakers could also worship freely. Rhode Island, which still embraced the principles of religious liberty and separation of church and state, was home to various denominations, including Quakers, Baptists, and Separatists. From their founding, the middle colonies offered an open door to people of various backgrounds. In the late seventeenth century, according to one report, residents of New York City spoke eighteen languages. Philadelphia and its environs in the 1720s boasted organized meetings of many denominations. Though disputes occasionally arose between churches, the Quaker government upheld liberty of conscience throughout the colonial period. With few towns in the Chesapeake, the established Anglican church suffered from southern rural conditions, and ministers in Virginia faced serious obstacles in meeting the spiritual needs of their scattered congregations. Only half of the Anglican churches had regular preachers. Few planters were interested in converting their African slaves, who kept—and passed on to their children—many traditional African beliefs. The colony's laws against nonconformity prevented most dissent, so only a few Presbyterians and Quakers worshipped openly.

The Great Awakening shattered the existing church structure of the colonies, as congregations wakened to the teachings and vigorous preaching style of revivalist, or New Light, ministers. Religious diversity grew in provinces where established churches, with government support, dominated religious life—especially Puritan churches in Connecticut and Massachusetts and the Anglican establishment in Virginia. As a result of the revivals, religious life in these colonies became more like that in Rhode Island, New York, and Pennsylvania.

In Massachusetts, revivals began in 1734, when minister Jonathan Edwards of Northampton preached a series of sermons on salvation, inclining many of his parishioners to believe they were saved. They went through the process of self-judgment—first feeling despair as sinners who were damned to hell, then rejoicing in the conviction that God had rescued them from this fate. Edwards wrote to a colleague that "this town never was so full of Love, nor so full of Joy, nor so full of distress as it has lately been." Over the next few years, the revival spread to other towns along the Connecticut River.

Revivalism Takes Fire

Beginning in 1739, the Great Awakening gained strength throughout the British mainland colonies after a young Anglican minister, **George Whitefield,** arrived from England to tour the middle colonies. Called the Grand Itinerant, he had a magnificent voice, ranging from a whisper to a roar, that could be heard by large crowds in fields and city streets. Benjamin Franklin calculated that twenty-five thousand people could easily hear the spectacular preacher at one time.

Whitefield found adherents across denominational lines and among native-born Americans and immigrants alike. In 1740, Jonathan Edwards invited Whitefield to Northampton, prompting the itinerant to travel through New England, where he attracted crowds as large as eight thousand in Boston. Other New Light ministers followed, including Gilbert Tennent and James Davenport, a Puritan preacher of Southold, Long Island.

The full force of the Awakening hit the South later than New England and the Middle Atlantic states. During the 1740s, Presbyterian missionaries set up churches on the southern frontier. The new settlements were a fertile field for the revivalists because few regular clergy had migrated west. The more explosive Baptist revivals began in the 1750s, when itinerants traveled through Virginia and North Carolina making converts and forming churches. The Baptists believed that individuals should be saved before they were baptized. With their

Doing History Online

The Enlightenment and the Great Awakening

Go to the CourseMate website for this chapter and link to Primary Sources. Based on Documents 1 through 4, in what ways do you think the Enlightenment and the Great Awakening complement each other? Do you see them as antagonistic toward each other at all? How?

www.cengagebrain.com

Whitefield, George (1714–1770) Anglican minister who arrived from England in 1739. Called the Grand Itinerant, he promoted the Great Awakening by touring and encouraging New Lights throughout the colonies.

George Whitefield. George Whitefield, the itinerant English evangelist, had a spellbinding effect on his listeners, as portrayed here by John Wollaston.

emotional religious style and challenge to the Anglican establishment in Virginia, they appealed particularly to ordinary white farm families and enslaved African Americans. Lacking formal churches, Baptists met in fields and homes. The ministry was open to all, even women and slaves, with no requirement for college training.

The Awakening's Impact

The revivals proved to be socially divisive, and many communities split into two groups: the "New Lights" and the "Old Lights." The style of most New Light preachers was to give impassioned, extemporaneous sermons that contrasted dramatically with the closely reasoned sermons of their opponents, the rationalist Old Light ministers. New Lights believed that salvation was more important than religious training; they required a "saved" ministry, with a dynamic preaching style. Congregations responded by fainting, shrieking, and shedding tears. Old Light clergymen, who defended their advanced education in theology, Greek, Hebrew, and ethics, resented accusations that they were unsaved. In turn, they charged the revivalists with being unlearned.

Bitter disputes ensued within colonial congregations and colleges alike, spilling what had begun as a religious controversy into the courts and politics. Where strong established churches existed—as in Massachusetts, Connecticut, and Virginia—the New Lights challenged political as well as religious authority. In response, the Connecticut Assembly, for example, passed the Anti-Itinerancy Act, which made it illegal for a clergyman to preach in another's parish without his permission, and repealed the 1708 law permitting religious dissent. Yale College was at the center of the intense religious and political battles in Connecticut. When the New Haven church separated, a large number of students followed the New Lights: they skipped classes to attend revivals, challenged Yale's curriculum, and questioned whether their teachers were saved. As in many other congregations, people eventually found ways to heal the bitterness and division that the Great Awakening had caused.

A more lasting effect of the revivals was the founding of new colleges. Until the mid-1740s, only Harvard, William and Mary, and Yale—all with ties to established churches—existed in the British colonies. Between 1746 and 1769, the revivalists founded the College of New Jersey (now Princeton), the College of Rhode Island (Brown), Queen's College (Rutgers) in New Jersey, and Dartmouth College in New Hampshire. Anglicans established King's College (Columbia) in New York City, and a group of civic leaders, headed by Benjamin Franklin, started the College of Philadelphia (University of Pennsylvania) on a nonsectarian basis. Though most of these new schools were tied to a specific religious denomination, all accepted young men of various faiths and adopted the new curricula in mathematics, science, and modern languages.

❖ Cultural Diversity and Expansion

Between 1720 and 1760, the population of British North America grew from 466,000 to 1.6 million. Much of this growth came from natural increase, but new arrivals also spurred population growth, as thousands of Germans and **Scots-Irish** immigrated and slave traders continued to import blacks (see Table 4.1). The newcomers brought ideas, religious beliefs, skills, and ways of life that significantly altered the cultural mix of the British colonies. The immigrants from the European continent and the British Isles sought a new beginning in

Scots-Irish Ulster Scot Presbyterians who settled in New York, Pennsylvania, Delaware, western Maryland, and the southern backcountry.

TABLE 4.1
Population Growth of the British Mainland Colonies, 1630–1760

1630	4,646
1640	26,634
1650	50,368
1660	75,058
1670	111,935
1680	151,507
1690	210,372
1700	250,888
1710	331,711
1720	466,185
1730	629,445
1740	905,563
1750	1,170,760
1760	1,593,625

"the best poor man's country": many disembarked in the middle colonies, traveling west to settle the backcountry from Pennsylvania south through the Shenandoah Valley to the Carolinas. Others went directly to Georgia, which reformers started in 1732 as a haven for the poor. The population explosion and demand for new lands brought the British colonists face to face with the Spanish in Florida, the French in Canada and the Ohio Valley, and Native Americans all along the frontier.

MAP 4.1
Ethnicity in Colonial British America, c. 1755
Europeans who came in large numbers to the British colonies included the Germans and Scots-Irish, who established farms outside the first English settlements. Many entered ports on the Delaware River, moved north and west in Pennsylvania, then moved south through western Maryland, the Shenandoah Valley of Virginia, and North and South Carolina. Enslaved Africans and bound British convicts also made up a significant proportion of migrants to North America.

German and Scots-Irish Immigrants

More than one hundred thousand Germans left their homelands for America during the century after 1683. Some were forced out by religious persecution, oppressive regulations, and war; others sought economic opportunity. Promoters told Germans of cheap fertile land and moderate government in the British colonies. Many immigrants paid their own passage. Those who could not signed on as "redemptioners," the equivalent of indentured servants, whose labor would be sold for a number of years upon arrival. Some Germans remained in Philadelphia, but the majority headed for the Pennsylvania hinterland and south through the backcountry of Maryland, Virginia, and the Carolinas (see Map 4.1).

Cultural exchange between the Germans and English enriched American society. Pennsylvania was the heart of German America, because the colony's religious freedom allowed a multitude of sects and churches to flourish: the Mennonites, Amish, Brethren, Moravians, Schwenkfelders, Lutheran, and Reformed. Immigrants retained their native German in churches and homes, but used English in business, the courts, and politics. German American decorative arts proliferated by the 1740s, in house ornaments, furniture, and elaborately illustrated documents. German farm women did much heavier fieldwork than most English wives but otherwise played a similar role in maintaining domestic culture. Large numbers of Scots, Scots-Irish, and Irish Catholics also came during the eighteenth century, settling in New York, Pennsylvania, Delaware, western Maryland, and the southern backcountry. Most were Ulster Scots (or Scots-Irish, as they were called in America)—Presbyterians whose families had migrated during the 1600s from Scotland to northern Ireland in search of economic opportunity. There they had combined tenant farming and weaving until the early eighteenth century, when their leases expired. Rising rents, poor harvests, and downturns in the linen industry compelled waves of immigrant groups toward America starting in 1717. In the colonies, the Scots-Irish achieved a reputation as tough defenders of the frontier. They came into frequent contact with Native Americans, often with violent results. One Pennsylvania frontiersman, not recognizing the Indians' rights, echoed the early Puritans when he argued that it was contrary to "the laws of God and nature, that so much land should be idle, while so many Christians wanted it to labor on, and to raise their bread."

The Founding of Georgia

Oglethorpe, James (1696–1785) Along with John Viscount Percival, Oglethorpe sought a charter to colonize Georgia, the last of the British mainland colonies. Upon royal approval, he founded the colony with the intention of establishing a society of small farmers, without slavery or hard liquor.

The last of the British mainland colonies, Georgia lured many German and Scots-Irish immigrants, as well as Scots and English. Animated by Enlightenment ideals of human progress and freedom, **James Oglethorpe** and John Viscount Percival, members of the Associates of the Late Doctor Bray, a philanthropic society, sought a charter to establish a colony to both help the poor and create a buffer between Spanish Florida and South Carolina. George II granted the charter, placing control of the colony in the hands of trustees, or proprietors, who could neither receive financial benefits from the province nor own land within its boundaries. The double function of Georgia as a haven for the poor and a military outpost shaped the terms under which settlers immigrated. The trustees intended to create a peaceful, moral society of small farmers in which all except indentured servants worked for themselves. The proprietors wanted to avoid duplicating lowland South Carolina, where large plantation owners lived off the toil of their slaves.

In February 1733, the first settlers arrived and built the first town, Savannah, on a high bluff overlooking the river. Oglethorpe purchased land from the Native Americans and pledged to prevent price gouging in trade, a significant complaint of the Indians against South Carolina merchants. He established alliances with Lower Creeks, Cherokees, and Chickasaws against Spanish Florida, not least because English traders offered better merchandise than their rivals. The Georgia Trustees, led by Oglethorpe, set three significant policies: they prohibited importation of hard liquor, banned slaveholding, and limited landownership to five hundred acres or less. Each free male immigrant was granted land at no charge, but no one could buy or sell real estate, and only men could inherit land.

Many settlers in Georgia believed that the prohibitions on liquor, land sales, and slavery were unreasonable, but they could do little to change the colony's direction because they lacked a representative assembly. The embargo on rum, a major Caribbean commodity, prevented expansion of trade with the West Indies, a ready market for their abundant lumber. The bans on slavery and large landholdings were also unpopular with many settlers, who coveted the grander lifestyle of planters north of the Savannah River, in South Carolina. In consequence, some settlers left almost immediately, and so Georgia grew slowly. The trustees gradually recognized their failure, and they allowed the importation of rum in 1742 and land sales and slavery in 1750. The Georgia population swelled as South Carolinians migrated across the Savannah River, transforming Georgia into a slave society. By 1773, the province had thirty-three thousand inhabitants, of whom 45 percent were enslaved blacks. Despite its halting start before 1750, Georgia attracted settlers of a variety of nationalities and religions, including Spanish and German Jews and German-speaking Lutherans.

The Growth of the African American Population

The failure of the trustees to create a free society in Georgia was symptomatic of the entrenchment of slavery in America. Like the Germans and Scots-Irish, Africans helped diversify the American population and shape its culture. Although the number of African Americans grew naturally in many places, slave traders imported more than two hundred thousand people between 1720 and the Revolution, most from West and Central Africa. In 1750, blacks were one-fifth of the population of the mainland colonies, including about 40 percent in the Chesapeake and the Lower South (see Map 4.2).

Gullah Creole tongue that evolved in the Lower South from English and various languages from southern Nigeria, the Gold Coast, Angola, and Senegambia.

As the number of African Americans increased and slave societies matured, blacks created patterns of community, work, and culture. Extended kinship networks structured community life on large plantations, and even in places where slaves lived in small households, such as in northern cities, family ties remained paramount. Blacks were most successful in perpetuating African language and customs in regions where they were most numerous, particularly the South Carolina low country and, later, Georgia. Africans melded African and European forms together, influencing evolving mainstream cultures, especially in the South.

The opportunity of slaves to engage in independent activities varied with the amount of time they had to spend working for their master. In South Carolina, blacks labored by the task; each slave received a certain amount of work to perform each day—a field to hoe, thread to spin, a fence to build. Those who completed their assignments quickly had time to raise their own crops and livestock. Consequently Carolina slaves participated in trade, selling their goods at the "Negro market" in Charleston on Sundays. As in Africa, women were responsible for marketing the family's goods. In the Chesapeake, most slaves on plantations labored for a specified number of hours or worked in gangs until the overseer told them to stop. As a result, they had little time to work for themselves.

The persistence of African culture was conspicuous in language, food, music, dance, and religion. Some newly arrived Africans knew Dutch, Spanish, Portuguese, French, or English from former contacts in Africa or the West Indies, but to communicate with other slaves and with Europeans, most adopted Creole speech, a combination of English and African languages. In the Lower South, for instance, the Creole tongue known as **Gullah** evolved from English and various languages from southern Nigeria, the Gold Coast, Angola, and Senegambia. Some African words became part of American vocabulary, including *cola, yam, goober* (peanut), and *toting* (carrying) a package. Blacks contributed to the food and material culture of British America, popularizing new foods such as okra, melons, and bananas. They made clay pipes, pottery, and baskets with African designs, and carved eating utensils, chairs, and other useful objects from wood. Although masters discouraged Africans from drumming because of the potential to call others to revolt, whites enjoyed the music of black fiddlers. Slaves helped create the Virginia jig, a fusion of African and European elements, accompanied by banjos and fiddles.

Along with whites during the Great Awakening, Africans shaped the forms of worship in southern Baptist churches. Blacks retained traditional African concepts of the hereafter, where the deceased reunited with ancestors, combining these beliefs with European views of heaven. Funerals remained important to African Americans throughout the colonies; mourners buried the dead facing Africa, with traditional rituals, music, and dance. Blacks also passed down African medical practice, a combination of physical and psychological treatment including magic. More African American women than men were doctors, practicing midwifery as well as nursing and providing cures.

Despite cultural exchange and indications of human understanding, the antagonism and economic exploitation inherent in slavery poisoned relationships

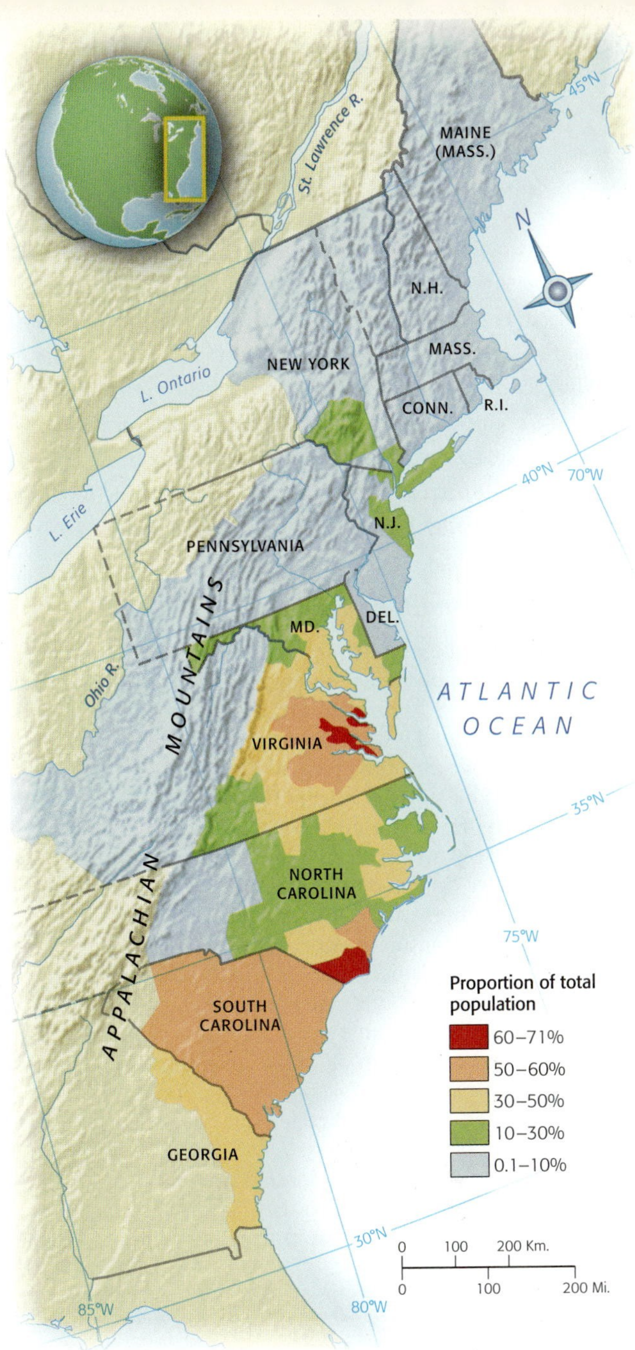

MAP 4.2
African American Population in Colonial British America, c. 1760
A much higher concentration of enslaved African Americans lived in colonies south of Pennsylvania. Notice, however, that the percentage of slaves in parts of New York and New Jersey was as high as in portions of the Chesapeake region and North Carolina. Uniform data for South Carolina mask the fact that the population of African Americans was much larger along the seacoast than in the upcountry.

Doing History Slave Resistance

These documents provide examples of the ways in which enslaved Africans and Native Americans grappled for freedom. Venture Smith, who was born in West Africa, captured at age six by an enemy army, then sold as a slave in Rhode Island, published his autobiography in 1798 after he had purchased freedom for himself and his family. The excerpt below graphically depicts his attempt to escape and the consequences of his failure. The second document is a newspaper advertisement placed by a slave owner for two escaped slaves: a Native American man and African American woman. The third is a report of the Stono uprising of 1741, excerpted from the Georgia colonial records.

Venture Smith Resists Slavery

After I had lived with my master thirteen years, being then about twenty-two years old, I married Meg, a slave of his who was about my own age. My master owned a certain Irishman, named Heddy, who about that time formed a plan of secretly leaving his master. . . . I at length agreed to accompany him. Heddy next inveigled two of his fellow-servants to accompany us. The place to which we designed to go was the Mississippi. Our next business was to lay in a sufficient store of provisions for our voyage. We privately collected out of our master's store, six great old cheeses, two firkins of butter, and one batch of new bread. When we had gathered all our own clothes and some more, we took them all about midnight and went to the water side. We stole our master's boat, embarked, and then directed our course for the Mississippi River.

We mutually confederated not to betray or desert one another on pain of death. We first steered our course for Montauk Point, the east end of Long Island. After our arrival there, we landed, and Heddy and I made an incursion into the island after fresh water. . . . [Later Heddy] went directly to the boat, stole all the clothes in it, and then travelled away for East Hampton. . . . I advertised Heddy and sent two men in search of him. They pursued and overtook him at Southampton and returned him to the boat. I then thought it might afford some chance for my freedom, or at least be a palliation for my running away, to return Heddy immediately to his master, and inform him that I was induced to go away by Heddy's address. . . . I informed my master that Heddy was the ringleader of our revolt. . . .

Not a long time passed after that before Heddy was sent by my master to New London jail. At the close of that year I was sold to a Thomas Stanton, and had to be separated from my wife and one daughter, who was about one month old.

Source: Venture Smith, *A Narrative of the Life and Adventures of Venture, a Native of Africa: But Resident Above Sixty Years in the United States of America* (New London, CT: C. Holt, 1798).

among whites and blacks. Whites believed that African Americans were an inferior race, and masters used their power in the slave system to control their human property with harsh punishments. Nevertheless, blacks refused to accept their subordinate position; increasing numbers ran away or were truant for weeks at a time.

Some enslaved Africans adopted violent means, killing their masters or setting fire to fields and homes. In 1739, a group of more than fifty slaves revolted near the Stono River in South Carolina. When armed planters defeated the rebels in battle, some of the slaves regrouped and headed for St. Augustine, Florida. But the South Carolina militia pursued the insurgents, putting to death everyone suspected of being involved. The **Stono uprising** sent shock waves throughout the American colonies.

Stono uprising (1739) Revolt of enslaved Africans against their owners near the Stono River in South Carolina.

The South Carolina legislature enacted a harsh slave code in an effort to prevent future revolts and limited slave importation for a decade. Most of the core group who planned the Stono rebellion were African-born slaves who hoped to escape to Florida, where Spanish authorities offered them religious sanctuary and freedom. By 1740, about a hundred former Carolina slaves had built the village

Escaped Slave Advertisement,
October 11, 1739

RUN away on the 20th of Aug. past, from the Subscriber near the Head of Bush River in Baltimore County, Maryland, an Indian Man, named Pompey, aged about 24 Years, of middle Stature, well set, speaks nothing but English, very much scarrified on the Body with whipping in Barbadoes; he had on his Neck when he went away an Iron Collar, but its suppos'd he has got it off. Also a lusty Negro Woman named Pegg, aged about 22 Years, this Country born and speaks plain English; They carried away with them a striped Duffle Blanket, an old Ticken Jacket and Breeches with black Buttonholes, a Felt Hat near new, a coarse linnen Bag, a new white Linsey woolsey Petticoat and other coarse Negro Apparel. Whoever secures the said Indian and Negro so that their Master may have them again, shall have Five Pounds Reward and reasonable Charges paid by Richard Ruff.

Source: Billy G. Smith and Richard Wojtowicz, *Blacks Who Stole Themselves: Advertisements for Runaways in the* Pennsylvania Gazette, *1728–1790* (Philadelphia: University of Pennsylvania Press, 1989), 19.

Stono Uprising, South Carolina, *1741*

On the 9th day of September last being Sunday which is the day the Planters allow them to work for themselves, Some Angola Negroes assembled, to the number of Twenty; and one who was called Jemmy was their Captain, they suprized a Warehouse belonging to Mr. Hutchenson at a place called Stonehow [sic]; they there killed Mr. Robert Bathurst, and Mr. Gibbs, plundered the House and took a pretty many small Arms and Powder, which were there for Sale. . . . They then turned back and marched Southward along Pons Pons, which is the Road through Georgia to [St.] Augustine, they passed Mr. Wallace's Tavern towards day break, and said they would not hurt him, for he was a good Man and kind to his Slaves. . . . They marched on towards Mr. Rose's resolving to kill him; but he was saved by a Negroe, who having hid him went out and pacified the others. Several Negroes joyned them, they calling out Liberty, marched on with Colours displayed, and two Drums beating, pursuing all the white people they met with, and killing Man Woman and Child when they could come up to them. Collonel Bull Lieutenant Governour of South Carolina, who was then riding along the Road, discovered them, was pursued, and with much difficulty escaped & raised the Countrey.

Source: Allen D. Candler, ed., *The Colonial Records of the State of Georgia* (Atlanta: Charles P. Byrd, 1913), 22:233–234.

QUESTIONS for REFLECTION

1. What do we learn from Venture Smith's autobiography that is not available in the other documents?
2. What can we find out from the newspaper advertisement that Smith does not reveal?
3. What details included in the Stono account suggest the beliefs and goals of the rebels?

of Gracia Real de Santa Teresa de Mose, called Mose, two miles north of St. Augustine (see *Doing History: Slave Resistance*).

Native American Worlds in the Mid-Eighteenth Century

As the British colonies grew, Native Americans chose strategies to maintain their communities and cultures. Those who remained within the British provinces were called by white Americans "settlement Indians," "domestic Indians," or "little Tribes." Many lived among European Americans and worked as servants, slaves, day laborers, mariners, artisans, and tenant farmers, assimilating some parts of English culture but rejecting others. Others, such as the Mashpees in Massachusetts, Lenapes (or Delawares) in New Jersey, and Catawbas in South Carolina, lived on remnants of traditional lands. They continued to hunt, fish, gather berries and wood, and raise corn while also trading with neighboring whites. Indians peddled venison and turkeys to the colonists or crafted baskets and brooms for sale.

(Colonial Williamsburg Foundation)

Virginia Tobacco Wharf. This illustration on a 1751 map drawn by Joshua Fry and Peter Jefferson, father of Thomas, demonstrates the significance of enslaved Africans in the Chesapeake labor force.

Dr. Alexander Hamilton, a recent immigrant from Scotland, recorded many encounters with Indians in 1744 as he traveled through the settlements from Maryland to Maine. The Native Americans he met varied greatly in status, from an Indian sachem who had established himself as a wealthy planter to those on the margins, who tried to hold on to native traditions within an alien culture. During worship in a Boston church, Hamilton sat near several Native Americans. He met an Indian at Princeton, New Jersey, who saluted him with, "How' s't ni tap," and, in New York, he watched "about ten Indians fishing for oysters . . . stark naked" near his tavern. Although most native people who stayed in white settled areas had given up political autonomy, they had not surrendered all of their traditions. Many spoke English in addition to their native language but did not learn to read and write.

Native Americans who intended to preserve their political independence moved west, a strategy that worked temporarily. From 1660 to the 1740s, for example, Iroquois, Shawnees, and Lenapes relocated in the eastern part of the Ohio Valley, from Pennsylvania and western New York to west-central Ohio. Some of the Lenapes left the East as a result of the Walking Purchase of 1737, when two of William Penn's sons, the proprietors, used an alleged 1686 deed to cheat the Indians out of their territory on the Pennsylvania side of the Delaware River. The deed, of which only a copy survived, ceded lands as far as a man could walk in one and a half days. Coerced by an alliance between the Penns and the Iroquois, the Lenapes agreed to comply. The Penns sent runners in relay to cover more than sixty miles of land in a day and a half, a deception the Lenapes could not fail to remember; in 1754, with the outbreak of war on the Pennsylvania frontier, many sought revenge.

The Ohio Valley became the focus of conflict in the 1740s as the British and French competed for trade. Some Pennsylvania traders took up residence in the multi-ethnic towns such as Chiningue (or Logstown), where Iroquois, Lenapes, Shawnees, Ottawas, and other Indians lived. The Ohio Valley, as one Indian leader said, was "a country in between" the English and the French, unfortunately a country that the Europeans craved. From 1754 to 1814, the Native Americans fought the British and Americans to keep their lands, forging pan-Indian alliances to meet the Anglo threat.

MAP 4.3

European Occupation of North America, to 1750

Great Britain, France, and Spain claimed the indicated areas just before the Seven Years' War. While waves of immigrants from Germany and the British Isles had expanded settlement in the British provinces since 1700 (see Map 3.4), the French colonies still consisted primarily of trading posts, forts, and relatively small agricultural areas. Native Americans controlled much of the territory that France claimed.

❖ Wars for Empire, 1739–1765

For a quarter century beginning in 1739, the British colonies took part in conflicts between Great Britain and Spain, France, and Native Americans. The War of Jenkins' Ear (1739–1744) against Spain; King George's War (1744–1748) against France; the Seven Years' War, called the French and Indian War in the colonies (1756–1763); and the Indian war for autonomy in the Ohio Valley (1763–1765) all required British colonists to participate more actively in defending the empire.

The Southern Frontier

The colonies along the southern tier—British South Carolina and Georgia, Spanish Florida, French Louisiana, and Spanish Texas and New Mexico—competed for trade with Native Americans and control of territory (see Map 4.3). Except for war between Georgia and Florida in the early 1740s, the most important battles along the southern rim were commercial, a competition the British traders often won because they had more plentiful and cheaper goods. They exchanged tools, clothing, scissors, guns, ammunition, and rum in return for slaves, deerskins, and furs from the Indians. In comparison with the English provinces, the Spanish and French colonies remained small and badly supplied by their parent nations. In 1760, Florida had approximately three thousand Spanish settlers, Texas had twelve hundred, and New Mexico about nine thousand; Louisiana counted four thousand whites and five thousand enslaved Africans. In contrast, in the same year, South Carolina and Georgia had a population of about forty-five thousand whites and fifty-nine thousand black slaves.

Governor James Oglethorpe of Georgia tried to use the outbreak of the War of Jenkins' Ear to eject the Spanish from Florida. As part of the 1713 Treaty of Utrecht, Britain had obtained the *asiento*, the right to sell a specified number of African slaves and commodities to the Spanish provinces. This opening led to British smuggling, which the Spanish countered with heavy-handed searches of British ships. Accounts of Spanish brutality inflamed the British public, especially when Captain Robert Jenkins displayed one of his ears, which he claimed the Spanish cut off when they caught him smuggling. In 1740, Oglethorpe attacked Florida with seven ships and two thousand troops. They captured several Spanish forts and Mose, the village of escaped Carolina blacks, but failed to conquer Fort San Marcos, which was resupplied by Cuba; Oglethorpe finally retreated. After a number of other conflicts, both sides gave up, bringing calm to the Georgia–Florida border.

King George's War, 1744–1748

The British avoided further conflict with Florida because they began hostilities with France in 1744, in the War of the Austrian Succession, known to the colonists as King George's War. The war began in Europe, but spilled into North America when, provoked by French attacks on Nova Scotia, Governor William Shirley of Massachusetts launched an attack on Louisbourg, which controlled access to the St. Lawrence River. In April 1745, four thousand New England farmers and fishermen assaulted the French garrison, which surrendered in June. New Englanders considered Louisbourg a great victory, even after many of their troops succumbed to disease. The war degenerated into a series of debilitating border raids. In spring 1746, a fleet of seventy-six ships left France to retake Louisbourg, but after fighting disease and Atlantic storms for three months, they returned to France empty-handed.

Despite this reprieve, New Englanders had little to celebrate, for they faced another threat—this one from their own imperial navy. During the war, Parliament had permitted naval officers to impress sailors without the permission of colonial authorities. The Royal Navy used impressment, or involuntary recruitment, because many seamen fled the harsh conditions on naval vessels. In 1747, several thousand Bostonians protested when a British press gang from the fleet of Admiral Charles Knowles swept up men along the waterfront. The mob surrounded the governor's house and burned a British barge in his courtyard. When the governor called up the militia, the troops refused to move. Knowles threatened to shell the town, but he eventually released the impressed men.

As the colonists became more involved in imperial politics, they learned that their interests held little sway. To their shock, the British government restored Louisbourg to the French in the Treaty of Aix-la-Chapelle (1748), and the combatants agreed to return all North American territories seized during the war. Despite heavy human and financial costs, the war brought no change in the power balance between Great Britain and France in North America.

Albany Plan of Union (1754) Plan proposed to the Albany Congress of 1754 by Benjamin Franklin to unite the colonies for common defense. The Congress approved the design for an intercolonial government empowered to tax, pass laws, and supervise military defense, but the colonies and British government rejected it.

The Seven Years' War, 1756–1763

During King George's War, the British and Iroquois had evicted French traders from the Ohio Valley. The Canadians returned, however, backed by a government determined to force out the British colonists. The Ohio Company of Virginia, which had received the rights to half a million acres from the British government, in 1749 made preparations to sell land in the region of present-day Pittsburgh, Pennsylvania (see Map 4.4). In response, the French constructed

MAP 4.4

The Seven Years' War in North America, 1754–1760

The war began in the Ohio Valley, an area Virginians claimed and hoped to sell to settlers. To do so, they had to force out the French, who sent troops to establish ownership; defeat the Delawares and Shawnees, who had built towns along the Allegheny and Ohio rivers; and prevail over Pennsylvania's competing charter claims. The English captured Quebec in 1759 and Montreal in 1760, defeating France in North America.

forts to stop the incursion of Anglo-American traders and Virginia's land speculators. In 1754, the governor of Virginia sent a young militia officer, George Washington, with about 160 troops to defend the colony's interests. When hostilities resulted, the Virginians were defeated at Fort Necessity by a superior force of French and Indians.

Recognizing that war was imminent, seven colonies sent delegates to a congress at Albany, New York, where they negotiated unsuccessfully with the Iroquois for an alliance against the French. The Albany Congress also adopted the **Albany Plan of Union** devised by Benjamin Franklin to unite the colonies for common defense. The plan for an intercolonial government empowered to tax, pass laws, and supervise military defense needed endorsement by each colony and the Crown. When the delegates returned home with the proposal, not one of the provincial assemblies approved it.

The British decided to destroy French forts even before a formal declaration of war. In early 1755, Major General Edward Braddock landed in the colonies with two British regiments. Joined by hundreds of provincial soldiers, the army marched through the Virginia backcountry to capture Fort Duquesne (now Pittsburgh). The British troops were unprepared for frontier fighting. Ten miles short of Fort Duquesne, the French and allied Indians ambushed Braddock's army, killing or wounding two-thirds of the British force. The general himself was mortally wounded. George Washington, his uniform ripped by bullets, led the retreat.

Doing History Online

The French and Indian War

Go to the CourseMate website for this chapter and link to Primary Sources. Read Documents 11 through 16. If you were a young white man living in Virginia or Massachusetts, what motivation would you have for joining the British forces to fight the French and Indians?

www.cengage.brain.com

Pitt, Sir William (1708–1778) British political leader and orator who directed his country's military effort during the Seven Years' War.

Wolfe, James (1727–1759) British general during the Seven Years' War. He defeated the French at Quebec (1759) but was mortally wounded in the battle.

The 650 Native Americans who fought with the French included their traditional allies and some Delawares and Iroquois of the Ohio Valley who had previously supported the British. By 1754, some Ohio Indians were convinced that Britain and its colonies posed a greater threat to their lands than the French; with the defeat of Braddock, many more joined the French. Between 1755 and 1757, Delawares, Shawnees, Iroquois, and many others attacked the white frontier from Pennsylvania to Virginia, burning settlements and killing or capturing thousands of colonists.

In 1756, the struggle in North America became part of the larger European conflict known as the Seven Years' War, in which Great Britain supported Prussia against Austria, Russia, and France. The French penetrated into New York, seizing Fort William Henry and two thousand soldiers at Lake George. The tide changed after the British statesman **Sir William Pitt** took command of the war effort. He poured money and men into the American theater, expecting colonial legislatures to do the same. The new generals, Jeffery Amherst and **James Wolfe,** with an army of almost ten thousand men, captured Louisbourg in July 1758. The French then pulled their troops out of the Ohio Valley to protect Quebec and Montreal, allowing the British to take control of the west. Without French supplies and devastated by smallpox, the Native Americans ended their war on the frontier.

In 1759, the British and provincial armies had even greater success, leading some of the Iroquois of New York to abandon neutrality to join their side. The British reestablished control of New York, while from Louisbourg, General Wolfe sailed up the St. Lawrence to Quebec, where after several months his forces pierced the defenses of the well-fortified city. The next year, Amherst's army seized Montreal, thus ending French control of Canada. While the defeat of Canada marked the cessation of war in North America, the Seven Years' War continued off the coast of France, in India, and in the West Indies. When Spain entered the conflict as France's ally in 1762 in return for the promise of lands west of the Mississippi River, the British captured Manila in the Philippines and Havana, Cuba.

During the Seven Years' War, thousands of colonists joined the British army, and many more served in the provincial forces. Ordinary settlers came into close contact with the imperial authorities—and many loathed the experience. The British army contained professional soldiers drilled rigorously in military tactics, cleanliness, and order. British officers, from the upper classes, maintained discipline with punishments of death for major offenses such as desertion and up to a thousand lashes for lesser crimes. The British officers disdained the colonial units, while some colonial soldiers thought the British regulars were immoral, profane men who needed to be controlled with brutal discipline.

The British colonists welcomed the Treaty of Paris in 1763, which finally ended the war. Under the treaty, France lost all of its territory in North America but retrieved the valuable sugar islands of Guadeloupe and Martinique. Spain relinquished Florida to get back Cuba and the Philippines and, because the British lacked interest in the region, acquired French territory west of the Mississippi and New Orleans, located on the east side of the river. The Treaty of Paris gave the British colonists security from France and Spain; the home government received two unprofitable colonies, Canada and Florida. The provincials celebrated the victory with patriotic fervor: New York City raised a statue of George III, who had taken the throne in 1760 at age twenty-two. Many colonists, especially New England ministers, viewed the victory as a sign that God favored Protestant Britain and its colonies. One Massachusetts clergyman declared, "Here shall our indulgent Mother [Britain], who has most generously rescued and protected us, be served and honoured by growing Numbers, with all Duty, Love and Gratitude, till Time shall be no more."

The Indians Renew War in the Ohio Valley, 1763–1765

For Native Americans, the Seven Years' War was a disaster. The Treaty of Paris seriously undermined their position east of the Mississippi whether they had fought for the British or French or had remained neutral. Françe's defeat meant that they could no longer play one European nation off the other. British traders ended the custom of giving annual presents, charged high prices, stopped selling rum, and reduced the amount of ammunition sold. Furthermore, with the end of the Seven Years' War, white settlers streamed west into Indian lands, ignoring treaties that colonial governments had made with the Native Americans.

The altered British trade policies and land grabbing drove many Delawares, Shawnees, Iroquois, and others to renew the fighting. They gained spiritual unity from the Delaware prophet **Neolin,** one of a line of spiritual leaders among the Delawares and Shawnees who preached that Indians must reject Christianity and European goods, particularly rum, and revitalize their ancient culture. Neolin warned his followers, "If you suffer the English among you, you are dead men. Sickness, smallpox, and their poison will destroy you entirely." Many Indians throughout the Ohio Valley adopted Neolin's strategy, boycotting the fur trade by hunting only for their own food and personal needs. In 1763, Native Americans from western Pennsylvania through the Great Lakes region launched a pan-Indian assault on British garrisons known as Pontiac's War. A follower of Neolin and leader of the Ottawas, Pontiac laid siege unsuccessfully to the British fort at Detroit, while other Indians defeated thirteen British outposts. Although the British army established military dominance in the Ohio Valley by the end of 1763, fighting continued for two more years.

Neolin Delaware prophet who preached in the 1760s that Indians must reject Christianity and European goods, particularly rum, and revitalize their ancient culture.

In addition to armed force, the British government tried to end the war by keeping white settlers out of the Ohio Valley. The king issued the **Proclamation of 1763,** requiring colonists to stay east of a line drawn along the crest of the Appalachian Mountains from Maine to Georgia. But land speculators continued their operations and immigrants demanded farms. The British government, weighed down by debt from the Seven Years' War, failed to supply manpower to enforce the law.

Proclamation of 1763 In an attempt to keep white settlers out of the Ohio Valley, the Proclamation of 1763 drew a line along the crest of the Appalachian Mountains from Maine to Georgia and required all colonists to move east of the line.

❖ The British Provinces in 1763

The end of the Seven Years' War brought pivotal changes in British North America. For more than a century and a half, colonists had traded with the Native Americans, built farms and businesses, and developed networks of Atlantic commerce. They dealt with crises, from economic slumps to rebellions, becoming ever more confident of their position as semi-independent societies. During the last quarter-century, with greater involvement in imperial affairs and rising importation of consumer goods, the provincials felt more a part of the British empire than ever before. They believed that they were equal to the residents of Great Britain and possessed the rights of English people.

The Economy

In 1763, the mainland provinces still operated within the system of British mercantilism, which consisted of regulations on colonial trade and manufactures. For mercantilism to work to Britain's benefit, the colonies had to produce raw materials and agricultural staples needed by the home economy and serve as a market for its manufactured goods. The basic laws establishing the British mercantilist system were the seventeenth-century Navigation Acts, which Parliament supplemented from time to time. Although most colonial trade conformed to the law by the eighteenth century, smuggling of colonial products such as tobacco and furs occurred often enough to prompt demands within the British government for strict enforcement. In particular, colonial shippers bribed customs officials to ignore the Molasses Act (1733), which levied prohibitive duties on foreign sugar products, including a tax of sixpence per gallon on molasses.

Grey's Inn Creek Shipyard. *Grey's Inn Creek Shipyard,* by an unknown artist, c. 1760. Shipbuilding, at this Maryland shipyard as well as in northern seaports, was a major industry in the British colonies.

(Maryland Historical Society)

Other laws passed by Parliament prior to 1763 had a significant but uneven impact on colonial economic growth. British legislation, combined with lack of investment capital, limited the development of most manufactures. Some laws prohibited the export of machinery and the migration of skilled craftsmen from Britain to America. The Iron Act (1750) allowed duty-free import of colonial bar iron into Britain but forbade fabrication of iron goods in the colonies. Nevertheless, crude iron production received substantial investment, as did shipbuilding and rum distilling. Unhampered by mercantilist regulation, North American shipbuilders produced nearly 40 percent of vessels in the British-owned merchant fleet.

Despite these laws, the wealth of the British colonies increased between the 1720s and 1760, as trade flourished with the West Indies and, after 1750, with southern Europe, where crop failures and population growth swelled demand for wheat and flour. The middle colonies, already expanding with German and Irish immigration, were well situated to supply new markets. Philadelphia became the largest city in the British colonies: its wealthy merchants invested in ships, built mansions, purchased coaches and other luxuries, and speculated in western lands from the profits of trade. To the south, large planters in the Chesapeake and Carolinas accumulated great estates, while ordinary farmers more modestly improved their standard of living. All along the eastern seaboard, after 1740, white families indulged in what has been called a "consumer revolution," purchasing cloth, clothing, carpets, paper, gloves, mirrors, clocks, silverware, china tea sets, pottery, and books. The colonies became major markets for textiles, metalware, and other items, which under the Navigation Acts they could import only from Britain. The consumer revolution made the British more attentive to their North American provinces; at the same time, the imports helped to create a more standardized English culture in America. Affluent colonists became aware of the latest fashions in England and complained when they received out-of-date merchandise.

The economic upswing of the 1750s gave way to a depression after 1760, as the Seven Years' War moved to the Caribbean and military spending dropped. The seaport towns, having attracted workers during the wartime boom, faced deepening poverty and rising demands for relief. With depressed wages and long periods of unemployment, families found survival difficult. The resumption of immigration from Europe after the war intensified economic hardships and contributed to unrest in the backcountry.

Politics

The year 1763 marked the end of an era of political stability that had prevailed since the late 1720s in the British mainland provinces. As part of Britain's empire, the eighteenth-century colonists believed themselves among the most fortunate people on earth. The Glorious Revolution of 1688–1689, which removed James II, had ended the long, bitter contest between king and Parliament. The monarch's power was subsequently limited by the national legislature, composed of the House of Lords, which represented the aristocracy, and the House of Commons, which in theory represented everyone else. As a result of the 1689 settlement, Parliament's consent was necessary for taxes, new courts, raising an army in peacetime, and foreign invasions. Parliament gained control over its own meetings, and after 1707, the Crown lost veto power over legislation.

The balance of powers, political theorists argued, prevented domination by a single segment of society: the monarch, aristocracy, or common people. Thus, the British avoided forms of government considered destructive of liberty: rule by a single despot (tyranny), corrupt and self-serving rule by a group of aristocrats (oligarchy), and uncontrolled rule by the mob (democracy). The prevailing colonial structure of governor, appointed council, and elected lower house of the assembly reflected the English model.

The British provinces were the only European settlements in North America where ordinary people could vote for representative legislatures. An estimated 50 to 75 percent of white men were qualified to vote in the British colonies, the result of much broader property ownership than in England, where about 15 to 30 percent of adult males had the franchise. The British believed that a person needed a certain amount of property to vote or hold office. Servants, slaves, children, and unpropertied men were beholden to someone else, so they could not make independent decisions. By tradition, women also lacked the franchise, whether or not they owned property or were married. The colonists favored direct representation, requiring their legislators to live in the area from which they were elected and to advocate the interests of their constituents, unlike England, where members of the House of Commons did not have to reside in their electoral districts. The British believed that Parliament represented all of the people of the empire whether they elected delegates or not, a concept known as virtual representation.

English political theory also recognized the right of common people to resort to crowd action to withstand tyranny or seek needed protection. The people theoretically had this right as long as violence was limited—directed at property rather than at persons. At various times, colonial mobs protested to prevent grain from being exported when food was in short supply, to destroy houses of prostitution, and to stop the British navy from impressing men into the king's service, as with the 1747 Knowles riot in Boston.

(The Granger Collection, New York)

King George III. *Portrait of George III in 1771* by Johann Zoffany.

The most important and sustained political development in British America during the first half of the eighteenth century was the rise of the elected lower houses of assembly. The legislatures acquired greater power and assumed more functions—most significant, the right to initiate bills to raise taxes and disburse public funds, that is, the power of the purse. They also gained the authority to initiate other legislation, choose their own leadership, and settle disputed elections.

The political stability and rise of the assemblies that marked the mid-eighteenth century resulted from a number of factors, including the long period of economic growth that began in the 1720s. Prosperity supported the formation of cohesive elites—mostly second-, third-, and fourth-generation Americans with inherited wealth, large estates, and enslaved Africans or servants to meet their domestic needs, and (consequently) sufficient leisure time for politics. Many studied the law: the growth of the colonial bar accompanied the professionalization of politics. Economic prosperity inclined ordinary whites to defer to the elites as long as opportunity was good and they had crops to tend or other work to do. Their deference to social and economic superiors became most visible after 1725, when participation at the polls declined among eligible voters, and incumbent assemblymen won reelection year after year.

The provincial elites also benefited after 1720 from the British decision to administer the colonies with a light touch, allowing royal governors to accommodate the assemblies. And although riots occurred during the 1740s and 1750s over land claims and impressment, none threatened social disorder on the level of the seventeenth-century rebellions. Indeed, most ordinary whites feared attacks by Native Americans and slave revolts more than misuse of governmental power by elites. By the end of 1763, the British colonists of North America had reason to be optimistic about their future as Englishmen.

CHAPTER REVIEW, 1720–1763

SUMMARY

- In the colonies, the Enlightenment created new educational opportunities, promoted scientific research, and encouraged the development of new political theories.
- Between 1720 and 1760, the Great Awakening, a series of religious revivals that emphasized emotionalism and personal salvation, swept across British America.
- The population of the colonies became increasingly diverse as the African American population grew, through both natural increase and increased importation, and from a significant influx of German and Scots-Irish immigrants.
- Between 1744 and 1765, colonists participated in a series of wars waged by Britain against Spain, France, and their Native American allies. By the end of these conflicts, France had withdrawn from the North American mainland.
- Involvement in British wars and integration into Atlantic trade networks fostered among many colonists a strong sense of English identity and feelings of entitlement to the rights of Englishmen.

IDENTIFICATIONS

inoculation
Enlightenment
Isaac Newton
John Locke
natural philosophy
Benjamin Franklin
midwives
Dr. William Shippen, Jr.
Great Awakening
George Whitefield
Scots-Irish
James Oglethorpe
Gullah
Stono uprising
Albany Plan of Union
William Pitt
James Wolfe
Neolin
Proclamation of 1763

MAKING CONNECTIONS: LOOKING AHEAD

Chapter 5 looks at how the year 1764 marked a major change in British government policy toward its North American colonies, a change that led to revolution a dozen years later.

1. Why did London impose the series of "reforms" beginning with the Sugar and Currency acts?
2. Why was Boston the center of colonial resistance?
3. How did events in the Spanish borderland colonies of Louisiana, Texas, and New Mexico compare with the unfolding crisis in the British provinces?

RECOMMENDED READINGS

Anderson, Fred. *Crucible of War: The Seven Years' War and the Fate of Empire in British North America, 1754–1766* (2000). A convincing analysis of the significance of the Seven Years' War.

Bailyn, Bernard, and Morgan, Philip D., eds. *Strangers Within the Realm: Cultural Margins of the First British Empire* (1991). Important essays on specific groups, including Native Americans, Scots-Irish, African Americans, Germans, and Dutch.

Beeman, Richard R. *The Varieties of Political Experience in Eighteenth-Century America* (2004). A wide-ranging overview of politics and ideology in the British colonies.

Carson, Cary, et al., eds. *Of Consuming Interests: The Style of Life in the Eighteenth Century* (1994). Excellent essays on topics ranging from housing and art to consumer behavior.

Daunton, Martin, and Halpern, Rick, eds. *Empire and Others: British Encounters with Indigenous Peoples, 1600–1850* (1999). Significant essays on relations between Natives and English in eastern North America and elsewhere.

Harper, Steven Craig. *Promised Land: Penn's Holy Experiment, the Walking Purchase, and the Dispossession of Delawares, 1600–1763* (2006). Analyzes the transition of Pennsylvania's relations with the Delawares from peace to war.

Morgan, Philip D. *Slave Counterpoint: Black Culture in the Eighteenth-Century Chesapeake and Lowcountry* (1998). A comprehensive study of African American work and culture in the South.

Richter, Daniel K. *Facing East from Indian Country: A Native History of Early America* (2001). Approaches significant events in relations between Indians and settlers from Native perspectives.

Steele, Ian K. *Warpaths: Invasions of North America* (1994). Examines the Seven Years' War as one of a series of European invasions of Indian territory during the colonial period.

Sweet, John Wood. *Bodies Politic: Negotiating Race in the American North, 1730–1830* (2003). Explores the intersection of racial ideology and political culture in New England.

PASSAGES 1764 to 1814

5 Wars for Independence, 1764–1783
6 Toward a More Perfect Union, 1783–1788
7 The Federalist Republic, 1789–1799
8 The New Republic Faces a New Century, 1800–1815

During the American Revolution, sixteen-year-old Dicey Langston of the South Carolina frontier left home in the middle of the night, by herself, to warn her brother's unit about Tory troop movements. As a historian later described Langston's journey,

> Many miles were to be traversed, and the road lay through woods, and crossed marshes and creeks where the conveniences of bridges and foot-logs were wanting. She walked rapidly on, heedless of slight difficulties; but her heart almost failed her when she came to the banks of the Tyger—a deep and rapid stream, rendered more dangerous by the rains that had lately fallen. . . . But the energy of a resolute will, under the care of Providence, sustained her.*

Dicey Langston's effort, like those of thousands of other Americans, was emblematic of her country's passage from a collection of British provinces in 1764 to a stable republic with some international standing a half-century later. The thirteen mainland colonies, proud of their contribution to victory in the Seven Years' War, were stunned by Britain's program to curtail their rights. Stretching from the mountains of northern New England to the rice fields of coastal Georgia, diverse in economics, religion, ethnicity, and politics, the colonies mustered enough unity to organize a revolutionary congress, stop British imports, raise an army, obtain help from France, and win the war.

The states refused to create a unified nation, however, and instead established, under the Articles of Confederation, thirteen separate republics joined loosely by a representative Congress. Without power to tax or raise troops, the Congress faced severe postwar problems in demobilizing the army, paying the war debt, protecting the frontiers, and unifying a populace divided by war. In the wake of bankruptcy and insurrection, nationalists in 1787 called together a constitutional convention. Through a series of compromises, the framers drafted the new Constitution, which gave more authority to the central government yet retained considerable power in the states. Americans ratified the document with the understanding that amendments to protect individual liberties and states' rights would be approved.

After the first national elections, the Constitution's proponents, the Federalists, controlled the new government, with George Washington as president. Having agreed on the frame of government, they were unprepared for the bitter factionalism that forged political parties in the 1790s. Nor were they ready for the foreign entanglements that resulted from two decades of war between Great Britain and postrevolutionary France. Only after the United States declared war on the British in 1812 and held its own as the conflict ended in stalemate did the nation finally demonstrate its independence. By 1814 most of the men who led the American Revolution had passed from power—though James Madison would remain president for several years—and a new generation was taking control.

The heroic story of the young nation surmounting difficulties—two wars against Great Britain, a constitutional crisis, several internal rebellions, an undeclared conflict with France, and constant fighting in the backcountry—masks other narratives—those of women, African Americans, and Native Americans, who failed to achieve autonomy. Thousands of sisters, mothers, and wives, like Dicey Langston, risked their lives during the Revolution, but after the war, women still lacked basic legal and political rights to hold property after marriage, vote, and take part in government. And, although revolutionary rhetoric against slavery resulted in abolition in the North and many private manumissions in the Chesapeake region, most African Americans

*Elizabeth F. Ellet, *Domestic History of the American Revolution* (1850), 234.

Bombardment of Fort McHenry, War of 1812. The successful American defense in 1814 against British bombardment of Fort McHenry in Baltimore harbor was the inspiration for Francis Scott Key's poem, "The Star Spangled Banner."

remained enslaved, a condition perpetuated by the new Constitution and development of cotton. Even most free blacks had little opportunity to acquire property, and they were denied suffrage and participation in government.

For Native Americans, the success and growth of the new nation meant their decline. Despite revitalization movements to restore traditional cultures led by Neolin, Handsome Lake, Tenskwatawa, and others, and destructive wars to defend their homelands in Alabama, Tennessee, Kentucky, and Ohio, by 1814 the United States dominated most of the territory east of the Mississippi River. Native Americans tried various routes to survive and retain as much of their autonomy as possible: adoption of white culture, cession of some lands for the promise they could keep others, alliances with Great Britain and Spain, and pan-Indian war. But in the face of unremitting westward settlement and continuing disease, the Indian peoples of eastern North America became remnants of formerly powerful nations.

CHRONOLOGY

	1760	1775	1780
POLITICS AND DIPLOMACY	**1765**: Stamp Act protest **1766–1771:** Regulator movements in North and South Carolina **1767:** John Dickinson's "Farmer" letters against Townshend Act **1768:** Nonimportation movement **1769:** Spanish colonize California **1770:** Boston Massacre **1772:** Committees of Correspondence **1773:** Boston Tea Party **1774:** Coercive Acts; port of Boston closed First Continental Congress	**1775:** Battles of Lexington and Concord Lord Dunmore's proclamation to servants and slaves **1776:** Thomas Paine's *Common Sense* Declaration of Independence **1777:** Burgoyne surrenders to Americans at Saratoga **1778:** Alliance with France Iroquois attacks in New York and Pennsylvania	**1780**: Pennsylvania law for gradual abolition of slavery **1781:** Articles of Confederation ratified Surrender of Cornwallis at Yorktown **1783:** Treaty of Paris **1787:** Shaysites attack Springfield, Massachusetts, arsenal Northwest Ordinance Constitution sent to states for ratification **1789:** Inauguration of President George Washington
SOCIETY AND CULTURE	**1765:** First American medical school **1766:** Queens College (Rutgers) New Southwark Theatre in Philadelphia **1769:** The *American Magazine* (Philadelphia) published Benjamin West's *Death of General Wolfe* American scientists observe transit of Venus **1770:** Equestrian statue of George III installed in New York **1771:** Benjamin Franklin starts Autobiography **1772:** John Singleton Copley's portrait of Samuel Adams **1773**: Phillis Wheatley's *Poems on Various Subjects, Religious and Moral*	**1776:** Jemima Wilkinson becomes Public Universal Friend **1779:** John Murray's American Universalist Church	**1780s:** Northern blacks start separate churches and societies **1783:** Noah Webster's American spelling book First daily newspaper, *Pennsylvania Evening Post* **1784:** Judith Sargent Murray begins essays on women's status **1786:** Virginia statue for religious freedom Gilbert Stuart's portrait of Joseph Brant
ECONOMICS AND TECHNOLOGY	**1760s**: British American traders cross Mississippi River **1764:** Sugar and Currency acts	**1776:** Adam Smith's *The Wealth of Nations* **1778:** Captain James Cook explores the Pacific Northwest **1779:** Continental money becomes nearly worthless	**1780s:** Rapid settlement of Kentucky and Tennessee Oliver Evans automates grist mills **1781:** Bank of North America in Philadelphia **1783:** Great Britain closes West Indies to American ships **1784:** Spain closes port of New Orleans to Americans Debt crisis spurs protests in the U.S. **1788:** Pennsylvania Society for the Encouragement of Manufactures and the Useful Arts introduces spinning jennies

1790	1796	1800
1791: Bill of Rights ratified **1794:** Whiskey Rebellion **1795:** Jay Treaty	**1798:** Alien and Sedition Acts Quasi-War with France **1799:** Fries Rebellion	**1800:** Washington, D.C., becomes national capital Gabriel's rebellion Jefferson elected president **1803:** *Marbury v. Madison* case Louisiana Purchase **1804:** Lewis and Clark expedition **1809:** Tecumseh organizes pan-Indian confederacy **1812:** U.S. war with Great Britain **1814:** Treaty of Ghent
1791: Charles Willson Pearle's *Thomas Jefferson* **c. 1793:** Mary Woolstonecraft's *Vindication of the Rights of Women* circulates in the U.S. **1795:** Philadelphia Quaker women establish first female benevolent society in the U.S.	**1797:** Second Great Awakening begins in New England **1799:** Rise of Handsome Lake as Seneca prophet Charles Brockden Brown's *Wieland*	**1800s:** Tenskwatawa, the Shawnee Prophet, inspires a following **1800:** Library of Congress **1801:** Cane Ridge, Kentucky, camp meeting **1805:** Pennsylvania Academy of Fine Arts
1790: Samuel Slater builds first U.S. water-powered textile mill Congress passes patent law **1791:** Bank of the United States Excise tax on whiskey Alexander Hamilton's plan for promoting manufactures **1793:** British blockade of French West Indies Eli Whitney's cotton gin **1795:** Great Britain opens West Indies to U.S. trade	**1796:** Spain opens navigation on Mississippi River Alexander Hamilton's industrial town in New Jersey fails **1798:** Eli Whitney attempts to manufacture guns with interchangeable parts **1790s:** U.S. international trade soars with European conflict Cotton expands Southern slavery Northern cities become magnets for African Americans	**1802:** Oliver Evans's high pressure steam engine **1806:** Non-Importation Act **1807:** Embargo Act **1808:** Federal ban on international slave trade **1809:** Giles's Enforcement Act Embargo repealed; replaced with Non-Intercourse Act **1811:** Charter of national bank expires

5 Wars for Independence

1764–1783

MAKING CONNECTIONS

LOOKING BACK

Chapter 4 showed that between 1720 and 1763 the thirteen British provinces underwent considerable change as a result of German and Scots-Irish immigration, the intellectual challenges of the Enlightenment, religious developments of the Great Awakening, and economic expansion within the Atlantic world. Before starting Chapter 5, you should be able to answer the following questions:

1. How did American colonists participate in the Enlightenment?
2. How did the Great Awakening affect colonial society?
3. In what ways did Native Americans respond to the expansion of British America?
4. What economic restrictions did the British government place on the colonies prior to 1763?

The treaty of 1763 that ended the Seven Years' War forced Spain and Great Britain to reassess their North American colonies. Both nations had relatively new kings: Charles III had taken Spain's throne in 1759, and George III had become the British monarch in 1760. For the Spanish, the borderlands in North America were of secondary importance, serving as a buffer to protect the Mexican silver mines. For Britain, however, the mainland provinces had become increasingly significant as a source of revenue and market for consumer goods. The Seven Years' War marked Britain's ascendancy to world power, but it resulted in a national debt of £130 million. Annual interest payments alone amounted to £4.5 million, equal to more than half of the government's yearly expenditures prior to the war.

When Parliament imposed levies on the American colonies to help pay expenses, the colonists protested vehemently that they should not be taxed without their consent. Beginning in 1764, the Americans petitioned, rioted, boycotted British goods, destroyed tea, and ultimately defied George III and parliamentary leaders when they sent troops. The colonists' belief that they possessed the same rights as the English was something for which many were willing to fight. Nevertheless, the consensus to declare independence did not come quickly, nor was independence easily won. Americans who disagreed that the British actions warranted insurrection remained loyal to the king. These **loyalists,** also called Tories after the pro-monarchy faction in England, tried to subvert the Revolutionary governments and formed loyalist militia units to fight alongside British troops. They found allies in many Native Americans and African Americans who conducted wars of independence of their own. The Revolution touched everyone: colonial leaders, Native Americans, women, and enslaved blacks, as well as the white men who served as most of the armed forces. The cause of the patriots—or **Whigs,** as the American revolutionaries called themselves, after the English party that had opposed the Crown—depended on the efforts of many people.

loyalists Residents of the British colonies who remained loyal to Great Britain during the American Revolution. Also called Tories after the pro-monarchy faction in England.

Whigs (Revolutionary era) Residents of the British colonies who opposed Great Britain during the American Revolution. Also called patriots, they took the name Whigs from the English party that had opposed the Crown.

❖ Imperial Realignments, Reform, and Resistance, 1764–1775

The peace of 1763 required Spain to withdraw from Florida, assume the government of Louisiana, and rethink its defenses in Texas and New Mexico (see Map 5.1). The Spanish considered Britain's enhanced power and the soaring population of the British colonies as a threat to their American empire. Yet British leaders were confronting problems of their own, including a soaring national debt. Their attempts to push the debt load onto their colonial subjects in North America, which seemed reasonable to most Britons, pushed the colonists to the brink of revolt.

CHAPTER TIMELINE 1760 | 1765 | 1770 | 1775 | 1780 | 1785

POLITICS AND DIPLOMACY

- 1765 Stamp Act protests begin
- 1770 Boston Massacre occurs
- 1766–1771 North Carolina Regulators protest taxation and lack of representation
- 1776 Declaration of Independence is adopted
- 1774 First Continental Congress is established
- 1763 Treaty of Paris is signed
- 1778 Alliance with France is negotiated

SOCIETY AND CULTURE

- 1765 First American medical school is founded
- 1769 Scientists observe transit of Venus

ECONOMICS AND TECHNOLOGY

- 1764 Sugar and Currency Acts pass
- 1776 Adam Smith's *The Wealth of Nations* is published
- 1779 Continental currency is nearly worthless

(Copyright © Cengage Learning)

MAP 5.1

North America in 1764

Significant changes in European claims to regions in North America resulted from the Seven Years' War. The Treaty of Paris of 1763 divided former French territory between Great Britain to the east of the Mississippi River and Spain to the west. The British also gained Spanish Florida.

Realignments in the Spanish Borderlands

Spain ordered all of its subjects to leave Florida when Britain took control. Although the British promised religious freedom to the Catholic Floridians, some 200 Christian Indians, 79 free African Americans, 350 slaves, and nearly all of the 3,000 Spanish departed, selling their property at a loss to British bargain hunters. To avoid being enslaved by the English, the free blacks of Mose, near St. Augustine, accepted Spain's offer of homesteads in Cuba.

Acquisition of Louisiana, including all French territory west of the Mississippi River and New Orleans on the east bank, gave Spain an extensive region to administer. Concerns about British expansion became all too real as interlopers spanned the Mississippi River to trade with Indians on the Great Plains. Indeed, within a decade, four thousand British colonists and their fifteen hundred African American slaves were living on the Gulf Coast and eastern shore of the Mississippi.

The more immediate challenge for Spanish authorities in Louisiana, however, was asserting political control of the province. For several years, the French government remained; even after the first Spanish governor, **Antonio de Ulloa,** arrived in 1766, he tried to govern jointly with the last French governor. Adhering to Charles III's instructions, Ulloa left the French administration and legal system intact, even allowing the French flag to fly over the capitol. Ulloa did not extend this leniency to commerce, however: he tried to stop business with France and Great Britain and restricted the Native American trade to certain dealers. Like the thirteen British provinces on the Atlantic coast, and at about the same time, merchants protested the new restrictions, then in October 1768 issued a declaration of loyalty to the king of France. With few Spanish troops at his disposal, Governor Ulloa left for Cuba. When the French refused to intervene, the colony became independent, but only for a year.

Ulloa, Antonio de (1716–1795) First Spanish governor of Louisiana, who arrived in 1766 and tried to govern jointly with the last French governor.

The Spanish regained Louisiana when General Alexander O'Reilly, an Irishman with a successful career in the Spanish army, arrived in 1769 with more than two thousand soldiers. O'Reilly raised the Spanish flag and within a year ended the French government, changed the legal system, made Castilian the official language, and outlawed trade with other nations. Despite the merchants' fears, the economy flourished as smuggling continued with Britain, and Spanish markets welcomed their goods. St. Louis, established in 1764, became the thriving center of trade with Native Americans of the Illinois and Missouri countries. Louisiana remained culturally French, as the numbers of French settlers far surpassed the Spanish.

With ownership of Louisiana, the Spanish could alter their defenses along the frontier in Texas and New Mexico. During the 1760s and 1770s, in the face of constant assaults by Apaches and Comanches who refused to submit to Spanish rule or Christianity, Spain tried to reform its administration and improve the colonies' defenses. From 1766 to 1768, the Marqués de Rubí, a high-level military official from Spain, inspected the fortifications and missions of the Southwest. He discovered badly located **presidios** (or forts) and soldiers suffering from lack of food and clothes because of their commanders' greed. Rubí recommended building new presidios and relocating others to create an orderly cordon of military

presidios Forts in colonial Spanish America built in an effort to defend the colonists and missions from Native American opponents.

bases situated about a hundred miles apart. The presidios would extend from the Gulf of California to the Gulf of Mexico, along a line that was close to today's boundary between the United States and Mexico. The borderlands officials also received more autonomy to deal with local problems, but they lacked sufficient troops to conquer the Apaches and Comanches.

The British Sugar and Currency Acts of 1764

In Britain's colonies, which experienced few restrictions before 1763, trouble began when George III appointed George Grenville as first minister, with responsibility for solving the debt crisis that resulted from the Seven Years' War. Grenville decided that Americans should pay more taxes because they benefited from the war and began his program in 1764 with the **Sugar Act,** which initiated a new policy of charging duties primarily to raise revenue rather than to regulate trade. It reduced the duty on foreign molasses from sixpence to threepence per gallon, which was further reduced to one penny in 1766. Grenville assumed merchants would pay the lower tariff rather than risk smuggling and bribery, as they had been doing. The law also added timber, iron, and hides to the list of enumerated goods. In addition, the law gave increased powers to the vice-admiralty courts, expanded the use of **writs of assistance** (search warrants), empowered the Royal Navy to inspect ships, and required endless bureaucratic paperwork from colonial shippers. Parliament also passed the Currency Act (1764), which forbid colonies from issuing paper money, thus creating a shortage of currency.

Sugar Act (1764) British law that initiated the policy of charging duties primarily for revenue rather than for regulating trade. The act reduced the duty on foreign molasses; added timber, iron, and hides to the list of enumerated goods; and increased the powers of vice-admiralty courts.

writs of assistance General search warrants; a writ of assistance authorized customs officials to search for smuggled goods.

Stamp Act (1765) British law requiring colonists to purchase a stamp for official documents and published papers, including wills, newspapers, and pamphlets.

Coming in the midst of an economic depression, this legislation stirred up colonial protest. Provincial assemblies sent petitions to England requesting relief. Merchants feared that if imports of foreign molasses were cut off, their provision trade to the Spanish and French West Indies would be lost. Without foreign credits, they could not pay for British manufactures. The Americans cut back their orders from Britain and encouraged home industry, arousing opposition to Grenville's policies from English businessmen.

The Stamp Act Protests

Passed by Parliament in 1765, the **Stamp Act** provoked an even greater storm of protest. The law departed entirely from the confines of mercantilist policy, because its purpose was to raise an internal revenue, which would be used to pay troops in the colonies. All publications, including deeds, liquor licenses, court documents, playing cards, newspapers, and official transactions were to be subject to this special stamp and tax. The tax could be paid only in gold or silver specie, an onerous requirement because colonists generally used paper money and credit. The vice-admiralty courts would enforce the act, confiscating any land or property involved in transactions conducted without the stamps.

Colonists of all walks of life found the Stamp Act offensive. Because Parliament, not their own provincial assemblies, passed the act, Americans considered it a violation of their rights as British subjects. As they understood the British constitution, the people must consent to taxes through their representatives. The provinces could not send delegates to Parliament, so that body should not tax them to raise revenue. As one Philadelphia merchant said succinctly, "The point in dispute is a very

(LC-USZ61-449)/Library of Congress Prints and Photographs Division Washington, D.C. 20540 USA)

Stamp Act Riots. A woman and African American man are prominently portrayed in this illustration of the Stamp Act riots in Boston, 1765.

Important one, if the Americans are to be taxed by a Parliament where they are not nor can be Represented, they are no longer Englishmen but Slaves." Only tariffs to regulate trade such as the 1733 duty on molasses, many colonists believed, were constitutionally valid. Thus, provincial assemblies formally protested the Stamp Act. In the Virginia House of Burgesses, the newly elected **Patrick Henry,** only twenty-nine years old, convinced the assembly to approve a series of moderate resolutions that defended the colonists' right to tax themselves.

Henry, Patrick (1736–1799) Elected to the Virginia House of Burgesses at age twenty-nine, Henry introduced fourteen resolves against the Stamp Act. He was a brilliant speaker and served as governor of Virginia during the Revolution.

When newspapers spread word of Virginia's action, other provinces responded, challenging British efforts to assert control. Rhode Island instructed its officials to ignore the stamp tax; Massachusetts, Connecticut, New York, New Jersey, Pennsylvania, Maryland, and South Carolina passed resolves similar to Virginia's. In October 1765, representatives from nine colonies traveled to New York City to attend the Stamp Act Congress. In resolutions and petitions to Parliament, the congress upheld the power of representative assemblies, not Parliament, to tax the colonists. Further, the congress defended trial by jury, which the expanded authority of the vice-admiralty courts threatened.

Ordinary colonists joined the challenge, drawing on the tradition of the mob to protest what they considered tyranny. The anti–Stamp Act riots began in Boston on August 14, 1765, when a group who called themselves the Loyal Nine organized a demonstration to hang in effigy the appointed stamp collector for Massachusetts, Andrew Oliver, and damaged his home. Oliver resigned his commission. Days later, a Boston mob attacked the houses of several other officials, gutting the mansion of Lieutenant Governor Thomas Hutchinson.

News of Oliver's resignation prompted protesters all along the Atlantic seaboard to prevent stamp distribution, scheduled to begin November 1. By the end of 1765, distributors in every colony except Georgia had resigned. The men who led the crowds called themselves **Sons of Liberty.** They were mostly propertied men—small merchants, shopkeepers, and craftsmen—who also established networks to organize boycotts of British goods. Merchants and retailers in New York City, Philadelphia, and Boston signed pacts to stop imports until Parliament repealed the act. By early 1766, the Sons of Liberty had coerced customs officials and judges to open the ports and resume court business without stamps. The American resistance aimed to expunge the stamp tax, not end British authority, and they succeeded in 1766, when Parliament repealed the Stamp Act. Suffering from postwar economic depression and unemployment, the British textile industry faced even worse times with an American boycott. British merchants clearly understood the growing significance of the colonial market.

Sons of Liberty Groups of small merchants, shopkeepers, and craftsmen who successfully opposed the Stamp Act in 1765–1766 by establishing networks to organize boycotts of British goods.

Doing History Online

The Stamp Act

Go to the CourseMate website for this chapter and link to Primary Sources. Read Documents 1 to 7 on reactions to the Stamp Act. What specifically upset the colonists so much? Did they overreact to the act?

www.cengagebrain.com

In the Carolinas, the Stamp Act resistance spawned revolts against colonial elites. To blacks, the radicals' oft-spoken argument that the English government intended to deprive white Americans of freedom—to make them slaves—seemed ironic. Yet such statements also gave them hope, for the Revolutionary movement spotlighted the institution of slavery and its immorality and injustice. In January 1766 in Charleston, South Carolina, fourteen hundred seamen and a group of black slaves threatened serious disorder. The sailors became restless because the customs agents refused to release ships from port without stamped documents. The people of Charleston were even more concerned, however, when a group of enslaved men marched through the town shouting "Liberty!" The city armed itself against a slave revolt, and the South Carolina assembly became so frightened that it restricted slave imports for three years.

The Regulator movement in North Carolina also began in 1766, inspired by the uproar against the Stamp Act, but it targeted the colonial elite, not Britain. Western farmers, who became known as **Regulators,** demanded confirmation of land titles and protested corrupt local officials, excessive court fees and taxes, and lack of adequate representation in the North Carolina legislature. The North Carolina Regulators refused to pay taxes and closed several courts. In 1771, when

Regulators Name used in the late 1760s by the North Carolina Regulator movement and the South Carolina Regulators. Both groups demanded fair representation in the state legislatures but otherwise had distinct goals and membership.

the government sent the eastern militia, two thousand Regulators met them at Alamance Creek but were dispersed.

Most of the grievances of the South Carolina Regulators were similar to the grievances of the North Carolina Regulators. They were planters who wanted to bring order—"to regulate" the backcountry, where there were no courts or jails. Bandits roamed freely, stealing horses and cattle, destroying property, and sometimes torturing and killing their victims. The Regulators resorted to vigilante "justice," capturing and whipping suspected felons. They finally ceased their activities in 1769 when the legislature established a circuit court system for the entire province.

The Townshend Revenue Act, 1767

In other British mainland colonies, attention focused on imperial tensions rather than on regional disputes. The British government and American radicals emerged from the Stamp Act crisis with conflicting views: the Americans celebrated the Stamp Act's repeal, but the British yielded no authority. In the Declaratory Act, passed with the repeal in March 1766, Parliament affirmed its power "to make laws and statutes of sufficient force and validity to bind the colonies and people of America, subjects of the crown of Great Britain, in all cases whatsoever." The act generated little response in the colonies but should have, for it laid the basis for subsequent restrictions.

In June 1767, Parliament passed three more laws affecting the Americans: an act establishing the American Board of Customs Commissioners to enforce legislation against illegal trade, the New York Restraining Act, and the **Townshend Revenue Act.** The Restraining Act threatened to dissolve the New York Assembly for refusing adequate supplies to British soldiers stationed in the province. Instead, the New York legislators gave in, pledging additional funds for the troops. The Townshend Revenue Act placed duties on tea, glass, paper, lead, and paint to pay the salaries of governors and judges, thus removing their dependence on the provincial legislatures. The act also required colonial courts to provide customs officials with writs of assistance to search houses and businesses for smuggled merchandise. To American Whigs, the Townshend Act was a step toward tyranny because it raised revenue without the approval of colonial assemblies and removed royal officials from the lawmakers' control.

Townshend Revenue Act (1767) Conceived by Charles Townshend, the British chancellor of the exchequer, the act placed duties on tea, glass, paper, lead, and paint to help pay British colonial administrative and military costs in North America.

At first, colonial reaction to the Townshend Act was restrained. Then, in December 1767, a few weeks after the act went into effect, John Dickinson, a Philadelphia lawyer and owner of a Delaware plantation, began publishing a series of twelve letters signed "A Farmer." Soon reprinted by newspapers throughout the thirteen colonies and published in pamphlet form as *Letters from a Farmer in Pennsylvania* (1768), Dickinson's arguments galvanized opposition to the Townshend duties. He rejected the position that the colonists should accept external taxes (duties) but not internal taxes (like the stamp tax), stating that only elected representatives could legally impose any revenue tax. Dickinson predicted, "If we can find no relief from this infamous situation . . . we may bow down our necks, with all the stupid serenity of servitude, to any drudgery which our lords and masters shall please to command." Dickinson urged the colonies to petition for repeal; if that failed, they should once again boycott British goods.

Massachusetts responded to the Townshend Act first. In early 1768, its assembly petitioned George III for redress and then dispatched a "circular letter," or communication, to the other twelve colonies suggesting they do the same. The new English secretary of state for the colonies, Lord Hillsborough, realized that the circular letter was a call to unified resistance and ordered the Massachusetts assemblymen to rescind their circular letter. They refused. When he directed

Doing History Opposing Views of the Stamp Act

When news arrived in 1765 that Parliament had passed the Stamp Act, the colonists protested the internal tax. In the Virginia assembly, Patrick Henry introduced resolutions accusing Parliament of attempting to destroy "American freedom." Of the seven resolutions published in newspapers, the Virginia legislators passed the first four listed below, which were more moderate than the rest. Not all Americans opposed the Stamp Act. The second document is an excerpt from a pamphlet by Martin Howard, Jr., a Rhode Island lawyer, who believed that the colonies obtained rights from their charters, which did not exempt them from parliamentary law.

Virginia Resolves Against the Stamp Act, *1765*

Resolved, That the first adventurers and settlers of this His Majesty's Colony and Dominion of Virginia brought with them, and transmitted to their posterity, and all other of His Majesty's subjects since inhabiting this His Majesty's said Colony, all the liberties, privileges, franchises, and immunities, that have at any time been held, enjoyed, and possessed, by the people of Great Britain.

Resolved, That by two royal charters, granted by King James the First, the colonists aforesaid are declared entitled to all liberties, privileges, and immunities of denizens and natural subjects, to all intents and purposes, as if they had been abiding and born within the realm of England.

Resolved, That the taxation of the people by themselves, or by persons chosen by themselves to represent them, who can only know what taxes the people are able to bear, or the easiest method of raising them, and must themselves be affected by every tax laid on the people, is the only security against a burthensome taxation, and the distinguishing characteristick of British freedom, without which the ancient constitution cannot exist.

Resolved, That His Majesty's liege people of this his most ancient and loyal Colony have without interruption enjoyed the inestimable right of being governed by such laws, respecting their internal polity and taxation, as are derived from their own consent, with the approbation of their sovereign, or his substitute; and that the same hath never been forfeited or yielded up, but hath been constantly recognized by the kings and people of Great Britain.

Resolved therefore, That the General Assembly of this Colony have the only and sole exclusive right and power to lay taxes and impositions upon the inhabitants of this Colony, and that every attempt to vest such power in any person or persons whatsoever other than the General Assembly aforesaid has a

colonial governors to dissolve assemblies that responded to the letter, most legislatures sent petitions and were disbanded. Simultaneously, Hillsborough reassigned military units from the Ohio Valley to Florida, Nova Scotia, Quebec, and the mid-Atlantic region, where they could be called on to control the defiant provinces. In June 1768, he sent British regiments to Boston when the customs commissioners demanded protection against rioters. As the troops disembarked in October, they heard cries of protest but met no armed resistance.

During 1768, Boston residents signed a nonimportation agreement, using the same strategy against the Townshend Act that had proved successful against the Stamp Act. Most of the city's merchants pledged to stop importing goods from Great Britain after January 1, 1769, unless the Townshend duties were repealed. The nonimportation movement soon spread to New York City, where artisans supported the merchants by agreeing to boycott any retailer who imported British goods. In Virginia, George Washington supported the boycott. He wrote, "At a time when our lordly masters in Great Britain will be satisfied with nothing less than the deprivation of American freedom, it seems highly necessary that some thing should be done to avert the stroke and maintain the liberty which we have derived from our Ancestors."

manifest tendency to destroy British as well as American freedom.

Resolved, That His Majesty's liege people, the inhabitants of this Colony are not bound to yield obedience to any law or ordinance whatever, designed to impose any taxation whatsoever upon them other than the laws or ordinances of the General Assembly aforesaid.

Resolved, That any person who shall, by speaking or writing, assert or maintain that any person or persons other than the General Assembly of this Colony, have any right or power to impose or lay any taxation on the people here, shall be deemed an enemy to His Majesty's Colony.

Source: Max Beloff, ed., *The Debate on the American Revolution, 1761–1783: A Sourcebook* (New York: Harper & Row, 1960), 70–72.

A Rhode Island Lawyer Supports British Power: Martin Howard, Jr., *1765*

But to bring this argument down to the most vulgar apprehension; The common law has established it as a rule or maxim, that the plantations are bound by British acts of parliament, if particularly named: and surely no Englishman, in his senses, will deny the force of a common law maxim. One cannot but smile at the inconsistency of these inherent, indefeasible men: If one of them has a suit at law, in any part of New-England, upon a question of land, property, or merchandize, he appeals to the common law, to support his claim, or defeat his adversary; and yet is so profoundly stupid as to say, that an act of parliament does not bind him: when, perhaps, the same page in a law book, which points him out of a remedy for a libel, or a slap in the face, would inform him that it does. In a word, The force of an act of parliament, over the colonies, is predicated upon the common law, the origin and basis of all those inherent rights and privileges which constitute the boast and felicity of a Briton.

Source: Jack N. Rakove, *Declaring Rights: A Brief History with Documents* (Boston: Bedford Books, 1998), 50–54.

QUESTIONS for REFLECTION

1. The Virginia Assembly passed only the first four of Patrick Henry's seven resolutions. What are the main arguments of these four "moderate" resolves?
2. What are the chief arguments of the three more "radical" of Henry's propositions that the legislators failed to approve?
3. How does Martin Howard, Jr., contest the view that provincial assemblies, not Parliament, had the right to impose internal taxes on the colonists?

The boycotts, which were unofficial agreements without the force of law, met uneven success. Between 1768 and 1769, American imports from England declined by 38 percent (see Figure 5.1). As the months passed, however, importers wavered as their incomes fell. In contrast, craftspeople—beyond their concern for liberty—often benefited from the boycott because it created a demand for their products. Some artisans organized into street groups to threaten merchants and customs officials who tried to undermine the nonimportation pacts. Women participated as both purchasers of goods and producers. Many "Daughters of Liberty" gave up imported tea and clothing, signing agreements to avoid the banned goods.

Crisis in Boston

During the years 1769 to 1775, Boston became the powder keg of the Revolution. In 1769, violence began to break out frequently between the Bostonians and British redcoats, whose chief responsibilities were to protect the despised customs commissioners and help them collect duties. The soldiers became even more unpopular when they took low-paying jobs during their off-duty hours, thus throwing city laborers out of work. On March 5, 1770, the bloodiest conflict occurred, the so-called **Boston Massacre.**

Boston Massacre (1770) Pre-Revolutionary incident growing out of the resentment against the British troops sent to Boston to maintain order and to enforce the Townshend Act.

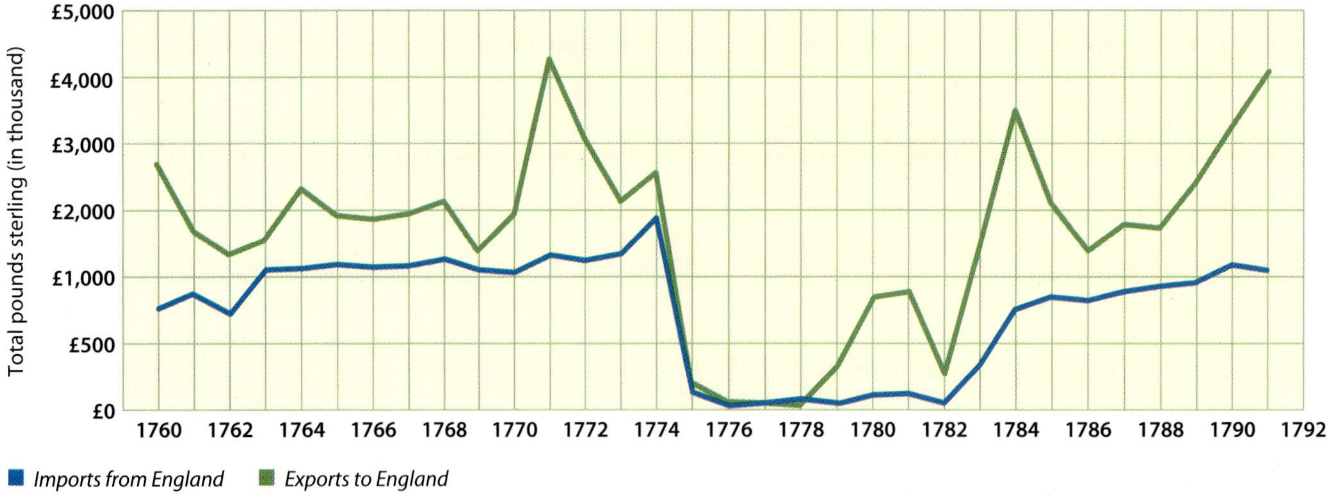

FIGURE 5.1

Trade Between 13 Colonies/ United States and England, 1760–1791

Though trade with England was only part of American commerce, this chart suggests the Revolution's impact. British imports spiked between 1769 and 1771, after Parliament partially repealed the Townshend Act. Imports and exports then plummeted during the Revolution, rising unevenly after 1782. The trade imbalance led to political unrest such as Shays's Rebellion (see Chapter 6).

Source: *Bureau of the Census, Historical Statistics of the United States Colonial Times to 1970,* Part 2 (Washington, D.C., 1975), 1176.

A young apprentice taunted the British sentry at the Customs House, who hit the boy with his gun. When a rowdy crowd gathered, Captain Thomas Preston led seven soldiers to defend the sentry. The crowd grew larger, throwing snowballs, ice, and sticks at the soldiers. Then someone hit a redcoat with a club, knocking the gun out of his hands. Preston's men fired, killing five townspeople and wounding six. The dead became martyrs, with March 5 commemorated as "Massacre Day" in the years ahead.

Just as the crisis in Boston came to a head in spring 1770, the British government decided on partial repeal of the Townshend Act, removing its duties except that on tea. The duties had raised less than £21,000 in revenues, but they had cost hundreds of thousands of pounds sterling in trade as a result of the nonimportation movement. As in the case of the Stamp Act, British officials backed away from a specific revenue measure without abandoning their right to levy taxes. Following Parliament's action, merchants in New York City and other colonial ports, eager to resume trade, cancelled their boycotts except on tea. Imports into the thirteen colonies from England rebounded over the next several years, increasing from £1.3 million in 1769 to £4.2 million in 1771.

For two years, the conflict between Great Britain and the colonies abated, but in 1772, it flared again in Rhode Island, when more than a hundred men burned the British schooner *Gaspée*, wounding its commander. Avidly enforcing the Sugar Act, the *Gaspée* had harassed merchant vessels sailing through Narragansett Bay. The Crown named a Commission of Inquiry to locate the perpetrators and send them to England to be tried for high treason. Although none were tracked down, colonists viewed the Commission as a serious threat to their constitutional rights. In response, the Virginia assembly appointed a Committee of Correspondence to monitor British policy and facilitate communication among the provinces. Within a year, Committees of Correspondence in all colonies coordinated opposition to Britain's restraints.

The Coercive Acts, 1773–1774

The final showdown began in 1773 when Parliament passed the Tea Act to bail out the nearly bankrupt East India Company. The boycott on tea was still in effect, so many colonists purchased smuggled Dutch tea instead. To sell the company's huge surplus, the government dropped a heavy import duty into England on tea headed for America, but it retained the Townshend duty, which Lord North insisted on keeping to uphold Parliament's power to tax the

Massacre in Boston, 1770. Paul Revere's engraving of the clash between British soldiers and Boston residents circulated soon after the event and helped intensify the crisis.

colonies. The Tea Act was doubly offensive to American Whigs: it renewed opposition to the duty and caused outrage over favoritism and privilege. When three ships of tea arrived in Boston, members of the Boston Committee of Correspondence prevented them from unloading. On the cold night of December 16, 1773, radicals disguised as Mohawks boarded the ships and dumped the tea in the harbor.

For the British, the Boston Tea Party required stern action. George III decried the Americans' actions as "quite subversive of the obedience which a colony owes to its Mother Country." In 1774, Parliament passed four **Coercive Acts:** they closed the port of Boston until residents paid for the destroyed tea and altered the provincial charter to limit the power of town meetings and create a Crown-appointed, instead of elected, provincial council. Further, the acts expanded the governor's control over the courts, allowed the removal of trials of royal officials to England or to another colony, and permitted quartering of troops in private buildings if a colony failed to provide suitable barracks. The Crown appointed General Thomas Gage, commander of the British army in North America, as governor of Massachusetts, thus threatening the colonists with military force.

Coercive Acts (1774) Passed by the British Parliament in 1774 in response to the Boston Tea Party, the acts closed the port of Boston, limited the power of town meetings, expanded the governor's control over the courts, and permitted quartering of British troops in private buildings.

Americans also considered the Quebec Act (1774) intolerable, though London did not intend it to punish the Bostonians. The Quebec Act helped keep the loyalty of French Canadians by confirming religious freedom to Roman Catholics in the province, allowing them to hold public office. Residents of the thirteen colonies abhorred the act because it extended rights to "papists" and gave control of the Ohio Valley to the Quebec government, thus curbing the ambitions of speculators in other colonies.

The First Continental Congress, 1774

Although the British government expected the Coercive Acts to isolate Boston and convince other provinces to be obedient, the policies actually pushed Americans toward more unified resistance. After the port of Boston closed, residents faced severe unemployment and food shortages. Neighboring towns provided supplies and harbored refugees looking for work, while other provinces suggested a Continental Congress to consider what action to take. A meeting in Philadelphia began on September 1, 1774, to which all of the thirteen colonies except Georgia sent delegates. The fifty-five representatives included Richard Henry Lee, Patrick Henry, and George Washington of Virginia; Sam and **John Adams** of Massachusetts; and John Dickinson and Joseph Galloway of Pennsylvania.

Adams, John (1735–1826) First vice president (1789–1797) and second president (1797–1801) of the United States. He was a major figure during the American Revolution: he helped draft the Declaration of Independence and served on the commission to negotiate the Treaty of Paris (1783).

The primary purpose of the First Continental Congress was to obtain repeal of the Coercive Acts and other restrictions. The Congress wanted Parliament to recognize the rights of Americans but was not ready to declare independence. Some of its leadership, notably Galloway (who later became a loyalist), argued for a moderate course, but the Congress was committed to action. It passed a set of resolves that blasted the Coercive Acts as "gross infractions of those rights to which we are justly entitled by the laws of nature, the British constitution and the charter of this province." Everyone qualified to fight should learn "the art of war as soon as possible, and . . . appear under arms at least once a week." The Continental Congress also passed resolutions that ended all trade with Great Britain and Ireland and exports to the West Indies. It also banned importation of slaves. Congress set up the Continental Association to enforce the ban on trade through elected local committees, called Committees of Observation and Inspection or Committees of Safety. Almost every town and county in the colonies elected these committees, which soon took on other functions of local government, including raising militias and collecting taxes. This was revolutionary: Americans were now vesting sovereignty in themselves rather than in Parliament. If the British had hoped to divide the colonies by closing Boston, the plan backfired.

❖ Resistance Becomes a War for Independence, 1775–1776

Over the winter of 1774–1775, the rift widened between the thirteen colonies and Great Britain. George III and his ministers considered the colonies in rebellion, yet the colonists themselves were unprepared to declare independence.

Lexington and Concord

The British government instructed General Gage to take forceful action. Headquartered in Boston, he decided to seize the patriots' stores of food and ammunition at Concord, twenty miles to the west, which he had learned about from an informer. Militant Bostonians discovered Gage's plan and spread the alarm on the night of April 18, 1775, alerting leaders Sam Adams and John Hancock in Lexington, on the route to Concord (see Map 5.2). The Massachusetts Provincial Council had resolved to resist any advance by Gage's troops.

As the British marched toward Concord, they heard church bells and saw lights in windows. Soon after sunrise on April 19, they reached Lexington, where they met about seventy armed militia, nearly half of the town's adult males. The Lexington company, led by Captain John Parker, had formed only a few weeks earlier, but the men were willing to defend, in the words of their town meeting,

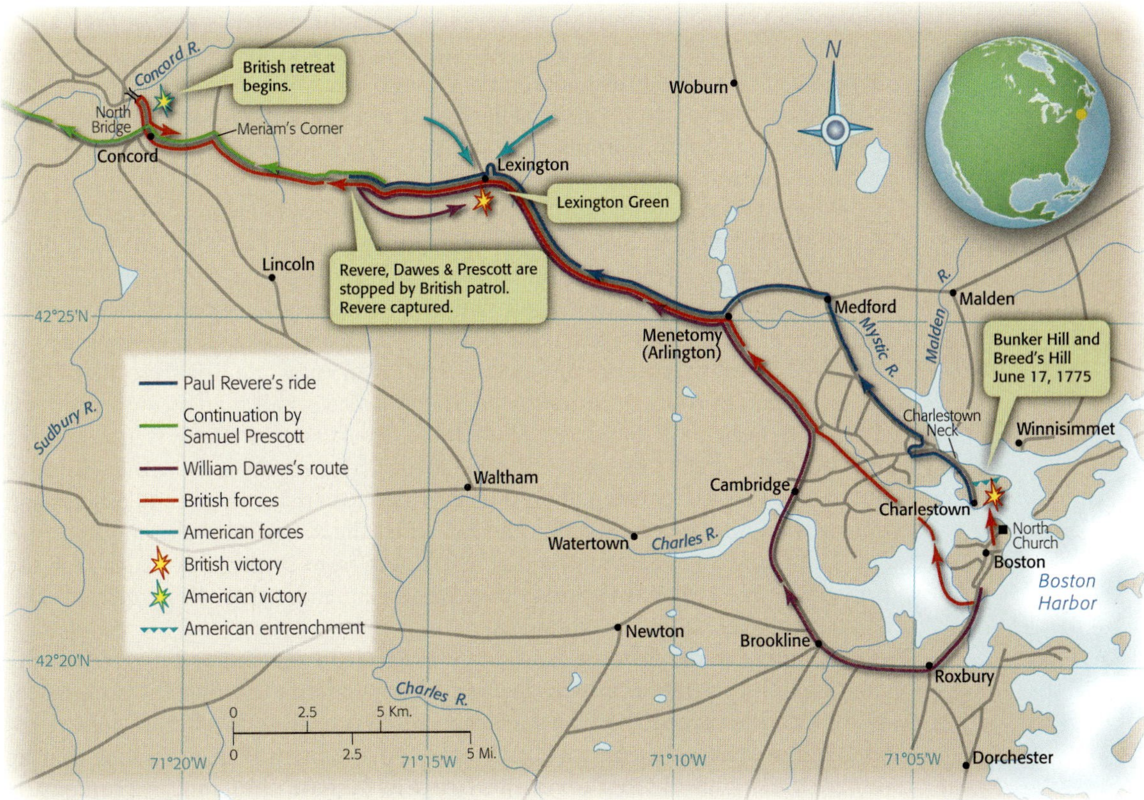

MAP 5.2
Battles in Eastern Massachusetts, April–June 1775
Paul Revere and William Dawes left Boston during the night of April 18, 1775, to alert colonial leaders that the British troops were marching to destroy military supplies at Concord. The map also shows the location of the Battle of Bunker Hill two months later.

their "natural, constitutional and chartered rights." In the face of six companies of British infantry, Captain Parker attempted to disperse his troops. The British officer, Major John Pitcairn, wanted to disarm the Americans, not engage in battle. But as the British advanced, a shot rang out, then several more. Pitcairn tried to stop his troops, but the shooting continued for fifteen to twenty minutes, leaving eight Lexington men dead and ten wounded. Only one British soldier was wounded and none killed.

The British reached Concord at about eight o'clock in the morning, long after the patriots had hidden most of their military stores. Following a brief skirmish in which the Americans inflicted more casualties than the British did, the redcoats headed back to Boston in a harrowing flight for their lives. Hundreds of colonial militia from throughout the Massachusetts countryside used guerrilla tactics, shooting from behind trees, walls, rocks, and buildings. The British countered by sending advance parties to clear houses along the route. Using their famed skills with the bayonet, the redcoats killed the occupants and set fire to the homes. By the end of the day, British losses totaled seventy-three dead and two hundred wounded or missing, and Massachusetts counted forty-nine killed and forty-three wounded and missing. In the days that followed the battles of April 19, New England went to arms. More than twenty thousand volunteers streamed to Cambridge, across the river from Boston.

The Second Continental Congress

On May 10, 1775, the Second Continental Congress met in Philadelphia, facing the prospect of executing a war already in progress. To ensure that all of the colonies backed the war and to place the military under the control of Congress, they appointed George Washington of Virginia as commander in chief of the Continental army. Washington was a delegate to Congress and steadfastly committed to civilian control of the armed forces. Despite his limited military experience, Washington proved to be an excellent choice. His military bearing, determination, dignity, physical stamina, and ability to learn from his mistakes suited his role as commander in chief.

Before Washington could arrive in Massachusetts, his troops engaged in the Battle of Bunker Hill. Learning that the British planned to seize the hills overlooking Boston, a detachment of the patriot army began to fortify the Charlestown Heights. General Gage and the man who would soon replace him as commander of British forces, William Howe, foolishly allowed the Americans to complete their fortifications and obtain reinforcements. The British regulars lined up in proper European formation to storm Breed's Hill, and Boston residents climbed to their roofs to watch. While the redcoats shot as they advanced up the hill—to little effect—the patriots waited until the enemy was within range of their guns. The redcoats failed on their first two assaults, losing many officers and troops; then reinforcements took the hill when the Americans' ammunition gave out. The patriots retreated, pounded by artillery from British ships. Although the British won the battle, their losses were staggering: more than 40 percent of their combatants were killed or wounded.

Despite the violent battles in eastern Massachusetts, many delegates to the Continental Congress opposed declaring independence. During the summer of 1775, Congress asked the king for peace while preparing for war. In July, it approved a petition to George III, called the Olive Branch Petition, asking that he resolve the dispute with Parliament. Upon its receipt, the king proclaimed the thirteen provinces in "an open and avowed rebellion." In December, Parliament cut off all trade with the colonies, making American ships and any vessels engaging in commerce with the mutinous provinces subject to confiscation. For many Americans, these actions proved that the British government meant to crush the colonies militarily and economically.

The Continental Congress further alienated the British by ordering General Philip Schuyler to invade Canada and spark rebellion there as well (they also wanted to prevent a northern attack). But Schuyler, suffering from illness and indecision, assembled troops and provisions too slowly. Brigadier General Richard Montgomery took charge in September and moved the army north via Lake Champlain. When the combined American forces finally attacked Quebec in a blinding December snowstorm, they were defeated with heavy casualties; Montgomery was among the dead. The army remained in Canada until May 1776, when British reinforcements arrived, pushing the patriots back into New York. For Congress, the campaign was a disastrous error.

Taking Sides

The deepening conflict forced colonists to decide whether to support the Revolutionary Whigs. Some people, like the pacifist Quakers, remained neutral, while Tory loyalists rejected the Revolution for a variety of motives. Tories included Crown officials, Anglican clergy, and merchants with close ties to Britain. Some of the best-known loyalists were wealthy gentlemen and officeholders, such as Governor Thomas Hutchinson of Massachusetts, and Joseph Galloway, speaker of the Pennsylvania Assembly. Other Tories were not wealthy: the tenants of New York manors, for example, took the opposite side of their Whig landlords. In eastern Maryland and throughout the South Carolina backcountry, farmers suffering from economic decline and lack of political power regarded the patriot elites as their enemies.

(The Granger Collection, New York)

Sketch of Soldiers. Antoine De Verger's sketch of American army uniforms reflects the military role of African Americans.

Of considerable concern to white Americans were the loyalties of enslaved African Americans. Of the 2.5 million people in the thirteen colonies in 1775, about 500,000 were blacks. As the rhetoric of revolution reached African American slaves, increasing numbers escaped. A chief source of unrest, the patriots believed, was the November 1775 proclamation of Lord Dunmore, royal governor of Virginia, declaring "all indented [sic] servants, Negroes, or others [owned by rebels] free, that are able and willing to bear arms, they joining His Majesty's Troops." Whigs considered this proclamation an attempt to start an insurrection and increased slave patrols, threatening death to rebellious slaves. Nevertheless, African Americans aided the British by joining the army and employing their firsthand knowledge of the Chesapeake Bay. Some served as pilots along its tributaries; others delivered fresh provisions to the British ships by foraging plantations at night.

Other African Americans supported the Revolution, but they received little welcome from the Whigs. Initially, slaves and even free blacks were prevented from enlisting in the Continental Army and state militias. By 1777, however, when recruiters found it difficult to fill their quotas, northern states began accepting free blacks and slaves. Officially Virginia took only free African Americans, but some masters sent slaves as substitutes for themselves. An estimated five thousand African Americans served in the Continental army and state militias or at sea on American privateers. At the end of their service, many of the enslaved African Americans who fought for independence received freedom, but other masters did not fulfill their promises.

Estimates of the total number of Americans who joined the Whig forces range from 100,000 to 250,000. Most signed up for tours of duty lasting several months or a year, not for the duration of the war. Thus, Washington and his generals constantly faced the problem of expiring enlistments. The inability of Congress

Doing History Online

Women in the Revolution

Go to the CourseMate website for this chapter and link to Primary Sources. Drawing on Documents 7, 14, 16, and 17, describe the range of female wartime experiences. What other perspectives or experiences can you imagine that are not represented in these documents?

www.cengagebrain.com

to pay soldiers adequately also hindered recruitment and retention of troops. As time went on, the American troops became better trained and disciplined, but by 1778, most states had to adopt conscription to fill their quotas. Men were drafted by lottery but could pay a fine or hire a substitute, loopholes that contributed to disproportionate service by the poor.

Women took part in the American war effort by operating farms and businesses in their husbands' absence, defending their homes and families against marauding enemy soldiers, supplying food and clothing for the troops, and even joining the army. Perhaps several hundred women put on uniforms to become soldiers. These troops included Deborah Sampson of Massachusetts, who fought in battle but was discovered when she became wounded; after the war, she collected an army pension. Others performed unofficial short-term service as spies. The most substantial contribution of women to the American military was that of the **Women of the Army**, as George Washington called them. Numbering perhaps twenty thousand over the course of the war, they served as nurses, cooks, laundresses, and water carriers. They were regular members of the army who drew rations and were subject to military discipline. Some saw action in battle, particularly women in artillery crews who carried water to swab out the cannon after each firing.

Women of the Army Name given by General George Washington to the approximately twenty thousand women who served in the Continental Army as nurses, cooks, laundresses, and water carriers. They drew rations and were subject to military discipline.

Independence and Confederation, 1776

During the winter and spring of 1776, fighting continued between Great Britain and the thirteen colonies. Although the Canada campaign was a disaster, the Americans met success in their siege of Boston. They sledged heavy guns from Fort Ticonderoga about three hundred miles, installing them in March 1776 on the Dorchester Heights overlooking Boston. Instead of storming the artillery, the British withdrew from the city, sailing to Nova Scotia in preparation for an invasion of New York City.

In 1776, London undertook a huge effort to put down the revolt. It sent across the Atlantic Ocean 370 transports with supplies and thirty-two thousand troops, of whom many were German mercenaries (called Hessians, because the largest proportion came from the principality of Hesse-Cassel). The British intended these soldiers to join General William Howe's ten thousand troops from Nova Scotia, take New York City, and destroy Washington's army. The British navy would bombard seaports and wreak havoc on colonial shipping.

As the British military descended on New York in midsummer 1776, the Continental Congress finally declared independence. The force of events propelled most moderate delegates to cast their vote for a complete break. In January 1776, Thomas Paine, a recent immigrant from England, had published ***Common Sense*** to argue the case for independence. "We have it in our power to begin the world over again," he wrote. Pragmatically, Paine argued that the colonists must break their ties with London if they expected aid from France and Spain. He pointed out the importance of American exports, which "will always have a market while eating is the custom in Europe." He exclaimed, "'TIS TIME TO PART . . . there is something very absurd, in supposing a continent to be perpetually governed by an island." *Common Sense* sold more than one hundred thousand copies within a few months, reaching hundreds of thousands of people as copies changed hands and many listened to Paine's words read aloud, becoming convinced of the need for independence.

***Common Sense* (1776)** Published by Thomas Paine in January 1776, Common Sense convinced the American public of the need for independence.

Through the spring of 1776, sentiment for independence increased. News that the British had engaged German mercenaries heated the debate. Congress appointed a committee to draft the **Declaration of Independence**, of which Thomas Jefferson, a wealthy thirty-three-year-old Virginia planter and lawyer,

Declaration of Independence (1776) The document, drafted primarily by Thomas Jefferson, that declared the independence of the thirteen mainland colonies from Great Britain and enumerated their reasons for separating.

was the principal author. A graduate of the College of William and Mary and a serious intellectual, he had been an active opponent of British policies since first elected to the Virginia assembly in 1769.

The declaration set forth Congress's reasons for separating from the government of George III; the revolutionaries focused on the king's offenses because they had already denied the sovereignty of Parliament. It held "these truths to be self-evident: That all men are created equal; that they are endowed by their Creator with certain unalienable rights; that among these are life, liberty, and the pursuit of happiness." (See the Appendix for the full text.) Employing the philosophy of John Locke and other Enlightenment writers, Jefferson continued, "That, to secure these rights, governments are instituted among men, deriving their just powers from the consent of the governed; that whenever any form of government becomes destructive of these ends, it is the right of the people to alter or to abolish it, and to institute new government." Congress placed the blame for the breach on the king, listing his misdeeds: refusing to approve necessary laws passed by the colonial assemblies, dissolving legislatures and courts, stationing a standing army, interrupting trade, and imposing taxes without colonial consent. In reference to Lord Dunmore's proclamation, the congressmen accused the king of exciting "domestic insurrection among us." For these reasons and more, the Continental Congress declared the thirteen colonies, now to be called the United States of America, "free and independent states" having "full power to levy war, conclude peace, contract alliances, establish commerce, and do all other acts and things which independent states may of right do."

On July 2, 1776, all delegations to the Continental Congress approved independence except New York's, which had not received new instructions and so was forced to abstain. Completing revisions two days later, the Continental Congress adopted the Declaration of Independence. For many Americans, independence ended the problem of fighting a government that they continued to recognize as sovereign. When the Continental troops heard the Declaration read

Declaration of Independence. In this painting, *The Declaration of Independence,* by John Trumbull, the drafting committee stands at center: from left to right, John Adams, Roger Sherman, Robert Livingston, Thomas Jefferson, and Benjamin Franklin.

(© Bettmann/CORBIS)

on July 9, they cheered, as did civilians throughout the states. However, the battles to defend this independence still lay ahead. General Washington cautioned "every officer and soldier . . . that now the peace and safety of his Country depends (under God) solely on the success of our arms."

Articles of Confederation (1781) First Constitution of the United States. Adopted by the original thirteen states in 1781, it remained the supreme law until 1789.

To mount sufficient military force to win the war, the states needed unity. In mid-July 1776, the Continental Congress began debating the **Articles of Confederation,** a plan for permanent union, which it approved and sent to the states for ratification more than a year later. The chief disagreement among the congressmen was one that remained central to American politics for two centuries: the power of the national government versus that of individual states. The Articles permitted less centralized authority than would the Constitution, which was drafted a decade later. Under the Articles, the "United States" meant thirteen sovereign states joined together by a Congress with specific functions. Congress could conduct foreign affairs, make war and peace, deal with Native Americans residing outside the states, coin and borrow money, supervise the post office, and negotiate boundary disputes between states. However, Congress could neither tax nor raise troops, but could only assess quotas on the states, a serious disadvantage in time of war. Even so, the Articles of Confederation were not ratified until 1781, when the last of the states finally approved them. In the meantime, Congress attempted to govern within the limits of the unratified Articles of Confederation, but its inability to raise revenue and draft troops obstructed the American war effort.

❖ War in the North, 1776–1779

For the American patriots, the Revolution was a defensive war. It lasted eight years, from 1775 to 1783, longer than any other in U.S. history until the Vietnam War. The Continental army was often outmatched, for it remained smaller than General Washington wanted; his troops constantly needed training as veterans left and new recruits arrived. But as the theater of war moved from one region to another, American generals obtained reinforcements from state militias and local volunteers. The sheer expanse of the thirteen states and the three thousand miles distance from England made the British army's task extremely difficult, despite its formal training, assistance from Tory loyalists, and Britain's larger population and wealth.

Invasions of New York

To conquer New York, and thus divide New England from the rest of the states, British troops landed on Staten Island in July 1776. In August, they attacked Washington's army at Brooklyn Heights (see Map 5.3). The redcoats defeated the Americans soundly, pushing them back to Manhattan Island and then to White Plains. But they failed to take advantage of Washington's mistakes, which could have allowed them to surround his troops. In November, however, the British did hand Washington a humiliating defeat by capturing the twenty-nine hundred defenders of Manhattan's Fort Washington.

The Continental army retreated across New Jersey with the British and their German allies at its heels. The patriots crossed the Delaware River into Pennsylvania, allowing the British to occupy New Jersey towns. The British gathered Tory support by offering a pardon to anyone who would take a loyalty oath within sixty days. For the Whigs, as Thomas Paine wrote, these were "times that try men's souls." The army was in retreat, and the New Jersey government had dispersed; citizens who were skeptical of Washington's abilities rallied to the British.

MAP 5.3

The War in the North, 1776–1778

The major Revolutionary battles of these years took place in New York, New Jersey, and Pennsylvania. In 1776, the British invaded Long Island and New York City, pushing Washington's troops across New Jersey until they won crucial battles at Trenton and Princeton. In 1777, the British were defeated at Saratoga, New York, but captured Philadelphia.

Before the end of the year, however, fortunes changed. British plundering across New Jersey turned indifferent farmers into radical Whigs, who became guerrillas, ambushing the enemy and stealing supplies. Meanwhile, Washington attacked fourteen hundred Hessians at Trenton on Christmas night, capturing more than nine hundred men. In early January, Washington took the offensive once again, eluding a superior British army under Lord Cornwallis and defeating a smaller force at Princeton. General William Howe withdrew most of his army to New York. In the words of one British officer, the Americans had "become a formidable enemy."

In 1777, as the British made plans to suppress the rebellion once and for all, their strategy became confused. General Howe intended to take Philadelphia not by crossing New Jersey, but by means of his brother Admiral Richard Howe's fleet. At the same time, London organized an invasion from Canada to win back Fort Ticonderoga and divide the states. The campaigns were not coordinated, and in June, British General "Gentleman Johnny" Burgoyne led his force of more than seven thousand by boat down Lake Champlain. True to his reputation,

Burgoyne overburdened his troops with baggage, including cartloads of personal clothing and champagne. His men easily took Fort Ticonderoga, then headed for Albany. But the American forces under Philip Schuyler had felled trees and rolled boulders into the path of Burgoyne's heavy column. Covering twenty-three miles of terrain took the British army twenty-four days. Short on supplies and horses, Burgoyne sent eight hundred troops to Bennington, Vermont, where General John Stark and his militia ambushed them by pretending to be Tories. British troops returned to Canada when they heard that Benedict Arnold was headed west to intercept them. The rebel forces burgeoned with volunteers as British soldiers pillaged the countryside. In September, near Saratoga, Burgoyne encountered the American army under General Horatio Gates, who had replaced Schuyler. The Americans surrounded the enemy as Burgoyne sent for help from New York City, but Howe had long since sailed with most of his troops to Philadelphia. Burgoyne's 5,800-man army surrendered at Saratoga on October 17, 1777.

Occupation and Alliance

As Burgoyne marched toward disaster in New York, General Howe more successfully reached Philadelphia. In July, his thirteen thousand soldiers departed from New York City aboard a fleet of 260 ships, but instead of disembarking within a week along the Delaware River, they sailed south to the Virginia capes, then up the Chesapeake Bay to Head of Elk. Their voyage lasted more than a month, costing Howe valuable time that might have permitted him to assist Burgoyne. Washington tried unsuccessfully, with an army of eleven thousand at Brandywine, to block Howe's advance through southeastern Pennsylvania. The British occupied Philadelphia, dividing their forces between Germantown and the capital. On October 4, 1777, Washington attacked the British encampment at Germantown, inflicting serious damage, though he was once again defeated.

Even so, in 1777, the British had failed to put down the American rebellion during yet another season of war. Upon hearing that Burgoyne's army had surrendered, the Howe brothers resigned. General Henry Clinton became the new commander of British forces in North America. The redcoats wintered in relative comfort at Philadelphia while Washington's troops nearly starved and froze to death at Valley Forge, to the west of the city. In February 1778, Continental soldiers lacked adequate clothing and received just three pounds of bread and three ounces of meat to last a week. Some ate only "fire cakes," baked from a paste of flour and water. Nevertheless, they became a disciplined army at Valley Forge under the Prussian officer Baron von Steuben, who rigorously trained the Americans in the European art of war.

Although February 1778 brought despair to the Americans, it also brought hope—in the form of an alliance with France. Already supporting the United States with economic and military assistance, the French government hoped to recoup the international status it had lost during the Seven Years' War. Convinced by the victory at Saratoga that the former colonies could win the war, the French signed the Treaty of Amity and Commerce and the military Treaty of Alliance. France renounced claims to its former colonies in North America but could retain any of the British West Indies that it conquered. In supporting the Americans, the French renewed their long struggle with Great Britain that had been suspended in 1763. France's entry widened the war, placing greater focus on the West Indies, whose sugar production made them more valuable than the North American mainland to the British. The following year, Spain allied with France but only provided limited financial aid. Unlike France, the Spanish viewed the Americans as potentially dangerous competitors.

The Wartime Economy

Despite significant economic assistance from France and a much smaller contribution from Spain, the United States had grave economic problems during the war. The loss of British markets devastated farmers, merchants, and fishermen, because the embargo closed crucial ports in the West Indies and British Isles. The Royal Navy attacked and blockaded American harbors and ravaged ships at sea. On land, the armies laid waste to farms and towns.

For Congress, the chief economic problem was paying for the war. Without the power to tax, it printed money—a total of almost $200 million in paper bills by 1779. The states printed a similar amount, despite their ability to tax, primarily because printing money was easier than trying to collect revenues from a financially strapped populace. However, as the war continued year after year, the demand for military equipment, food, medical supplies, clothing, and soldiers' wages persisted, sending prices soaring. By 1779, the paper money was nearly worthless.

The depreciation of currency resulted in popular unrest, and a group of Philadelphia militia in 1779 demanded a more equitable military draft and regulation of food prices. The protesters, according to one broadside posted along the streets, blamed "a few overbearing Merchants, a swarm of Monopolizers and Speculators, an infernal gang of Tories" for the spiraling costs. In the so-called Fort Wilson Incident of October 1779, armed members of the Philadelphia militia gathered at the house of lawyer James Wilson. Eventually, shots rang out and a melee ensued. After cavalry broke up the battle, six people lay dead and seventeen wounded, the majority of them militia. The Fort Wilson Incident terrified many because lower-class patriots had directed armed force against the Whig elite, protesting the policies of their own government.

❖ The War Moves West and South

The failure of the British army to defeat Washington's troops and the entry of France into the war led the imperial government to rethink its military strategy. Protection of Caribbean sugar islands from the French navy gained top priority. With redeployment of forces to the West Indies, British General Clinton had to consolidate his army, so in June 1778, he pulled his occupation forces out of Philadelphia, marching across New Jersey toward New York. Washington's army caught up with Clinton at Monmouth Courthouse, where the battle, fought in traditional European style with soldiers in rank and file, was indecisive. The British escaped to New York.

The Frontier War

In the West, from New York to Georgia, fighting devastated the backcountry. When the Revolution broke out, many Indians supported the British, who still held garrisons in the West and had more gunpowder and provisions than the patriots did. Yet Native Americans responded in various ways to "this dispute between two brothers," as neutral Iroquois called the Revolution in 1775. Within some tribes, factions separated those who favored the British or the Americans or wanted to avoid any involvement. The militant Indians who sided with Great Britain considered the threat of white settlers crossing the Appalachians as most dangerous to their future. Many attempted to form pan-Indian alliances to fight their own wars of independence against land grabbers from the East.

Beginning in 1776, Indians attacked Anglo-Americans from the Georgia frontier to the Great Lakes. The Cherokees raided the southern backcountry and planned a major assault on Whig militia in Tennessee, but they ran short of gunpowder and were defeated. Many Cherokees, Choctaws, Creeks, Shawnees, Iroquois, and others regrouped, and in 1779 planned "a general invasion of the Frontiers" coordinated by Henry Hamilton, the British lieutenant governor of the Illinois country. George Rogers Clark, a surveyor, heard of plans for the Indian and British offensive and assaulted Fort Vincennes with a small force, obtaining British surrender and ending the pan-Indian campaign.

Despite Clark's victory at Vincennes, the frontier remained embattled throughout the war. In Pennsylvania and New York, most Iroquois and Delawares abandoned their neutrality to ally with the British. In 1778 and 1779, Major John Butler, his son, Captain Walter Butler, and the Mohawk leader, Theyendanegea, also known as Joseph Brant, led Tory and Native American forces against white settlements. The loyalists and Iroquois destroyed property and killed or captured settlers over a wide swath of frontier. In summer 1779, General Washington sent General John Sullivan with four thousand troops, who retaliated by burning Iroquois villages, orchards, and fields of corn. At Newtown, New York, Sullivan defeated a contingent of about seven hundred loyalists and Indians. His scorched-earth policy seriously damaged most of the Iroquois towns, displacing Indians, who suffered through the winter of 1779–1780 on short rations. But the next spring they had renewed their assaults.

Because many Anglo-Americans had trouble distinguishing between Indian friends and foes, Native Americans who allied with the United States or remained neutral throughout the war often fared little better with the Whigs than those who sided with the British. In March 1782, frontier militia massacred ninety-six pacifist Indian men, women, and children at the Moravian mission of Gnadenhutten in Ohio. The Catawbas of South Carolina were better treated. They performed extensive service for the patriots, searching for loyalists and escaped slaves, supplying food to the rebels, fighting the Cherokees in 1776, and battling the British, who destroyed their town in retaliation. After the war, the South Carolina assembly compensated them for their loyalty, refusing to abet the governor's plan to lease out their reservation.

The Southern Campaigns

Although the Revolution ravaged the frontier, the main theater of war remained east of the Appalachians, where the British inaugurated a new southern strategy in 1778, counting on loyalist and African American support in Georgia, the Carolinas, and Virginia to restore colonial governments to the Crown. In November 1778, British General Clinton sent thirty-five hundred troops under Lieutenant Colonel Archibald Campbell to Georgia, where they joined two thousand soldiers from Florida (see Map 5.4). They captured Savannah and Augusta, but had trouble conquering the backcountry. Then, with ten thousand troops, the British turned to Charleston, where in May 1780 they compelled the American general Benjamin Lincoln to surrender fifty-five hundred men. In July 1780, the American general Horatio Gates arrived to build a new southern army. Disaster struck once again when Gates placed too much responsibility on untrained militia in action against Lord Cornwallis at Camden, South Carolina. The battle was a rout; even the regular Continentals were dispersed, and Gates, the hero of Saratoga, was disgraced.

The tide turned after General Nathanael Greene replaced Gates as commander of the southern army. The British contributed to the turnaround, as they became more insistent in demanding oaths of allegiance from Carolinians but withdrew protection from the people who took the oaths, thus exposing them to punishment by the Whigs. The redcoats and Tories also plundered, outraging many southerners and pushing them into the American camp. Most notorious

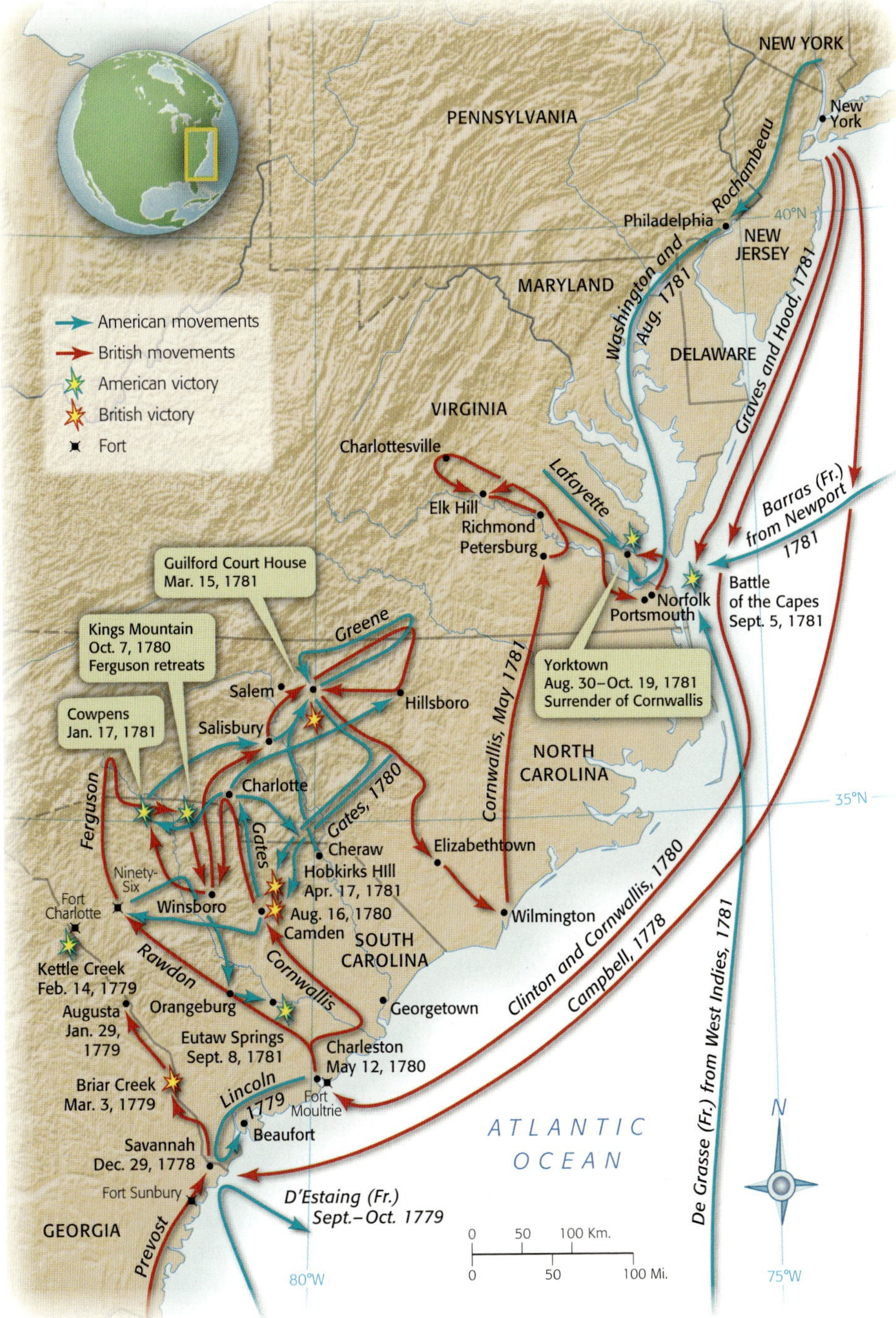

MAP 5.4

The War in the South, 1778–1781

In late 1778, the British decided to invade the South, where they were no more successful in ending the war. They agreed to peace after their defeat by the Americans and French at the Battle of Yorktown in Virginia.

was Banastre Tarleton's Tory Legion, which executed prisoners of war and destroyed houses and fields, leaving many families homeless. Southerners joined Greene's army or the smaller irregular brigades led by Thomas "The Gamecock" Sumter, Colonel Andrew Pickens, and Francis Marion, the "Swamp Fox." During 1780 and 1781, Greene rebuilt the southern army using both traditional and guerrilla forces.

Although African American slaves were not welcome as soldiers in South Carolina and Georgia, they played an important role in the southern campaigns, acting as spies and counterspies for each side. Throughout the South, African

Americans provided much of the supporting labor for both armies. American officers complained about the chronic shortage of black laborers, because Whig slave owners jealously guarded their strongest and most talented slaves to work on their plantations. Further, thousands of African Americans took advantage of General Clinton's 1779 proclamation offering freedom to those who joined the king's service.

A practice of rebel leaders that highlighted their ability to dissociate their own fight for liberty from the plight of enslaved African Americans was to offer recruits enlistment "bounties" in slaves, much as other states promised bounties in land. In South Carolina, Thomas Sumter offered one African American bondman or bondwoman to each private who would enlist for ten months. A colonel would receive three mature blacks and one child. Because sufficient numbers of African Americans owned by Tories were lacking, regiments reported "pay" in arrears, some with grotesque precision. One payroll noted a deficit of 93 3/4 mature slaves and "Three Quarters of a Small Negro."

In fall 1780, Lord Cornwallis decided to head north, believing that the time had come to conquer the entire South. As his forces marched toward North Carolina, however, they met heavy resistance. In several battles, the conflict became a civil war as Americans fought on both sides. In October 1780, just to the south of the state line at King's Mountain, Whig frontier units defeated an enemy force, of which only Patrick Ferguson, the commander of the loyalists, was British. In January 1781, at Cowpens, General Daniel Morgan crushed Tarleton's Tory Legion by making the most of his sharpshooting frontiersmen. When Cornwallis learned that Tarleton's legion was lost, he chased the Americans into North Carolina, abandoning most of his equipment and supplies to move quickly. In March, Cornwallis met Greene at the Guilford Courthouse. Although the battle ended indecisively, one-fourth of Cornwallis's troops lay wounded or dead. Having discarded tents, medical equipment, and food—and cut off from his base in South Carolina—the British general withdrew to the North Carolina coast, where he sought naval support.

(LC-USZC4-1306)/Library of Congress Prints and Photographs Division Washington, D.C. 20540 USA)

Evacuation of New York by the British, 1783.
An nineteenth-century print celebrating the centennial of the British evacuation of New York City in November 1783.

Meanwhile, Greene moved south to regain South Carolina and Georgia, where the British still had eight thousand men in arms. Because these troops were spread out in numerous towns and forts, Greene's fifteen hundred Continental soldiers and the guerrilla brigades of Sumter, Pickens, and Marion could pick off the garrisons one by one. By July, the Americans had pushed the redcoats and Tories back to a narrow strip of territory between Charleston and Savannah. Despite initial disastrous defeats, the Whigs prevailed in the Carolinas and Georgia by recruiting irregular forces and employing them strategically. The great sweep of territory controlled by the former colonies proved impossible for the British army to subdue.

The surrender of Cornwallis at Yorktown in October 1781 effectively ended the war. The general had moved into Virginia in April 1781, replacing Benedict Arnold as commander of the British forces there. Arnold, the former American officer, had turned traitor, joined the British army, and most recently captured Richmond. With an army of about eight thousand men, Cornwallis intended to concentrate British military efforts in Virginia, so he requested more troops from New York. General Clinton refused. Their squabbling and delay allowed the Americans and the French to surround Cornwallis's camp on the Virginia peninsula by land and sea. Soldiers under the Comte de Rochambeau and French fleets commanded by the Comte de Grasse and Comte de Barras played a decisive role in defeating Cornwallis. Washington's army marched south from New York. With seventeen thousand men and heavy artillery, the American and French forces won the British surrender, finally winning American independence.

The Peace Settlement, 1783

In negotiating the peace, the United States had to reckon with both its adversary, Great Britain, and its ally, France, which in turn was beholden to Spain. American peace commissioners Benjamin Franklin, John Jay, and John Adams shrewdly worked one European nation against the other to obtain a desirable settlement. In violation of the 1778 treaty with France, the American diplomats negotiated separately with the British, obtaining recognition of independence and most other provisions they requested.

The British and American peacemakers approved preliminary articles of peace on November 30, 1782; the **Treaty of Paris** signed on September 3, 1783, was essentially unchanged. The new nation would extend from approximately the present-day U.S.–Canada boundary on the north, to the Mississippi River on the west, to the thirty-first parallel on the south (today's Georgia–Florida state line and due west). The American diplomats also secured fishing rights off Newfoundland and the St. Lawrence River, of particular interest to New Englanders. Further, the British agreed to evacuate their troops promptly from the United States. For its part, Congress would urge state governments to return confiscated property to the loyalists, and prewar debts owed by citizens of each country to citizens of the other would be honored.

Treaty of Paris (1783) Signed on September 3, 1783, the Treaty of Paris established the independence of the United States from Great Britain. It set specific land boundaries and called for the evacuation of British troops.

The treaty was a success on paper for the United States, but left France and Spain dissatisfied and pro-British Native Americans "thunderstruck." In coming decades, the Americans would struggle to enforce its provisions. The French gained little from the war except the separation of the mainland colonies from Great Britain. The Spanish had wanted to keep the Americans out of the Mississippi Valley and hoped to obtain the return of Gibraltar from the British. They instead accepted East and West Florida and the Mediterranean island of Minorca. Native Americans were furious that their British allies had signed away their lands.

While U.S. possession of the trans-Appalachian region remained disputed for decades, the provision that most immediately caused trouble was the one dealing with enslaved African Americans. Thousands of African Americans had fled behind British lines to find freedom, and some had fought against their former masters. The British ruled that blacks who sought refuge before the signing of the provisional treaty in November 1782 could not be considered the property of Americans because they were already free, but slaves who escaped after that date would be returned to their masters. At least twenty thousand African Americans, including those who accompanied loyalist owners as well as the ex-slaves of Whigs, left with the British military. Some went to Nova Scotia, where they received a generally unfriendly welcome; many newly freed blacks were quickly reenslaved in the West Indies.

Although the War of Independence was a success, the coming years would present a series of challenges to the new republic. Establishing a stable government became imperative in the 1780s as conflicts and uncertainty followed the peace settlement with Britain.

CHAPTER REVIEW, 1764–1783

SUMMARY

- Discontent with British rule arose among colonists primarily because of British efforts to impose taxation without representation in Parliament. To resist British policy, colonists boycotted British goods, circulated petitions, held meetings, and participated in riots.
- Colonial resistance culminated in the Boston Tea Party. In response to this act of rebellion, Britain passed the unpopular Coercive Acts, which further exacerbated tensions between the colonies and the mother country.
- The Revolutionary War began in 1775. Despite Britain's superior military strength, the colonies, with crucial support from the French, won their independence in 1783.
- After gaining independence, Americans created a confederation of sovereign states, claimed vast lands in the trans-Appalachian territories, and built a society that granted new rights and freedoms to propertied white men.
- Not all members of society benefited equally from American independence. Under the new government, Native American land rights were not respected, and the institution of slavery became more firmly entrenched.

IDENTIFICATIONS

loyalists
Whigs
Antonio de Ulloa
presidios
Sugar Act
writs of assistance
Stamp Act
Patrick Henry
Sons of Liberty
Regulators
Townshend Revenue Act
Boston Massacre
Coercive Acts
John Adams
Women of the Army
Common Sense
Declaration of Independence
Articles of Confederation
Treaty of Paris

MAKING CONNECTIONS: LOOKING AHEAD

In Chapter 6 we examine the problems facing the new United States under the Articles of Confederation and the steps that nationalists took to remedy what they perceived to be the government's ills.

1. What were the chief economic problems of the new nation?
2. How, if at all, did the status of women change after the Revolution?
3. Did the Constitution of 1787 fulfill the promise of the Revolution? Why or why not?

RECOMMENDED READINGS

Bailyn, Bernard. *To Begin the World Anew: The Genius and Ambiguities of the American Founders* (2003). An illustrated collection of thought-provoking essays on Jefferson, Franklin, and other Revolutionary leaders.

Breen, T. H. *The Marketplace of Revolution: How Consumer Politics Shaped American Independence* (2004). Demonstrates the role of consumerism and consumer boycotts in developing popular support for the Revolution.

Calloway, Colin G. *The American Revolution in Indian Country: Crisis and Diversity in Native American Communities* (1995). Focuses on eight Indian communities to demonstrate the diversity of Native American experiences during the Revolutionary War.

Hoffman, Ronald, and Albert, Peter J., eds. *Women in the Age of the Revolution* (1989). Very good essays on women's status and contributions to the War of Independence.

In Search of Early America: The William and Mary Quarterly, 1943–1993, comp. Michael McGiffert (1993). Compilation of classic essays published in a major journal of early American history.

Morgan, Edmund S., and Morgan, Helen M. *The Stamp Act Crisis: Prologue to Revolution*, 2nd ed. (1996). A close examination of a crucial episode in the pre-Revolutionary decade.

O'Shaughnessy, Andrew Jackson. *An Empire Divided: The American Revolution and the British Caribbean* (2000). Evaluates the differences that led West Indies planters to stay within the empire while mainland colonists rebelled.

Pencak, William, Dennis, Matthew, and Newman, Simon P., eds. *Riot and Revelry in Early America* (2002). Innovative essays that span the colonial and early national eras including a chapter on pre-Revolutionary Boston.

Quarles, Benjamin. *The Negro in the American Revolution*, 2nd ed. (1996). The classic text on African Americans during the war.

Van Buskirk, Judith L. *Generous Enemies: Patriots and Loyalists in Revolutionary New York* (2002). Demonstrates the complexity of community relationships that existed in wartime New York.

CourseMate Go to the CourseMate website at www.cengagebrain.com for additional study tools and review materials for this chapter.

6

Toward a More Perfect Union

1783–1788

MAKING CONNECTIONS

LOOKING BACK

Chapter 5 focused on the period from 1764 to 1783, when the thirteen colonies moved from relatively peaceful resistance to outright war against Great Britain. Before starting Chapter 6, you should be able to answer the following questions:

1. Why did the colonists oppose the Sugar, Currency, and Stamp acts when they had posed no political complaint against the Molasses Act?
2. What was the role of African Americans during the Revolution?
3. How did the patriots achieve the unity necessary to wage the War for Independence?
4. How significant was the loyalist opposition?
5. What was the impact of the Revolution on Native Americans?

The American patriots had won victory on the battlefield and, at least on paper, in negotiating the peace. The new country soon discovered, though, that independence brought severe tests as well as opportunities. In 1786, former patriot Dr. Benjamin Rush of Philadelphia argued in a pamphlet:

> The American war is over: but this is far from being the case with the American revolution. It remains yet to establish and perfect our forms of government; and to prepare the principles, morals, and manners of our citizens, for those forms of government.

Americans' first government was a confederation of small republics in which property-holding white men elected representatives. But questions remained about how to avoid the opposite evils of tyranny and anarchy—questions that inspired fiery debates and even rebellion during the 1780s.

With limited powers under the Articles of Confederation, Congress faced challenges in demobilizing the army, conducting trade outside the confines of British mercantilism, paying the war debt, coexisting with Spanish colonies in Louisiana and Florida, dealing with Native Americans, and supervising white settlement in the

West. Despite Congress's competent action on some of these issues, the need for a more powerful central government became clear. In 1787, just four years after the conclusion of the war, delegates from the states met in Philadelphia to draft the new Constitution, which became law on ratification in 1788. This Constitution has endured, with relatively few amendments, for more than two centuries.

❖ Politics and Change in the New Republic

Benjamin Rush thought the revolution had to continue because the government was not yet "perfect"—the states had too much power relative to the nation, leading to disunity and inertia. Other Americans wondered: To what extent did the War of Independence bring about basic changes in politics and society? The war was revolutionary for propertied white men, but less so for women, African Americans, religious minorities, and the poor.

Republican Politics

Under the Articles of Confederation, the United States consisted of thirteen sovereign states rather than one nation. Only state assemblies, elected by the voters, could impose taxes; the central government, or Congress, was an agent of the states. This decision was based on republican theory, which held that only in a small republic could representatives act according to the will of its citizens. Furthermore, state officials were wary of losing power to a remote central government. Each state had an equal vote in Congress and sent delegates "appointed in such manner as the legislature of each State shall direct." The U.S. Congress had responsibility to conduct foreign affairs, declare war and peace, and coin money, but it could not levy taxes or raise troops. During the 1780s, its dependence on the states for funds brought the Confederation to a standstill. For years, Congress sought an amendment of the Articles of Confederation to permit a national tax but failed to obtain the required unanimous consent of the states.

The structure of the state governments reflected their framers' concept of republicanism. Most of the state constitutions resembled the old colonial

Great Seal of the United States. The Great Seal of the United States, adopted by Congress in 1782, incorporated as symbols of the new nation the thirteen stars and stripes, the eagle with the olive branch of peace and arrows of war, and the motto E Pluribus Unum, Latin for "Out of Many, One."

CHAPTER TIMELINE 1783 1784 1785 1786 1787 1788

POLITICS AND DIPLOMACY
- 1784 Rhode Island and Connecticut pass gradual abolition laws
- 1785 Treaty of Fort McIntosh is signed
- 1786–1787 Shays's Rebellion
- 1787–1788 Constitution is ratified by 11 states
- 1787 Constitutional Convention convenes

SOCIETY AND CULTURE
- 1780s African Americans found separate churches
- 1786 Virginia statute for religious freedom becomes law

ECONOMICS AND TECHNOLOGY
- 1783 British West Indies is closed to American ships
- 1784 Debt crisis spurs protests
- 1784 New Orleans is closed to Americans

governments but incorporated changes that made them more responsible to the people. Most had two-house legislatures and a governor but gave the largest share of power to the lower house of assembly, elected annually by the voters. The Pennsylvania constitution of 1776, more democratic than others, included no governor or upper house of assembly (senate). Even states that retained the governor eliminated his veto over legislation or allowed the assembly to override with a two-thirds vote. All of the states produced written constitutions as a protection against the kind of changes they believed the British had made in their unwritten constitution before the Revolution.

Constitutional Convention (1787) Fifty-five delegates met in Philadelphia in May 1787 to reform the U.S. government. They chose to draft a new constitution rather than revise the Articles of Confederation.

During the late 1770s and 1780s, as Americans formulated and revised state constitutions, they also developed the method by which frames of government were written and approved—the **Constitutional Convention.** Pennsylvania radicals called the first state convention in 1776, explaining that its members would be "invested with powers to form a plan of government only, and not to execute it after it is framed." Then, in 1780, Massachusetts voters demanded a convention to write a new constitution rather than accept a document their assemblymen had prepared. The constitution was ratified by the people (voters), who thus claimed to be sovereign—the ultimate source of political power—because the frame of government originated with them. Within a few years, other states adopted the same process.

State constitutions also provided some protection for the liberties many Americans had defended in the Revolution. Virginia included a model Declaration of Rights that other states copied loosely. Most state constitutions offered freedom of worship, required search warrants, and banned excessive fines and quartering of troops in private dwellings. Only some of the states, however, guaranteed trial by jury and the rights of free speech, press, and assembly.

The state constitutions were radical in the context of eighteenth-century politics because they vested power in the voters and lower houses of assembly. Remarkably, in Massachusetts in 1780, every free man, even those without property, could vote on the new constitution. However, the document they approved limited suffrage to propertied men, and the definition of who was qualified to cast ballots and hold office remained traditional. John Adams spoke for most politicians of his time when he wrote that only property holders should be counted among the sovereign people who could choose and serve as magistrates because the purpose of government was to safeguard property. "It is dangerous," Adams wrote, ". . . to alter the qualifications of voters. There will be no end to it. New claims will arise. Women will demand a vote. Lads from 12 to 21 will think their rights not enough attended to, and every man, who has not a farthing, will demand an equal voice." Voters, according to republican theory, must have a stake in society. Wives, slaves, servants, and unpropertied laboring men were dependent on others and thus unqualified for suffrage. Yet in most places, women and free African Americans who owned property were also barred from voting by law or by informal pressure. One exception was New Jersey, where the 1776 state constitution extended the vote to "all free inhabitants" who held sufficient property; in 1807, the legislature fell into line with other states by disenfranchising all women and blacks.

The Question of Abolishing Slavery

The revolutionary rhetoric of freedom and self-determination unleashed a public debate over the legitimacy of slavery. During the war, some African Americans escaped to the British and others served in the American army. In doing so, African Americans made whites more aware of the hypocrisy of fighting a war of independence while they kept other human beings in chains.

In the North, the first significant opposition to slavery had developed among Pennsylvania and New Jersey Quakers well before the Revolution. Since the seventeenth century, individual members of the Society of Friends had argued that black bondage violated basic Christian concepts, particularly the belief that all humans are equal in the eyes of God. After 1750, the Society of Friends became the first American religion to denounce perpetual bondage as a sin and to prohibit members from holding slaves. The Quakers then spearheaded an emancipation movement that gained strength among other whites in the 1770s and 1780s, contributing to the growth of free black communities in Philadelphia, New York, and other northern cities. In addition, by the 1780s, slavery was less important economically in northern states than in the South. Thus, the combination of religious conviction, natural rights concepts of liberty and equality, and pressure by African Americans undercut the viability of slavery in the North. Northern employers instead hired workers from among the growing numbers of free laborers, including many African Americans.

In Pennsylvania and New England, state governments had acted against slavery by the mid-1780s. The Pennsylvania assembly passed the first abolition law in 1780, declaring, "We conceive that it is our duty, and we rejoice that it is in our power, to extend a portion of that freedom to others." The act was less comprehensive than its heartiest supporters wished. As a result of compromises required for passage, the Pennsylvania act abolished slavery gradually—so gradually that under its provisions, no black Pennsylvanian would achieve freedom until 1808. But the Pennsylvania act was more effective than expected because many enslaved blacks, exasperated that the law failed to free them, escaped their masters, while hundreds of slaveholders voluntarily manumitted (freed) their slaves. Also significant was the work of the **Pennsylvania Abolition Society**, which tested the limits of the 1780 abolition act by providing legal counsel to African Americans to defend their liberty. The number of slaves in Pennsylvania declined from almost 7,000 in 1780 to 795 in 1810.

Pennsylvania Abolition Society Organization founded in Philadelphia during the revolutionary period that advocated expansion of the state's 1780 act for gradual abolition and provided legal counsel to African Americans to defend their liberty.

Elsewhere in the North, the Massachusetts Supreme Court in 1783 decided that slavery was incompatible with the state's 1780 constitution, which said all men are free and equal, though it did not specifically outlaw perpetual bondage.

(© Francis G. Mayer/CORBIS)

***The Residence of David Twining,* by Edward Hicks.** Although northern Quakers had emancipated their slaves by the late 1780s, most free African Americans, like the man at the plow, continued to work for others as indentured servants, because, as former slaves, they lacked funds to establish their own shops and farms.

As blacks sued for freedom, the courts ruled on their behalf, and so by 1790 Massachusetts reported no slaves on the federal census. The Connecticut and Rhode Island legislatures in 1784 followed Pennsylvania's example by passing gradual abolition laws, and Vermont and New Hampshire also banned the institution. New York and New Jersey passed gradual abolition acts in 1799 and 1804, respectively.

During the 1780s, considerable support for abolition developed in the Chesapeake region, though enslaved African Americans composed almost 40 percent of the population. Southern states, like their northern counterparts, had continued the First Continental Congress's prohibition of the slave trade. Some people expected that cessation of the trade to result in the gradual death of slavery in Virginia and Maryland, which turned out to be a mistaken belief because the African American population there grew naturally by reproduction. Involuntary bondage would persist without positive action for abolition. Thomas Jefferson exemplified the troubled and confused state of mind of many white Americans about slavery. Although he remained a slaveholder throughout his life and held racist beliefs, Jefferson claimed to support a strategy for gradual abolition in Virginia. The plan, never considered by the assembly, would have freed and educated African American children born after the plan went into effect and, when they became adults, removed them to a separate territory.

Efforts for general abolition failed south of Pennsylvania, yet some progress occurred when Virginia (in 1782), Delaware (in 1787), and Maryland (in 1790) made private manumission easier. New laws permitted slaveholders who were inspired by antislavery beliefs to free their slaves. A private abolition movement took fire in areas of the Upper South, where Quakers and Methodists were numerous and planters were changing from tobacco to wheat as their chief crop, thus requiring fewer field hands. But some slaveholders merely sold their slaves to the Carolinas and Georgia, where abolitionist sentiment had little impact. Another measure of opposition to slavery was the rise in the number of free African Americans in the Upper South: the free black population in Virginia rose to nearly thirteen thousand. Even with impressive numbers of manumissions, however, emancipated blacks in 1800 made up just 8 percent of all African Americans in the region.

> **Doing History Online**
>
> **Gradual Abolition of Slavery in the North**
>
> Go to the CourseMate website for this chapter and link to Primary Sources. Read Document 2 (Pennsylvania Act for the Gradual Abolition of Slavery) and Document 5 (essay by Anthony Benezet). According to Section I of the Pennsylvania act, for what reasons did the Pennsylvania Assembly enact gradual abolition? How did their rationale compare with Benezet's reasoning against slavery?
>
> www.cengagebrain.com

Defining Religious Liberty

The issue of religious freedom also confronted the architects of the new state governments. Revolutionary ideals led many to challenge laws that forced people to attend and financially support an established church. Before the Revolution, opinions in the colonies had varied widely about the relationship between church and state. Congregational churches were supported by taxes in Massachusetts, New Hampshire, and Connecticut; the Church of England (Anglican) was established in the Carolinas, Virginia, Maryland, and New York. In contrast, Rhode Island, New Jersey, and Pennsylvania protected a great diversity of religions, giving none of them public funds. All of the colonies, however, limited service in political office to members of certain religions.

The break with Great Britain had the greatest impact on the established Church of England, called the Protestant Episcopal church in the United States after the Revolution. With independence, some of its parishes dissolved as missionaries departed because the church hierarchy in England stopped paying their salaries. Many Anglican clergymen and laypeople in New England and the mid-Atlantic region had been loyalists, which helped fuel the Whig movement for disestablishment. Upon independence, all of the states in which the Anglican church was established promptly ended government support except Virginia, which finally acted in 1786. Its assembly passed Thomas Jefferson's **statute for religious freedom,** stating, "No man shall be compelled to frequent or support any religious worship, place or ministry whatsoever, nor shall be enforced, restrained, molested, or burthened in his body or goods, nor shall otherwise suffer on account of his religious opinions or belief."

statute for religious freedom (1786) Virginia legislation written by Thomas Jefferson and passed in 1786 that disestablished the Episcopal (Anglican) Church in Virginia.

Nevertheless, the movement to end discrimination stalled, and in the 1780s, religious tests for political office remained common. The states most resistant to disestablishment were the old Puritan strongholds in New England. Massachusetts, New Hampshire, and Connecticut required tax support for Protestant churches well into the nineteenth century (see *Doing History: Religious Liberty*).

❖ Challenges to the Confederation

Despite the dominance of the states, the Confederation Congress had important functions that required far more unity and power than it possessed. Of all Congress's difficulties, the inability to tax was most damaging, resulting in the Confederation's demise.

Military Demobilization

One of the most remarkable aspects of the American revolutionary experience—in the light of revolutions since that time—was the absence of a serious military challenge to civilian control. George Washington was committed to popularly elected government and thus ignored suggestions that he become a military ruler. Even so, the United States faced two problems concerning the armed forces. During the war, Congress failed to pay or supply the army properly, but it had promised generous pensions and bounties to entice men to sign up for the duration of the war. The second question confronting Congress was whether to establish a peacetime army, an issue that had both ideological and financial significance.

For two years after the Battle of Yorktown in 1781, the Continental army continued to exist, with Washington encamped at Newburgh, New York, where his troops monitored the British army still in New York City. American officers and enlisted men voiced grievances because they needed food, clothing, and wages. Soldiers rioted and insulted their officers, while many simply went home with no compensation except their weapons. Officers at Newburgh drew up a list of complaints for Congress, demanding as much of their back pay as possible and a full reckoning of the entire sum they were owed. They seemed so disgruntled that Washington remained at Newburgh instead of going home to Mount Vernon as he had planned.

In what became known as the Newburgh conspiracy, **Robert Morris** of Philadelphia and Gouverneur Morris and Alexander Hamilton of New York hatched a plan to use the officers' protests to strengthen the Confederation and compel states to give Congress authority to tax. The crisis ended when Washington pledged to negotiate for their back pay and pensions and the officers swore their loyalty to Congress. For its part, Congress agreed to pay troops three months' wages at discharge, and officers would receive pensions of five years' full pay in government bonds. Dissatisfied, a group of eighty enlisted men stationed at Lancaster, Pennsylvania mutinied and marched on Philadelphia, barricading the State House where Congress met. Although the soldiers backed down without violence, the frightened congressmen fled to Princeton.

Morris, Robert (1734–1806) American Revolutionary politician and financier. A signer of the Declaration of Independence, he raised money for the Continental Army, attended the Constitutional Convention (1787), and was financially ruined by land speculation.

Restitution of military pensions, back wages, and bounties took until the 1790s because Congress lacked the funds to discharge its debts. Soldiers who had

Doing History Religious Liberty

The three documents that follow demonstrate the progress of the law regarding religious freedom during the 1780s. The first excerpt is a petition from the Philadelphia Jewish community. Although Pennsylvania was renowned for religious liberty, its constitution limited election to the state assembly to Christians. The new Pennsylvania constitution adopted in 1790 removed this religious test. The Virginia statute of 1786, drafted by Thomas Jefferson, was a major breakthrough. Although itself an act of legislation rather than part of the state constitution, the law affirmed religious liberty as a natural right. Amendment I of the U.S. Constitution, part of the Bill of Rights, prohibited Congress from establishing a religion.

Petition of Philadelphia Jews for Equal Rights, *1783*

To the honourable the Council of Censors, assembled agreeable to the Constitution of the State of Pennsylvania. The Memorial of . . . the Synagogue of the Jews at Philadelphia. . . .

That by the tenth section of the Frame of Government of this Commonwealth, it is ordered that each member of the general assembly of representatives of the freemen of Pennsylvania, before he takes his seat, shall make and subscribe a declaration, which ends in these words, "I do acknowledge the Scriptures of the old and new Testament to be given by divine inspiration." . . .

Your memorialists beg leave to observe, that this clause seems to limit the civil rights of your citizens to one very special article of the creed; whereas by the second paragraph of the declaration of the rights of the inhabitants, it is asserted without any other limitation than the professing the existence of God, in plain words, "that no man who acknowledges the being of a God can be justly deprived or abridged of any civil rights as a citizen on account of his religious sentiments." . . .

—Your memorialists cannot say that the Jews are particularly fond of being representatives of the people in assembly or civil officers and magistrates in the State; but with great submission they apprehend that a clause in the constitution, which disables them to be elected by their fellow citizens to represent them in assembly, is a stigma upon their nation and religion. . . .

The Jews of Pennsylvania in proportion to the number of their members, can count with any religious society whatsoever, the Whigs among either of them; they have served some of them in the Continental army; some went out in the militia to fight the common enemy; all of them have cheerfully contributed to the support of the militia, and of the government of this State; they have no inconsiderable property in lands and tenements, but particularly in the way of trade, some more, some less, for which they pay taxes. . . .

been promised land bounties in the West had to wait fifteen years for surveys, in large part because Native Americans refused to give up the territory. By the 1790s, most veterans had long since sold their rights to speculators for a fraction of their worth.

standing army After the American Revolution, the issue of a standing, or peacetime, army pitted revolutionary ideology against the need for defense.

The issue of a **standing army** squared revolutionary ideology against the need for defense. One of the chief causes of the Revolution had been the peacetime quartering in New York and Boston of the British army, which patriots called a "MONSTER of a standing ARMY." But now the United States faced threats from the Spanish in Florida and Louisiana, the British in Canada, and Native Americans everywhere along the frontier. In April 1783, Congress appointed a committee to consult Washington and other generals on military requirements. The commander in chief argued that the United States had to be prepared against its enemies. He suggested retaining twenty-six hundred Continentals and advised Congress to organize a national citizens' militia that would stay in training for ready defense. In 1784, Congress dismissed Washington's plan for reasons of principle and finance, virtually disbanding the army during an interval of peace—a pattern the nation would follow well into the twentieth century.

And your memorialists humbly pray, that if your honours, from any consideration than the subject of this address, should think proper to call a convention for revising the constitution, you would be pleased to recommend this to the notice of that convention.

Source: Richard D. Brown, ed., *Major Problems in the Era of the American Revolution 1760–1791* (Lexington, MA: D. C. Heath and Company, 1992), 358–359.

Virginia Statute for Religious Freedom, *1786*

Be it enacted by the General Assembly, That no man shall be compelled to frequent or support any religious worship, place, or ministry whatsoever, nor shall be enforced, restrained, molested, or burthened in his body or goods, nor shall otherwise suffer on account of his religious opinions or belief; but that all men shall be free to profess, and by argument to maintain, their opinion in matters of religion, and that the same shall in no way diminish, enlarge, or affect their civil capacities.

And though we well know that this assembly elected by the people for the ordinary purposes of legislation only, have no power to restrain the acts of succeeding assemblies, constituted with powers equal to our own, and that therefore to declare this act to be irrevocable would be of no effect in law; yet we are free to declare, and do declare, that the rights hereby asserted are of the natural rights of mankind, and that if any act shall be hereafter passed to repeal the present, or to narrow its operation, such act will be an infringement of natural right.

Source: Merrill D. Peterson and Robert C. Vaughan, eds., *The Virginia Statute for Religious Freedom: Its Evolution and Consequences in American History* (Cambridge: Cambridge University Press, 1988), xvii–xviii.

The Bill of Rights, *1791*

Amendment I

Congress shall make no law respecting an establishment of religion, or prohibiting the free exercise there-of; or abridging the freedom of speech, or of the press; or the right of the people peaceably to assemble, and to petition the Government for a redress of grievances.

Source: "The Constitution of the United States of America." See the Appendix for the full text.

QUESTIONS for REFLECTION

1. During the colonial period, how did Pennsylvania compare with other provinces regarding religious liberty?
2. What arguments did Philadelphia Jews employ to challenge the religious test to serve in the assembly?
3. What was the significance of the Virginia Statute for Religious Freedom of 1786 and Amendment I of the U.S. Constitution?

Economic Troubles

The Confederation Congress failed to solve the problem of its war debt, which by 1790 amounted to an estimated $10 million owed to other countries and $40 million owed to Americans. During the war, the government had issued **paper currency** to pay for goods and services. It abandoned this policy because of rampant inflation. Congress turned to the states, which refused to contribute sufficient funds, and then borrowed from France and from American merchants and farmers for military provisions.

paper currency After the Revolution, Americans hotly debated the issue of paper currency because it had resulted in inflation during the war, when the government used it to pay for goods and services. Many farmers favored issuing paper currency through a land office, which would provide capital based on the value of their land.

One long-lasting consequence of the war's inflationary crisis was conflict between urban and rural interests over public finance. The spiraling cost of food and fuel in the late 1770s had hurt city residents much more than farmers. In public debate over currency and credit, farmers wanted access to government loans based on the value of their land, similar to the colonial land banks that had allowed them to use real estate as collateral for loans. Although the provincial currency issued by the land banks had been fairly stable, merchants and urban artisans in the 1780s recalled the more recent inflation of the Revolution. They believed that paper currency based on real estate would send prices soaring. At the same time, merchants knew that the economy would stagnate if specie (gold and silver) were required for every transaction, so they embraced an alternative method of generating paper currency, the bank.

Bank of North America (1781) The first bank in the United States, modeled on the Bank of England, helped to solve the wartime fiscal crisis. Instead of issuing paper currency through a land office, as farmers wanted, the bank issued money in the form of short-term loans backed by gold and silver plate.

The first bank in the United States was the **Bank of North America,** chartered in 1781 in Philadelphia by both the Congress and state of Pennsylvania. Robert Morris proposed the institution, based on the Bank of England, as a way to help solve the wartime fiscal crisis. Instead of issuing paper currency through a land office, as farmers wanted, the bank issued currency in the form of short-term loans to merchants. These bank notes were backed by gold and silver that investors deposited in return for a share of the bank's profits. The attraction for stockholders was that formerly idle gold and silver assets could now earn interest. Bank advocates believed that once a few people tested its soundness and received specie, others would trust the bank and accept the bank notes as currency. The Bank earned regular profits during its first two decades.

The Bank of North America's conservative course kept it solvent financially but made it unpopular with many people. The bank's manager, Thomas Willing, lent money only to good credit risks in the mercantile community, thus angering artisans and farmers who viewed the bank as a monopoly created by Congress to benefit the commercial elite. Also, Willing refused to liberalize the bank's loan policy as confidence in the bank's strength increased. Instead of expanding the money supply as later banks did, the Bank of North America made loans only up to the amount of specie in its vaults. Despite its flaws, the Bank of North America helped the mercantile community through a time of uncertainty as merchants lost trading connections with partners in Great Britain but also gained release from the restrictions of British mercantilism.

Although being part of the mercantilist system had brought advantages, it also brought constraints. To Great Britain and its colonies, the United States was now a foreign country. Americans could sell provisions in the British West Indies and purchase rum, sugar, and molasses, but everything had to be carried on British ships. West Indies planters complained because this resulted in higher prices. For its part, Britain was eager to purchase tobacco from the Chesapeake and sell to Americans all the manufactures they would buy. U.S. merchants had access by treaty to ports in France and the French colonies, but were barred from trading in New Spain. Gradually Americans developed trade with Germany, the Netherlands, Scandinavia, and even China. By the end of the 1780s, U.S. exports recovered to approximately their pre-Revolutionary level.

The road to recovery was rocky, however, because in the immediate post-war years, American demand for British manufactures far outstripped exports. During the Revolution, American artisans had attempted to supply metal goods and textiles, but had been unable to match British quality and prices. With peace, British manufacturers extended generous credit to American consumers for clocks, watches, furniture, textiles, clothing, mirrors, and other goods. When depression hit in fall 1783 because of the loss of the West Indies market, American farmers, merchants, and shopkeepers found themselves seriously in debt. In New England, for example, the balance of trade with Great Britain was so uneven that exports covered only 13 percent of imports. Although the economy improved after mid-1785, many farmers had difficulty escaping from debt.

Jay, John (1745–1829) American diplomat and jurist who served in the Continental Congress and helped negotiate the Treaty of Paris (1783). He was the first chief justice of the U.S. Supreme Court (1789–1795) and negotiated the agreement with Great Britain that became known as the Jay Treaty.

Indeed, estimates of the gross national product suggest that the Revolution had an extended negative impact on the American economy. Data available for 1774 and 1790 indicate that income declined by more than 40 percent, close to the decrease Americans experienced during the Great Depression of the 1930s.

Foreign Affairs

Though the United States had won the war, its leaders soon learned that they received little respect among European nations. Despite the boundary provisions of the Treaty of 1783, Spain and Great Britain took advantage of the Confederation's weakness to trespass on territory in the West, gaining allies among Native Americans who were losing their lands to the steady stream of white settlers crossing the Appalachians (see Map 6.1).

During the 1780s, Spain tried to restrict expansion of the United States. With settlers rapidly filling the region between the Appalachians and the Mississippi River, Spain feared for its control of Louisiana and East and West Florida. Its military retained forts north of the thirty-first parallel, which the United States claimed as its southern border, and in 1784, the Spanish government closed the port of New Orleans to Americans. Settlers in the trans-Appalachian region protested vigorously because they needed access to the New Orleans market for their goods. Some threatened to secede from the United States unless Congress convinced Spain to reverse its decision. Congress directed **John Jay**, the secretary of foreign affairs and a New Yorker, to negotiate with Spanish diplomat Diego de Gardoqui to reopen the port. With the permission of Congress, Jay agreed to a treaty that provided commercial advantages for eastern merchants but closed New Orleans to westerners for a generation. The West and South erupted in opposition, blocking approval of the Jay-Gardoqui Treaty. The lower Mississippi River remained closed until 1788, when the Spanish permitted Americans to use New Orleans on payment of duties.

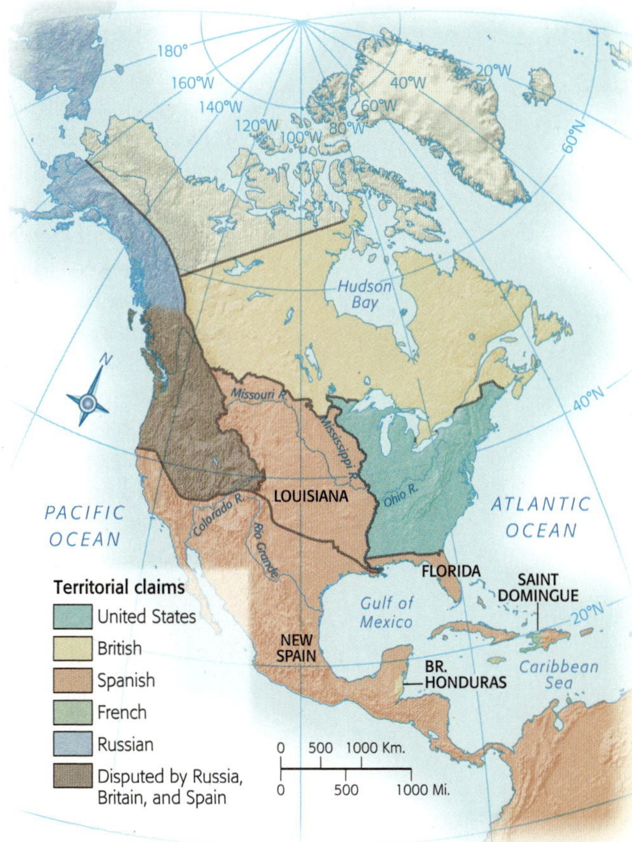

MAP 6.1
North America in 1783
The peace treaty ending the American Revolution gave the United States most of the territory from the Atlantic Ocean to the Mississippi River, south of the St. Lawrence River and Great Lakes, and north of Spanish Florida. Several borders remained vague, however, causing ongoing negotiations with European nations as well as Native American leaders.

The Spanish government also cooperated with Native Americans to slow the influx of Anglo-American settlers into contested territory. Contrary to Spain's traditional policy of considering Native Americans as subjects to the Crown, its colonial officials in 1784 signed written treaties of alliance with the Indians. Most threatening of these pacts to the United States was the one with the Creeks, which their leader, **Alexander McGillivray**, arranged. The son of a Scottish trader and a French-Creek woman and educated in Charleston, McGillivray could negotiate his way in both European and Indian societies. To protect Creek lands from settlers streaming in from Georgia, he offered the Spanish "a powerful barrier in these parts against the ambitious and encroaching Americans" in return for an alliance and weapons. With Cherokees and Shawnees to the north, the Creeks battled Anglo-Americans through the 1780s, thus slowing settlement on the southwest frontier.

McGillivray, Alexander (1759?–1793) Son of a Scottish trader and a French-Creek woman, McGillivray served as a Creek leader and allied with Spain to prevent white settlement on Creek lands during the 1780s.

The Confederation government also had difficulty establishing its claims against the British and the Indians of the Ohio Valley. In the Treaty of 1783, the British had promised to remove their troops from forts in the Great Lakes region. Through the 1780s, however, they refused to withdraw, hoping for return of the territory. They barred American ships from the Great Lakes and allied with Native Americans who wanted to halt white settlement. British diplomats justified these actions with the excuse that Americans had failed to pay prewar debts to British creditors and return confiscated loyalist property.

Great Britain's neglect of its Indian allies in negotiating the peace led the U.S. government to treat them as a conquered people. With great bravado, considering the Confederation's small army, American commissioners said to the Ohio Indians, "You are mistaken in supposing that . . . you are to become a free and independent nation, and may make what terms you please. . . . You are a subdued people." Under threat of arms, a group of Iroquois yielded rights in the Northwest with a series of treaties signed between 1784 and 1786, but many Native Americans refused to recognize them because their negotiators lacked authority and had been forced to sign.

Soon frontier warfare made U.S. officials realize that they were the ones who were "mistaken" in presuming that the Indians had been "subdued." Theyendanegea (Joseph Brant), the pro-British Mohawk leader, rallied Indians against white settlement in the Northwest. In 1786, he urged potential allies, "The Interests of Any One Nation Should be the Interests of us all, the Welfare of the one Should be the Welfare of all the others." Their resistance convinced Secretary of War Henry Knox that the United States must change its tactics or risk a general Indian war. He suggested that Congress return to the policy of purchasing lands instead of demanding them by conquest. The congressmen agreed, incorporating into the Northwest Ordinance of 1787 the futile promise that the Indians' land "shall never be taken from them without their consent."

The Northwest Ordinances of 1785 and 1787

Despite war with the Indians and the presence of British troops, the Confederation Congress moved forward with legislation to create the Northwest Territory. The issue of western lands had divided the thirteen states even during the Revolution since different states made overlapping claims, as in the region north of the Ohio River, which Virginia claimed in its entirety and Connecticut and Massachusetts claimed in part. States lacking rights to western lands believed that all should be ceded to the Confederation. Virginia, whose charter rights were oldest, resolved the issue in 1781 by agreeing to transfer to the United States the region north and west of the Ohio River, the area that later became the states of Ohio, Indiana, Illinois, Michigan, Wisconsin, and part of Minnesota (see Map 6.2). Virginia offered cession on the condition that the territory eventually be divided into states that would join the Confederation on an equal basis with the original thirteen. The trans-Appalachian lands south of the Ohio River remained temporarily under the control of Virginia, North Carolina, and Georgia.

Congress passed three ordinances to establish guidelines for distributing land and governing the Northwest Territory. Thomas Jefferson was principal author of the first ordinance, which passed Congress in 1784. This law gave settlers a great deal of autonomy in establishing a territorial government. The Northwest would be divided into seven districts, with the settlers of each to govern themselves by choosing a constitution and laws from any of the existing states. When any district reached the population of the smallest of the original thirteen states, it would be admitted as a state to the Confederation on equal terms. Congress retained responsibility for selling the public lands.

The second ordinance, passed in 1785, set the rules for distributing lands and was influenced by wealthy speculators who had purchased rights from Native Americans. The minimum price of a lot was $640, payable in specie or its equivalent, a sum far beyond the means of many potential settlers. All property would be surveyed before sale, laid out in townships 6 miles square (see Map 6.3). Each lot would contain 640 acres, sold at a minimum of $1 per acre, with better land offered at a higher price. The government retained lots for public schools and for distribution to Revolutionary War veterans. Because of the relatively high cost, Congress found few individual buyers. In fact, many land-hungry squatters simply set up their farms without government approval, sometimes purchasing rights

MAP 6.2
Western Land Cessions, 1782–1802
A number of states claimed territory west of the Appalachians based on their colonial charters. For example, under Connecticut's charter, which defined the Pacific Ocean as its western boundary, residents claimed part of Pennsylvania as well as western lands.

from neighboring Indians, sometimes not. So Congress accepted a deal offered by a group of New England speculators, the Ohio Company, agreeing to sell them 1.5 million acres for $500,000 in depreciated bonds, or less than ten cents per acre in hard money. Given the Confederation's debt, the sale was welcome.

Congress further cooperated with the Ohio Company in drafting the **Northwest Ordinance of 1787.** In response to speculators' demands, the law established firmer congressional control over the territory, providing settlers less self-government than under the 1784 ordinance. Initially a governor, secretary, and three judges appointed by Congress would administer the government. When five thousand adult males resided in the territory, they could elect an assembly, but the governor held a veto over its actions. Men were eligible to vote if they owned at least fifty acres of land. Three to five states would be created from the Northwest Territory, with each state qualified to enter the Union when its population reached sixty thousand. New states would have equal status with the original thirteen. The ordinance of 1787 also included provisions for individual rights that the Congress and the Ohio Company hoped would attract purchasers from New England. The ordinance protected private contracts, religious liberty, trial by jury, and habeas corpus (protection against illegal imprisonment). It prohibited slavery from the region forever. Thus, while catering to the interests of speculators, the Northwest Ordinance also extended rights won during the Revolution to new settlers in the West and limited the spread of slavery.

Northwest Ordinance (1787) Adopted by the Congress to establish stricter control over the government of the Northwest Territory ceded to the United States by the states. The ordinance was the most significant achievement of Congress under the Articles of Confederation.

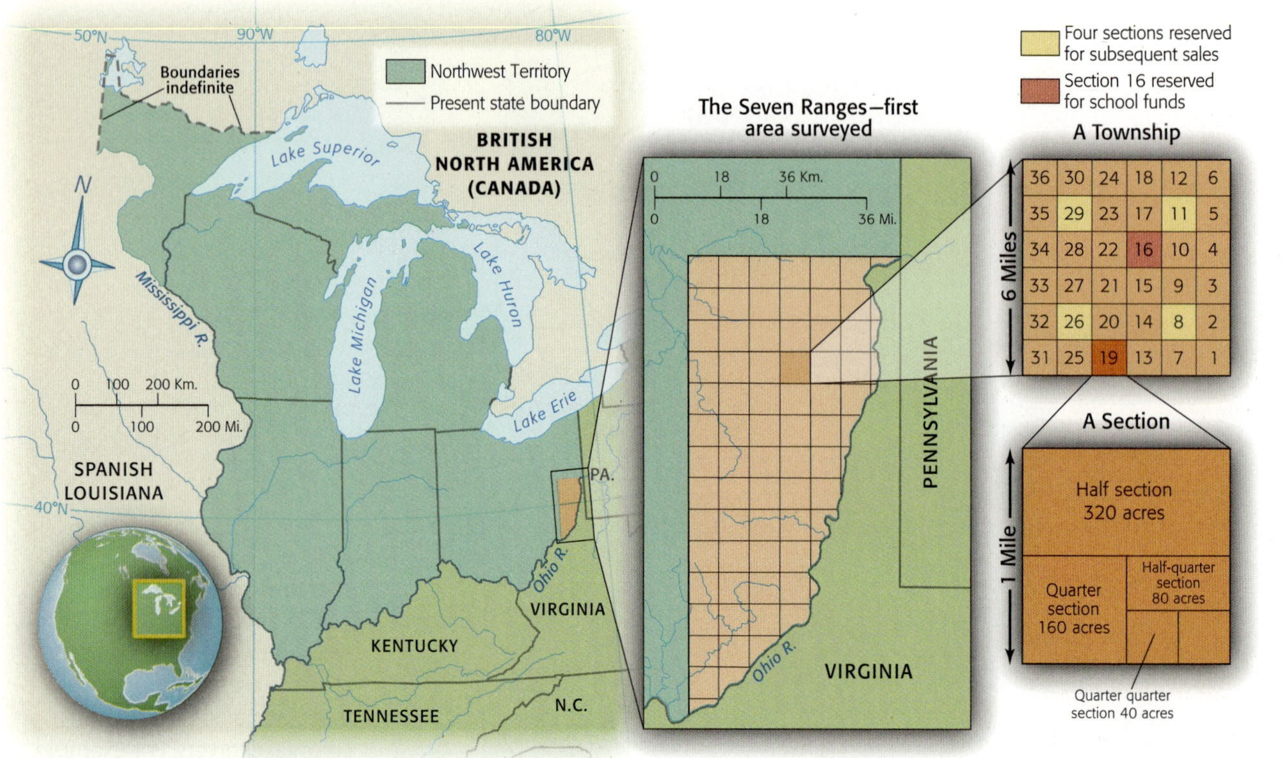

MAP 6.3
The Northwest Territory, 1785–1787
The map to the left shows the boundaries of the Northwest Territory, which later became the states of Ohio, Indiana, Illinois, Michigan, Wisconsin, and part of Minnesota as they met population requirements. The center and right diagrams illustrate the plans for dividing land in eastern Ohio into townships and lots. The minimum price was $1 per acre.

❖ Political and Economic Turmoil

Political strife under the Articles of Confederation disappointed Americans who had high hopes for their republic. Instead of harmony, economic interests clashed; the states failed to satisfy everybody. Many elites thought the United States was becoming too democratic and anarchic. As farmers revolted, government failed to control the violence, and some legislatures approved the insurgents' demands.

Creditors Versus Debtors

As a result of the postwar depression, farmers throughout the United States faced economic hardship. Many had eagerly purchased British manufactures, expecting to pay for the new clothes and consumer goods by selling their grain and livestock to the West Indies. British merchants offered easy credit to stimulate sales; American merchants and shopkeepers passed the credit on to farm families, who would pay with the fall crop. This house of cards collapsed when the British government closed the West Indies to American ships. English mercantile houses called in their debts in specie only, starting a chain of default that extended from London to the frontier. In many places, the number of debt cases rose dramatically. For example, in Hampshire County, Massachusetts, almost one-third of the county's adult males were prosecuted for insolvency.

State governments aggravated the situation by imposing taxes to repay war bonds in full, a policy that worked to the advantage of wealthy speculators who had bought up the bonds from farmers and artisans at a large discount. The Massachusetts government particularly favored mercantile interests, levying on farmers high taxes that also had to be paid in specie. When farmers defaulted, the courts sold their land and cattle, often at only one-third to one-half value. If their assets failed to cover the debts and back taxes, the farmers were imprisoned until they or someone else paid the sum.

Angry at the threats of imprisonment and the loss of property, protesters mobilized as they had in the pre-Revolutionary period. In Massachusetts, they demanded changes in the state constitution to make the government more responsive to their needs and less costly to run. They wanted abolition of the state senate, which represented the commercial elite; lowering of property qualifications to hold office; and transfer of the capital from Boston to a more central location. The farmers also demanded paper money and tender laws, the latter enabling them to settle debts and taxes with goods rather than specie. During the Revolution, the yeomen had benefited from inflation and were able to pay off prewar debts with cheap dollars. While they stopped short of demanding a return to high inflation, they hoped for a gentle upswing in prices and a larger money supply to help them settle their debts.

Shays's Rebellion, 1786–1787

When state governments failed to help, debtors in New England, New Jersey, Pennsylvania, Maryland, Virginia, and South Carolina protested militantly. Events moved furthest in Massachusetts. In fall 1786, armed Massachusetts farmers closed down county courts to prevent further hearings for debt. They were called Shaysites when Daniel Shays, a forty-year-old veteran of Bunker Hill and Saratoga, emerged as their leader. The government frantically requested aid from Congress, which complied by requisitioning $530,000 and 1,340 soldiers from the states. When the states failed to cooperate, the powerlessness of the Confederation was clear.

Lincoln, Benjamin (1733–1810) Revolutionary War general who in 1786–1787 successfully led the army funded by Boston merchants against the Shaysites in western Massachusetts.

The Massachusetts government acted on its own, taking measures that further alienated angry farmers. The assembly passed the Riot Act, which prohibited armed groups from gathering in public and permitted sheriffs to kill rioters who refused to disband. The legislature also suspended habeas corpus, allowing officials to jail suspected insurgents without showing cause. The farmers refused to back down; they protested that the suspension of habeas corpus was "dangerous if not absolutely destructive to a Republican government." Nevertheless, in November 1786, the state government sent three hundred soldiers to arrest rebel leaders. When that failed to stop the farmers from closing the courts, Boston merchants raised private funds to outfit forty-four hundred troops. Revolutionary general **Benjamin Lincoln** commanded the army; in January 1787, they marched to Worcester to protect the county court.

(Bettmann/CORBIS)

Shays's Rebellion. Illustration of a fight outside a courthouse during Shays's Rebellion.

Lincoln's army forced the Shaysites to choose between submission and armed rebellion, for a middle ground of petitions and court closings was no longer viable. The farmers amassed their own troops, estimated at twenty-five hundred men, with Shays in charge of one regiment. They unsuccessfully attacked the federal arsenal at Springfield for weapons to assault Boston, then regrouped to await the merchants' army. Shays was convinced that their cause was just; in a newspaper interview, he confidently stated that he "knew General Lincoln was coming against him, but as he would bring with him nobody but shopkeepers, lawyers, and doctors, he could easily defeat him." Lincoln attacked Shays by surprise in a blizzard, dispersing the rebels within half an hour.

The aftermath of Shays's defeat was more divisive and bloody than the engagements between the armies. The assembly declared a state of "open, unnatural, unprovoked, and wicked rebellion," giving the governor the power to treat the Shaysites as enemies of the state. The legislators passed the Disqualification Act, which barred people implicated in the revolt from voting and holding office for three years, teaching school, or keeping inns and taverns. Many of the insurgents fled to other states, while others were imprisoned. As a result of the uprising and repression, voter turnout skyrocketed in the April 1787 election. A much greater number of western Massachusetts towns sent delegates to the legislature than they had in previous years, making the new assembly somewhat more responsive to rural debtors. While refusing to approve paper money, it enacted a tender law and quickly restored the civil rights of the insurgents.

❖ The Movement for Constitutional Reform

The Confederation's helplessness in response to the spreading armed rebellions strengthened the hand of nationalists like Robert Morris and Alexander Hamilton, who had been arguing for a more powerful central government. By 1787, Congress had lost much of its authority, and representatives stopped attending, often preventing action for lack of a quorum. Furthermore, the Confederation was broke. In 1785, Congress stopped interest payments on its French debt and in 1787 ended those on the principal. Nor could it reimburse American creditors. In 1787, Congress transferred responsibility for the national debt to the states.

The Philadelphia Convention

In September 1786, when Shays's Rebellion was still gathering steam, representatives gathered for a convention in Annapolis, Maryland, to discuss amending the Articles to give Congress power to regulate trade. The convention failed when only five state delegations arrived on time. Several of the delegates, including Alexander Hamilton, James Madison, and John Dickinson, called for another convention to meet in May 1787 at Philadelphia to consider a more thorough revision of the Articles. By early 1787, the disorder in Massachusetts and the growing concern about state emission of paper money built support for constitutional reform. In February, Congress endorsed a change in the Articles. Twelve states—all but Rhode Island, where farmers controlled the legislature—sent delegates to Philadelphia.

Madison, James (1751–1836) Fourth president of the United States (1809–1817). Member of the Continental Congress (1780–1783) and the Constitutional Convention (1787), he strongly supported ratification of the Constitution and was a contributor to *The Federalist*.

The convention started on May 25, 1787. One of the Virginia delegates was **James Madison**, a thirty-six-year-old planter, slaveholder, and intellectual who had served in the Virginia assembly and Congress. A shy man who avoided public speaking, Madison nevertheless took a dominant role in the proceedings, for which he was later called the "Father of the Constitution." Propelled by the breakdown of Congress and the problems he witnessed in state government, Madison wanted to create a stronger central government. He believed that state constitutions with powerful assemblies were too democratic, giving too much influence to the common people. As a consequence, these legislatures collaborated with debtors by circulating paper money, which Madison considered an attack on property. The common people should be represented adequately, Madison thought, but their power must be constrained. The United States needed a new constitution that would place authority in the hands of well-educated, propertied men. Another Virginia delegate was George Washington, who lent his popularity and prestige to the proceedings but participated little in the debates.

Fifty-five men, most of whom supported the idea of a stronger national government, served at the Constitutional Convention for four months of debate. Twenty-one were practicing lawyers, another thirteen had been educated in the law, seven were merchants, and eighteen were farmers or planters; nineteen owned African American slaves. Most were relatively young men under the age of fifty, and many had served in the Revolution and had held political office. Benjamin Franklin, now eighty-one years old and ailing, was a member of the Pennsylvania delegation. Several heroes of the Revolution were absent, including Thomas Jefferson and John Adams, who were serving as ministers to France and Great Britain, respectively. Samuel Adams was not chosen as a delegate, and Patrick Henry refused to participate because he "smelt a rat."

The Great Compromise

During the first seven weeks, the matter overshadowing all discussion was the power of large versus small states. Madison, who thought the Confederation beyond repair, moved the convention along with a document he had drafted in advance, called the **Virginia Plan,** which scrapped the Articles and proposed a powerful central government, dominated by the National Legislature of two houses (bicameral). The lower house would be elected by qualified voters and would choose the members of the upper house from nominations by state legislatures. The number of delegates from each state would depend on population. This bicameral National Legislature would be empowered to appoint the executive and judicial branches of the central government and to veto state laws.

Virginia Plan Constitutional proposal written by James Madison, the Virginia Plan proposed a powerful central government dominated by a National Legislature of two houses (bicameral). It also favored a system of greater representation based on a state's population.

Several states opposed the Virginia Plan because it gave greater representation in the National Legislature to states with large populations. Delaware, Maryland, New Jersey, and Connecticut feared the power of Virginia, Pennsylvania, and Massachusetts, which together contained almost one-half of the American people. If the Virginia Plan were adopted, just four states could dominate the legislature. In dividing on this issue, states considered the possibility of future population expansion as well as existing size. Thus, states with

(Independence National Historical Park)

The Constitutional Convention. This painting of the Constitutional Convention of 1787 by an unknown artist shows George Washington presiding. Because the convention met in secrecy, the artist used his imagination to paint the scene.

New Jersey Plan Proposal for the U.S. Constitution drafted by William Paterson, it provided for a one-house (unicameral) Congress in which states had equal representation.

unsettled territories mostly sided with the large states, while those without room for growth chose the opposite camp. In mid-June, William Paterson introduced the **New Jersey Plan,** which proposed a one-house, or unicameral, Congress in which the states had equal representation. Congress would appoint an executive council, which would choose a supreme court. As in the Virginia Plan, the authority of Congress was much enlarged, with powers to tax, regulate commerce, and compel states to obey its laws. The large states objected to this plan, arguing that Delaware (population 59,000) should not have as much power as Virginia (population 748,000).

Great Compromise (1787) At the Constitutional Convention, plan proposed by the Connecticut delegation for a bicameral Congress with a House of Representatives, with representations based on a state's population, and the Senate, in which each state would be represented equally. Also known as the Connecticut Compromise.

The debate over representation in Congress brought the convention to an impasse until Connecticut formally proposed what has become known as the **Great Compromise.** The plan established a bicameral Congress, with representation in the lower house based on population. This body, called the House of Representatives, would be elected directly by the voters every two years and have the sole right to initiate revenue bills. Thus, the idea that all people with a stake in society should elect the representatives who taxed them was incorporated into the document. In the upper house, called the Senate, states would have equal representation; each state legislature would choose two senators for six-year terms. The bicameral Congress resolved the division between the small and large states and also satisfied those who wanted to limit the influence of ordinary voters. Senators were expected to come from the wealthier, more established segments of society; their long terms and appointment by state legislators would shield them from public opinion and thus provide a stabilizing influence. Both houses of Congress had to approve legislation.

The compromise between the large and small states created a government that was both national and federal. It was national because the House of Representatives was popularly elected, with not more than one representative per thirty thousand people. Upon ratification, the United States would become a single nation rather than a confederacy of states. By expanding legislative powers, the sovereign people vested more authority in the central government. Congress received the powers to tax, coin and borrow money, regulate commerce, establish courts, declare war, and raise armed forces. States were specifically forbidden from keeping troops without the permission of Congress, making treaties, coining money, and issuing paper currency. At the same time, the new Constitution established a federal government—one in which the states retained rights, including equal representation in the Senate. Congress was forbidden from giving one state preference over another when levying taxes and regulating trade, and it could not impose export duties, prohibit the slave trade until 1808, or carve a new state from any state's territory without permission. Approval by three-fourths of the states would be necessary to amend the Constitution.

The Executive, Slavery, and Commerce

Once the question of state representation was solved with the great compromise, the convention made greater headway. Factions within the convention shifted from one debate to the next.

The power of the executive was a concern to people living in a world dominated by kings and princes. Delegates wanted to ensure that their government remained a republic, that it would not become a monarchy or dictatorship. At the same time, they believed that the executive branch should serve as a check on the legislature and ultimately chose a single president with a four-year term, without specifying the number of times the president could be reelected. The question of how the president would be chosen was divisive, with some preferring direct election by the people and others wanting Congress or the state legislatures to make the choice. A committee appointed by the convention devised a complicated formula to satisfy all sides: an **electoral college** was empowered to elect the president and vice president, with each state allotted as many votes as it had representatives and senators. Thus, even the smallest state received three votes and the large states were represented according to population. The state legislatures could determine how to choose the electors. The electoral college would never meet together as a group. The electors of each state gathered within their states to cast votes, which they sent to Congress for counting. If no candidate received a majority, the House of Representatives made the selection from among the five candidates with the most votes.

electoral college The group that elects the president. Each state received as many electors as it had congressmen and senators combined.

Of the Philadelphia convention's decisions on the executive, most crucial to the endurance of the Constitution was the balance of power between the executive and legislative branches. The convention gave the president a veto power over laws passed by Congress. The legislators could override the veto if two-thirds of both houses approved. Congress also had authority to remove the president by impeachment and trial for treason, bribery, and "other high Crimes and Misdemeanors." Whereas Congress received power to declare war and raise troops, the president served as commander in chief. Only with the "advice and consent" of the Senate could the chief executive negotiate treaties and appoint ambassadors, Supreme Court justices, and other officials.

Slavery was a major factor in the convention's deliberations, though the words *slavery, slave,* and *slave trade* appeared nowhere in the 1787 Constitution. African American bondage affected the debates on representation in Congress, the election of the president, and the regulation of commerce. The southern states wanted to include slaves in a state's population when computing delegates to the House of Representatives and votes in the electoral college. Because slaves made up significant portions of the population in southern states (see Table 6.1), northerners protested that this would give white southerners an unfair advantage. They argued that slaves should not be counted because they could not vote. As part of the Great Compromise, the convention decided that five enslaved Americans would count as three free persons for apportioning representation and direct taxes among the states. Since three-fifths of slaves living in the Chesapeake and Lower South numbered 380,000 people, the power of white voters south of Pennsylvania was significantly increased by this compromise.

Political bargaining resulted in additional provisions that upheld slavery. The convention approved a **fugitive slave clause,** which prevented free states from emancipating slaves who had escaped from masters in other states. The delegates also adopted a provision that forbade Congress from prohibiting slave importation for twenty years (with no requirement that it ban the slave trade after that time). North and South Carolina and Georgia demanded the option of importing people from Africa because they expected settlement to continue into western Georgia and what are now the states of Alabama, Mississippi, and Tennessee. Northern delegates did almost nothing to promote the abolition of slavery.

fugitive slave clause (1787) Provision of the U.S. Constitution that prevented free states from emancipating slaves who had escaped from masters in other states.

The Philadelphia convention created a Constitution that shifted important powers to a national government but still vested a great deal of authority in the states. The framers painstakingly created checks and balances among the branches of government. They required direct popular election of only the House of Representatives, giving that body the right to initiate taxes. The convention incorporated flexibility into the document, which had been absent in the Articles of Confederation, by permitting amendment with approval of two-thirds of both houses of Congress and three-fourths of the states.

TABLE 6.1
Enslaved Population in the United States, 1790

	Total	Slaves
New England	1,009,206	3,763
Middle Atlantic	1,017,087	45,210
Maryland and Virginia	1,067,338	395,663
Lower South	726,626	237,141

Source: U.S. Bureau of the Census, *A Century of Population Growth from the First Census of the United States to the Twelfth, 1790–1900* (Washington, DC: U.S. Government Printing Office, 1909), 57, 133.

Doing History Online

The Constitution

Go to the CourseMate website for this chapter and link to Primary Sources. Read Documents 8 to 12, 15, and 16. Why were Virginia and New York so important to the ratifying process and the "more perfect union"?

www.cengagebrain.com

The document shielded some individual rights, though critics argued that many were omitted. The Constitution protected trial by jury in criminal cases and habeas corpus. It banned religious tests for holding office under the United States, ex post facto (retroactive) laws, and bills of attainder, which extinguished a person's civil rights on sentence of death or as an outlaw. While codifying the principles of self-government and individual liberties, however, the convention denied them to almost one-fifth of the American population by embedding slavery within the fabric of the new government.

Ratification, 1787–1788

ratification Process by which the Constitution of 1787 and subsequent amendments must be approved. The original document required ratification by nine state conventions; states that refused to ratify could remain independent or unite under another frame of government.

After the delegates to the Philadelphia convention signed the Constitution on September 17, 1787, they quickly sent it to the Confederation Congress, which forwarded it to the states after little debate. One congressman from Virginia, Richard Henry Lee, tried to bury the document by adding amendments, but he was overruled. Article 7 of the document required **ratification** by nine state conventions. States refusing to ratify could remain independent or unite under another frame of government. Advocates of ratification knew that prompt action was necessary to forestall an effective opposition movement.

The group favoring ratification was not particularly well organized but had advantages over its opponents. James Madison, Alexander Hamilton, John Jay, and other supporters of the Constitution argued in favor of the federalist provisions that reserved powers to the states as well as the nationalist elements of the prospective government. While others denounced the Constitution because it transferred too much power to the national government from the states, the Federalists claimed the document provided balance. The critics were obliged to take the negative name of Antifederalists, which misrepresented their position in favor of states' rights.

The second advantage of those favoring ratification was that many advocates of a strong central government resided in the coastal cities and towns, where public opinion was easier to mobilize than in outlying areas. Most newspapers supported the Constitution. For example, in New York, where the ratification battle became intense, Hamilton, Madison, and Jay published in the newspapers a series of eighty-five essays that provided a detailed argument in favor of the Constitution. The essays also gained wide attention outside New York, and in spring 1788, the authors published them in book form as ***The Federalist,*** which is still considered a major work in American political theory.

Federalist, The Alexander Hamilton, James Madison, and John Jay wrote a series of eighty-five essays in support of the Constitution. First published in newspapers, they appeared in book form as *The Federalist* in the spring of 1788.

Most Federalists were merchants, shopkeepers, professionals, artisans, and commercial farmers. As creditors and consumers, many favored the Constitution because it stopped state emission of paper currency. Federalists desired a government that would foster the growth of a market economy and facilitate trade with other countries. They believed a national government would provide the

(Courtesy, American Antiquarian Society)

The Federal Pillars. The Federal Pillars, from the *Centinel* (Boston, Massachusetts), August 2, 1788, illustrates ratification of the Constitution of 1787.

stability and strength that were lacking under the Confederation, enabling the United States to gain stature among the nations of Europe. Some frontier settlers, seeking military defense against Native Americans, also supported the Constitution.

The Federalists, who viewed commercial development more favorably than the Antifederalists did, thought the purpose of government was to arbitrate among opposing interests. They believed that society benefited when people pursued their own individual goals. They considered elusive the republican ideal of a community in which citizens could reach a consensus because they had similar needs. Madison argued in *Federalist No. 10* that people possess different interests because they have unequal abilities and thus varying success in accumulating property. People by nature also have "different opinions concerning religion, concerning government, and many other points." In a free society, they form factions on the basis of their conflicting ideologies and "the various and unequal distribution of property." Madison claimed that the Constitution would be beneficial because a large republic contained more safeguards than a small one. In an extended polity, so many factions exist that the ability of a single interest to monopolize power is reduced. With the national government, "You take in a greater variety of parties and interests; you make it less probable that a majority of the whole will have a common motive to invade the rights of other citizens."

Antifederalists disagreed with this analysis, both because they favored small, homogeneous republics and because they feared the actions of men who would likely dominate the central government. Small farmers, many of them debtors who considered the mercantile elite their enemies, believed that power should remain in the states. The Antifederalists understood that despite equal representation in the Senate, the new government was fundamentally different from that under the Articles. They believed the new central government would be too large and too remote, that the interests of citizens of the thirteen states were too diverse. A congressman could never know the will of thirty thousand constituents; with so few persons elected to Congress and such large electoral districts, affluent, well-known candidates would have the advantage over ordinary men who ran for office. To the Antifederalists, the Constitution also lacked sufficient barriers against corruption and abuse of power; they argued for term limits and more frequent elections.

Antifederalists also pointed to the omission of a bill of rights as cause for rejecting the Constitution. They advocated freedom of speech, press, assembly, and religion; jury trials for civil cases; judicial safeguards such as the right to a speedy trial and to confront accusers and witnesses; and prohibitions against unwarranted searches and seizures. The Federalists answered that a bill of rights would be superfluous because state constitutions offered these protections (some did, but in no case was protection comprehensive), and because a bill of rights was needed against a powerful king, not when the people themselves were sovereign. This latter argument ignored the vulnerability of the individual to the will of the majority.

Nevertheless, ratification proceeded rapidly at first as state legislatures called elections for the state ratifying conventions. Delaware was the first to ratify when its convention approved the Constitution unanimously on December 7, 1787 (see Map 6.4). In Pennsylvania, where resistance was potentially heavy in the backcountry, Federalists moved quickly, securing approval by a two-to-one margin. New Jersey and Georgia then ratified unanimously. When Connecticut accepted the new government in January 1788 by a three-to-one vote, five states had joined the Union. All of these states except Pennsylvania were relatively small and recognized the advantages of joining a union in which they had equal representation in the Senate.

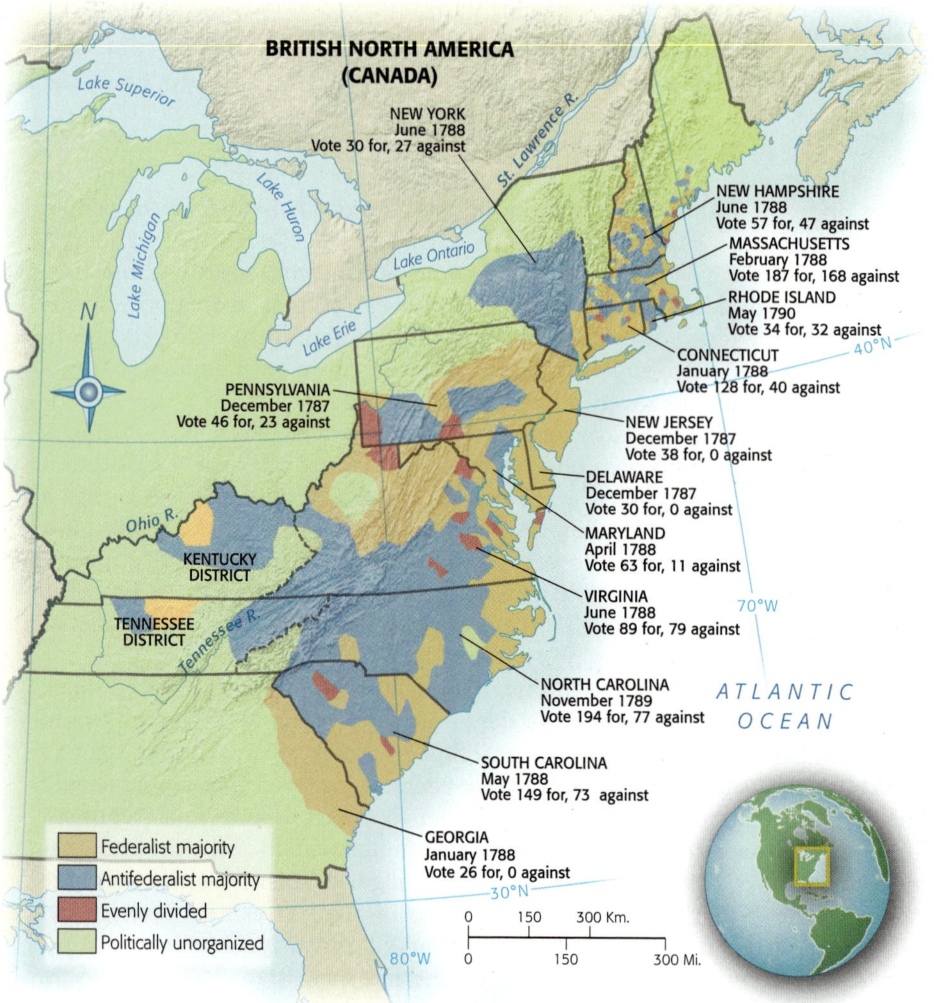

MAP 6.4
Ratification of the Constitution, 1787–1790
The pattern of support by relatively small states is visible in the votes of Delaware, New Jersey, Georgia, and Connecticut. In Pennsylvania, Massachusetts, and New York, the more populated urban areas supported ratification.

Then the conventions became more acrimonious. North Carolina and Rhode Island rejected the document outright, and New Hampshire put off its decision. Maryland and South Carolina ratified easily, but the vote in Massachusetts was close, as animosities from Shays's Rebellion colored the debate. The convention barely ratified the document by a vote of 187 to 168, recommending a series of amendments to protect individual rights and limit the powers of Congress. In June 1788, New Hampshire finally acted, becoming the ninth state to ratify, the number required to establish the new government. Nevertheless, two states remained crucial: Virginia and New York, whose size and economic importance made their approval necessary if the Constitution were to succeed. Virginia ratified in late June after a fierce debate, recommending to the first Congress a series of amendments, including a bill of rights. New York finally approved in late July 1788. With ratification by eleven states, the United States began a new experiment in Republican government.

CHAPTER REVIEW, 1783–1788

SUMMARY

- The United States based its new government on the republican principles of small government and the sovereignty of independent property owners.
- The Articles of Confederation created a weak central government that proved unable to raise money, repel border challenges from Britain and Spain, or resolve land disputes with Native Americans.
- The young republic suffered from a postwar economic depression that caused the proliferation of paper money, widespread debt, and economically motivated uprisings such as Shays's Rebellion.
- The Constitutional Convention was characterized by contentious debates over states' rights, proportional representation and slavery, and the proper powers of the national government.
- Opposition to the Constitution of 1787 arose from doubts about the new powers the document gave to the central government and the lack of a bill of rights.

IDENTIFICATIONS

Constitutional Convention
Pennsylvania Abolition Society
statute for religious freedom (Virginia)
Robert Morris
standing army
paper currency
Bank of North America
John Jay
Alexander McGillivray
Northwest Ordinance of 1787
Benjamin Lincoln
James Madison
Virginia Plan
New Jersey Plan
Great Compromise
electoral college
fugitive slave clause
ratification
The Federalist

MAKING CONNECTIONS: LOOKING AHEAD

Chapter 7 examines the process by which the Federalists created the national government as required by the Constitution. Although the election of George Washington as president offered stability, many issues remained unresolved. Differences within the ranks of former revolutionaries and supporters of the Constitution resulted in political parties.

1. How did Washington's administration address the problem of the Revolutionary War debt?
2. What was the new government's policy toward Native Americans?
3. Why did former allies such as Alexander Hamilton and James Madison create opposing political parties?

RECOMMENDED READINGS

Beeman, Richard, Botein, Stephen, and Carter, Edward C., eds. *Beyond Confederation: Origins of the Constitution and American National Identity* (1987). These essays provide an excellent introduction to the Confederation period and the making of the Constitution.

Doerflinger, Thomas M. *A Vigorous Spirit of Enterprise: Merchants and Economic Development in Revolutionary Philadelphia* (1986). A very good study of Philadelphia merchants and their impact on economic growth in the emergent United States.

Gellman, David N. *Emancipating New York: The Politics of Slavery and Freedom, 1777–1827* (2006). Engaging study of New York's debates on gradual abolition during the post-Revolutionary era.

Greene, Jack P. *Peripheries and Center: Constitutional Development in the Extended Polities of the British Empire and the United States, 1607–1788* (1986). Links the constitutional structure of England and its colonies to the Constitution of 1787.

Hamilton, Alexander, Jay, John, and Madison, James. *The Federalist Papers* (1788). Defense of the Constitution of 1787; seminal treatise of American political thought.

Hoffman, Ronald, et al., eds. *Native Americans and the Early Republic* (1999). Essays focusing on the impact of the Revolution and founding of the new republic on white–Indian relations.

Kenyon, Cecilia M. "Men of Little Faith: The Anti-Federalists on the Nature of Representative Government." *William and Mary Quarterly*, 3d ser., 12 (1955): 3–43. Insightful essay on the men who opposed ratification of the Constitution of 1787.

Kerber, Linda K. *Women of the Republic: Intellect and Ideology in Revolutionary America* (1980). Evaluates the impact of the Revolution on attitudes toward women.

Rhoden, Nancy L., and Steele, Ian K., eds. *The Human Tradition in the American Revolution* (2000). Biographical essays of famous and more ordinary Americans during the Revolutionary era.

Richards, Leonard L. *Shays's Rebellion: The American Revolution's Final Battle* (2002). A study of the western Massachusetts revolt that challenges earlier interpretations.

CourseMate Go to the CourseMate website at www.cengagebrain.com for additional study tools and review materials for this chapter.

7 The Federalist Republic

1789–1799

MAKING CONNECTIONS

LOOKING BACK

In 1783 the American patriots had won independence from Great Britain and achieved a favorable treaty, yet they faced many problems in establishing the new nation. The Articles of Confederation failed to provide the framework by which the thirteen states could pay the war debt and provide national defense. Before starting Chapter 7, you should be able to answer the following questions:

1. What were the chief problems facing the Confederation Congress in 1783?
2. Why did Massachusetts farmers rise in Shays's Rebellion?
3. Should the Northwest Ordinance of 1787 be considered a success of the Confederation Congress? Why or why not?
4. Why has James Madison been called the Father of the Constitution?
5. What were the most important differences between the Articles of Confederation and the Constitution of 1787?

After ratification of the Constitution, the **Federalists** took leadership in creating the new government. Everyone expected George Washington to become president. The three authors of *The Federalist*, Alexander Hamilton, James Madison, and John Jay, who had been so important in the creation and ratification of the Constitution, went on to play a central role in making it work. John Adams and Thomas Jefferson, who were serving as ministers to Great Britain and France during the convention, returned home to become, respectively, vice president and secretary of state.

Although many Federalists disagreed with specific parts of the Constitution, they accepted compromise and knew the weak Confederation had to be replaced. In the flush of victory over the Antifederalists, they set to the task of remedying the nation's ills. Differences soon became clear, however, between Hamilton on the one side and Madison and Jefferson on the other, as the first administration tackled the national debt and foreign policy. Out of their conflicts over policy, varying interpretations of the Constitution, and competition for power, the nation's first political parties developed.

❖ The New Government, 1789–1790

Federalists Name assumed by the supporters of the U.S. Constitution of 1787 during the contest for ratification. Also the group supporting policies of Alexander Hamilton that evolved into a political party during the 1790s.

The first national elections went well from the Federalist point of view, considering the strong Antifederalist opposition to the Constitution. The great majority of representatives and senators in the first Congress were Federalists. They fulfilled Madison's image of well-to-do men of national reputation and experience in politics; just a few came from lower-class backgrounds. Although the first congressmen were revolutionaries, they were also elites who wanted a stable government to foster economic growth.

George Washington Becomes President

The choice of George Washington as president was a forgone conclusion: in February 1789, members of the electoral college met in their state capitals to cast unanimous votes for the former commander in chief. Washington's leadership during the war, his dignity and character, and his support for republican government made him the obvious choice. The first president's commitment to the success of the Constitution ensured the nation's survival during the early years. John Adams, elected vice president, received fewer than half as many votes as Washington. On April 23, 1789, Washington arrived in New York City, the temporary federal capital, on a festooned barge, welcomed by thousands of cheering New Yorkers. He took the oath of office a week later.

The president and Congress, aware that they were setting precedent, initially placed a great deal of emphasis on titles and the comportment of officials. In this republic, in a world of monarchies, how should they be addressed? Should the president keep his door open to the public or remain detached? Although the questions may seem trivial, they indicate the novelty of this republican experiment. After much debate, Congress dropped the notion of titles, preferring a more republican style. Washington and his successors have been addressed simply as "Mr. President."

Beyond titles, Congress and the president needed to establish executive departments and courts, and draw up a bill of rights to fill gaps in the written Constitution. In creating executive departments, which included War, Treasury, State (foreign affairs), and the attorney general, the most crucial constitutional question concerned who would be able to remove the heads of departments from office. Some senators hoped to restrict the president's power by requiring Senate

CHAPTER TIMELINE 1789 · 1791 · 1793 · 1795 · 1797 · 1799

POLITICS AND DIPLOMACY
- 1789–1797 George Washington presidency
- 1791 Bill of Rights is ratified
- 1794 Whiskey Rebellion occurs
- 1795 Jay Treaty is ratified
- 1798–1800 Quasi-War with France
- 1798 Alien and Sedition Acts pass

SOCIETY AND CULTURE
- c. 1793 Wollstonecraft's *Vindication* circulates
- c. 1795 First female benevolent society is formed

ECONOMICS AND TECHNOLOGY
- 1790 Samuel Slater builds textile mill
- 1791 Bank of the United States is founded
- 1793 Eli Whitney invents cotton gin

approval before officeholders could be fired, thus making them more accountable to the legislature. In rejecting this proposal and allowing this authority to reside with the president, Congress clarified one aspect of the Constitution's balance of powers.

Judiciary Act of 1789 Congressional legislation that established the U.S. Supreme Court of six justices and a system of federal inferior courts, which were restricted primarily to consideration of federal crimes. State courts retained original jurisdiction in most civil and criminal cases, with the U.S. Supreme Court taking appeals from the highest state courts.

With the **Judiciary Act of 1789**, Congress put some flesh on the skeleton outlined in Article III of the Constitution, which stated that the "judicial power of the United States shall be vested in one Supreme Court, and in such inferior courts as the Congress may from time to time ordain and establish." The Judiciary Act, the result of compromise, established a Supreme Court of six justices and a system of federal inferior courts, which were few in number and restricted primarily to consideration of federal crimes. State courts retained original jurisdiction in most civil and criminal cases, with the U.S. Supreme Court taking appeals from the highest state courts. John Jay became the first chief justice.

The Bill of Rights

Bill of Rights (1791) The first ten amendments to the Constitution. These contain basic protection of the rights of individuals from abuses by the federal government, including freedom of speech, press, religion, and assembly.

During its first months, Congress took up the question of amending the Constitution to satisfy criticisms voiced during ratification that basic rights were not protected, objections that by the summer of 1789 still kept North Carolina and Rhode Island out of the Union. James Madison became the chief proponent of what became known as the **Bill of Rights** in Congress despite his earlier advocacy of the Federalist position that the amendments were unnecessary. But Antifederalist leaders who wanted to scrap the Constitution entirely now denied support to the Bill of Rights because they knew protection of individual freedoms would garner popular support.

After much negotiation between the Senate and the House, on September 25, 1789, Congress sent to the states for ratification a total of twelve amendments. By December 15, 1791, three-quarters of the states had approved the ten amendments known as the Bill of Rights, thus putting them into effect. Of the Bill of Rights, Articles 1 through 8 enumerated basic individual rights, while the intention of Article 9 was to protect any personal freedoms omitted from this list. Article 10 directed that "powers not delegated to the United States by the Constitution, nor prohibited by it to the States, are reserved to the States respectively, or to the people." It addressed concerns that the national government might assume powers that were not mentioned in the Constitution. Passage of the Bill of Rights by Congress attracted enough support to bring in the two remaining states; North Carolina ratified the Constitution in November 1789, and Rhode Island followed suit in May 1790.

The First Census, 1790

Congress promptly ordered a census of the American population, which the Constitution required within three years of Congress's first meeting and every ten years subsequently. The census, the founders expected, would provide an accurate enumeration for apportioning delegates to the House of Representatives and electoral college. Congress set August 1790 as the date of the first census, appointing marshals to complete their work within nine months, which actually stretched to eighteen.

Census of 1790, U.S. To fulfill the constitutional requirement for a decennial census, Congress ordered a population count to provide an accurate enumeration for apportioning delegates to the House of Representatives and electoral college.

Although it was sketchy and incomplete, the **U.S. Census of 1790** served as a baseline for measuring the growth of a dynamic, expanding people. President Washington reported to Congress a total of 3.9 million people, of whom 60,000 were free blacks and almost 700,000 were slaves (see Table 7.1). During the 1780s, the white population of the country had swelled by an extraordinary 44 percent, mostly through reproduction; in the 1790s, the increase remained high, at 36 percent. After the Treaty of Paris, European immigrants once again

TABLE 7.1
Population of the United States, 1790

United States	Total 3,929,625	Slaves 697,624
New England	1,009,206	3,763
Maine (part of Massachusetts)	96,643	0
New Hampshire	141,899	157
Vermont	85,341	0
Massachusetts	378,556	0
Rhode Island	69,112	958
Connecticut	237,655	2,648
Middle States	1,017,087	45,210
New York	340,241	21,193
New Jersey	184,139	11,423
Pennsylvania	433,611	3,707
Delaware	59,096	8,887
Southern States and Territories	1,903,332	648,651
Maryland	319,728	103,036
Virginia	747,610	292,627
North Carolina	395,005	100,783
South Carolina	249,073	107,094
Georgia	82,548	29,264
Kentucky	73,677	12,430
Tennessee	35,691	3,417

Source: U.S. Bureau of the Census, *A Century of Population Growth from the First Census of the United States to the Twelfth 1790–1900* (Washington, DC: U.S. Government Printing Office, 1909), 57, 133.

began crossing the Atlantic Ocean, with the majority coming from Ireland. From 1783 to 1799, 156,000 Europeans entered the United States: 69 percent were Irish; 14 percent were English, Scottish, or Welsh; and 6 percent were German. The African American population also grew quickly during the 1780s and 1790s, at a rate of 32 percent per decade, but was strikingly small in New England and Pennsylvania compared with the southern states.

❖ Opposing Visions of America

Almost immediately during Washington's first administration, political divisions arose between sides favoring commerce versus agriculture. Two divergent conceptions of the nation's future emerged among supporters of the Constitution. During the early 1790s, two political parties—sometimes called factions—developed, despite a general belief that parties were detrimental to unified republican government. As events unfolded in foreign and domestic affairs, the two parties contested one issue after another.

Hamilton Versus Jefferson

Alexander Hamilton, appointed by Washington as secretary of the treasury, saw the future greatness of the United States in commerce and manufacturing. Born in the West Indies, Hamilton attended King's College in New York City, then

Hamilton, Alexander (1755–1804) First U.S. secretary of the treasury (1789–1795), he established the national bank and public credit system. In 1804 he was mortally wounded in a duel with his political rival Aaron Burr.

served as Washington's aide-de-camp during the Revolution. Highly intelligent and energetic, he was a major proponent of the new Constitution. Appointment to the treasury allowed Hamilton to promote his concept of a strong nation modeled on Great Britain, but his efforts to foster commerce and manufacturing aroused resistance and led to bitter partisan disputes.

(Thomas Jefferson Portrait (1791) By Charles Wilson Peale Oil on Canvas/Independence National Historical Park Collection; Philadelphia, PA)

Thomas Jefferson. *Thomas Jefferson*, 1791, by Charles Willson Peale. The first secretary of state, who favored an agrarian republic, strict construction of the Constitution, and the French, quickly became Hamilton's chief opponent.

Adherents of Hamilton's policies became known as Federalists. They favored commercial development, a national bank, high tariffs to spur manufacturing, and a strong central government based on a loose interpretation of the Constitution, which allowed expansive powers to Congress and the president. The Federalists favored the British, abhorred the French Revolution after 1792, and were generally suspicious of power wielded by ordinary folk. They were somewhat critical of slavery, however, and gained the allegiance of free blacks. Because their power base lay in New England and the Middle Atlantic states, the Federalists had little enthusiasm for western expansion and sometimes supported the right of Native Americans to retain their lands.

The **Republican Party**, in contrast, favored a strict interpretation of the Constitution, opposing a strong central government and federal privileges for manufacturing and commerce. Republicans thought Hamilton's plans for funding the national debt, the bank, and protective tariffs infringed on states' rights and helped the "few" at the expense of the "many." It disdained the British model and charged Hamilton with advocating a return to monarchy. With their power base in the South, the West, and northern cities, the Republicans rejected efforts to abolish slavery and were ardent expansionists on the frontier. They had little sympathy for Indian rights.

Republican Party (1790s) Led by Thomas Jefferson and James Madison, the party favored a strict interpretation of the Constitution and opposed Alexander Hamilton's vision of a strong central government and federal privileges for manufacturing and commerce.

Jefferson, Thomas (1743–1826) Third president of the United States (1801–1809). As a member of the second Continental Congress, he drafted the Declaration of Independence (1776). His presidency was marked by the purchase of the Louisiana Territory (1803) and the Embargo of 1807.

Thomas Jefferson became the chief spokesman for the Republican Party, though James Madison collaborated in its growth. Jefferson, a wealthy planter and slaveholder, author of the Declaration of Independence, former minister to France, and now Washington's secretary of state, argued that Hamilton wanted too much national power. He believed that the United States, with limitless land, should foster an agrarian society of small producers. A virtuous republic was one made up of small farmers whose goal was to produce enough to support their families. Commerce should exist primarily to allow them to sell their surplus in Europe and purchase manufactured goods in return. The farmers should be educated to participate wisely in republican government. Their self-sufficiency and education would encourage them to act for the good of society rather than solely for their own gain.

Paradoxically a large proportion of the Republicans were not small farmers. Many of the leaders were southern plantation gentry like Jefferson and Madison or old Antifederalist elites. The party drew together people who had opposed ratification of the Constitution as well as those who favored it, but abhorred the government's direction under Washington and Hamilton. The Republicans received solid backing from farmers, especially in the South and West, and from urban craftsmen and small traders who watched wealthy speculators and merchants benefit from Hamiltonian policies.

Funding the National Debt

As secretary of the treasury, Alexander Hamilton's primary challenge was the Revolutionary War debt. The United States owed $10 million to foreigners, particularly to the French, and $40 million to Americans. The states also owed $25 million in domestic debts. To continue the War of Independence when funds were depleted, Congress and the states had issued certificates to merchants, artisans, and farmers for supplies and to soldiers for wages. After the war, many ordinary folks could not wait for the government to pay—or lost hope that the money was forthcoming—so they sold their certificates to wealthy speculators for a fraction of face value. Often the sellers received only 10 to 15 percent, rates that reflected the risk speculators were taking during the shaky Confederation period.

In his **Report on Public Credit** of January 1790, Hamilton formulated a plan that would both enlarge national power and resolve the financial hurdle of debt. This funding proposal would honor at face value all Revolutionary War debts, including those of the states, and exchange new federal securities for the old debt certificates. Hamilton planned to pay off foreign creditors as soon as possible but retain the domestic debt, paying only interest and a small amount of the principal each year. A customs duty on imports and an excise tax on whiskey would cover the interest; post office income would gradually reduce the principal. Hamilton's funding plan would tie wealthy Americans to the new government through their continuing investment and the loyalty of investors from the states to the nation.

Report on Public Credit (1790) Alexander Hamilton's plan for funding all Revolutionary War debts, including those of the states, by paying the interest with an import duty and excise tax on whiskey.

Congress eventually passed Hamilton's proposal, though with great opposition. Many people, including Madison, argued that funding allowed speculators to benefit from the hardships of farmers, who had lost money when they sold their war bonds and who would pay again through import duties and the excise tax. Opponents also feared the expansion of national power and became convinced that the treasury secretary was upsetting the balance between the central government and the states. The assumption of state debts was also controversial: Massachusetts and South Carolina were keen on having the federal government assume their large debts, whereas Virginians opposed the plan because they had nearly paid theirs off. Despite these divisions, the funding and assumption program passed Congress in July 1790 as part of a bargain struck by Hamilton, Jefferson, and Madison to situate the nation's permanent capital on the Potomac River, in Maryland and Virginia.

Planning Washington, D.C.

Although everyone agreed that a central location for the nation's capital was necessary, regional interests surfaced as congressmen recognized its potential economic and political benefits. The complicated negotiations over funding and assumption resulted in moving the temporary capital from New York to Philadelphia, as well as locating the new city on the Potomac. President Washington and his fellow Virginians supervised the development of the capital. The Residence Act of 1790 gave the president authority to choose land on both sides of the river that included Alexandria in Virginia and Georgetown in Maryland. Washington appointed a surveyor, three commissioners to manage the project, and **Pierre Charles L'Enfant** to design the layout of the capital and its major buildings. L'Enfant's grandiose street plan and Greek and Roman architecture expressed an exalted vision of the republic. The commissioners named the federal city "Washington" and the entire district "Columbia."

L'Enfant, Pierre Charles (1754–1825) French-born American architect, who designed Washington, D.C., and its major buildings. His grandiose street plan and Greek and Roman architecture expressed an exalted vision of the republic.

The president expected to finance construction by selling lots in the capital, thinking that land prices would skyrocket as citizens valued proximity to the seat of government. Instead, land sold poorly, and lack of money undermined the project. When the commissioners suspended construction temporarily for insufficient funds, L'Enfant protested and was fired. His plan for grand boulevards, public squares, fountains, and imposing buildings was retained, but for a decade, the enterprise limped along, saved by grants from Maryland and Virginia. In 1800, when the government moved to Washington, the president's mansion was still unfinished, and only one wing of the Capitol had been built.

The National Bank

Bank of the United States (1791–1811) National bank established as part of the system proposed by Alexander Hamilton to hold the federal government's funds and regulate state banks. Its chief purpose was to expand the money supply, thus encouraging commercial growth.

The cornerstone of Hamilton's new commercial order was a national bank, to be patterned after the Bank of England. The **Bank of the United States** and its branches would hold the federal government's funds and regulate state banks. The chief purpose of the national bank was to expand the money supply, thereby encouraging commercial growth.

The Bank of the United States, which Congress chartered in 1791 for twenty years, would have assets of $10 million, including $2 million in government deposits. Private investors could purchase the remaining $8 million in stock. As the bank prospered, stockholders would receive dividends on their funds. Thus, Hamilton created a way for wealthy Americans, who had just profited from funding the Revolutionary War debt, to benefit further. Because the government was a major stockholder, it also received dividends that could be used to pay off the national debt. To Hamilton and his commercial backers, the Bank's ability to increase the supply of money was essential for economic growth. The majority of the House of Representatives agreed, by a vote of 39 to 20, but the tally indicated important regional differences. Among northern congressmen, 33 voted for the bank and 1 against, whereas only 6 southern delegates supported and 19 opposed Hamilton's bill.

The plan had many opponents, who variously considered the bank immoral, monopolistic, or unconstitutional. The wild frenzy to purchase the bank's stock—in which twenty-five thousand shares sold in two hours and then the shares were bid up to 1,300 percent of their face value—reinforced fears that the national bank would undermine republican virtue. Jefferson called the bank's stock "federal filth." Others charged the bank with monopoly, complaining that merchants could secure short-term loans to finance their commercial ventures, but farmers and artisans could not obtain mortgages for purchasing property or making improvements.

In Congress, Madison opposed the national bank on the constitutional grounds that the federal government lacked the power to create corporations, a strict interpretation of the Constitution. In particular, Madison said, the Tenth Amendment would deny the central government any power not expressly given. Hamilton and his supporters countered that some powers of the federal government are implied. In the case of the bank, for example, the Constitution delegated to Congress and the president the power to lay and collect taxes, pay debts, regulate commerce, and coin and regulate money. It also provided the authority to "make all laws which shall be necessary and proper for carrying into execution the foregoing powers." Hamilton argued that the bank was a method by which the United States could fulfill its functions, and because some means were necessary, the power to establish the bank was implied. Though President Washington was initially unsure, he accepted Hamilton's reasoning and approved the bill.

Jefferson, like Madison, was convinced that the national bank was unconstitutional. By 1791, the secretary of state realized the political and economic consequences of the funding act—channeling more power to the federal government and more money to the rich—and thought the bank could only further these trends. He said he had been "duped" by Hamilton and "made a tool for forwarding his schemes" in accepting the assumption of state debts in return for the capital on the Potomac. He now believed that the treasury secretary's program "flowed from principles adverse to liberty." Hamilton chafed at this criticism, stating "that Mr. Madison, cooperating with Mr. Jefferson, is . . . in my judgment, subversive of the principles of good government and dangerous to the Union, peace, and happiness of the country."

Technology and Manufacturing

Slater, Samuel (1768–1835) British-born textile pioneer in America. He oversaw construction of the nation's first successful water-powered cotton mill (1790–1793).

Whitney, Eli (1765–1825) American inventor and manufacturer whose invention of the cotton gin (1793) revolutionized the cotton industry. He also established the first factory to assemble muskets with interchangeable parts.

Evans, Oliver (1755–1819) American inventor who developed the first application of steam power in an industrial setting. He also developed a method of automating flour mills that had become standard in U.S. mills a generation later.

Although the treasury secretary won congressional support for the bank and funding the national debt, he was much less successful in his plan for industry. In the 1790s, U.S. manufacturing remained on a small scale. Americans appreciated the quality of British imports; what they did not import, they produced themselves or purchased from neighboring artisans. Although some master craftsmen enlarged their shops and hired more workers, mechanized factories with mass production still lay in the future.

During the colonial and revolutionary periods, urban entrepreneurs had attempted large-scale textile manufacturing to provide employment for poor women and independence from British imports, but these efforts were short lived and not mechanized. The "factories" had consisted of workhouses in which large numbers of impoverished widows produced thread and yarn at traditional spinning wheels. Other businessmen used a "putting-out" system, whereby they distributed flax and wool for spinning at home.

Samuel Slater, a twenty-two-year-old millworker and recent immigrant from Great Britain, instituted a new phase in American cloth production in 1790 by building a textile mill in Pawtucket, Rhode Island, using water power to run the spinning machines. From memory he constructed a spinning frame, a machine that produced stronger threads than regular spinning wheels. He had left Britain illegally; to keep its advantage in textile making, the government prohibited emigration of craftworkers or export of drawings of the machines. No satisfactory power loom yet existed, so Slater's mill performed only the first two steps of cloth production: carding, or preparing the cotton fibers for spinning, and spinning the thread. Slater then used the putting-out system of distributing the thread to families, who produced the cloth on looms at home. Though Slater established additional mills in Rhode Island and Massachusetts, his workforce stayed fairly small, with about one hundred millworkers in 1800.

The United States made some progress during the 1790s toward industrialization. In 1790, Congress passed patent legislation, giving inventors exclusive rights to their work for seventeen years, and Slater initiated water-powered textile manufacture, as described above. Then, in 1793, while visiting a Georgia plantation, **Eli Whitney**, a New Englander, built the cotton engine, or gin. The device, which separated cotton fibers from husks and seeds, greatly increased the productivity of cotton cultivation, swelling the demand for African American slaves and fertile land in the Southwest and spurring cloth production in the North. Because the gin could be duplicated easily, Whitney failed to make a fortune from the machine. In 1798, he further laid the basis for industrial growth by attempting to manufacture guns with interchangeable parts. At this early date, however, such rigid standards were impossible to meet, and as a result, parts needed filing to fit together smoothly.

(National Museum of American History, Smithsonian Institution)

Model of Eli Whitney's Cotton Gin. In 1794, Eli Whitney was awarded one of the first U.S. patents for the cotton gin. He used models like this in court cases to defend his rights to the invention against manufacturers who were selling similar machines.

In 1772, at age seventeen, Delaware-born artisan **Oliver Evans** heard that the Scottish inventor James Watt had improved the steam engine a few years earlier. Evans began building his own model, but thirty years passed before he actually installed a high-pressure steam engine in his gypsum fertilizer factory in Philadelphia. This was the first application of steam power to an industrial setting. In the 1780s, Evans also developed the idea of automating grist mills, devising water-powered machinery that allowed one worker instead of three to supervise all the steps of producing flour. With insufficient capital, however, he was unable to pursue many of his designs, including steam carriages and trucks, a machine gun, refrigeration, central heating, and gas lighting.

❖ Expansion and Conflict in the West

While Alexander Hamilton's financial policies aided commerce in the East, dynamic growth also occurred in the West. The westward movement of settlers challenged the ability of the new government to keep their loyalty. In particular, Hamilton's excise tax on whiskey weighed heavily on westerners. The young nation also contended with Native Americans who were losing lands to the settlers; the British military, who kept forts in the Northwest; and the Spanish, who contested U.S. territorial claims and rights to navigate the Mississippi.

Kentucky and Tennessee

During the 1780s, the region west of the Appalachians and south of the Ohio River developed quickly as families left Virginia and North Carolina in search of fertile land and lower taxes. White settlement of Kentucky and Tennessee proceeded quickly as state governments, speculators, and frontiersmen defeated the Cherokees, who claimed ancestral rights to the territory. Believing that they were renting the land out rather than selling it, in 1775 a group of Cherokee leaders had traded twenty-seven thousand square miles to Richard Henderson and his associates for a cabin of consumer goods. Called Henderson's Purchase, the sale involved most of Kentucky and was illegal in Indian and English law. With the outbreak of the Revolution, most Cherokees joined the British, fighting for return of their lands. Receiving little help from Britain, the Cherokees were defeated in 1777 and forced to sign away even more territory.

Chickamaugas Militant Cherokees who allied with Creeks and Shawnees against settlers along the frontier from Kentucky to Georgia during the 1780s and early 1790s.

In the 1780s and early 1790s, militant Cherokees, called **Chickamaugas,** allied with Creeks and Shawnees against settlers along the frontier from Kentucky to Georgia. On both sides, fighting was vicious, with men, women, and children burned, scalped, and shot; and as in so many other cases, the whites failed to distinguish between enemy Indians and those who wanted peace. The Washington administration attempted to end the hostilities with the Treaty of Holston in 1791, but it gave responsibility for negotiating with the Cherokees to Governor **William Blount** of the Tennessee Territory, a land speculator the Indians called "dirt king" for his greed after land. Blount ignored Washington's promise to the Cherokees that if they ceded territory on which the whites had settled, the United States would guarantee their remaining lands. The treaty fell apart and war continued. In 1794, after their leader Dragging Canoe died and the Spanish stopped supplying the Indians because of war in Europe, the Chickamaugas met defeat.

Blount, William (1749–1800) Governor of the Tennessee Territory and a land speculator the Indians called "dirt king" who, after the Treaty of 1791, ignored President George Washington's guarantee to the Cherokees that they could retain their remaining lands.

By the end of the war, parts of Kentucky and Tennessee had passed the initial stages of settlement. Early on, groups of settlers had gathered in frontier stations consisting of two-story log houses connected by a high wall to create a fort against Indian attack. As the population grew and the threat from Native Americans declined, families moved away from the stations. One Kentucky pioneer described how "the women the first spring we came out, wo'd follow their cows to see what they ate, that they might know what greens to get. My Wife and I had neither spoon, dish, knife, or any thing to do with when we began life. Only I had a butcher knife." The settlers grew corn, tobacco, hemp, cotton, vegetables, and fruits; raised cattle, sheep, horses, and pigs; and hunted and fished. Soon they produced a surplus to trade for necessities they could not make themselves, such as nails, rifles, ammunition, needles, tools, and salt, as well as to pay taxes and fees. As fertile lands such as Kentucky's Bluegrass region yielded bountiful crops, farmers sought markets by way of the Mississippi River and the port of New Orleans. But transporting crops overland through the mountains was much more difficult and expensive than sending them downstream, so southwestern farmers demanded that the federal government convince Spain to end its restrictions on lower Mississippi shipping.

Although the population increased and a market economy developed in the 1790s, the trans-Appalachian region had few schools or church buildings. Most children, if taught at all, learned reading and arithmetic at home. In towns where schools existed, boys might attend for a few months, but girls did not. The exceptions were the children of wealthy families, who entered academies with secondary school curricula. Religion was the frontier's chief cultural institution. Throughout the region, Presbyterian, Baptist, and Methodist ministers held services in private homes. Baptist lay ministers farmed beside their neighbors through the week, then led services on Sunday. Methodist circuit riders traveled from one congregation to another, conducting worship services, baptisms, marriages, and prayer meetings. The churches expected members to avoid sin, including fighting, excessive drinking, adultery, and even celebrating the Fourth of July. If members committed offenses and failed to express regret, they were expelled, a serious consequence for people who had few social outlets.

The Ohio Country

White settlement moved more slowly north of the Ohio River, partly because the U.S. government kept tighter control in the Northwest Territory, but more because Native Americans resisted strongly. Delawares, Shawnees, Iroquois, and many others refused to cede lands that the federal government wanted to sell to land-hungry easterners. In the 1780s, the United States obtained a series of cessions, but from just some of the people who owned the land. Indians who were not party to the agreements rejected them. Forming a confederacy to withstand U.S. invasion, Ohio Indians attacked whites who risked settling in the region. This northern Indian confederacy allied with the Chickamaugas and Creeks in the South, establishing a pan-Indian defensive that gained help from the Spanish in the South and the British in the North.

In the early 1790s, President Washington challenged the northern confederacy by sending two expeditions, both of them unsuccessful. Arthur St. Clair, governor of the Northwest Territory, was defeated in the second invasion of 1791. Regrouping with federal rather than militia troops, in 1794, he defeated the Native Americans decisively at the Battle of Fallen Timbers (see Map 7.1). Though the British had customarily given aid to the Ohio tribes, this time they closed the gates to Fort Miami, denying refuge to the retreating Indians. A year later, when it became clear to the Native Americans that their alliance with the British had ended, they signed the Treaty of Greenville, ceding to the United States the land south and east of the treaty line, most of it in present-day Ohio.

(National Archives)

Signatures of Native Americans on the Treaty of Greenville, 1795. Indian leaders commonly used symbols such as diagrams of animals to sign deeds and treaties.

The Whiskey Rebellion, 1794

In 1794, the Washington administration also sent troops against western Pennsylvania farmers, who since 1791 had resisted the whiskey tax. Farmers throughout the West resented the tax on spirits, because distilling whiskey from

MAP 7.1

Conflict in the Northwest Territory, 1790–1796

Native Americans continued to resist U.S. settlement in the Ohio region. They defeated U.S. forces in 1790 and 1791 but lost the Battle of Fallen Timbers in 1794. British forts in the Northwest Territory supported the Ohio Indians until that time.

Whiskey Rebellion In the early 1790s western Pennsylvania farmers resisted the whiskey tax: they held protest meetings, tarred and feathered collaborators, and destroyed property. In 1794 the Washington administration sent thirteen thousand troops to restore order, but the revolt was over by the time they arrived.

grain made their produce less bulky, and thus less expensive to transport to eastern markets. Washington and Hamilton decided to demonstrate the power of the new federal government by targeting resisters in western Pennsylvania. In what became known as the **Whiskey Rebellion,** farmers tarred and feathered collaborators, burned barns, and destroyed stills of people who paid the tax. The insurgents understood their fight as a struggle for "the virtuous principles of republican liberty." But the whiskey tax was only one of the farmers' complaints, which included failure to open up the Ohio country and removal of Spanish trade restrictions on the Mississippi.

Events came to a climax in July 1794. When officials continued to collect the tax and arrest resisters, five hundred men surrounded the excise inspector's home, exchanged gunfire that killed several people, and burned the house. The official and his family escaped. In the days that followed, demonstrations and violence spread to central Pennsylvania, Virginia, Maryland, and Ohio. Washington called up thirteen thousand eastern militia, who marched west with the president briefly in command. By the time the soldiers reached western Pennsylvania, the revolt was over, as the show of force intimidated the rebels. The administration had demonstrated that armed resistance to federal policies would not be tolerated.

The Spanish Frontier

As settlers from the United States migrated across the Appalachians and traders extended their commercial networks, they came into contact with the Spanish. The 1790s marked the high point of Spain's control in North

America, its provinces extending from East Florida across the Gulf Coast to Louisiana, Texas, New Mexico, and California (refer back to Map 6.1). The Spanish government continued to view these borderlands of their empire as a buffer against American and British designs on Mexican silver. Spanish officials regarded the phenomenal population growth of the United States warily: one warned that Americans were "advancing and multiplying . . . with a prodigious rapidity."

(Courtesy of the Bancroft Library, University of California, Berkeley)

California Indians. California Indians are lined up at the Spanish mission in Carmel to greet French visitors.

Nevertheless, the Spanish decided to open their territory to Americans, hoping to bolster the small settler populations. Spain offered free land in the Floridas and Louisiana, and even changed official policy to allow Protestants to keep their religion as long as they took an oath of allegiance to the Crown and had their children baptized Catholic. Because Spain could not provide desired consumer goods or adequate markets, it also relaxed mercantilist restraints, allowing plantation owners in the borderlands to sell their sugar, cotton, and indigo in the United States. These new immigration and economic policies facilitated later U.S. acquisition of the Floridas and Louisiana. Jefferson said prophetically, in 1791, that Spain had provided "the means of delivering to us peaceably, what may otherwise cost us a war."

Farther west in New Mexico, the Spanish finally achieved peace with the Comanches and Apaches and signed a treaty recognizing their sovereignty. The Indians had forced the Spanish to set aside the goal of complete domination and to provide tribute, but the Spanish sent prisoners of war to Cuba and settled others on reservations called *establecimientos de paz*, or peace establishments. While many Apaches resisted, the fighting eventually stopped, making Texas, New Mexico, and Arizona safer for travel and economic development.

For several decades, fearing Russian and British incursions along the Pacific coast, Spain had expanded settlement in California. The government sent missionaries and soldiers north from Baja California in 1769 to set up missions and presidios along the coast from San Diego to San Francisco. José de Gálvez organized the effort, enlisting **Junípero Serra,** a zealous Franciscan priest, to establish the missions. Though fewer than a thousand Hispanics lived in California by 1790, the missions controlled most of the arable land along the Pacific. As elsewhere in North America, the California Indians declined sharply in population after contact with Europeans. According to one missionary, "they live well free but as soon as we reduce them to a Christian and community life . . . they fatten, sicken, and die." The native population in the mission region along the Pacific coast declined from approximately sixty thousand in 1769 to thirty-five thousand at the end of the century.

The Spanish also looked to the Pacific Northwest, which they explored in 1774, four years earlier than the British explorer Captain James Cook. After Cook publicized the trade for sea otter furs, however, British and American merchants sailed to Nootka Sound, at Vancouver Island, challenging the Spanish claim to the area north of San Francisco. The traders made huge profits by purchasing the silky black otter pelts from the Tlingit, Haida, Nootka, and Chinook peoples, to sell in China for tea, porcelain, and silk. When the Spanish seized two British ships, England threatened war. Spain signed the Nootka Convention (1790), yielding its sole claim to the Pacific Northwest and returning the confiscated vessels. During the 1790s and beyond, the countries tried but failed to negotiate a northern boundary of California.

Doing History Online

Rebellion and Government

Go to the CourseMate website for this chapter and link to Primary Sources. Using your book and Documents 2, 7 through 10, and 13, compare the official responses to Shays's Rebellion and to the Whiskey Rebellion. What does the comparison reveal about the Articles of Confederation and the Constitution and the evolution of the national government?

www.cengagebrain.com

Serra, Junípero (1713–1784) Franciscan missionary who in 1769 established Spanish missions along the Pacific coast from San Diego to San Francisco.

❖ Foreign Entanglements

In 1789, the United States rejoiced when the French abolished noble privileges and formed a constitutional monarchy. Americans believed that France had followed their example, for during the first phase of the French Revolution, its moderate leaders included friends of the United States, notably the Revolutionary War hero the Marquis de Lafayette. In 1792, however, radicals took control; they executed King Louis XVI the next year. The international situation became perilous when the French Republic declared war on Britain and Spain. The king's execution and thousands of deaths by guillotine during the second phase of the French Revolution cost the French support in the United States, particularly among Federalists, who feared the consequences of ordinary people, "the mob," taking power. Republicans did not defend the excesses, but they remained sympathetic toward France because they hated monarchical Britain more.

Neutrality

The European war presented Americans with a tricky situation, for they had potentially dangerous connections with both France and Britain. The U.S.–France commercial and military alliance of 1778 remained in force. It did not require the United States to enter the war, but the French Republic expected favorable trade policies and informal military assistance. Though Secretary of State Jefferson favored France and despised Britain, he agreed that neutrality was essential. American commerce was closely tied with Britain, whose navy could sweep U.S. ships from the sea. President Washington issued his Proclamation of Neutrality in April 1793. The message warned citizens to avoid hostile acts against either side, including sales of weapons and privateering.

Genêt, Edmond (1763–1834) French ambassador who enlisted American mercenaries to assist the French against the British. Genêt's move threatened relations between the United States and Britain.

American neutrality quickly hit shoals with the activities of **Edmond Genêt,** the new minister from France. Citizen Genêt, as he was called in republican France, had arrived in Charleston several weeks before Washington proclaimed neutrality. He enlisted American mercenaries to man privateers and obtained ships to sail under the French flag against British shipping. The privateers, with largely American crews, seized British vessels, taking them to U.S. ports, where French consuls sold the ships and their cargoes, paying the mercenaries with part of the proceeds. The French claimed this right under the 1778 alliance. The Washington administration, fearful of British reprisals and outraged by this violation of U.S. sovereignty, closed the ports to Genêt's privateers, requested his recall, and prohibited foreign belligerents from arming vessels in U.S. ports.

The Washington administration soon faced an even greater challenge: protecting the nation's sovereignty from British aggression. In the early 1790s, the Royal Navy began impressing—recruiting by force—U.S. citizens from merchant ships. Then in November 1793, the British ordered a total blockade of the French West Indies: any ship intending to trade there would be confiscated. The British kept the blockade a secret until after U.S. ships headed for the Caribbean. Over the winter, their navy seized more than 250 American vessels, whether they were aimed for French, British, or neutral ports. The British impounded ships, cargoes, and even the sailors' possessions. Exacerbating the crisis was the British refusal to vacate their forts and their aid to Native Americans in the Ohio country. Britain also helped Native Americans resist settlement in the West. In 1794 the governor of Canada, Lord Dorchester, told a group of Indians that they could expect war to break out between the United States and Britain within a year.

(The Granger Collection, New York)

Preparation for War. *Preparation for War to Defend Commerce* (1800), illustrating construction of the frigate Philadelphia. During the 1790s the United States tried to remain neutral in the European wars while prospering from international trade.

The Jay Treaty, 1795

The crisis abated when the British ended their total blockade of the French islands, permitting Americans to trade foodstuffs and consumer goods but not war material. Rather than take retaliatory action, the president sent John Jay, chief justice of the Supreme Court, as special envoy to England. Jay's instructions were to convince the British to evacuate their forts in the West, pay for African American slaves who had left with their army after the Revolution, end impressment, open the British West Indies trade to American ships, and compensate recent shipping losses in the Caribbean.

Jay was unable to secure compensation for slaves, convince the British to stop impressment, or obtain recognition of all the neutral rights that Americans demanded. He did gain British withdrawal from the western forts by June 1, 1796, payment for confiscated ships in the Caribbean, and the opening of trade in the British West Indies to American vessels of 70 tons or less. He agreed, however, that American shippers would not export from the United States certain tropical products, including cotton, molasses, sugar, coffee, and cocoa, and that Americans would repay British creditors for pre-Revolutionary debts.

Jay Treaty (1794) Treaty between the United States and Great Britain negotiated by John Jay. It settled difficulties arising from violations of the Treaty of Paris of 1783 and regulated commerce and navigation.

Washington received the **Jay Treaty** in March 1795, keeping its contents secret until the Senate debate in June. The Federalists struck the provision forbidding U.S. merchants from exporting tropical crops. If they had agreed to this section, American trade would have faced a serious obstacle, particularly with the development of cotton. Twenty Federalist senators voted to ratify, while ten Republicans refused. Thus, the Senate approved the treaty by exactly the two-thirds needed and sent it to the president, who signed the treaty as amended. When the treaty became public, Republicans expressed fury over Jay's failures on impressment, neutral rights, and compensation for slaves. The Jay Treaty greatly hastened the growth of political parties, as Republicans gained support from former Federalists, particularly in the South. John Jay was burned in effigy; mass meetings, petitions, and demonstrations protested the treaty throughout the country.

By spring 1796, however, the tumult was over, in part because news arrived that Thomas Pinckney had concluded an agreement with Spain the previous October. The Treaty of San Lorenzo opened the Mississippi River to free navigation, allowed Americans to use the port of New Orleans without charge, and fixed the boundary between the United States and West Florida at the thirty-first parallel as specified in the Treaty of Paris.

Washington Retires

With the threat of war temporarily eased, the West open for settlement and trade, and a flourishing economy, the success of the republic seemed more certain than before. General Wayne's defeat of the Ohio Indians, the Jay Treaty, and Pinckney's diplomatic success gave westerners—and westward-looking Americans—resolution of their major problems: cession of lands in Ohio, removal of the British from the forts, free access to the Mississippi, and the right of deposit at New Orleans. Eastern merchants and farmers benefited from the lifting of trade restrictions in the British West Indies. Wartime demand for provisions in Europe and the Caribbean drove up farm prices and stimulated production. By the end of the century, American exports and shipping profits were almost five times their 1793 level. With increased transportation profits, merchants invested more heavily in ships. The shipbuilding boom created demand for lumber, rope, and other supplies; wages for craftsmen and laborers rose, and Americans took advantage of their newfound prosperity to buy British imports, which in turn paid tariff income toward the national debt. Hamilton's funding plan was a success—the nation's credit was firm—despite resistance to the whiskey tax.

As the election of 1796 approached, George Washington announced his retirement, raising the question of his successor. The president had served two terms, his health had declined, and the battle over the Jay Treaty had left him exhausted and angry. In his Farewell Address, Washington surveyed the accomplishments of his administration and gave the nation advice. The United States should avoid as much as possible becoming entwined in international affairs, he counseled. The European war demonstrated how perilous such involvement could be and how difficult it was to escape. "The great rule of conduct for us in regard to foreign nations is, in extending our commercial relations to have with them as little *political* connection as possible," Washington urged. His other major argument concerned factions. In lamenting "the spirit of party," Washington blamed the Republicans for failing to support his administration. They had undercut his authority and the ideal of a consensual republic.

❖ The Adams Presidency, 1797–1801

Although Washington's successors appreciated the wisdom of his "great rule" of foreign policy, they had less enthusiasm for his advice on factions. In 1796, the parties lacked full-scale national organization, and candidates did not campaign. But the contest was very much alive: Federalists supported the policies of Hamilton and Washington, and Republicans opposed them.

Election of 1796

In the third presidential election under the Constitution, both parties had sufficient cohesion to offer national tickets: the Federalist candidates were John Adams for president and Thomas Pinckney for vice president; the Republicans put up Thomas Jefferson for president and Aaron Burr, a senator from New York, for the second spot. The results of the electoral college vote were close: Adams 71, Jefferson 68, Pinckney 59, Burr 30, and a number of other candidates totaling 48. As specified by the Constitution, Adams became president and Jefferson vice president. Americans quickly realized the problem of this procedure for electing the executive, because the president represented one party and the vice president the other. In any event, the Federalists kept control of the presidency, though barely, and they increased their votes in Congress by a small margin, to sixty-four Federalists versus fifty-three Republicans.

For many Americans, John Adams possessed credentials from service in the Revolution and the new republic that made him a worthy heir to Washington. He had contributed to pre-Revolutionary agitation in Boston, served as a delegate to the Continental Congress, promoted the Continental navy, and assisted Jefferson in drafting the Declaration of Independence. He had helped negotiate the 1783 Treaty of Paris, and in 1785 he became the first U.S. minister to Great Britain. Adams was a skilled diplomat, an avid student of government, and entirely honest, but he lacked Washington's charisma, military bearing, and understanding of executive leadership.

Like Washington, Adams denounced parties. He began his administration with the hope, soon abandoned, that he might bridge the gulf between Federalists and Republicans. Jefferson rebuffed the chief executive's peace overture and directed the Republican opposition from his post as vice president. After the first few days of the Adams administration, the president and vice president never consulted one another.

"Quasi-War" with France

The second president inherited an international situation that had worsened by the time he assumed office in March 1797. The French, now ruled by a dictatorial executive board called the Directory, declared that the Jay Treaty revoked the 1778 alliance with the United States. They confiscated American merchant ships and cut off diplomatic relations. Once again, the United States seemed headed for war.

Called into special session in May 1797 by Adams, Congress authorized the mobilization of eighty thousand militia, completion of three war vessels, and fortification of harbors. Adams also appointed a commission of three men to negotiate with France: John Marshall of Virginia, Elbridge Gerry of Massachusetts, and Charles Cotesworth Pinckney of South Carolina. Their assignment was to prevent war, stop the confiscation of American ships carrying nonmilitary cargoes, and obtain compensation for recent losses. In France, the U.S. commission corresponded with French Foreign Minister Talleyrand through three intermediaries, who later became known to the American public as X, Y, and Z. The French agents told the commissioners that, like other petitioners to the Directory, they must pay a bribe even to be heard. The amount specified in this case was $250,000. The Directory also required an apology from Adams for criticizing France, a huge loan, and assumption by the U.S. government of any unpaid debts owed by France to American citizens. The commission refused these conditions and returned home. Their experience became known as the **XYZ Affair.**

XYZ Affair (1797–1798)
Diplomatic incident in which the French government demanded, through three agents known to the American public as X, Y, and Z, that the U.S. government pay a bribe and apologize for criticizing France.

In spring 1798, Adams received delayed correspondence that his envoys had been rebuffed. When he called for additional troops and warships, Congress responded by giving him more than he requested. Jefferson denounced the military buildup as "insane"; Republicans demanded to see evidence of France's treachery. When Adams made the commission's dispatches public, war fever engulfed the nation. Congress expanded the regular army and war fleet, established the Department of the Navy, authorized naval vessels to protect American merchant ships, suspended commerce with France, and revoked the French alliance. George Washington assumed command of the army, with Alexander Hamilton in charge of field operations. To pay for all of this, Congress levied a direct tax of $2 million on dwelling houses, land, and slaves.

Without declaring war, the United States engaged France in hostilities from 1798 to 1800. In what was known as the Quasi-War, the U.S. navy dominated the French, defeating their warships and sinking privateers. The British navy helped by protecting U.S. carriers. Although some congressmen feared a French invasion and thereby justified further military preparations, French naval losses to Great Britain and the United States quickly removed that threat.

The Alien and Sedition Acts of 1798

The Federalists rode the crest of patriotism in 1798, using their majority in Congress to pass a series of acts that limited the rights of immigrants and critics of the administration. Congressional sponsors argued that the laws were necessary wartime measures. The Federalists tried to take advantage of the Quasi-War to link their opponents with the enemy. This strategy worked in the short term, as the pro-French Republicans lost votes in the 1798 congressional election, but it proved suicidal for Adams's party after the fear of invasion had passed.

The Federalist design resulted in four restrictive laws. The Naturalization Act of 1798 lengthened the period of residence needed for citizenship from five to fourteen years. The legislation was intended to stop the flow of Irish immigrants who, because they were anti-British and pro-French, swelled the number of Republican voters. The Alien Enemies Act established procedures in the event of declared war or invasion for jailing and deporting citizens of the enemy nation who were considered likely to spy or commit sabotage. The Alien Act, which had a term of two years, allowed the president to deport any non–U.S. citizens "he shall judge dangerous to the peace and safety of the United States, or shall have reasonable grounds to suspect are concerned in any treasonable or secret machinations against the government thereof." Like the Naturalization Act, this law potentially threatened Irish immigrants, but Adams refrained from using it.

The fourth law, the Sedition Act, made it illegal for "any persons [to] unlawfully combine or conspire together, with intent to oppose any measure or measures of the government of the United States" or to interfere with the execution of a law. Nor could a person "write, print, utter or publish . . . any false, scandalous and malicious writing or writings against the government of the United States, or either house of the Congress . . . or the President." In effect, this law permitted imprisonment and fines for criticizing the government, an obvious infringement on freedom of speech and freedom of the press. The term of the law lasted until March 3, 1801, the day before the next president would be inaugurated. Thus, the Federalists ensured that if the next chief executive were a Republican, he would not be able to retaliate without obtaining a new statute.

The administration enforced the law with serious results. Adams believed that the Sedition Act was constitutional, that people who censured his policies threatened the future of the republic. The prime targets for prosecution were Republican newspapers, and the official authorized to administer the act was Secretary of State Timothy Pickering, a staunch Federalist who methodically reviewed the Republican papers for actionable offenses. Under the law, the Federalists indicted and tried at least seventeen people for sedition. They timed the cases to reach court in the fall of 1799 or the following spring, with the goal of silencing the Republican press during the 1800 election. Some papers folded and others closed temporarily while their editors were imprisoned. All but one of the cases were prosecuted in New England and the Middle Atlantic states, where the Federalists controlled the courts and could pack juries (see *Doing History: Controversy over the Sedition Act of 1798*).

The Republican Opposition Grows, 1798–1799

Passage of the Alien and Sedition acts and the jailing of Republican spokesmen shifted the political winds. In late 1798, the Kentucky and Virginia legislatures approved resolutions that protested the acts on the grounds that they were unconstitutional. The Kentucky and Virginia resolutions, drafted anonymously by Thomas Jefferson and James Madison, respectively, argued that these laws violated the First Amendment and granted powers to the national government not delegated by the Constitution. Virginia and Kentucky sent their resolutions to other legislatures, none of which agreed that states could declare a federal law unconstitutional. But the resolutions contributed toward a theory of "nullification," the idea that a state had the right to veto a federal law it considered unconstitutional. This theory was based on the strict interpretation of the Constitution that denied, as in the controversy over the national bank, implied powers to the central government.

With the Alien and Sedition acts, the Federalists had made a strategic error. Where formerly the Republicans could be branded as a faction creating animosity and disunity, they now became seen as legitimate defenders of Revolutionary principles. The Republican Party justified its opposition by warning that the Federalists were on the road to tyranny. The administration fanned the flames of indignation with its heavy-handed reaction to a tax rebellion among German Americans in eastern Pennsylvania, a group who had previously favored the Federalists or stayed out of politics entirely. The Republicans added the administration's unwarranted use of force to their arsenal of charges against the Federalists, whose excessive actions inadvertently legitimized the party system in the eyes of many Americans.

Doing History Online

Development of Political Parties

Go to the CourseMate website for this chapter and link to Primary Sources. Using the textbook and Documents 5 and 6, determine what major issues contributed to party development

www.cengagebrain.com

Doing History Controversy over the Sedition Act of 1798

These documents present excerpts from the Sedition Act of 1798, the Virginia Resolutions drafted by James Madison, and counterresolutions from Rhode Island. The Federalists passed the Alien, Sedition, Naturalization, and Alien Enemies acts to restrict opposition during the Quasi-War. Madison and Thomas Jefferson particularly opposed the Sedition Act for its limitation on First Amendment freedoms of speech and the press.

The Sedition Act, *July 14, 1798*

Sec. 1. Be it enacted . . . , That if any persons shall unlawfully combine or conspire together, with intent to oppose any measure or measures of the government of the United States, . . . or to intimidate or prevent any person holding a place or office in or under the government of the United States, from undertaking, performing or executing his trust or duty; and if any person or persons, with intent as aforesaid, shall counsel, advise or attempt to procure any insurrection . . . he or they shall be deemed guilty of a high misdemeanor. . . .

Sec. 2. That if any person shall write, print, utter, or publish, or shall cause or procure to be written, printed, uttered or published, or shall knowingly and willingly assist or aid in writing, printing, uttering or publishing any false, scandalous and malicious writing or writings against the government of the United States, or either house of the Congress of the United States, or the President of the United States, with intent to defame . . . or to bring them, or either of them, into contempt or disrepute; or to excite against them, or either or any of them, the hatred of the good people of the United States, or to stir up sedition within the United States . . . then such person, being thereof convicted before any court of the United States having jurisdiction thereof, shall be punished by a fine not exceeding two thousand dollars, and by imprisonment not exceeding two years.

Source: *United States Statutes at Large,* 1:570, 596–597.

Virginia Resolutions, *December 24, 1798*

Resolved, . . . That this Assembly doth explicitly and peremptorily declare, that it views the powers of the Federal Government as resulting from the compact to which the states are parties, as limited by the plain sense and intention of the instrument constituting that compact, as no further valid than they are authorized by the grants enumerated in that compact; and that, in case of a deliberate, palpable, and dangerous exercise of other powers, not granted by the said compact, the states, who are parties thereto, have the right, and are in duty bound, to interpose, for arresting the progress of the evil, and for maintaining, within their respective limits, the authorities, rights, and liberties, appertaining to them. . . .

That the General Assembly doth particularly PROTEST against the palpable and alarming infractions of the Constitution, in the two late cases of the "Alien and Sedition Acts," passed at the last session of Congress; the first of which exercises a power nowhere delegated to the Federal Government; . . . and the other of which acts exercises, in like manner, a power not delegated by the Constitution, but, on the contrary, expressly and positively forbidden by one of the amendments thereto,—a power which, more than any other, ought to produce universal alarm, because it is levelled against the right of freely examining public characters and measures, and of free communication among the people thereon, which has ever been justly deemed the only effectual guardian of every other right.

Counter Resolutions of the Rhode Island Legislature, *February 1799*

Certain resolutions of the Legislature of Virginia . . . being communicated to this Assembly,—

1. Resolved, That, in the opinion of this legislature, the second section of the third article of the Constitution of the United States, in these words, to wit,—"The judicial power shall extend to all cases arising under the laws of the United States,"—vests in the Federal Courts, exclusively, and in the Supreme Court of the United States, ultimately, the authority of deciding on the constitutionality of any act or law of the Congress of the United States.

2. Resolved, That for any state legislature to assume that authority would be—

   2nd. Blending together legislative and judicial powers;

   2d. Hazarding an interruption of the peace of the states by civil discord; . . .

3. Resolved, That, although, for the above reasons, this legislature, in their public capacity, do not feel themselves authorized to consider and decide on the constitutionality of the Sedition and Alien laws, (so called,) yet they are called upon, by the exigency of this occasion, to declare that, in their private opinions, these laws are within the powers delegated to Congress, and promotive of the welfare of the United States.

Source: Richard Hofstadter, ed., *Great Issues in American History: A Documentary Record*, vol. 1 (New York: Vintage Books, 1958), 182–185.

QUESTIONS for REFLECTION

1. Why did the Federalists believe it necessary to pass the Alien and Sedition acts?
2. On what basis does James Madison contend in the Virginia Resolutions that a state has the right and duty, when warranted, to declare a federal law unconstitutional? On what basis does the Rhode Island legislature disagree?

CHAPTER REVIEW, 1789–1799

SUMMARY

- After the ratification of the Constitution, Americans worked to create a new government. Members of the electoral college unanimously elected George Washington to be the nation's first president. Congress and the states amended the Constitution with a Bill of Rights designed to protect individuals against government abuses of authority.
- During the 1790s, two opposing factions arose within American politics, one led by Alexander Hamilton, which favored strong central government and commerce, the other led by Thomas Jefferson, which favored weak national government and agriculture.
- Increased expansion into the West caused tensions between white settlers and the Spanish and Native American peoples who already inhabited these territories.
- The new republic attempted to remain neutral in the conflicts that raged between Britain and France between 1793 and 1815. The 1778 alliance between the United States and France, however, and ongoing trade relations with both nations made neutrality impossible to maintain.
- John Adams's administration was characterized by an increase in partisan feeling, growth in sentiment against the Federalists, the buildup of the military, and the passage of the unpopular Alien and Sedition acts.

IDENTIFICATIONS

Federalists
Judiciary Act of 1789
Bill of Rights
U.S. Census of 1790
Alexander Hamilton
Republican Party (1790s)
Thomas Jefferson
Report on Public Credit
Pierre Charles L'Enfant
Bank of the United States
Samuel Slater
Eli Whitney
Oliver Evans
Chickamaugas
William Blount
Whiskey Rebellion
Junípero Serra
Edmond Genêt
Jay Treaty
XYZ Affair

MAKING CONNECTIONS: LOOKING AHEAD

In Chapter 8, we will see that the year 1800 marked a watershed in American politics because the Federalists lost control of the federal government and declined in power. For most Americans, however, national politics held little importance as they focused on building communities and churches and pursued their daily lives.

1. Why were the Republicans, under Thomas Jefferson, able to win the election of 1800?
2. To what extent did Jefferson adhere to his vision of an agrarian republic?
3. How did the Jefferson administration deal with the continuing foreign entanglements of war between Great Britain and France?

RECOMMENDED READINGS

Cayton, Andrew R. L., and Teute, Fredrika J., eds. *Contact Points: American Frontiers from the Mohawk Valley to the Mississippi, 1750–1830* (1998). Essays about Indian–white relations in the backcountry from the pre-Revolutionary period through the early republic.

Chernow, Ron. *Alexander Hamilton* (2004). Comprehensive study of Hamilton's life, including his achievements in Washington's administration.

Elkins, Stanley, and McKitrick, Eric. *The Age of Federalism* (1993). Detailed narrative of the Washington and Adams administrations.

Hackel, Steven W. *Children of Coyote, Missionaries of Saint Francis: Indian–Spanish Relations in Colonial California, 1769–1850* (2005). Interesting examination of relations between the California Indians and Spanish missionaries.

McCullough, David. *John Adams* (2001). An excellent biography of the second president.

McGaw, Judith A., ed. *Early American Technology: Making and Doing Things from the Colonial Era to 1850* (1994). Original essays on technology from agriculture to turnpikes.

Najar, Monica. *Evangelizing the South: A Social History of Church and State in Early America* (2007). A convincing interpretation of the role of Baptist congregations in community formation during the late eighteenth and early nineteenth centuries.

Schutt, Amy C. *Peoples of the River Valleys: The Odyssey of the Delaware Indians* (2007). Exemplifies Native American community evolution through the history of the Delawares before the Treaty of Greenville.

Sharp, James Roger. *American Politics in the Early Republic: The New Nation in Crisis* (1995; reprint ed.). A thoughtful analysis of party formation during the 1790s and the election of 1800.

Slaughter, Thomas P. *The Whiskey Rebellion: Frontier Epilogue to the American Revolution* (1986). An excellent book on the struggle between Alexander Hamilton and western Pennsylvania farmers over excise taxes.

CourseMate Go to the CourseMate website at www.cengagebrain.com for additional study tools and review materials for this chapter.

8

The New Republic Faces a New Century

1800–1815

MAKING CONNECTIONS

LOOKING BACK

Within the context of world history, with governments that regularly rise and fall, the longevity of the American republic is remarkable. As discussed in Chapter 7, the decade following ratification of the Constitution was critical. Despite conflicts such as the Whiskey Rebellion, growing opposition from the Republicans, and the Alien and Sedition Acts, the Washington and Adams administrations established strong precedents for constitutional rule. Before starting Chapter 8, you should be able to answer the following questions:

1. What were the most important challenges that George Washington faced as he assumed the presidency?
2. What fueled the acrimony between Alexander Hamilton and Thomas Jefferson?
3. Why did James Madison spearhead the effort to approve the Bill of Rights?
4. How did international affairs, particularly the war between Great Britain and France, affect U.S. domestic politics?
5. Was Hamilton's plan for an economy based on manufacturing realistic in 1790? Why or why not?

Americans confronted the nineteenth century with a variety of fears. For the Federalists, the growing Republican opposition warned that the evils of democracy and anarchy stood ready to take control. For the Republicans, the Alien and Sedition acts and Federalist repression of the whiskey rebels underscored the need for change. Both parties, still members of the revolutionary generation, thought in terms of the ideals for which they had fought against the British. They also measured events against what was transpiring elsewhere in the world. By 1800, the excesses of the French Revolution and Napoleon Bonaparte's rise to power dismayed Americans. The never-ending European war threatened to involve the United States for twenty years, and it finally did in 1812. The 1791 revolt by slaves in the French West Indies horrified southern slave owners.

Although Thomas Jefferson's presidency would prove to be less revolutionary than many Federalists feared, the new century brought indelible changes to American politics and society. The Federalist Party shriveled and died, the Louisiana Purchase expanded the nation's territory to the Rocky Mountains and beyond, slavery became more firmly embedded in the southern economy, and the republic fought once more against Great Britain. The Second Great Awakening, the series of religious revivals that began in the late 1790s and gained steam after the turn of the century, influenced the ways in which many people interpreted these events.

❖ Religion in American Society

During the first decade of the nineteenth century, religion absorbed the energies of many different groups: frontier settlers and Native Americans caught up in revivals, organizations to provide welfare relief in towns and cities, new sects like the Shakers, and free African Americans who built separate churches as the cornerstone of their communities. Many people believed that renewed emphasis on religion would transform the nation through individual faith and communal action.

The Second Great Awakening

As the century began, people throughout the country sought spiritual renewal. Among New England Congregationalists, the revivals spread from one town to another between 1797 and 1801. The national Methodist conference of 1800 held in Baltimore witnessed an outpouring of religious fervor. These flames heralded a series of revivals—the **Second Great Awakening**—which lasted into the 1830s. In accepting the message of revival, large numbers of Americans embraced evangelicalism—the belief that they must take their message of salvation to others. They expected to create a more godly nation through conversion and good works.

Second Great Awakening Protestant religious revivals that began in 1797 and lasted into the 1830s.

In particular, evangelical ministers feared for the nation because so many westerners were "un-churched." The clerics expressed their dread in terms of millennialism, the belief that the millennium—Christ's second coming—was at hand, as foretold in Revelation, the last book of the Bible. Pastors urged their

CHAPTER TIMELINE 1799 1803 1807 1811 1815 1819

POLITICS AND DIPLOMACY

- 1801–1809 Thomas Jefferson presidency
- 1812–1815 War of 1812
- 1800 Gabriel's rebellion occurs
- 1808 Federal ban on slave importation
- 1803 *Marbury v. Madison* case is decided
- 1804–1806 Lewis and Clark expedition
- 1809–1817 James Madison presidency
- 1809–1811 Tecumseh organizes pan-Indian resistance

SOCIETY AND CULTURE

- 1799 Rise of Handsome Lake's influence as a prophet
- 1801 Cane Ridge, Kentucky, camp meeting takes place

ECONOMICS AND TECHNOLOGY

- 1807 Embargo Act passes
- 1811 Bank of the United States charter expires

(The Granger Collection, New York)

Methodist Camp Meeting. *Methodist Camp Meeting*, engraving by E. Clay. During the Second Great Awakening, itinerant preachers held outdoor revivals that often lasted for several days.

congregations to prepare for the millennium by supporting missionary efforts in the West. Circuit preachers and missionaries traveled throughout the frontier; the churches they started were often the first social organizations in new communities. The great western revivals of 1800 to 1815, which built on this work, began when several Presbyterians summoned the first camp meeting, a religious gathering held outside over the course of several days. People came together, miles from their homes, to hear revivalist preachers. The most famous of the early camp meetings took place in August 1801 at Cane Ridge, Kentucky, where Presbyterian, Methodist, and Baptist clergy preached for about a week to a throng numbering about twenty thousand. From wagons and crude tents, the crowds listened to the message that Jesus Christ could save all people from their sins. People reacted emotionally and physically to this message, some jerking their heads or entire bodies, others falling to the ground in a faint.

Reminiscent of the Great Awakening in the South during the 1750s and 1760s, the camp meetings spread throughout Kentucky, Tennessee, and southern Ohio, gathering new congregations. The Methodist and Baptist churches, which placed less importance on the fine points of religious doctrine and a well-educated clergy than did the Presbyterians, benefited most from the revivals.

Religion was also important to black Americans, whether they remained enslaved or had achieved freedom. In the South, African Americans responded enthusiastically to revivalist preachers. The Methodists and Baptists welcomed free and enslaved blacks into their congregations as equals in spirit though not in governing the church. In hostile northern cities, free black communities depended on separate churches for leadership and communal fellowship.

The period around 1800 also witnessed the expansion of several dissenting sects, including the Shakers and the Universalists. They are called *sects*, rather than *denominations*, because they were new and fairly small. They held distinctive beliefs that set them apart from mainstream religions yet had a significant influence on the intellectual and social movements of their times.

The Shakers, whose official name was the United Society of Believers in Christ's Second Coming (the Millennial Church), came to America in 1774, when Mother **Ann Lee** arrived from Britain with eight disciples. They left England to escape mob attacks and imprisonment. The group grew slowly at first, but expanded after Lee's death in 1784 as they reaped followers from revivals, especially Baptists. The sect offered an avenue for people who had been spiritually reborn in the Awakening and sought a distinctive way to represent that rebirth in their lives. The Shakers believed in salvation by confession of sin, equality regardless of sex or race, opposition to slavery and war, and assistance to the poor. They abstained from sexual relations.

Lee, Ann (1736–1784) Founder of the Shakers in the United States. The sect believed in salvation by confession of sin, equality regardless of sex or race, opposition to slavery and war, sexual abstinence, and assistance to the poor.

Another sect, the **Universalists,** rejected the Calvinist belief that only a minority of people, the elect, could attain salvation. They preached that "it is the purpose of God, through the grace revealed in our Lord Jesus Christ, to save every member of the human race from sin." The American Universalist church, established in 1779 by an Englishman, John Murray, found a sympathetic audience among ordinary people caught up in the Second Great Awakening in New England and on the frontier. Its message of universal salvation had wide influence, though the Universalist church itself remained small.

Universalists Protestant denomination established in 1779 by an Englishman, John Murray. Its message of universal salvation had wide influence, though the Universalist church itself remained small.

Revivalism Among Native Americans

While the Second Great Awakening and dissenting sects claimed the imagination and souls of white and black Americans, a new wave of revivals drew together Native Americans. Among the Iroquois living on reservations in western New York and the Shawnees, Creeks, Cherokees, and other nations retaining lands in the trans-Appalachian region, prophets warned of imminent doom unless people changed their ways. Native Americans had continued to lose lands to whites throughout the area from the Appalachians to the Mississippi; by 1812, settlers in the region dwarfed the Indian population by seven to one. Decline in the numbers of fur-bearing animals caused economic hardship, and conflict over whether to cooperate with the United States created political factions within tribes.

The nativists blamed loss of land and power on the Indians' failure to maintain traditional rituals and on their adoption of practices from the whites such as drinking rum. Among many prophets, **Handsome Lake** of the Senecas (a nation of the Iroquois) and **Tenskwatawa** of the Shawnees wielded the greatest influence in the first decade of the nineteenth century.

Handsome Lake (1735–1815) Seneca spiritual and political leader. He advocated peace, the U.S. acculturation policy, abstinence from drinking alcohol and practicing witchcraft, and return to ancestral rituals.

Handsome Lake, a respected warrior and leader of the Allegany Senecas, became a leader of the Iroquois Confederacy from 1801 to 1803. In a series of revelations over several years, Handsome Lake, who claimed to see visions, received a message of impending catastrophe and a means to salvation. He told his people to stop drinking alcohol and practicing witchcraft; instead they should perform their ancestral rituals. The prophet also advocated peace. Handsome Lake's spiritual message remained strong for many years, particularly his drive against liquor. A former heavy drinker himself, the Seneca prophet advised, in the words of a white observer, that "the Whiskey is the great Engine which the bad Spirit uses to introduce Witchcraft and many other evils amongst Indians."

Tenskwatawa (1768–1834) Called the Shawnee Prophet, he became prominent among the people of the Great Lakes and Ohio Valley. With his brother, Tecumseh, he inspired a nativist movement to resist the U.S. government's acculturation policy and land seizure.

Also influential was Tenskwatawa, called the Shawnee Prophet, who became prominent among the people of the Great Lakes and Ohio Valley. With his brother, Tecumseh, he inspired a nativist movement to resist the U.S. government's acculturation policy and land grabbing. To avoid fiery destruction, Tenskwatawa warned, Indians must revitalize their traditional ceremonies, avoid liquor, and reject new gender roles. One of the prophet's visions promised that the whites would be destroyed if his people obeyed these instructions.

❖ African Americans

As slavery ended in the North, free blacks faced discriminatory practices that kept the racial caste system in place, including segregation in churches and schools and restriction from politics and many occupations. Despite this racism, northern blacks created new lives, institutions, and communities that offered a potent draw to African Americans in the South. Some southern blacks also considered more violent means to end bondage.

Free Blacks in the North

Allen, Richard (1760–1831) Reverend Allen was a former slave who founded the African Methodist Episcopal church and was a leader of the Philadelphia black community.

St. Domingue French West Indies colony in which blacks led by Toussaint L'Ouverture, a former slave, defeated local whites and invading European armies. Napoleon failed to regain control of the island and, in 1804, the victorious rebels established Haiti as an independent nation.

By 1800, Pennsylvania, New York, and all of New England had passed gradual abolition acts or ended slavery outright. New Jersey in 1804 became the last northern state to pass a law for gradual emancipation, which, like those of other states, freed children henceforth born to slave mothers but retained slaves born before the date of the law in perpetual bondage. Despite the gradual nature of these emancipation laws, slavery declined rapidly in the northern states (see Table 8.1). Responding to their slaves' requests for freedom and to the spirit of the abolition acts, many owners freed people whom the laws left in bonds. In 1805, a New York slave, Margaret, obtained her owner's pledge of freedom in eight years if she behaved "as she always has done in an orderly manner as a servant ought to do." When masters proved recalcitrant, blacks often forced the issue by running away.

The northern cities became magnets for escaped slaves. Philadelphia and New York City became centers of free African American culture, with churches

TABLE 8.1
Number of Enslaved African Americans, 1800 and 1810

	1800	1810
New England	1,339	418
New York	20,903	15,017
New Jersey	12,422	10,851
Pennsylvania	1,706	795
Delaware	6,153	4,177
Maryland and District of Columbia	107,707	115,056
Virginia	346,968	394,357
North Carolina	133,296	168,824
South Carolina	146,151	196,365
Georgia	59,406	105,218
Kentucky	40,343	80,561
Tennessee	13,584	44,535
Mississippi Territory	3,489	17,088

Source: U.S. Bureau of the Census, *A Century of Population Growth from the First Census of the United States to the Twelfth 1790–1900* (Washington, DC: U.S. Government Printing Office, 1909), 133.

fostering autonomous community growth (see Table 8.2). In Philadelphia, responding to hostility from whites, freed men and women organized separate black congregations in the 1780s and 1790s. Reverend **Richard Allen**, for example, led black worshippers from St. George's Methodist Episcopal Church when whites insisted on segregated seating. By 1803, Allen's black Methodist church, which he called Bethel, had 457 members, the result of revivals and Allen's fervent preaching. In 1816, Philadelphia's Bethel became the first congregation of the African Methodist Episcopal church when differences with the white Methodist church hierarchy became irreconcilable.

TABLE 8.2
Free Black Population in Northern Cities

	1790	1800	1810
Pennsylvania	1,849	6,028	8,942
New York City	1,078	3,499	8,137
Boston	761	1,174	1,464

Source: Gary B. Nash and Jean R. Soderlund, *Freedom by Degrees: Emancipation in Pennsylvania and Its Aftermath* (New York: Oxford University Press, 1991), 18; U.S. Bureau of the Census, *A Century of Population Growth from the First Census of the United States to the Twelfth 1790–1900* (Washington, DC: U.S. Government Printing Office, 1909), 84; Leonard P. Curry, *The Free Black in Urban America 1800–1850* (Chicago: University of Chicago Press, 1981), 250.

Urban black churches like Bethel provided mutual aid, fellowship, and avenues for leadership. One benefit of belonging to a New York congregation became obvious to an eighty-year-old woman after a fire destroyed her home. When asked where she would find shelter, she answered, "O a sister in the church has promised to take me in." Other freed men and women formed mutual benefit societies. The names African Americans chose for these organizations demonstrated pride in their African heritage, though many of the founders were two, three, or even four generations removed from ancestral lands. Philadelphians, for example, formed the Free African Society, Daughters of Ethiopia, Angola Society, Sons of Africa, and many others. The official purpose of these societies was to collect dues to provide relief to poor widows and children, but just as important, the groups facilitated community involvement.

With little money or access to capital, few African Americans, perhaps one in ten, scraped together the funds to purchase a house, shop, or farm. In the first decades of the nineteenth century, many blacks were still completing terms of servitude; others, though free, lived and worked in white households as domestic servants. Even if they established their own households, women generally washed clothes or performed domestic service for others. Most men were mariners or common laborers. The African American community provided additional opportunity by employing its own. Residents supported black shoemakers, carpenters, food retailers, hucksters, barbers, hairdressers, seamstresses, tailors, cooks, bakers, schoolteachers, and ministers. In Philadelphia, a few African Americans achieved considerable wealth and fame. By 1807, James Forten employed thirty men—blacks and whites—to produce sails for the city's shipbuilders.

African Americans in northern cities also knew of recent struggles by slaves in St. Domingue and elsewhere; a large number of blacks in Philadelphia and New York City had come from the French island with their masters who had fled the black revolt. During the 1790s, blacks on **St. Domingue** led by Toussaint L'Ouverture, a former slave, had defeated local whites and the French, Spanish, and British armies. In 1802, Napoleon tried to regain control of the island but failed when disease decimated his forces. In 1804, the victorious rebels of St. Domingue established Haiti as an independent nation. Most white Americans dreaded the importation of black revolt. After St. Domingue erupted, Georgia and the Carolinas declared black émigrés from the West Indies a threat, prohibiting their entry.

(The Granger Collection, New York)

Reverend Richard Allen. Reverend Richard Allen, a former slave, was founder of the African Methodist Episcopal Church and a leader of the Philadelphia black community.

Slave Rebellion in the South

With more than 850,000 enslaved blacks in the American South in 1800, one-third of the population, whites had reason to be concerned about slave insurgency. In August 1800, their worst fears were nearly realized when an enslaved blacksmith named Gabriel organized an armed march against the capital of Virginia. With about six hundred supporters from Richmond and surrounding counties, Gabriel planned a full-scale insurrection. His strategy included seizing guns from an arsenal, taking Governor James Monroe hostage, and forcing concessions from town officials. Gabriel expected poor whites to join him because they, like slaves, lacked political power. The attack failed when a torrential rainstorm washed out bridges, making travel impossible. Gabriel was arrested and hanged, as were twenty-six others implicated in the plot.

White Americans still held the revolutionary belief that all men and women desired freedom, so masters took seriously the threat of slave revolt. After Gabriel's rebellion, Governor Monroe observed about enslaved African Americans, "Unhappily while this class of people exists among us we can never count with certainty on its tranquil submission." In 1802, Virginians discovered additional conspiracies, with rumors of more violence heightening tensions. In 1805, after four whites had been poisoned in North Carolina, officials burned a slave woman alive, hanged three other slaves, and whipped and cut off the ears of another. The St. Domingue uprising, Gabriel's plot, and what appeared to be an upsurge of murders and arson by blacks convinced southern lawmakers to enact more stringent slave codes. On a more positive note, as the twenty-year constitutional restriction on prohibiting the slave trade expired, Congress officially banned the importation of slaves after January 1, 1808.

❖ Jefferson's Republic

In 1800, the federal government moved from Philadelphia to an unfinished village on the Potomac: Washington, D.C. The ruling party also changed, as voters voiced their dissatisfaction with the Federalists by electing Thomas Jefferson and a Republican Congress. Jefferson's promise of reduced government and taxes appealed to a populace concerned about other things besides national politics—their finances, their souls, and local communities. Events prevented the young nation from wrapping itself in isolation, however, for its economic prosperity was threatened by the ongoing European war.

The Election of 1800

Shortly before the election of 1800, the United States had been involved in the Quasi-War with France, in which the French navy initially ravaged the American merchant fleet. Congress had expanded the army, authorized the U.S. Navy to protect commercial ships, and revoked unilaterally the American–French treaty of 1778. The Federalists had swept the congressional elections of 1798 on the crest of anti-French fervor and had tried to use war fever against the Republicans through the Alien and Sedition acts. Instead, the backlash of concern about civil liberties swelled the opposition.

As the 1800 election approached, many Federalists expected to take advantage of the unresolved difficulties with France in continuing to paint the Jeffersonian Republicans as pro-French, and hence un-American. Nevertheless, President John Adams moved to end hostilities. He nominated a commission to make peace with France, but the diplomats received instructions that proved impossible to fulfill: their mission was to obtain French agreement that the 1778 alliance had ended and indemnities for confiscated American ships. Napoleon had no intention of paying compensation, so the commissioners reached an accord only by ignoring their instructions. The **Convention of 1800**, signed in France in October and ratified reluctantly by the U.S. Senate in February 1801, called for "a firm, inviolable, and universal peace," but it voided the defensive alliance of 1778, eliminating the French claim to U.S. support against Great Britain. The pact also included a vague confirmation by the French of neutral rights in international trade, but it provided no restitution to American shippers, a failing that opponents said made the convention worthless. Still, the agreement normalized relations between the two countries.

Convention of 1800 Negotiated with France by a three-man commission appointed by President John Adams, the convention echoed provisions of the 1778 commercial treaty but voided the defensive alliance, thus eliminating the French claim to U.S. support against Great Britain.

The chief beneficiary of reduced tensions with France was Thomas Jefferson, named in May 1800 as Republican nominee for president, with Aaron Burr of New York for vice president. John Adams received the Federalist nomination for reelection, with Charles Cotesworth Pinckney of South Carolina as his running mate. Many Federalists opposed Adams for making peace with France. When the electoral votes were tallied, Jefferson and Burr each received 73 votes, Adams 65, Pinckney 64, and John Jay 1 (see Map 8.1). In lining up votes in the electoral college, the Republicans had failed to take account of the constitutional election procedures that lacked provision for party slates. The Constitution directed that each elector cast two votes, with the candidate receiving the highest number elected president and the runner-up vice president. The electors had no way of designating which candidate they supported for president and which for vice president.

The tie sent the election to the House of Representatives, which had a Federalist majority from the previous election. Each state delegation received one vote. Alexander Hamilton opposed Burr vigorously, advising his party to make a deal with Jefferson to keep the system of public credit and the navy, retain Federalist appointees in office, and remain neutral in the war between Britain and France. The House of Representatives required thirty-six ballots over six days before the Federalist delegate from Delaware, James A. Bayard, shifted his position from Burr to Jefferson to break the tie. Jefferson became president and Burr vice president.

1800

Candidate (Party)	Electoral Vote		Popular Vote
Jefferson (Republican)	73	53%	
Burr	73	53%	
Adams (Federalist)	65	47%	
Pinckney	64	46%	
Jay	1		

MAP 8.1
The Election of 1800
The election Thomas Jefferson called "the revolution of 1800" was close, with Jefferson receiving 73 votes to John Adams's 65. The Federalist ticket, headed by Adams and Charles Cotesworth Pinckney, obtained considerable support from the Carolinas and the mid-Atlantic states, as well as New England.

Jefferson's "Revolution"

The third president assumed a conciliatory stance toward the Federalists as he took office. On March 4, 1801, Jefferson delivered his inaugural address to the new Congress, which the Republicans now dominated in the House by 69 votes to 36 and in the Senate by 18 to 13. The speech reflected his Republican beliefs: emphasis on the power of state governments, freedom of religion and the press, majority rule but protection of minority rights, low government expenditures, and reduction of the federal debt. Jefferson upheld the Convention of 1800 with France implicitly by stating that he desired amity and trade with foreign nations and "entangling alliances with none." His most famous statement, "We are all Republicans, we are all Federalists," attempted to get beyond the partisan battles that had bedeviled his two predecessors. He later described his election as "the revolution of 1800." Despite bitter political enmity, American leaders had created a party system by which power could be contested in elections rather than through bloodshed. With the election of 1800, the Constitution passed a crucial test, with peaceful transfer of power from one party to its opponents.

The new president worked to put his principles into action and create an agrarian republic in which the federal government kept its role to a minimum. The location in Washington, D.C., seemed the ideal setting for a weak government. In 1800, the town had fewer than four hundred dwellings, which one government official described as mostly "small miserable huts." The Capitol was incomplete, with wings for the Senate and House but no center. The president's house was not yet finished in 1814 when the British burned it. Cows grazed on what later became the Mall; hogs ran through the city's streets. In 1802, federal personnel throughout the country numbered under ten thousand, of whom sixty-five hundred served in military posts. The president and Supreme Court each had one clerk, Congress employed thirteen, and the attorney general had none. The central government had relatively little to do, for state and local governments or voluntary associations took primary responsibility for keeping law and order, maintaining roads and bridges, supervising the militia, and providing welfare relief and schools.

Jefferson's lack of attention to building Washington, D.C., revealed his approach to the presidency. In contrast to Federalist efforts to reflect the grandeur of European courts and capitals, he adopted informality and frugality. Jefferson dealt with members of Congress and foreign diplomats personally, inviting small groups for dinner and conversation. He avoided making speeches, instead sending written messages to Congress. With only one clerk, he handled many documents himself.

The change of political power from the Federalists to the Republicans raised questions about office holding and political spoils. At the highest level of executive appointments, the cabinet, Jefferson assumed his right to appoint trusted supporters. He named James Madison of Virginia, his closest ally, as secretary of state and Albert Gallatin of Pennsylvania as secretary of the treasury. The question of whether to retain bureaucrats was more difficult. Jefferson supported the idea of a civil service in which public officers held their positions on the basis of merit, but when he learned that Washington and Adams had appointed only six Republicans to about six hundred positions, the new president replaced about half of the Federalists with Republicans. Most infuriating to Jefferson were the "**midnight appointments**," as Jefferson characterized them—the appointments Adams made as a lame duck after he knew that the election was lost.

midnight appointments Federal judicial officials appointed to office in the closing period of a presidential administration. The Republicans accused Adams of staying awake until midnight in order to sign the commissions for Federalist officeholders.

Jefferson and Gallatin placed high priority on decreasing government expenditures, taxes, and the national debt. Gallatin opposed all spending by the federal government, including the military. With the support of the Republican Congress, the administration cut the defense budget in half. It repealed all excise taxes, including that on whiskey, relying primarily on import duties for income.

Jefferson's plan to reduce the navy and remain clear of international conflicts hit a snag when Yusuf Karamanli, the leader of Tripoli in North Africa, demanded payments from the United States to "protect" American merchant carriers from pirates. To end this extortion, in 1801 Jefferson sent naval vessels to blockade Tripoli and protect shipping. The United States experienced a major loss when the ship *Philadelphia* ran aground while pursuing pirates, but when a small force of U.S. Marines and Arab mercenaries seized the port city of Derna, the Tripolitans agreed to peace. The war had propelled military expenditures upward, however, and convinced Jefferson of the navy's value, thus hindering somewhat the administration's plans for reducing spending.

(The Architect of the Capitol)

Chief Justice John Marshall. During his tenure to 1835, the chief justice established federal judicial authority, in particular the Court's power to decide the consitutionality of laws.

The Judiciary

Although the Republicans had captured the presidency and Congress in 1800, the judiciary remained firmly in the hands of the Federalists. Adams and the outgoing Congress had tried to solidify their party's power in the courts with the Judiciary Act of 1801, which amended the Judiciary Act of 1789. By appointing additional federal judges, the new law ended the onerous requirement for Supreme Court justices to ride from state to state to convene circuit courts twice a year. The act also reduced the number of justices on the Court from six to five, thereby denying Jefferson the opportunity to make an appointment when a seat became vacant. The Republican Congress repealed this law in early 1802, reinstating the Judiciary Act of 1789, thus forcing some federal judges out of their jobs and the Supreme Court back to the circuit.

Jefferson's bitter relationship with the Supreme Court resulted in part from his antipathy toward Chief Justice **John Marshall**, his distant cousin, whom Adams had named to the bench in early 1801. Like Jefferson, Marshall was tall, informal in manner, and a native of Virginia. He had joined the patriot forces in 1775, serving until 1781. Marshall began a successful law practice after the war, served as a Virginia assemblyman, supported ratification of the federal Constitution, then became the leading Federalist in his state. In the legal environment of the new republic, many colleagues appreciated his originality in building cases on logic and natural law rather than depending on English precedent. On the Supreme Court, too, Marshall followed his own lights, creating the legal basis on which the power of the Court still rests. During his long, illustrious career, which lasted until 1835, Marshall solidified the authority of the judicial branch of the federal government.

Marshall, John (1755–1835) American politician and jurist. As chief justice of the United States (1801–1835), he helped establish the doctrine of judicial review.

Marbury v. Madison (1803) The first decision by the Supreme Court to declare unconstitutional and void an act passed by Congress that the Court considered in violation of the Constitution. The decision established the doctrine of judicial review, the authority of courts to declare statutes unconstitutional.

Marshall's most important decision, ***Marbury v. Madison* (1803)**, commenced in a suit by William Marbury, nominated by Adams as a justice of the peace but not commissioned by the Jefferson administration. Marbury sued under the Judiciary Act of 1789, which granted the Supreme Court the power to require Secretary of State Madison to hand over Marbury's commission. Given the partisanship involved, most observers expected Marshall and his Federalist court to direct Madison to comply. Instead, the chief justice said that he could not remedy Marbury's situation, though he wished to do so, because the Congress had erred in giving the Court such authority. Marshall declared the provision of the 1789 Judiciary Act unconstitutional, thus establishing the Supreme Court's power of judicial review.

Jefferson decided that the federal judiciary, still dominated by Federalists and growing in power under Marshall, had to be controlled. Because federal judges constitutionally held their seats for life, "during good behavior," the president suggested to congressional Republicans that they start impeachment proceedings against objectionable Federalists. The Republicans impeached John Pickering, an official of the federal district court of New Hampshire, who was an alcoholic and insane but who had not to anyone's knowledge committed any high crimes. The Senate found him guilty anyway and removed him from his position. Next, in January 1805, the House of Representatives impeached Samuel Chase of Maryland, an associate justice of the Supreme Court and extreme Federalist who had castigated Jefferson's administration. But the prosecution failed to convince two-thirds of the Senate that Chase should be expelled from office for misconduct and other charges.

Domestic Politics

Jefferson and the Republicans gained in popularity as they steered a course more moderate than the "revolution" of 1800 had promised. The president had reduced taxes and attempted to limit the judiciary, but did not dismantle the Federalist edifice of national power, including the military and the national bank. He mixed republican theory, based on a nation of small farmers, with practical politics aiding commerce. His policies, combined with booming exports, steadily increased Republican support, as many Federalist voters switched parties. In the election of 1802, the Republicans won 102 seats to the Federalists' 39 in the House of Representatives; the Republican margin in the Senate was 25 to 9.

Looking forward to the next presidential election, Congress acted promptly to avoid the deadlock that had occurred in 1800. The Republicans wanted a formal way to keep the Federalists from conspiring once again to elevate the Republican candidate for vice president to the presidency. The **Twelfth Amendment** to the Constitution, which required the electors to draw up distinct lists for president and vice president, was ratified by September 1804, and soon thereafter, Jefferson was reelected, defeating the Federalist presidential candidate, Charles Cotesworth Pinckney, by 162 electoral votes to 14.

Twelfth Amendment (1804) Constitutional amendment requiring electors to draw up distinct lists for president and vice president, thus avoiding the deadlock of 1800 in which Thomas Jefferson and Aaron Burr tied for the presidency.

Jefferson had replaced Aaron Burr as his running mate with George Clinton, also of New York, while Burr ran for governor of New York against the Republican candidate, Morgan Lewis. He lost by a landslide when Alexander Hamilton actively campaigned against his long-time enemy. Burr challenged Hamilton to a duel. When the two faced each other at Weehawken, New Jersey, in July 1804, Burr shot Hamilton to death. In doing so, the vice president ended his own political career, as well as the life of one of the architects of the American nation-state.

❖ The Louisiana Purchase

Jefferson had boosted his popularity prior to the 1804 election with the **Louisiana Purchase**, which marked the greatest success of his presidency. In pursuing the deal with France, he deviated from one of his beliefs—in limited power of the central government—to obtain land for his agrarian republic. Long interested in the West, he scored a diplomatic coup that doubled the size of the United States and reduced Spain's dominance west of the Mississippi River.

Louisiana Purchase (1803) The acquisition of the Louisiana Territory west of the Mississippi River and New Orleans by the United States from France for $15 million.

Diplomatic Negotiations

The chain of events leading to the Louisiana Purchase began in 1800, when France signed a secret treaty with Spain to recover the lands in western North America it had ceded to Spain in 1763. When Jefferson and Madison heard in 1801 of the impending transfer, they sent the new U.S. minister to France, Robert R. Livingston, with instructions to prevent the exchange or at least obtain West Florida. The Americans wanted to prevent France from controlling the Mississippi Valley; the dilapidated Spanish empire had caused trouble enough. In October 1802, the Spanish suspended once again the right of Americans to deposit goods for export at New Orleans. The Americans thought, incorrectly, that Napoleon was behind the ban. Many wanted to take New Orleans by force, but Jefferson pushed for negotiations, not war.

In response to Livingston's overtures, Napoleon decided to sell the entire Louisiana Territory to the United States. The French leader's zeal to construct an American empire had cooled with the loss of his army in St. Domingue. In documents dated April 30, 1803, the United States agreed to pay France $15 million, respect the rights of the French and Native Americans living in the territory, and recognize the French residents as American citizens. Jefferson worried, as a strict constructionist, that the Louisiana Purchase was unconstitutional because the federal government had no specific power to acquire territory. He put aside these concerns, however, confident that the Louisiana Purchase would extend the life of the republic by providing space for generations of virtuous, independent farmers. Although some Federalists disagreed, most Americans celebrated the end of friction over the Mississippi River and New Orleans. Western farmers could get their products to market while eastern merchants prospered from the trade.

When U.S. officials gained formal possession of Louisiana in December 1803, the Spanish were not pleased; they had only recently transferred control to the French. The entire white population of the Louisiana Territory—approximately fifty thousand—was a diverse mix of French, Spanish, Germans, English, and Americans. The establishment of boundaries quickly raised diplomatic conflicts with Spain. Thomas Jefferson pushed for the most generous interpretation for the United States, demanding West Florida as well as all of Texas and part of New Mexico, and in the Northwest to the Rocky Mountains. Spain, however, said the Louisiana Territory included only a constricted region along the west bank of the Mississippi from northern Missouri to the Gulf of Mexico (see Map 8.2). The United States eventually conceded, but continued to eye these regions hungrily.

Doing History Online

Jefferson and the Louisiana Territory, 1804

Go to the CourseMate website for this chapter and link to Primary Sources. Based on his letter to Governor Claiborne (Document 2), what appear to be Jefferson's concerns regarding governance of the Louisiana Territory?

www.cengagebrain.com

The Lewis and Clark Expedition, 1804–1806

To strengthen U.S. claims to the West, Jefferson sponsored an exploratory mission to the Pacific Ocean. Several times since 1783, he had tried to organize expeditions for scientific knowledge and promote American interests in the region. As president, he now had the authority and financial resources to support this major undertaking. By the early nineteenth century, however, others had surveyed parts of the territory. In 1792, an American sea captain, Robert Gray, explored the Columbia River, and George Vancouver, a British naval officer, sailed the Northwest coast. A few years later, fur traders working for the Spanish government ascended the Missouri River to present-day North Dakota, and British traders from Canada began moving west.

Even before buying Louisiana, the president had decided to send an expedition west; the purchase gave the project greater urgency. He appointed his private secretary, Meriwether Lewis, captain of the enterprise. Jefferson wanted "a person who to courage, prudence, habits & health adapted to the woods, & some familiarity

MAP 8.2

The Louisiana Purchase and Western Exploration, 1803–1807

At about the same time that Meriwether Lewis and William Clark led the Corps of Discovery along the northern route to trade with Native Americans, explore the natural resources, and locate a northwest passage, Zebulon Pike traveled north along the Mississippi River and west to the Rocky Mountains.

with the Indian character, joins a perfect knoledge of botany, natural history, mineralogy & astronomy." Lewis chose his friend William Clark to be his partner in what became known as the **Lewis and Clark expedition.** Lewis and Clark had served in the army together in the Old Northwest, so both were familiar with frontier conditions.

Jefferson had a long list of goals for his explorers. They were to travel to the source of the Missouri River to find the elusive Northwest Passage, fill in huge blanks in geographic knowledge of the West, and bring back descriptions of species of plants and animals thus far unknown. He also hoped they would make peaceful contact with Native Americans to expand commercial networks for fur traders. Lewis and Clark more than fulfilled their assignment, keeping daily journals of their experiences, including descriptions of Indian societies and culture, systematic weather records, and observations of flora and fauna, as well as a detailed map of their journey. Their relations with the people of the Northwest were for the most part amicable.

Lewis and Clark received commissions as army officers to lead the Corps of Discovery of about forty men who departed from St. Louis in May 1804. During that summer and fall, they traveled up the Missouri River and eventually arrived in the Mandan and Hidatsa villages of what is now North Dakota, where they spent the winter of 1804–1805. In April 1805, the Lewis and Clark expedition set out with a Shoshone woman, **Sacagawea,** and her French husband and infant son. They proceeded up the Missouri River, made an arduous crossing of the Rockies, and reached the mouth of the Columbia River before winter. On the way back, the Corps of Discovery divided in two. They joined forces once again in North Dakota and returned to St. Louis by September 1806.

Lewis and Clark Expedition From 1804 to 1806 Meriwether Lewis and William Clark led the Corps of Discovery from St. Louis to the Pacific coast and back. They informed Native Americans that the United States had acquired the territory from France and recorded geographic and scientific data.

Sacagawea (1787?–1812?) Shoshone guide and interpreter who accompanied the Lewis and Clark expedition (1805–1806).

Spies, Infiltrators, and Traitors

Lewis and Clark had been away so long that many assumed they had been killed by the Spanish or Native Americans. Spanish officials in fact had tried to intercept

Lewis and Clark, whom they correctly suspected of making allies for the United States among the western Indians. General James Wilkinson, commander of U.S. troops in the West, governor of the Louisiana Territory, and a double agent known to the Spanish as "Agent 13," had tipped off New Spain about the expedition. One Spanish party nearly intercepted Zebulon Pike, whom Wilkinson had dispatched to explore and spy in the region that is now Kansas, Colorado, and New Mexico. When Pike became lost in the southern Rockies, he was rescued by Spanish soldiers, who arrested, and then released, him.

The United States and Spain knew they were playing for high stakes. The United States could use exploration of the West and alliances with Native Americans to help confirm its claims to broad boundaries of the Louisiana Territory. The Spanish had by far superior documentation for Texas, New Mexico, Arizona, California, and western Colorado. But they also denied American rights to what is now western Louisiana. Concerned about protecting their silver mines in Mexico, the Spanish took steps to increase settlement in Texas. They welcomed Indian exiles—Cherokees, Choctaws, and Alabamas—from lands overrun by American settlers east of the Mississippi, but the Hispanic population failed to grow significantly. New Spain officials barred U.S. citizens from Texas: one Spanish official warned that Americans "are not and will not be anything but crows to pick out our eyes." Anglo-American traders continued to infiltrate Texas, however, to trap animals and bargain for horses with the Comanches and other Indians.

(The Granger Collection, New York)

Meriwether Lewis. A portrayal of Meriwether Lewis during the western expedition. C.B.J.F. de Saint-Memin produced the print in 1816, after the explorer's death.

Meanwhile, Aaron Burr, who in 1804 had mortally wounded Alexander Hamilton in a duel and was estranged from Jefferson, conceived a plot to create a separate nation in the West. He contacted the double agent James Wilkinson, various unhappy politicians, and representatives of foreign governments, suggesting a variety of plans to those who would listen, including an invasion of New Spain, an attack on Washington, D.C., and secession of the West. Wilkinson cooperated with Burr at first, then turned informer when the conspiracy became public knowledge. Burr tried to escape to Europe but was captured and taken to Richmond, Virginia, where he was tried in 1807.

The Burr conspiracy case, presided over by Chief Justice Marshall and involving three prosecutors and six defense lawyers, might have been called the trial of the century. The principal actors in the trial were Marshall, who ignored his responsibility as an impartial judge to favor the defense, and Jefferson, who directed the prosecution from afar. Because Marshall upheld a definition of treason that required actual gathering of troops, not just conspiracy, the case against Burr collapsed. Jefferson blamed Marshall and considered trying to impeach him, but he found insufficient congressional support.

❖ More Foreign Entanglements

The renewal of war in 1803 between Great Britain and France portended trouble for the United States. American merchants flourished as they took advantage of neutrality and wartime demand for provisions in Europe and the West Indies. But their ships became vulnerable to the British navy and French privateers.

A Perilous Neutrality

Great Britain and France each wanted to prevent the United States from provisioning the other. In the *Essex* case of 1805, British courts stiffened export rules, allowing the Royal Navy to step up its confiscations of American ships. Then, in 1806 and 1807, the British and French blockaded each other's harbors, in combination eliminating neutral trade with Europe and the British Isles. Napoleon's Berlin and Milan Decrees banned trade with Britain and threatened neutrals who obeyed the British rules with seizure.

After the British destroyed the French and Spanish navies in 1805 at Trafalgar, off the coast of Spain, the British restrictions and impressment of sailors were by far the more troublesome to Americans. Many Federalists and some Republicans cried for war, but Jefferson and the congressional majority looked for ways to avoid hostilities. Congress passed the Non-Importation Act (1806) banning specified British goods, and the president opened negotiations with Great Britain to end impressment and recognize neutral trading rights. No agreement satisfactory to both sides could be reached. Then in June 1807, the British ship *Leopard* fired on the American frigate *Chesapeake* for refusing to submit to a search for British deserters. The *Chesapeake*, hit twenty-two times, managed to respond with only a single shot. The *Leopard* boarded her, impressing four men.

The Embargo of 1807

As Americans clamored for war in response, Jefferson closed U.S. ports and territorial waters to British vessels and recalled American ships from the Mediterranean, where they would have been trapped had war begun. The British refused to stop impressing American sailors, and they challenged Jefferson's port closure by firing on coastal towns in Maine and sailing into Chesapeake Bay.

Embargo Act (1807) Passed by Congress in response to British restrictions on U.S. trade and impressment of American sailors, the act prohibited exportation to all other countries. The policy had serious economic repercussions and was widely violated.

At the urging of President Jefferson and Secretary of State Madison, Congress passed the **Embargo Act** in December 1807, which prohibited exportation to all other countries. A by-product of nonexportation would be a severe drop in imports of British manufactures. Jefferson and Madison argued that the boycott would hurt all warring parties but Britain the worst. During 1808, the administration faced difficulty enforcing the embargo because ships, especially from New England, left harbor pretending to sail to American coastal ports but headed for foreign destinations instead. The trade with the British West Indies continued illegally. Federal agents also had little success in preventing smuggling into Canada. In January 1809, the government resorted to an extreme measure, Giles's Enforcement Act, which empowered the president to use the militia against smugglers. The act effectively ended trade.

The embargo had considerable impact on the U.S. economy, particularly in New England. Agricultural prices declined, leading to farm foreclosures. According to official records, exports declined by 80 percent in 1808, though smuggling certainly cushioned the effect. The U.S. Treasury suffered a loss in customs revenue, its chief source of income. However, the embargo stimulated further technological development of the textile industry, particularly in weaving cotton cloth with power looms. With stern enforcement of Giles's Act, New Englanders became strident in their demands for termination of the embargo. On March 1, 1809, Republicans in Congress replaced the embargo with the Non-Intercourse Act, which reopened trade with all countries except Great Britain and France. Although the new law banned trade with major markets, loopholes offered generous opportunities for smuggling.

Congress made this shift just days before the close of Jefferson's presidency. Jefferson thus ended his administration without solving the nation's international troubles. As he returned to Monticello, however, the president could reflect favorably on the goals he had achieved: lower taxes and national debt, smaller government, open doors to immigrants, and peace. He also took pride in an accomplishment he had not foreseen in 1801: the purchase of the Louisiana Territory. Jefferson's administration was remarkable for what it did—and for what it did not do, considering his opposition to Hamiltonian policies in the 1790s.

Under Jefferson, the Republicans left intact the national bank, the federal administrative structure, and the armed forces. Considering the war-torn world in which the young nation found its way, however, the Republican commitment to minimal government left the United States militarily unprepared.

❖ Madison and the War of 1812

When Britain continued to impress American sailors and seize ships, the United States was faced with two choices: accept humiliation or declare war on Great Britain. The British argued that they acted from necessity, as Napoleon conquered Europe. Americans upheld their rights as neutrals to sell provisions to both sides. They considered British impressment of six thousand seamen as a violation of national sovereignty and human rights. Between 1809 and 1812, these conflicts developed into war.

The Election of 1808

Despite the embargo, Jefferson retained enough popularity to win a third term, had he chosen to run. Instead, he declined and designated James Madison, the secretary of state, as his successor. James Monroe, who had served as governor of Virginia and minister to Great Britain, challenged Jefferson's choice, but congressional Republicans endorsed Madison. The Federalists put up Charles C. Pinckney and Rufus King, hoping that the effects of the embargo might reverse their party's decline. Although they improved on their performance in 1804 and 1806, gaining twenty-four seats in Congress, the electoral vote for president was 122 for Madison and 47 for Pinckney. Americans suffered from the embargo, but most were unprepared to desert the Republicans. In electing the new president, citizens ratified Jefferson's political philosophy and policies, which Madison had helped formulate.

In another way, however, the new administration represented a real departure. The diminutive Madison brought his elegant wife, Dolley Payne Madison, with him to the executive mansion, which was still unfinished when they arrived. They made a remarkable couple, as one observer admiringly described Mrs. Madison: "There was a frankness and ease in her deportment, that won golden opinions from all, and she possessed an influence so decided with her little Man." The first lady transformed the president's house into a proper executive mansion. She served as hostess to frequent teas and dinner parties, inviting Federalists and Republicans to socialize together.

Heading for War

After Madison's election, the European struggle continued to embroil the United States. Although both Britain and France were hostile to free trade, the British dominated the seas and had a particular impact on U.S. commerce. Over the period to 1812, as Napoleon pushed across Europe, invaded Russia, and met defeat, he became an inconsequential threat. In West Florida, Anglo-Americans, who had earlier pledged allegiance to Spain, in 1810 commandeered the Spanish fort at Baton Rouge, declared independence, and petitioned Madison for annexation by the United States. The president promptly claimed West Florida as part of the Louisiana Purchase, and U.S. troops occupied Baton Rouge. When Louisiana became a state in 1812, it included the western part of West Florida from Baton Rouge to the Pearl River.

In 1811, Madison appointed James Monroe, his former rival for the presidency, as secretary of state. Monroe took office hoping to reach an accord with the British, but events soon convinced him otherwise. Great Britain adhered to its Order in Council that American exports go to England before shipment to Europe; the Royal Navy continued to impress American seamen. When Napoleon partially lifted his blockade in 1811, the United States resumed trade with France, but the British disrupted it with frequent attacks on American ships. Events in the West also intensified anger toward Britain, because Anglo-Americans believed that the British in Canada were stirring up Native American discontent. In fact, whereas some Indians traded with the British, many natives distrusted the whites of both Canada and the United States. An alliance between militant Indians and the British took time to evolve, as each group moved independently toward war with the Americans.

Tecumseh (1768?–1813) Shawnee leader who attempted to establish a confederacy to unify Native Americans against white encroachment. He sided with the British in the War of 1812 and was killed in the Battle of the Thames.

Harrison, William Henry (1773–1841) While governor of the Indiana Territory, he attacked and burned the nativist village of Prophetstown in 1811. The ninth president of the United States (1841), he died of pneumonia after one month in office.

The nativist message of Tenskwatawa, the Shawnee Prophet, and his brother **Tecumseh** found widespread support as a result of the Louisiana Purchase, expanding white settlement, and sales by accommodationist Indian leaders of a large proportion of native lands still remaining east of the Mississippi. The Treaty of Fort Wayne (1809), which turned over 2.5 million acres to the United States, was the last straw. Tecumseh met with **William Henry Harrison**, governor of the Indiana Territory, to request that the treaty be annulled. Failing that, the Indian leader went south to seek support from the Creeks, Cherokees, and Choctaws. He found allies among militant factions of Creeks and Seminoles called the Red Sticks. Tecumseh's effort to create a pan-Indian movement throughout the trans-Appalachian West ultimately failed, however, because by 1811, large white populations in Tennessee, Kentucky, and Ohio formed a barrier between northern and southern Indians (see *Doing History: Native Americans and the New Republic*).

In November 1811, William Henry Harrison decided to cut short Tecumseh's efforts for unity. The governor did not believe the Indian leader's assurance that whites were "unnecessarily alarmed at his measures—that they really meant nothing but peace—the United States had set him the example by forming a strict union amongst all the fires that compose their confederacy." Harrison led a force against Prophetstown, a village Tenskwatawa had founded several years before on the Tippecanoe River. Before Harrison struck, the prophet attacked the encamped soldiers at night, but suffered casualties and withdrew. Harrison also lost men, but burned the town and claimed victory in what became known as the Battle of Tippecanoe. The nativists subsequently rebuilt their settlement; Harrison's action had little effect except to drive them closer to the British.

The War of 1812 Begins

When news of the battle reached Washington, many officials interpreted it as evidence that a British–Indian alliance already existed. The outcome, they mistakenly believed, showed that the British were weak, incapable of sustaining their allies. "War Hawks" in Congress, including the newly elected Speaker of the House, Henry Clay of Kentucky, and Representative John C. Calhoun of South Carolina, advocated preparations for war. They represented a new generation who, in Calhoun's words, had to prove to "the World, that we have not only inherited that liberty which our Fathers gave us, but also the will and power to maintain it." By April 1812, President Madison agreed. The Federalists, only one-fourth of Congress and primarily from New England, opposed conflict with Great Britain in part to obstruct administration policy, in part for commercial interests. The Republicans were divided.

Doing History Online

The United States Enters the War of 1812

Go to the CourseMate website for this chapter and link to Primary Sources. Based on your reading of Documents 8 and 9, what effect did the foreign crises of the early 1800s, culminating in the War of 1812, have on Americans' sense of nationhood?

www.cengagebrain.com

The nation was ill prepared when Madison issued his war message on June 1. Military funding would prove difficult because the charter of the Bank of the United States had been allowed to expire in 1811 due to politics and state

MAP 8.3

The War of 1812

Many of the battles occurred in the Great Lakes region, on the U.S.–Canadian border. In 1814, the British failed in their attempt to defeat the United States by taking Washington, D.C. Their attack on New Orleans occurred after the Treaty of Ghent.

banking interests, leaving state banks, but no central agency as a source of loans. Lack of federal taxes beyond import duties, which fell sharply when the British blockaded the Atlantic coast, further limited the country's resources. The failure of New England leaders to provide their share of funds particularly hampered the war effort, and the governors of Massachusetts and Connecticut even refused to send their militia. Not everyone in New England opposed the war, however, for the majority of representatives from Vermont, New Hampshire, and Maine (still part of Massachusetts) voted in favor of the June 1812 declaration of war. Large numbers of the region's young men enlisted in the army.

Despite military deficiencies and lack of national unity, the Madison administration pushed forward into battle, targeting Canada, with only five thousand regular British soldiers. U.S. military leaders planned three advances: one from Lake Champlain to Montreal, a second at the Niagara River, and the third from Fort Detroit east through Upper Canada (see Map 8.3). With American victories, they hoped, Canada would fall, forcing Britain to recognize U.S. rights.

The Americans moved first in the West, where they expected more support from local militia than from New England. General William Hull received orders to lead about two thousand troops against Fort Malden, opposite Detroit, under

Doing History Native Americans and the New Republic

The following documents give two views—among many others—of U.S. westward expansion during the first decade of the nineteenth century. The entries from the journals of Meriwether Lewis and William Clark record information about their initial contact with Native Americans along the upper Missouri River. Tecumseh, in contrast, presents the case of Native Americans of the Great Lakes region, who lost 2.5 million acres of land with the Treaty of Fort Wayne (1809).

The Journals of Meriwether Lewis and William Clark, *1805*

[Clark] 14th January 1805 Monday.

This morning early a number of Indians men women children dogs &c. &c. passed down on the ice to join those that passed yesterday, we sent Sergt Pryor and five men with those Indians to hunt (several men with the venereal caught from the Mandan women). One of our hunters sent out several days [ago] arrived & informs that one man (Whitehouse) is frost bit and can't walk home.

[Lewis] 8th February Friday 1805. This morning was fair wind S.E. the weather still warm and pleasant. Visited by the Black-Cat the principal chief of the Roop-tar-he, or upper Mandan village. This man possesses more integrity, firmness, intelligence and perspicuity of mind than any Indian I have met with in this quarter, and I think with a little management he may be made a useful agent in furthering the views of our government. The Black Cat presented me with a bow and apologized for not having completed the shield he had promised alleging that the weather had been too cold to permit his making it. I gave him some small shot 6 fishing-hooks and 2 yards of ribbon. His squaw also presented me with 2 pair of moccasins for which in return I gave a small looking glass and a couple of needles.

[Lewis] 11th February Monday 1805 . . . about five o'clock this evening one of the wives of Charbonneau [Sacagawea] was delivered of a fine boy. It is worthy of remark that this was the first child which this woman had borne, and as is common in such cases her labor was tedious and the pain violent; Mr Jessome informed me that he had frequently administered a small portion of the rattle of the rattle-snake, which he assured me had never

the command of British General Isaac Brock and reinforced by Tecumseh and his men. Hull moved too slowly, though, and not only failed to take Fort Malden, but also surrendered Detroit. The British and Native Americans then took control of much of the region by capturing Fort Michilimackinac, to the north, and Fort Dearborn, at the present site of Chicago. Another blow came for the United States in October when the army lost the Battle of Queenston, opposite Fort Niagara, after the New York militia refused to leave American soil to assist the regular troops. William Henry Harrison, commissioned a general, reinforced Fort Wayne against Indian attack, and undermined Tecumseh's war effort by destroying Indian towns and cornfields in Ohio, Indiana, and Illinois.

During the frustrating campaign against Canada, James Madison stood for reelection. His opponent was DeWitt Clinton, a New York Republican who ran as a Federalist. Clinton tried to gain support from both political parties by criticizing Madison's war effort, but in contrast to the army's failures in 1812, the tiny U.S. fleet had surprising success against the mighty Royal Navy. These victories, including the U.S.S. *Constitution*'s sinking of the British *Guerrière* in August, greatly bolstered public opinion. The president won by an electoral tally of 128 to 89; he obtained substantial Republican majorities in the House and Senate.

failed to produce the desired effect, that of hastening the birth of the child; having the rattle of a snake by me I gave it to him and he administered two rings of it to the woman. . . . Whether this medicine was truly the cause or not I shall not undertake to determine, but I was informed that she had not taken it more than ten minutes before she brought forth.

Source: Gary E. Moulton, ed., *The Journals of the Lewis and Clark Expedition*, vol. 3 (Lincoln: University of Nebraska Press, 1987).

Tecumseh Opposes Land Cessions, *1810*

It is true I am a Shawnee. My forefathers were warriors. Their son is a warrior. From them I only take my existence; from my tribe I take nothing. I am the maker of my own fortune; and oh! that I could make that of my red people, and of my country, as great as the conceptions of my mind, when I think of the Spirit that rules the universe. I would not then come to Governor Harrison, to ask him to tear the treaty, and to obliterate the landmark; but I would say to him, Sir, you have liberty to return to your own country. The being within, communing with the past ages, tells me, that once, nor until lately, there was no white man on this continent. That it then all belonged to red men, children of the same parents, placed on it by the Great Spirit that made them, to keep it, to traverse it, to enjoy its production, and to fill it with the same race. Once a happy race. Since made miserable by the white people, who are never contented, but always encroaching. The way, and the only way to check and stop this evil, is, for all the red men to unite in claiming a common and equal right in the land, as it was at first, and should be yet; for it never was divided, but belongs to all, for the use of each.

Source: Albert L. Hurtado and Peter Iverson, eds., *Major Problems in American Indian History*, 2nd ed. (Boston: Houghton Mifflin Company, 2001), 202–203.

QUESTIONS for REFLECTION

1. What kind of interaction occurred between the Mandans and the Lewis and Clark Expedition?
2. Can we gain understanding of the Mandans' opinions of the explorers from these diary entries? Why or why not?
3. What is Tecumseh's view of the experience of Native Americans as a result of European American settlement?

Victories and Losses, 1813–1814

Despite the naval successes, on land 1813 began with another disaster for the Americans: the British and Native Americans killed or captured nearly an entire force of nine hundred troops at Frenchtown, south of Detroit. The U.S. army managed to hold Fort Meigs and Fort Stephenson in northern Ohio but needed naval support to destroy British control of Lake Erie. The United States began building ships at Presque Isle, Pennsylvania (now Erie), and on September 10, 1813, Oliver Hazard Perry defeated the British squadron at Put-in-Bay, establishing American dominance of the lake. This naval victory cleared the way for General Harrison to attack Fort Malden, from which the British and Indians hastily retreated toward Niagara. The Americans caught up with them at Moraviantown on October 5, winning a decisive victory known as the Battle of the Thames. Tecumseh died on the battlefield; his brother Tenskwatawa continued to fight alongside the British during the rest of the war, but with little success. To the east, the U.S. Army had burned York (Toronto), the capital of Upper Canada. But the Americans met defeat in an offensive against Montreal and lost Fort Niagara.

(The Granger Collection, New York)

Burning of Washington, D.C., 1814. A colored engraving of the British destruction of Washington produced two years later in England.

In the Mississippi Territory, the nativist Red Sticks waged civil war against Creek leaders who accommodated Anglo-American demands for land. The fratricidal conflict became a war against the United States in July 1813 when 180 American militia struck a much smaller group of Red Sticks. A month later, the nativists killed about 250 settlers who had taken cover in a stockade called Fort Mims. The Red Sticks, with four thousand warriors but lacking adequate arms, faced overwhelming odds against the combined forces of U.S. troops, accommodationist Creeks, and Cherokee allies. Three armies entered Red Stick territory, destroying homes and dispersing families. The turning point came in March 1814 when General **Andrew Jackson**, with three thousand militia and Indian allies, defeated a thousand Red Sticks in the Battle of Horseshoe Bend, killing eight hundred of them. The surviving militants escaped to Florida, where they joined nativist Seminoles and continued to fight, while the Creeks were forced to cede more than 20 million acres of land.

Jackson, Andrew (1767–1845) U.S. general and seventh president of the United States (1829–1837). In the War of 1812, he defeated the Red Sticks at Horseshoe Bend (1814) and the British at New Orleans (1815). As president he denied the right of individual states to nullify federal laws and increased presidential powers.

In the summer of 1814, the British turned greater attention to the war in America, having defeated Napoleon in April. They sent ten thousand experienced redcoats to Canada, threatening New York until a American naval victory on Lake Champlain in September cut short the British invasion. Britain also sent forces to Chesapeake Bay, where in August they attacked the nearly defenseless Washington, D.C. Redcoats burned the Capitol and the president's mansion shortly after the Madison household fled, saving official documents and the Gilbert Stuart portrait of George Washington. The enemy promptly left the capital, and the U.S. government returned.

The British then assaulted Baltimore. Despite heavy bombardment of Fort McHenry by the Royal Navy, the redcoats failed to take the city. James Monroe, by then secretary of war as well as secretary of state, took credit for Baltimore's stand. Francis Scott Key memorialized the scene of flaming rockets and exploding bombs in his poem "The Star Spangled Banner," which was later set to the tune of a popular English song and became the national anthem in the early twentieth century. The British sailed south to the Gulf Coast, intending to block off the Mississippi River. In late 1814, Andrew Jackson captured Pensacola, Florida, and then organized the defense of New Orleans.

1814: The Hartford Convention and the Treaty of Ghent

Over the course of the war, sentiment had grown in New England for secession as the British tightened their blockade of the region and occupied the Maine coast. In late 1814, a group of Federalists organized the **Hartford Convention** to remedy their loss of power within the Union. The Hartford delegates called for significant amendments to the Constitution: removal of the three-fifths clause that counted slaves in apportioning delegates in the House of Representatives and electoral college; a two-thirds majority in Congress to declare war and admit new states; a one-term limit on the president and ban on residents from the same state succeeding one another in the office (obviously targeted at Virginia); and prohibition of naturalized citizens, who were largely Republican, from federal positions. However, these proposals fell on deaf ears when news of a peace treaty arrived from Europe. An outpouring of postwar patriotism eroded the stature of the Federalist party.

Hartford Convention (1814) Gathering of Federalists in 1814 that called for significant amendments to the Constitution and attempted to damage the Republican party. The Treaty of Ghent and Andrew Jackson's victory at New Orleans annulled any recommendation of the convention.

Peace came as both the British and the United States recognized that they had little hope of victory. Britain might continue its blockade and smother U.S. commerce, but to what purpose? Conquest of the former colonies, now expanded into the West, would require huge expenditures of manpower and funds. British victory at New Orleans would plug the Mississippi, but in late 1814 success was still uncertain. As the British considered terms for peace, news arrived that the Americans had repelled the offensives at Lake Champlain and Baltimore. Although some Britons desired revenge, more wanted to resume trade.

Madison authorized John Quincy Adams, Albert Gallatin, Henry Clay, and two others to meet a British peace delegation in August 1814 at Ghent, in what is now Belgium. After several months of stalemate, the negotiators agreed on Christmas Eve, 1814, to return to the status quo at the outbreak of war. The British dropped their demands for part of Maine and an independent Indian territory north of the Ohio River, and the Americans stopped insisting that the British renounce impressment, which had ceased.

Battle of New Orleans, 1815

Bad weather in the Atlantic delayed the ship bringing news of the Treaty of Ghent until February. In the meantime, British forces prepared to move against the Gulf Coast. A fleet of sixty ships and fourteen thousand men planned to attack Mobile, seize control of the coast and the rivers, and then move against New Orleans.

For Americans unaware of the peace treaty, such a plan posed a serious threat. New Orleans, distant and disconnected from the cities of the East Coast, lay vulnerable to invasion. A British invasion threatened to bring free and enslaved African Americans, French and Spanish settlers, Native Americans, and even pirates into the conflict throughout the Gulf territories, igniting rebellions against white farmers and traders. The commander in charge of the American forces, Andrew Jackson, was especially sensitive to the dangers settlers faced on the Gulf Coast. A Tennessee lawyer, planter, and militia leader, he had defeated the Red Sticks at Horseshoe Bend. He repelled the British at Mobile, then raced to New Orleans before the British troops could arrive. The Americans got there first, in December 1814. When six hundred free blacks volunteered to help defend the city, Jackson gratefully accepted their offer.

A series of attacks by the British damaged the American forces but did not take New Orleans. The British general in charge, Sir Edward Pakenham, unleashed a frontal assault on January 8, 1815. Jackson's troops, dug in behind earthworks, fired directly into the charging British troops; wave after wave of the onslaught fell as American troops took turns firing and reloading. In less than an hour, it was over: Pakenham and two of his generals lay dead, along with more than two thousand of their troops. The Americans suffered only thirteen dead and a few dozen wounded or missing. Nearly a month later, word of Jackson's remarkable success reached the nation's capital. "ALMOST INCREDIBLE VICTORY!!!" headlines trumpeted. Nine days later word of the Treaty of Ghent, ratified two weeks before the Battle of New Orleans, arrived in Washington. The Atlantic world was at peace once again.

CHAPTER REVIEW, 1800–1815

SUMMARY

- In the late eighteenth and early nineteenth centuries, new Christian sects such as the Shakers were founded, Native Americans and whites experienced religious revivals, and African Americans established their own churches.
- Free African Americans developed distinctive cultural institutions and networks in northern cities. In the South, slave rebellions caused widespread anxiety among the white population and led to the development of harsher slave codes.
- In 1800, Thomas Jefferson was elected president. Although committed to the republican ideal of limited government, Jefferson relaxed his strict construction of the Constitution to extend the republic's landholdings through the Louisiana Purchase.
- The impressment of American men into the British navy caused tensions between the two nations, which Americans sought to diffuse through economic sanctions such as the Embargo of 1807.
- Between 1812 and 1815, Britain and America engaged in the War of 1812. Although the war did not bring significant gains to either side, it inspired nationalism in the United States.

IDENTIFICATIONS

Second Great Awakening
Ann Lee
Universalists
Handsome Lake
Tenskwatawa
Richard Allen
St. Domingue
Convention of 1800
midnight appointments
John Marshall
Marbury v. Madison
Twelfth Amendment
Louisiana Purchase
Lewis and Clark Expedition
Sacagawea
Embargo Act
Tecumseh
William Henry Harrison
Andrew Jackson
Hartford Convention

MAKING CONNECTIONS: LOOKING AHEAD

With the War of 1812 behind them, Americans expanded westward, building turnpikes and canals to facilitate trade. As will be discussed in Chapter 9, under President James Monroe, the government entered a period of reduced factionalism.

1. What was the impact of U.S. expansion on Native Americans during the period from 1815 to 1828?
2. Why were the years of Monroe's administration known as the "Era of Good Feelings"?
3. How did the Supreme Court assist economic development?

RECOMMENDED READINGS

Andrews, Dee E. *The Methodists and Revolutionary America, 1760–1800: The Shaping of an Evangelical Culture* (2000). An excellent study, including important chapters on the role of women and African Americans.

Dowd, Gregory Evans. *A Spirited Resistance: The North American Indian Struggle for Unity, 1745–1815* (1992). Demonstrates the significance of religion in Native American resistance.

Ellis, Joseph J. *American Sphinx: The Character of Thomas Jefferson* (1996). A highly readable study of a complex president.

Freeman, Joanne B. *Affairs of Honor: National Politics in the Early Republic* (2001). A provocative study of the means of political conflict, including dueling.

Kukla, Jon. *A Wilderness So Immense: The Louisiana Purchase and the Destiny of America* (2003). Examines the significance of the Louisiana Purchase within international and domestic politics.

McCoy, Drew R. *The Elusive Republic: Political Economy in Jeffersonian America* (1980). Insightful exploration of Jeffersonian politics and thought.

Nash, Gary B. *Forging Freedom: The Formation of Philadelphia's Black Community, 1720–1840* (1988). Insightful study of the challenges of freedom for one community of African Americans in the North.

Smelser, Marshall. *The Democratic Republic, 1801–1815* (1992). A useful, lively overview of the period.

Smith, Billy G., ed. *Down and Out in Early America* (2004). Essays spanning the seventeenth to early nineteenth centuries on the meaning and depth of poverty for many Americans.

Waldstreicher, David. *In the Midst of Perpetual Fetes: The Making of American Nationalism, 1776–1820* (1997). Study of popular political culture, including the ways in which African Americans and women participated in celebrations yet were excluded from voting.

CourseMate Go to the CourseMate website at www.cengagebrain.com for additional study tools and review materials for this chapter.

PASSAGES 1815 to 1855

The United States redefined itself during the forty years after 1815. The boundaries of the nation, the character of its population, the nature of its economy, and the religious beliefs of its people all took new shape. Some of the changes confirmed what the architects of the young nation had expected several decades before; other changes proved to be surprises and the bitterest of disappointments. The speed and scale of transformation astonished everyone.

In 1815, the young United States held only eighteen states, with Louisiana standing exposed at the western boundary, Florida in the hands of the Spanish, and an unsettled line between Canada and the United States. The western half of the continent remained only vaguely known to Anglo-Americans and seemed too far away to be of importance any time soon. Even within the country's sketchy borders, Native Americans populated large and rich areas in both the North and the South.

Four decades later, the continental boundaries of the nation had expanded beyond recognition. Florida had come into the Union from Spain. War with Mexico had brought in vast territories from Texas to California. Negotiation with Great Britain had defined the northern boundary from Maine to Oregon. Military and economic pressure on the Native American nations had driven them across the Mississippi River. A new state entered the Union about every two and a half years; by the end of the 1850s, thirty-three states, including two on the Pacific coast, claimed a place in the nation.

The population exploded. The number of Americans grew from 8.4 million in 1815 to 31.4 million by the end of the 1850s. Nearly 4 million of those people were held in slavery, while 3 million had crossed the Atlantic from Europe in a mixture of hope and desperation. People spread out across the expanse of the burgeoning country, establishing farms and towns far from the older cities of the East. About half the population of an average town moved every ten years. By the end of the period, the United States claimed 5 million more people than England, and the new country boasted eight cities of more than 150,000 inhabitants—more than any other country in the world.

Large changes altered the scale of life, tying people together as few could have imagined in 1815. Steamboats transformed water transportation in the 1810s, canals boomed in the 1820s, and railroads arrived in the 1830s. The United States claimed over thirty-five thousand miles of railroad track by the end of the era. In the 1840s, the first telegraph wires carried information from one city to another in a clatter of keys; by the late 1850s, telegraph wires stretched across the Atlantic Ocean. Novels sold tens of thousands of copies in a few months. Newspapers, confined to just a few major cities in 1815, became staples of American life in the 1830s and 1840s, read and published in hundreds of communities of every size. Daguerreotypes and colorful lithographs decorated homes that had been empty of pictures a generation earlier.

The United States became integrated ever more tightly into the international economy. The capacity of ships arriving in American ports doubled in the 1830s, doubled again in the 1840s, and then again in the 1850s. American vessels plied the Atlantic with cargoes of cotton and wheat for England and Europe. Clipper ships sailed around South America and into the Pacific, carrying prospectors and immigrants along with tea. The United States, anxious about

(Library of Congress)

St. Louis, Missouri. Spurred by the growth of trade and agricultural production in the West and served by the new steamboat traffic, small towns along the Mississippi River and its tributaries quickly grew into booming young cities like St. Louis.

European intervention in Latin America and the Caribbean, claimed the hemisphere as a place under its jurisdiction and protection.

Americans created lodges, clubs, and societies of every sort. Baptists, Methodists, and Presbyterians vied with one another for converts. Reform groups emerged to stamp out alcohol and war, encourage education and humane treatment of the unfortunate, improve diet and health, and end slavery. Women accounted for many members of these organizations, lending their energy and intelligence to activities beyond the home. Political parties mobilized nearly all adult white men, sweeping them up as Democrats, Whigs, Free-Soilers, Know-Nothings, and Republicans. Men swore allegiance to their party, expressing their passions and beliefs in slogans, songs, and parades. On election days, as many as eight out of ten eligible voters went to the polls, publicly proclaiming support for their candidates.

The expansion of the United States was the expansion of the largest and most powerful slave society in the modern world. Slavery grew stronger with each passing decade, embracing an ever larger part of the continent to the south and west, holding more people within its bonds, accounting for a larger share of the nation's exports. As the years passed, the discussions in churches, reform organizations, and political parties increasingly turned to sectional conflict. Rivalry and distrust between the North and the South infected everything in the public life of the country.

The years between 1815 and 1855, then, did not witness a smooth passage through an "industrial revolution" or "growth of the common man" or "westward expansion." Rather, these years marked a passage filled with rapids and countercurrents and waterfalls. Panics and depressions, internal and external wars, massive migration and immigration, freedom and slavery: all came tumultuously.

CHRONOLOGY

	1815	1823	1831
POLITICS AND DIPLOMACY	**1815:** Battle of New Orleans **1816:** Monroe elected president "Era of Good Feelings" begins Clay calls for "American System" Indiana admitted to the Union **1817:** Mississippi admitted to the Union **1818:** Jackson invades Florida Illinois admitted to the Union **1819:** Transcontinental (or Adams-Onís) treaty with Spain Alabama admitted to the Union **1820:** Missouri Compromise Monroe elected president Maine admitted to the Union **1821:** Missouri admitted to the Union **1822:** Denmark Vesey rebellion planned in Charleston	**1823:** Monroe Doctrine **1824:** Contested election of John Quincy Adams **1828:** Tariff of Abominations Calhoun's *South Carolina Exposition* Election of Andrew Jackson **1829:** Mexico tries to abolish slavery in Texas **1830:** Indian Removal Act Anti-Masonic Party holds first national party convention **1831:** Nat Turner's rebellion Jackson reorganizes cabinet	**1832:** Nullification crisis Virginia debates over slavery Jackson reelected **1833:** Force bill against South Carolina Compromise Tariff Slavery abolished in British Empire **1834:** Whig party organized **1835:** Arkansas admitted to the Union Revolution breaks out in Texas Abolitionists' postal campaign War against Seminoles and runaway slaves in Florida begins **1836:** Congress imposes gag rule Battle of the Alamo; Texas Republic established
SOCIETY AND CULTURE	**1816:** American Colonization Society founded American Bible Society founded **1819:** Auburn penitentiary established	**1824:** Lafayette's visit American Sunday School Union founded **1825:** American Tract Society founded **1829:** David Walker's *Appeal* **1830:** *The Book of Mormon* Charles Finney's revivals begin in Rochester, New York	**1831:** Garrison's *The Liberator* Mormons migrate from New York to Ohio **1833:** Formation of American Anti-Slavery Society **1837:** Grimké sisters lecture to mixed audiences Horace Mann becomes first secretary of Massachusetts' Board of Education Ralph Waldo Emerson, "The American Scholar" **1839:** Daguerreotypes introduced to the United States
ECONOMICS AND TECHNOLOGY	**1815:** *Enterprise* first steamboat from New Orleans to Pittsburgh **1816:** Second Bank of the United States chartered **1818:** Erie Canal begun National Road completed **1819:** *Dartmouth College v. Woodward* *McCulloch v. Maryland* Financial panic and depression	**1824:** *Gibbons v. Ogden* **1825:** Completion of Erie Canal **1828:** Tariff of Abominations	**1831:** John Bull locomotive begins railroad operation **1832:** Bank War begins **1833:** Compromise Tariff **1834:** National Trades Union formed Cyrus McCormick patents reaper **1837:** Financial panic *Charles River Bridge v. Warren Bridge* **1839:** Depression worsens

1840	1845	1850
1840: William Henry Harrison elected president Frederick Douglass escapes from slavery American Anti-Slavery Society splits James G. Birney runs for president as candidate for Liberty Party **1841:** Harrison dies; John Tyler becomes president *Amistad* case heard before the Supreme Court **1844:** James K. Polk asserts the United States' claim to "all Oregon"	**1845:** Texas and Florida admitted to the Union **1846:** Mexican war begins Stephen Kearny occupies Santa Fe; Zachary Taylor takes Monterey Border between Canada and United States established at 49th parallel Wilmot Proviso ignites sectional conflict Bear Flag Republic in California proclaimed by John C. Frémont **1847:** Taylor defeats Santa Anna at Buena Vista; Winfield Scott captures Vera Cruz and Mexico City **1848:** Treaty of Guadalupe Hidalgo Attempt to buy Cuba from Spain Free-Soil Party runs Van Buren for president Zachary Taylor elected president **1849:** California seeks admission to the Union	**1850:** Nashville Convention attempts to unify South Taylor dies; Millard Fillmore becomes president Compromise of 1850, includes controversial Fugitive Slave Law **1851:** Woman's rights convention in Akron, Ohio Indiana state constitution excludes free blacks **1852:** Franklin Pierce elected president **1853:** Gadsden Purchase **1854:** Know-Nothings win unexpected victories Whig Party collapses Republican Party founded Kansas-Nebraska Act Ostend Manifesto encourages acquisition of Cuba
1840: Washingtonian temperance movement emerges **1841:** Brook Farm founded P.T. Barnum opens the American Museum **1842:** Edgar Allan Poe, "The Murders in the Rue Morgue" **1844:** Methodist Episcopal church divides over slavery Edgar Allan Poe, "The Raven"	**1846:** Hiram Powers completes statue *The Greek Slave* **1847:** Mormons reach Great Salt Lake **1848:** Seneca Falls Convention Oneida community established	**1850:** Nathaniel Hawthorne, *The Scarlet Letter* **1851:** Herman Melville, *Moby Dick* Maine adopts prohibition **1852:** Harriet Beecher Stowe, *Uncle Tom's Cabin* **1854:** Henry David Thoreau, *Walden*
1840: Congress passes Independent Treasury Act **1841:** California sees arrival of first wagon train Oregon fever **1843:** Oregon sees arrival of first wagon trains **1844:** Baltimore–Washington telegraph line Samuel F. B. Morse patents the telegraph	**1848:** Gold discovered in California Regular steamship trips between Liverpool and New York City **1849:** Forty-niners race to California Rising cotton prices invigorate South	**1854:** High point of immigration Railroad reaches Mississippi River

9 Exploded Boundaries

1815–1828

MAKING CONNECTIONS

LOOKING BACK

Chapter 8 considered the religious context in which Americans—native whites, African Americans, new immigrants, and Indians—shaped their communities and interpreted political affairs. The Republican administrations of Thomas Jefferson and James Madison, while taking action for national expansion and defense, reflected the desire of many Americans for limited government. Before starting Chapter 9, you should be able to answer the following questions:

1. Why was religion so important to Americans on the frontier and in developing cities?
2. Was Jefferson's administration consistent with the Republican principles he had stated prior to his election? Why or why not?
3. Did Madison make the right decision to go to war against Great Britain? Why or why not?
4. Why did the Federalists decline?

The sudden climax of the War of 1812 surprised everyone. The leaders of the United States had wondered whether a large and lightly governed republic could survive in the rough-and-tumble world of international conflict. When the new country held its own in the war against England, the most powerful military force on earth, Americans gained a new confidence.

James Monroe, another in a long line of Virginia Republican presidents, easily won the national election of 1816. He bore the reputation of being an honest and dependable man, though less intellectually distinguished than Jefferson or Madison. Monroe and his wife set a new tone for the presidency, with greater emphasis on style, entertaining, and celebrating the new national stature of the United States. The Monroes had the executive mansion painted a brilliant white to cover the smoke stains from its burning during the war with England; the residence became known as the "White House." Newly secure, the United States entered a period of territorial expansion and economic growth no one could have foreseen just a few years earlier.

❖ New Borders

The borders of the United States had been fluid and in doubt throughout the nation's brief history. In every direction, other nations and peoples contested American boundaries. To the north, English power loomed in Canada. To the west, American Indians resisted efforts by whites to buy or seize their ancestral lands. To the south, the Spanish held on in Florida. Moreover, many states had little economic dealing with one another, trading instead with England, Europe, and the Caribbean. As a result, states defended sharply conflicting policies, and their economies did not connect with one another very effectively. The peace after 1815 provided an opportunity for the United States to establish its borders more securely and to integrate itself more fully.

Monroe, James (1758–1831) Fifth president of the United States (1817–1825), whose administration was marked by the acquisition of Florida (1819), the Missouri Compromise (1820), and the Monroe Doctrine (1823).

Native Peoples

President Monroe worked to establish clearer borders for the young nation. He succeeded in his dealing with Great Britain when the two countries clarified the boundaries between the United States and Canada. The Rush-Bagot Treaty of 1817 calmed conflict on the Great Lakes, and the Convention of 1818 fixed the border with Canada at the **forty-ninth parallel** (see Map 9.1).

forty-ninth parallel Line of latitude established as the border between the United States and Canada by the Treaty of 1818; extended to the Pacific by President Polk's secret negotiation of the Oregon Treaty in 1846.

Relations with Native Americans proved much more challenging. By the early nineteenth century, many Native Americans had lived in contact with European culture for more than two hundred years. They had long combined their ancient practices with newer ones. The intermingling worked both ways, for considerable numbers of English and Scots traders lived among native peoples or their trading partners. Many men of European background adopted Native American dress and language and married into native families. African Americans, too, often took refuge with the Creeks and **Seminoles.**

Seminoles Native American people made up of various primarily Creek groups who moved into northern Florida during the eighteenth and nineteenth centuries, later inhabiting the Everglades region as well.

The removal of the British troops after the War of 1812 dealt a strong blow to the hopes of the Native Americans. Now that the alliance with England had been destroyed, the United States quickly sought to exert firm control over the eastern half of the continent. Andrew Jackson, triumphant general in the war, was placed in charge of negotiating with the Creek, Cherokee, Chickasaw, and Choctaw nations of Alabama, Florida, and Mississippi after the peace of 1815. Jackson used heavy-handed treaties to force Native Americans from their former lands.

CHAPTER TIMELINE 1808 — 1812 — 1816 — 1820 — 1824 — 1828

POLITICS AND DIPLOMACY

- (1809)–1817 James Madison Presidency
- 1817–1825 James Monroe presidency
- 1820 Missouri Compromise admits Missouri without restriction on slavery
- 1822 Denmark Vesey Rebellion planned
- 1823 Monroe Doctrine asserts the Americas are free of Eurpean colonization
- 1825–(1829) John Quincy Adams presidency

SOCIETY AND CULTURE

- 1816 American Colonization Society founded
- 1819 Auburn penitentiary is established
- 1824 Lafayette received as a hero in the United States

ECONOMICS AND TECHNOLOGY

- 1815 First steamboat from New Orleans to Pittsburgh
- 1818–1825 Erie Canal construction
- 1818 National Road completed to Wheeling
- 1819 Financial panic and depression

MAP 9.1
Redrawing the Nation's Boundaries
A series of land purchases and treaties expanded the nation's boundaries significantly between 1783 and 1819.

Many resisted the removal, objecting that the treaties Jackson had extracted had been signed by leaders who had no authority to make such concessions.

The various native peoples identified themselves by the location of their villages, their languages, and their traditional enemies, and they often fought with one another, but whites nevertheless insisted on lumping these diverse people into groups that could be more easily dealt with. Jackson and other officials relied on particular Native Americans as allies in war but then deliberately punished all the tribes in the region regardless of earlier promises. Such policies weakened the power of native leaders and left their people little choice but to accept bribes and annual grants of money in return for their lands. As soon as Jackson managed to secure lands from the Creeks, Cherokees, and Chickasaws, white settlers rushed into the territories, hungry for the fertile land and the fortunes it could build (see Map 9.2 and *Doing History: The Future of Native Americans*). Such incursions occurred across millions of acres in North Carolina, Kentucky, and Tennessee, as well as in Alabama, Mississippi, and Georgia; in each state, the native peoples were pushed to the hilly and mountainous lands least desirable for farming.

As in the South, white settlement in the Northwest was made possible by the subjugation of the native peoples. After northern Native Americans' disastrous losses in the War of 1812, they posed little threat to white settlers. The U.S. government quickly established a series of forts throughout the Northwest to intimidate any Native Americans in the area and to make sure that the British did not regain a foothold. The growing numbers of white farmers made it difficult for Native Americans to hunt for a living.

At the encouragement of the federal government, some Native Americans adapted to white ways. The Cherokees, in particular, won praise for their customs that whites considered "civilized." One Cherokee, Sequoyah, devised an alphabet in his people's language in 1821. The wealthiest Cherokees purchased African American slaves and built substantial cotton plantations. No matter

MAP 9.2
Lands Ceded by Native Americans
The United States negotiated one treaty after another with Native Americans in the decades after 1815, acquiring land and pushing the natives of these areas to the west.

what accommodations they made, however, they suffered repeated conflicts with whites, who relied on sheer numbers, trickery, violence, and the law to dispossess them of their land claims.

The Spanish in Florida

Like the Native Americans, the Spanish who remained in Florida after 1815 had become vulnerable. Without the assistance of the British, they found it nearly impossible to resist American incursions into their territory. White Americans, for their part, felt they had a right to drive the Spanish from the mainland, in part because Anglo Protestants had a long tradition of distrusting the Catholic, monarchical Spanish. To make relations even more volatile, sixty miles from the southern border of the United States stood the so-called Negro Fort near Pensacola, occupied by runaway slaves and their Indian allies.

Spain was eager, in fact, to be rid of the fort as well, but it did not have the military power to overthrow it. The Spanish feared that Jackson would use the

Doing History The Future of Native Americans

In the first document, from 1824, a prestigious religious group argues before the U.S. Congress that American Indians have suffered for generations at the hands of the United States. The only way to atone for these "national sins," the commissioners argue, is to educate the Indian people in the ways of white Americans. The document shows the goodwill that many white Americans held toward the Native Americans—and the limits of their understanding of the Indians' culture.

In the second document, from 1836, American Indians speak for themselves. In this case, a delegation of Cherokees protests a treaty that would remove them from their homes in the east to the Indian Territory of Oklahoma. They plead that they have done everything white Americans have asked.

The American Society for Improving Indian Tribes, *1824*

The history of our intercourse with Indians, from the first settlement of this country, contains many facts honorable to the character of our ancestors, and of our nation—many, also, too many, which are blots on this character. . . . We here allude to the neglect with which these aboriginal tribes have been treated in regard to their civil, moral, and religious improvement. . . . It is desirable that our Indians should receive such an education as has been mentioned, we conceive, because the civilized is preferable to the savage state; because the Bible, and the religion therein revealed to us, with its ordinances, are blessings of infinite and everlasting value and which the Indians do not now enjoy. It is also desirable as an act of common humanity. . . . There is no place on the earth to which they can migrate, and live in the savage and hunter state. The Indian tribes must, therefore, be progressively civilized, or *successively* perish.

Source: American Board of Commissioners for Foreign Missions, Memorial to the Senate and the House of Representatives, in *American Society for Improving Indian Tribes, First Annual Report*, 1824, pp. 66–68.

Memorial and Protest of the Cherokee Nation, *1836*

The Cherokees were happy and prosperous under a scrupulous observance of treaty stipulations by the government of the United States, and from the fostering hand extended over them, they made rapid advances in civilization, morals, and in the arts and sciences. Little did they anticipate, that when taught to think and feel as the American citizen, and to have with him a common interest, they were to be *despoiled by their guardian,* to become strangers and wanderers in the land of their fathers, forced to return to the savage life, and to seek a new home in the wilds of the far west, and that without their consent. An instrument purporting to be a treaty with the Cherokee people, has recently been made public by the President of the United States, that will have such an operation, if carried into effect. This instrument, the delegation aver before the civilized world, and in the presence of Almighty God, is fraudulent, false upon its face, made by unauthorized individuals, without the sanction, and against the wishes, of the great body of the Cherokee people.

Source: *Memorial and Protest of the Cherokee Nation*, June 22, 1839. Executive Document No. 286, 24th Congress, 1st session, pp. 1–2.

QUESTIONS for REFLECTION

1. Are the two documents making the same arguments? What assumptions underlie both of them?
2. Could the desires of the U.S. government, and the white men it represented, have been reconciled to the desires of the American Indians? Explain your reasoning.
3. What argument could the U.S. government make in response to the Cherokee protest?

refuge as a pretext to invade Florida. Indeed, in 1816 the Americans sent an expedition against the fort; a projectile hit a powder magazine, killing 270 men, women, and children inside. Two years later, Jackson's forces also punished groups of Seminoles, who, with their Creek allies, had launched raids against white settlers in south Georgia and then fled into Florida. Although his authorization from Washington was doubtful, Jackson invaded Spanish territory and executed a Creek prophet and two British men he accused of abetting the Indian cause. While some in Congress called for hearings to punish Jackson for his unauthorized attack, the hearings had little effect except to make Jackson suspicious of the men in power in Washington.

Meanwhile, American and Spanish officials negotiated. The U.S. delegation was led by the brilliant and tenacious John Quincy Adams, son of the former president. With Jackson's military victories giving force to his words, Adams held out until the Spanish, in return for $5 million in compensation for private claims, ceded to the United States all territories east of the Mississippi River. In this, the **Adams-Onís Treaty** of 1819, the Spanish kept the vast territory from Texas to present-day California, while the United States claimed a northern border that ran unbroken to Oregon and the Pacific Ocean. Adams called his handiwork the Transcontinental Treaty, for it stretched the borders of the United States from the Atlantic to the Pacific (see Map 9.1).

Adams-Onís Treaty (1819) Negotiated by John Quincy Adams, this treaty gave the United States control of Spanish Florida and the Oregon Territory, and recognized Spanish authority over southwestern territories from Texas to California.

❖ Building a National Economy

Leading members of the Republican Party, long known for their opposition to federal power, began to view the central government more favorably after the victory over Britain in 1815. Young Republicans such as **Henry Clay** of Kentucky and **John C. Calhoun** of South Carolina urged Congress and the president to encourage the growth of enterprise with the aid of the government, creating roads, canals, a strong navy, and a national bank. The future of the country, Clay and Calhoun believed, lay in commerce and industry. These nationalists dubbed their vision the **American System** and called for tariffs that would protect American manufacturing, federal roads to tie the newly expanded markets and farms together, and a system of canals to connect the United States' abundant rivers and lakes.

Clay, Henry (1777–1852) American statesman and a founder of the Whig party. He pushed the Missouri Compromise through the U.S. House of Representatives (1820) in an effort to reconcile free and slave states and served as secretary of state under John Quincy Adams (1825–1829).

Calhoun, John C. (1782–1850) Vice president of the United States (1825–1832) under John Quincy Adams and Andrew Jackson. In his political philosophy he maintained that the states had the right to nullify federal legislation that they deemed unconstitutional.

American System Political program developed by Henry Clay and John C. Calhoun to strengthen the federal government and promote commerce and industry through a national bank, a strong navy, federally sponsored internal improvement projects, and protective tariffs.

Banks, Corporations, and Law

No other country needed credit more than the United States. Because far too little cash was spread across its vast and growing territory, much business within the country rested on nothing more than trust and promises. Credit relations became tangled and fragile; the fall of one borrower could bring down a chain of lenders. Throughout the years before and during the War of 1812, states had chartered banks to help alleviate the problems caused by a shortage of cash. More than two hundred such banks had been founded by 1815 and nearly four hundred by 1818, issuing notes that served as currency in cash-starved areas.

Many influential men, including the recently elected President Monroe, supported a new national bank to stabilize the economy and distribute scarce money more uniformly. Advocates of the bank argued that the notes of state banks varied far too much in soundness and value, making the economic system dangerously unstable. The expanding country's economic system needed a central institution to coordinate the flow of money. Accordingly, in 1816 Congress chartered the

Second Bank of the United States (1816–1836) New national bank created to stabilize the economy and distribute scarce money across the country. President Jackson believed the bank had too much power, and he vetoed the rechartering of the bank in 1836.

Second Bank of the United States. Based in Philadelphia, it was authorized to establish branches wherever it wished, and handled the funds of the federal treasury without fees. The new national bank was an amalgam of public and private enterprise: the federal government deposited its funds in the bank and appointed a fifth of the directors, but the bank ran as a private business. The bank pumped large amounts of paper currency into the system in an attempt to feed the voracious hunger of the postwar economy, especially in the new states of the West, where speculation in land fueled demands for access to easy credit.

The local, state, and federal courts also encouraged the growth of business after the peace of 1815. Those who wanted to dam rivers for factories or build roads enjoyed increasing precedence over farmers and landowners threatened by floods, fires, or disruption caused by development. The courts assumed that the public good from the growth of business outweighed the stability favored by older notions of justice. Because many people bitterly protested this shift in emphasis, state legislatures sometimes sought to curb the power of business interests.

***Gibbons v. Ogden* (1824)** Supreme Court case that overturned a steamboat monopoly granted to Robert Fulton and Robert Livingston by New York State. The decision established federal authority over interstate navigation, as an extension of the federal power to regulate interstate commerce.

***McCulloch v. Maryland* (1819)** Supreme Court case striking down Maryland's efforts to tax notes issued by the Bank of the United States. The decision established the constitutionality of the bank, the supremacy of federal over state laws, and the principle that the federal government possessed powers implied by but not enumerated in the Constitution.

The Supreme Court under Chief Justice John Marshall issued a number of important decisions following the War of 1812 that also hastened economic development. One decision of 1819 made bankruptcy laws more uniform across the country; another, *Dartmouth College v. Woodward*, sheltered corporations from legislative interference; and yet another, ***Gibbons v. Ogden***, limited the rights of states to interfere in commerce with either special favors and monopolies or restrictive laws. "In all commercial regulations," Marshall pronounced, "we are one and the same people." In ***McCulloch v. Maryland***, which established the constitutionality of the Bank of the United States and protected it from state taxation, the Supreme Court ruled that the laws of the federal government "form the supreme law of the land." In this new legal environment, increasingly emulated by state courts and legislators, business flourished.

Roads, Canals, and Steamboats

National Road Federally sponsored road running from the Potomac River at Cumberland, Maryland, to the Ohio River at Wheeling, [West] Virginia, by 1818; extended to Vandalia, Illinois, by 1839.

Americans threw themselves into a frenzy of road and turnpike building after 1815. Investors, states, and even the federal government built thousands of miles of private roads, called turnpikes, that charged tolls to offset the roads' notoriously high maintenance costs. In 1818, the U.S. government opened the **National Road**, connecting the Potomac River at Cumberland, Maryland, with Wheeling, Virginia (now West Virginia), on the Ohio River. The road was the best that technology could provide at the time, with excellent bridges and a relatively smooth stone surface. It attracted so much business, however, that traffic jams slowed movement to a crawl, and the road quickly fell into poor condition.

Erie Canal First major American canal, stretching two hundred fifty miles from Lake Erie across the state of New York to Albany, where boats then traveled down the Hudson River to New York City. Begun in 1818, it was completed in 1825.

Private corporations and state governments began to plan dependable canals with controllable locks and a steady flow of water. In New York, an ambitious plan to connect the Hudson River with Lake Erie would result in a canal ten times longer than any other then in existence: 364 miles through swamps and solid rock. Year after year, the canal edged toward Lake Erie, transforming the countryside along the way. As soon as workers completed a segment, boats crowded on its waters, the tolls they paid financing the portions yet unfinished. The **Erie Canal** was completed in 1825, and by 1834, approximately nine boats passed through its major locks each minute.

Yet the Erie and other canals reached only a limited part of the vast North American continent. Rivers, especially the Mississippi, Missouri, and Ohio, offered faster and cheaper travel than over land, but they could be dangerously fast in some seasons and so slow as to be impassable in others. They often froze for months in the winter. Strong currents ran in only one direction. Not surprisingly,

(The Granger Collection, New York)

Erie Canal. The Erie Canal, connecting the Hudson River with Lake Erie, demanded a monumental engineering effort. It soon paid its way, however, as shippers and farmers rushed to use the new waterway.

people dreamed of using steam engines to drive riverboats. By 1811, Robert Fulton managed to build a steamship intrepid enough for the rigors of the Mississippi. Dozens of other craft soon joined his, competing with one another. In 1819, the journey from New Orleans to Louisville had been reduced from several months to fourteen days. "If any one had said this was possible thirty years ago," a journalist marveled, "we should have been ready to send him to a mad-house."

The increasing speed and frequency of the steamboats encouraged the growth of villages and towns along the rivers, such as Louisville, Pittsburgh, and Cincinnati.

❖ Regional Growth

As the American economy grew, different parts of the country began to specialize economically. Enslaved people in the South produced cotton that fueled the growth of the Northeast's textile factories and provided a large market for the farms of Ohio, Illinois, and Indiana.

The Creation of the Cotton South

The demand for cotton in England took off after the War of 1812, when cotton became, for the first time, the clothing of choice for large numbers of the world's people. No other place in the world was as prepared to supply the burgeoning demand for cotton as the American South. Small farmers as well as planters from the older states of the southern seaboard saw opportunity in the new states of Alabama and Mississippi further west (this region is sometimes called the Old Southwest). The steamboat and the cotton gin gave planters in the **Cotton South** powerful new tools, while the South's slaves could clear and cultivate land for new plantations far more quickly than would have been possible otherwise. Slave owners in the older states of the Atlantic seaboard, faced with what they considered a surplus of labor, eagerly sold slaves to planters moving to the "new" lands. As a result, the price of slaves, which had been stagnant or declining before 1815, began to rise.

Cotton South Southeastern United States; became a major cotton-producing region following the invention of the cotton gin in 1793 and the eviction of Native Americans from their lands in the decades after 1815. The spread of cotton cultivation led to the development of a vast interstate slave trade.

(The Granger Collection)

Cotton Cultivation. Planters used giant presses to force cotton into tight bales for easier transportation.

Hundreds of thousands of slaves endured forcible migration to the new states of the Old Southwest in the 1810s and 1820s. Some moved in groups along with their owners to new plantations, but many were sold as individuals to slave traders in the East, who then shipped or marched them to slave markets in New Orleans, Mobile, and other cities in the Southwest. This domestic trade, a complex network of traders, provisioners, and insurers, constituted as much as 13.5 percent of the total southern economy.

The movement west was not a simple march from the East; instead it followed the geographic and political contours of areas recently acquired from Native Americans. The first settlements began along the rivers that made it possible to transport cotton to market and in those places where the Creeks and other Native Americans exercised no claims. The new plantation districts were disconnected from one another, centering on Montgomery in Alabama, Jackson in Mississippi, and Memphis in Tennessee, all areas taken from the natives of the region since 1814. Small farmers occupied the land farthest from the rivers, supporting themselves with hunting and foraging as well as with growing small amounts of cotton. Young planters, lawyers and newspaper editors headed out for the Southwest as well, eager to make their mark. They sought to build a world as much as possible like those of Virginia or Carolina, only more prosperous. The combined population of Alabama, Mississippi, and Louisiana more than tripled between 1810 and 1820.

Emergence of the Old Northwest

The area west of the Appalachians, north of the Ohio, and east of the Mississippi—the Old Northwest—was growing even faster than the Southwest. "Old America seems to be breaking up, and moving westward," one man wrote in 1817 as he watched people move down the Ohio River. In the first two decades of the new century, the trans-Appalachian population grew from about 300,000 inhabitants to more than 2 million. This immigration in the North bore considerable similarities to its southern counterpart. Many of the settlers to the Old Northwest came from the states of the Upper South; large parts of southern Ohio, Indiana, and Illinois were settled by people from Virginia, Kentucky, Tennessee, and North Carolina. Some southern migrants to the North professed themselves eager to move out of states with slavery, while others merely followed the easiest routes to good land. People from New England and New York filled the towns and farms of the northern parts of the new states. People often emigrated in family or community groups.

Most white settlers proved dissatisfied with the first land they claimed; about two out of three migrants moved again within a few years. Rumors always circulated about richer land a bit farther west, about a new town certain to develop into a major city, about opportunity just over the horizon. Those who remained in a community became its leading citizens, consolidating land into larger farms, setting up gristmills and sawmills, running for office, establishing the small towns that served as county seats and trading centers. In many cases, storekeepers were among the first to arrive and among those whose fortunes flourished best. Courthouses were built early on to formalize land sales and taxation.

Doing History Online

The Rise of the Market Economy

Go to the CourseMate website for this chapter and link to Primary Sources. Read Documents 2, 6, and 11. What do they say about cotton and the economy? What social and economic changes do the authors attribute to the cotton boom?

www.cengagebrain.com

Farm and Factory in the Northeast

While the economies of the West and the South were being transformed by settlers and slaves, the economy of the East underwent its own fundamental change. Since the colonial years, people outside the major cities—more than nine out of ten Americans—had made in their own homes much of what they needed. This local production grew stronger when trade dried up during the war with England; in the war's wake, more than two-thirds of the clothes Americans wore were made in their own homes. Household manufacturing peaked in 1815. Local blacksmiths, tailors, cobblers, and other artisans supplied what families could not produce for themselves, and local mills processed crops and lumber.

Farms averaged a little over a hundred acres, about half cultivated and the other half occupied by wood lots for fuel and timber. Women and men, children and adults shared and divided the work among themselves. Farm families reaped flax in June, enjoyed a brief respite in August, and then pushed hard for the fall harvest. In winter, men and boys cut wood, while women and girls spun thread and wove cloth for clothes. The garden and dairy for the family's use and local sale were the responsibility of women and girls, the major cash crops the responsibility of men. Farmers, chronically short of cash, bartered among themselves and with merchants.

After 1815, the farms in many parts of New England, New York, and Pennsylvania would be tied ever more tightly to the economies of the towns and cities. Farm families produced more cash crops and bought more goods with money rather than through barter. Women, especially widows and other single females, worked in their homes to produce palm hats, portions of shoes, or articles of clothing that merchants from nearby cities gathered and had assembled in workshops. These women added such **piecework** to their farm work, laboring in the evenings and throughout the winters. With so many young men leaving New England for the West, many communities found themselves with considerable numbers of young women who might never marry, as well as older women who could not count on the support of sons. Piecework offered these women a chance to add scarce cash to their household economies.

Although it would be generations before cities and factories dominated the economies of the Northeast, farms, towns, and small factories grew ever more interconnected. The textile industry of New England stood as the most dramatic example of industrial growth. The cost of cotton clothing fell faster than the cost

Doing History Online

Improving Female Education

Go to the CourseMate website for this chapter and link to Primary Sources. Read Documents 1, 3, 5, and 13. How does Emma Willard justify education for women? What are some of the rights and responsibilities of women, according to Huntington, Crocker, and Willard? How do they justify education for women? What limitations do they see on women's political and intellectual involvement?

www.cengagebrain.com

piecework Early manufacturing system in which clothing, hats, and portions of shoes were sewn by women, generally working in their own homes, then sent to merchants in nearby cities for assembly and sale.

(The Granger Collection, New York)

Early Textile Mills. Young women who were familiar with fabrics and thread were considered especially suited to work in textile mills. Although the work was exhausting and often dangerous, women's wages gave them a measure of independence and helped support families back home.

MAP 9.3
Early Cotton Mills in the Northeast, 1810–1840
The cheap cotton of the South combined with the cheap labor and abundant waterpower of the Northeast to create the United States' first industrial economy in small towns and cities located on streams.

for any other product as machinery and cheaper cotton lowered the price. Francis Cabot Lowell of Boston designed a power loom in 1813, re-creating from memory a machine he had seen on a recent trip to England. The same year, Lowell and a partner, Nathan Appleton, spent more than $400,000 to open the first factory in the United States that could integrate all the steps of making cloth under a single roof: the Boston Manufacturing Company, in Waltham, Massachusetts, where a waterfall with a ten-foot drop offered free power. An expanded group of investors in the enterprise—the Boston Associates, they were called—pooled the resources of the city's most prominent merchant families.

Unlike earlier factories, the Boston Associates used unskilled labor and machines even for weaving, the most expensive part of the process. Lowell and Appleton, concerned that the introduction of factories into the United States might create the same alienated and despised working class they saw in England, recruited young New England farm women and girls as operatives. The operatives, unlike British laborers, considered millwork a three- or four-year commitment before they married and began families of their own. They worked fourteen hours a day, six days a week. The factory was unlike anything the young women had ever confronted. "You cannot think how odd everything seemed," one mill girl recalled; even those who had spun and woven for years could not be prepared for the "frightful" sight of "so many bands, and wheels, and springs in constant motion" (see Map 9.3).

❖ Consequences of Expansion

The enlarged boundaries of the American nation, as exciting and promising as they seemed, brought consequences few could have imagined. The newly integrated economy proved vulnerable to fluctuations in currency and outside pressure. The rapid spread of slavery in the South threatened northerners, who did not want to see the institution expand into new territories in the West. The resulting political fight over the future of slavery inspired slaves to launch a revolt in South Carolina. The leaders of the United States came to feel that their new status in the world called for an emboldened foreign policy, one that proclaimed an enlarged role for the United States in its hemisphere.

The Panic of 1819

In 1819, a series of events abroad and at home combined to bring a sudden halt to some of the economic growth in the United States. Prices for cotton lands in the Southeast skyrocketed as world demand for cotton cloth increased every year. Southern cotton prices rose to such an extent that in 1818 and 1819, British manufacturers turned to other cotton sources, especially India, and as they did, American cotton prices tumbled, along with the value of the land that produced it. The panic of 1819 had begun.

The panic proved a sudden and sobering reminder of just how complicated and interdependent the economy of the nation was becoming. The cities were hit the hardest. About half a million workers lost their jobs as business ground to a halt. Americans shuddered to see "children freezing in the winter's storm—and the fathers without coats and shoes." Charitable groups opened soup kitchens, while many families who had moved to towns and cities returned to the countryside to live with relatives. Many people, including congressmen, began to call for the revocation of the charter of the Second Bank of the United States, objecting to what they considered its dictatorial power. Several states tried to limit that power by levying extremely high taxes on the branches of the bank in their states, but they were overruled by the Supreme Court in *McCulloch v. Maryland.*

Despite the panic, James Monroe was reelected to the presidency in 1820 in one of the quietest and most lopsided elections in the nation's history. The Federalist Party, fatally crippled by its opposition to the War of 1812, offered no effective opposition. Neither did Monroe face an organized contest from others within his own party, which was divided along sectional lines. Most Americans seemed to blame someone other than President Monroe for the panic of 1819 and the lingering hard times that followed it. The **Era of Good Feelings,** so called for the near-absence of party politics, somehow managed to survive for the president, it turned out, but not Congress.

Era of Good Feelings Period in U.S. history (1817–1823) when, the Federalist party having declined, there was little open party feeling.

The Missouri Compromise, 1820

The recent admission of the new states of the Southwest and Old Northwest had left a precarious balance in the Senate between slave states and free, though northern states held a strong, and growing, preponderance in the House of Representatives. The Missouri Territory posed a special challenge to the balance. Slavery had quickly spread in Missouri, stretching along the richest river lands. If Missouri were admitted with slavery, as its territorial legislature had decreed, then the slave states would hold a majority in the Senate. Slavery in Missouri, an area of the same latitude as much of Illinois, Indiana, and Ohio, seemed to violate the assumption long held by many northerners that slavery, if it grew at all, would expand only to the south. Furthermore, the three-fifths clause of the Constitution, these northerners complained, gave the slave states twenty more members of Congress and twenty more electors for the presidency than they would have if only white populations were counted. The South seemed to be getting extra representation unfairly.

The debates over slavery in Missouri in 1819 and 1820 were not between fervent abolitionists in the North and fervent proslavery advocates in the South. Neither of those positions had yet been defined. Instead, white northerners and southerners of all political persuasions agreed that blacks and whites could not live together in the United States once slavery had ended. That was the message of the **American Colonization Society**, founded in 1816 and based in Washington, D.C. The society bought land in Africa, naming the new country "Liberia," and sent about twelve thousand free African Americans there over the next fifty years. Disease in Liberia took a terrible toll, however, and many died. As time went by, fewer African Americans migrated. In Philadelphia, many even staged protests against the notion of colonization.

American Colonization Society Founded in 1816 to colonize freed slaves on land purchased in Africa and called "Liberia." Members included white slaveholders and opponents of slavery, as well as free African Americans.

In the meantime, slavery caused problems for the political system. A New York congressman, James Tallmadge, Jr., introduced an amendment to the bill that would admit Missouri as a state only if it admitted no more slaves and if those slaves in the territory were freed when they became twenty-five years old. More than eighty of the North's congressmen supported the Tallmadge amendment and only ten opposed it. In the Senate, though, the slave states prevailed by two votes. A deadlocked Congress adjourned in March 1819, to meet again in December.

During the months in between, politicians worked behind the scenes to prepare for the debates and decisions of December. The Union, so celebrated and expansive in the wake of the war with Britain, so peaceful for whites since the Creeks, Seminoles, and Cherokees had been quelled, now seemed in danger of breaking apart from within. Both northern and southern politicians talked openly of ending the Union if need be. White southerners thought northerners irresponsible and unrealistic to attack it as the proposed Tallmadge amendment did.

Doing History Online

Charles Pinckney's Speech to Congress

Go to the CourseMate website for this chapter and link to Primary Sources. What are Pinckney's major problems with northerners' attitudes toward slavery (see Document 11)? Based on what you've read about cotton and the market economy, are his claims justified?

www.cengagebrain.com

In northern states, people began to oppose the institution publicly. Furious meetings erupted in towns and cities across the North, turning out antislavery petitions and resolutions in large numbers. Slavery, these petitions thundered, was a blot on the nation, a violation of the spirit of Christianity, an abomination that must not spread into places it had not already ruined. The antislavery advocates of the 1820s expected colonization and abolition to occur simultaneously and gradually, but they were determined to stop the spread of slavery in the northern states and territories.

After weeks of debate, the **Missouri Compromise** emerged from the Senate: Missouri, with no restriction on slavery, should be admitted to the Union at the same time as Maine, thereby ensuring the balance between slave and free states. Slavery would be prohibited in all the lands acquired in the Louisiana Purchase north of the southern border of Missouri at 36°30' latitude (see Map 9.4). Such a provision excluded the Arkansas territory, where slavery was already established, but closed to slavery the vast expanses of the Louisiana Territory—the future states of Iowa, Minnesota, Wisconsin, the Dakotas, Nebraska, and Kansas. Any slaves who escaped to the free states would be returned. Many northern congressmen who voted for the measure found themselves burned in effigy back home and defeated when it came time for reelection. Southerners were no more satisfied than the northerners; they were furious to hear themselves vilified in the national capital they had long dominated.

Missouri Compromise (1820–1821) Congressional legislation that ended the first of a series of crises concerning the extension of slavery.

Northern and southern politicians had become as wary and distrustful of one another as they had never been before. In a real sense, the debates over slavery in Missouri created "the North" and "the South," uniting the new states of the

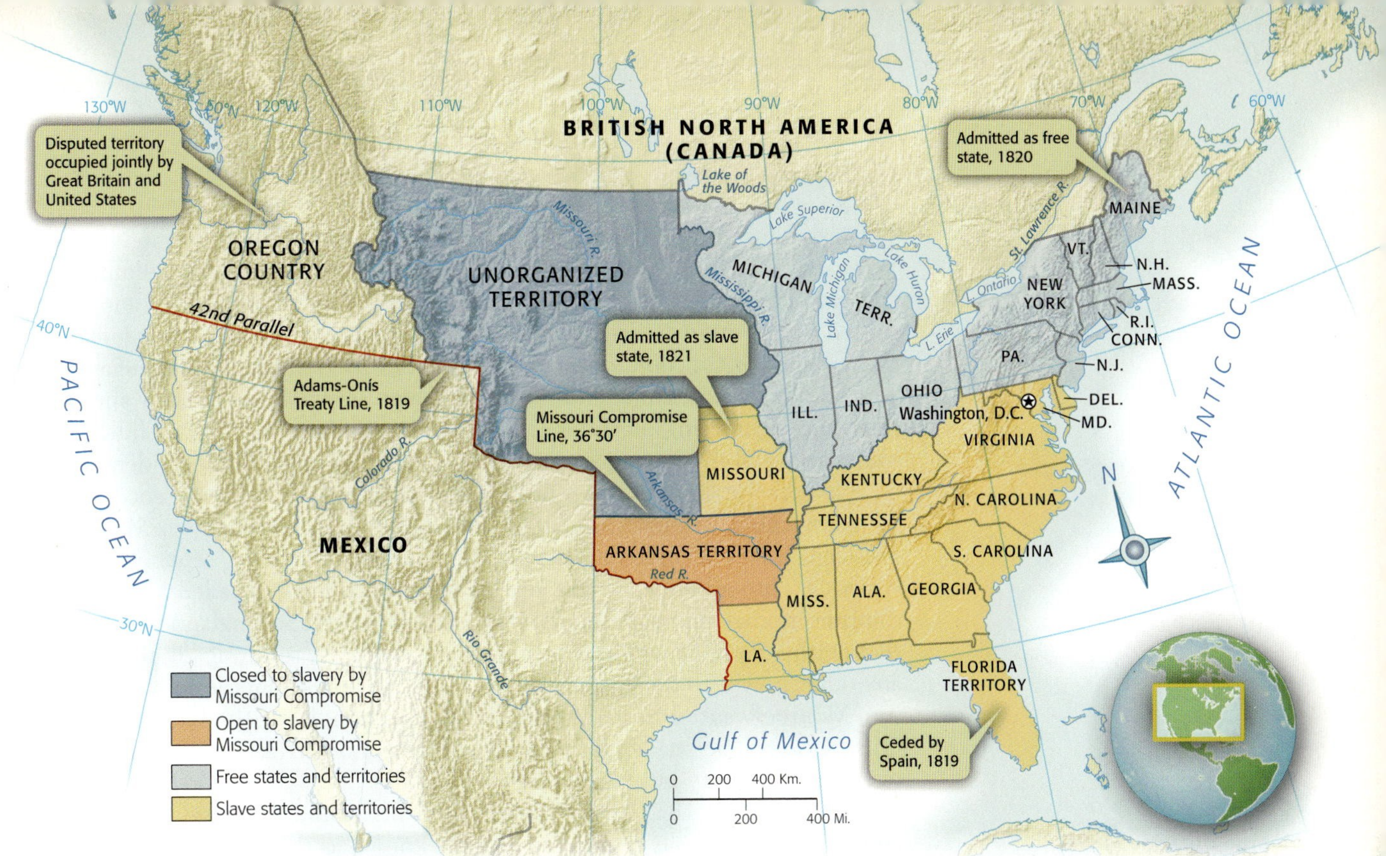

MAP 9.4
The Missouri Compromise, 1820
The conflict over the fate of slavery in Missouri proved the first great sectional conflict over the issue. Under the provisions of the Missouri Compromise, Missouri entered the Union as a slave state while Maine entered as a free state. Slavery was prohibited in the remainder of the Louisiana Territory.

Northwest with the states of New England, New York, and Pennsylvania, and forging a tighter alliance among the new states of the Southwest and Virginia, the Carolinas, and Georgia.

In Charleston, South Carolina, the heart of South Carolina's richest plantation district, a free black man named **Denmark Vesey** had followed in the papers the debates over the Missouri controversy. What he read there reinforced what he had seen in the Bible and the documents of the American Revolution: slavery was immoral. Vesey, a middle-aged man of large stature who had bought his freedom twenty years earlier, stood as a commanding presence among the African American people of the Low Country. Vesey traveled up and down the coast and into the interior with a powerful ally, Gullah Jack, who projected an aura of spiritual authority. Gullah Jack, an Angolan, had arrived in South Carolina near the turn of the century, one of the forty thousand slaves brought into the state right before the end of the legal slave trade in 1807.

Vesey, Denmark (1767?–1822) American insurrectionist. A freed slave in South Carolina, he was implicated in the planning of a large uprising of slaves and was hanged. The event led to more stringent slave codes in many southern states.

Vesey, Gullah Jack, and their followers conspired to seize the city's poorly protected guardhouse, stores, and roads before the whites could gather themselves in opposition. House slaves would kill their white owners. Once Charleston was secure, the rebels, Vesey planned, would sail to Haiti, where Toussaint L'Ouverture had staged a black rebellion decades earlier and where slavery had been abolished. But a house servant alerted Charleston whites to the danger only two days before the revolt planned for June 16, 1822. The governor ordered out five military companies, and Vesey called off the attack. Over the next two months, white authorities hanged thirty-five alleged conspirators and banished thirty-seven more from the state. Few of the rebels would reveal the names of their allies, going to their deaths with the secrets of the revolt secure. Denmark Vesey was one of those executed. White southerners blamed Vesey's rebellion on the agitation against slavery in the Missouri debate.

The Monroe Doctrine, 1823

The instability of the Spanish regime in Europe, exacerbated by the Napoleonic Wars, sent aftershocks into the colonies in the New World. Throughout the first and second decades of the nineteenth century, one struggle after another disrupted Latin America. Seeing Spain vulnerable in Europe and abroad, leaders in the colonies of the Western Hemisphere—Simón Bolívar in Venezuela, José de San Martín in Argentina, and Miguel Hidalgo in Mexico—pushed ahead with their long-simmering plans for national independence. By 1822, Chile, Mexico, Venezuela, and the Portuguese colony of Brazil had gained independence.

Neither the United States nor Great Britain wanted to see France or Russia fill the vacuum left by Spain in the New World. Accordingly, in March 1822, President Monroe urged Congress to recognize the new republics of Latin America. Throughout the next year, as the French army invaded Spain, the U.S. minister in England proposed that the United States and England jointly declare that neither country would annex any part of Spain's tottering empire or permit any other power to do so. Encouraged by former presidents Jefferson and Madison, Monroe wanted to make the joint declaration, but Secretary of State John Quincy Adams persuaded him that it would be more fitting for the United States to declare its policy independently.

Monroe Doctrine (1823) U.S. foreign policy statement presented to Congress by James Monroe, declaring U.S. opposition to European interference in the Americas.

In December 1823 the president used his annual message to Congress to announce what would eventually become known as the **Monroe Doctrine:** "The American continents, by the free and independent conditions which they have assumed and maintained, are henceforth not to be considered as subjects for future colonisation by any European power." The North American republic had exerted its first claim to recognition by the great powers of the world, making a show of acting independently even though Great Britain was the real power. Though the Russians and Spanish denounced the American policy, they tolerated it because the European powers, exhausted by wars among themselves, had little desire to expand their involvement on the other side of the world. The leaders of the Latin American revolts welcomed the warning to the European powers, but they were less certain about the intentions of the United States toward Latin America.

❖ The Reinvention of Politics, 1824–1828

Few eligible voters had bothered to cast a ballot when James Monroe was reelected in 1820 virtually without opposition. But bitter debates over slavery and the role of the national government that followed set off a new era of political partisanship. The election of 1824 showed that Americans had become far more divided than had seemed possible only four years earlier.

John Quincy Adams and the Elections of 1824 and 1828

With five strong contenders eying the presidency in 1824, politicians and observers expected a more interesting contest than four years earlier. There were five candidates: William Crawford, secretary of the treasury, a Georgian and apparent heir to the Virginia dynasty; John Quincy Adams, the secretary of state and son of President John Adams; John C. Calhoun of South Carolina, secretary of war; Henry Clay of Kentucky, Speaker of the House of Representatives; and war hero Andrew Jackson of Tennessee.

Several of these men realized they did not command sufficient national support to win the election outright. They hoped, however, to prevail if the election went into the House of Representatives, where the top three candidates would vie if no candidate won a majority in the electoral college. Cliques spread rumors, and alliances of convenience flourished. Openly partisan newspapers sang the praises of their man and published lacerating rumors about his opponents. Many American voters seemed disenchanted with the crass politicking, though, and relatively few voted in 1824. Jackson's popular vote nearly equaled that of Adams and Crawford combined, but the election was indeed thrown into the House of Representatives to choose among the top three candidates: Jackson, Adams, and Crawford.

Since his fourth-place finish put him out of the running, Clay, the Speaker of the House, sought to strike the best deal he could with the other candidates, assuring himself of maximum power. Clay, considering Jackson unworthy of the post and a potential military despot, discussed his future with Adams. When the vote came to the House of Representatives in early 1825, Adams won the presidency, taking the three states Clay had won in the electoral college. Two weeks later, Henry Clay received the appointment of secretary of state. Throughout the muddy little city of Washington, people speculated about the promises the upright John Quincy Adams had made to win the presidency.

(Collection of the New-York Historical Society)

Lafayette's Return. Even as the 1824 election revealed divisions within the country, Americans united to welcome the marquis de Lafayette, French hero of the American Revolution. Lafayette's visit united the country with bonds of memory and celebration, commemorated with memorabilia such as this snuffbox.

Adams wanted a stronger national government, internal improvements, and a tariff to protect American industry, but he could not mobilize public or political support for his positions. Adams refused to use patronage to persuade or coerce people to go along with his plans. His administration bogged down in factionalism and paralysis, with his supposed "corrupt bargain" with Clay darkening his reputation.

In the meantime, New York politicians sought to harness ambition into organized forms in the 1820s, pioneering the development of the party system. DeWitt Clinton invented the "spoils system," in which it became the expectation that an incoming officeholder would remove those appointed by his predecessor and put his own supporters in their place. Martin Van Buren, a young lawyer and politician from New York nicknamed the "Little Magician," created a powerful statewide organization. He used newspapers in Albany and New York City to spread the word of the party to the fifty small newspapers he controlled throughout the state, and built a large network of party men, many of them lawyers, who traveled widely and knew many of their counterparts. Van Buren's goal was to combine party unity with personal advancement for party members, creating a powerful and self-reinforcing cycle.

Van Buren opposed John Quincy Adams in the presidential contest of 1824 because Adams's nationally sponsored canals, roads, education, and other services would cut into the power of state government, elevating what Van Buren saw as dangerous federal power over power closer to home. Partly for this reason, Van Buren cast his lot in 1824 and the years thereafter with Andrew Jackson, who shared Van Buren's preference for localized power. As the next presidential election came closer, Van Buren, now a senator, worked ever more energetically for Jackson, hoping to spread the model of New York politics to the nation as a whole.

Supporters of Andrew Jackson of Tennessee, John C. Calhoun of South Carolina, and William Crawford of Georgia gradually joined forces in anticipation of the election of 1828, when they hoped to unseat Adams and his vision of an active and centralized government. The struggle, Calhoun wrote to Jackson, was between "power and liberty." After some jockeying, Andrew Jackson emerged as the man to challenge Adams.

Adams's supporters warned of the dangers of electing a raw and rough "military chieftain" such as Andrew Jackson to the presidency and distributed a handbill marked with eighteen coffins, each one representing a man Jackson had supposedly killed in a duel or ordered executed under his military command. The most incendiary charge, however, was that Jackson had married a woman married to another man. The facts of the case were unclear—it appears that Rachel Jackson was a religious woman, trapped in a bad marriage, who thought she had received a divorce when she married Jackson—but the anti-Jackson forces made the most of any suspicions to the contrary.

The Anti-Masons Organize

Charges of conspiracy and corruption raged throughout American politics in the 1820s. Some of the suspicions seemed confirmed by events in New York. As the economy of that state prospered along with the Erie Canal, so did fraternal organizations of every sort. The Ancient Order of Masons did especially well, claiming almost 350 lodges in the state, but many non-Masons felt that their strict secrecy contradicted American ideals of democracy.

Suspicion of the Masons exploded when a brother named William Morgan turned against the order and published its secret rituals. Local Masonic leaders used their influence with county officials to harass and jail Morgan, who disappeared in September 1826. Many said he had been murdered. The investigation soon stalled, however, as Masonic law enforcement officers and others dragged their feet. Despite twenty trials and three special prosecutors, only a few convictions resulted. Congregations split and communities divided into warring factions over the Masons.

By 1827, nearly a hundred "Morgan committees" had met and formed in New York and began to spread across the entire northern half of the country, attracting men of reputation and prestige. Within two years, the "Anti-Masons" had established more than a hundred newspapers. They held public meetings and launched lobbying campaigns, devoting themselves to mobilizing people against a powerful entrenched force. They succeeded: Masonry lost more than half its members and created virtually no new lodges for the next fifteen years.

Birth of the Democrats

Even while the struggle over the Masons unfolded, Martin Van Buren traveled throughout the United States, hammering out a new coalition of ambitious state politicians willing to back Andrew Jackson. The members of the coalition called themselves "Democratic Republicans," eventually shortened to "Democrats." Their candidates did extremely well in the off-year congressional elections of 1827, exploiting people's disapproval of the ineffectual Adams administration. The Democrats controlled both the House and the Senate.

In preparation for Jackson's contest with Adams, Van Buren and the other party leaders organized voters as they had never been organized before. Although Jackson himself was a prominent Mason, Van Buren adopted techniques not unlike those pioneered by the Anti-Masons in these same years. Using every strategy at their disposal—bonfires, speeches, barbecues, parades, professional writers, and the first campaign song—these Jacksonians claimed that they had found a true man of the people. In towns across the country, "Old Hickory"—Jackson was supposedly as hardy as that toughest of trees—was celebrated with hickory poles, brooms, sticks, and trees. The National Republicans, as Adams's supporters became known, sniffed at what they considered the unseemly display that diverted attention from real issues, but they could not deny the power of the new methods to win voters' attention.

In the meantime, American politics became more democratic and inclusive. Most legislatures across the Union lowered property requirements for voting and

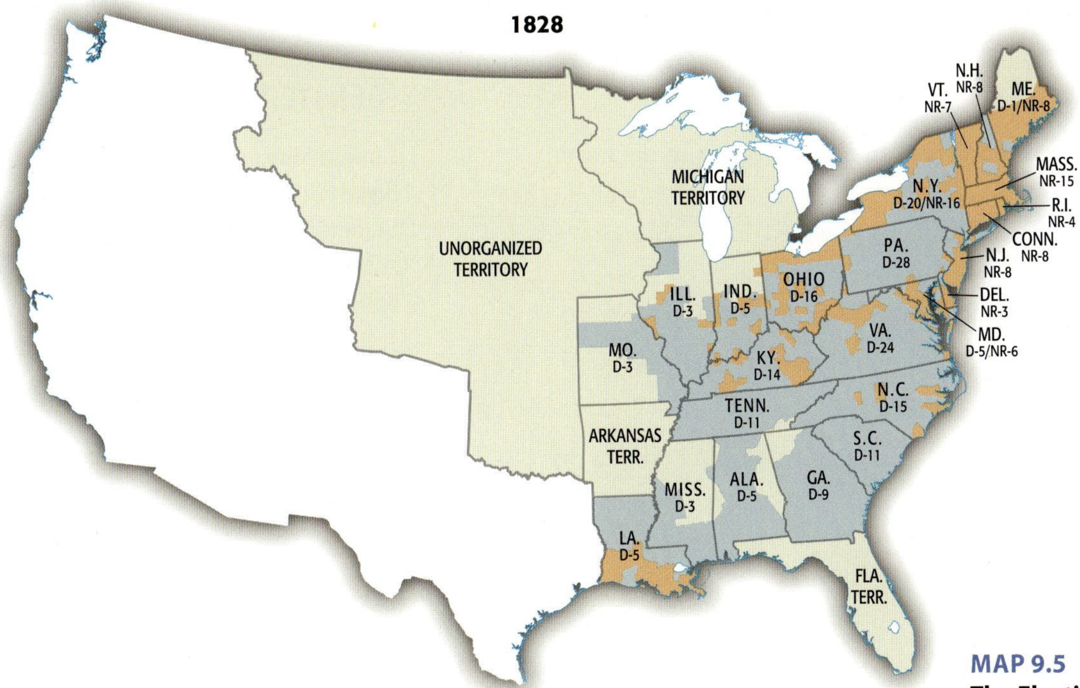

Candidate (Party)	Electoral Vote		Popular Vote	
Jackson (Democrat)	178	68%	647,286	56.0%
J.Q. Adams (National Republican)	83	32%	508,064	44.0%

Territories, unsettled, etc.

MAP 9.5
The Election of 1828
Andrew Jackson overwhelmed John Quincy Adams almost everywhere except in Adams's native New England.

made judicial offices elective rather than appointed. Citizens seemed restless, hungry for someone to give direction and force to public life. As a result, voter turnout in 1828 was double that of the 1824 election. The dramatic confrontation of men and styles contributed to widespread voter interest, and politicians at every level and on both sides made sure voters went to the polls. Jackson's supporters wanted no repeat of the last electoral controversy or chance for victory to be stolen by insider politics.

Jackson won easily over Adams, winning 178 of the 261 electoral votes and capturing the critical mid-Atlantic states and all the states of the South except Louisiana and Kentucky (see Map 9.5). The election proved bittersweet for Jackson, though: his wife died soon afterward. Jackson blamed the slanderers of the other party for Rachel's death, for she had fallen ill after seeing an editorial denouncing her. The president-elect passed the weeks before his inauguration in sadness and bitterness.

CHAPTER REVIEW, 1815–1828

SUMMARY

- Treaties established new borders of the United States to the north, west, and south.
- A newly integrated national economy emerged, based on improved roads, canals, and steamboats.
- The first major financial panic shook the entire country.
- Cotton drove the aggressive expansion of slavery across the South.
- Factories developed in the Northeast.
- The Missouri Compromise redefined the relationship between the North and the South.
- The first major national political party, the Democrats, was forged by Martin Van Buren and Andrew Jackson.

IDENTIFICATIONS

James Monroe
forty-ninth parallel
Seminoles
Adams-Onís Treaty
Henry Clay
John C. Calhoun
American System
Second Bank of the United States
Gibbons v. Ogden
McCulloch v. Maryland
National Road
Erie Canal
Cotton South
piecework
Era of Good Feelings
American Colonization Society
Missouri Compromise
Denmark Vesey
Monroe Doctrine

MAKING CONNECTIONS: LOOKING AHEAD

Chapter 10 will show how the compromises and reforms of the 1820s, designed to balance conflicting political interests, would shape political and economic development in future years.

1. Why did lawmakers believe that the Missouri Compromise could offer a long-term solution to conflicts between the North and the South? Were they right?

RECOMMENDED READINGS

Buchanan, Thomas C. *Black Life on the Mississippi: Slaves, Free Blacks, and the Western Steamboat World* (2004). An in-depth look at the lives of slaves and free blacks on the Mississippi through the nineteenth century.

Cashin, Joan E. *A Family Venture: Men and Women on the Southern Frontier* (1991). The compelling story of the southwestern migration.

Frank, Andrew K. *Creeks and Southerners: Biculturalism on the Early American Frontier* (2005). An examination of the concepts of race and cultural interactions between Creeks and Anglo-Americans.

Horwitz, Morton J. *The Transformation of American Law, 1780–1860* (1977). A strong and controversial argument about the law and commerce.

Larson, John Lauritz. *Internal Improvement: National Public Works and the Promise of Popular Government in the Early United States* (2001). The best treatment of this important subject.

Martin, Scott C., ed. *Cultural Change and the Market Revolution in America, 1789–1860* (2005). Essays that examine how ordinary Americans, black and white, reacted to changes in the economy.

Rohrbough, Malcolm J. *The Trans-Appalachian Frontier: People, Societies, and Institutions, 1775–1850* (1978). A complex story told well.

Rothman, Adam. *Slave Country: American Expansion and the Origins of the Deep South* (2004). Offers an engaging analysis of the development of the cotton frontier and its connections to international capitalism.

Saunt, Claudio. *A New Order of Things: Property, Power, and the Transformation of the Creek Indians, 1733–1816* (1999). Makes comprehensible the great complexities in the lives of American Indians in these crucial decades.

Sheriff, Carol. *The Artificial River: The Erie Canal and the Paradox of Progress, 1817–1862* (1996). A compelling account of the canal's origins, building, and effects.

CourseMate Go to the CourseMate website at www.cengagebrain.com for additional study tools and review materials for this chapter.

10

The Years of Andrew Jackson

1829–1836

MAKING CONNECTIONS

LOOKING BACK

Chapter 9 showed that the expansion of the United States after the War of 1812 unleashed a series of unanticipated challenges to the new nation. Before starting Chapter 10, you should be able to answer the following questions:

1. Could the spread of slavery into the southern territories have been avoided? Explain your reasoning.
2. How might relations between the U.S. government and Native Americans have followed a different path?
3. What role did governments play in the growth and spread of the economy?

Tumultuous change came to the United States in the years Andrew Jackson served as president. Elections became sweeping public events that involved white men of every class. Voters and leaders hotly debated and contested the role of government in American life. Religious revivals swept up entire communities in devotion and prayer. Working people created labor unions, and abolitionists launched a bold crusade against slavery.

Growing democracy was not the full story of these years, however. The people of the Creek, Choctaw, Cherokee, Seminole, Sac, and Fox nations were driven from their homes in the South and in the Old Northwest. A crisis threatened to ignite a military struggle between South Carolina and the federal government. The revolt of Nat Turner and debates over slavery in Virginia unleashed a proslavery reaction throughout much of the South. The defeat of Mexico by the Republic of Texas opened a vast new territory to slavery as well as to the settlement of free Americans. Few other decades in American history have witnessed such important and fundamental changes.

Accompanying this rapid expansion of boundaries of every sort was considerable anxiety that American society threatened to spin out of control. People worried that many Americans had moved beyond the influence of church, family, school, or employer. Some Americans began to suggest antidotes for the consequences of change, offering political compromise, reform societies, and new ideals of the home.

❖ Andrew Jackson Takes Charge

Andrew Jackson, still wearing black after the recent death of his beloved wife, Rachel, traveled by steamboat from Nashville, Tennessee, to Washington in the winter of 1829 to begin his presidency. The entire nation watched to see what sort of changes this new kind of leader might make.

The People's President

Once he arrived in Washington, Jackson began to assemble his cabinet, balancing North, South, and West. Martin Van Buren, the leader of Jackson's successful 1828 campaign, became secretary of state, a position traditionally reserved for the man next in line for the presidency. Vice President John C. Calhoun, ambitious for the presidency himself, chafed at the appointment but could do little to change it; he and his wing of the party had to satisfy themselves with the appointment of one of their number as secretary of the treasury. The most controversial appointment, however, proved volatile for reasons that had little to do with political partisanship. Jackson wanted a close friend in the cabinet, someone in whom he could confide, and he chose an old Tennessee associate and influential newspaper editor, John Eaton, as his secretary of war.

Eaton, a widower in middle age, had married Peggy O'Neal Timberlake, an attractive and witty twenty-nine-year-old daughter of a well-known innkeeper in

CHAPTER TIMELINE 1824 1827 1831 1833 1835 1837

POLITICS AND DIPLOMACY

- (1825)–1829 John Quincy Adams presidency
- 1829–(1837) Andrew Jackson presidency
- 1829 David Walker's *Appeal*
- 1830 Indian Removal Act
- 1831 Nat Turner's Rebellion
- 1832 Nullification crisis
- 1832 Virginia debate over slavery
- 1834 Whig Party organized
- 1836 Battle of the Alamo; Texas Republic established

SOCIETY AND CULTURE

- 1830 *The Book of Mormon*
- 1830 Charles Finney's revivals begin in Rochester, New York
- 1831 William Lloyd Garrison establishes *The Liberator*
- 1833 Formation of American Anti-Slavery Society

ECONOMICS AND TECHNOLOGY

- 1831 John Bull locomotive begins railroad operation
- 1832 Bank War begins
- 1834 National Trades Union formed

Washington. She was rumored to have driven her last husband to suicide, forcing him to defraud the government to pay debts she had run up, and was considered promiscuous. Eaton had asked Jackson's opinion of the marriage beforehand, receiving the old general's blessing; the president liked outspoken women and knew from bitter experience the power that unfounded rumors could hold. Jackson, in a gesture of friendship and support as the gossip flew, offered Eaton the cabinet position. The decision electrified Washington.

Despite his rambunctious youth, Jackson disdained official Washington's fondness for strong drink, endless banquets, and overheated social life. He considered himself an outsider determined to reform Washington and make the city worthy of the nation it was supposed to serve. As the inauguration day of March 4 neared, Washington's population doubled as men who considered themselves important in General Jackson's election arrived in the city to claim their fair share of glory, excitement, and jobs. At the inauguration, thirty thousand people crowded in to see the new president. They surged into the White House, spilling barrels of orange punch, standing with muddy boots on expensive chairs to get a better look at the proceedings, and smashing thousands of dollars worth of china. Jackson, suffocated by admirers and disgusted by the scene, climbed out a rear window and went for a steak at a boardinghouse.

Jackson and the Spoils System

As the new administration got under way, Jackson and his advisers cleaned house in the federal government, removing officials whose competence, honesty, or loyalty to Jackson and the Democrats was suspect. Although such a policy had become established practice in several major states, including Van Buren's New York, Jackson was the first president to make such sweeping changes on the federal level. He envisioned himself purging an arrogant bureaucracy of corruption and establishing the democratic practice of rotation in office. As officeholders quaked and fretted, Jackson's lieutenants decided which customhouses and federal offices would be cleansed. Some of the incumbents clearly deserved to lose their jobs, but others were guilty only of being active partisans for the other side in the recent election.

Jackson further infuriated opponents by appointing partisan newspaper editors to important posts, leading to charges that Jackson was corrupting, rather than cleansing, American government. Over the course of Jackson's two terms, he replaced only about 10 percent of all officeholders, not many more than his predecessors had, but did so in an especially brash spirit. One Jackson supporter unwisely announced to the Senate that the Jacksonians saw "nothing wrong in the rule that to the victors belong the spoils of the enemy." This proclamation gave an enduring notoriety to what from then on would be called the **spoils system**, a system that Jackson envisioned as reform, not cynical politics.

spoils system Initiated by President Andrew Jackson, civil service system by which the victorious political party rewarded its supporters with government jobs.

The festering conflict within the administration over the so-called Eaton affair proved just how important matters of symbolism could be. The wives of the other cabinet members, Vice President Calhoun's wife, and even Emily Donelson—Jackson's daughter-in-law and hostess of the White House—refused to be in the same room with **Peggy Eaton.** But Jackson would not be swayed in his support for the Eatons. The new cabinet found itself bitterly divided, and though Jackson labored to mend fences, nothing proved effective. Martin Van Buren, a widower, cemented his friendship with the president by treating Mrs. Eaton with ostentatious respect. Jackson, embittered by the refusal of his other advisers to stand by Mrs. Eaton, largely abandoned his official cabinet and relied instead on an informal group of advisers, his so-called Kitchen Cabinet, and on Van Buren.

Eaton, Peggy (1799–1879) Wife of John Eaton and the central figure in a controversy that divided President Jackson's cabinet into pro- and anti-Eaton factions.

(The Granger Collection, New York)

Peggy Eaton. The young wife of Secretary of War John Eaton became the center of a scandal that rocked Washington during Andrew Jackson's first term.

❖ Struggles over Slavery

Several issues surrounding slavery came to a head in the years around 1830. Leaders in the southern states, worried about the rapidly growing population and power of the North, sought to define the limits of federal power. Feeling themselves neglected and abused by northern interests, South Carolina's leaders tried to secure greater autonomy. At the same time, free blacks in both the North and the South worked to replace the colonization movement with a campaign to end slavery and create freedom for African Americans in the United States. Even as these struggles unfolded, one of the largest slave revolts in the history of the United States erupted in Virginia. Combined, these events demonstrated that slavery would bedevil the confident and boisterous young country.

The Tariff of Abominations, Nullification, and States' Rights, 1828–1833

Before the election of 1828, Martin Van Buren and other Democrats had sought to broaden support for Jackson, whose strength lay in the South, by passing a tariff favorable to the economic interests of New Englanders and westerners. After elaborate deal making, the Democrats enacted the major tariff. But it came with a high cost: southerners were furious with what they called this "tariff of abominations," for it raised the price they would have to pay for manufactured items and threatened markets for southern cotton abroad. John C. Calhoun, like other South Carolina planters, feared not only that the tariff would bleed the state dry economically but that it would set a regulatory precedent for antislavery forces, who might gain control of the federal government at some future date.

Accordingly, in the summer and early fall of 1828, a few months before he would take office as Jackson's vice president, Calhoun sought to find a principled way to reconcile his national ambitions and his local concerns. Rather than argue only against the tariff itself, Calhoun asserted the general rights of individual states within the Union. Rather than merely letting the majority run roughshod over the minority, Calhoun believed, it made more sense to let a state "nullify" a national law within its own borders. Such **nullification** was constitutional, he said, because the federal system did not locate sovereignty in any one place, but rather divided it among the states and the nation. Should three-fourths of the states agree that a law must apply to all the country, then that clear majority could overrule the nullification. Calhoun thought he was finding a way to preserve order in an increasingly contentious Union. The document in which he laid out his ideas, the *South Carolina Exposition*, appeared in December 1828; the pamphlet was published anonymously because it was too politically dangerous for the vice president of the United States to be publicly on record for nullification.

nullification (1828–1833)
Argument between leaders in South Carolina and in Washington, D.C., especially President Andrew Jackson, over the relationship between federal and state power. Theorists of nullification, especially John C. Calhoun, argued that a state had the authority to "nullify" a federal law within its own boundaries. The precipitating issue was a tariff, but the debate—eventually settled by compromise over the tariff and a threat of force by the federal government over the issue of authority—was seen as a trial case regarding slavery.

South Carolina planters had watched with growing alarm as newspapers told of the success of British abolitionists in ending slavery in the British West Indies—the place from which many elite white South Carolina families had come generations earlier. With the memory of Denmark Vesey's plan of 1822 and an 1829 revolt in the Low Country still fresh in their memory, white South Carolinians felt they could display no weakness on the slavery issue. Throughout the state, raucous crowds gathered to call for a fight against the federal government on the tariff. South Carolinians who favored a more conciliatory stance toward the federal government could not generate nearly as much support for their position.

President Jackson had no sympathy for nullification, and the leaders of the movement in South Carolina were surprised and disappointed to garner no support from other southern states in resisting federal authority. Jackson considered the tariff to be for the good of the nation as a whole. The tariff provided money for defense and prevented federal debt. The South Carolina challenge would limit the power of the U.S. government to make law for the country in matters that transcended state boundaries. Jackson did not believe the United States could afford to permit such divisiveness to impair its strength in the world of nations. Congress passed a "force bill" to permit him to use military power to keep South Carolina in line and collect the tariff duties. After much debate, Congress, under the leadership of Henry Clay, offered a compromise in early 1833: the tariff would be slowly but steadily lowered over the next decade. South Carolina's leaders declared victory and accepted the compromise tariff.

Free Blacks and African American Abolitionism

Even as the white leaders of South Carolina struggled to define the extent of their powers within the Union, free blacks and slaves struggled to define their freedom. Communities of several thousand free blacks lived in every major northern city, establishing their own churches, newspapers, schools, and lodges. More numerous still were free African Americans in the Upper South slave states, especially Maryland and Virginia, and in all major cities on the Atlantic and Gulf coasts of the South. These free blacks communicated through newspapers, letters, and word passed by the many black sailors who plied the eastern seaboard. In the 1820s, they debated the merits of leaving the United States altogether, and many whites encouraged them to do. But few black Americans were willing to be shipped to a place that they had never seen, the colony of Liberia. Moreover, African Americans came to see in colonization an attack on their hard-won accomplishments in the United States. Rather than spending moral energy and money on removing black people, they argued, Americans should work instead on making the United States a fairer place.

David Walker proved to be an important figure in this movement that sought to improve the plight of black Americans. Walker had lived in Charleston at the time of Denmark Vesey's conspiracy in 1822 and was familiar with the long tradition of revolt and resistance in the Carolina Low Country. After the suppression of Vesey, Walker moved to Boston. There, he established a used-clothing store, one of the few businesses open to African Americans in the North. Walker did well in the business, bought a home, joined the African Methodist church, and became a black Mason, an organization that fought against slavery and the slave trade. He gave his support to *Freedom's Journal*, an anticolonization paper published by black people in Boston and New York City between 1827 and 1829.

Walker, David (1785–1830) African American abolitionist and author of *Walker's Appeal . . . To the Coloured Citizens of the World* (1829), an early and powerful call for black self-awareness and opposition to slavery.

In 1829, Walker released his *Appeal . . . to the Coloured Citizens of the World*. (See *Doing History: What Slavery Means*.) Americans, whatever their skin color, had never read such a document. Walker denied that slaves felt or owed any bond to their masters. He called for black spiritual self-renewal, starting with African Americans' recognition of just how angry they were with their lot in the United States. He called for black Americans to be full Americans in both government and the economy. Walker accused those supporting colonization of concocting a "plan to get those of the colored people, who are said to be free, away from those of our brethren whom they unjustly hold in bondage, so that they may be enabled to keep them the more secure in ignorance and wretchedness. . . . For if the free are allowed to stay among the slaves, they will have intercourse together, and . . . the free will learn the slaves *bad habits*, by teaching them that they are MEN . . . and certainly *ought* and *must* be FREE."

Within weeks of its publication, Walker's *Appeal* appeared in Savannah, where it was seized, then in Georgia's capital, Milledgeville, and then in Virginia, North Carolina, South Carolina, and New Orleans. The *Appeal* created panic and repression wherever it appeared. Southern whites worried at this evidence of invisible networks of communication and resistance among the slaves, free blacks, and, perhaps, sympathetic whites in their midst. Events in Virginia bore out their worst suspicions.

The Crisis of Slavery in Virginia, 1831–1832

Nat Turner was a field hand, born in 1800, who felt that God had called him for more than the lot of a slave. Well known even in his youth for his intellectual abilities and his effectiveness as a preacher, on Sundays Turner traveled throughout the countryside around Southampton County, Virginia, coming to know most of the slaves and free black people who lived there. Praying and fasting, Turner claimed that he saw visions that foretold a slave revolt, of the time "fast approaching when the first should be last and the last should be first." Turner, unlike Gabriel in Richmond in 1800 and Vesey in Charleston in 1822, chose to build his revolt around a small group of select lieutenants rather than risk spreading the word broadly. Their plan was to begin the rebellion on their own and then attract compatriots along the way.

Turner, Nat (1800–1831) American slave leader who organized about seventy followers and led a rebellion in Virginia, during which approximately fifty whites were killed (1831). He was then captured and executed.

On August 22, 1831, Turner and his band began their revolt. They moved from one isolated farmhouse to the next, killing all the whites they found inside, including children, and then taking the horses and weapons there. As the night wore on, Turner's men killed about seventy people, starting with the family of Turner's master. By morning, word had rushed to Richmond of the unimaginable events in Southampton. Whites huddled together in Jerusalem, the county seat, and troops arrived to put down the revolt. Blacks, many of whom had no connection with the rebellion, were killed by infuriated and frightened whites hundreds

Doing History What Slavery Means

David Walker, a free black man who lived in both the South and the North, wrote his scathing account of the injustices done to African Americans for an African American audience in 1829. Drawing on a wide reading of world history, Walker argued that American slavery was among the worst the world had ever seen and that God would exercise harsh judgment on white Americans for their acts.

Daniel R. Hundley, a white southerner living in Chicago, wrote his account to a largely white northern audience, trying to explain the nature of the South and to rebut what he saw as extremists on both sides. Publishing his book in 1860, Hundley repeated the most far-reaching argument used to defend slavery.

David Walker, Walker's Appeal . . . to the Coloured Citizens of the World, *1829*

Americans! . . . you have and do continue to treat us more cruel than any heathen nation ever did a people it had subjected to the same condition that you have us . . . we must and shall be free. . . . You may do your best to keep us in wretchedness and misery, to enrich you and your children, but God will deliver us from under you. And wo[e], wo[e], will be to you if we have to obtain our freedom by fighting. Throw away your fears and prejudices then, and enlighten us and treat us like men . . . and tell us now no more about colonization, for America is as much our country, as it is yours.

Source: David Walker, *Walker's Appeal, in Four Articles; Together with a Preamble to the Coloured Citizens of the World* . . . (Boston, September 28, 1829).

Daniel R. Hundley, Social Relations in Our Southern States, *1860*

We are well persuaded that many good men, pious men—men of earnest natures and delicate sensibilities, not in the North alone but even in the South—do honestly look upon slavery as both a great moral evil and an equally great social curse. . . . In our folly, we do not consider that Jehovah never would have permitted the first human-freighted ship to leave the shores of Africa for the New World, had he not designed a beneficial result should flow from the introduction of the sable children of the tropics into the fruitful fields of our own temperate latitude. Yes, Madam, with our conception of the Deity, we can not believe that the All-wise Ruler would purposely allow a great evil to grow and increase to such magnitude, as to become the very centre and pivot of the world's commerce . . . when he might have crushed it in the beginning without harm to a single individual.

Source: Daniel R. Hundley, *Social Relations in Our Southern States* (New York: Henry B. Price, 1860), 288–289.

QUESTIONS for REFLECTION

1. What do these two documents have in common?
2. In the context of the Second Great Awakening, does their appeal to God provide hope for common understanding or persuasion? Explain your reasoning.
3. What response would slavery's defenders make to Walker? What response would slavery's attackers make to Hundley?

of miles away from Southampton. Turner's troops were all captured or killed, but Turner managed to escape and hide in the woods for two months. Once captured, he narrated a remarkable "confession" in which he told of his visions and prophecies. At his hanging in November, he showed no signs of remorse.

Nat Turner's Rebellion. Nat Turner's raid unleashed terror throughout southeastern Virginia, far from Southampton County.

White southerners saw in Nat Turner their worst nightmares. Here was a literate slave, allowed to travel on his own and proselytize on the Bible to dissatisfied slaves. The crackdown was not long in coming: delegates to the state assembly gathered in Richmond a month after Turner's execution. In a series of remarkable debates, these white Virginians, some of them sons and grandsons of Thomas Jefferson, John Marshall, and Patrick Henry, openly admitted the debilitating effect of slavery on Virginia. They worried most about slavery's influence on whites, worried that slavery kept the economy from developing as it did in the North. Delegates from western Virginia, where relatively few slaves lived, expressed their misgivings most freely, but even large slaveholders from the East admitted slavery had negative effects. Petitions flowed into Richmond urging the legislators to take a decisive step to rid Virginia of slavery. Defenders of slavery warned that the **Virginia slave debates,** published in the newspapers and discussed on the streets and in shops and homes across the state, might result in more revolts. Enslaved Virginians were not an "ignorant herd of Africans," one delegate warned, but an "active, intelligent class, watching and weighing every movement of the Legislature, with perfect knowledge of its bearing and effect."

Virginia slave debates (1831–1832) Debates in the Virginia state legislature following Nat Turner's Revolt over proposals to end slavery in Virginia. Although the legislature decided against abolition, the debates revealed white fears and divisions.

The disparate regions of Virginia found themselves in deep conflict; some discussed separating themselves from the rest of the state if one policy or another were followed. The lawmakers, starkly divided, ultimately decided that it was "inexpedient" to take any step at all against slavery at that time, that it would be left for subsequent legislatures to begin the process that would free Virginia from slavery. In the meantime, they passed harsher laws to limit the movement and gathering of free blacks and slaves.

❖ The Election of 1832 and Expansionist Tensions

Andrew Jackson made fervent enemies as well as devoted followers throughout his presidency. No one could be neutral about him, for he seemed to touch everything in American life. The election of 1832 saw voters and leaders mobilize in opposition to or support of Jackson, latching on to a wide range of issues: the economy, states' rights, and morality. The nation had never seen such political conflict.

Taking Sides

In September 1830, the first national political convention in U.S. history met in Baltimore, convened by the Anti-Masons. Despite their origins and their name, the Anti-Masons were concerned with the state of American politics in general, not merely with the threat posed by the Masons. They attracted an impressive list of ambitious and accomplished young men to their convention, including many who believed that Jackson, a Mason, was too prosouthern and too callous toward Native Americans. The Anti-Masons promised to become a powerful third party, a wild card in an already tumultuous American political scene.

Economic resentment also fueled the conflict of the early 1830s. As prices and rents rose more quickly than wages, urban working people found themselves falling behind. These working men and women felt their contributions slighted in the new economy. Workers formed unions to defend their rights in cities from New York to Kentucky. They sponsored newspapers, lobbied legislatures, and supported one another during strikes. By the mid-1830s, between one hundred thousand and three hundred thousand men and women belonged to unions. Some unions became deeply engaged in politics and put forward their own candidates. Although union members generally liked Andrew Jackson's blows against monopoly, they believed he pulled up short in his attack on economic privilege.

The Bank War, 1832–1834

Doing History Online

Jackson Takes Office

Go to the CourseMate website for this chapter and link to Primary Sources. Based on your readings of the text and Documents 4 to 8, what kind of president did Americans expect Andrew Jackson to be? Were those expectations fulfilled? Did Jackson's eight years in the presidency hold surprises for his supporters?

www.cengagebrain.com

Despite the tariffs intended to serve their interests, most people in the Northeast viewed Andrew Jackson with distrust and growing anger, perceiving in Old Hickory an enemy to moral and commercial progress. The fate of the Second Bank of the United States stood as the key issue. Many merchants and businessmen, worried about stabilizing the American economy, supported the Bank of the United States and its president, Nicholas Biddle. The bank ensured that state banks kept plenty of metal currency—specie—on hand with which to pay the national bank when asked to do so. Such rules kept the state banks from putting out too many notes, which would inflate the currency with paper money unsupported by gold or silver. When the economy fell into trouble, Biddle and the Bank of the United States would lessen their demands on the state banks, preventing panics and deflation.

While businessmen appreciated this role of the bank, many other Americans distrusted it. In their eyes, this largely private institution enjoyed far too much power for its own good or the good of the country. For many voters, objections to the Bank of the United States were as much objections to banking and commerce in general as to any specific policies of the national bank. The whole business of banking seemed suspect, with its paper money, its profits seemingly without labor, its government-supported monopolies, and its apparent speculation with public money. Andrew Jackson shared these feelings of mistrust: he disliked monopoly, he disliked paper money, and he disliked the Bank of the United States.

Bank War (1832–1834) Attacks by President Andrew Jackson on the Second Bank of the United States. By vetoing the renewal of the bank's charter and removing federal funds to state banks, he effectively destroyed the central bank.

Jackson initiated what became known as the "**Bank War,**" vetoing a rechartering of the bank and proclaiming that the bank was "unauthorized by the constitution, subversive of the rights of the States, and dangerous to the liberties of the people." He moved all federal funds from the Bank of the United States to state banks. The Bank of the United States, deprived of government support, began a slow death.

Jackson's opponents saw the president, not the bank, as the usurper of American rights. Henry Clay and other opponents argued that his action posed a far greater threat to the American people than did the bank. If the president could force his way into the lawmaking process, the division of powers laid out in the Constitution would be violated and the Union would risk falling under the despotic rule of a president who would be king.

In the election of 1832, Jackson portrayed himself as the champion of the common man fighting against a bloated aristocracy of privilege and monopoly. Clay, the candidate of the National Republicans, characterized Jackson as a man who had disregarded morality and justice in his dealing with Native Americans, had corrupted the government with the spoils system, and had attacked the national bank. William Wirt, the candidate of the Anti-Masons, declared himself the opponent of all conspiracies, corruptions, and subversions.

Jackson won by a considerable margin. Emboldened by his majority at the polls, the president went on the offensive. Those opposed to Jackson began to call themselves "Whigs." Like their British namesakes, the American Whig party saw itself as the counterbalance to otherwise unchecked monarchical power—in this case "King Andrew I," "the most absolute despot now at the head of any representative government on earth."

"King Andrew the First." Fearing the president's growing power, Whigs began referring to Jackson as "King Andrew I."

Jackson and the American Indians

Andrew Jackson had announced, and acted on, his attitudes toward Native Americans years before he took office as president. The steady advance of the white population onto the rich lands of the Cherokees, Chickasaws, Creeks, Seminoles, and Choctaws, he thought, left the people of those nations with two choices: become "industrious Citizens" who accepted the sovereignty of the states that claimed the lands on which they lived, or "remove to a Country *where* they can retain their ancient customs, so dear to them, that they cannot give up in exchange for regular society."

White people had mixed feelings about Native Americans. Americans of European descent considered native peoples admirable in many ways, dignified and free, able to learn and prosper. Not a few "white" and "black" families were proud to claim some native ancestry. Many white Americans, including some in Congress, had long contributed time and money to the Native Americans, helping to build and staff schools, sending seed and agricultural implements to ease the transition to farming.

By the late 1820s, the "civilized tribes" had adapted themselves to the dominant society. Many of the tribes were led by chiefs of mixed descent, such as Cherokee leader **John Ross,** who negotiated land settlements and profited from such deals but also attempted to create systems of political representation and law. Ross joined the Methodist church and courted any political party he believed best advanced Cherokee interests. The wealthiest Native Americans, especially the Cherokees, bought African American slaves. The children of the Native American leaders and others went to schools established by white missionaries, who persuaded a considerable number of Native Americans to convert to Christianity. The Cherokees published a newspaper that included articles in both their own language and in English.

Ross, John (1790–1866) Cherokee chief who challenged Indian removals in *Cherokee Nation v. Georgia* (1831).

Despite their many adaptations, the Native Americans of the Southeast in the late 1820s showed no desire to leave the land on which they lived. In their view, they had already given up more land than they should have—millions of acres over the preceding twenty years—and were determined to hold on to what remained. Most whites, especially those who coveted the rich cotton lands under the Native Americans' control, bristled at the continuing presence of the native inhabitants.

Jackson told the Native Americans he was their friend, even their "father," but that he could do nothing to stop their mistreatment except to move them beyond the Mississippi River, where, he promised, they would be safe. The Native Americans and their supporters, mostly religious people in the North, responded bitterly to such claims, arguing for the constitutional rights of Native Americans. But the Jacksonians quickly pushed through the **Indian Removal Act** of 1830. Two Supreme Court decisions in favor of the Cherokees, in 1830 and in 1832, *Cherokee Nation v. Georgia* and *Worcester v. Georgia*, proved to be without effect, since they depended on the federal government to implement them. Jackson had no intention of doing anything of the sort.

Indian Removal Act (1830)
Congressional legislation that set aside land in the Oklahoma Territory for American Indians who were to be removed from the eastern United States. During the next eight years, tens of thousands of Choctaw, Chickasaw, and Cherokee people were transported from their homes on what the Cherokees called the "Trail of Tears."

In the face of the impending removal, most of the native peoples split into pro-assimilation, "progressive," factions and anti-assimilation, "conservative," factions. They debated fiercely and sometimes violently among themselves. Agents, some of mixed blood, swindled the Native Americans as they prepared for the removal (see Map 10.1). The Choctaws, the first to move, underwent horrific experiences, suffering greatly and dying in large numbers as they traveled in the worst winter on record with completely inadequate supplies. The Creeks too confronted frauds and assaults.

The Cherokee removal was the most prolonged. After years of negotiating, the government struck a bargain with a small and unrepresentative number of Cherokees in the Treaty of New Echota in 1836. While groups of several hundred at a time left, including some of the wealthiest, seventeen thousand refused to leave by the deadline. General Winfield Scott then led seven thousand troops

MAP 10.1
Removal of the Native Americans, 1830s
In the 1830s, the Native Americans of the North and South were "removed" to reservations in Oklahoma and Kansas.

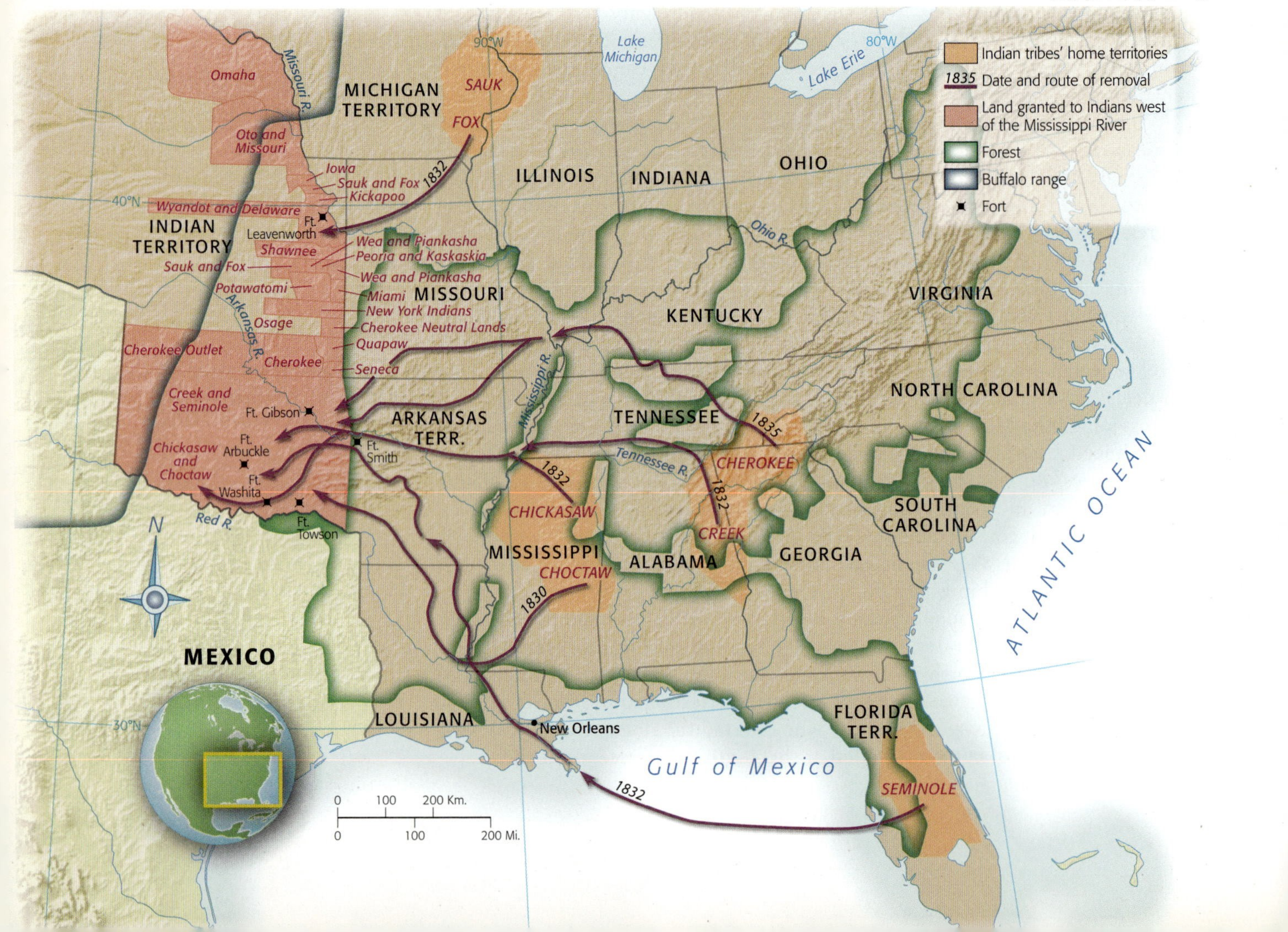

against them, driving people from their homes empty-handed, marching them to stockades, and shipping them out by rail and water. About a quarter of all eastern Cherokees died on what they called the **Trail of Tears.** The power of the eastern Indians was destroyed.

Trail of Tears Forced migration of Indians from southeastern states to what is now Oklahoma, in accordance with the Indian Removal Act (1830). Thousands died on the march known as the Trail of Tears.

Osceola (1800?–1838) Seminole chief who led opposition to Indian removal in the Second Seminole War.

The Seminoles fought against removal as long as they could. Led by **Osceola,** the son of an English trader and the husband of an escaped slave, the Seminoles tried to break the will of the whites by killing soldiers and civilians and burning their crops and homes. The Second Seminole War launched by the federal government to remove five thousand Native Americans began in 1835 and dragged on for nearly seven years. The conflict proved both unpopular and unsuccessful. Of the thirty-six thousand or so U.S. soldiers who fought, fifteen hundred died, and many more suffered debilitating disease. The federal government spent $20 million in the fight, even though few white people wanted to settle on the Seminoles' land. The United States captured Osceola only by deception at a supposed peace conference. He died in captivity a few months later, after which some Seminoles finally migrated to Oklahoma. But most of the Seminole people, able to live in the swampy landscape, were never driven out of Florida.

Fighting also erupted in the Illinois Territory between white settlers and the Sac and Fox natives. These people, under the leadership of Black Hawk, saw their lands along the Mississippi River violently taken over by whites while the Native Americans were on a hunting expedition in 1832. In retaliation, the Sac and Fox destroyed white settlements. A large contingent of volunteers (including a young Abraham Lincoln), regular troops, and allied Native Americans set out after Black Hawk and his people, eventually overtaking Black Hawk and killing nearly five hundred Native Americans as they tried to cross the Mississippi River. Taken prisoner, Black Hawk refused to repent, telling his captors that he "has done nothing for which an Indian ought to be ashamed. He has fought for his countrymen, the squaws and papooses, against white men who came, year after year, to cheat them and take away their land." Black Hawk's words and deeds, widely reported in the newspapers of the country, attracted considerable sympathy among whites in the East. Andrew Jackson met with Black Hawk and pardoned him; the warrior's autobiography became a best-seller.

Austin, Stephen F. (1793–1836) Virginian who led efforts to settle U.S. citizens in Texas, negotiated with the Mexican and U.S. governments, commanded Texas forces in the early period of the Texas Revolution, and served as secretary of state for the Republic of Texas.

(The Granger Collection, New York)

Osceola. The leader of the Seminoles, Osceola resisted the United States for years in hard fighting in Florida.

Conflict with Mexico

In the wake of the panic of 1819, speculators and settlers from the United States emigrated to Mexican Texas, where large swaths of Mexican land could be had on far better terms than the U.S. government offered. Prospective immigrants simply had to swear allegiance to the Mexican government, become Catholic, and present letters testifying to their good character. Mexico began inviting American settlers into its vulnerable northern border region in hopes of populating Texas, but soon clashed with the settlers over the issue of slavery. Mexico attempted to outlaw slavery at various times but found that Mexico City was too far from Texas to exercise effective control over the region.

A key leader in the American migration was **Stephen F. Austin,** a Virginia-born entrepreneur who first arrived in Mexico in 1821 on the heels of Mexican independence. Throughout the 1820s, Austin, negotiating with the changing Mexican governments, allotted and registered land grants and oversaw the settlement of hundreds of Americans. Most of these settlers came from the U.S. South and believed that slavery would be crucial for the development of Texas.

Santa Anna, Antonio López de (1794–1876) Mexican general and politician. Leader of Mexico at the time of the battle at the Alamo. Taken prisoner at San Jacinto, he signed the Treaties of Velasco, which granted Texas its independence and recognized the Rio Grande as the boundary.

General **Antonio López de Santa Anna** began consolidating power in Mexico during the early 1830s. His attempts to centralize control in Mexico City led to revolts throughout Mexico, including the Yucatan, Zacatecas, and Texas. Settlers increasingly came into conflict with the Mexican government when provincial officials attempted to collect tariffs and slow immigration into the province. Austin and others petitioned the Mexican government to let them become a separate Mexican state under its own administration, but they were rebuffed when Santa Anna took control and sent in troops. In 1835, a convention of Texans created a provisional government, with Sam Houston as commander of the army, to fight against Santa Anna for their rights as Mexican citizens outlined in the Constitution of 1824. For many Texans, this was not a vote for independence; those seeking immediate independence were voted down thirty-three to fifteen. Austin was sent east, offering large parcels of land to all who would fight in the struggle.

Tejanos Mexicans in Texas who supported the revolt for independence from Mexico.

During the Texas Revolution, volunteers and money flowed from the United States to Texas; southern states in particular sent hundreds of men. Nevertheless, Texas army enlistments were greatly outnumbered by the Mexicans. When the Mexican army occupied San Antonio in early 1836, about two hundred rebels—including David Crockett of Tennessee, famous for his frontier exploits—took refuge in an old mission called the Alamo. Most of the people inside were American or European immigrants, but they were joined by ***Tejanos*** (Mexicans native to Texas) who allied themselves with the rebellion against Santa Anna. The defenders of the Alamo held out against nearly three thousand Mexican soldiers for two weeks, until the Mexicans finally stormed the mission and killed all inside except three white women, two white children, and an African American slave. On orders of Santa Anna, the Mexican army stripped the bodies of the insurrectionists and burned them. In the aftermath of the Alamo, Texans committed themselves to creating an independent state, as many American observers began to view the conflict as a moral struggle between the forces of freedom and autocracy.

Seguín, Juan (1806–1890) Tejano cavalry commander who played a key role in defeating Mexican troops at the Battle of San Jacinto, which secured the independence of Texas.

Santa Anna stood on the verge of destroying the Texas rebellion until Sam Houston's army surprised the larger Mexican force at San Jacinto in April 1836. A force of nine hundred Texans with *Tejano* cavalry commanded by **Juan Seguín** stormed Santa Anna's troops, winning decisively in only eighteen minutes. Santa Anna, captured a day after the battle, signed treaties removing Mexican troops from Texas, granting Texas its independence, and recognizing the Rio Grande as the boundary. The Mexican Congress, on hearing of this capitulation, renounced the treaty on the grounds that Santa Anna had signed under penalty of death.

Texans, and many Americans elsewhere, urged the U.S. government to annex the new republic before it could be reconquered by Mexico. The question of annexation unleashed a heated and protracted debate, most of which raged between southerners, who saw Texas as a vast new empire, and northerners who opposed annexation because it would lead to slavery's expansion. The fate of Texas would remain a central political issue for the next decade.

❖ Religion and Reform

The power and influence of Protestant churches surged to a new level in the Jacksonian era. Far more than in any previous generation, the churches took leading roles in every facet of life and in every part of the Union. Revivals pulled in scores of new members. Many of those who experienced the spiritual rebirth of the revivals sought to bring others closer to God through religious education and social reform. A radical new movement against slavery gathered force with stunning speed. Other Americans worked to reform asylums, orphanages, and penal institutions. Still others sought purer forms of religion itself.

Revivalism

Since the late eighteenth century, revivals led by the major Protestant denominations had periodically inflamed the United States. In those revivals, people who had never before declared their faith or had fallen away from the church made public expressions of their faith. Thousands of people gathered across the nation and along the frontier, in town and countryside, to pray and hear ministers tell them of God's love and forgiveness. The churches that devoted themselves to spreading the Gospel periodically experienced revivals, or "awakenings," when numbers of people expressed or renewed their faith in emotional public displays. This revivalism burst out again in the mid-1820s and became known as the Second Great Awakening.

As Americans looked about them in the 1820s, they became concerned that little seemed to be holding their society together. Men and women married at younger ages and left home far earlier than their parents had. The opening of land in the West undermined one of the principal forms of control exercised by fathers in earlier generations: the promise of passing on land to sons who stayed and worked at home. Daughters might marry earlier, begin families of their own, and move far away. The American population skyrocketed as so many young families established themselves.

The new economy also caused concern for many. Increasingly men and women seemed pulled in different directions, away from a sole focus on the family farm or family artisan shop. Young men often worked for wages for a number of employers rather than serving for many years with one master. Young women might move to mill towns, where they too lived among strangers, away from parental control. Revivals and reform movements responded to these dislocations and uncertainties.

Many ministers and churches across the country were swept up in the religious awakening of the 1820s, but one man embodied its new and aggressive spirit: **Charles Grandison Finney.** Finney, a young attorney from Utica, New York, who had not regularly attended church until encouraged to do so by his

Finney, Charles Grandison (1792–1875) American evangelist, theologian, and educator. Licensed to the Presbyterian ministry in 1824, he had phenomenal success as a revivalist in the Northeast, converting many who later became noted abolitionists.

(The Granger Collection, New York)

Revival during the Second Great Awakening. To outside observers, the revivals of the Second Great Awakening appeared as frightening scenes of chaos and unsettled relations between men and women.

fiancée, suddenly found himself struck with the power of God's love. "An overwhelming sense" of his wickedness brought Finney to his knees. "I wept aloud like a child [and] the Holy Spirit descended upon me in a manner that seemed to go through me body and soul," he recalled. Finney spread the word of the Bible in the plain and straightforward language of everyday life. He told people that they had it within their power to take the first step toward God and that God would listen.

Finney found a receptive audience in the new cities of western New York. The churches, these people believed, had grown cold in the hands of the established ministry and needed a revival of spirit. Finney's influence grew in strength and numbers as women prayed with one another. The district of upstate New York that lay along the path of the Erie Canal became known as "the burned-over district," as one revival after another blazed through its towns and farms.

Women's prayer groups met daily and traveled from home to home in efforts to bring the word of Jesus. Women pleaded with their husbands to listen to the Reverend Finney. Employers made it clear to the men who worked under them that it would be noticed whether they attended the revival. These efforts, combined with Finney's masterful sermons and hopeful message, brought hundreds of people into the church who had not come before and reclaimed many who had strayed. All of the Protestant denominations worked together, setting aside for a while their doctrinal differences.

Such a powerful revival seemed evidence to many people that America could be changed by faith. As they watched saloons shut down, families brought together, and shops and stores closed while the revival was in progress, it appeared that the way was being prepared for God's kingdom on earth. It was up to Americans themselves to purge their country of sin, to make themselves better, and then to help others see the way as well. Such faith bred a demand for immediate reforms.

The Birth of Mormonism

Smith, Joseph (1805–1844) American religious leader who founded the Church of Jesus Christ of Latter-Day Saints (1830). He led his congregation from New York State to western Illinois, where he was murdered by an anti-Mormon mob.

Like many other American families of these years, that of **Joseph Smith** could not find a secure place. His father, who dreamed of bringing his family out of poverty, moved them from one community to another. Young Joseph watched with concern for his soul as revivals came and went without his conversion. Smith reported that he felt the presence of an angel, however, who told him "that God had work for me to do, and that my name should be for good and evil among all nations, kindreds, and tongues." Smith claimed that an angel had directed him to the location of sacred writings, and he began to transcribe what he had found. *The Book of Mormon* took shape, telling of a struggle between the chosen ones and their persecutors, of a promised land reserved for the righteous.

After 1830 Joseph Smith and several followers traveled throughout New York selling copies of what they called the "Gold Bible." They were met with hostility virtually everywhere they went, but they slowly gathered converts to their Church of Jesus Christ of Latter-Day Saints. Many of the new members were poor, including some free blacks, but others had considerable resources. The most important converts were two brothers, Brigham and Joseph Young. As the movement gathered momentum, hundreds of people joined the church; entire congregations of churches of other faiths joined the Mormons and contributed everything they owned to the church's common fund. The faithful moved first to Ohio and then to what Smith believed to be the original Eden: Missouri. But other settlers made no secret of their disapproval of the Mormons: they fired shots, threw stones through windows, and burned the crops of the Latter-Day Saints. The Mormons gained followers but found no peace for the next decade.

Middle-Class Reform Movements

Americans looked to the new churches for guidance, but they also turned to families, and especially middle-class women, to create virtuous children and husbands. The lives of these middle-class women were undergoing a dramatic shift, especially in the towns and cities of the Northeast. Bakeries, butcher shops, clothiers, and candlemakers began to offer, more easily and cheaply than ever before, some of the things that women had long labored to produce at home. Schools became more common, providing a place for children to receive education beyond the bounds of the home. Young women from poorer backgrounds came into cities looking for jobs as maids and laundresses, taking away some of the household burden for women well off enough to hire them.

As ministers, journalists, and other opinion makers looked at the changing households, they began to articulate an ideal of what has been called "domesticity." Women, they said, should become the moral center of the household, the guardians of good thoughts, clean living, providers of a sense of safety for children and husbands. While the world beyond the household seemed increasingly threatening and disorienting, women could make the home a place of refuge and renewal. Many middle-class women welcomed this message and this mission, which fit well with their own experiences and their own aspirations. Domesticity asked something of men as well: men would have to make a greater investment in home life than had their fathers. Men needed to acknowledge the feelings of their wives more, speaking in tones of respect and affection, and provide a firm male model to accompany the softer nurture of their wives.

This ideal, however, remained beyond the reach of many Americans. Women who had to work for others all day had little time to devote to their own families, and men who could not be certain of their next day's wages could not afford to keep children out of the workforce into their late teens. Slave families struggled to stay together in any way they could. Nevertheless, this middle-class ideal was elaborated and celebrated in print and sermons across the growing young nation.

The same Americans who promoted the Christian middle-class home as their ideal looked to other institutions and reforms in the 1820s to help remake American society. They sought to extend the ideals of character, self-control, and education to those who seemed to fall beyond the good effects of family and household. They worried about hungry children, desperate fathers, and distraught mothers. They noticed increasing numbers of women selling themselves on the city streets. They decried bulging jails and streets full of people without homes. Groups of reform-minded people mobilized themselves to counter these problems.

The American Sunday School Union wrote and published materials for children to be used in Sunday schools across the country. Those schools, although based in churches, taught reading and writing as well as religion. The American Bible Society launched an ambitious drive to put Bibles in every American home, pioneering national systems of distribution, and ultimately issuing more than 32 million Bibles. The new organizations prided themselves on knitting Americans together with a common faith. They preached nothing controversial, claiming only to spread the good news of the Protestant Christian faith. They depended on the hard work of women, who filled the membership rolls and helped raise funds.

During these years, reformers created a new kind of institution—the "penitentiary"—for those apparently most in need of reform: criminals. In a penitentiary, unlike a common jail, criminals would be locked in individual cells, free from the contamination of others, alone with their consciences and the Bible. There, reflecting on their crimes, they would become "penitent" and would emerge as better people. Americans were proud of their penitentiaries, among the first in the world, holding them up as examples of what the enlightened new nation could do.

Alongside penitentiaries, asylums for the deaf and blind, for the insane, for orphans, and for the poor began to appear in the 1820s, replacing more informal kinds of care. **Dorothea Dix** became famous throughout the United States for her often lonely crusade on behalf of people otherwise forgotten. Dix lobbied ceaselessly for the construction of cleaner, healthier, and more hopeful kinds of institutions for those who could not care for themselves. Each institution placed its faith in strict order, moral teaching, and faith in the inherent goodness of human nature.

Dix, Dorothea (1802–1887) American philanthropist, reformer, and educator who took charge of nurses for the United States during the Civil War.

Abolitionism

Two hundred antislavery societies emerged in the early 1830s. Ground that had been prepared by the evangelical crusades of the preceding few years proved fertile for the antislavery cause. Some northern church members argued that it was the duty of good Christians to cast out slaveholders and work for immediate emancipation, to use the enormous power of the church as a force for freedom. These "immediatists" called for slaveholders to recognize the truth of what the abolitionists were saying, to free their slaves immediately, hire them as free workers, and help repay the former slaves for their years of unpaid toil.

In the late 1820s, **William Lloyd Garrison,** the young editor of a prohibition newspaper, attended antislavery meetings held by African Americans, including the group that published the first antislavery newspaper, *Freedom's Journal.* Garrison suddenly saw the limitations of the colonization movement as he witnessed the passion of people such as David Walker. In 1831, the balding and bespectacled young Garrison launched a paper of his own: *The Liberator.* It called for the immediate start toward emancipation, explicitly rejecting colonization. In its first year, the paper had only six subscribers, but it had acquired fifty-three, most of them African American, by the following year. "I *will* be as harsh as truth," Garrison announced, "and as uncompromising as justice. On this subject, I do not wish to think, speak, or write, with moderation. . . . I am earnest—I will not equivocate—I will not excuse—I will not retreat a single inch—AND I WILL BE HEARD." He was. *The Liberator* spread the news of abolition to many whites who had never seen a newspaper edited by black people. Ironically, Garrison's argument was spread even further by newspaper editors who denounced him.

Garrison, William Lloyd (1805–1879) American abolitionist leader who founded the antislavery journal *The Liberator* (1831–1865).

The American Anti-Slavery Society formed in Philadelphia in 1833. Looking to the example of Great Britain, where the major denominations supported the antislavery movement that was at that moment triumphing over slavery in the British West Indies, the members of the society expected American church leaders to take the lead against American slavery. Antislavery organizations held out the prospect of a free South, where 2 million freed slaves would constitute an "immense market" for the products of Northern "mechanics and manufacturers." These abolitionists spoke little of the competition the freed people might provide to the workers of the North. Similarly, the antislavery people believed a free South would prosper, with planters and free whites flourishing as they never had before; the South, they claimed, would "exhibit the flush of returning health, and feel a stronger pulse, and draw a freer breath." Far more than any other organizations in the United States at this time, the antislavery cause brought together male and female, black and white, patrician and working class, Quaker and Unitarian, Baptist and Methodist, radical and moderate, political and antipolitical people. Each of these groups had its own vision of how the abolitionists should spend their energies and influence. Black abolitionists, in particular, wanted the organizations to do more to help black communities in the North.

Doing History Online

Newspapers

Go to the CourseMate website for this chapter and link to Primary Sources. African Americans began publishing a newspaper in 1827 and the Cherokees did so in 1828. Just over a decade later, women working in New England factories started a number of papers, such as the *Factory Girl,* the *Voice of Industry,* the *Wampanoag and Operatives' Journal,* and the *Lowell Offering.* Based on Documents 2, 3, and 12, why did these groups turn to newsprint?

www.cengagebrain.com

(The Library Company of Philadelphia)

The Slave Trade and the Capitol. Abolitionists pointed to the irony of the slave trade taking place within sight of the U.S. capitol, the symbol of "aboasted free nation."

The antislavery societies used pamphlets, leaflets, and other literature as their major weapons. Rapid innovations in printing lowered the cost of producing such materials, which flooded post offices and streets. The postal campaign reached its peak in 1834 and 1835, when a million pieces went out through the mail, much of it to the South, where the abolitionists hoped to appeal directly to ministers and others who might be willing to listen to their pleas. That literature, white southerners furiously protested, virtually invited slaves to follow Nat Turner's example. Georgia slaveholders offered a $12,000 reward for the capture of wealthy merchant Arthur Tappan, who, along with his brother Lewis, funded much of the postal campaign against slavery. Arthur received a slave's severed ear in the mail. Mobs in Charleston seized sacks of mail from northern cities and burned them in the streets.

The pamphlets infuriated people in much of the North as well. Mobs, led by some of the wealthiest merchants of northern towns but constituted in large part by white working people, rose up violently against the abolitionists. In 1835 mobs destroyed the home of African Americans, pelted antislavery speakers, and dragged William Lloyd Garrison through the streets of Boston at the end of a rope. The leaders of that mob announced that they had assaulted Garrison "to assure our brethren of the South that we cherish rational and correct notions on the subject of slavery." Abolitionists' churches were blown up and their school buildings dragged into swamps.

The persecution, ironically, strengthened the abolitionist cause. Denunciation and harassment only made the abolitionists more certain of the need for their efforts, of the moral decay caused by slavery. The two hundred antislavery societies of 1835 grew to more than five hundred in 1836. The reformers flooded Congress with petitions calling for the end of slavery in the District of Columbia, sending more than three hundred petitions signed by forty thousand people. The acceptance of these petitions by the House, southerners argued, besmirched slaveholders' honor and threatened to incite slaves to rebellion; the southerners said the petitions should be rejected out of hand. Congress sought to avoid conflict by merely tabling the petitions without consideration, but the compromise pleased no one.

gag rule Congressional practice, starting in 1836, to ban consideration of antislavery petitions.

During the next decade, northerners of even a mild antislavery bent chafed at this **gag rule**, which they saw as a clear violation of American freedom in the interests of slavery. Former President John Quincy Adams fought back in 1837 by attempting to present a petition from twenty-two slaves. Representatives from Georgia and Alabama demanded that Adams be expelled and the petition "taken from the House and burnt or the southern states would withdraw from the House." In their fury to squelch any petitions to Congress on the subject of slavery, southern representatives failed to notice that the petition from the slaves did not advocate abolition.

CHAPTER REVIEW, 1829–1836

SUMMARY

- Andrew Jackson became the most active president the United States had yet seen.
- Slaves were involved in revolts in South Carolina and Virginia, leading to stricter slave codes.
- Slavery generated a debate over nullification in South Carolina and wide-ranging debate over the future of the institution in Virginia.
- The Bank of the United States became a major focus of political conflict.
- President Jackson led a determined and successful effort to remove eastern Native Americans to west of the Mississippi River.
- The Second Great Awakening shook the nation as many Americans sought spiritual refuge from tumultuous change and growth.
- A movement for the immediate abolition of slavery emerged in the North, and women led other reform movements as well that sought to improve American society.

IDENTIFICATIONS

spoils system
Peggy Eaton
nullification
David Walker
Nat Turner
Virginia slave debates
Bank War
John Ross
Indian Removal Act
Trail of Tears
Osceola
Stephen F. Austin
Antonio López de Santa Anna
Tejanos
Juan Seguín
Charles Grandison Finney
Joseph Smith
Dorothea Dix
William Lloyd Garrison
gag rule

and the United States during the past decade offered hope to inland cities. When New Jersey sponsored a bold rail and canal connection between New York and Philadelphia in 1831, it ordered a custom-built locomotive from an English company: the John Bull. The railroad became an immediate success, carrying more than 100,000 passengers in 1834. By 1841, ten American railroad companies had opened to meet the growing demand.

Railroads almost immediately became the key form of transportation in the United States. Rail transport grew cheaper as the network expanded, and trains could run when canals had frozen over. By 1840, American companies and states had spent $75 million to build thirty-three hundred miles of track, surpassing Great Britain; by 1850, the country claimed nearly nine thousand miles of railroad. New industries rose to serve the trains as iron, coal, timber, and steel manufacturing companies burgeoned with the railroads' demand.

Railroads appeared in every region of the United States but not in a uniform network (see Map 11.1). Beginning from many different entrepreneurial efforts and adapting to widely varying terrain, railroads did not adapt a standard distance between the rails (the gauge). As a result, trains could not travel rapidly across the nation; cargo had to be unloaded and reloaded. Trains connected coastal cities with inland plantations and farms in the South, while in the North and West, railroads ran from city to city, knitting together a network of economic development that benefited a wider area. In this way, railroads accelerated the growth of differences between the South and the rest of the country.

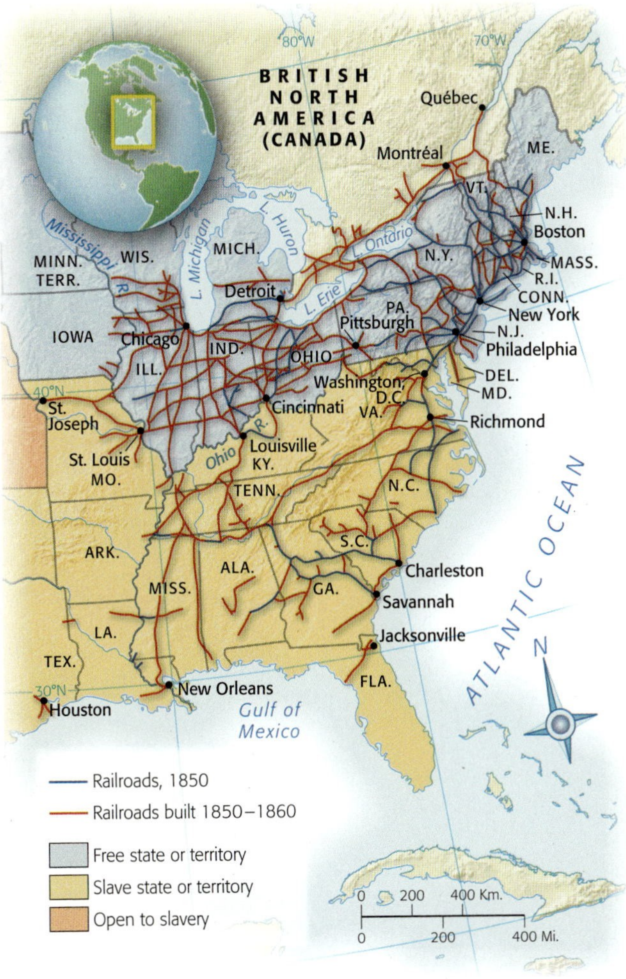

MAP 11.1
The Growth of Railroads, to 1860
A vastly expanded transportation network tied the United States together. The system exaggerated sectional differences by unifying the Northeast with the Northwest, creating the reality and perception of a "North" with interests different from those of a "South" stretching from the Atlantic to the Mississippi and beyond.

Telegraph poles marched alongside the railroads, their wires carrying news of train locations on single-track lines and preventing gruesome crashes while also speeding the flow of information just as the railroads sped the flow of people and goods. Like the locomotive, the telegraph was the product of inventors in several countries, but it received a major impetus from America. **Samuel F. B. Morse** patented his version of the electronic telegraph in 1840. Following its success, the telegraph spread across the country with great speed. In the four years after its initial test in 1844, more than five thousand miles of wire had been strung, with another three thousand under construction.

Morse, Samuel F. B. (1791–1872) American painter and inventor. He refined and patented the telegraph and developed the telegraphic code that bears his name.

❖ Life in the New Slave South

The South, increasingly dominated by slavery, remained an integral part of the United States. Southern cotton drove national economic growth, and southern politicians controlled much of the nation's government. Thanks to the rapid expansion of newspapers and the telegraph, white southerners took part in all of the national conversations about race, slavery, and politics. As northerners and southerners read the critical words often aimed across the Mason-Dixon line, though, distrust between the regions grew. The single profound difference between the North and South, slavery, became ever more significant.

African Americans and the South

By the 1830s, slavery had spread over an area stretching from Maryland to Texas (see Map 11.2). The domestic slave trade expanded at a feverish rate during the decade as the new planters of Mississippi, Alabama, and Louisiana eagerly imported slaves to clear land and plant cotton (see Figure 11.1). American slavery became ever more diverse as it expanded. In addition to cotton fields, enslaved people worked in hemp, wheat, rice, corn, sugar, and tobacco fields. They worked with livestock and racehorses, practiced trades such as carpentry and blacksmithing,

MAP 11.2
Paths of the Slave Trade, 1840–1860
The slave trade grew into a vast business in the years before the Civil War. The trade ran strongly from the Upper South to the Lower South, from east to west.

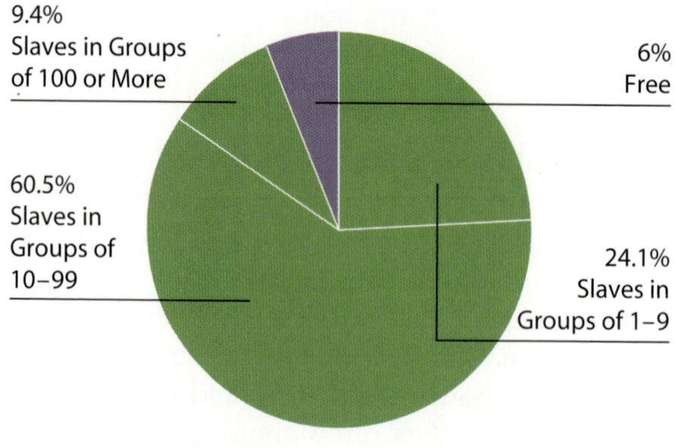

FIGURE 11.1
Patterns of Black Population in the South
Most black people lived on large plantations with more than ten other enslaved people; others were scattered on much smaller farms and in towns and cities.

and labored in factories and on the docks and in the shipyards of southern ports. Southern culture mixed English, African, Scots-Irish, Caribbean, French, Indian, and Hispanic influences into a rich and complex blend. Language, food, music, and religion took on new shapes as black and white cultures interacted.

Black culture remained distinct and vibrant, even as it influenced the larger American culture. African American families, often split apart by sale, tended to rely on a broader range of kin than did white families. Grandparents, aunts, and uncles often played significant roles in child rearing in black families. When people of blood relation were unavailable, southern slaves created "fictive kin," friends and neighbors given honorary titles of "brother" or "aunt" and treated as relatives. These arrangements permitted slave families considerable resiliency. African Americans often found wives or husbands on nearby farms, visiting one another on evenings and weekends.

Plantations and Farms

Most slave owners in the American South lived on the same farms as their slaves, but wealthier owners put day-to-day control of their plantations in the hands of professional overseers. These overseers were often ambitious young men of middling background who used the position as a steppingstone to purchasing their own plantations. On larger plantations, where slaves often worked in groups called gangs, trusted male slaves served as "drivers." Such drivers tended to be especially strong and skilled, commanding respect from whites as well as blacks. Although whites held the ultimate threat of force, they much preferred to keep the work moving smoothly, minimizing both potential conflict and their own exposure to heat and weather.

About three out of four enslaved people were field hands, though almost all enslaved people went to the fields during the peak times. Women and men also served in white households as cooks and domestics. Slaves' lives were by no means simple. Lines of power often became complicated and tangled on

(Collection of the New-York Historical Society)

Laborers Returning from Picking Cotton. Enslaved people of both genders and of all ages labored long hours to bring the South's valuable cotton crop from seed to bale.

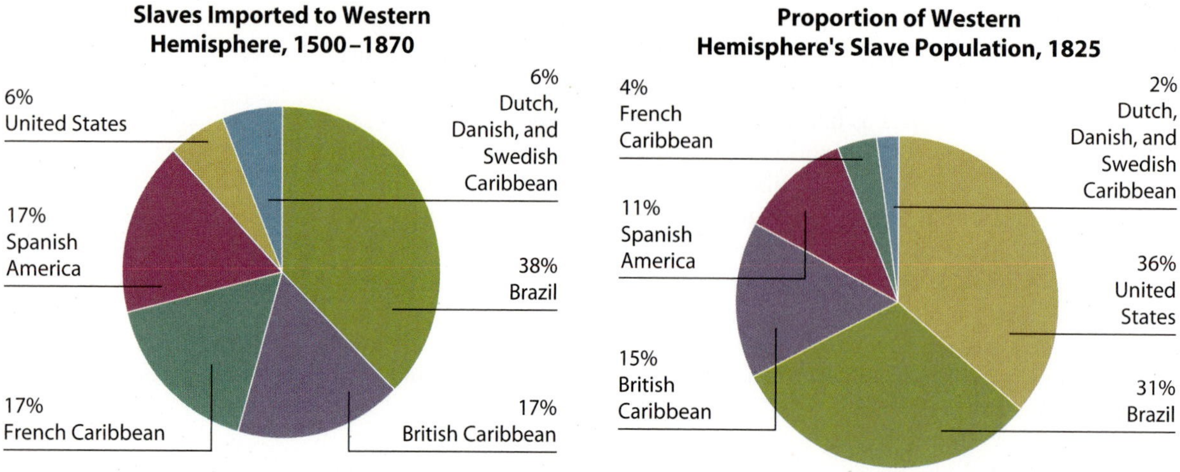

FIGURE 11.2

North American Slavery in Context

As these two graphs show, the United States accounted for a relatively small proportion of all enslaved people brought from Africa into the Western Hemisphere, but because of the longer life spans of North American slaves, over a third of the enslaved population of the New World lived in the United States in 1825.

plantations and farms, with slave owners, their children, overseers, and drivers claiming authority. Some slaves were respected as purveyors of healing or religious knowledge from Africa; some were admired for their musical ability; others won recognition for their ability to read and preach the Gospel. But white southerners frequently underestimated the abilities and character of the people among whom they lived.

Whites told themselves that they provided "their people" a better life than they would have known in Africa. Indeed, southern masters explained the justice of slavery to themselves and to the North by stressing their Christian stewardship for the slaves. As one clergyman wrote to his fellow slaveholders in the early 1840s, slaves "were placed under our control . . . not exclusively for our benefit but theirs also." Most masters would not permit their slaves to learn to read, but they did arrange to have Bible selections read to their slaves.

American slavery was a harsh institution. Many slave owners did not refrain from having their slaves whipped on small provocation, branded, shackled, or locked up in sweltering enclosures; female slaves especially suffered sexual abuse. Partly because expectant mothers were often kept in the fields until labor began, about a third of all black babies died before they reached their first birthday. Compared with slaves elsewhere in the hemisphere, those of the American South were relatively healthy (see Figure 11.2). Still, they lived with monotonous diets, ineffective or dangerous health care, continual fear of violence and sale, meager shelter—and the psychic costs of their status as human property.

(Library of Congress)

Slave Nurse and Child. Relationships between African Americans and the white people for whom they labored contained complicated elements of human emotion.

The Politics of the White South

White men in the South took their politics seriously and built much of it around slavery. America's commitment to slavery was grounded in a cold social and economic calculus. In southern cities such as Natchez, Mississippi, whites enjoyed among the highest per capita incomes in the nation, the finest homes, and access to music, theater, and public entertainment that rivaled any city in the country. In the South as in the North, the Whigs portrayed themselves as the party of progress and prosperity, appealing to lawyers, editors, merchants, and wealthy planters.

The Democrats found their strongest supporters among the middling farmers and aspiring planters of the South. These men tended to resent taxes on their lands and slaves. They admired the Democrats' aggressive approach to western expansion and removing the American Indians. Southerners distrustful of northern reformers and financial speculators found the small-government pronouncements of the Democrats appealing.

In the South, both the Whigs and the Democrats declared themselves the friends of southern slavery, but they differed in their emphases. Democrats pledged that they would protect slavery by extending the power of the federal government as little as possible. Whigs argued that the best way to protect slavery was for the South to develop its region's economy and build strong economic and political bridges to the North and Europe.

❖ Reform Takes Root

The wild economic swings of the 1830s, added to religious reform impulses, further drove Americans to improve their society. They could see dangers all around them, but they could also glimpse how things could be better. The news machinery of railroads, telegraphs, and printing presses held out exciting new possibilities for spreading reforms to wider audiences than ever before. (See *Doing History: Religion and Reform*.)

Education and Temperance

Many Americans had become dissatisfied with the way young people were schooled. No state had a statewide school system, and local districts ran their own affairs, often wretchedly. The rich attended private schools or employed tutors. Hundreds of districts, especially in the South and West, created no schools at all. Many American children never went to school in the 1820s and 1830s, and those who did often attended for only a short time, interrupted by the demands of family and farm. Reformers argued that unequal and inadequate education would not suffice in America, a country dependent on an informed democracy. These reformers wanted free public schools.

A Massachusetts lawyer and Whig politician, **Horace Mann** worked relentlessly to make rich citizens, especially manufacturers, see that a tax in support of schools was a wise investment. Think how much better workers would be, he argued, if they could read and calculate. Think to what good use women could be put as teachers, he argued, instilling future citizens with their virtues of cooperation and peacefulness. Mann gradually persuaded influential people in Massachusetts of the practicability of common schools. In 1837, he became the first secretary of the Massachusetts Board of Education and transformed that system during his tenure. The minimum school year stretched to six months, buildings and teacher training improved significantly, and teachers' pay increased by more than half.

Mann, Horace (1796–1859) Educational reformer and promoter of public school education; first secretary of the Massachusetts Board of Education.

Women teachers became common in the Northeast and Midwest. Females attended new "normal schools" that provided teacher training; they read educational journals, received professional supervision, and taught with uniform textbooks. These standards spread throughout the North and the West in the 1840s and 1850s, as did *McGuffey's Readers*. These books, which sold an astonishing 9 million copies between 1836 and 1850, celebrated Christian piety, the virtues of hard work, and patriotism.

Doing History Religion and Reform

Charles Grandison Finney, a young attorney from western New York who later became president of Oberlin College, helped spread the revivals of the Second Great Awakening. His sermons, delivered in a dramatic speaking style, were often reprinted in newspapers and published collections.

Massachusetts-born Ralph Waldo Emerson was a central figure in transcendentalism, which split from established religion believing that religious inspiration could be found in nature and within the individual. In this address, delivered to the graduates of Harvard Divinity School in 1838, Emerson argued that institutional religion failed to inspire an experience of the divine.

Charles Grandison Finney, "What a Revival of Religion Is," *1834*

Almost all the religion in the world has been produced by revivals. God has found it necessary to take advantage of the excitability there is in mankind, to produce powerful excitements among them, before he can lead them to obey. . . . A revival always includes conviction of sin on the part of the church. Backslidden professors cannot wake up and begin right away in the service of God, without deep searchings of heart. . . . Christians will have their faith renewed. . . . When they enter into a revival, they no longer see men as trees walking, but they see things in that strong light which will renew the love of God in their hearts. This will lead them to labor zealously to bring others to him. . . . They will have a longing desire for the salvation of the whole world. . . . Very often the most abandoned profligates are among the subjects. Harlots, and drunkards, and infidels, and all sorts of abandoned characters, are awakened and converted.

Source: Charles Grandison Finney, "What a Revival of Religion Is" (1834), in *Lectures on Revivals of Religion*, ed. William G. McLoughlin (Cambridge, MA: Belknap Press of Harvard University Press, 1960; reprint, New York: Leavitt, Lord & Co., 1835), 10, 15–17.

Ralph Waldo Emerson, Divinity School Address, *July 15, 1838*

Whilst a man seeks good ends, he is strong by the whole strength of nature. . . . The perception of this law of laws awakens in the mind a sentiment which we call the religious sentiment. . . . Through it, the soul first knows itself . . . showing the fountain of all good to be in himself, and that he, equally with every man, is an inlet into the deeps of Reason. . . . In how many churches, by how many prophets, tell me, is man made sensible that he is an infinite Soul; that the earth and heavens are passing into his mind; that he is drinking forever the soul of God? . . . The test of the true faith, certainly, should be its power to charm and command the soul, as the laws of nature control the activity of the hands,—so commanding that we find pleasure and honor in obeying. The faith should blend with the light of rising and of setting suns, with the flying cloud, the singing bird, and the breath of flowers.

Source: Ralph Waldo Emerson, "An Address Delivered Before the Senior Class in Divinity College, Cambridge, Sunday Evening, July 15, 1838," in *The Complete Works of Ralph Waldo Emerson: Nature Addresses and Lectures*, Vol. 1 (Boston: Houghton, Mifflin, 1903–1904), 124–125, 136–137.

QUESTIONS for REFLECTION

1. What concerns do these two documents share?
2. What demands does religious experience place on believers for Finney and Emerson?
3. How would Emerson react to Finney's emphasis on the church's role in religious experience?

Washingtonian temperance movement Nineteenth century reform movement that encouraged the reduction or elimination of alcoholic beverage consumption.

Americans had long waged campaigns against intemperance, but the fight against drink took on a new urgency in the depression years of the late 1830s and early 1840s. Many people, religious and otherwise, saw alcohol as the scourge of American life. Men drank at work, farmers routinely turned their surplus grain into whiskey, and rum was a major part of New England commerce. The **Washingtonian temperance movement**, named in honor of George Washington, gave great force and visibility to a crusade against alcohol. Older reform attempts had been largely the efforts of men, but now women became active.

The Washingtonians began in Baltimore in 1840, when six drinkers pledged to one another to quit drinking and persuade other drinkers to do the same. Word of the new movement quickly spread up the eastern seaboard, and by 1843 the Washingtonians claimed millions of adherents. Unlike earlier temperance efforts led by upper-class or religious leaders, Washingtonians prided themselves on an egalitarian ethos. Partly as a result of the new organization and partly from the growing stigma attached to drunkenness, Americans' consumption of alcohol plummeted in the 1840s.

Women's "Martha Washington" societies also grew rapidly, challenging the men's movement in both size and in fervor. They helped families in distress get back on their feet and reminded men that it was the wives and children of drunkards who suffered most from their neglect, cruelty, and financial irresponsibility.

Doing History Online

Age of Reform

Go to the CourseMate website for this chapter and link to Primary Sources. Historians have long tried to explain the flurry of reform efforts during the 1830s and 1840s. Based on your reading of Documents 5 to 7, 11, and 12 and the textbook, in this and other chapters, what explanation would you offer?

www.cengagebrain.com

Abolitionism Strengthened and Challenged

By the late 1830s, the American Anti-Slavery Society claimed more than a quarter of a million members, primarily in the Northeast and Midwest. The first female abolitionist speakers, **Angelina and Sarah Grimké,** were prize recruits into the antislavery ranks, for they were the daughters of a prominent South Carolina slave-owning planter. By relating their own own experiences with slavery to New England audiences, the Grimkés held a credibility that white northern abolitionists could not match. "*All moral beings have essentially the same rights and the same duties,* whether they be male or female," Angelina Grimké admonished an audience. The female slaves of the South, who "now wear the iron yoke of slavery in this land of boasted liberty and law . . . are our countrywomen—*they are our sisters.*"

Grimké, Angelina (1805–1879) and Sarah (1792–1873) The first female abolitionist speakers; they were prominent figures in the antislavery movement of the late 1830s.

As it grew stronger, the antislavery cause met with more determined opposition. When abolitionist editor **Elijah P. Lovejoy** offended readers of his religious paper in St. Louis—by denouncing a local judge who prevented the trial of a mob who had burned a black man alive—citizens of Alton, Illinois, invited Lovejoy to move to their town. Alton prided itself on being a progressive place, but soon mobs destroyed two of his presses and vowed to tar and feather him. In November 1837, as a replacement press arrived, a battle erupted, and Lovejoy was killed as he and his assistants fought the crowd. The mob shattered his press, and local law officers arrested the defenders of Lovejoy for inciting the violence.

Lovejoy, Elijah P. (1802–1837) Abolitionist editor, killed by proslavery advocates in an attack on his printing press in Alton, Illinois.

Abolitionists debated the proper response to such opposition. William Lloyd Garrison, editor of the antislavery newspaper *The Liberator,* counseled his allies to offer no resistance to violence. He and his supporters renounced all allegiance to the established parties and churches, which had long since shown themselves tolerant of slavery. Other abolitionists, by contrast, used whatever means they could to bring slavery to an end, including political parties.

The differences among the abolitionists came to a head at the annual meeting of the American Anti-Slavery Society in 1839. They differed most visibly in their attitudes toward the role of women. Women constituted perhaps half of all members of the antislavery organizations, but some male abolitionists sought to keep females in a subordinate role and prevent women members from voting, speaking publicly, or serving on committees with men. Unable to resolve their differences, the abolitionists split. The more conservative group, based in New York, created the **Liberty Party** to run a candidate for president in the upcoming election of 1840, seeking gradual emancipation. Garrison's organization, the Friends of Universal Reform, maintained a more radical stance on the role of women and sought immediate emancipation of slaves.

Liberty Party U.S. political party formed in 1839 to oppose the practice of slavery; it merged with the Free-Soil party in 1848.

Whatever their differences, abolitionists barraged Congress with petitions demanding that slavery be ended in the District of Columbia. Former President John Quincy Adams, now a congressman from Massachusetts, used all of his parliamentary skill to fight the gag rule that prevented Congress from recognizing antislavery petitions; he finally succeeded in getting it overthrown in 1845. Adams also successfully defended Africans who had seized a slave ship, the ***Amistad,*** bound for Cuba and landed it in Connecticut. Supported by a large network of abolitionists, Adams took the case before the U.S. Supreme Court and in 1841 won not only the acquittal of the Africans for murdering the ship's captain but their freedom as well.

Amistad Cuban slave ship on which forty-nine Africans rebelled in 1839 off the Cuban coast. The ship sailed to Long Island Sound where Spanish authorities demanded they be turned over for punishment. A group of American abolitionists, led by former President John Quincy Adams, won their freedom in 1841. The thirty-five who survived returned to Africa.

Black antislavery speakers greatly strengthened the antislavery cause. Abolitionists such as Henry Brown, Henry Bibb, Solomon Northup, Sojourner Truth, **Harriet Tubman,** and Ellen Craft electrified audiences. Although white abolitionists valued the contributions of their black compatriots, African American abolitionists chafed under the restrictions they faced from fellow reformers and enemies alike; they demanded greater rights for northern as well as southern blacks.

Tubman, Harriet (c. 1820–1913) Escaped slave who returned to the South and led hundreds of enslaved people to freedom in the North. Active throughout the 1850s, Tubman became famous as the most active member of the Underground Railroad.

One of the most remarkable Americans of the nineteenth century burst into visibility in the early 1840s. **Frederick Douglass** had grown up in Maryland. He learned to read from one mistress, though it was against the law for her to teach him. Sent to Baltimore by his owner, Douglass worked in the shipyards, continued to read widely, and plotted his escape to freedom. After several attempts, Douglass finally borrowed the papers of a free black sailor and rode a train to freedom in 1840. Douglass found himself in New York City, alone and without any notion of what he should do. Fortunately he met a black man who introduced the young runaway to the New York Anti-Slavery Society. After white abolitionists saw the skill with which he spoke, they sent Douglass to lecture throughout the North with William Lloyd Garrison.

Douglass, Frederick (1817–1895) American abolitionist and journalist who escaped from slavery (1838) and became an influential lecturer in the North and abroad. He wrote *Narrative of the Life of Frederick Douglass* (1845) and cofounded and edited the *North Star* (1847–1860), an abolitionist newspaper.

❖ Development of an American Culture

European visitors had long scoffed at the failure of the United States to create anything they considered culture. During the first desperate decades of the nation's experience, filled with war, economic panic, and political conflict, few Americans found opportunity to write novels, produce ambitious paintings, or carve sculptures. But in the 1830s and 1840s, the new country experienced a sudden outburst of creativity in everything from philosophy to popular amusements.

Doing History Online

Slavery

Go to the CourseMate website for this chapter and link to Primary Sources. Read Document 13. Why do you imagine a fugitive slave would correspond with his or her former master? Why might it be risky to contact a former master?

www.cengagebrain.com

Transcendentalism, Romanticism, and the American Landscape

Leading American thinkers saw the possibilities of improvement everywhere. Several emerged from the Unitarian Church, a form of liberal Christianity especially strong in New England. Unitarianism encouraged people to emphasize feeling rather than dogma. Several young people raised within the Unitarian church took these ideas further than their elders intended, arguing that belief in the literal truth of the Bible trapped religion in the past. Better to appeal directly to the heart from the very beginning, turning to nature for inspiration and transcending the limits of churches and denominations.

Women played an active role in the effort to create a tradition of American philosophy, with Margaret Fuller becoming especially important. Fuller, raised in the Unitarian church in Cambridge, Massachusetts, received a fine education. But she felt herself adrift, full of "unemployed force," after her male classmates went on to college. She read widely and taught school with two other important figures in the revolt against Unitarianism: Elizabeth Peabody and Bronson Alcott. These three argued that school, like church, should not be permitted to get in the way of people's natural connection with nature and with one another.

Emerson, Ralph Waldo (1803–1882) American writer, philosopher, and central figure of American transcendentalism. His poems, orations, and especially his essays, such as *Nature* (1836), are regarded as landmarks in the development of American thought and literary expression.

They soon took their lead from **Ralph Waldo Emerson,** who had grown up near Concord, Massachusetts. Though descended from a distinguished ministerial family, he was raised by a widowed mother and forced to work his way through Harvard College. Uncomfortable as a minister and dissatisfied as a schoolteacher, Emerson set out for Europe, where he met English intellectuals whose stirring ideas influenced him deeply: Samuel Coleridge, Thomas Carlyle, and William Wordsworth. These writers, caught up in European romanticism with its rejection of the austere logic of the Enlightenment, provided Emerson with a perspective far removed from the cool Unitarianism on which he had been raised. Emerson perceived humankind as deeply tied to nature, filled with its rhythms and longings. He published such ideas in his first book, *Nature* (1836), which gained him considerable attention from like-minded young people of New England.

But it was Emerson's address before the Phi Beta Kappa initiates at Harvard in 1837 that announced his arrival to a larger audience. Emerson worried over the state of the nation after the panic of 1837. In his speech, "The American Scholar," Emerson argued that the scholar should be a man of action, a man of nature, a man of risk and endeavor. Books and poetry held tremendous power, Emerson admitted, but it was in activity, in striving, that the scholar became truly American. It was time to set the teachings of Europe aside long enough to find America's own voice, Emerson told the graduates.

Doing History Online

Ralph Waldo Emerson on the American Scholar, 1837

Go to the CourseMate website for this chapter and link to Primary Sources. Read the excerpted passages from Ralph Waldo Emerson's "The American Scholar" (Document 2) and Horace Mann's report to the Massachusetts Board of Education (Document 7). Why did each consider education so important for all Americans?

www.cengagebrain.com

Echoes of these ideas were also heard in the South. **William Gilmore Simms,** a leading essayist, novelist, poet, and proslavery advocate from South Carolina, lectured and wrote on diverse topics. Americans anxiously promoted their political and economic independence, Simms wrote, yet "our people have taken too little interest in the productions of the American mind. . . . A nation . . . must do its own thinking as well as its own fighting" or risk falling "a victim to that genius of another, to which she passively defers." Speakers like Emerson and Simms developed these ideas throughout the late 1830s, enjoying growing fame and influence through public lectures. Americans flocked to the lectures for personal improvement and social camaraderie.

Simms, William Gilmore (1806–1870) Prominent southern essayist, novelist, poet, and proslavery advocate.

Emerson's home in Concord became the gathering place for a group who came to be called the **transcendentalists:** they sought to "transcend" the mundane into the mystical knowledge that every human possessed if he or she would but listen to it. Margaret Fuller became the editor of the *Dial*, the transcendentalist magazine, and Elizabeth Peabody opened a bookstore catering to the interests of the group. Bronson Alcott and about eighty others founded Brook Farm, one of the many utopian experiments of the 1830s and 1840s. Brook Farm put people to work in the fields in the morning and on their books in the afternoon. The community produced both crops and an impressive weekly newspaper, and its schools stood as examples of enlightened education. The experiment failed economically after a few years, but for a while, Brook Farm offered the possibility of combining intellectual excitement, physical work, and social responsibility in a way the transcendentalists craved.

(Thomas Cole, American, 1801–1848, *Distant View of Niagara Falls*, 1830. Oil on panel. Friends of the American Art Collection, 1946.396. Photograph by Robert Hashimoto. Reproduction, The Art Institute of Chicago.)

American Romanticism. Thomas Cole's *Distant View of Niagara Falls* celebrated the power and beauty of nature as well as the uniqueness of the American landscape.

Because the transcendentalists believed that people should establish a close connection to nature, Henry David Thoreau decided to conduct an "experiment in human ecology." He wanted to see—and show—how a modern man could live in harmony with nature. In 1845, he built an isolated house in the woods near Concord's Walden Pond, where he strove to be self-sufficient and self-contained. Thoreau published reflections on his experience as *Walden: Life in the Woods* (1854).

transcendentalists Members of an intellectual and social movement of the 1830s and 1840s that emphasized the active role the mind plays in constructing what we think of as reality. A loose grouping of intellectuals in Massachusetts sought to "transcend" the limits of thought in conventional America, whether religious or philosophical.

Hudson River School Group of mid-nineteenth-century landscape painters, including Thomas Cole, Asher Durand, and Frederic Edwin Church, whose work was influenced by Romanticism and known for its stirring depictions of American landscapes.

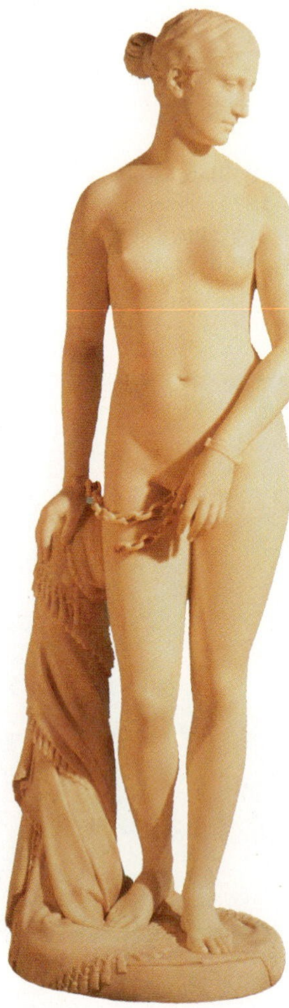

(The Newark Museum/Art Resource, NY)

The Greek Slave. Hiram Powers's statue *The Greek Slave* became an American sensation, attracting large crowds and many imitators.

The transcendentalists were not alone in their search for spiritual intensity through connection with nature. American painters, sculptors, and writers found an increasing audience for their works in the 1830s. Thomas Cole, a key figure in the emergence of American painting, was born in England and moved to the Ohio frontier as a small child. Cole taught himself to paint but went to England and Italy to perfect his art. He returned to New York's Hudson River Valley in the late 1830s and early 1840s to paint its dramatic and uniquely American landscapes. Soon younger painters, such as Asher Durand and Frederic Edwin Church, joined Cole in their fascination with the stirring American landscape, creating what became known as the **Hudson River School.**

Other important artists followed their own paths through the American landscape. Beginning in the 1830s, George Catlin lived among the Native Americans of the Great Plains, making hundreds of drawings and paintings. As a young man he was moved by the sight of a Native American delegation visiting Philadelphia and vowed that "nothing short of the loss of my life shall prevent me from visiting their country and becoming their historian." Audiences could also view vanishing wildlife in the remarkable watercolors of John James Audubon, who set out on daunting journeys to record the environment and appearance of the birds of the young nation. After ten years of work, Audubon produced *The Birds of America, from Original Drawings, with 435 Plates Showing 1,065 Figures* in four immense volumes, completing the project in 1838.

The most popular artistic production of antebellum America, however, was a statue: Hiram Powers's *The Greek Slave,* completed in 1846. The young woman represented, Powers said, a Greek girl captured by the Turks in the Greco-Turkish war. As such, she represented Christianity and whiteness, unbowed by the evil and darkness surrounding her. *The Greek Slave* served as the model for hundreds of miniature copies that appeared in the drawing rooms of the finest homes.

Emergence of a Popular Culture

The same drawing rooms also began to display a novelty of the age: daguerreotypes. This form of photography developed in France but arrived in the United States in 1839 soon after its creation. Within a few years, more than eighty young photographers practiced their craft in New York City alone, and by 1850 as many as ten thousand daguerreotypists had set up shop. Engravings based on paintings and photographs soon filled the publications coming off the presses. For the first time, illustrations could be produced cheaply. Magazines, incorporating short stories and illustrations, became tailored to children, farmers, women, sportsmen, and other specialty audiences.

Seeing the opportunity afforded by this emergence of a popular audience for print, American writers worked hard to fill the hunger. One especially gifted author, Edgar Allan Poe, wrote short stories, the kind of writing most in demand, but he brought to the form a kind of self-consciousness few had demonstrated before. Poe tapped into a widespread fascination with the occult, crime, séances, and ghosts. Throughout the 1840s, Poe published stories such as "The Masque of the Red Death," "The Pit and the Pendulum," and "The Tell-Tale Heart" and poetry such as "The Raven." Plagued by ill health, however, Poe did not survive the decade.

P. T. Barnum also exploited public fascination with the macabre and fanciful when he opened his American Museum in New York in 1841. Unlike earlier museum curators, Barnum frankly offered entertainment, including magicians and midgets such as the famous Tom Thumb and the Feejee Mermaid, actually a monkey torso attached to the body of a large fish. The fact that the "curiosities" were often attacked as fakes by scientists did not seem to deter visitors: Barnum's American Museum flourished for the next twenty years and habituated Americans to a culture of celebrity and publicity stunts.

❖ The Transformation of American Politics, 1840–1842

Popular politics had expanded in the United States since the 1820s, when Andrew Jackson electrified the electorate and states lowered the obstacles to political participation. The two major parties, the Democrats and the Whigs, had experimented with ways to mobilize voters and retain the power they won. The system grew throughout the 1830s, but no one was prepared for what happened in 1840.

The Election of 1840

election of 1840 Whig innovations in campaign slogans, large rallies, and efforts to involve women supporters in this election marked a new style of political campaigning. The election, between Democrat Martin Van Buren and the Whig party's William Henry Harrison, was won by Harrison.

The **election of 1840** should have offered an easy contest for the Whigs, given the Democrats' challenges. Much of the nation remained mired in depression. Democratic President Van Buren offered little effective leadership during the economic crisis, and many people held him to blame for the hard times. But the Whigs were not as strong as they might have been. Their party had been built piece by piece in the 1830s in reaction to Andrew Jackson. As a result, it was a crazy quilt of interests and factions. In 1836, the party had permitted three candidates to run against Van Buren because no one man could command the party's full allegiance. Party leaders vowed that they would not make the same mistake in 1840.

The Whigs were determined to find a candidate who stood for the common beliefs that unified Whigs beneath their surface differences. Those beliefs turned around faith in commerce, self-control, Protestantism, learning, and self-improvement. They found such a man in William Henry Harrison. Harrison had made his name as a general in the Old Northwest—most notably for his defeat of an Indian confederacy in the Battle of Tippecanoe in 1811—and later served in the House of Representatives and the Senate. He had won fame without gathering many political liabilities and was identified with no particular position.

Seeking to balance their ticket, the Whigs chose Senator John Tyler of Virginia. Tyler shared few beliefs with his fellow Whigs, but his embrace of slavery helped mollify southerners. Moreover, his name made a nice pairing in the phrase that soon became famous: "Tippecanoe and Tyler, Too."

The Democrats considered Harrison a nonentity; one reporter commented sarcastically that if Harrison were merely given some hard cider and a small pension, he would contentedly sit out the rest of his days in a log cabin. (He actually lived in a mansion and was a rich man.) The sarcasm backfired, though, for many Americans, still living in rural homesteads, saw log cabins and home-brewed cider as evidence of American virtue and self-reliance. The Whigs, long frustrated at their reputation as snobs and elitists, seized on hard cider and log cabins as symbols of their party's loyalty to the common American.

All over the country, Whig speakers displayed paintings, signs, flags, and models of log cabins at huge outdoor rallies while freely dispensing cider to thirsty crowds. Harrison himself went out on the campaign trail, the first presidential candidate to do so. A new kind of American political style was being forged. For the first time, women became prominent at these rallies, encouraging their husbands, fathers, and suitors with smiles, waving kerchiefs, and riding in parades with pro-Harrison banners they had sewn. The Whigs embraced causes many women supported, such as temperance and church attendance.

The Democrats had no idea of how to respond to the hard cider and log cabin campaign. Martin Van Buren's portly figure and penchant for silk vests and doeskin gloves made the Democrats' long-standing claims of representing the

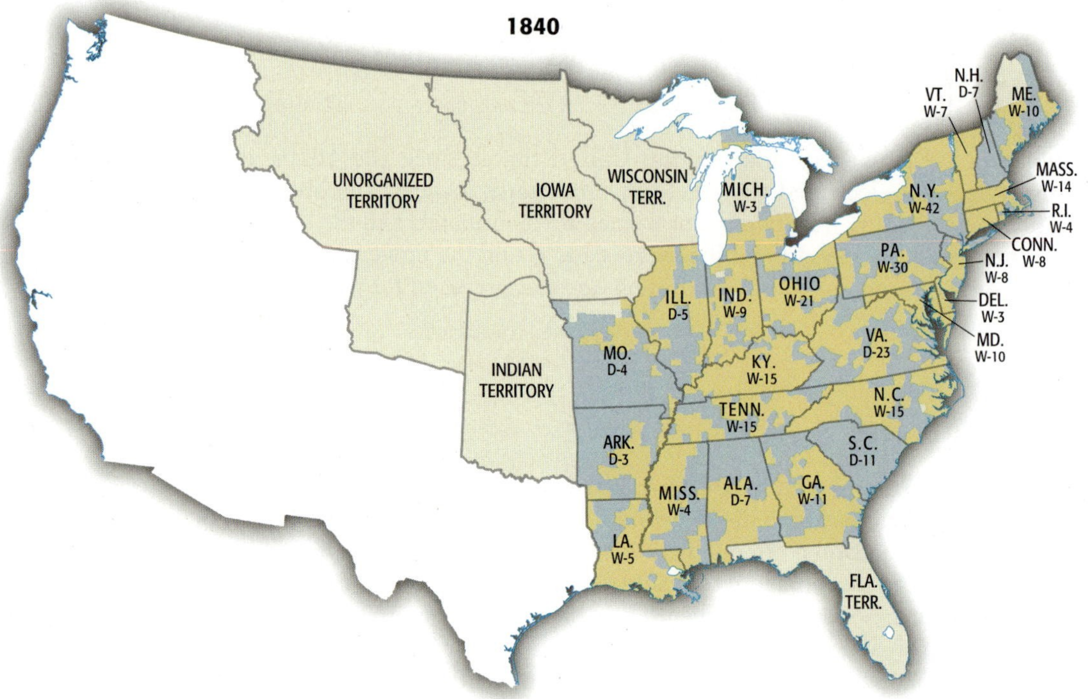

Candidate (Party)	Electoral Vote		Popular Vote	
Harrison (Whig)	234	80%	1,274,624	53.1%
Van Buren (Democrat)	60	20%	1,127,781	46.9%

Territories, unsettled, etc.

MAP 11.3

The Election of 1840

Although William Henry Harrison won resoundingly in the electoral college, Whig and Democratic support balanced each other among voters in most states. National leaders had to appeal to both proslavery and antislavery voters if they were to remain in power.

common man look hypocritical. Harrison won nineteen of the twenty-six states, bringing about half a million new voters to the Whigs (see Map 11.3). Voter turnout surged to a level almost unimaginable just a decade earlier: eight of every ten eligible voters went to the polls. After 1840, electoral success would demand the same combination of active campaigning, potent symbols, and boisterous public displays.

Tyler, Webster, and Diplomacy

The Whig celebration did not last long. Harrison, determined to prove his fitness despite his age, expounded the longest inaugural speech in American history in March 1841, in bitterly cold weather. He contracted pneumonia and died exactly a month after taking office. John Tyler had become president even though he shared few of the prevailing ideals of the Whigs in Congress. Efforts on the part of Whig leaders to expand the power and reach of government with tariffs, banks, and internal improvements proved fruitless in the face of Tyler's opposition. Whig leaders in Congress responded by gathering in the Capitol gardens and excommunicating him from the party. Whig newspapers denounced him as "His Accidency" and the "Executive Ass." All but one member of the cabinet Tyler inherited from Harrison resigned in protest.

The only member to stay on, Secretary of State Daniel Webster, did so because he was in the midst of important negotiations with England over the boundary between the United States and Canada. In 1837, armed men had fought along the border as Americans aided a rebel movement trying to overthrow British control of Canada; later, Canadian militia burned an American steamboat carrying supplies for the insurgents, generating intense anger in the northern United States. Conflict had also long been building between the British and the Americans over the African slave trade. Great Britain insisted that its vessels be permitted to search American ships off the coast of Africa to prevent the transportation of slaves to British colonies, where slavery had ended in 1832; Americans refused. The issue threatened to explode in 1841, when American slaves seized a slaving ship, the ***Creole,*** which was taking them from Virginia to New Orleans. The slaves steered the vessel to the Bahamas and claimed their freedom under British law. Much to the anger of southern whites, the British gave sanctuary to the slaves.

Creole Slaving ship sailing from Virginia to New Orleans in 1841 when it was seized by captives and sailed to the Bahamas, a British colony. Britain, which had recently emancipated its own slaves, gave sanctuary to the slaves.

Daniel Webster met with the British representative, Lord Ashburton, to settle these issues before they flamed up into a war that neither nation wanted. After extensive debate, the United States and Great Britain decided on a new boundary that gave each about half of what each had claimed in Maine and in the area to the west of Lake Superior. The Webster-Ashburton Treaty also established joint American-British patrols to intercept ships carrying slaves from Africa, but in practice the Americans did not pursue the illegal trade vigorously. By 1850, the U.S. Navy had captured only seven slavers, while the British had captured more than five hundred ships and freed more than thirty-eight thousand Africans.

❖ The Challenge of the West

Americans kept their eyes to the West. Railroads, telegraphs, canals, and roads strained in that direction, and population restlessly flowed there. But thoughtful people recognized that the lack of borders and limits posed threats as well as opportunities.

The "Wests"

The hard times in the East made moving west seem an increasingly attractive option. Horace Greeley, the most influential newspaper editor of the day, warned people looking for jobs in the midst of the depression not to come to the city but rather to "go to the Great West." To people in New England, migration to the West in the 1840s often meant migration to the lands of the northern plains and surrounding the Great Lakes. To people from Virginia and Kentucky, migration to the West might mean heading to the free states of Ohio, Indiana, or Illinois or, more often, to Mississippi, Louisiana, and Texas. For people from the cities of the East, the destination might be a booming new city such as Indianapolis, Chicago, or Detroit (see Map 11.4).

(George Catlin, *The Female Eagle-Shawano,* 1830. Paul Mellon Collection, image courtesy of the Board of Trustees, National Gallery of Art, Washington)

Catlin, The Female Eagle-Shawano. In his paintings, George Catlin sought to convey the dignity and individuality of his vanishing American Indian subjects.

One "West" that captured the imagination of Americans in these years lay in Oregon and Mexican California, word of whose beauty and wealth had slowly filtered east throughout the preceding decade. Although crossing the Rockies and what was called "The Great American Desert" was grueling, a growing stream of families decided to take the chance. Most gathered in northern Missouri or southern Iowa, setting out in early May across undulating plains, with water and fuel easy to find, their wagons pulled by oxen. The settlers would gradually ascend to Fort Laramie, at the edge of the Rockies,

MAP 11.4

Population Expansion, 1850

The population of the United States moved steadily westward at the same time that the Northeast became ever more densely settled. The population of the South remained thinner because plantations did not concentrate people as the family farms and towns of the North did.

and reach the Continental Divide, the point at which rivers on one side flowed to the east and those on the other flowed to the west, by July.

From the divide, the settlers heading to California split off from those going to Oregon. Both faced enormous difficulties in the remainder of their trip. They raced early mountain snowstorms and navigated treacherous mountain passes so steep that wagons had to be dragged up one side and let down the other with ropes, chains, and pulleys. Finally, by October, two thousand miles and six months after they had left Missouri or Iowa, the settlers crossed one last ridge and looked down on the sparkling valleys of Sacramento or the Willamette River (see Map 11.5).

Migration to the Pacific began slowly, with only a few dozen families making the treacherous journey between 1840 and 1842. The numbers mounted between 1843 and 1845, when more than five thousand people passed through Utah on their way to Oregon and California. Throughout the 1840s, the great majority of migrants chose Oregon over Mexican California as their destination. Oregon came to seem a respectable place for literate and upright Protestant families to settle, whereas California seemed a gamble, attractive mainly to single men willing to take their chances in a foreign country.

Manifest Destiny

In 1842, the Great United States Exploring Expedition returned from an ocean journey of 87,780 nautical miles. It had circumnavigated the globe, located Antarctica, and explored the Pacific coast. The captain of the expedition reported that Oregon was a treasure trove of "forests, furs, and fisheries." If the

MAP 11.5

Trails to the West, 1840s

The trails to Oregon and California looked straightforward enough on a map but proved immensely challenging, even deadly, in practice.

United States did not use its military to occupy the territory all the way to the 54°40' boundary, it would be risking much more than the Oregon Territory itself. California might throw off the light Mexican rule under which it rested and join with an independent Oregon to create a nation "that is destined to control the destinies of the Pacific." The Tyler administration sought to downplay this report, not wanting to disrupt negotiations still pending on the boundary of Maine and Wisconsin.

The forces of expansion proved too strong for the administration to contain, however. In 1845, newspaper editor John Louis O'Sullivan announced that it was the "**manifest destiny**"—the clear and unavoidable fate—of the United States "to overspread the continent allotted by Providence for the free development of our yearly multiplying millions." In other words, God intended white Protestant Americans to fill in every corner of the continent, pushing aside Native Americans, Mexicans, English, and anyone else. The Democrats in Congress and President Tyler supported this expansion, focusing first on Texas. If the United States did not quickly annex Texas, Democrats contended, it might fall under the sway of the British and become not only a barrier to further American migration but also a bastion of antislavery. For their part, midwestern Democrats agreed that westward expansion was essential to the American future. The country simply could not afford to have major ports and potential markets sealed off. These Democrats had their eye on Oregon.

manifest destiny Idea proposed by newspaper editor John L. O'Sullivan in 1845 that the United States was destined to grow from the Atlantic to the Pacific and from the Arctic to the tropics. Providence supposedly intended for Americans to have this area for a great experiment in liberty.

Politics in Turmoil, 1844–1845

In 1844, James K. Polk, a former governor of Tennessee, received the Democratic nomination for president after an acrimonious convention and nine ballots. The Democrats appealed to both northerners and southerners with a program of aggressive expansion, attempting to counter fears of slavery's growth not by rejecting Texas but by embracing Oregon as a free territory.

The Whigs nominated Henry Clay for president on a platform opposed to expansion. The apparently clear-cut choice between Clay and Polk soon became complicated, however. Clay announced that he would not oppose Texas annexation if it could be done peacefully and by consensus. His strategy backfired, attracting few advocates of expansion but alienating antislavery advocates and opponents of expansion.

At the same time, the abolitionist Liberty Party won sixty-two thousand votes in 1844. In New York, in fact, the Liberty Party's strong showing took enough votes from Clay to give the state to Polk. And those electoral votes proved the difference in the national election. Although Polk won only 49.6 percent of the vote, he entered office with a clear vision of annexing large areas of Mexican territory, Texas, and Oregon.

Even before Polk took office, the Senate voted to annex Texas, an independent republic since 1836, as soon as Texas consented. Texas gave its approval in the fall of 1845 and won its vote for annexation in Washington at the end of that year. The Democrats sought to quiet concerns among northerners by simultaneously annexing Oregon as a free territory. Although Americans, including some northern Democrats in Congress, clamored for all of Oregon to its northernmost boundary with Russian territory, chanting "Fifty-Four Forty or Fight," Polk secretly negotiated with Britain to set the boundary at the forty-ninth parallel, an extension of the northern U.S. boundary from the east. Northern Democrats who had supported Polk on Texas felt betrayed and cheated by this southern conspiracy to "strangle Oregon."

Meanwhile, the early 1840s witnessed bloody battles over religion. A growing stream of immigrants from Ireland, the great majority of them Roman Catholic, flowed into northern cities, causing many Protestant Americans to perceive a direct threat to American institutions. In 1844, a huge anti-Catholic riot broke out in Philadelphia; several Catholic churches burned to the ground while local firemen, rather than fight the blaze, simply hosed down the surrounding buildings to prevent the fire from spreading. Because the Democrats proved far more sympathetic to the Irish than did the largely Protestant Whigs, the political differences between the parties now became inflamed with religious and ethnic conflict.

Slavery too led to religious schisms. In 1844, the Methodist church divided over slavery, and the Baptists split the following year. Southern church leaders were angry that many of their northern brethren refused to believe that American slavery was part of God's plan and bitterly resented their northern brethren's passage of a clause demanding no communion with slaveholders. Five hundred thousand southerners formed the Methodist Episcopal Church, while Baptists from nine southern states created the Southern Baptist Convention. Questions about slavery moved beyond laws and the Constitution into debates about sin, evil, and God's plan for the nation.

CHAPTER REVIEW, 1837–1845

SUMMARY

- The United States experienced the largest economic depression it had ever seen.
- Railroads began to spread over large parts of the country.
- The Washingtonian movement against alcohol gathered momentum.
- Abolitionism spread, but so did violent reactions against abolitionists.
- Major figures of philosophy emerged in the transcendentalist movement, and the United States saw its first original artists.
- The election of 1840 redefined electoral politics.
- Many Americans followed trails to the Pacific Coast.

IDENTIFICATIONS

Martin Van Buren
Panic of 1837
Charles River Bridge **case**
Samuel F. B. Morse
Horace Mann
Washingtonian temperance movement
Angelina and Sarah Grimké
Elijah P. Lovejoy
Liberty Party
Amistad
Harriet Tubman
Frederick Douglass
Ralph Waldo Emerson
William Gilmore Simms
transcendentalists
Hudson River School
election of 1840
Creole
manifest destiny

MAKING CONNECTIONS: LOOKING AHEAD

Chapter 12 will show that after the hard times of the early 1840s, the United States entered a period of rampant expansion, political mobilization, and economic growth.

1. How did the election of 1840 influence every campaign that followed? Were those changes positive, negative, or mixed?
2. What legacy did the major cultural events of the late 1830s and early 1840s leave on American culture?

RECOMMENDED READINGS

Applegate, Debby. *The Most Famous Man in America: The Biography of Henry Ward Beecher* (2006). An engaging look at the minister, abolitionist, and brother of Harriet Beecher Stowe.

Balleisen, Edward J. *Navigating Failure: Bankruptcy and Commercial Society in Antebellum America* (2001). A compelling portrait of the financial turmoil of these years.

Blue, Frederick J. *No Taint of Compromise: Crusaders in Antislavery Politics* (2005). Examines the politics of the period through compelling biographies of ten antislavery activists.

Downey, Tom. *Planting a Capitalist South: Masters, Merchants, and Manufacturers in the Southern Interior, 1790–1860* (2006). Offers a fresh interpretation of the relationships among southern planters, merchants, and industrialists.

Ely, Melvin Patrick. *Israel on the Appomattox: A Southern Experiment in Black Freedom from the 1790s Through the Civil War* (2004). A wonderfully evocative portrayal of free black life in the slave South.

Fehrenbacher, Don E. *The Slaveholding Republic: An Account of the United States Government's Relations to Slavery* (2001). Offers a magisterial overview of this important subject.

Genovese, Eugene. *Roll, Jordan, Roll: The World the Slaves Made* (1974). The most powerful portrayal of American slavery.

Johnson, Walter. *Soul by Soul: Life Inside the Antebellum Slave Market* (1999). The best study of the vast domestic slave trade.

Kimball, Gregg. *American City, Southern Place: A Cultural History of Antebellum Richmond* (2000). A highly readable study of commerce, industrialization, and race relations in a southern city.

Reiss, Benjamin. *The Showman and the Slave: Race, Death, and Memory in Barnum's America* (2001). Tells the fascinating story of the connection between popular culture, commerce, and race.

CourseMate Go to the CourseMate website at www.cengagebrain.com for additional study tools and review materials for this chapter.

12 Expansion and Reaction

1846–1854

MAKING CONNECTIONS

LOOKING BACK

As Chapter 11 showed, the years surrounding 1840 presented Americans of all descriptions with the biggest economic challenge the country had yet seen, combining a sharp panic with long-term changes in the fundamental structures of the American economy. Before starting Chapter 12, you should be able to answer the following questions:

1. How did the business cycle shape people's lives in ways they may not have perceived at the time?
2. How much did reform movements grow from optimism and how much from fear of social disorder? Why did they tend to be stronger in the North than in the South?

The years of territorial expansion, population growth, and prosperity that followed victory in a war with Mexico also proved to be years of unprecedented foreboding for the United States. Positive changes were accompanied by discouraging consequences. Heightened expectations of a transcontinental American empire led to bitter political fighting; the immigration of working people from Europe fueled social conflict; and writers, reformers, and ordinary Americans grappled with the questions raised by these upheavals.

❖ The Mexican-American War, 1846–1848

The immense Spanish territory to the south and west of the United States had been a major concern for generations. Throughout the 1820s, American leaders had struggled with Mexican independence; throughout the 1830s and 1840s, Americans had aided Texans in their fight against the Mexican army and fought with each other over the **annexation of Texas** to the Union. Americans longed for the territories Mexicans controlled in western North America, but Mexico pledged to keep those lands. No one could be at all certain that the United States could defeat Mexico in a large-scale war, but President Polk seemed determined to find out.

The United States at War

The Mexican government had never recognized the independence of Texas, which Texans claimed as a result of their victory over Santa Anna in 1836. President James K. Polk raised the stakes by insisting that the border between Texas and Mexico lay at the Rio Grande, not at the Nueces River farther north, the accepted southern border of Texas. Even before the formal annexation of Texas was ratified in July 1845, Polk ordered American troops under the command of General **Zachary Taylor** to cross the Nueces.

Mexico, already furious over annexation, claimed that the decision to move U.S. troops across the Nueces constituted an invasion of Mexican territory. With four major factions struggling for control of the Mexican government, no leader could ignore the U.S. advance. Yet the army lacked funds, effective weapons, and training. Mexican president José Joaquín de Herrera ordered troops to assemble on the south side of the Rio Grande and wait.

Polk prepared for war, ordering John C. Frémont, leading an army expedition to map rivers within U.S. borders, to California. Frémont supported the "Bear Flag Rebellion," an armed struggle in 1846 by American settlers against the Mexican government. Disrupted, Polk hoped the Mexican provinces might be sacrificed more easily and more cheaply to the United States. But it was a skirmish in April 1846 between Mexican and American troops north of the Rio Grande in Texas that gave Polk an excuse for war. He declared that Mexico had "invaded our territory and shed American blood on the American soil." Although northern Whigs denounced the war and its motives, Whig congressmen believed they had to support soldiers in the field. The final vote for war was overwhelming, with only fourteen Whig congressmen and two senators opposed. Although unpopular in New England, the war stirred widespread support in the South and West, where residents hoped a victory over Mexico would open new land for American settlement.

The war with Mexico unfolded across an enormous area (see Map 12.1). Sixteen hundred American troops took Santa Fe in New Mexico with no casualties late in the summer of 1846. California proved to be a greater struggle, partly because Mexican settlers there put up more of a fight and partly because Frémont provoked fights and stimulated enraged Californios to drive the Americans from Los Angeles. Nevertheless, with seizure of the territory's ports, the American forces won control of California a few months after they had taken New Mexico. The U.S. Army, under Zachary Taylor and Winfield Scott, achieved a startling

annexation of Texas (1845) Incorporation of Texas into the United States as the twenty-eighth state. The Republic of Texas invited U.S. annexation following the Texas Revolution but annexation was delayed by disputes with Mexico. Annexation was hotly debated among supporters and opponents of slavery's expansion.

Taylor, Zachary (1784–1850) U.S. general and twelfth president (1849–1850), he defeated Mexico in the Mexican-American War. As Whig president, he tried to avoid entanglements of both party and region.

CHAPTER TIMELINE

1846 1848 1850 1852 1854 1856

POLITICS AND DIPLOMACY

(1845)–1849 James K. Polk presidency
1846–1848 War with Mexico
1848 Seneca Falls Convention
1849–1850 Zachary Taylor presidency
1850 Compromise of 1850
1850–1853 Millard Fillmore becomes president upon Taylor's death
1853–(1857) Franklin Pierce presidency
1854 Kansas-Nebraska Act

SOCIETY AND CULTURE

1847 Mormons reach Great Salt Lake
1850 Nathaniel Hawthorne's *The Scarlet Letter*
1851 Herman Melville's *Moby Dick*
1852 Harriet Beecher Stowe's *Uncle Tom's Cabin*
1854 Henry David Thoreau's *Walden*

ECONOMICS AND TECHNOLOGY

1848 Gold discovered in California
1849 Rising cotton prices invigorate the South
1854 Railroad reaches the Mississippi River

series of victories in Mexico itself in 1846 and 1847, including an impressive amphibious landing at Vera Cruz by Scott's forces in 1847 that ended in the conquest of Mexico City.

The Mexican-American War forged the careers of military leaders like Ulysses S. Grant, Jefferson Davis, and Robert E. Lee, who would play pivotal roles in the Civil War. These well-trained leaders commanded something less than a polished army, however. As many as 40 percent of recruits were recent immigrants, and 35 percent were illiterate. Conditions of service were harsh, with savage discipline, irregular pay, and poor supply. At any period during the Mexican-American War, one-third of the men on the muster rolls had deserted, the highest rate of desertion among American wars.

The Consequences of War

Many northerners worried about the expansion of slavery and southern political power that might accompany victory over Mexico. To put such concerns to rest, David Wilmot, a first-term Pennsylvania Democrat in favor of the war, made a bold move: when a bill to appropriate $2 million to end the war and purchase California and Mexican territory north of the Rio Grande came before Congress in 1846, Wilmot offered a "proviso," or condition, that declared slavery could not

MAP 12.1

War with Mexico, 1846–1848

The war between the United States and Mexico ranged over an enormous territory, though the main battles occurred deep within Mexico. While the navy blockaded Mexican coastlines, General Winfield Scott landed at Vera Cruz, marched more than two hundred miles inland, and seized the capital, Mexico City, forcing a negotiated settlement to the war.

(LC-USZC2-656)/Library of Congress Prints and Photographs Division)

The Battle of Cerro Gordo, April 17–18, 1847. American forces under the command of Winfield Scott prevailed against Mexican General Antonio Lopez de Santa Anna and his troops.

be established in any territory the United States might win from Mexico as a result of the war. Northern Democrats saw the proviso as "our declaration of independence from southern dictation, arrogance, and misrule." It passed the House by a vote of 83 to 64, with congressmen, with few exceptions, voting along regional rather than party lines. The Wilmot Proviso eventually went down to defeat in the Senate, but from 1846 on, regional divisions would threaten party unity.

The war with Mexico limped to a conclusion in late 1847 and early 1848. American troops controlled Mexico City, the Gulf Coast, and all the northern provinces claimed by the United States, but the Mexican government refused to settle on terms of peace. American politicians were also divided: some urged Polk to lay claim to all of the conquered country, others insisted that the United States should seize no territory at all from the war, and many, such as Senator John C. Calhoun, driven by racial fears, wanted to limit seized territories to the sparsely settled regions to prevent "the fatal error of placing these colored races on an equality with the white race." The Treaty of Guadalupe Hidalgo brought the negotiations to an end in February 1848: Mexico, for $15 million and the abandonment of American claims against the Mexican government and its people, agreed to sell California, New Mexico, and all of Texas above the Rio Grande. Though popular support for the war had declined and politicians were still divided on many issues, they swallowed their disagreements long enough to ratify the treaty in March. A prominent newspaper pronounced the treaty "a peace which every one will be glad of, but no one will be proud of." The Mexicans signed the treaty in May, surrendering nearly 600 million acres of territory to the United States.

The Election of 1848

James K. Polk did not seek reelection in 1848. The Democrats, scrambling to find someone to unite the northern and southern branches of the party, decided on Lewis Cass of Michigan. He called for **popular sovereignty**, allowing people in the territories to make their own policies on slavery, and spoke for northern

popular sovereignty The concept that settlers of each territory would decide for themselves whether to allow slavery.

Democrats who sympathized with white southerners' determination to keep black people enslaved.

Outraged antislavery Democrats walked out of the Democratic convention and called their own convention in Buffalo, New York, where they nominated former president Martin Van Buren as the Free-Soil candidate for the presidency. Abolitionists who had earlier supported the failed Liberty Party and antislavery "Conscience Whigs" also threw their support behind Van Buren. These various groups forged a working alliance for the election of 1848, declaring their solidarity behind the **Free-Soil Party** and its stirring motto: "fight on and fight forever" for "free soil, free speech, free labor, and free men." This opposition to slavery's expansion into the West fractured old party loyalties developed in the Jacksonian era.

Free-Soil Party U.S. political party formed in 1848 to oppose the extension of slavery into the territories; merged with the Liberty Party in 1848.

The mainstream Whigs found themselves in an awkward spot, for they had fervently opposed the Mexican War but now sought to capitalize on the popularity of General Zachary Taylor, whom they nominated for the presidency. Taylor, a Virginian, was a slaveholding planter who had opposed the war with Mexico before he had been sent there to lead American troops. With his lack of connection to recent bitter party squabbles, Taylor appealed to voters in both sections who desired a less partisan style of political leadership.

Taylor won the election in the electoral college, but the popular vote revealed little consensus. Taylor, with 1.36 million votes, won eight slave states and seven free ones. Cass won eight free states and seven slaveholding ones, with 1.22 million votes (see Map 12.2). Although the Free-Soilers' prospects as a third party appeared bleak, Van Buren came in second in several important states, and his vote total was large enough to gain the notice of northern Democrats and send twelve men to Congress.

MAP 12.2

The Election of 1848

The balanced strength of the two-party system across the entire country was demonstrated by the 1848 election, in which candidates Taylor and Cass won northern and southern states in almost equal numbers.

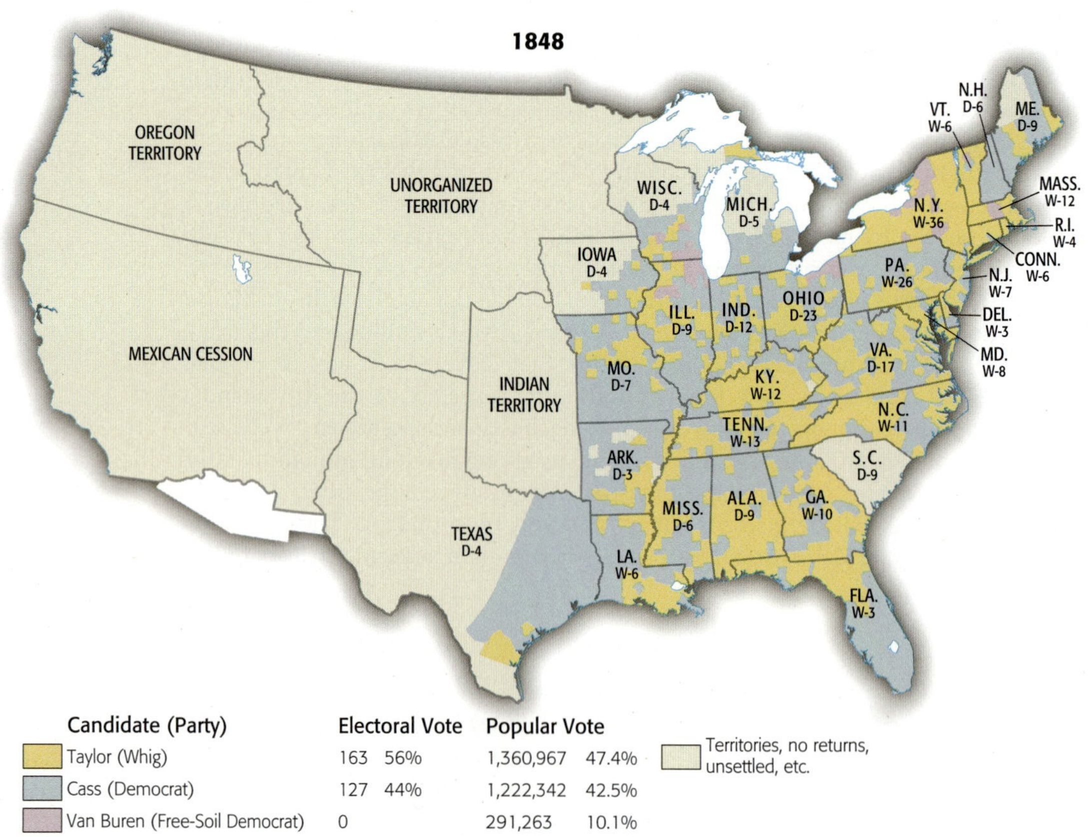

❖ Americans on the Move

Americans moved in massive numbers in the years around 1850. As the economy improved, transportation developed, boundaries became settled, and gold beckoned, people flooded to the states of the Old Northwest and the Old Southwest as well as to Texas, Oregon, and California. The suffering of Ireland and political conflict within Germany drove millions across the Atlantic, filling the cities and farms of the East.

Rails, Sails, and Steam

In the late 1840s and early 1850s, the United States had the fastest growing rail lines and the fastest ships in the world. Private investors poured tens of millions of dollars into rail expansion, and the federal government aided railroads with free surveys and vast grants of land. Railroads flourished in New England and New York, where the density of population and manufacturing permitted the new technology to work most efficiently. Midwestern states such as Ohio, Illinois, and Indiana also showed themselves well suited to the railroads, flat and fertile. Chicago had no railroads at all in 1850, but by 1860 twelve lines converged in the city.

Rural areas as well as cities immediately felt the effects of the railroad. Farmers now found it profitable to ship their produce to cities a hundred miles away. Farmers began to specialize, becoming dairymen, vegetable growers, or fruit producers. Corn, wheat, hogs, and cattle flowed out of Ohio, Illinois, Indiana, and Wisconsin. The older farms of New England, New York, and Pennsylvania turned to specialty products such as cheese, maple sugar, vegetables, and cranberries. These products rode the railroad tracks to market, tying countryside and city together.

In the South, still recovering from failed improvement schemes and loan repudiation after the economic crises of the late 1830s, railroad building trailed off in the 1840s. While spending levels did not match those of the North, states such as Virginia aggressively pursued rail construction beginning in 1847 and had spent more than $15 million by 1860 in loans to corporations and the building of two state-owned lines. North Carolina reversed decades of opposition to state-supported improvements in 1849, building a major line and subsidizing plank roads, private rail lines, and navigational aids. Despite this progress, most southerners relied instead on the steamboats that plied the Mississippi and other major rivers. The riverboats grew in size and number throughout the period.

Elsewhere, packet steamships carried mail, freight, and passengers up and down the eastern seaboard, over the Great Lakes, and as far west as the rivers allowed. More than 57 million newspapers, pamphlets, and magazines and nearly 48 million letters crisscrossed the nation in 1847. Beginning in 1848, Americans could count on regular steam-powered travel between New York and Liverpool, England. These innovations in transportation, exciting as they were, came at a steep cost. Accidents were frequent on the new railroads and steamboats. "I never open a newspaper that does not contain some account of disasters and loss of life. This world is going on too fast. Oh, for the good old days of heavy post-coaches," one diarist observed.

The Gold Rush

The natives of California had long known of the gold hidden in the rocks and creeks of that vast territory. White American settlers too had found gold deposits in the early 1840s. But it was a discovery by Swiss immigrant John Sutter in January 1848 that changed everything. While building a large fort, trading post,

(The Granger Collection, New York)

San Francisco, 1849. Ships filled the harbor of the small town of San Francisco as "forty-niners" descended on nearby goldfields.

and wheat farm near Sacramento, one of his workers noticed "something shining in the bottom of the ditch": a gold nugget. When word of the discovery spread to San Francisco, sailors abandoned their ships, soldiers deserted their barracks, and clerks left their shops to look for gold along the American River. Newspapers stopped publishing and local governments shut down as Mexicans, Native Americans, and white Americans in California rushed to the foothills. By the end of 1848, these men had gathered nuggets and dust worth about $6 million.

Back east, people remained skeptical about the discovery until 230 ounces of almost pure gold went on display in the War Department in Washington, D.C. The gold rush was on. "The coming of the Messiah, or the dawn of the Millennium could not have excited anything like the interest," one newspaper marveled. By the end of 1849, more than seven hundred ships carrying more than forty-five thousand easterners sailed to California. About fifty-five thousand settlers followed the overland trails cut across the continent. Whether they went by sea or land, participants in the gold rush were quite different from other immigrants to the West. The **forty-niners** tended to be either single men or groups of men from the same locality. Most of the men who flooded into California had little interest in settling there permanently: they intended to find their share of the gold and move on. Once in California, men of all classes, colors, and nations worked feverishly alongside one another in the streams and mountainsides. Disease, violence, and miserable living conditions hounded them, sending thousands to their deaths.

forty-niners Prospectors and others, mostly men, lured to California by the gold rush of 1849.

When some Chinese men returned home from California flush with American riches and stories of the "Golden Mountain," the fever spread in Asia. About 70 percent of the Chinese immigrants came from Guangdong Province, where many peasants and artisans had become impoverished and desperate enough to undertake the dangerous journey to California. Young men, in particular, thought California might offer a way to attain the wealth they needed to acquire a farm and a wife back in China. Migrants could buy tickets from brokers on credit, with high interest. Upon their arrival in California, the Chinese immigrants discovered that they had to borrow yet more money from Chinese merchants in San Francisco to be transported to the goldfields. The miners worked continuously in hopes of paying off that debt.

California held hope for African Americans too. Most of the black migrants to California left from the coastal cities of New England. California beckoned with the promise of an American West where color might not matter so much. Although abolitionists, black and white, warned that even California might not be safe for black migrants, several thousand African Americans took the chance.

Whatever their race, few miners discovered a fortune, but California as a whole flourished. The average miner in 1848 found about an ounce of gold a day, worth around $20, or about twenty times what a laborer back east made with a daily wage. As the number of competing miners skyrocketed during the next few years, however, the average take declined until it reached about $6 a day in 1852. Mining became more mechanized, and soon the biggest profits went to companies that assaulted the riverbeds and ravines with battalions of workers, explosives, and crushing mills. Men who tired of mining turned instead to farming, teaching school, or building houses. The largest fortunes were made supplying the miners: Levi Strauss, a dry goods salesman from New York, created tough denim jeans, and Collis P. Huntington, later founder of the Central Pacific Railroad, met arriving ships and bought all the shovels on board for marked-up sale to miners. By 1850, San Francisco had grown into a brash and booming city of thirty-five thousand diverse residents.

The Mormon Migration

A different kind of westward movement was already in full force as the California gold rush got under way. These migrants were members of the Church of Jesus Christ of Latter-Day Saints, or Mormons. In the face of relentless persecution, Joseph Smith, the founder of the church, had led his flock to Illinois. There they established the town of Nauvoo, which by the mid-1840s had become the largest city in Illinois, with more than fifteen thousand people. But conflict erupted among his followers when Smith decreed that polygamy was God's will and that leading men within the church would marry several wives. When Smith ordered the destruction of a Mormon press that printed a poster condemning polygamy, the paper's owners signed warrants for his arrest. In June 1844, a mob of non-Mormons broke into the jail where Smith was being held and killed him and his brother.

After a struggle among the elders, **Brigham Young**, a young loyalist of Joseph Smith, emerged as the new leader of the Mormons. Young decided to move to the Great Salt Lake, a region cut off from the east by mountains and from the west and south by deserts. The Mormons abandoned Nauvoo in the spring of 1846 as anti-Mormons pounded the town with cannon, destroying the Great Temple. When fifteen thousand Mormons began to arrive at the Great Salt Lake in 1847, the valley presented a daunting picture of rock and sagebrush. The settlers irrigated the land and turned it into a thriving community.

Young, Brigham (1801–1877) Mormon leader after the death of Joseph Smith; he led his followers to the Great Salt Lake.

Even though frosts, insects, and drought ruined much of the crop in the spring of 1848, Young led the construction of an ambitious city with wide streets surrounding a temple that would "surpass in grandeur of design and gorgeousness of decoration all edifices the world has yet seen." As some non-Mormons settled at the Great Salt Lake, Young decided that a form of government other than the church must be established. He oversaw the creation of a state called "Deseret" and began a successful campaign to attract new converts from Europe, Asia, and Latin America. In 1849, the residents of Deseret, with Brigham Young as territorial governor, petitioned Congress for admission into the Union as a new state—a status it was not to achieve for another half-century because of conflict over polygamy.

Although polygamy was practiced by no more than 15 percent of Mormons, the church decreed in 1852 that plural marriage was a fundamental church doctrine. The pronouncement provoked outrage across the country.

Irish and German Immigration

As Americans moved west, a vast immigration from Ireland surged into the eastern United States. Irish immigration was not new; about a million people had left Ireland for the United States between 1815 and 1844. But the situation in Ireland changed much for the worse beginning in 1845, when a blight struck healthy potato fields, turning the leaves black almost overnight and filling the air with "a sickly odor of decay." This, the Great Potato Famine, which would last for nearly a decade, destroyed the basic food for most of the Irish people. More than 1 million people died; another 1.8 million fled to North America. The Irish immigrants tended to be young, single, poor, unskilled, and Catholic; they came over with virtually no money or property and lived from day to day on whatever money they could earn. Most men worked on docks, others in canal and railroad construction; women worked as domestics and as unskilled laborers in textile mills.

The high tide of Irish immigration occurred just before the peak of German immigration (see Figure 12.1). More than 1 million Germans came to America between 1846 and 1854, many of them dislocated by a failed revolution in Germany in 1848. The Germans tended to be farmers who brought some money with them and established farms in the Midwest. They, more than the Irish, were divided by wealth, generation, politics, regional background, and religion. Combined, the Irish and German immigrants accounted for almost 15 percent of the population of the United States in the 1850s.

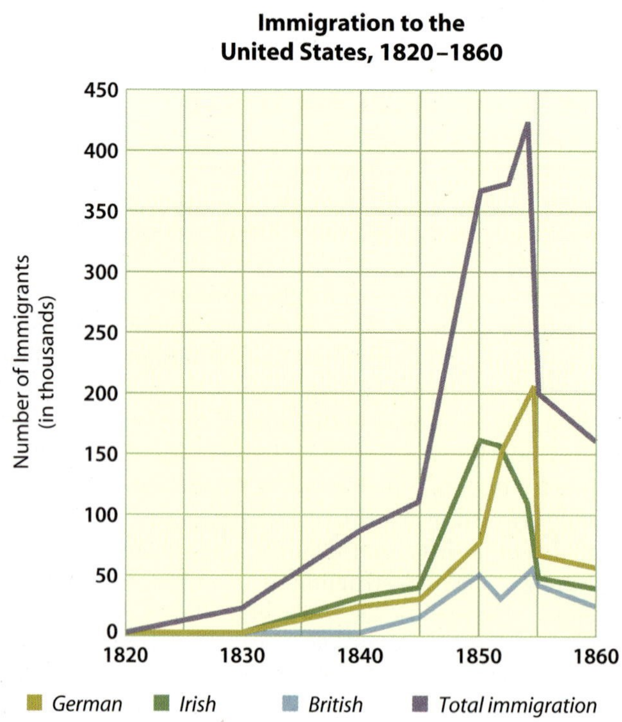

FIGURE 12.1
Immigration to the United States, 1820–1860
The number of immigrants from Ireland grew markedly in the late 1840s and early 1850s as a result of the Great Potato Famine. Immigration from Germany reached its peak a few years later as political turmoil erupted there.

❖ Social Movements and Culture

Although the late 1840s and early 1850s were relatively peaceful and prosperous, reformers continued working to mitigate the evils they saw in American society. Some became so disenchanted that they established utopian communities where they could experiment with alternative ways of organizing labor, power, and sexuality. Others, building on the ideas of the abolitionist movement, launched a crusade for woman's rights.

Perfect Communities

Most of the hundred or so utopian communities created in the United States between the Revolutionary War and the Civil War were founded in the 1840s. Some communities were secular in origin and some religious. Like the Transcendentalists at Brook Farm, they all insisted that people truly dedicated to social improvement had to flee corruption and compromise.

The most notorious American communal experiment emerged in 1848, when John Humphrey Noyes and his 250 followers created the **Oneida Association** in upstate New York. Like other religious thinkers of the day, Noyes had become convinced that it was possible for humans to be "perfected," that is, made free of sin. More controversially, he argued that people in a state of perfection should not be bound by conventional monogamous marriages; all belonged to one another sexually in "complex marriage." Oneida also experimented with economic cooperation. Everyone performed the full range of labor. The women of the group cut their hair short, wore pantaloons rather than skirts, and played sports with their male compatriots. Unlike other utopian communities, Oneida focused its energies on manufacturing rather than farming and eventually evolved into a profitable business corporation specializing in silverware.

Oneida Association Utopian community established in 1848 in upstate New York by John Humphrey Noyes (1811–1886) and his followers; practiced "complex marriage," economic cooperation, and gender equality of labor; also known for the community's steel manufacturing.

The utopian communities testified to the freedom the United States offered. People took advantage of the isolation offered by the enormous space of the young country to experiment with communities based on religious, sexual, or philosophical principles. The proliferation of such communities also revealed, however, how full of longing many Americans seemed for communal relations in a society changing from the influences of immigration, technological advances, and political conflict.

Women's Rights

The seeds for the organized movement for women's rights in the United States had been planted in 1840 when women attending the World's Anti-Slavery Convention in London, England, found themselves consigned to seats in a separate roped-off area. One of the delegates was **Elizabeth Cady Stanton,** who felt "humiliated and chagrined" by the experience. Stanton discovered an important ally at the London meeting: Lucretia Mott, a devout Quaker and feminist. The two women vowed that they would start a movement back in the States for women's rights, but they did not soon find the opportunity they sought. Stanton devoted her time to raising her family in Boston. In 1847, she moved with her family to Seneca Falls, New York.

Stanton, Elizabeth Cady (1815–1902) American feminist and social reformer who helped organize the first woman's rights convention, held in Seneca Falls, New York (1848), for which she wrote a Declaration of Rights and Sentiments calling for the reform of discriminatory practices that perpetuated the subordination of women.

While living in Seneca Falls, Stanton grew frustrated with the narrowness of life in a small town and the limitations placed on women there. Meeting with Lucretia Mott again, Stanton told her friend how miserable she had become. The two women joined with three of Mott's Quaker friends to plan a convention in July in Seneca Falls. They decided to model a "Declaration of Rights and Sentiments" on the Declaration of Independence. The document demanded women's right to vote and insisted on women's full equality with men in every sphere of life, including property rights, education, employment, divorce, and in court. (See *Doing History: Gender and Power*.) Of those men, the most prominent was Frederick Douglass, whose newspaper, the *North Star*, was one of the few papers to give the convention a positive notice. The organizers of the **Seneca Falls Convention** succeeded in their major role: getting Americans to talk about women's rights. Word of the declaration spread among the many women's groups and reform organizations.

Seneca Falls Convention (1848) First major gathering of women's rights advocates, held in Seneca Falls, New York.

At one such meeting in Akron, Ohio, in 1851, a black woman spoke. She had escaped slavery in New York in 1827 and supported her family by working as a domestic. In 1843, she had a vision in which she was commanded to carry the word of God; she renamed herself "**Sojourner Truth.**" But the campaign for women's rights developed a complex relationship with abolition and African Americans. White women's rights advocates generally phrased their demands for equal rights in terms of education and refinement that neglected black women and their needs.

Truth, Sojourner (1797–1883) Former slave who became an advocate for abolitionism and for woman's rights.

Not all activist women dedicated themselves to woman's suffrage. More conservative women, usually from middle- or upper-class families, devoted their energies to acquiring public funds for orphanages or shelters for "fallen" women and the poor, using their connections to important men in state legislatures, on city boards, and in prosperous businesses to raise money and garner support. They asked for laws to criminalize seduction and change property laws, oppose Indian removal, restrict slavery, support colonization of free blacks to Africa, and stop the sale of liquor. Southern women in particular rejected the cause of women's suffrage, in part because it was linked so closely to abolitionism. Woman "has no need to make her influence felt by a stump speech, or a vote at the polls," fumed Louisa S. McCord. "The woman must *raise* the man, by helping, not by rivalling, him." These women often achieved success through indirect means of influencing powerful men, and they saw little need to agitate for the vote.

(The Granger Collection, New York)

Sojourner Truth. Sojourner Truth, a former slave from New York, embodied for many people the pride and strength of black women, for she spoke out for both her gender and her race.

Mass Appeal

The ever-growing acceleration of printing presses and railroads in the 1850s meant that Americans enjoyed increasing access to books, newspapers, plays, and lectures every year. Several authors, now forgotten, reached remarkably large audiences with their writing. Some achieved success by playing on the nativism and anti-Catholicism of these years with polemics such as *Maria Monk's Awful Disclosures*, supposedly by one Maria Monk of a nunnery in Montreal. That titillating volume, imagining sordid behavior by priests and nuns, sold more than three hundred thousand copies in the first twenty-five years after its publication in 1836.

Other authors used the new capacities of mass printing to produce an ever-growing flood of self-help books. Catherine Beecher reprinted an edition of her *Treatise on Domestic Economy* every year in the 1840s and into the 1850s. The book offered a comprehensive guide to women on how to live their lives in the

Doing History Gender and Power

Sixty-eight women and thirty-two men signed the Declaration of Rights and Sentiments, *produced at Seneca Falls in 1848. Modeled on the Declaration of Independence, this document provided a touchstone for the women's movement throughout the rest of the century and beyond.*

Harriet Beecher Stowe's remarkable novel, Uncle Tom's Cabin *(1852), captured the moral energy of the antislavery movement and focused the eyes of the nation on the morality of slavery. In the episode here, the evil New England–born Simon Legree is confronted by the unbending Christian strength of Uncle Tom.*

Declaration of Rights and Sentiments of the Woman Suffrage Movement, *1848*

The history of mankind is a history of repeated injuries and usurpations on the part of man toward woman, having in direct object the establishment of an absolute tyranny over her. To prove this, let facts be submitted to a candid world.

He has never permitted her to exercise her inalienable right to the elective franchise.

He has compelled her to submit to laws, in the formation of which she had no voice.

He has withheld from her rights which are given to the most ignorant and degraded of men—both natives and foreigners. . . .

He has monopolized nearly all the profitable employments, and from those she is permitted to follow, she receives but a scanty remuneration. . . .

He has denied her the facilities for obtaining a thorough education, all colleges being closed against her. . . .

He has endeavored, in every way that he could, to destroy her confidence in her own powers, to lessen her self-respect, and to make her willing to lead a dependent and abject life.

Now, . . . in view of the unjust laws above mentioned, and because women do feel themselves aggrieved, oppressed, and fraudulently deprived of their most sacred rights, we insist that they have immediate admission to all the rights and privileges which belong to them as citizens of the United States.

Source: Elizabeth Cady Stanton et al., *History of Woman Suffrage*, Vol. 1 (Rochester, NY: Fowler and Wells, 1889), 58–59.

Harriet Beecher Stowe, Uncle Tom's Cabin, *1852*

"And now," said Legree, "come here, you Tom. You see I telled ye I didn't buy ye jest for the common work; I mean to promote ye and make a driver of ye; and tonight ye may jest as well begin to get your hand in. Now, ye jest take this yer gal and flog her; ye've seen enough on't to know how."

"I beg Mas'r's pardon," said Tom, "hopes Mas'r won't set me at that. It's what I an't used to—never did—and can't do, no way possible."

"Ye'll larn a pretty smart chance of things ye never did now before I've done with ye!" said Legree, taking up a cowhide and striking Tom a heavy blow across the cheek, and following up the infliction with a shower of blows.

"There!" he said, as he stopped to rest, "now will ye tell me ye can't do it?"

"Yes, Mas'r," said Tom, putting up his hand to wipe the blood that trickled down his face. "I'm willin' to work night and day, and work while there's life and breath in me, but this yer thing I can't feel it right to do; and, Mas'r, I never shall do it—never!"

Tom had a remarkably smooth, soft voice, and a habitually respectful manner that had given Legree an idea that he would be cowardly and easily subdued. When he spoke these last words, a thrill of amazement went through everyone; the poor woman clasped her hands and said, "O Lord!" and everyone involuntarily looked at each other and drew in their breath, as if to prepare for the storm that was about to burst.

Source: Harriet Beecher Stow, *Uncle Tom's Cabin* (Boston: J. P. Jewett, 1852), 419–423.

QUESTIONS for REFLECTION

1. Were the demands of the Declaration of Rights and Sentiments radical ideas? Fundamentally American ideas?
2. Why was it significant that the author of *Uncle Tom's Cabin* was a woman? Would a man have been likely to see things from this angle?
3. Why were feminists and abolitionists so deeply tied together? What did they share? Where did they differ?

new domestic world, providing tips on topics as diverse as etiquette and how to wash feathers (carefully). The book was more than a how-to compilation, however; it told women that their work stood at least equal in importance to the work their husbands did outside the home.

In their popular reading, Americans showed themselves both excited and frightened by the large social changes through which they were living. Whether the books fed fear and suspicion or offered strategies for dealing with the new challenges—or both—Americans liked stories told in bold colors.

Doing History Online

Frances Gage Remembers Sojourner Truth Appearing at the Akron Convention, 1851

Go to the CourseMate website for this chapter and link to Primary Sources. What evidence is there in this piece (Document 9) that Frances Gage, like other white women's rights activists of the day, held a condescending attitude toward black women like Sojourner Truth?

www.cengagebrain.com

Hawthorne, Melville, and Whitman

While popular authors dealt with the changes around them in melodramatic and obvious ways, more enduring writers also captured key elements of the American mood in the 1850s. Nathaniel Hawthorne's *The Scarlet Letter* (1850) and Herman Melville's *Moby-Dick* (1851) were ironic, dark, and complex allegories, but Walt Whitman's *Leaves of Grass* (1855) evoked a hopeful vision. Their lives as well as their work bore the unmistakable marks of the times in which they lived.

Hawthorne, Nathaniel (1804–1864) Massachusetts writer whose novels were mostly set in colonial New England, including *The Scarlet Letter* (1850) and *The House of Seven Gables* (1851).

Nathaniel Hawthorne of Massachusetts, fascinated by the lingering consequences of sin, turned to the history of New England as the setting for his best work, finding there an allegory for the struggles of his own age. Hawthorne wrote for Democratic newspapers and won a patronage post in the Salem customhouse, but his Whig opponents tried to remove him from his job and charged him with corruption. Perhaps not coincidentally, Hawthorne wrote *The Scarlet Letter,* a story about revenge and its costs, at this point in his life. Though set in the colonial era, the novel opened with a biting portrayal of the Salem customhouse and its petty Whig politicians. The novel propelled Hawthorne into literary fame.

Melville, Herman (1819–1891) Author of *Moby-Dick* (1851), often considered the greatest American novel of the nineteenth century.

Another young author from Massachusetts, **Herman Melville,** left school at the age of fifteen and tried his hand at writing, but he eventually went to sea to find work. His experiences abroad would provide him with the subjects for most of his writing. Melville's masterpiece, about a ship captain's search for the great white whale named Moby-Dick, created a peculiarly American idiom: part Old Testament, part adventure story, part how-to book, part encyclopedia. Good and evil swirled together in *Moby-Dick.* Unlike *The Scarlet Letter, Moby-Dick,* published in 1851, did not do well on the market. Melville, disenchanted, made his work more cynical and biting. His greatest fame and affirmation would come posthumously.

Whitman, Walt (1819–1892) Visionary poet who wrote *Leaves of Grass* (1855), inventing a new American idiom.

A bit farther south, in Brooklyn, **Walt Whitman** labored on an epic work, *Leaves of Grass,* throughout the early 1850s. This collection of poems reflected America at midcentury in all its diversity, roughness, innocence, and exuberance. This poetry included everything and everyone, speaking in a language stripped of classical allusion and pretension. As Whitman wrote in the preface to this book, anyone who would be a poet in the mid-nineteenth century must "flood himself with the immediate age." His poetical style matched his kaleidoscopic vision of American life. Both his life and his poem would be "A Song of Myself": Whitman self-published the first edition in 1855.

Initially, *Leaves of Grass* came out to no public recognition whatsoever. Whitman sent a few copies to people he admired, however, including Ralph Waldo Emerson. The reply could not have been more heartening: "I find it the most extraordinary piece of wit and wisdom that America has yet contributed." But most leading literary critics considered it vulgar, even obscene, shapeless, and crude. The hopeful words of *Leaves of Grass* soon became lost in years when a darker vision of the United States prevailed.

(The Granger Collection, New York)

(The Granger Collection, New York)

(© Bettmann/CORBIS)

Development of an American Literature. Nathaniel Hawthorne (top left) and Herman Melville (bottom left) grappled with questions of good and evil, sin and regret, while Walt Whitman (right) celebrated New York, America, and his connection to common people.

❖ Slavery and Political Chaos, 1850–1854

The 1850s began with many signs of change and progress as the economy kicked into high gear. People flooded to the recently acquired territories of California and Oregon while clipper ships, steamships, and railroads tied the nation together even more tightly. Yet a persistent undercurrent of anxiety wore at even the most privileged Americans when they read their newspapers.

The Crisis of 1850

Some of Americans' worry emanated from the new golden land of California, where lawlessness became rampant. The men who had left everything to come to the goldfields showed little respect for the property rights—or lives—of the Mexicans, Native Americans, and white men who were there before them. As gold fever spread, the military governor urged the president to grant the territory a government as soon as possible. A territorial convention created such a government in 1849, helping to restore order, but one of the provisions of the new constitution created political disorder back east. The new constitution declared that "neither slavery nor involuntary servitude . . . shall ever be tolerated in this state."

This straightforward statement exacerbated conflicts that had been brewing in Washington ever since the Wilmot Proviso three years earlier. White southerners of both parties considered the admission of a free California a grave threat to their own status in the Union, giving the Senate a free-state majority. John C. Calhoun, the most vocal and extreme spokesman for the South, argued that if southerners did not unite, they would be overwhelmed by the numbers and the energy of the free states of the North and the West. Southern congressmen talked of commercial boycotts, even of secession.

Southern Whigs had supported Zachary Taylor for the presidency in 1848, assuming that as a southerner himself, he would support the expansion of slavery. To the disbelief and disgust of southerners, however, Taylor urged that California be admitted as it wished to be admitted, without slavery. Outraged southern politicians argued that to deny the South an equal representation in the Senate was to risk war between North and South. To give in on California was to lose the sectional balance on which their very safety rested.

In January 1850, the three most famous legislators of the first half of the nineteenth century—John C. Calhoun, Henry Clay, and Daniel Webster—assumed leading roles in the great national debate on California. Calhoun played the role of the southern protagonist, delivering fiery warnings and denunciations on behalf of the white South; Clay reprised the role of the Great Compromiser that had made him famous in the Missouri controversy thirty years earlier; Webster played the role of the conciliator, persuading the angry North to accept, in the name of the Union, the South's demand for respect.

Douglas, Stephen A. (1813–1861) American politician who served as U.S. representative (1843–1847) and senator (1847–1861) from Illinois. He proposed legislation that allowed individual territories to determine whether they would allow slavery (1854), and in the senatorial campaign of 1858 he engaged Abraham Lincoln in a famous series of debates.

Clay's bold plan addressed in one inclusive "omnibus" bill all the issues tearing at the United States on the slavery issue (see Map 12.3). Balance the territory issue, he suggested, with other concerns that angered people about slavery. Keep slavery legal in the District of Columbia, but abolish the slave trade there. Provide a stronger law to capture fugitive slaves in the North, but announce that Congress had no power to regulate the slave trade among the states. Admit California as a free state, but leave undetermined the place of slavery in the other territories won from Mexico.

Advocates on both sides hoped the compromise would buy time for passions to cool, but the arguments went on for months. In March, Webster, trying to put the conflict to rest, claimed to speak "not as a Massachusetts man, nor as a northern man, but as an American." He was widely denounced in the North as a traitor. President Taylor—like Clay and Webster, a Whig—refused to support the compromise.

Although the omnibus bill in Congress appeared doomed, a series of unanticipated events brought compromise. Calhoun passed away; Millard Fillmore, now president, supported the omnibus bill. Webster resigned to serve as Fillmore's secretary of state, and the elderly Clay, after seventy addresses to the Senate defending the omnibus bill, left Washington to recover. Younger, less prominent, members of Congress, most notably **Stephen A. Douglas,** a promising young Democrat from Illinois, steered the various components of the compromise through committees and votes. The majority of northern and southern senators and representatives voted against one another, but each part of the compromise passed because a small group of conciliatory congressmen from each side crafted shifting coalitions large enough to pass each section. By September the various components of the **Compromise of 1850** had become law.

The problem of slavery, of course, would not go away. The **Fugitive Slave Act** of 1850 proved especially troubling because it directly implicated white northerners in the capture of runaway slaves. Marshals and sheriffs could force bystanders, including abolitionists, to help capture accused fugitives. The commissioners who decided the fate of black Americans accused of being runaway slaves received $10 if an accused fugitive were returned to his or her

Compromise of 1850 Congressional compromise intended to balance demands among slave and free states. It admitted California as a free state but left the question of slavery open in other new territories; abolished the slave trade in Washington, D.C., but kept slavery legal there; declared that Congress had no power to regulate the interstate slave trade; and created a stronger fugitive slave law.

Fugitive Slave Act (1850) Part of the Compromise of 1850, the federal law that provided for the return of escaped black slaves to their owners in the South.

MAP 12.3

The Compromise of 1850

The Compromise of 1850, the result of elaborate and bitter negotiation, brought California into the Union as a free state, leaving the territories of Utah and New Mexico open to the (slight) possibility of slavery.

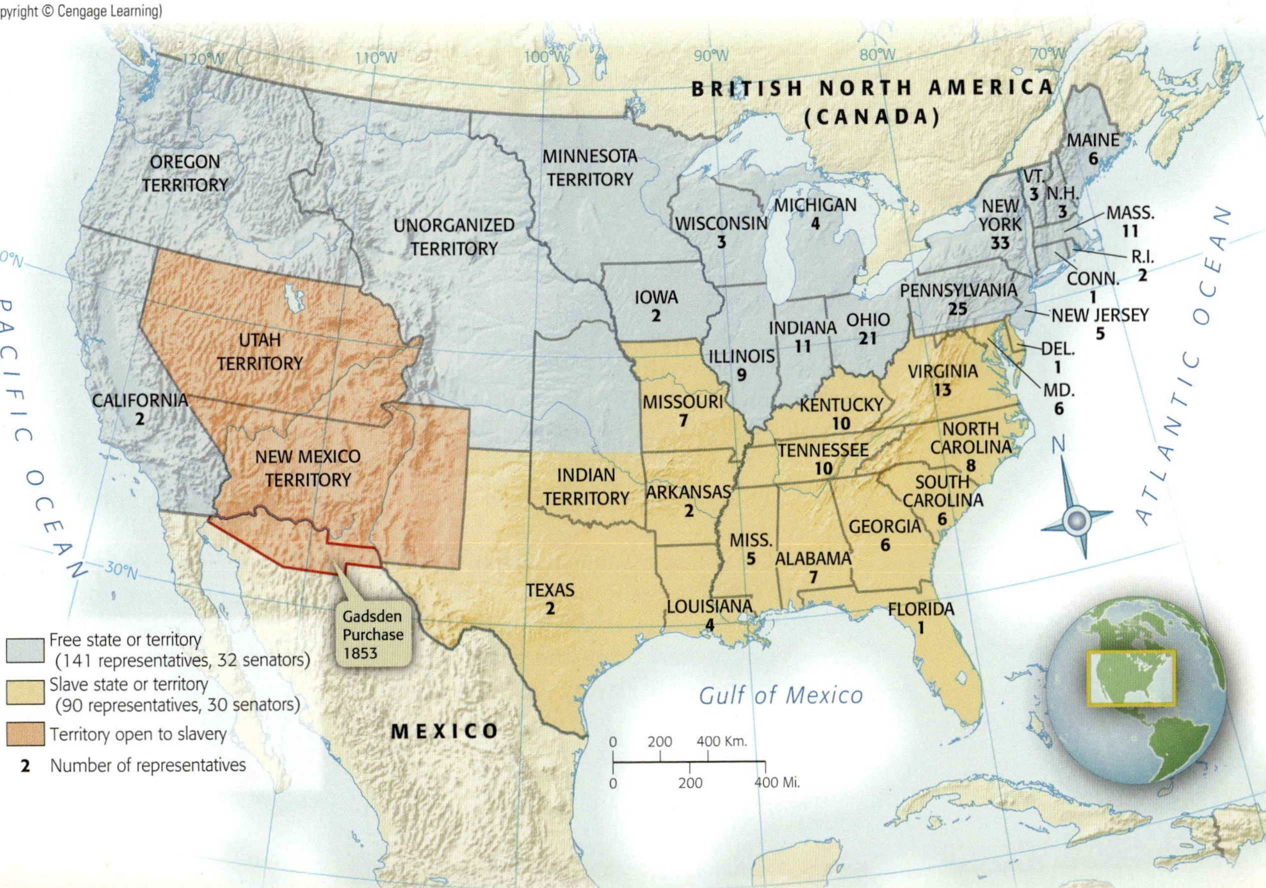

master but only $5 if freed. The alleged runaway could not testify in his or her own defense or call witnesses. And no matter how long it had been since slaves had escaped, no matter how settled or respectable they had become, they could be captured and sent back into bondage. Most of the two or three hundred alleged fugitives prosecuted under the law were ruled to be runaways and sent south.

Abolitionists raged at the Fugitive Slave Law, and they were not alone. Armed opposition to the slave catchers immediately arose in cities across the North; mobs broke into jails to free ex-slaves; one slave owner who came north to claim his property was shot. The Fugitive Slave Law, far from calming the conflict between North and South, embittered it.

African Americans and the White North

Another troubling development of the early 1850s was the growing popularity of minstrel shows. These traveling performers offered the strange ritual of white men in blackface simultaneously ridiculing and paying homage to the creativity of African American culture. White people of all classes and backgrounds attended the minstrel shows, and the quick-paced, humorous, and flashy skits and songs offered a comforting dramatization of white racial superiority and a way to associate imaginatively with carefree and fun-loving "black" people.

White northerners revealed ambivalence about African Americans in other ways. Those who argued for "free soil" in the new territory of the West frequently insisted on the exclusion of free blacks. Ohio, Indiana, Illinois, and Oregon passed laws barring free blacks from entering or settling within their boundaries. The great majority of northern whites showed little interest in attending abolition rallies.

Stowe, Harriet Beecher (1811–1896) Author of *Uncle Tom's Cabin* (1852), the most important abolitionist novel.

Harriet Beecher Stowe's *Uncle Tom's Cabin or Life Among the Lowly* helped change some of these white attitudes toward African Americans. Stowe put her objections to the Fugitive Slave Law and its effects into a story printed serially in a moderate antislavery newspaper, the *National Era*, beginning in June 1851. She based her portrayals on the African Americans she had known in Cincinnati, where they worked for her as domestic servants. They told Stowe of the terrors of being sold south to Louisiana, of their vulnerability to sexual exploitation. Stowe also drew on firsthand narratives of escape. She made a woman, Eliza, the active heroine and a man, Uncle Tom, the one left behind to endure slavery. The image of Eliza crossing the partially frozen Ohio River, baby in her arms, grew into one of the most powerful and familiar scenes of American culture.

The novel's 300,000 copies drove eight steam presses night and day to meet the demand in 1852 alone; eventually more than 6.5 million copies sold in the United States and around the world. It was the best-selling novel of the nineteenth century. *Uncle Tom's Cabin* became the subject of the most popular play in American history. Readers and theatergoers were shocked at stories of cruelty, violence, and sexual abuse. Stowe used techniques commonly found in domestic novels—the sanctity of the family, the power of religion, the triumph of endurance—to dramatize the moral argument against slavery.

That *Uncle Tom's Cabin* and minstrel shows reached their peak of popularity at the same time gives some idea of the confusion and ambivalence with which white northerners viewed African Americans in the early 1850s. Meanwhile, the coming years would bring the most violent conflicts the nation had yet seen between the forces of slavery and antislavery.

The Know-Nothings

The presidential election of 1852 revealed the growing erosion of party unity. Franklin Pierce, the Democratic candidate for president, was a northerner friendly to the white South. Pierce's Whig opponent, Winfield Scott, proved to be unimpressive despite his fame as a general in the war with Mexico. Pierce crushed Scott in every state except four. "General opinion seems to be that the Whig party is dead and will soon be decomposed into its original elements," one diarist commented in the wake of the election.

Many influential Whigs took the 1852 election as a sign that the Democrats would always succeed by appealing to the lowest common denominator. The issues that had originally shaped the two parties—banks, the tariff, and internal improvements—no longer distinguished them from one another. Neither did slavery and sectional issues sharply define the two parties, for each tried to appease voters in both the North and the South. Even the broader cultural orientation of the two parties had blurred in 1852, as the Whigs appealed to the burgeoning foreign-born vote.

The high tide of immigration in the early 1850s unleashed a political backlash as nativists organized themselves against the newcomers from Ireland and Germany. In the eyes of many white Protestants, the new arrivals, especially from Ireland, appeared impossible to assimilate. "They increase our taxes, eat our bread, and encumber our street," commented one American diarist. The immigrants threatened to drive down wages because they were willing to work for so little. They often received the right to vote in state and local elections soon after they landed, with Irish Catholics supporting the Democratic Party and opposing the prohibition of alcohol, and English, German, and Irish Protestants supporting the Whigs and frequently voting in favor of prohibition.

In the face of perceived challenges to their values and power, "native Americans" organized against the immigrants. The most powerful manifestation of nativism appeared in New York City in 1849, when Charles Allen founded the Order of the Star Spangled Banner, its membership restricted to native-born white Protestants sworn to secrecy. When asked about the order by outsiders, members were instructed to say "I know nothing"—and thus they became popularly known as the "Know-Nothings." The order grew slowly at first, but its appeal to deeply held and deepening prejudices grew as existing political parties seemed too corrupt to stem the flood-tide of immigration.

The **Know-Nothings** moved into politics in 1854 in a way few expected. Mobilizing as many as 1.5 million adherents, they did not announce their candidates beforehand but wrote them in on the ballots, taking incumbents by complete surprise. In Massachusetts, the Know-Nothings won virtually all the seats in the legislature, the governor's chair, and the entire congressional delegation with this strategy. By 1855, they dominated much of New England and displaced the Whigs as the major opponents to the Democrats through the Middle Atlantic states, in much of the South, and in California. Democrat and Whig leaders denounced "the 'Know Nothing' fever" that disrupted the campaigns and strategies of the parties.

Know-Nothings Popular name for the American party, an anti-immigration party of the mid-1850s, derived from members' response to any question about their activities: "I know nothing."

No one in the major parties had anticipated such a turn of events. The Know-Nothings offered a revitalized political party, one more receptive than the Whigs to the anti-Catholic and anti-immigrant desires of its constituents and one that would attack problems rather than compromise on them. Many rural districts voted heavily for the Know-Nothings as a way to get back at the cities that had dominated the major parties for so long. The appearance of the Know-Nothings reflected nothing less than a deep-seated change in the American political system. The party system began disintegrating at the local and state level, with the Whigs fading in some states as early as 1852 and in others not until three years later. Voters defected from the Whigs and Democrats to both the Know-Nothing and Free-Soil parties.

A Hunger for Expansion

The same forces of commerce and transportation that tied together the vastly expanded United States in the late 1840s and early 1850s pulled Americans into world affairs. American ships set out for South America, Asia, Australia, New Zealand, and Tahiti, as well as Europe. The ships carried lumber and hides, tea and silks, missionaries and scientists. American whaling ships patrolled the South Pacific, stopping for fuel and food at islands scattered over a vast territory. American traders eager to break into the Asian market appeared in Japanese ports.

Some well-placed Americans gazed at yet more Mexican territory with covetous eyes, urging the Pierce administration to acquire Baja California and other parts of northern Mexico. Mexico was not interested. Proponents of expansion had to settle for much less than they had wanted: after long wrangling, in 1853 the United States paid $15 million for a strip of Mexico to use as a route for a southern transcontinental railroad. This was the **Gadsden Purchase,** named for the American diplomat who negotiated it. The purchase defined the final borders of the continental United States.

Gadsden Purchase (1854) A piece of land, 29,670 square miles, purchased from Mexico in 1853 to provide a southern route for a transcontinental railroad; final extension of the southern U.S. border.

Cuba seemed the most obvious place for further expansion. Many Americans believed that Cuba should be part of the United States. It was rich from sugar production, its slave trade flourishing even after the slave trade to the United States had ended. Abolitionists and others talked of freeing Cuba from both slavery and the Spanish, whereas white southerners talked of adding this jewel to the slave empire.

The United States offered to buy Cuba from Spain in 1848 but met a rude rebuff. Franklin Pierce, pressured by the southerners in his party and in his cabinet, renewed the effort to "detach" Cuba from Spain in the early 1850s. American diplomats in Europe created a furor in October 1854 when they clumsily wrote the "Ostend Manifesto," a statement of the policy they wanted the administration to follow: gain Cuba peacefully or by force. When the "manifesto" was leaked to the press, the Pierce administration was widely vilified. London newspapers derided the manifesto as the "pursuit of dishonorable objects by clandestine means." Pierce publicly renounced any intention of taking over Cuba. The movement to expand the United States into the Caribbean came to a temporary halt.

Kansas-Nebraska Lets Loose the Storm

As the Cuban episode revealed, Franklin Pierce proved to be an ineffectual president and a weak leader. The best hope for the Democrats, according to Senator Stephen A. Douglas, was to deflect attention to the West. Douglas called for two kinds of action: organizing the territories of the West, especially the Kansas and Nebraska area, and building a railroad across the continent to bind together the expanded United States with the route running through his home state of Illinois. The two actions were interrelated, for the railroad could not be built through unorganized territory. Partly to get southern votes for the territorial organization and partly because he believed that slavery would not survive in the northern territories, Douglas wrote a bill invalidating the Missouri Compromise line. In 1854 he proposed that the people of the new territories should decide for themselves whether their states would permit slavery. Adopting the phrase others had used to describe such territorial self-determination, "popular sovereignty," Douglas put it forward in the **Kansas-Nebraska Bill** (see Map 12.4).

Kansas-Nebraska Bill (1854) Congressional legislation drafted by Stephen A. Douglas that provided that people of new territories could decide for themselves whether or not their states would permit slavery.

Douglas's plan unleashed political and sectional resentments that had been bottled up by prior compromises. Six prominent Free-Soil senators, including Salmon P. Chase, Charles Sumner, and Joshua Giddings, denounced the plan as a plot by a "Slave Power" to make Nebraska a "dreary region of despotism, inhabited

MAP 12.4
Kansas-Nebraska and Slavery, 1854
The Kansas Territory, adjacent to slaveholding Missouri but well north of the Missouri Compromise line, stood as a place that both slaveholders and Free-Soilers felt they could claim as their own.

by masters and slaves." Northern ministers publicly protested the pending legislation in their sermons, and newspapers throughout the North scornfully attacked the proposal. Despite the widespread opposition, however, the opponents of the Kansas-Nebraska Bill could not coordinate their efforts sufficiently to stop its passage.

The fight over the Kansas-Nebraska Bill inflamed northern resentment as never before. Many northerners determined that they could no longer trust southerners to keep a bargain and that northerners were no longer obligated to enforce the Fugitive Slave Act because the Kansas-Nebraska Bill had nullified the Missouri Compromise of 1820. Attempts to arrest and extradite Anthony Burns, a fugitive slave in Boston, created such a turmoil that the mayor called out fifteen hundred militia to line the streets along the route between the courthouse and the ship that was to take Burns back to slavery in Virginia.

The Kansas-Nebraska Bill sparked a chain reaction: it divided the Democratic Party across the North; provided a set of common concerns to unite disgruntled northern Whigs, Democrats, Free-Soilers, and abolitionists; and upset the fragile balance of power between North and South in Congress. Northern voters punished Democrats who had supported the Kansas-Nebraska Bill; the party lost sixty-six of the ninety-one free-state House seats it had gained in 1852. As northern Democrats lost seats, southerners gained control of the party, fueling further resentment of southern dominance. Know-Nothings took advantage of the widespread disillusionment with the two major parties to campaign against Catholics, immigrants, and corruption—issues apparently unrelated to slavery.

During the next two years the northern political system lurched along as voters looked for a party that would reflect their concerns and also have a chance of winning power. The Know-Nothings began to fade almost as quickly as they had emerged. Violent gangs that terrorized immigrants under the Know-Nothing

Anthony Burns. This illustration tells the story of Anthony Burns's sale, escape, arrest, and return to slavery in Virginia. His highly publicized case further inflamed the conflict between the North and the South in the mid-1850s.

(© CORBIS)

banner alienated many voters, and Know-Nothing legislators proved unable to restrict Catholic influence as they had promised.

In 1854, a party was founded in Wisconsin to unite disgruntled voters. The new party appealed to former Whigs, Free-Soilers, Know-Nothings, and even Democrats fed up with their prosouthern party. This new party called itself the "Republican" Party. Its platform announced that it would not permit slavery in the territories or in new states. People wondered whether the new party could finally unite the North against the South.

CHAPTER REVIEW, 1846–1854

SUMMARY

- The United States went to war with Mexico, winning enormous territory as a consequence.
- A gold rush in California drove hundreds of thousands of people to the West.
- Mormons moved to the Great Salt Lake.
- Movements for women's rights emerged.
- American authors like Melville and Whitman produced the first great novels and poetry of the young nation.
- The Compromise of 1850 and the Kansas-Nebraska Act galvanized the politics of the nation, sharpening the divisions caused by slavery.
- A nativist movement—the Know-Nothing party—won much support throughout the country.

IDENTIFICATIONS

annexation of Texas
Zachary Taylor
popular sovereignty
Free-Soil Party
forty-niners
Brigham Young
Oneida Association
Elizabeth Cady Stanton
Seneca Falls Convention
Sojourner Truth
Nathaniel Hawthorne
Herman Melville
Walt Whitman
Stephen A. Douglas
Compromise of 1850
Fugitive Slave Act
Harriet Beecher Stowe
Know-Nothings
Gadsden Purchase
Kansas-Nebraska Bill

MAKING CONNECTIONS: LOOKING AHEAD

In Chapter 13 we will see that many Americans hoped that the crisis of 1850, and the resulting compromise, would put an end to the bitter fight over slavery. In fact, it did just the opposite.

1. Did the Kansas-Nebraska Bill make it a certainty that the North and the South would collide repeatedly over slavery, or was there hope that things might die down once that crisis had passed?
2. What role did *Uncle Tom's Cabin* play over the years that followed its publication in mobilizing white northerners against slavery?

RECOMMENDED READINGS

Anbinder, Tyler. *Nativism and Slavery: The Northern Know-Nothings and the Politics of the 1850s* (1992). A full and balanced account.

Faragher, John Mack, and Robert V. Hine. *The American West: A New Interpretive History* (2000). A superb synthesis.

Fehrenbacher, Don E. *The Slaveholding Republic: An Account of the United States Government's Relations to Slavery* (2001). Carefully analyzes this troubling issue.

Foos, Paul. *A Short, Offhand, Killing Affair: Soldiers and Social Conflict During the Mexican-American War* (2002). A dark work on a neglected war.

Griffith, Elisabeth. *In Her Own Right: The Life of Elizabeth Cady Stanton* (1984). Tells the compelling story of this crucial leader of the woman suffrage movement.

Hedrick, Joan D. *Harriet Beecher Stowe: A Life* (1994). Gives a detailed portrait of the author of *Uncle Tom's Cabin.*

Libura, Krystana M., Luis Gerado Morales Moreno, and Jesus Valasco Marquez. Trans. Mark Fried. *Echoes of the Mexican War* (2004). Reveals both Mexican and American points of view from the 1830s through the end of the Mexican War.

Miller, Kerby A. *Emigrants and Exiles: Ireland and the Irish Exodus to North America* (1985). Contributes a full account of the origins and impact of this migration.

Reynolds, David S. *Beneath the American Renaissance: The Subversive Imagination in the Age of Emerson and Melville* (1988). A brilliant exploration of the "classic" era of American literature.

Salerno, Beth A. *Sister Societies: Women's Antislavery Organizations in Antebellum America* (2005). Discusses the role of women in the antislavery movement, including their participation in earlier reform activities and issues that split the movement.

CourseMate Go to the CourseMate website at www.cengagebrain.com for additional study tools and review materials for this chapter.

PASSAGES 1855 to 1877

Americans of the 1850s had no idea that the Civil War awaited them. They could not imagine that a vast war, larger than any Europe had known, could overwhelm the new republic. New farms and plantations, after all, spread rapidly in expectation of more boom years like the 1850s. Villages and workshops developed throughout the North, while cities, fed by millions of immigrants from Europe, grew at harbors and along railroads and rivers. In the South, cotton and slavery created a per capita income for white Southerners higher than that of any country in Europe except England. Slavery, it was clear, would not collapse of its own contradictions any time soon; the institution had never been more profitable. Telegraphs, newspapers, steamboats, and railroads tied the North and South together more tightly every year.

The North and South viewed each other as aggressive and expansionist, intent on making the nation all one thing or another. The North claimed that the slaveholding South would destroy the best government on earth rather than accept the results of a fair election. The white South claimed that the arrogant and greedy North would destroy the nation rather than acknowledge what the Constitution had established. Both sides were filled with righteous rage, accepting violence to gain the upper hand, whether that involved capturing fugitive slaves or applauding John Brown's failed insurrection. Americans could not stop the momentum they had themselves created. Despite desperate efforts at compromise and delay, war came. And once it could no longer be avoided, most people threw themselves into the conflict alongside their neighbors, regardless of whatever doubts they had held before.

Confident that the war would be brief, young men on both sides enlisted to teach their enemies a lesson. Both the North and the South proved excellent at war. They innovated freely and successfully, fought relentlessly, discovered effective generals, and mobilized women as well as men. Indeed, the North's strengths and the South's strengths balanced so that the war went on for four years, killing 630,000 people, a proportion of the population equivalent to 5 million people in the United States today and a number larger than the country has ever sacrificed in another war.

Throughout the conflict, from Lincoln's election to his death, the role of slavery remained both powerful and unclear. Lincoln announced that the war was fought to preserve the Union, not for abolition. The Confederacy announced that the war was for independence, not merely slavery. Enslaved Americans in the South, however, forced slavery as an issue on both the Union and the Confederacy, risking their lives to flee to Union camps and undermining plantations and farms. Lincoln and much of the North came to see that ending slavery would end the Confederacy and help redeem the death and suffering. Two hundred thousand black men enlisted as soldiers and played a key role in bringing Union victory.

The North and the South struggled with themselves even as they fought one another. The North broke apart along lines of class, ethnicity, party, and locale. By 1864, a considerable portion of the Northern population wanted the war to end, with compromise if necessary. Lincoln's opponents expected to overwhelm him in the election that fall and even Lincoln shared that expectation. The white South broke apart along lines of class, locale, and gender. Poor soldiers deserted; upcountry communities shielded the deserters and resisted the Confederate government; impoverished white women rioted and resisted. Slaves rushed to the Union army at the first opportunity, every escape weakening the Southern economy and Confederate morale.

Events on the battlefield, through ten thousand conflicts large and small, exerted their own logic and momentum. The Union army grew stronger as the Confederate army thinned and weakened. The

(LC-USZC4-7985)/Library of Congress

Company A Eighth, New York Militia. In both the North and South, unprecedented numbers of men fought and died in the Civil War. Units were often raised locally, so men served alongside friends and family who wrote of their exploits—courageous or otherwise—to family back home.

victories of Grant and Sherman in 1864 destroyed the South's best hope of a negotiated peace. The relentless spread of the Union army throughout the South divided the Confederacy into smaller and smaller pieces, each helpless to aid the others. When Lee's army fell to defeat, the Confederate nation dissolved almost immediately.

Whatever Lincoln's plans for reuniting the nation, those plans ended at Ford's Theater in April 1865. Lincoln's successor, Andrew Johnson, took the most cautious route possible, limiting the scope of black freedom in every way he could. The white South's resolve, indeed, seemed greater than any power the Union wielded in the South. African Americans struggled to make their freedom real: they mobilized politically, founded churches and schools, and reconstituted families. They demanded rights as Americans and did all they could to secure those rights. Black Southerners found many white Northern allies but many more white Southern enemies who quickly turned to violence, as well as white Northerners who supported or tolerated the violence. The years 1866 and 1867 were full of a promise and a terror no one could have imagined ten years before. In many ways, the Civil War had not yet ended; its consequences had hardly begun.

For the next decade, Reconstruction in the South gradually receded. The process left blacks with greater political rights in law because of the Fourteenth and Fifteenth amendments, but a more limited role in the day-to-day process of governing. The presidency of Ulysses S. Grant was a disappointment as the hero of the war proved unable to provide effective leadership, sectional reconciliation, or honest government. An economic collapse in 1873 helped the Democrats restore the national political balance and hasten the end of Reconstruction. The disputed election between Rutherford B. Hayes and Samuel J. Tilden in 1876 saw the abandonment of black Southerners to the rule of those who believed in white supremacy. The Civil War had preserved the Union and abolished slavery, but the unsettled problem of race cast a long shadow into the future.

CHRONOLOGY

	1855	1861	1862
POLITICS AND DIPLOMACY	**1855:** Proslavery and free-soil forces clash in Kansas **1856:** John Brown's raid in Kansas James Buchanan elected president Congressman Preston Brooks canes Senator Charles Sumner **1857:** *Dred Scott* decision Lecompton Constitution **1858:** Lincoln-Douglas debates **1859:** John Brown's raid on Harpers Ferry Kansas ratifies free-soil constitution **1860:** Democratic convention divides Abraham Lincoln elected president South Carolina secedes from the Union	**1861:** Mississippi, Florida, Alabama, Georgia, Louisiana, and Texas secede Montgomery Convention creates Confederate States of America Jefferson Davis elected president of Confederacy with six-year term Lincoln inaugurated Firing on and surrender of Fort Sumter Arkansas, Tennessee, Virginia, and North Carolina secede Confederate victory at Bull Run (Manassas) Union navy seizes Confederate commissioners Mason and Slidell from British ship *Trent*	**1862:** Confederates surrender Fort Donelson to Grant Grant wins dramatic victory at Shiloh New Orleans surrenders to Admiral Farragut Jackson's Shenandoah Valley Campaign Lee takes command of Army of Northern Virginia Lee drives McClellan from Richmond in Seven Days' Battles Confederate victory at Second Bull Run (Manassas) Battle of Antietam (Sharpsburg) Preliminary Emancipation Proclamation Burnside replaces McClellan as commander of Army of the Potomac Lee overwhelms Burnside at Fredericksburg
SOCIETY AND CULTURE	**1855:** Massachusetts desegregates public schools **1857:** Religious revivals Hinton R. Helper, *The Impending Crisis of the South*	**1861:** U.S. Sanitary Commission founded Dorothea Dix becomes superintendent of nurses for the Union army Vassar College founded to provide higher education for women **1861–1865:** Women enter war effort in aid societies, hospitals, factories, and government positions	**1862:** First missionaries arrive at Port Royal, South Carolina, to provide aid to freedmen
ECONOMICS AND TECHNOLOGY	**1857:** Financial panic and depression Baltimore–St. Louis rail service completed	**1861:** Suspension of specie payments Mathew Brady begins photography of Civil War	**1862:** Legal Tender Act in North authorizes "greenbacks" Homestead Act passed by Union Congress *Monitor v. Virginia* initiates new era of naval warfare

1863	1865	1868
1863: Final Emancipation Proclamation Union begins recruiting African American soldiers Lee defeats Hooker at Chancellorsville Grant's successful campaign in Mississippi Death of Stonewall Jackson Union victory at Gettysburg Vicksburg surrenders to Grant Black troops fight at Fort Wagner, South Carolina Union victory at Chattanooga **1864:** Grant assumes command of all Union forces Battle of the Wilderness in Virginia Sherman captures Atlanta Lincoln reelected president Beginning of Sherman's march from Atlanta to the Atlantic	**1865:** Congress passes Thirteenth Amendment, abolishing slavery Congress creates Freedmen's Bureau Lee surrenders to Grant at Appomattox Court House Lincoln assassinated; Andrew Johnson becomes president Former Confederate states hold constitutional conventions through December; pass "black codes" **1866:** Congress passes Civil Rights Act and Freedmen's Bureau renewal over Johnson's veto Congress approves Fourteenth Amendment Ku Klux Klan formed **1867:** Congress passes Reconstruction Act and Tenure of Office Act Johnson dismisses Secretary of War Stanton, triggering impeachment proceedings First elections in South under Reconstruction Act Passage of Reconstruction Act	**1868:** Andrew Johnson impeached and acquitted U.S. Grant elected president **1869:** Fifteenth Amendment passes Congress Woman suffrage starts in Wyoming Territory **1870:** Ku Klux Klan conducts terror raids in South **1871:** Tweed Ring exposed in New York City **1872:** Grant reelected **1873:** Salary Grab and Crédit Mobilier scandals **1874:** Democrats gain in congressional elections **1875:** Civil Rights Act passes Congress **1876:** Hayes and Tilden in disputed election **1877:** Hayes declared president after compromises settle election dispute
1863: Lincoln's Gettysburg Address New York City draft riots	**1866:** Riots in New Orleans and Memphis American Equal Rights Association founded to seek black and woman suffrage **1867:** Horatio Alger begins publishing series of books for young boys	**1868:** Louisa May Alcott publishes *Little Women* **1869:** Licensing of women lawyers begins First intercollegiate football game played between Princeton and Rutgers **1871:** Cable car invented **1873:** Mark Twain and Charles Dudley Warner, *The Gilded Age* Comstock law prohibits use of mail to distribute birth control information and products **1874:** Women's Christian Temperance Union founded **1875:** Cornell University admits first female students **1876:** Centennial Exposition in Philadelphia
1863: Confederate Congress passes Impressment Act Union Congress passes National Bank Act Bread riot in Richmond **1864:** Confederate Congress assumes new powers of taxation, impressment of slaves George Pullman invents sleeping car	**1866:** National Labor Union organized **1867:** Patrons of Husbandry (Grange) founded	**1868:** First eight-hour day for federal workers **1869:** Gold Corner scheme of Jay Gould and Jim Fisk Transcontinental railroad completed **1870:** Standard Oil Company of Ohio organized **1873:** Panic of 1873 starts depression **1874:** Sale of typewriters begins Tomkins Square riot of unemployed in New York City

13 Broken Bonds

1855–1861

MAKING CONNECTIONS

LOOKING BACK

Chapter 12 showed that in the years following the war with Mexico the United States found itself pulled apart by the forces of economic growth, massive immigration, territorial expansion, and conflict over slavery. Before starting Chapter 13, you should be able to answer the following questions:

1. Could the United States have avoided war with Mexico? Explain your answer.
2. Under what conditions might the Whig party have been able to survive the 1850s?
3. Why did slavery seem such an issue in the North in the early 1850s?

The United States had never seemed stronger than at the beginning of 1855. The economy was booming, settlers pushed into the West, railroads spread at a relentless rate, and immigrants streamed into American farms and factories. Churches, schools, and reform organizations grew faster than ever.

But the danger signs were not hard to see. The conflict to control the national future grew more bitter with each passing political crisis. Disputes broke out in the Kansas Territory, in the village of Harpers Ferry, and finally in the contest for president. Parties and politicians, weakened by nativism and loss of faith by voters, seemed powerless to stop the disintegration.

❖ North and South Collide, 1855–1857

Conflict had been a staple of American politics for decades before 1855. Territories proved a persistent problem, but Americans also argued over tariffs, nominees for high office, and the role of religion. The arguments grew hot, but eventually calmed down until the next outbreak. Events of the late 1850s, however, broke the pattern. New crises came before the old ones could cool. The crises suddenly engulfed every political, economic, moral, and practical difference among Americans. Citizens were under pressure to prove their loyalties and defend their vision of America's future course—slave or free. The time for compromises and moderation was over.

The White South Fortifies Itself

Slavery had never been stronger in the United States than it was in the 1850s. The 3.5 million slaves of the South extended over a vast territory stretching from Delaware to Texas and north to Missouri. Theorists devised ever more elaborate and aggressive defenses of slavery, no longer depicting it merely as a necessary evil or an unfortunate inheritance from the English. Rather, they claimed, slavery was an instrument of God's will, a means of civilizing and Christianizing Africans otherwise lost to barbarism. Southern physicians went to great lengths to "prove" that Africans and their descendants were physically and intellectually inferior to whites.

Some defenders of slavery argued that slavery was more humane and Christian than free labor. If the hypocritical and self-righteous men of the North would admit it, white Southerners argued, free labor exacted a great cost. Men, women, and children went hungry when unemployment, ill health, or old age struck. In the South, by contrast, slaveholders cared for their slaves even when those slaves had grown too old or feeble to work. The South's relative lack of schools, orphanages, asylums, and prisons, the defenders of the region insisted, testified not to backwardness but to a personalized society where individual responsibility replaced impersonal institutions. Most white Southerners wanted to keep and protect what they had, not jeopardize slavery by brashly expanding it. The white South prided itself on having created a stable and prosperous society during its two and a half centuries of slavery and did not want to endanger that society.

Moreover, the slave economy boomed in the late 1850s. Planters took advantage of improved cotton gins, riverboats, railroads, and new kinds of seed to double, in the 1850s alone, their production of cotton. The claim of Southern politicians that "Cotton Is King" proved no empty boast. Even though Northern factories and farms grew rapidly in the 1850s, cotton accounted for a growing proportion of U.S. exports—more than half in 1860. Without cotton, many thousands of Northern and British workers would have had no jobs.

The prosperity created by the cotton boom resonated throughout the Southern economy. Slaves proved to be adaptable to both factories and cities. Southern cities grew quickly, attracting immigrants and businesses. Although the South

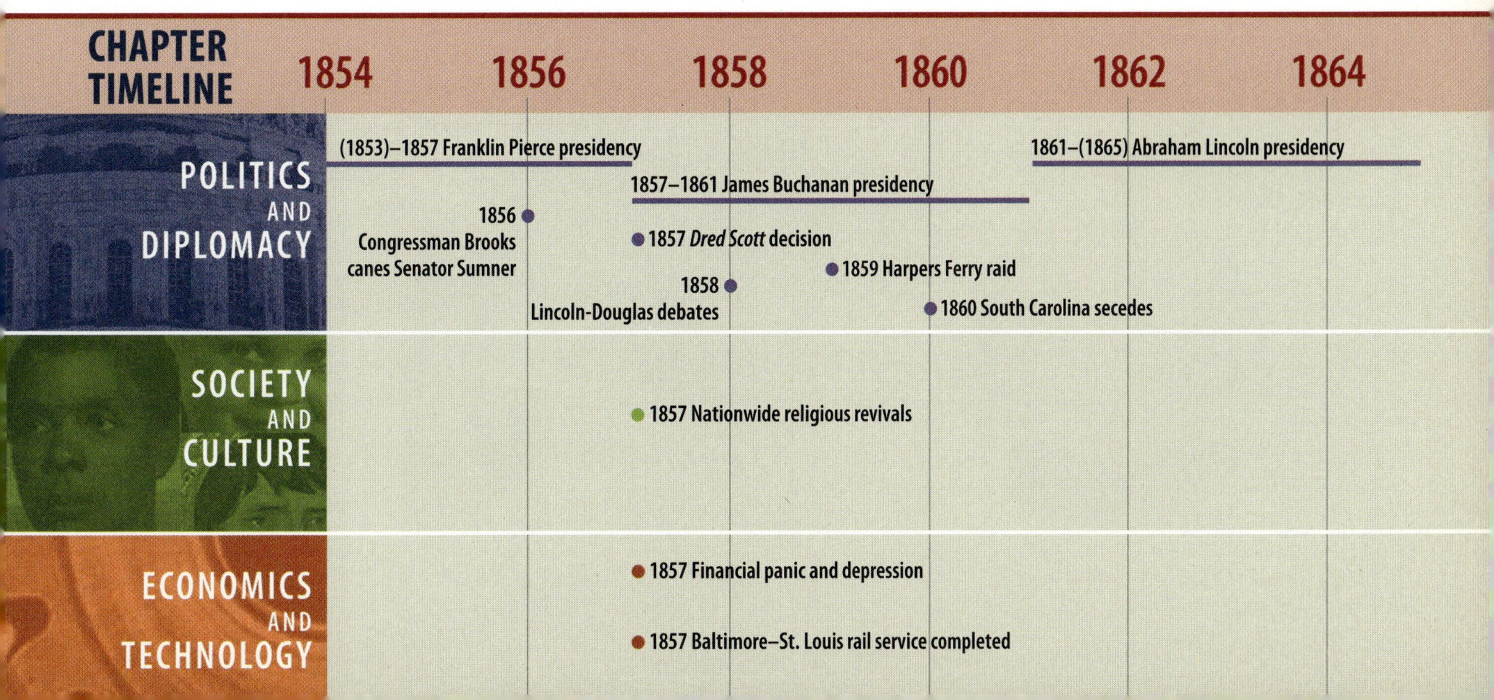

could not keep up with the North, it actually did quite well by international standards. Considered as a separate economy, the South stood second in the world in the number of miles of railroad, sixth in cotton textile factories, and eighth in iron production. Nevertheless, the South was not urbanizing or industrializing nearly as quickly as the North. It did not create a large class of entrepreneurs or skilled workers, nor did the region invest much money in machinery to make its farms and plantations more efficient. The Southern plantation economy, in effect, was too profitable for its own good. The short-term gains of the 1850s, reflected in the escalating value of slaves, dissuaded wealthy Southerners from investing in businesses that might have held greater potential for long-term development.

Critics of the South argued that slavery victimized not only slaves but also "poor whites." In the antislavery portrayal, the **Slave Power's** domination began at home, where haughty self-proclaimed aristocrats lorded over ignorant whites, bullying them into supporting parties and policies that worked against their own interests. Antislavery advocates charged that slaves degraded white labor in the South and substituted a cheap sense of racial superiority for actual accomplishment.

Slave Power Before the Civil War, term referring to the disproportionate power that Northerners believed wealthy slaveholding politicians wielded over their constituents and, as a result, over national political decisions.

Most Southern whites, however, saw slavery as an avenue for advancement. Slave owners included women, shopkeepers, industrialists, lawyers, ministers, and even a few free blacks. No investment seemed to offer a more certain return than a slave, especially in the 1850s when slave prices rose rapidly. Although that rise in prices meant that a growing proportion of white people could not afford slaves, many Americans' livelihoods depended on servicing the slave trade, through insurance, manufacture of slave shoes and clothing, medical care, and transport. Often Southerners who could not afford to purchase slaves or did not need slave labor year-round hired slaves to do specific tasks (see Figure 13.1). The slave trade generated tens of millions of dollars in the antebellum economy. (See *Doing History: White Southerners Without Slaves*.)

Politics reinforced the sense among Southern white men that they lived in a fair and democratic white society. Although many nonslaveholders in mountainous districts across the South voted against the large slaveholding districts, most Southern white men voted in concert with the richest men in their immediate neighborhoods. In the eyes of poorer whites, their wealthy neighbors could act as spokesmen and brokers for the community in the state capital. Whites held black people in contempt, despite their knowledge that many African Americans were more intelligent, hard working, and Christian than many whites. To be white was to be the inheritor of all the accomplishments of the ancients, of Christendom and of the modern world. Such attitudes were reinforced at every level, from the daily rituals of life to the writings of leading thinkers from Europe.

FIGURE 13.1
Slave Owning in the South
About three-fourths of Southern white families owned no slaves in 1860. More than half of those who did possess slaves claimed four or fewer.

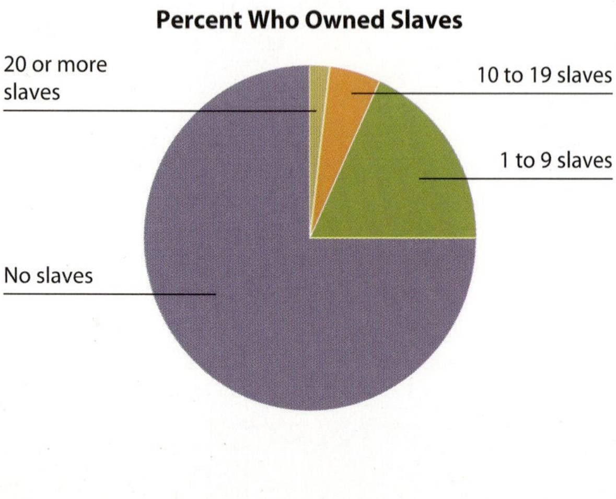

Doing History White Southerners Without Slaves

Hinton Helper's book of 1857, which argued that the South's growth, prosperity, and cultural development were being held back by slavery, became a national sensation. The Republican Party seized on the book as a revelation from inside the slave power's empire, arguing that it revealed the secret resentments of the white majority. To the Republicans' surprise and dismay, however, the book bred anger against the North instead of Republican recruits in the South.

Hinton Helper, The Impending Crisis of the South, *1857*

The lords of the lash are not only absolute masters of the blacks, who are bought and sold, and driven about like so many cattle, but they are also the oracles and arbiters of all the non-slaveholding whites, whose freedom is merely nominal, and whose unparalleled illiteracy and degradation is purposely and fiendishly perpetuated. . . . [The nonslaveholders] must be as mum as dumb brutes, and stand in awe of their august superiors, or be crushed with stern rebukes, cruel oppressions, or downright violence. If they dare to think for themselves, their thoughts must be forever concealed. The expression of any sentiment at all conflicting with the gospel of slavery, dooms them at once in the community in which they live, and then, whether willing or unwilling, they are obliged to become heroes, martyrs, or exiles. . . . Never were the poorer classes of a people, and those classes so largely in the majority, and all inhabiting the same country, so basely duped, so adroitly swindled, or so unpardonably outraged.

Source: Hinton R. Helper, *The Impending Crisis of the South* (New York: A. B. Burdick, 1859), 40–43.

J. D. B. DeBow was a former superintendent of the U.S. Census whose influential New Orleans periodical, DeBow's Review, *promoted the economic development of the South. Here he argues that slavery actually helped the nonslaveholding white Southerner.*

James B. D. DeBow, "The Interest in Slavery of the Southern Non-Slaveholder"

[How does slavery benefit the non-slaveholding white man?]

The non-slaveholders, as a class, are not reduced by the necessity of our condition, as is the case in the free States, to find employment in crowded cities and come into competition in close and sickly workshops and factories, with remorseless and untiring machinery.

The non-slaveholder is not subjected to that competition with pauper labor, which has degraded the free labor of the North. . . .

The non-slaveholder of the South preserves the status of the white man, and is not regarded as an inferior or dependent.

The non-slaveholder knows that as soon as his savings will admit, he can become a slaveholder, and thus relieve his wife from the necessities of the kitchen and the laundry, and his children from the labors of the field.

The large slaveholders and proprietors of the South begin life in great part as non-slaveholders. . . .

Without the institution of slavery, the great staple products of the South would cease to be grown, and the immense annual results, which are distributed among every class of the community, and which give life to every branch of industry, would cease.

Source: "The Non-Slaveholders of the South," in DeBow and others, *The Interest in Slavery of the Southern Non-Slaveholder: The Right of Peaceful Secession. Slavery in the Bible* (Charleston: Evans and Cogswell, 1860), 3–5, 7–12.

QUESTIONS for REFLECTION

1. How could both Helper and DeBow use statistics to make their arguments?
2. What parts of life in the South did Helper focus on? DeBow? Could they both be right? Which argument is more persuasive?

fire-eaters Before the Civil War, Southerners who enthusiastically supported Southern rights and, later, secession.

border ruffians Missouri settlers who crossed into Kansas to lend support for proslavery issues (1855).

Despite the solidarities of racial thinking, important political differences divided Southerners. At one extreme were the so-called **fire-eaters,** virulent defenders of the South and slavery. These men argued that the abolitionists and their Republican supporters intended to destroy the South. The only sane response, they believed, was to agitate the slavery issue constantly, to refuse to yield an inch in the territories or anywhere else. At the other end of the political spectrum in the South were the former Whigs and Know-Nothings, men who considered themselves a "thoughtful, sedate, constitution-abiding, conservative class of men." The many Unionists in the Upper South, in cities, and in some of the richest plantation districts of the cotton South warned that those who boasted of slavery's power would unify the white North against slavery. Caution and compromise, these men argued, were the best friends of slavery.

Bleeding Kansas, 1855–1856

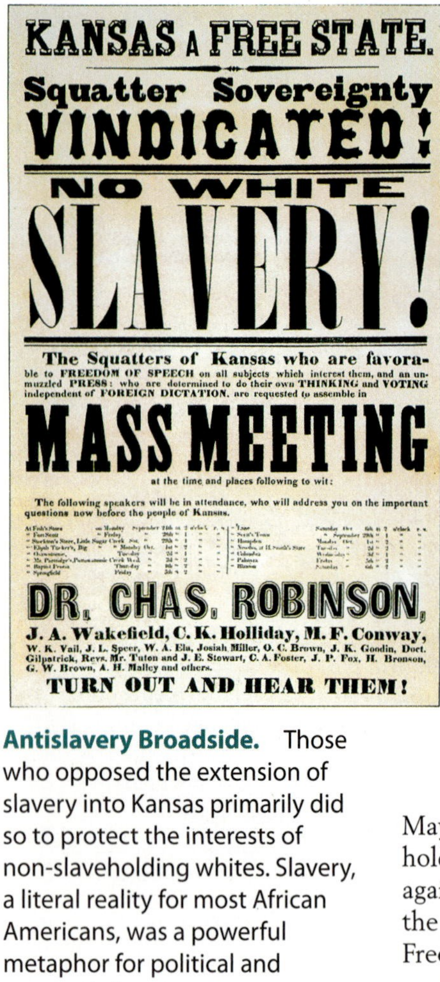

(The Granger Collection, New York)

Antislavery Broadside. Those who opposed the extension of slavery into Kansas primarily did so to protect the interests of non-slaveholding whites. Slavery, a literal reality for most African Americans, was a powerful metaphor for political and economic impotence among whites as well.

The Kansas-Nebraska Act declared that settlers would decide for themselves, by "popular sovereignty," what kind of society they would create. But partisans from both the North and the South determined to fill the territory with settlers of their own political persuasion.

The Massachusetts Emigrant Aid Company announced that it planned to raise \$5 million to aid and encourage settlement in Kansas to ensure that the embattled territory became a free state. Proslavery advocates in Missouri, for their part, flooded across the border to vote in support of proslavery candidates, casting roughly thirty-four hundred more ballots than there were eligible voters. This action by the **border ruffians,** as the Northern press quickly labeled them, was not necessary, for Southerners already accounted for six of every ten men settled in Kansas by 1855. The proslavery forces took control of the territorial legislature in Lecompton and passed a series of aggressive laws against free-soil advocates. Forbidding antislavery men to serve on juries or hold office, the legislature also decreed the death penalty for any person who assisted a fugitive slave.

Antislavery Kansans decided that their only recourse was to establish a rival government. They worked through the summer and fall of 1855 in Topeka to write a constitution of their own. Over the winter, the free-soil advocates "ratified" their constitution and elected their own legislature and governor. Antislavery forces in New England and New York sent rifles to Kansas to arm what they saw as the side of righteousness. Southerners, in turn, organized an expedition of three hundred young men to reinforce their comrades.

Not surprisingly, this volatile situation soon exploded into violence. On May 21, 1856, a group of slave-state supporters marched into the free-soil stronghold of Lawrence, Kansas, to execute warrants from the proslavery territory court against free-state leaders and two newspapers. They threw printing presses into the river, fired cannon at the Free State Hotel, and burned the hotel to the ground. Free-soilers labeled the episode the "sack of Lawrence."

Sumner, Charles (1811–1874) U.S. senator from Massachusetts (1851–1874), he was a noted orator with an uncompromising opposition to slavery.

The next day, in Washington, D.C., Representative Preston Brooks of South Carolina searched out Senator **Charles Sumner** of Massachusetts. Sumner had delivered a series of bitter speeches against slavery, attacking Brooks's relative and fellow South Carolinian, the elderly Senator Andrew P. Butler, for taking "the harlot, slavery" as his "mistress." As Sumner wrote letters at his Senate desk, Brooks, defending the honor of his family and his state, struck Sumner repeatedly about the head with a heavy rubber cane. By attacking with a cane, a punishment usually reserved for servants or slaves, Brooks implied that Sumner was unworthy of a gentleman's challenge to a duel. Because of the severity of his injuries,

(The Granger Collection, New York)

Caning of Sumner. Preston Brooks's attack on Charles Sumner in the U.S. Senate electrified the nation in the spring of 1856—even though this artist apparently did not have an image of Brooks from which to work.

Sumner did not return to his seat for two and a half years, and his empty seat became a symbol in the North of Southern brutality.

The next day, an event back in Kansas intensified the conflict. The episode swirled around **John Brown,** a free-soil emigrant to Kansas. Brown had been a supporter of abolitionism since 1834 and followed five of his sons to Kansas in 1855. There, he became furious at the proslavery forces. He accompanied a group of free-state supporters to defend Lawrence, but they heard of the hotel's destruction before they arrived. Brown persuaded four of his sons and a son-in-law, along with two other men, to exact revenge for the defeat. The band set out for Pottawatomie Creek. There, acting in the name of the "Army of the North," they took five men from three houses and split their skulls with broadswords. The men had been associated in some way with the territorial district court, but no one was sure of Brown's precise motives. He was never punished for the killings.

Brown, John (1800–1859) American abolitionist who, in 1859 with twenty-one followers, captured the U.S. arsenal at Harpers Ferry as part of an effort to liberate Southern slaves. His group was defeated, and Brown was hanged after a trial in which he won sympathy as an abolitionist martyr.

In the wake of the "sack of Lawrence," the caning of Sumner, and the "Pottawatomie massacre"—exploding in just a three-day period in May 1856—the territory became known as **Bleeding Kansas.** The legitimacy of the territorial government remained an issue of heated contention, and the symbolic value of Bleeding Kansas would long endure.

Bleeding Kansas Nickname given to the Kansas Territory in the wake of a number of clashes between proslavery and antislavery supporters in 1856.

The Republicans Challenge the South: The Election of 1856

Democrats were still divided in the wake of their stunning losses in the congressional elections of 1854. To many Southerners, the Democrats seemed a mere tool of Stephen Douglas and his Northern allies; to many Northerners, it seemed that Douglas's call for popular sovereignty was a cover for slaveholder dominance. President Franklin Pierce seemed incapable of leadership. The Democrats, needing someone who had not been tarnished by the events of the preceding two years, turned to **James Buchanan** to run for president in 1856. As minister to England, Buchanan had conveniently been out of the country during the crisis in Kansas.

Buchanan, James (1791–1868) Fifteenth president of the United States (1857–1861). He tried to maintain a balance between proslavery and antislavery factions, but his views angered radicals in both the North and South.

Although Know-Nothings were able to agree at the local and state levels on issues of corruption and anti-Catholicism, slavery split them as they attempted to organize a presidential campaign, and they failed to develop consensus on sectional issues. Southerners who had voted with the Know-Nothings had nowhere to turn but to the Democrats, while Northern Know-Nothings were attracted to the new Republican Party.

Frémont, John C. (1813–1890) Republican presidential candidate in 1856; western explorer who had supported the Bear Flag Revolt in California during the Mexican-American War.

To represent their 1856 presidential platform, the Republicans bypassed their most outspoken antislavery men and nominated **John C. Frémont,** famed as an explorer of the West. Frémont had taken almost no public positions and had accumulated little political experience, but Republicans thought they had found just the sort of vague candidate who would offend the least number of voters. These men avoided talking about race. Republicans stood for the goodness of the North, a place where hard-working white men could build a life for their families free from competition with powerful slaveholders. They denied any intention of ending slavery in the South and even resurrected talk of colonization, the movement abolitionists had abandoned twenty-five years earlier. But the Republicans did warn of the "Slave Power," a political conspiracy by slaveholders to dominate the national government. Republicans saw everything from the three-fifths clause to the bloodshed in Kansas as the fruit of the Slave Power. Kansas and the caning of Sumner showed that the Slave Power, a Cincinnati paper raged, "cannot tolerate free speech anywhere, and would stifle it in Washington with the bludgeon and the bowie-knife, as they are now trying to stifle it in Kansas."

Fillmore, Millard (1800–1874) Thirteenth president of the United States (1850–1853), who succeeded to office after the death of Zachary Taylor. He struggled to keep the nation unified but lost the support of his Whig party.

Nativist sentiment again reared its head during the 1856 campaign. Many Republicans attacked Catholics, repeating the charges that nativists had made for decades about the undemocratic power of the pope, priests, and nuns. Ironically, rumors that Frémont was a Catholic quickly surfaced and refused to subside. Former president **Millard Fillmore** ran under the banner of the American Party, as the Know-Nothings called themselves in a vain attempt to resurrect themselves as a national party. Fillmore hoped that the three-way election would split the electorate so that the final decision would rest with the House, where he would appear as a compromise candidate.

On election day, 83 percent of eligible voting men went to the polls, one of the highest turnouts of the era (see Map 13.1). Although Buchanan won all Southern states except Maryland, he received only 45 percent of the overall popular vote. A difference of a few thousand votes in a few states would have denied Buchanan the election. The Democrats had won, but they were filled with anxiety; the Republicans had lost, but they were filled with confidence. The American political system was clearly in flux.

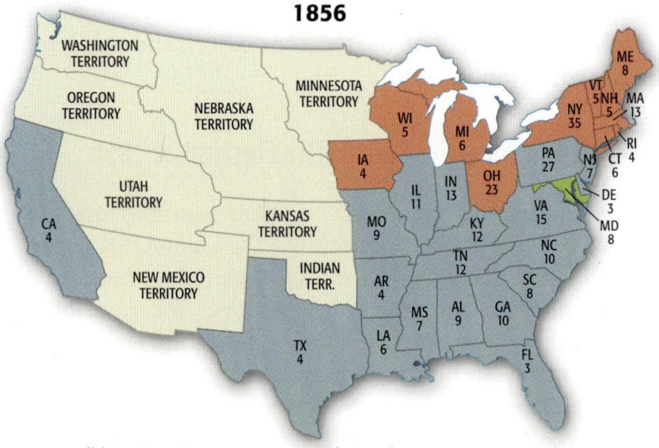

Candidate (Party)	Electoral Vote		Popular Vote	
Buchanan (Democrat)	174	59%	1,832,955	45.3%
Frémont (Republican)	114	38%	1,339,932	33.1%
Fillmore (American)	8	3%	871,731	21.6%
Territories				

MAP 13.1

The Election of 1856

By 1856, none of the national political parties proved able to bridge the growing sectional divide. Buchanan won all Southern states except Maryland, although Fillmore's American Party also made a strong showing throughout the South. The newly formed Republican Party dominated much of New England and the Upper North.

Observers of all political persuasions believed that James Buchanan had it within his power to strengthen the Democrats in both the North and the South. His party, after all, still controlled the Senate. The Republicans, moreover, had drawn much of their power from the chaos in Kansas. Once Kansas had peacefully entered the Union as a free state under the banner of popular sovereignty, Democrats happily observed, no other territory awaited in which similar conflicts might be expected. Slavery, everyone seemed to agree, had no chance in Oregon, Nebraska, Minnesota, Washington, Utah, or New Mexico. The territorial issue that had torn at the country since 1820 might finally die down.

Dred Scott, 1857

In his inaugural address, James Buchanan mentioned a case pending before the Supreme Court, a case regarding a slave. Dred Scott, born a slave in Virginia around 1800, had in the 1830s been taken by his master, an army surgeon named John Emerson, to territories far in the Upper Midwest. Scott had married Harriet Robinson, the slave of a federal Indian agent. Dr. Emerson bought Harriet and thus owned the two daughters she bore with Scott. When Emerson died in 1843, Scott and his family became the property of Emerson's widow, who moved to St. Louis. In 1846 the Scotts petitioned for their freedom, claiming that their residence in the free territory entitled them to free status.

A long series of postponements and delays dragged the case on into the early 1850s, just as the legal environment had become especially divided by

FRANK LESLIE'S ILLUSTRATED NEWSPAPER

No. 82.—VOL. IV.] NEW YORK, SATURDAY, JUNE 27, 1857. [PRICE 6 CENTS.

TO TOURISTS AND TRAVELLERS.

VISIT TO DRED SCOTT—HIS FAMILY—INCIDENTS OF HIS LIFE—DECISION OF THE SUPREME COURT.

(The Granger Collection, New York)

Dred and Harriet Scott, *Leslie's Illustrated*. The *Dred Scott* case attracted the attention of the entire country in 1856. This northern newspaper depicted Scott and his family sympathetically, emphasizing family ties and the women of the family.

slavery. Democratic judges and lawyers worked to deny the Scotts their freedom on the grounds that such a precedent would undermine the right of Southerners to take slaves into the territories. A Republican lawyer agreed to carry the Scotts' case before the Supreme Court to counter the Democrats' aggressive claims. Unfortunately for the Republicans and the Scotts, five Southern Democrats sat on the Court, along with two Northern Democrats, one Northern Whig, and one Northern Republican. Presiding was Chief Justice **Roger B. Taney** (pronounced "tawney"), an eighty-year-old Marylander appointed to the Court by Andrew Jackson in 1835.

Taney, Roger B. (1777–1864) Chief Justice of the United States (1836–1864). In the *Dred Scott* decision (1857) he ruled that slaves and their descendants could not become citizens of the United States.

***Dred Scott* case (1857)** An enslaved man sued for his freedom in 1847, leading to a crucial Supreme Court decision in 1857 in which the Court ruled that African Americans held no rights as citizens and that the Missouri Compromise of 1820 was unconstitutional. The decision was widely denounced in the North and strengthened the new Republican party.

The ***Dred Scott* case** came before the Supreme Court during the superheated months of 1856, when Kansas, the Brooks/Sumner affair, and the presidential election commanded the country's attention. Although the case could have been decided on relatively narrow grounds, the Democratic members of the Court wanted to issue a sweeping pronouncement that would settle once and for all the question of slavery in the territories. President-elect Buchanan pressured a fellow Pennsylvanian on the Court to side with the Southerners. Two days after Buchanan took office in March 1857, the Court announced its decision in the *Dred Scott* case.

It took Chief Justice Taney two hours to read the opinion. He spent an hour denying that Scott had the right to bring a case in the first place. Black people, Taney decreed, could not become citizens of the United States because "they were not included, and were not intended to be included, under the word 'citizens' in the Constitution." Taney declared that at the time the Constitution was written, throughout the "civilized and enlightened portions of the world," members of the "negro African race" were held to be "altogether unfit to associate with the white race . . . and so far inferior, that they had no rights which the white man was bound to respect." Therefore, Dred Scott had never been a citizen of Missouri and had no right to sue his mistress. Taney also decreed that Congress had never held a constitutional right to restrict slavery in the territories and that therefore the Missouri Compromise of 1820 was invalid. Two justices dissented from the majority's opinion, but the decision stood as the law of the land.

Southerners and many Northern Democrats exulted that they had been vindicated by the *Dred Scott* decision, that the Republicans' demand for territories free of slavery was simply unconstitutional. Republicans, however, publicized the dissenting opinions in the *Dred Scott* case and denounced the decision in the state legislatures they controlled throughout the North. If the *Dred Scott* decision were followed to its logical conclusion, they warned, the United States would reopen the slave trade with Africa and even extend slavery into Northern states, where it had been banned. Republicans recognized that outrage over the decision would strengthen their own party.

❖ American Society in Crisis, 1857–1859

The American economy boomed in the mid-1850s. Not only did cotton do well, but so did the farms, factories, railroads, and cities of the North and West. People cheered the laying of a telegraphic cable across the Atlantic Ocean, an incredible feat that triggered celebrations in towns across the nation, including wild fireworks in New York City that set city hall ablaze. Currier and Ives prints became the rage, brightening homes around the country with charming scenes of American life. The sale of newspapers, books, and magazines surged. Working people's organizations staged a comeback. Churches and schools spread with remarkable speed. The mileage of railroads tripled to more than thirty thousand miles.

But underlying this prosperity ran a deep current of unease. Some people worried that Americans were growing soft and self-indulgent. Others felt guilt that as the economy boomed, slavery became stronger. Others despaired at the state of American politics, which seemed in disarray. The conflict between the North and the South embodied all of these anxieties, giving them concrete shape.

Financial Panic and Spiritual Revival, 1857

Late in the summer of 1857, people warned that there had been too much speculation recently, that companies and individuals had borrowed too much money. The end of the Crimean War in Europe seemed ominous for the United States, for now the countries of the Old World could turn their energies toward growing their own food, undermining the heavy demand for American farm products that had buoyed the economy for several years. When a major insurance company went under in 1857, a panic spread among New York banks, and railroad stocks plummeted along with western land values. Soon banks and companies across the country began to fail.

Working people of all ranks lost their jobs, from unskilled laborers, domestics, and millworkers to educated bookkeepers and clerks. Across the North, hundreds of thousands of people had no income, and many were forced to rely on charity to feed and clothe themselves. Workers tried to organize, but employers shut down the mills and factories. As winter approached, starvation threatened many families. Southerners blamed Northern financiers for bringing on the **Panic of 1857.** Though the white and free black working people of Southern cities suffered along with their counterparts in the North, white Southerners boasted that their slaves, unlike white workers, never starved or went without a roof over their heads.

Panic of 1857 Financial crisis resulting from decreased European demand for American produce and decreased European investment following the Crimean War. The panic led to a wave of bank suspensions, individual bankruptcies, and a two-year depression.

A wave of religious revivals that emerged in response to the panic lasted for over a year, sweeping back and forth across the country. Unlike earlier revivals, the religious spirit emerged not in rural districts but in the largest cities of the Northeast, and they attracted a conspicuously large number of men as well as women. Middle-class men in the commercial districts of larger cities met for daily prayer meetings. The Young Men's Christian Association expanded rapidly during this time, providing young single clerks a venue for creating a "businesslike piety." It seemed to many people that the revivals were the most heartening and significant in American history.

The Agony of Kansas

Most of the settlers who arrived in Kansas in 1856 and 1857 were nonslaveholding migrants from the Upper South and did not appear eager to establish slavery in Kansas. An open election therefore would likely install a constitutional convention in favor of free soil at the time Kansas became a state. The proslavery legislature elected in the earliest days of the territory, however, still controlled Kansas in 1857. The constitution they drafted permitted voters to choose between the constitution with slavery or without slavery. In either case, slave owners already in Kansas would be permitted to keep their slaves.

This "Lecompton Constitution" unleashed serious problems for Democrats across the country. Northern members of the party could not support it without appearing too sympathetic to the South; they could not oppose it without alienating the Southern Democrats who made up the bulk of the party's strength. President Buchanan knew well that 112 of his 174 electoral votes had come from the South and that 100 of the 165 Democrats in both houses of Congress were Southerners.

Stephen Douglas refused to endorse the Lecompton Constitution because it was a violation of popular sovereignty, but President Buchanan urged its adoption. The president persuaded himself that the constitution was a moderate compromise, letting Kansas enter the Union as a free state in the long run while protecting the slaveholders who were already there. Once Kansas was a state, Buchanan reasoned, its legislature could decide what to do with those slaves. Most Northerners saw the matter differently: though it was obvious that the great majority of Kansans wanted to enter the Union as a free state, antislavery Kansans would be forced to accept slavery.

Republicans could hardly believe that Buchanan had handed them such an easy way to portray him as a tool of the South. And moderate Southern and Northern Democrats warned that the South was destroying its only hope for continued success: a strong Democratic Party in the North. When Kansas voters overwhelmingly rejected the Lecompton Constitution in 1858, they rejected Buchanan and the South as well. The Democrats suffered widespread defeat in the state elections that spring and lost control of the House. Stephen Douglas faced a tough election battle, and Buchanan did everything he could to destroy this rival in his own party. Running against a promising Republican candidate, **Abraham Lincoln,** Douglas needed all the help he could get.

Lincoln, Abraham (1809–1865) Sixteenth president (1861–1865), his election triggered Southern secession. He led the United States throughout the Civil War, strengthened the power of the presidency, and signed into law the Emancipation Proclamation. He was assassinated two days after Lee's surrender.

The Lincoln–Douglas Debates, 1858

Abraham Lincoln was very much the underdog in the Illinois senatorial race of 1858. As a Whig in a heavily Democratic state, Lincoln had lost many elections, occupying national office just once: elected to the House of Representatives in 1846, Lincoln lasted only one term. Returning to Springfield, he made a good living as a lawyer, drawing on his own abilities and the connections that came with his marriage to Mary Todd, a member of a prominent family. Lincoln's modest beginnings on the Kentucky and Illinois frontier lay comfortably in the past. Still, he longed for a major public office.

Though the short, portly, pragmatic, and famous Stephen Douglas seemed the opposite of the tall, thin, inexperienced, principled, and obscure Abraham Lincoln, the two men shared their constituents' moderate positions on most national issues. Illinois's population was composed of many New England migrants in the northern half of the state, upcountry Southern migrants in the lower half, and German and Irish immigrants in Chicago. Both the factories and the farms of Illinois prospered in the 1850s, as did abolitionists, Know-Nothings, Whigs, and Southern-leaning Democrats. The Illinois senatorial election of 1858 promised to throw all of these groups into contention. At stake was this question: Could the Democrats survive as a national party, with Douglas as their leader, or were they doomed to become a party of the South?

Douglas, though reluctant to give the relatively unknown Lincoln a share of attention, finally agreed to hold seven joint debates in the late summer and early fall. The unprecedented debates gained a national audience as the two candidates articulated each party's position. Lincoln repeatedly brought up the *Dred Scott* decision from the previous year, arguing that it would permit slavery to spread into lands where Illinois men or their sons would otherwise migrate. The West must remain a region where "white men may find a home . . . where they can settle upon some new soil and better their condition in life." Douglas countered that slavery would not spread anywhere the majority of the white population did not want it to. A far greater and more immediate threat, Douglas argued, was that the Republicans would drag moral issues into political contexts. Let the sovereign white people of each state decide for themselves whether they would have slavery, Douglas counseled. Douglas did not defend slavery, but he declared, "I care more for the great principle of self-government, the right of the people to rule, than I do for all the negroes in Christendom."

Lincoln took the offensive, making Douglas appear more of a defender of slavery than at heart he was. He charged that Douglas's strategy merely postponed an inevitable reckoning between the slave states and the free states. Notwithstanding Douglas's efforts to dismiss the morality of slavery as beside the point, that morality repeatedly surfaced in the debates. Lincoln argued that he, not Douglas, was the one defending true self-government. Douglas's policy permitted the forces of slavery to grow stronger and more aggressive, whereas Lincoln's would place slavery on the path toward "ultimate extinction." It would likely be several generations before that extinction occurred, Lincoln believed, but the process could begin in 1858.

The election was close, but the state legislature, which elected U.S. senators in these decades, went to the Democrats, and they returned Douglas to Washington. But Lincoln had become identified as the spokesman for a principled yet restrained antislavery. All across the North, in fact, the Republicans made impressive gains in 1858. In every state, many people wanted the nation to find some compromise. But the political environment did not have a chance to calm in 1859, for it was then that John Brown returned to the national scene.

John Brown and Harpers Ferry, 1859

John Brown had become famous in the three years since he had burst into prominence in Bleeding Kansas in 1855. Antislavery people back east, assured by journalists that Brown had not personally killed anyone at Pottawatomie, admired the hard man for his firsthand opposition to slaveholders. Thus, as he toured New England in search of funds to carry on the cause, he found willing listeners and

(© Bettmann/ CORBIS)

John Brown. The campaign launched by John Brown and twenty-one black and white allies in 1859 failed in its immediate aims of unleashing a rebellion of the enslaved but succeeded in heightening the moral and political debate over slavery.

Harpers Ferry Virginia town that was the site of John Brown's raid in 1859, a failed attempt to lead a slave insurrection. It ignited public opinion in both the North and the South.

open hands. Brown wrote letters to wealthy abolitionists requesting assistance for "an important measure, in which the world has a deep interest." Throughout 1857 and 1858, Brown planned an attack on the federal arsenal at **Harpers Ferry,** Virginia. He had a thousand iron pikes forged to arm the slaves he believed would rise in rebellion once he and his men triggered the revolt. He tried to win the support of Frederick Douglass, who, while sympathetic, thought the plan doomed. But Brown pressed on.

The assault on Harpers Ferry started in earnest in the summer of 1859, when Brown rented a farm seven miles away and assembled his men and munitions. To his disappointment, he could recruit only twenty-one men, five of them African Americans. The raid began easily enough on Sunday, October 16, as Brown's men quickly seized the arsenal and a rifle-manufacturing plant and waited for word to spread among the slaves of Virginia that their day of liberation had come. The word spread instead among local whites, who quickly surrounded Brown's men in the armory building, killing or capturing eight of them. Militia from Virginia and Maryland arrived the next day, followed soon after by federal troops that rushed the armory. Ten of the abolitionist force were killed, five (including Brown) wounded, and seven escaped. Brown was tried within two weeks and found guilty. He was sentenced to be hanged exactly a month later, on December 2.

The entire episode, from the raid to Brown's execution, took only about six weeks to unfold. Yet during those six weeks, opinion in both the North and the South changed rapidly. Public opinion, mixed at first, crystallized into sharply opposing viewpoints. Even Northerners who were appalled at the violence were shocked at the speed with which Brown was tried and condemned. Even Southerners who read with reassurance early denunciations of Brown in the North were appalled when they realized that many Northerners refused to condemn the raid. The many people of moderate sympathies on both sides watched, dismayed, as common ground eroded beneath their feet.

❖ The North and South Call Each Other's Bluff, 1860–1861

Everyone knew the election of 1860 held enormous meaning for the United States, but no one could be sure what that meaning might be. Would this be the election that brought all to their senses? Would the border states control the election? Would Northern voters suddenly realize the South meant what it said? The actual events proved far more complex than most Americans had believed possible.

The Election of 1860

John Brown's raid at Harper's Ferry had a polarizing influence on both national parties. White Southerners automatically linked John Brown with the Republicans; in turn, Southern exultation at his execution made the Republicans more attractive among Northern voters than before. The Democrats' ability to remain attractive to both Southern and Northern voters was sorely tested. In a series of nomination meetings throughout 1860, the Democrats could not agree on a candidate. When Northern Democrats nominated Stephen Douglas, the Southern

Democrats declared themselves the "purified" Democratic party and nominated **John C. Breckinridge** of Kentucky.

Before the Democrats convened again in June, Unionists in both the North and the South tried to avert catastrophe by nominating a compromise candidate. Calling themselves the Constitutional Union Party, they settled on **John Bell** of Tennessee. Many of these Unionists were former conservative Whigs and Know-Nothings who no longer had a political home. They advocated an end to agitation over slavery, "the Union as it is, the Constitution unchanged," to safeguard the "priceless heritage of our fathers." They counted on the other candidates to create a deadlock that would have to be settled in the House of Representatives. There, the Unionists hoped, legislators would gratefully turn to their compromise candidate.

Breckinridge, John C. (1821–1875) Born in Kentucky, vice president under James Buchanan (1857–1861), and presidential candidate of the Southern wing of the Democratic Party in 1860.

Bell, John (1797–1869) Tennessee-born slaveholder who became the presidential candidate of the Constitutional Union Party, which was founded as a compromise party in 1860.

As the Democrats tore themselves apart, the Republicans met in Chicago. There, in efforts to put Southern concerns at rest, the Republicans announced their belief in the right of each state to decide for itself whether it would have slavery. In a much stronger position than in 1856, the Republicans cemented their appeal to voters unconcerned with the slavery issue by calling for protective tariffs, internal improvements, and free homesteads for western settlers. Party strategists calculated that they need only win Pennsylvania and one other state they had lost to the Democrats in 1856 to wrap up the election. The states they needed to take were Illinois, Indiana, or New Jersey—all of them on the border with the South and all of them far more moderate on the slavery question than states farther east or north. Thus, the Republicans turned to a moderate who was a favorite son of one of the crucial states: Abraham Lincoln of Illinois.

The election of 1860 was actually two separate elections: one in the North and one in the South. Lincoln made no attempt to explain himself to the South; Breckinridge made little attempt in the North. They never met face to face. Bell spoke mainly to the already converted. Douglas, breaking with tradition, spoke from New England to Alabama, trying to warn people what could happen if they voted along sectional lines. While campaigning across the Deep South, he endured having rotten fruit thrown at him, insults, and injuries from a collapsed platform. Yet despite such unruliness, Americans in the North and South seemed to have grown accustomed to overheated political rhetoric. Few men were willing to believe their opponents would have the nerve to act on their threats.

On election day, November 6, Lincoln won in every Northern state except New Jersey, which divided between Douglas and Lincoln. Douglas won outright only in Missouri. Breckinridge won the entire South except the border states of Virginia, Tennessee, and Kentucky, which went with Bell. Even at this late stage of sectional division, voters did not fit into easy categories. It was hardly a contest between a rural South and an industrial urban North, for Northern cities tended to vote for compromise candidates, not for Lincoln. Similarly, more than half of Southerners voted for Bell or Douglas, supporting the Union over the South.

Once the election returns were in, these complications seemed to evaporate (see Map 13.2). Although Lincoln won only in the North, the election was not even close in the electoral college, where Lincoln won 180 electoral votes to Breckinridge's 72, Bell's 39, and Douglas's 12. In Southern eyes, the North had arrogantly placed its own interests above those of the Union, insisting on electing a man who did not even appear on Southern ballots. In Northern eyes, the South, walking out of nominating conventions and talking of disunion, was to blame. The election of 1860 completed the estrangement of North and South.

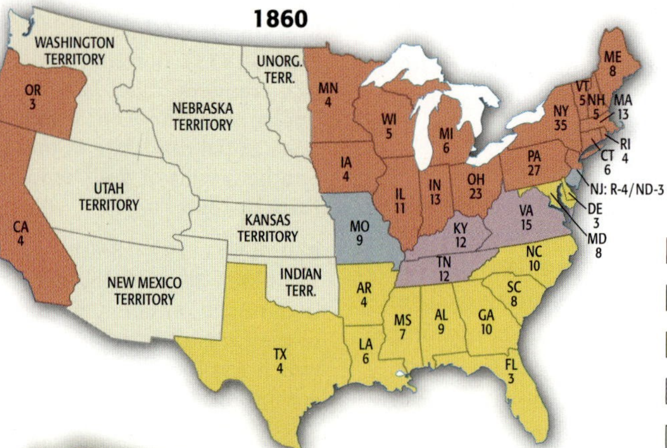

Candidate (Party)	Electoral Vote		Popular Vote	
Lincoln (Republican)	180	59.4%	1,865,593	39.8%
Douglas (Northern Democrat)	12	3.9%	1,382,713	29.5%
Breckinridge (Southern Democrat)	72	23.8%	848,356	18.1%
Bell (Constitutional Union)	39	12.9%	592,906	12.6%
Territories, no returns				

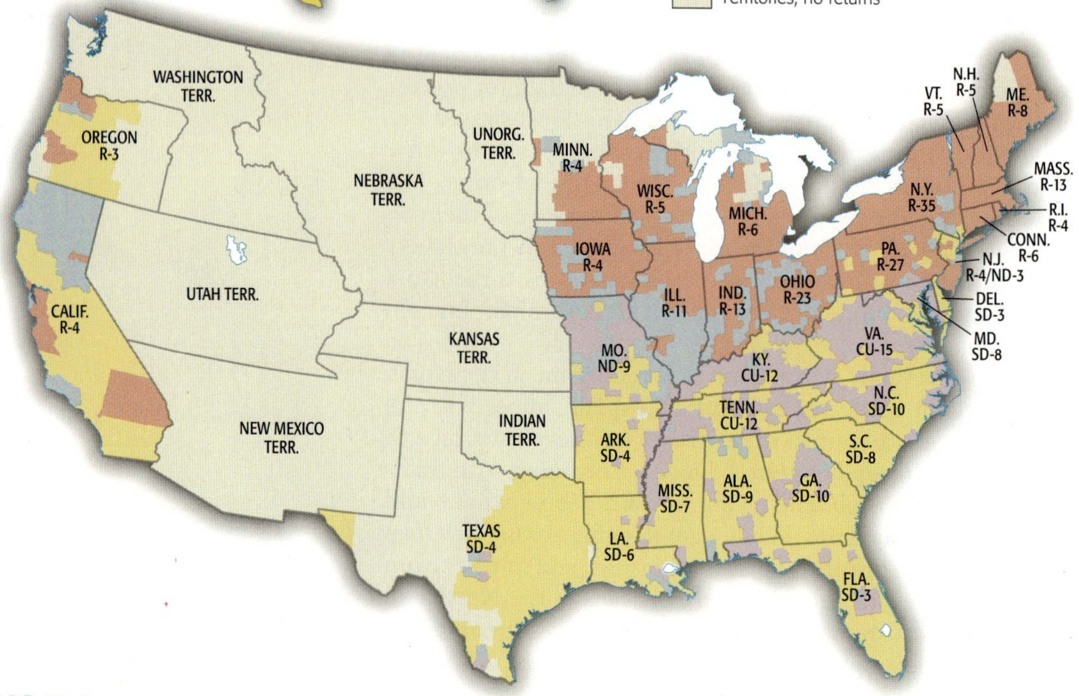

MAP 13.2
The Election of 1860
This four-way election saw the North divided between Lincoln and Douglas, the South divided between Bell and Breckinridge.

The South Debates Independence

The fire-eaters declared Abraham Lincoln's 1860 victory a sign that the North valued neither the Union nor the Constitution on which it was based. The South, they said, had every right, every incentive, to leave the Union. Although the Republicans claimed to work within the political system, Lincoln's supporters had violated an honored tradition of compromise.

Even though the Democrats still controlled the Senate and the Supreme Court, Southerners believed that Lincoln would use the patronage of the federal government to install Republican officials throughout the South and possibly entice nonslaveholders with their free labor doctrines. Such officials could undermine slavery from within, eroding the authority of slave owners. For years, Lincoln had talked of "a house" that had to be unified, of a nation that had to be all slave or all free. Would he not act to undermine slavery now that he was in power?

The nation's eyes turned to South Carolina. Influential men there, after all, had talked of secession since the nullification crisis nearly thirty years earlier. They believed that the same states that had created the Union could also dissolve that Union when it no longer served their purposes. The South Carolina legislature met on the day after Lincoln's election but did not secede immediately. Its members called for an election two months later to select delegates who would then decide the course the state should follow. In the meantime, they hoped, support for secession would grow. The next day, a local paper blustered, "The tea has been thrown overboard; the revolution of 1860 has been initiated."

States of the Deep South quickly lined up behind South Carolina. Carolina leaders, heartened by the response, seceded earlier than they had planned, on December 20. Southerners serving in Buchanan's cabinet began resigning, and by the administration's annual New Year's Day reception, the Southerners in attendance refused to shake Buchanan's hand or acknowledge the president. By February 1, Mississippi, Florida, Alabama, Georgia, Louisiana, and Texas had joined the secession movement. On February 4, delegates from these states met in Montgomery, Alabama, and created a provisional constitution, similar to that of the United States except in its explicit guarantee of slavery and states' rights. On February 18, the convention inaugurated a provisional president, Jefferson Davis of Mississippi, and a vice president, Alexander H. Stephens of Georgia. Davis was a strong states' rights advocate but not a fervent secessionist. With an eye toward the crucial states of Virginia, North Carolina, Kentucky, and Tennessee, leaders of the new Confederacy portrayed themselves as a calm and conservative people, not wild-eyed revolutionaries.

Many thousands of white Southerners resisted secession. Some argued that secession was treason. Others warned that the South was committing suicide. A few argued that the Southern states should wait until they could cooperate with one another more formally and fully. By presenting a united front to the North, these "cooperationists" insisted, the South would not need to secede at all. The North, recognizing that the South was not bluffing, would grant concessions protecting slavery forever. The arguments against immediate secession appealed to a large portion of Southerners, particularly in the Upper South. Even in the Southern states that rushed to secede in January 1861, almost half of all votes went to delegates who had not supported immediate secession. More than a month after the first seven states seceded, secession lost in Virginia by a two-to-one margin. The secessionists were also stymied in Tennessee, North Carolina, and Arkansas.

Recognizing the need to convince the border states to join the secession movement, five states from the Lower South dispatched agents to the Upper South to advocate for disunion. These commissioners wrote numerous letters and spoke to legislatures, public meetings, and private gatherings of community leaders in their efforts to cajole and persuade. These conversations among Southerners emphasized the importance of race and slavery, warning that the Republican Party's future vision of America "destroys the property of the South, lays waste her fields, and inaugurates all the horrors of a San Domingo servile insurrection, consigning her citizens to assassinations and her wives and daughters to pollution and violation."

Northerners too remained quite divided at the beginning of 1861. Many recent immigrants viewed the conflict as none of their business. Northern Democrats called for conciliation with the South. Many black Northerners warned that a war for the Union alone did not deserve black support. A war to end bondage would be worth fighting, they argued, but in 1861 only the most aggressive white abolitionists spoke of such a cause. After the first flush of secessionist victory at the beginning of 1861, people throughout the nation watched and waited to see what would happen when Lincoln officially assumed office on March 4. In the meantime, no one appeared to be in charge.

Most Republicans, including Lincoln, viewed the rhetoric and even the votes for Southern secession as negotiating strategies rather than actual steps toward dissolving the Union. The Republicans showed no inclination to bargain with the South over what remained the key issue: federal support for slavery in the territories. The tensions that had built up in the 1850s, Lincoln thought, could no longer be avoided. "The tug has to come," he argued, "and better now, than any time hereafter."

❖ The First Secession, 1861

In the winter of 1861, the center of the conflict between the North and the South gradually shifted to two obscure forts in the harbor of Charleston, South Carolina. A Kentucky-born U.S. Army officer, Major Robert Anderson, worried that secessionists would attack his small federal force at Fort Moultrie in Charleston. Determined to avoid a war, Anderson moved his small garrison to **Fort Sumter** on December 26, a facility occupying a safer position in Charleston harbor. When South Carolina guns drove away a ship President Buchanan had sent with supplies for Anderson and his men, Buchanan chose not to force the issue. Meanwhile, South Carolina troops strengthened their position around the harbor.

Fort Sumter Fort in the harbor of Charleston, South Carolina, that was fired on by the Confederacy on April 12, 1861, triggering the Civil War.

Lincoln Becomes President

Men from both the North and the South worked frantically, but fruitlessly, to find a compromise during these weeks. Some urged the passage of a new constitutional amendment that would permit slavery forever; some urged the purchase of Cuba to permit slavery to expand; some urged that war be declared against another country to pull the United States together again. All of the compromises were designed to placate the South. Abolitionists viewed such maneuvering with disgust and told their countrymen to let the South go. "If the Union can only be maintained by new concessions to the slaveholders," Frederick Douglass argued, "then . . . let the Union perish." Such views were not popular. Mobs attacked antislavery advocates throughout the North.

On February 11, Abraham Lincoln began a long and circuitous railway trip from Illinois to Washington, covering nearly two thousand miles and using twenty separate rail lines, pausing frequently along the way to speak to well-wishers. At first, he downplayed the threat of secession: "Let it alone," he counseled, "and it will go down of itself." But as the train rolled on and the Confederate convention in Montgomery completed its provisional government, Lincoln became more wary. Warned of attempts on his life, he slipped into Washington under cover of darkness.

Lincoln assembled his government under the growing shadow of war. He sought to balance his cabinet with men of various backgrounds. The two most formidable cabinet members were Secretary of State William H. Seward, a moderate Republican, and Secretary of the Treasury Salmon P. Chase, a radical Republican inclined to take a harder line with the South. Fort Sumter stood as the most pressing issue facing the new administration. Any show of force to reclaim the fort from South Carolina, Southern Unionists warned, and the secessionists would sweep border states such as Virginia into the Confederacy.

Lincoln, with Seward's advice, offered a conciliatory tone in his inaugural speech in March. He told the South that he had no intention of disturbing slavery where it was already established, that he would not invade, that he would not attempt to fill offices with men repugnant to local sensibilities. But he also warned

(The Granger Collection, New York)

Firing on Fort Sumter. South Carolina troops fire cannons at federal forces under the command of Major Robert Anderson. Although no one was killed in the assault, the shots opened the Civil War.

that secession was illegal. It was his duty to maintain the integrity of the federal government, and to do so he had to "hold, occupy, and possess" federal property in the states of the Confederacy, including Fort Sumter. Lincoln pleaded with his countrymen to move slowly and let passions cool. But people heard in Lincoln's inaugural what they chose to. Republicans and Unionists in the South thought it a potent mixture of firmness and generosity, while skeptics focused on the threat of coercion at Fort Sumter.

The Decision at Fort Sumter, April 12–14, 1861

There was less time than Lincoln realized. On the very day after Lincoln's speech, Major Anderson reported to Washington that he would be out of food within four to six weeks. Initially unsure as to the wisdom of retaining the fort, Lincoln finally decided that he had to act: he would send provisions but not military supplies to Fort Sumter. By doing so, Lincoln would maintain the balance he promised in his inaugural speech, keeping the fort but not using coercion unless attacked first.

Meanwhile, Jefferson Davis and his government already had decided that any attempt to reprovision the fort would be an act of war. Davis believed that no foreign power would respect a country, especially one as new and tenuous as the Confederate States of America, if it allowed one of its major ports to be occupied by another country. The Union's resupply of the fort would mean the Union still controlled it.

The Confederate government decided that its commander in Charleston, P. G. T. Beauregard, should attack Fort Sumter before the relief expedition had a chance to arrive. The leaders understood the risks. The Confederate secretary of state, Robert Toombs, warned Jefferson Davis that the attack would "lose us every friend at the North" and "wantonly strike a hornet's nest which extends from

Doing History Online

Broken Bonds, 1855–1861

Go to the CourseMate website for this chapter and link to Primary Sources. After reading Documents 1 to 18, evaluate the following statement: the Civil War was a conflict that was inevitable, a struggle that was bound to occur.

www.cengagebrain.com

mountains to ocean, and legions, now quiet, will swarm out and sting us to death. It is unnecessary; it puts us in the wrong; it is fatal." Nevertheless, on April 12, at 4:30 in the morning, Beauregard opened fire on the Union garrison. The shelling continued for thirty-three hours. Anderson held out for as long as he could, but when fire tore through the barracks and his ammunition ran low, he decided the time for surrender had come.

The events in South Carolina could not go unanswered. Lincoln issued a call for seventy-five thousand volunteers to defend the Union. Southerners agreed that they would have no choice but to come to South Carolina's aid if the North raised a hand against their fellow Southerners. The time for a peaceful resolution had run out.

CHAPTER REVIEW, 1855–1861

SUMMARY

- Bleeding Kansas and the *Dred Scott* decision fed the growth of the new Republican Party.
- Abraham Lincoln and Stephen Douglas engaged in famous debates that sharply defined the place of slavery in American politics.
- John Brown's raid horrified the South and mobilized the North in response.
- The election of 1860 pitched four candidates against each other, and Abraham Lincoln emerged victorious because of his victories across the North.
- The states of the Gulf South formed the Confederate States of America and then fired on Fort Sumter in Charleston.

IDENTIFICATIONS

Slave Power
fire-eaters
border ruffians
Charles Sumner
John Brown
Bleeding Kansas
James Buchanan
John C. Frémont
Millard Fillmore
Roger B. Taney
***Dred Scott* Case**
Panic of 1857
Abraham Lincoln
Harpers Ferry
John C. Breckinridge
John Bell
Fort Sumter

MAKING CONNECTIONS: LOOKING AHEAD

Chapter 14 will show how the events of 1860 quickly spun out of control and began what would become a vast war.

1. What kind of conflict would Americans in both the North and the South have predicted lay ahead of them when South Carolina seceded in December 1860?
2. Why were both Northerners and Southerners so confident in 1860?

RECOMMENDED READINGS

Dew, Charles B. *Apostles of Disunion: Southern Secession Commissioners and the Causes of the Civil War* (2001). Excellent coverage of debates among Southerners about secession.

Etcheson, Nicole. *Bleeding Kansas: Contested Liberty in the Civil War Era* (2004). The fullest and most recent account of this complicated story.

Fehrenbacher, Don E. *The* Dred Scott *Case: Its Significance in American Law and Politics* (1978). The classic account of this complex episode.

Freehling, William W. *The Road to Disunion: Volume 2: Secessionists Triumphant* (2007). Offers a wide-ranging interpretation of events leading up to the Civil War.

Gudmestad, Robert H. *A Troublesome Commerce: The Transformation of the Interstate Slave Trade* (2004). Examines the South's increasing commitment to slavery and the slave trade in the face of abolitionist arguments.

Martin, Jonathan D. *Divided Mastery: Slave Hiring in the American South* (2007). Examines an important facet of the Southern economy and experience of enslaved laborers.

Morrison, Michael A. *Slavery and the American West: The Eclipse of Manifest Destiny and the Coming of the Civil War* (1997). A subtle and up-to-date survey of this critical topic.

Pierson, Michael D. *Free Hearts and Free Homes: Gender and American Antislavery Politics* (2003). A provocative interpretation of connections between gender and the antislavery movement in antebellum politics.

Reynolds, David S. *John Brown, Abolitionist: The Man Who Killed Slavery, Sparked the Civil War, and Seeded Civil Rights* (2005). Brings a modern edge to this important story.

Zarefsky, David. *Lincoln, Douglas, and Slavery: In the Crucible of Public Debate* (1990). Recasts our understanding of these famous political debates.

CourseMate Go to the CourseMate website at www.cengagebrain.com for additional study tools and review materials for this chapter.

14 Blood and Freedom

1861–1865

MAKING CONNECTIONS

LOOKING BACK

As Chapter 13 showed, in the late 1850s and early 1860s, voters in the United States faced the most important elections in the country's history. Those elections turned around the meaning that slavery held for white Americans. Before starting Chapter 14, you should be able to answer the following questions:

1. Why did the sectional crisis peak when it did?
2. Were there times when events could have taken a different turn and the United States could have avoided secession? When might that have happened?
3. Did long-term economic and social changes push the United States toward war, or were the causes located firmly in political events?

At the beginning of 1861, Americans could not imagine anything like the war that would soon consume the entire nation. Events piled on one another in ways that no one could have anticipated: the outcome of a battle could win an election or trigger a riot, while events at home affected the leaders' decisions of when and where to fight. In the North, strong political opposition to Abraham Lincoln exerted a constant pressure on his conduct of the war. In the South, slaves abandoned plantations, and white families' hardships led soldiers to rethink their loyalties.

The outcome of the Civil War was not predetermined by the North's advantages of population and resources. Deep into the war, events could have taken radically different turns. Slavery might have survived the conflict had the Confederacy won at particular junctions, or had the United States lost the will to insist on its abolition. Even with the war's end, the future course of the nation remained in doubt as Americans confronted the greatest rupture in their history.

❖ North and South Face Off

Neither the Union nor the Confederacy was ready for conflict in the spring of 1861. A number of states had yet to declare their loyalties; other states, communities, and families were divided among themselves. In a matter of months, both the North and the South had to prepare for war.

Two days after the Confederate flag went up over Fort Sumter on April 15, 1861, President Lincoln declared South Carolina in rebellion against the United States and called for seventy-five thousand militiamen to help put the rebellion down. The president sought to blend firmness and conciliation, demanding that forces gathering from the states of the Lower South "disperse and retire peacefully." But Southern states saw the call to the militia as an act of aggression, and they replied to Lincoln's requests for troops with defiance. Virginia seceded two days later, refusing to supply soldiers to confront another slaveholding state. Recognizing the importance of moving President **Jefferson Davis** and his government closer to their armies, the Confederacy immediately voted to move its capital to Richmond in May 1861. Meanwhile, in Northern cities, hundreds of thousands gathered to protest Southern acts of aggression. In Chicago, Democrat Stephen Douglas proclaimed, "There are only two sides to the question. Every man must be for the United States or against it. There can be no neutrals in this war, only patriots—or traitors."

Davis, Jefferson (1808–1889) United States senator, secretary of war, and then president of the Confederacy (1861–1865). He was captured by Union soldiers in 1865 and imprisoned for two years. Although he was indicted for treason (1866), he was never prosecuted.

The States Divide

Arkansas, Tennessee, and North Carolina quickly followed Virginia's example and joined the new Confederacy. The Oklahoma Territory, too, aligned itself with the Confederacy. There, leaders of the Five Civilized Tribes, slaveholders themselves, used the opportunity to fight against the U.S. government that had dispossessed them from their homes three decades earlier.

State leaders elsewhere frantically struggled with one another. Maryland was bitterly divided: the southern portion of the state sympathized with the Confederacy while Baltimore and the western portion generally supported the

CHAPTER TIMELINE 1861 1862 1863 1864 1865 1866

POLITICS AND DIPLOMACY

- 1861–(1865) Abraham Lincoln presidency
- 1861 Southern states secede, establishing Confederate States of America
- 1861 Jefferson Davis elected president of Confederacy
- 1861 First Bull Run
- 1862 Union victory at Shiloh
- 1862 New Orleans surrenders to Admiral Farragut
- 1863 Final Emancipation Proclamation; Union begins recruiting African American soldiers; Union victories at Gettysburg, Vicksburg; New York City draft riots
- 1864 Confederacy passes Impressment Act
- 1865–(1869) Andrew Johnson presidency
- 1865 Thirteenth Amendment abolishes slavery; Lee surrenders to Grant at Appomattox Courthouse

SOCIETY AND CULTURE

- 1861 U.S. Sanitary Commission founded; Dorothea Dix becomes superintendent of nurses for the Union army
- 1861–1865 Walt Whitman composes *Drum Taps*
- 1861–1865 Matthew Brady photographs Civil War
- 1863 Gettysburg Address

ECONOMICS AND TECHNOLOGY

- 1862 Homestead Act
- 1862 Legal Tender Act in North allows printing of paper money
- 1862 Battle of Ironclads *Virginia v. Monitor* initiates new era in naval warfare
- 1863 Inflation rampant in Confederacy
- 1863 Bread riot in Richmond

writ of habeas corpus
Constitutional provision allowing prisoners to petition against unlawful detention. The writ was suspended by Lincoln as a wartime measure to prevent the release of prisoners accused of aiding the Confederacy.

Union. Should the United States lose Maryland, the District of Columbia would be completely surrounded by Confederate territory. Accordingly, Lincoln acted quickly to keep Maryland in line, jailing secession advocates and suspending the **writ of habeas corpus**, which allowed prisoners to petition against unlawful detention, so they could not be released. Kentucky, after months of determined attempts to remain neutral, decided for the Union in September after Confederate troops entered the state. Missouri officially remained in the Union but was ravaged from within by brutal violence for the next four years. In the mountains of western Virginia, delegates from fifty counties met in Wheeling to renounce the Virginia secession convention, begin the gradual abolition of slavery, and declare their loyalty to the Union. After a series of conventions and elections, the state of West Virginia came into being in 1862 and joined the Union the following year.

As it turned out, the Union and the Confederacy divided about evenly (see Map 14.1). Virginia, Tennessee, North Carolina, and Arkansas all joined the Confederacy only after Lincoln requested their troops to assist in suppressing insurrection in the Lower South. Those states accounted for half of all manufacturing and half of all food production in the Confederacy. Maryland, Kentucky, and Missouri might well have joined the Confederacy; had they done so, the Union cause would have been weakened, perhaps fatally. Although Abraham Lincoln was criticized from every angle in these months, he managed to bring into the Union the states he had to win. Had he lost these struggles, he might well have failed in all the other struggles that awaited him.

Comparing Advantages and Disadvantages

In retrospect, the cards seemed heavily stacked in the North's favor. The Union, after all, had vastly greater industrial capacity, railroads, canals, food, draft animals, ships, and entrepreneurial experience, and four times as many white residents as

MAP 14.1
Southern Secession, 1860–1861
The states of the Deep South were the first to secede. Immediately after Lincoln called for troops to suppress the rebellion, Virginia, Arkansas, North Carolina, and Tennessee departed the Union. The other slave states—Kentucky, Maryland, Delaware, and Missouri—remained in the Union.

the South. Although the 3.5 million enslaved people who lived in the Confederacy were vitally important, everyone recognized that the slaves could become equally valuable allies for the North.

Since the South acknowledged the North's advantages, many people then and since assumed that the Confederates must have been driven by either irrational rage or heedless bravery. Neither the Confederates nor the Unionists, however, expected the secession crisis to turn into a full-fledged war, much less a four-year war. When Lincoln called for the seventy-five thousand militia, he called them for only ninety days' service. Since both sides believed that their opponents were weak and divided, Northerners and Southerners thought the conflict would likely come to a swift, and peaceful, resolution.

The initial military strategies of both sides sought to minimize actual fighting. The South saw itself as purely on the defensive; it would wait for Northern armies to invade and then defeat them. The North, for its part, counted on General Winfield Scott's **Anaconda Plan**, named after the large snake that squeezes its prey to death. That plan depended on sending an overpowering force down the Mississippi River in the fall, dividing the South in two. At the same time, the Union navy would seal off the South from outside supplies. Ground troops and land battles would be kept to a minimum.

The Confederacy possessed considerable military advantages. It occupied an enormous geographical area, including dozens of harbors and ports, and was connected by an excellent system of rivers and an adequate network of railroads. The Confederacy's long border with Mexico made it difficult to seal off outside supplies. The Confederacy could wage a defensive war, moving its troops internally from one point to another, whereas the Union had to move around the perimeter. The many country roads of the South, known only to locals, would provide routes for Confederate surprise attacks or strategic retreats. Southerners considered the American Revolution a useful model: like the Patriots, the Confederates did not have to win every battle or conquer Northern territory. Southerners thought they had only to keep fighting long enough for the North's political, economic, regional, and ethnic divisions to overwhelm its temporary unity.

On the matter of leadership, in 1861 many observers would have given the advantage to the Confederates. Abraham Lincoln, after all, had held public office for only two years before he assumed the presidency, and his only military experience had been a brief service in the militia during Black Hawk's War. Jefferson Davis, by contrast, had distinguished himself in the war with Mexico and wielded military knowledge and experience. He had been secretary of war under Franklin Pierce and had served in the U.S. Senate. Both Lincoln and Davis assembled cabinets that balanced geography, political faction, personality, and expertise. Davis ran through several secretaries of war and secretaries of state before finding the two men on whom he felt he could rely, James A. Seddon and Judah P. Benjamin. Lincoln's cabinet ended up containing men whom he barely knew.

Southern generals also had more experience: the average age of the Union generals in 1861 was thirty-eight; of

Doing History Online

Secession

Go to the CourseMate website for this chapter and link to Primary Sources. After reading Documents 1 to 6, consider the following: If you had lived in Virginia in 1861, do you think your sympathies would have rested with the Union or the Confederacy?

www.cengagebrain.com

Anaconda Plan Term given to the strategy employed by the North during the Civil War in which the Confederacy would be slowly strangled by a blockade.

(The Granger Collection, New York)

(© CORBIS)

Civil War Generals. Prominent generals included Ulysses S. Grant of the Union and Robert E. Lee of the Confederacy.

Lee, Robert E. (1807–1870) U.S. and Confederate general. He led the Army of Northern Virginia in the American Civil War.

Confederate generals, forty-seven. **Robert E. Lee** of Virginia had served as an engineer, an officer in the Mexican War in the 1840s, and superintendent of West Point in the late 1850s. He resigned his U.S. military commission, along with about two-thirds of all Southern-born officers, and accepted command of Virginia's forces. About a third of Union generals and half their Confederate counterparts had not been professional soldiers, though most had some military training.

Mobilization and the First Conflicts

Battles began before anyone was ready. Soon after Lincoln's call for troops in April 1861, Confederate troops managed to recover valuable gun-making machinery, artillery, naval stores, and ships at Harpers Ferry and Norfolk, Virginia. A few weeks later, battles broke out along the B&O Railroad in what would become West Virginia, while nearly four thousand Confederates, most of them from Texas, pushed into New Mexico. They hoped to win the mineral riches discovered in Colorado in 1857 for the Southern cause.

These struggles showed that both sides were far from ready to fight in 1861. Guns and uniforms were scarce, and combat experience was rare. The militia who first responded to the calls of the Union and Confederacy had scarcely been trained. The U.S. Army contained only about sixteen thousand men, and nearly twelve thousand of those were scattered across the vast territory west of the Mississippi River.

Both sides took immediate steps to create new armies. The Confederate Congress authorized 400,000 volunteers in May 1861, and in July 1861, the Union Congress authorized 500,000 troops, each signing on for three years. Despite many divisions among classes, occupations, religions, and ethnic groups in the North, both working men and wealthy men eagerly enlisted. Members of ethnic groups took pride in forming their own units; the Irish and Germans supplied more than 150,000 men each, with the total of foreign born in service totaling nearly half a million. Editor Horace Greeley hailed the transformation of Northerners from "a sordid, grasping money-loving people" to one in whom the "fires of patriotic devotion" still burned. Southern men were activated by the same impulses that drove their Northern counterparts. At this point in the war, white Southerners talked less about slavery than they had before or they would later. In their eyes, they fought to defend their homes from "foreign" invaders.

Editors, politicians, and citizens of both the North and the South demanded that the conflict be wrapped up immediately. "ON TO RICHMOND" ran the headline in Northern papers. Confident of victory, Southerners itched for the fight that would settle things once and for all. Only a few dissented: William T. Sherman predicted that this "is to be a long war—very long—much longer than any politician thinks."

With so many men eagerly signing on to fight, Northerners thought they should get the war over early, before the South had time to consolidate its forces. The Union already had thirty-five thousand men poised in northern Virginia, about twenty-five miles away from a Confederate force of twenty thousand under the command of P. G. T. Beauregard. Beauregard's troops protected the rail junction at Manassas, along Bull Run (a "run" is a stream). Confederate and Union troops also watched one another warily in the Shenandoah Valley, about fifty miles to the west. These troop deployments reflected a primary goal of each side in the early stages of the war: capturing the capital of its enemy.

Officers of both the Union and the Confederacy had learned strategy at West Point, and they usually attempted to concentrate their forces in hopes of overwhelming the enemy at the point of attack. The Union tried to take advantage of its greater numbers of men and resources; the Confederacy sought to use its interior lines, knowledge of the Virginia landscape, and aggressive maneuvers to

Doing History Online

Mobilization

Go to the CourseMate website for this chapter and link to Primary Sources. Read the documents in this module. To sufficiently mobilize for the war, what special demands may have been made on the Southern states?

www.cengagebrain.com

gain an advantage. Educated with the same texts and serving together in peace and war, leaders on both sides knew what the others hoped and planned to do.

In the first major battle of the war, the South's advantages outweighed the North's. Both sides attempted to coordinate their troop movements near Washington and in the Shenandoah Valley. The valley had long served as a major corridor between the North and the South. The Confederacy employed cavalry, under the command of the flamboyant young colonel James E. B. (Jeb) Stuart, to move quickly up and down the valley, keeping the North off balance. The Union, under the command of General Irvin McDowell, tried to concentrate most of its forces at Manassas by moving them from the valley. On July 21, the Northern troops were finally ready to attack. Congressmen and other spectators drove their carriages out from Washington to "see the Rebels get whipped." Union troops flooded over the battlefield, fording the creeks, flanking the strongest points in the Confederate lines. The Southern forces fell back. When it looked as if they were to be routed, a Southern general pointed out **Thomas J. Jackson** to his men, and shouted, "There is Jackson standing like a stone wall! Rally behind the Virginians!" "Stonewall Jackson," previously an undistinguished mathematics professor at the Virginia Military Institute, had been christened.

Jackson, Thomas J. "Stonewall" (1824–1863) Confederate general who commanded troops at both battles of Bull Run (1861 and 1862) and directed the Shenandoah Valley campaign (1862). He was accidentally killed by his own troops at Chancellorsville (1863).

Confederate reinforcements poured off a train at Manassas and gave Beauregard a renewed spirit. The Union forces suffered confusion when the lack of a common uniform led some Northerners to mistake Confederates for their own troops. They began to pull back and then to run, giving the South its first victory. Each side had engaged about eighteen thousand soldiers, making Bull Run by a considerable margin the largest battle ever waged in the United States up to that time, and each lost about six hundred men. Key parts of Confederate lore emerged from Bull Run: the Rebel yell and the Confederate battle flag. The yell was a high wail, unnerving and strange, and it served as the rallying cry for Southern troops for the rest of the war. The initial flag of the Confederacy looked a great deal like that of the United States, leading to confusion in the heat of battle. After Bull Run, Beauregard designed a new battle flag—a square banner, red with a blue cross and white stars—to ensure that Southern troops did not fire on one another.

Each side called this first battle of the war by different names. Northern forces generally named battles after physical features such as rivers and mountains; thus, they deemed this the Battle of Bull Run. Southerners usually named battles after nearby towns; they called this one Manassas.

Women and War

Women avidly followed the debates and war coverage in the newspapers. Within two weeks of the war's beginning, both Union and Confederate women alike formed over twenty thousand aid societies devoted to supplying their respective armies' needs. One such organization in Alabama provided, in just one month, "422 shirts, 551 pairs of drawers, 80 pairs of socks, 3 pairs of gloves, 6 boxes and one bale of hospital supplies, 128 pounds of tapioca, and a donation of $18 for hospital use." With the first battles, women claimed positions as nurses, even though previously only men had served as military nurses. Dorothea Dix, long known as the champion of the mentally ill and other neglected people in the antebellum era, became superintendent of nurses for the Union army, the highest executive appointment for a woman to date, organizing three thousand female volunteers.

Women's efforts soon became legendary. They labored until they could no longer stand, until their long dresses trailed blood from amputations and wounds. Kate Cumming and Phoebe Pember played leading roles in the Confederacy, and Clara Barton took her aid to the front lines of the Union and later founded the American Red Cross. As Northern farmers departed for the military, observers in the Midwest saw "more women driving teams" and more "at work in fields than men." (See *Doing History: Women and War.*)

Doing History Women and War

With so many men in the military, both sides began to employ women in government clerical positions. Women and children, some as young as nine years old, also manufactured uniforms and munitions. On March 13, 1863, more than forty women were killed in an explosion at the Confederate munitions factory on Brown's Island in Richmond.

Helen M. Linscott to Abraham Lincoln, "Letter," *November 14, 1864*

I am an orphan girl—dependent upon my own exertions for a livelihood. . . . I am anxious to—procure a situation as copyist, or to do writing in some of the Government offices in Washington.

Source: Helen M. Linscott to Abraham Lincoln, Monday, November 14, 1864, transcribed and annotated by the Lincoln Studies Center, Knox College, Galesburg, IL. Available at *Abraham Lincoln Papers at the Library of Congress,* Manuscript Division (Washington, DC: American Memory Project, 2000–2002), http://memory.loc.gov/ammem/alhtml/alhome.html.

Daily Richmond Examiner, *May 22, 1863*

Embowered in the deep shade of Brown's Island, with its busy colony of female operatives the laboratory works are well worthy a visit. Here the delicate hands of the southern maiden put up the little packet of powder and bullet, the thicker finger and unerring aim of the southern soldier sends on its mission of death into the breast and brain of the invader.

Source: "The Brown's Island Laboratory Works," *Daily Richmond Examiner,* May 22, 1863, p. 1.

Mary Darby De Treville, "Letter," *May 22, 1863*

Never will I forget the first day in that large, dingy room in Kinsler's Hall, the numberless steps to climb to reach the room where hundreds sat numbering and signing. I first had to take the Oath of Allegiance to the Confederate States; then had given me pens, pen holder, clamp with sponge, writing pad, etc. . . . Next–I was given a bundle of treasury notes; thus I became a government employee, a treasury note signer. . . . When pay-day came, the first time I had ever worked for wages, how mean I felt when I went up and signed for my pay. Rose Wilkinson, of New Orleans, was next to me and laughingly said, "Never mind, Mary, I too felt that way at first, but you will get beautifully over the feeling and find yourself going up demanding it as your right."

Source: Mary Darby De Treville, "Letter from Mary Darby De Treville," in United Daughters of the Confederacy, South Carolina Division, *South Carolina Women in the Confederacy,* vol. 2, ed. Mrs. James Conner et al. (Columbia, SC: State Company, 1907), 180–183.

J. Andrews Harris to Abraham Lincoln, "Letter," *January 23, 1863*

I venture to appeal to *you* directly . . . on behalf of about thirty thousand suffering . . . women who sew, *(on army work)*, and their children.

These women are now forced . . . to be at the mercy of contractors who give them sometimes not one half of the government rates. . . . These women are, very many of them, the wives or widows of American Soldiers. . . . The hand which by a stroke of the pen gave freedom to an oppressed race can, if you will, secure, at the least, *fair dealing* with those who are dear to men who left them at home, unprotected, to be able to back up your Emancipation proclamation at the risk of their lives. The prayers of a poor wife, a helpless widow, & destitute children, will surely call down a blessing from Heaven upon you if you will but interpose in their behalf.

Source: J. Andrews Harris to Abraham Lincoln, Monday, January 23, 1865, transcribed and Annotated by the Lincoln Studies Center, Knox College. Galesburg, Illinois. Available at *Abraham Lincoln Papers at the Library of Congress,* Manuscript Division (Washington, DC: American Memory Project, 2000–2002), http://memory.loc.gov/ammem/alhtml/alhome.html.

QUESTIONS for REFLECTION

1. How did their gender and participation in the war effort shape women's appeals for government protection?
2. How much did women feel that their roles were changing as a result of the war? Did they welcome these changes?

❖ Shifting Strategies

The war spread across the continent in the fall, winter, and spring of 1861–1862. Generals consolidated command and launched campaigns thousands of miles from their respective capitals. Governments transformed their economies, developed navies, conducted diplomacy, and cemented the loyalties of those at home. Families steeled themselves for a long conflict.

The North took from the embarrassing defeat at Bull Run a determination to fight more effectively. Volunteers flooded into recruitment offices. Lincoln removed the leaders responsible for that battle and replaced them with **George B. McClellan.** Although only thirty-four years old, McClellan had distinguished himself in the Mexican War and had studied military tactics in Europe. Moreover, he had already frustrated Confederate forces under Robert E. Lee in western Virginia. As he took command, the press lavished praise on the young general, who viewed Lincoln and his cabinet with contempt. McClellan wanted to make his army perfectly prepared before he risked it in battle against Confederates whose numbers his spies consistently exaggerated. Meanwhile, months dragged by, and Lincoln and newspaper editors became furiously impatient.

McClellan, George B. (1826–1885) Major general of the United States Army who led forces in Virginia in 1861 and 1862. He was widely blamed for not taking advantage of his numerical superiority to defeat the Confederates around Richmond. McClellan ran against Abraham Lincoln for president in 1864 on the Democratic ticket.

The War in the West Begins

There was to be no waiting in the West, as the situation in Missouri burst into chaos in July and August 1861. Four days after the battle at Bull Run, the Union had installed a new commander in charge of the forces in Missouri: John C. Frémont, the "pathfinder of the West" and former Republican presidential candidate. Confederate armies built up on the southern border, ready to attack, as guerrilla forces raged throughout the state. With the populace of Missouri divided in its loyalties, Frémont did not know whom to trust. Frantic, he declared the entire state under martial law, decreed the death penalty for captured guerrillas, and seized the slaves and other property of all Confederate sympathizers. Slaveholders in the border states of Kentucky and Maryland threatened to throw their allegiances to the South if Lincoln did not overrule Frémont. The president, desperate to keep the border states within the Union, requested that Frémont revoke his order. When Frémont resisted, Lincoln removed him from his post.

Events on the earliest battlefields proved to be a poor guide to the long term. Although the North had been shaken by Bull Run and Missouri, it had lost neither Washington nor the border states. And although the South had apparently won at Bull Run, the exhausted Confederate forces had not taken advantage of the situation to attack the Union capital. Although slaveholders in the border states fumed at Union leadership, they remained within it. As a result, the South was deprived of a key strategic advantage: access to the Ohio River and a defensible border with the North. The war was not to be won within a few months of the war's start.

Skirmish. Much of the Civil War turned around conflicts such as the one depicted in this painting, in which small groups of soldiers confronted one another and civilians far from the scenes of major battles.

The Economics of War

The Civil War immediately became breathtakingly expensive. Although the Union and the Confederacy were rich societies by any international standard, neither had ever supported a large army or an active government. Taxes on imported goods and the sale of apparently endless public lands paid for what government there was. Ever since the Bank War of the 1830s, the federal and state governments had done little to manipulate the currency. As a result, when the war came, the men responsible for paying for it had only a few options: loans, new taxes, or the creation of paper money. Loans met the least resistance, but borrowing could provide only a third of the cost of the war. Taxes proved even less effective. The Confederacy quickly decided that it had no choice but to print paper money and soon produced millions of dollars in the new currency. Accordingly, catastrophic inflation began to grow as early as the winter of 1861–1862.

In the North, taxes and bonds carried much more of the burden of financing the war, but the Union too was forced to issue paper money by 1862. People hoarded gold in anticipation of the deprivations a widened war would cause. In February 1862, the Union Congress reluctantly passed the Legal Tender Act, permitting the treasury to release up to $10 million of the new currency, quickly dubbed **greenbacks.** More than $450 million in paper notes circulated during the war, replacing the earlier system of state bank notes with the first unified national currency.

greenbacks Paper currency issued by the Union under the Legal Tender Act of 1862, replacing the notes of individual banks with a unified national currency.

Meanwhile, Southerners soon faced severe economic conditions. Many watched helplessly as armies stripped their farms of food and livestock. They ministered to the bleeding young men dragged into their parlors and bedrooms. Governors received letters from women, their husbands and sons gone, who worried that they faced starvation if they did not get help soon. Inflation ate away at the Confederacy like a cancer as its currency's value plummeted. The government issued war bonds that paid 8 percent interest per year at a time when inflation reached 12 percent per month in 1861, leading to rampant speculation. Farmers grew cotton because it stored well and was thought to fetch a high price after the war; as a result, land and labor that could have grown food bent under the weight of cotton. Managing slaves also got more challenging during wartime: many plantation mistresses discovered that slaves would not work when the master was off fighting.

Resentment against the wealthy—mediated during peacetime by family ties, common church membership, and democratic politics—quickly came to the surface in the context of war. Common people were quick to notice when plantation slaves labored over cotton rather than corn, when the well-to-do hoarded gold, received draft exemptions, or dodged taxes.

Diplomacy and Conflicts on the Water

The Union initially enjoyed a great naval advantage. By the end of 1861, more than 260 Union vessels patrolled the coasts, blockading 189 harbors and ports from Virginia to Texas and patrolling 3,500 miles of coastline. But such enormous territory obviously proved difficult to control. The South had virtually no ships at the beginning of the war, but the Confederate navy seized, acquired, or built roughly 125 ships each year, including more than 400 steam-powered vessels. Jefferson Davis authorized Southern sailors to attack Northern ships on the high seas and turn them in for a share of the booty. One such **blockade runner**, Raphael Semmes, seized 18 Union ships in 1861 before he was trapped at Gibraltar and forced to sell his ship and escape to England.

blockade runners During the Civil War, ships that smuggled war supplies and imported goods into the Confederacy during the Union blockade of its coastline.

In August 1861, at Cape Hatteras in North Carolina, federal ships shelled the forts there and cut off supplies that dozens of blockade runners had brought into the Confederacy. The most valuable seizure was Port Royal, South Carolina, which stood midway between the major Southern ports of Charleston and

Savannah. The seventy-seven ships and sixteen thousand sailors and soldiers dispatched to Port Royal were the largest combined force yet assembled in American warfare. One incident on the high seas, known as the ***Trent* affair,** escalated into a tense diplomatic predicament when a Union ship stopped a British mail packet, the *Trent,* as it traveled from Cuba to St. Thomas. The *Trent* carried two Confederate commissioners sailing to London and Paris to negotiate for international support. Charles Wilkes, the captain of the Union ship, boarded the British vessel, seized the Confederate emissaries, and met with a hero's welcome when his ship returned to Boston. Yet international law did not offer a clear ruling on whether Captain Wilkes had acted legally.

***Trent* affair (1861)** Diplomatic incident growing out of the Union seizure of two Confederate envoys aboard a British ship, which highlighted the question of whether European countries would recognize Confederate nationhood.

The *Trent* affair reflected the uneasy state of international relations created by the war. Most Europeans were conflicted on which side had the better claim to their ideological and economic sympathies; although many sympathized with the Confederacy's fight for self-determination, abolitionists in both nations were dismayed by its continued reliance on slavery. The Confederacy hoped that England or France, or even both, would come to its aid due to those nations' reliance on Southern cotton. However, British factories had stockpiled cotton in expectation of the war; industrialists had also begun investing heavily in Egyptian cotton production. In addition, neither the British nor the French were eager to upset the fragile balance of power between themselves by taking the first step in America. The *Trent* affair was settled through diplomatic evasion and maneuvering, but the international situation remained tense throughout the war.

While leaders of both Britain and France waited for events on the battlefields of North America to clarify issues, in 1862 Union generals in the West began to advance aggressively. Deprived of control of the Ohio River when Kentucky sided with the Union, the Confederates under Albert Sidney Johnston desperately needed to stop the Union. Troops under the command of **Ulysses S. Grant,** a relatively obscure general from Illinois, confronted a Confederate line of defense across southern Kentucky. Employing the Union's new river gunboats to great effect, Grant pushed down both the Tennessee and the Cumberland rivers across the Kentucky border into Tennessee.

Grant, Ulysses S. (1822–1885) U.S. general and eighteenth president of the United States (1869–1877). He commanded the Union Army during the Civil War.

Important Confederate forts stood on both rivers, but Grant hoped to overwhelm them by combined attacks on water and land. He assaulted Fort Henry on the Tennessee River in early February, easily overcoming the fort's defenses and then marching his men overland to Fort Donelson. There, the Confederates fought desperately, destroying several of the gunboats, but Grant ultimately overwhelmed the Southern troops and took control of the region. When the Confederate general in charge attempted to negotiate with Grant for their surrender, Grant brusquely responded: "No terms except an unconditional and immediate surrender can be accepted." Grant's phrase soon echoed through the Northern press. Within days, Union troops pushed into nearby Nashville, the capital of Tennessee, making it the first great conquest of the war.

At the same time, the Union navy continued its relentless attack on the eastern seaboard of the Confederacy. A well-planned amphibious assault allowed the Northern navy to consolidate its control of the North Carolina coast, and the blockade steadily tightened. Yet the Southern navy had reason for hope in early 1862. Confederate Secretary of the Navy Stephen Mallory had created an effective and innovative department, and he sought to take advantage of recent developments in shipbuilding and naval warfare, including iron-plated ships.

Virginia* and *Monitor Two ironclad vessels that fought in the harbor at Hampton Roads on March 9, 1862, in the first American battle between ironclads. Though neither won, the encounter established the importance of ironclads for the remainder of the war.

The Confederacy began building an ironclad almost from the very beginning of the war, adding walls of 2-foot-thick solid oak, covered with 2-inch-thick iron plate, to the hull of a Union frigate scuttled in Norfolk in April 1861. Engineers installed an iron ram on the front to rip through the wooden hulls of enemy ships and armed the ship with ten heavy guns. The Confederacy changed the ship's name from the U.S.S. *Merrimack* to the **C.S.S. *Virginia*.** The Union, for its part,

(First Battle of Iron Ships, LP102, The Mariners' Museum, Newport News, VA)

Battle of Hampton Roads. Traditional wooden vessels were helpless against the new ironclads, which could fire at close range without sustaining significant damage themselves. The battle between the U.S.S. *Monitor* and the C.S.S. *Virginia* foreshadowed the importance of ironclad ships to the remainder of the war.

hired a Swiss inventor to design a shallow-draft ship that would be mostly submerged except for a rotating turret on top. No one was sure it would stay afloat, much less fight effectively with its two guns. It was called the **U.S.S. *Monitor*.** On March 8, 1862, the Confederates unleashed their new weapon. The *Virginia* attacked several Union ships in the harbor at Hampton Roads, Virginia; their guns proved useless against the heavy iron sheathing.

In one of the more dramatic episodes of the young war, however, the Union happened to be sending its own ironclad to another Virginia port thirty miles away. On March 9, the *Virginia* and the *Monitor* engaged in battle and pounded one another for hours. Although neither iron ship actually won the battle, the advantages of the Northern *Monitor*'s innovative design quickly became evident. The imposing Southern ironclad had been neutralized, and the blockade would continue. The Union began a crash campaign to build as many ironclads as possible, using the *Monitor* as its model.

The Battles of Spring 1862

On the very day that the C.S.S. *Virginia* emerged at Hampton Roads, Abraham Lincoln gave his approval of General George McClellan's long-delayed plan to win the war in the East. Rather than fighting in northern Virginia, McClellan would attack Richmond from the south, using the peninsula between the James and York rivers as an invasion route and relying on the Chesapeake Bay as a supply route. By moving the war away from Washington, McClellan argued, he would lessen the threat to the nation's capital (see Map 14.2). Four hundred watercraft of every description began transferring one hundred thousand Union soldiers to the tip of the peninsula at Fort Monroe, about seventy miles from Richmond. McClellan took several more weeks to arrange his men in preparation for the expected triumph of taking the Confederate capital.

In the meantime, U.S. Grant and his fellow general William T. Sherman pushed their troops ever deeper into Tennessee. The Confederates, under Albert Sidney Johnston, planned to attack Grant to regain momentum and lost territory. Grant established his own base of operations only twenty miles away, at Pittsburgh Landing, Tennessee. To the surprise of the Union, Johnston attacked the larger Union force at Shiloh Church on April 6. The battle disintegrated into a series of brutal fights among desperate groups of scattered men with little coordinated leadership. Johnston, killed leading an attack, was replaced by Beauregard, who succeeded in

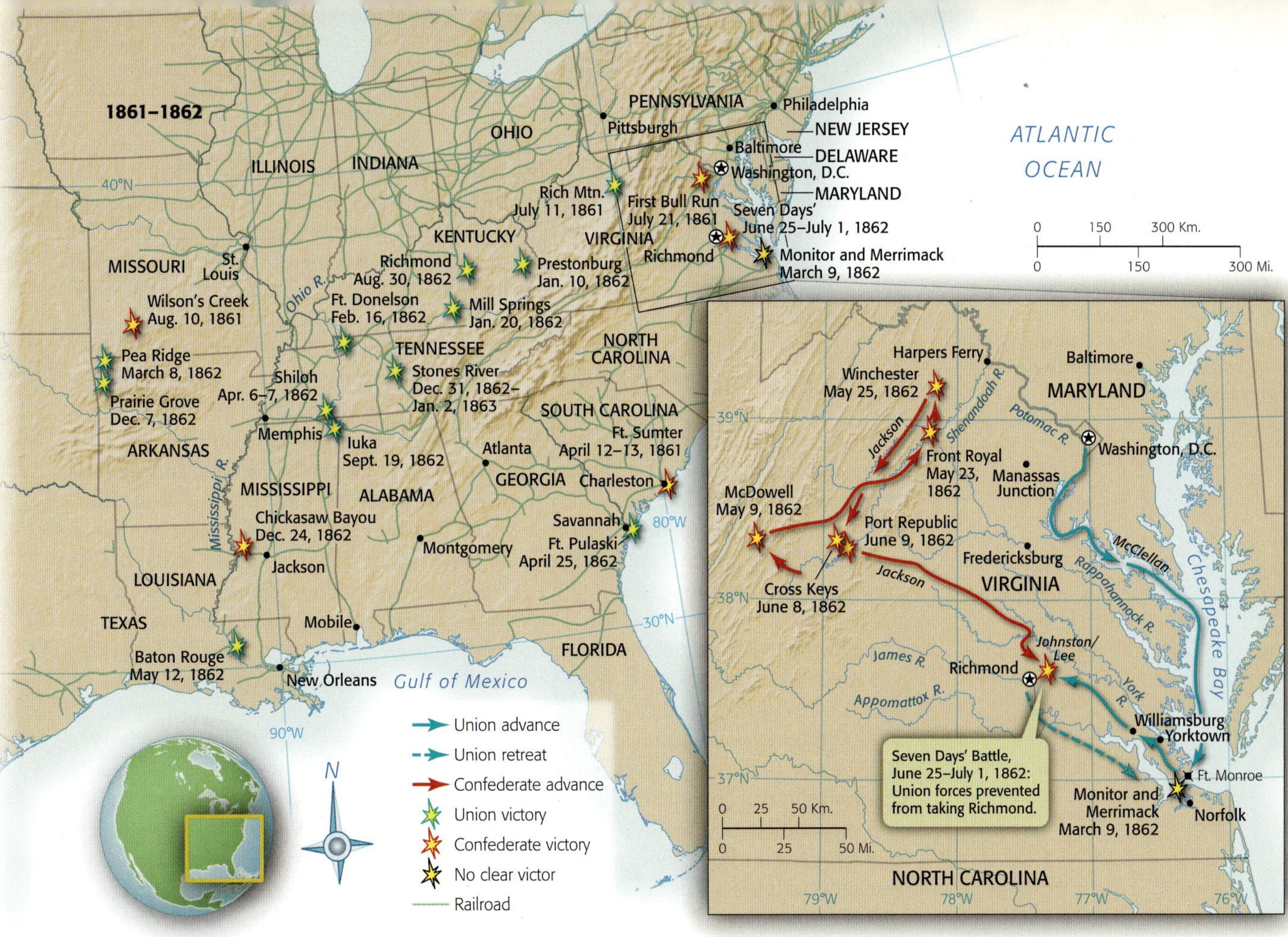

MAP 14.2

Eastern Battles of 1862

George McClellan's long-awaited campaign to take Richmond, Virginia, the capital of the Confederacy, began in March 1862. The vast maneuver unfolded over many months and ended with the brutal stalemate of the Seven Days' Battles. Stonewall Jackson's Valley Campaign kept the Union forces divided.

pushing the Union men back two miles. The Confederates' dominance proved short lived, however, for twenty-five thousand Northern reinforcements arrived overnight. The next day saw Grant and his army regain the ground they had lost, driving the Confederates back to Corinth. Though the Southern forces had been badly hurt, the Northern forces were too exhausted to pursue them.

The carnage at Shiloh exceeded anything anyone had ever seen. The bloodiest battle in the hemisphere up to that point, Shiloh exacted a horrible toll: about seventeen hundred killed and eight thousand wounded on each side. About two thousand of the wounded men in both the Union and the Confederacy forces would soon die. Newspapers and generals debated the outcome of the battle for months, but it eventually became clear that the Southern attempt to halt Northern momentum in the Mississippi Valley had failed.

Another drama occurred in New Orleans, where a Union naval force under David Farragut determined to overwhelm the Confederates' largest city and largest Gulf port. The city was stoutly protected by two well-armed forts as well as a river blocked with logs, barges, and thick cables. So safe did they consider New Orleans that Confederate troops abandoned the city to fight at Shiloh, leaving the port protected only by militiamen. Yet Farragut's forces were formidable: twenty mortar boats, seventeen ships with 523 guns, and fifteen thousand soldiers pounded the forts for days. Finally, before dawn on April 24, Farragut audaciously led his ships, single file, through a gap opened in the cables past the forts and Confederate ships. Once they had run this gauntlet, the Union ships sailed right up to the docks of New Orleans, confronting no resistance as four thousand Confederate troops withdrew from the city.

Vicksburg, battle of (1863)
Mississippi battle site under siege by Grant's army for six weeks. Before falling it became the symbol of Confederate doggedness and Union frustration.

Troops under the command of Benjamin Butler occupied New Orleans while Farragut continued to drive up the Mississippi River. He took Baton Rouge, Natchez, and Memphis, but was unable to overcome Confederate forces at **Vicksburg.** Northern forces could now use the river as a major supply route, as the Mississippi became a chasm separating one half of the Confederacy from the other.

The Bloody Summer of 1862

From the viewpoint of the battlefields in Tennessee and Mississippi, the Union seemed to be prevailing by the middle of 1862. In Virginia, only five miles separated George McClellan's troops, the pride of the Union and one hundred thousand strong, from Richmond. But it would not be easy for the Union troops to take the Confederate capital. The river assaults that had worked so well two months earlier in Tennessee failed in Virginia, where Confederates were able to attack the Union gunboats from high bluffs. Even the *Monitor* proved ineffectual when faced with an enemy a hundred feet above. Moreover, the Confederates had established imposing defenses around Richmond and concentrated many of their troops in the vicinity.

Defensive positioning proved more important in the American Civil War than in any prior conflict. Defenders gained their advantage from a new kind of weapon: the rifle. A rifle, unlike a musket, used a spiral groove in the barrel to put spin on a bullet, known as a Minié ball after the French inventor who developed it, giving the bullet much greater stability and accuracy than a musket ball. A musket had been accurate at only about eighty yards, but a rifle could hit a target at four times that distance. The rifle, along with ironclad ships, howitzers, and other advances in weaponry, contributed to the unprecedented casualties of the Civil War.

Lincoln and McClellan believed that Washington faced a direct threat from Confederate troops in the Shenandoah Valley under the command of the increasingly impressive Stonewall Jackson. For three months in the spring of 1862, Jackson maneuvered his men up and down the valley, creating the impression that his forces were larger and more nimble than they were. As a result, the Union divided its forces, undermining McClellan's plans for the assault on Richmond.

The Union and the Rebel forces tested one another around Richmond in May and June, inflicting heavy casualties in battles that settled nothing. Robert E. Lee replaced Joseph Johnston, wounded in battle, as general of the Confederate forces in Virginia, and quickly proved himself aggressive and daring. Lee almost immediately planned an attack against McClellan's larger force, sending out J. E. B. Stuart, his cavalry leader, who rode all the way around McClellan's troops, reconnoitering their position and stealing their supplies. Lee brought Jackson and his men to join in an assault. But the resulting prolonged conflict, which became known as the Seven Days' Battles, did not distinguish either side: the Confederates' offensive did not work as planned, and for the North's part, McClellan, though possessing far more troops, believed himself outnumbered and abandoned the attempt to take Richmond.

By July 1862, the war seemed to have reached a stalemate. The Union could draw little solace from McClellan's sluggish performance in the ferocious Seven Days' Battles outside Richmond in June. Lincoln placed Henry Halleck, who advocated a more aggressive stance, in charge of all Union troops, and put John Pope, who had been fighting in the West, in charge of the new Army of Virginia. McClellan still commanded troops, but his role was restricted.

The new Union leaders decided to remove McClellan's troops from the peninsula of Virginia and consolidate them, under the joint command of Pope, with troops from the Shenandoah Valley. The forces began to move from the peninsula in August, creating a temporary opportunity for the Confederacy. Lee decided to attack Pope's troops while McClellan's were withdrawing. His plan worked better than he could have expected, so Lee decided to push into Maryland seeking a major victory in Northern territory. Such an achievement, Lee felt certain, would prove that the South deserved the support of the European powers.

On September 17, Robert E. Lee and George McClellan fell into battle once more, this time at Antietam Creek, near Sharpsburg, Maryland. The Confederates had thirty-five thousand men to McClellan's seventy-two thousand, but the Southerners held the defensive ground. The terrible battle ended in confusion and stalemate. More men were killed, wounded, or declared missing on this day than on any other day in the Civil War: thirteen thousand for the Confederacy and twelve thousand for the Union. Lee had lost nearly a third of his army; McClellan, despite his numerical advantage, had been unable to shatter the enemy.

Neither side could be satisfied with the battle's outcome. The Confederacy decided that it would pull back into Virginia to fight another day. Lincoln, making the best of the situation, decided that **Antietam** represented enough of a victory to justify his announcement of the preliminary Emancipation Proclamation. The European powers decided that they would withhold their support for the Confederacy for the time being. Had Lee merely held his ground in Virginia after driving McClellan away from Richmond and Pope back into Washington, England and France might have offered mediation—and the North might well have accepted, again without the end of slavery. As it was, however, both the North and the South would fight again and again.

Antietam, battle of (1862) Civil War battle near Sharpsburg, Maryland, in September 1862 in which the Union Army stopped the Confederacy's drive into the North. With twenty-five thousand casualties, it was the bloodiest single-day battle of the Civil War.

Slavery Under Attack

As the war dragged into its second year, the issue of slavery became more urgent. Even Northerners who did not oppose slavery on moral grounds could see that slavery offered the South a major advantage: slaves in the fields meant more white Southerners on the battlefields. In addition, black Southerners themselves pressed slavery as a problem on the Union armies, fleeing to them as refugees wherever the soldiers advanced. The Union called the black people who made their way to the Union ranks **contrabands,** a term used to describe property that could be used in a war effort and was thus subject to confiscation. Although some Union officers returned slaves to their owners, others employed former slaves as local guides and camp laborers.

contrabands During the Civil War, term for slaves who made their way to Union lines. By defining the refugees as "contrabands of war," a term used to describe property that could be used in a war effort and was thus subject to confiscation, Union leaders justified the decision not to return escaped slaves to their masters.

Northern leaders confronted the problem of slavery most directly near **Port Royal,** South Carolina. The Sea Islands claimed some of the largest and richest plantations in the South, growing rare and expensive long-staple cotton. When Union forces overran the Sea Islands along the coast in 1861, the remaining whites who lived there fled, leaving behind ten thousand slaves. Almost immediately, various Northerners began to vie for the opportunity to reshape Southern society. Abolitionists journeyed from the Northeast to educate the freedmen, while others arrived to demonstrate that plantations run on the principles of free labor could be both productive and humane. Politicians, ministers, and newspapermen reported the progress made at Port Royal as a measure of what the end of slavery would mean for blacks and for the South. Abolitionist General David Hunter took advantage of his position in Port Royal in 1862 to organize a number of black military units and declare slavery abolished in South Carolina, Georgia, and Florida. President Lincoln, however, revoked Hunter's proclamation.

Port Royal South Carolina port; abandoned by Confederate slaveholders early in the war, this became the site of a well-publicized experiment in the shift from slave to free labor.

Though he detested slavery personally, Lincoln thought that it must end gradually, with payments to the slaveholders for their loss of property. Lincoln also initially resisted calls for enlisting black soldiers into the Union army. Republicans who supported the idea, often called "Radicals" for their support of black rights, passed laws that forbade Northern commanders to return refugee slaves to their former masters, and they ended slavery in the District of Columbia.

Many Northern Democrats firmly opposed such expansion of the war's purposes and means, warning that abolition would only embitter and embolden the Confederates. McClellan, a strong opponent of Radical Republicans, believed emancipation would "disintegrate our present armies." Democrats sympathetic to the South, called **Copperheads** by their opponents, marched under the motto, "The Constitution as it is and the Union as it was." They wanted slavery to remain in place so that the South would come back into the nation, and they were deeply hostile to ideas of racial equality.

Copperheads Derogatory term used by some Republicans to refer to Peace Democrats, implying that they were traitors to the Union. Peace Democrats thought that the war was a failure and should be abandoned.

Early in the war, Lincoln sought to steer a course between the Radicals and the Copperheads, but in the summer of 1862, he moved closer to an assault on slavery. The Union army had strengthened its position in Kentucky and Missouri, and it no longer appeared that the border states could effectively align themselves with the Confederates. The president wrote, "This government cannot much longer play a game in which it stakes all, and its enemies stake nothing. Those enemies must understand that they cannot experiment for ten years trying to destroy the government, and if they fail still come back into the Union unhurt." On July 22, 1862, Lincoln and his cabinet authorized federal military leaders to take whatever secessionist property they needed and to destroy any property that aided the Confederacy. That meant that Union officers could protect and employ the black men and women who fled to Northern camps.

Stalemate

By the summer and fall of 1862, many men had died to little apparent purpose. Lincoln finally decided to replace McClellan with Ambrose E. Burnside. In November, Burnside planned for yet another ultimately futile assault on Richmond. He moved his troops to Fredericksburg, Virginia, and launched an attack on a virtually impregnable Confederate position at Marye's Heights. With Southerners able to fire down on them at will from protected positions, more than twelve thousand Union soldiers were killed, wounded, or missing. Observing the suicidal Union charges, Robert E. Lee remarked to General Longstreet, "It is well that war is so terrible—we should grow too fond of it." At battle's end, both armies remained where they had been at the battle's beginning. The North fell into mourning, humiliation, and anger at this sacrifice. Despondent, Lincoln responded to defeat at Fredericksburg, "If there is a worse place than Hell, I am in it." The winter of 1862–1863 saw the North and the South precariously balanced, both against one another and within their own societies. Military victories would decide whether the South or the North would break first.

❖ Americans at War

By the spring of 1863, war had become a way of life. Both the South and the North had claimed military victories, but clarity did not come as the months passed. The waste of young lives made many question the conduct of the war. In the midst of all this suffering, President Lincoln sought to define a greater purpose for the war. He had come to realize that the Confederacy could not be defeated unless slavery, its bedrock, was destroyed. In the wake of Antietam, enough of a victory to call a victory, Lincoln announced the end of slavery in all areas held by the Confederacy by January 1, 1863. This **Emancipation** Proclamation was denounced throughout the South and in much of the North as well. Although the proclamation would free no slaves under Union control in the border states, it

emancipation The ending of slavery, initiated in the Emancipation Proclamation of 1863 but not accomplished in many places until the Confederate surrender in 1865.

ruled out compromise that would end the war and bring the South back into the Union with slavery.

Lincoln knew as well as anyone else, however, that without victories on the battlefield, nothing else would matter. Both Northerners and Southerners expected the spring of 1863 to bring the climax of the Civil War. Yet while generals and armies determined the result of battles, the women, slaves, workers, bureaucrats, draft dodgers, and politicians behind the lines would determine the outcome of the war.

Soldiers and the Meaning of War

Soldiers eventually adjusted to the miseries of sleeping on the ground, eating poorly cooked food, and marching through driving rain and endless mud. They learned to adapt to lice, gambling, drinking, and prostitution, and toughened themselves to the intermittent mails and the arrival of bad news from home. But they also faced diseases such as diarrhea, dysentery, typhoid, malaria, measles, diphtheria, and scarlet fever. As bloody as the battles were, disease killed twice as many men as died from the guns of the enemy. Many doctors of the Civil War era used the same surgical instruments on soldier after soldier, unwittingly spreading disease and infection. After every battle, screams filled the night as surgeons sawed off legs and arms, feet and hands, in often-vain hopes of stopping gangrene.

Despite the brutality of the war, soldiers acted courageously. They cared about the official political purposes for which they were fighting, but they also wanted to be admired by the people at home; they wanted to do their part for their comrades; they wanted to bring the war to a quicker end; and they grew to hate the enemy. A steady stream of letters flowed back and forth between the units and the families and neighbors back home; any soldier knew that his deeds in the war would live with him the rest of his life. Courage developed, too, out of hatred. People on both sides spread the worst stories and rumors about one another. The longer the war went on, the more people felt they had to hate one another to justify so much bloodshed.

The Confederate Government's Challenges

The South's challenges mounted throughout 1862 and into 1863. Although many of the battles of the spring of 1862 had been close, they all seemed to turn out in favor of the North. Despite its many extraordinary military accomplishments, the Confederacy would have a hard time keeping its men fighting.

The first yearlong enlistments in the Confederate army had run out in April of 1862, and many soldiers had returned home. The Confederate Congress, fearful that its armies would be short of men as the Union stepped up its attacks, decided that it had no choice but to initiate a compulsory draft. All white men between the ages of eighteen and thirty-five were required to fight for three years. But the Confederacy also exempted one white man for every twenty slaves he supervised with passage of the **"twenty negro law."** That law, necessary though it was, divided Southerners more profoundly than anything else in the Civil War. A Mississippi private deserted to return home, refusing to "fight for the rich men while they were at home having a good time." Desertion remained a major problem for the Confederacy throughout the remainder of the war.

Class conflict also broke out in the streets of the Confederate capital in the spring of 1863. Convinced that greedy merchants were holding supplies of flour until shortages and inflation drove prices even higher, poor women in Richmond broke open merchants' stores and took what they needed. The threat of violence and of arrest, as well as the promise of free supplies, broke up the **bread riot**, but

"twenty negro law" Confederate law exempting from military service one white man for every twenty slaves he supervised.

bread riots (1863) Riots in Richmond and other Southern cities, that occurred when poor women attacked the shops of merchants accused of hoarding food in order to profit from wartime inflation.

(Courtesy of the Library of Virginia)

Richmond Bread Riots.
This Northern portrayal of the Richmond bread riots imagined the rioters as fearsome, gaunt amazons; other accounts emphasized their respectability. In either case, they behaved in ways quite remarkable for any women in nineteenth-century America.

similar events occurred in several other Southern cities such as Atlanta, Columbus, and Augusta.

The rioters were not the only ones who took what they needed: Confederate officers in the field forced reluctant farmers to sell their crops to the army for an increasingly worthless currency. In the spring of 1863, the Confederate government attempted to curb exploitation of farmers in the **Impressment Act**, to little effect. Yet the Southern government could not afford to lose civilian support. Although the absence of political parties initially appeared to be a sign of the South's consensus, it meant that Jefferson Davis, without a party mechanism to discipline those who spoke out against him, could not remove enemies from office. Even his own vice president, Alexander Stephens, became a persistent and outspoken critic of the Confederate president's "tyrannical" policies.

The Confederate government faced a fundamental dilemma. The whole point of secession had been to move political power closer to localities, protecting slavery in particular and self-determination in general. The government of the Confederacy, however, had to centralize power. If soldiers were to be mobilized, fed, and clothed, if diplomats were to make a plausible case for the Confederacy's nationhood, then the Confederate government had to exercise greater power than its creators had expected or intended. Jefferson Davis continually struggled with this tension. For every Southerner who considered Davis too weak, another considered the president dangerously powerful.

The Northern Home Front

In the North, the war heightened differences between Democrats and Republicans. The Democrats won significant victories in congressional elections in 1862, testifying to the depth and breadth of the opposition to Lincoln's conduct of the war. Wealthy businessmen were eager to reestablish trade with their former Southern partners, whereas Irish immigrants wanted to end the risk of the draft and competition from freed slaves. Many citizens of Ohio, Indiana, and Illinois, whose families had come from the South, wanted to renew the Southern connections that had been broken by the war.

Impressment Act (1863) Confederate legislation that authorized the seizure of produce and slaves for military purposes, and provided the means for Confederate farmers to appeal unfair prices paid for property seized.

Conscription Act (1863) Union act instituting military draft; service could be avoided by hiring a substitute or paying a fee.

The Union passed its **Conscription Act** in March 1863 because disease, wounds, and desertion had depleted the ranks of soldiers faster than they could be replaced. When drafted, a man could appear for duty, hire a substitute to fight in his place, or pay a fee of $300 directly to the government. Poorer citizens resented the wealthy who could avoid service. Demonstrations broke out in Chicago, Pennsylvania mining towns, Ohio, rural Vermont, and Boston. State and federal governments often paid bounties—signing bonuses—to those who volunteered. More than a few men took the bounties and then promptly deserted and moved to another locality to claim another bounty.

Growing opposition to the Lincoln government raised crucial issues. With the North claiming to fight for liberty, what limitations on freedom of speech and protest could it enforce? A Democratic congressman from Ohio, Clement Vallandigham, tested those limits in the spring of 1863 when he refused to obey a general's orders to stop criticizing the Lincoln administration. He was arrested, tried before a military court, and sentenced to imprisonment for the rest of the war. Dismayed, Lincoln commuted Vallandigham's sentence, sending him to the Confederates in Tennessee, hoping to make Vallandigham appear a Southern sympathizer rather than a martyr to the cause of free speech. Vallandigham quickly escaped to Canada, however, where he continued his criticism. Ohio Democrats defiantly nominated Vallandigham for governor in the elections to be held in the fall of 1863.

African American Soldiers

Although Northern civilian and military leaders remained deeply divided and ambivalent about black freedom, many began to realize that black men could be of great value to the Union. In May 1863, the War Department created the Bureau of Colored Troops, charged with recruiting regiments not only in the North but among Southern slaves and free blacks as well. African American men rushed to enlist as soon as they heard of the new black regiments.

Confederate officials who expected **African American soldiers** to make reluctant or cowed fighters soon discovered otherwise. In May 1863, two black regiments stormed, seven times, a heavily fortified Confederate installation at Port Hudson, Louisiana. Soon after, black soldiers found themselves on the other side of the barricades. At **Milliken's Bend**, Louisiana, they fought Confederates hand to hand. Northern newspapers echoed the words of praise from generals in the field: "No troops could be more determined or more daring." Encouraged, African American men in the North signed up in great numbers. Frederick Douglass, the leading spokesman for black Americans, celebrated the enlistments: "Once let the black man get upon his person the brass letters, U.S.; let him get an eagle on his button, and a musket on his shoulder, and bullets in his pocket, and there is no power on earth which can deny that he has earned the right to citizenship in the United States."

(The Granger Collection, New York)

4th U.S. Colored Infantry, Company E, at Fort Lincoln, District of Columbia, 1865, Oil Over Photograph. More than 180,000 African American men fought for the Union. Their military service helped convince policymakers to extend American citizenship to black men.

❖ Turning Point

Despite unrest on the home fronts, everything seemed in place for a climactic culmination of the war in the summer of 1863. The Union had almost severed the western half of the Confederacy from the eastern; the federal army had penetrated deep into Tennessee and stood on the threshold of Georgia. Nevertheless, Confederate armies learned to make the most of their advantages.

African American soldiers Finally allowed to enlist in May 1863, African American soldiers accounted for more than one hundred eighty thousand troops and played a major role in the Union victory.

Milliken's Bend, battle of (1863) Battle on June 7, 1863, that turned to hand-to-hand combat between African American Union troops and Confederate soldiers during Grant's Vicksburg Campaign. The battle won Union recognition of African American soldiers' fighting abilities.

Vicksburg and Chancellorsville

In early 1863, Ulysses S. Grant and William T. Sherman remained frustrated in their goal of seizing Vicksburg; William S. Rosecrans faced Braxton Bragg in Tennessee; and Robert E. Lee's army had yet to be decisively defeated despite the men, resources, and determination thrown into battle against him. Lee would face General Joseph Hooker, whom Lincoln had chosen to replace Ambrose Burnside. Throughout the spring, "Fighting Joe" Hooker energized his men and repaired some of the damage inflicted at Fredericksburg. But no one knew if he would be able to handle Lee.

Vicksburg, heavily fortified by both geography and the Confederates, seemed most vulnerable to attack from the southeast, but to get there, Grant would have to find a way to move his men across the Mississippi River without landing them in swamps. Throughout the long, wet winter, Grant had tried one experiment after another, but nothing had worked. Grant finally decided on a bold move: he would run a flotilla of gunboats and barges past Vicksburg under the cover of night to ferry his men across the Mississippi south of the city (see Map 14.3). The guns of Vicksburg stood two hundred feet above the river, ready to fire down on

MAP 14.3

Vicksburg, April–July 1863

After months of frustration, Ulysses S. Grant and William T. Sherman found a way to attack Vicksburg from the south and east. Following a great struggle, the Union generals were able to take the city on July 4, 1863.

any passing craft, but the Union men covered their ships' boilers with sacks of grain and bales of cotton to protect them from the shelling. Most of the boats made it through. Grant had Sherman create a diversion, confusing the Confederates, and then ferried his entire army across the Mississippi. By mid-May, Grant had fought four battles, cost the South eight thousand dead and wounded, marched two hundred miles, and pinned thirty thousand Confederates within Vicksburg's fortifications.

In the same week Grant made his landing near Vicksburg, Hooker began his attack on Lee, still based in Fredericksburg (see Map 14.4). Hooker commanded 130,000 men. Unlike Burnside, however, he intended to outsmart Lee rather than try to overwhelm him with numbers. A large Union force would sweep around Lee and attack him from behind as another force attacked from the front, forcing Lee to emerge from his well-entrenched defensive position. But Lee met this bold move with an even bolder one: he divided his forces and sent Stonewall Jackson to attack Hooker's men from the rear, outflanking Hooker's own flanking maneuver.

On May 2, Jackson assaulted Hooker's troops near Chancellorsville, defeating the surprised Hooker. Southern jubilation, though, ended the very night of this triumph, for nervous Confederate soldiers accidentally shot Stonewall Jackson while he surveyed the scene near the front lines. The next day, while Jackson lay in his tent, fading in and out of consciousness, Lee managed to contain another assault on Fredericksburg and push the Union troops away from their positions. The losses had once again been staggering—thirteen thousand casualties, roughly 22 percent of the army—but Lee had overcome a larger opponent. After the last battles quieted, however, Jackson died. His death took with it Lee's most skillful general.

MAP 14.4

The War in the East, 1863

The Battle of Chancellorsville, not far from Fredericksburg, was a great victory for the Confederates. But it marked just the opening stage of a long summer of fighting that would culminate at Gettysburg two months later. In that battle, the Confederates sorely missed General Stonewall Jackson, accidentally killed by his own troops at Chancellorsville.

The Battle of Gettysburg, July 1–3, 1863

Despite his victory at Chancellorsville, Lee recognized that the Confederacy was in trouble. Rosecrans still threatened to break through Tennessee into Georgia, Grant clawed his way closer to Vicksburg, and the Union blockade drew an ever tighter net around the coast. Some of his generals urged Lee to rush with his troops to Tennessee to defend the center of the Confederacy and pull Grant away from Vicksburg. But Lee decided that his most effective move would be to invade the North again, taking the pressure off Virginia and disheartening the Union. A successful strike into the North might yet persuade Britain and France to recognize the Confederacy and give heart to Peace Democrats, Northerners who wanted to abandon the war effort.

In early June 1863, Lee began to move up through the Shenandoah Valley into southern Pennsylvania with seventy-five thousand men. When Hooker failed to react decisively, the president put General George Meade in charge. Meade had to decide how best to stop the greatest threat the Confederate army had yet posed to the North. Washington and Baltimore lay in danger, along with the cities, towns, and farms of Pennsylvania. There, the Confederate troops enjoyed taking food and livestock from the rich land. Free blacks and fugitive slaves were also seized and forced south into slavery. Still, Lee and his men found themselves in a dangerous situation. Lee had permitted Jeb Stuart's cavalry, his "eyes," to range too widely from the main army; as a result, the Confederates had little idea what the Union army was doing. For their part, Meade and his fellow officers decided to pursue Lee, but not too aggressively, looking for a likely time and place to confront the enemy.

On June 30, units from the Confederacy and the Union stumbled over one another at a small town neither side knew or cared much about: Gettysburg. On July 1, they began to struggle for the best defensive position, fighting over the highest land. It appeared at first that the Southerners had the better of the first day's battle, but as the smoke cleared, both sides could see that late in the day, the Union army had consolidated itself on the most advantageous ground. Meade's men, after fierce fighting at the ends of their line, occupied a fishhook-shaped series of ridges and hills that permitted them to protect their flanks. The second day saw the Confederates slowly mobilize their forces for assaults on those positions and launch attacks late in the afternoon. The resulting battles proved horrific—with thirty-five thousand men dead or wounded—but left the Union in control of the high ground.

Despite the Union's superior position, Lee decided on a frontal attack the next day. The Confederates hoped their artillery would soften the middle of the Union lines. The Confederates did not realize how little damage their guns had done until well-entrenched Union troops decimated waves of an attack led by George E. Pickett. It proved a disastrous three days for the Army of Northern Virginia, which lost twenty-three thousand men through death or wounds, about a third of its entire force. The Union lost similar numbers of men, but it had more to lose. The Southern side, short of supplies and men, had gambled on an aggressive assault, and lost. Elation swept the North. "The glorious success of the Army of the Potomac has electrified all," a Northerner exulted.

The next morning, a thousand miles away, Vicksburg surrendered to Ulysses S. Grant. Unlike Gettysburg, where the battle had been fought in a place no one considered strategically crucial, Vicksburg held enormous tactical and psychological importance. It had been the symbol of Confederate doggedness and Union frustration. After six weeks of siege and near starvation behind the Confederate defenses, Vicksburg fell. The Mississippi River now divided the Confederacy while it tied the Union to the Gulf of Mexico.

The New York City Draft Riots, July 13–16, 1863

On the very day that Lee struggled across the Potomac to safety, riots broke out in New York City. Northern working people had complicated feelings about the war. Many of those who labored in the North's factories, mines, farms, and railroads had come to the United States during the previous fifteen years. These people, mostly Irish and Germans, volunteered in large numbers to fight for the Union cause. Between 20 and 25 percent of the Union army consisted of immigrants, the great majority of them volunteers. But despite their patriotism, some immigrants viewed black Americans with dread and contempt. Many Catholic Irishmen, almost all of them Democrats, resented the draft and despaired at the losses among Irish American regiments. The effect of inflation on workers' wages, along with the fact that wealthy men could hire substitutes to fight in their places, exacerbated tensions.

When word came—just as the draft lottery was to take place in New York City on July 11, 1863—of the twenty-three thousand men lost at Gettysburg, the fury of working people rose, and on July 13, it exploded. Mobs began by assaulting draft officials, then turned their anger on any man who looked rich enough to have hired a substitute, then on pro-Lincoln newspapers and abolitionists' homes. They assaulted any African Americans they encountered on the streets, burning an orphanage, whipping men and women, and hanging victims from city lampposts. Lincoln was sickened by accounts of the riot and a city editor despaired, "Great God! What is this nation coming to?"

The police struggled for three days to control the riot. Eventually troops (including all-Irish units) rushed from the battlefields of Pennsylvania to aid the police. The troops fired into the rioters; more than a hundred people died, and another three hundred were injured. The working people got some of what they wanted: more welfare relief, exemptions from the draft for those whose families would have no other means of support, and an exodus of black people who feared for their lives.

Ironically, a few days after the **New York City draft riots,** scores of black troops died during a bold nighttime assault on **Fort Wagner** near Charleston, South Carolina. Despite the bravery of the African Americans, the assault failed. The Confederates made a point of burying the African American soldiers in a mass grave along with their white officer, Robert Gould Shaw, intending to insult him and his memory. Instead, they elevated him to a Northern martyr. The *Atlantic Monthly* marked a change in Northern attitudes toward black soldiers: "Through the cannon smoke of that dark night, the manhood of the colored race shines before many eyes that would not see."

New York City draft riots (1863) Riots, July 13–16, 1863, among working people of New York, many of them recent immigrants, following news of heavy losses at Gettysburg and efforts to replace troop losses through the draft lottery.

Fort Wagner Fort guarding the approach to Charleston Harbor, South Carolina. In the Union assault on July 18, 1863, nearly half of the 54th Massachusetts Volunteers leading the attack were killed, but their courage helped convince the North to continue recruiting African American soldiers.

Events slowed until September, when Union General William Rosecrans left Chattanooga, near the Georgia border, and began moving toward Atlanta. His opponent, Braxton Bragg, confronted Rosecrans's forces at Chickamauga Creek. The Confederates took advantage of Union mistakes, inflicting harrowing damage and driving Rosecrans back into Chattanooga, trapping his men with few routes of escape and limited supplies. The Northerners had gone from a position of apparent advantage to one of desperation. Lincoln, judging Rosecrans "confused and stunned" by the battle at Chickamauga, used this opportunity to put Grant in charge of all Union armies between the Appalachian Mountains and the Mississippi River. In the fall of 1863, Grant traveled to Chattanooga, where he was joined by Sherman and Hooker.

The Gettysburg Address

The North's victories at Vicksburg and Gettysburg aided Lincoln's popularity. The draft riots in New York City damaged the reputations of Democrats, whereas the bravery of black soldiers on the battlefields of Louisiana and South Carolina led Union soldiers and other white Northerners to rethink their prejudices. In the fall of 1863, the Republicans won major victories in Pennsylvania and Ohio. Lincoln determined to make the most of these heartening events. When he received an invitation to speak at the dedication of the cemetery at Gettysburg on November 19, he saw it as a chance to impart a sense of purpose to the Union cause.

Burial crews had been laboring for weeks on the Gettysburg battlefield. Thousands of horse carcasses had been burned; thousands of human bodies had been hastily covered with a thin layer of soil. Pennsylvania purchased 17 acres and hired a specialist to lay out the burial plots so that no state would be offended by the amount of space devoted to its fallen men. Only about a third of the reburials had taken place when Lincoln arrived; caskets remained stacked at the station.

Lincoln attempted to shift the purpose of the war from Union for Union's sake to Union for freedom's sake. His "remarks," as the program put it, lasted three minutes. Lincoln said virtually nothing about the details of the scene surrounding the twenty thousand people at the ceremony. Neither did he mention slavery directly. Seeking to salvage something from the deaths of the fifty thousand men at Gettysburg, Lincoln called for a "new birth of freedom," and spoke of equality as the fundamental purpose of the war. Democratic newspapers rebuked Lincoln for his claim, arguing that white soldiers had "too much self-respect to declare

Gettysburg Address (1863) Brief speech given by President Lincoln at the dedication of the Gettysburg Cemetery in November 1863 that declared that the Civil War was dedicated to freedom.

that negroes were their equals." But other Northerners accepted Lincoln's exhortation as the definition of their purpose. As years went by, the words of the **Gettysburg Address** would gain force and resonance.

Just four days after Lincoln's speech, Grant gave the North new reason to believe its ideals might triumph. On November 23, Grant's men overwhelmed the Confederates on Lookout Mountain outside Chattanooga; two days later, Union soldiers shocked the Confederates by fighting their way up the steep Missionary Ridge—Confederate artillery could not reach opponents coming up directly from below. The Union, now in control of the cities and rail junctions of Kentucky and Tennessee, had a wide and direct route into Georgia.

England and France finally determined in late 1863 that they would not try to intervene in the American war. First Britain, then France detained or sold to foreign powers warships intended for the Confederacy. The Northern public, encouraged by events on the battlefield, supported Republican candidates in the congressional elections of 1863 more vigorously than had seemed possible just a few months before.

The Winter of Discontent, 1863–1864

The battles of the summer had been horrific. Both sides held their victories close to their hearts and brooded over their losses. The resolve and fury of summertime faded into the bitterness and bickering of winter, as Americans steeled themselves for another bloody year of war.

Lincoln hoped to end the war as soon as possible, using persuasion as well as fighting to entice white Southerners back into the national fold. In early December 1863, he issued his proclamation of amnesty and reconstruction. To those who would take an oath of loyalty to the Union, Lincoln promised a full pardon and the return of all property other than slaves. Although he excluded Confederate leaders and high officers from this offer, Lincoln tried to include as many white Southern men as possible. As soon as 10 percent of the number of voters in 1860 had sworn their loyalty to the Union, he decreed, those Southerners could begin forming new state governments. Education and apprenticeship programs would aid former slaves in the transition to full freedom. He did not provide for African American participation in these new governments of the South.

However, Lincoln, Northern Republicans, and much of the public underestimated the depth of Southern bitterness at years of war and occupation. Even in areas under federal control such as Tennessee and Kentucky, guerrilla bands and raiders terrorized the local population and disrupted elections. Civilians were often caught between two odious threats: those who failed to aid Union forces were perceived as "enemies of mankind" with "the rights due to pirates and robbers," whereas those who actively aided the federals were liable to find crops trampled, barns burned, and vigilante justice enacted by neighbors.

Wade-Davis Bill (1864) Congressional legislation for reconstructing the South. The Radical Republicans proposed stringent conditions for states that had seceded to reenter the Union. The bill provided that a majority of citizens in the states sign oaths swearing that they had never supported secession. The bill passed in the Senate and House but was pocket-vetoed by President Lincoln, who favored a more lenient approach.

Yet abolitionists and their allies attacked Lincoln's reconstruction plan as far too lenient to Confederates and not helpful enough for former slaves. In the **Wade-Davis Bill** of February 1864, Republican congressmen attempted to enforce a standard set of laws across the South and to require 50 percent, rather than 10 percent, of the population to swear the loyalty oath, an oath of past as well as future loyalty. With an eye toward the upcoming election and the need to entice Arkansas and Louisiana to rejoin the Union, Lincoln refused to sign the Wade-Davis Bill.

Although Jefferson Davis did not have to worry about his own reelection in late 1863—the Confederacy had established the presidential term at six years—he did have to worry about congressional elections. They did not go well: 41 of the new 106 representatives expressly opposed Davis and his policies, and he

(© Bettmann/CORBIS)

Andersonville Prison Camp. This Confederate prisoner of war camp in Andersonville, Georgia, witnessed great brutality and appalling death rates from disease and hunger.

held only a slight majority in the Senate. Just as Northern Democrats called for compromise and peace, so did some Southerners. Editors savaged Davis as responsible for the South's worsening fortunes: "Had the people dreamed that Mr. Davis would carry all his chronic antipathies, his bitter prejudices, his puerile partialities, and his doting favoritisms into the Presidential chair, they would never have allowed him to fill it." The Confederacy stumbled through the winter and into the spring of 1864, desperately watching for signs that the North might be losing heart.

As the war ground on, conditions in military prisons became another contentious issue. Early in the Civil War, both sides had exchanged prisoners of war rather than maintaining prisons. Such arrangements worked well enough into 1863, but then the system began to break down. As African Americans began serving in the Union armies, Confederates decreed that any former slave captured would be executed or reenslaved, not taken prisoner. The Union refused to participate in any exchanges so long as this policy remained in effect, and Lincoln even threatened retaliation in kind against captured Confederates. Northerners became livid when they heard about conditions at the Confederate camp at Andersonville, Georgia. The camp, built for ten thousand men in an open, partly swampy field, soon held thirty-three thousand prisoners. Of the forty-five thousand men eventually held at Andersonville, thirteen thousand died from exposure, starvation, and brutality. The camp's commander, Colonel Henry Wirz, was the only Confederate official executed for war crimes after the war. Overall, about 16 percent of Northern soldiers and 12 percent of Southerners died in prison.

Union Resolve and the 1864 Presidential Election

In March 1864, Lincoln gave new direction to the Union effort by putting Ulysses S. Grant in charge of all Northern forces. Grant and Lincoln agreed that the Union had to use its superiority in materiel, manpower, and navy to attack the Confederacy on every front at once, forcing the South to decide what territory it would sacrifice. While Grant would fight in Virginia, Lincoln left **William T. Sherman** in charge in Chattanooga. Sherman would attack the railroad center of Atlanta, cutting the Gulf South off from the Upper South. The loss of Atlanta would chop the Confederacy into pieces too small to resist the Northern army.

Sherman, William T. (1820–1891) Union general under Ulysses S. Grant who took Atlanta and led the "March to the Sea."

The Confederates seemed to face overwhelming odds in 1864, yet Southerners recognized that everything turned on holding the Northerners off until the presidential election in the North. If the Southerners could inflict enough damage on the Union army, Northerners might elect someone willing to bring the war to an end through compromise. The Confederates knew that the three-year terms of the most experienced veterans in the Union army expired in 1864, and they also realized that Grant, new to his command, would be confronting Robert E. Lee, who was fighting with an experienced army. All things considered, it was by no means clear in 1864 that the Union would win the war.

African Americans played an increasingly large role in Union plans, for more than 180,000 black soldiers enlisted just when the North needed them most (see Map 14.5). By the spring of 1864, the means of recruitment, training, and pay for these soldiers had become well established. The Confederates, however, refused to recognize the same rules of warfare for black soldiers that they acknowledged for whites. In April 1864 at Fort Pillow in western Tennessee, Confederate cavalry under the command of Nathan Bedford Forrest shot down black Union soldiers and their white commander who attempted to surrender.

With the election clock running, Grant set out in May 1864 to destroy Lee's army. The Battle of the Wilderness near Chancellorsville saw brutal fighting and horrible losses. Fire in the tangled woods trapped wounded men, burning them alive. Grant lost more men than Hooker had in the battle of the previous year, but whereas Hooker treated such losses as a decisive defeat and retreated, Grant pushed onward.

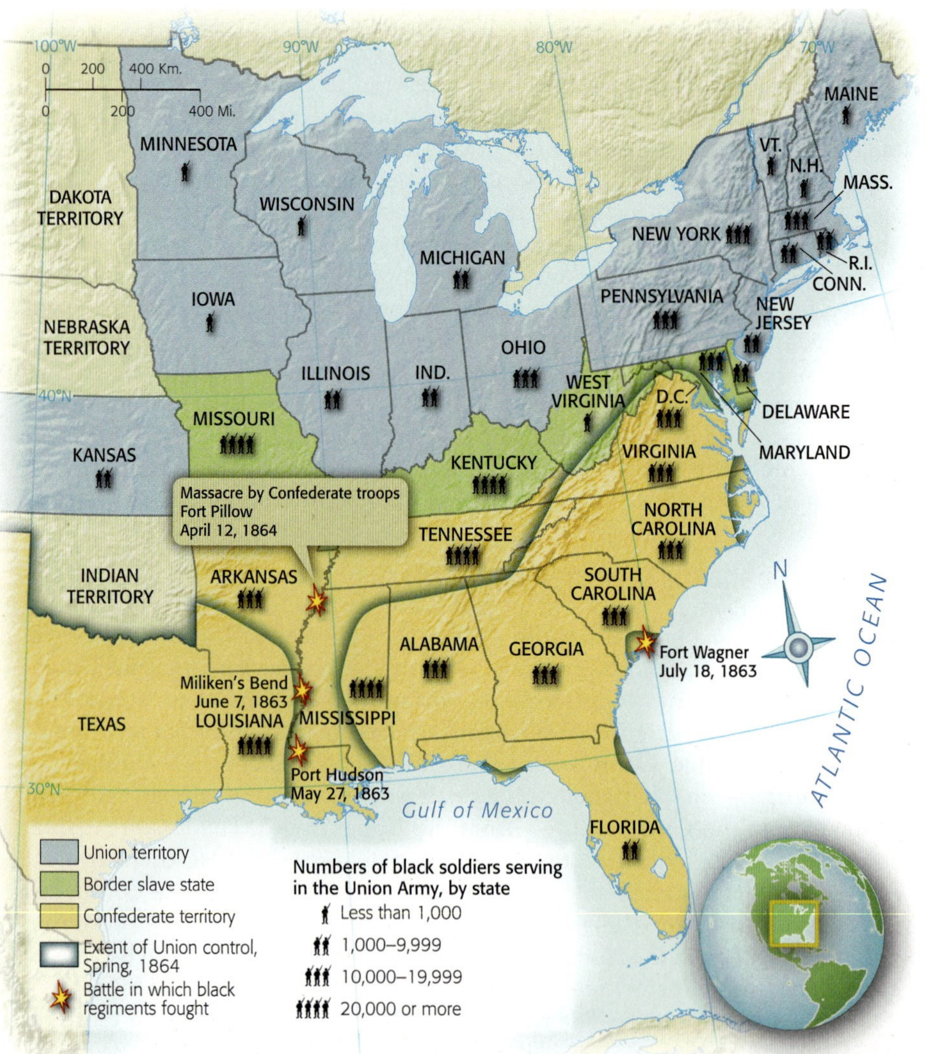

MAP 14.5
Black Soldiers in the Union Army
African American men streamed into the U.S. Army from all across the country, but they were especially prominent in the occupied South where they had been enslaved.

The two armies fought again and again over the next two months in the fields of Virginia. The Confederates turned the Union army back to the east of Richmond and rushed up the Shenandoah Valley to threaten Washington itself. The North repulsed the invasion and dispatched Philip Sheridan to make sure the Confederates did not regroup, while Grant pinned down Lee's main force around Richmond and Petersburg, forcing the Confederates to construct ever-longer lines of earthworks to protect the Confederate capital. In an attempt to break through Lee's defenses, Pennsylvania coal miners volunteered to tunnel under the fortifications and plant explosives. Throughout July, they dug; finally, at the end of the month, they detonated a charge and blew an enormous crater in the Confederate lines. The attack that followed the explosion, however, failed. Union soldiers piled into the crater, where the rallying Confederates trapped them.

(Neg. no 42793, Collection of The New-York Historical Society)

Union Party Campaign Poster. With the war driving to a culmination, the Republicans called themselves the **"Union Party,"** nominated a Unionist from Tennessee alongside Lincoln, and painted pictures of peace and prosperity in their campaign poster.

Fortunately for Lincoln and his reelection campaign, things were going better farther south. Throughout June and July, Sherman pushed relentlessly through north Georgia toward Atlanta. By the end of July, the Southern army had fallen back into Atlanta, preparing to defend it from siege. It seemed only a matter of time before the Union triumphed. But politically, the president had to fight off challenges even within his own party. The Republican Party tried to broaden its appeal to Democrats by nominating **Andrew Johnson**, a former Democrat from Tennessee, to the vice presidency.

In the meantime, the Democrats confidently moved forward. They knew that in the eyes of his critics, Lincoln had caused the war, trampled on constitutional rights, consolidated too much power, and refused to end the war when he had a chance. To take full advantage of such criticisms, the Democrats nominated General George McClellan as their candidate. McClellan and the Democrats portrayed themselves as the party committed to restoring the United States to its prewar unity and grandeur. McClellan said he would end the war if the South would reenter the Union—bringing slavery with it. It was a bargain that appealed to many in the North.

Johnson, Andrew (1808–1875) Seventeenth president of the United States (1865–1869); he succeeded the assassinated Abraham Lincoln.

Just when it appeared that the Democrats would unseat Lincoln, news from the battlefield changed everything: Sherman had swung around Atlanta and begun destroying the railroads that made the small city an important junction. The Confederates set much of Atlanta on fire and abandoned it. Sherman and his army marched into the city on September 2. Two weeks later, Sheridan attacked the Confederates in the Shenandoah Valley, systematically destroying the valley's ability to support the Southern army again.

❖ From Destruction to Reconstruction

Even with these military victories, Lincoln won only 55 percent of the popular vote. Contrary to expectations, Lincoln carried the large majority of the armies' votes. After three years of war, soldiers in the field, even those who considered themselves loyal to McClellan, would not support the Democratic peace platform. The Republicans also elected heavy majorities to both houses of Congress and elected the governor and legislative majorities in all states except New Jersey, Delaware, and Kentucky.

Sherman's March to the Sea

A week after Lincoln's election, Sherman set out across Georgia, provisioning his army along the way, taking the war to the Southern people themselves. Such a march would be as much a demonstration of Northern power as a military maneuver: "If we can march a well-appointed army right through [Confederate] territory," Sherman argued, "it is a demonstration to the world, foreign and domestic, that we have a power which Davis cannot resist." The triumphant army of sixty thousand made its way across the state throughout the fall of 1864. Large numbers of deserters from both sides, fugitive slaves, and outlaws took advantage of the situation to inflict widespread destruction and panic. Sherman arrived at Savannah on December 21. "I beg to present to you, as a Christmas gift, the city of Savannah," Sherman buoyantly telegraphed Lincoln. Contrasting with the devastation of the South, the president's annual message to Congress outlined a portrait of a North gaining strength with "more men now than we had when the war began."

Special Field Order 15 Issued by William T. Sherman in January 1865, this order reserved land in coastal South Carolina, Georgia, and Florida for former slaves. Those who settled on the land would receive forty-acre plots.

Thirteenth Amendment (1865) Constitutional amendment abolishing slavery.

Appomattox Small Virginia town where Confederate forces under Robert E. Lee surrendered to Ulysses S. Grant on April 9, 1865, generally recognized as bringing the Civil War to an end.

War's Climax

As the war ground to a halt in early 1865, Americans had to wonder if they remembered how to share a country with their former enemies. They had to wonder, too, how different the country would be with African Americans no longer as slaves. Of all the changes the United States had ever seen, emancipation stood as the most profound.

Events moved quickly at the beginning of 1865. In January, Sherman issued **Special Field Order 15,** which reserved land in coastal South Carolina, Georgia, and Florida for former slaves. Those who settled on the land would receive forty-acre plots. Four days later, the Republicans in Congress passed the **Thirteenth Amendment,** abolishing slavery forever. Antislavery activists, black and white, packed the galleries and the House floor, weeping and cheering. A congressman wrote his wife that "we can now look other nations in the face without shame."

At the beginning of February, Sherman's troops began to march north into the Carolinas. Columbia, South Carolina, was burned to the ground. Growing numbers of Confederate soldiers deserted from their armies. Lincoln met with Confederate officials at Hampton Roads on board the steamship *River Queen* to try to bring the war to an end, offering slave owners compensation for their freed slaves if the Southerners would immediately cease the war. Jefferson Davis refused to submit to the "disgrace of surrender."

At the beginning of March, Lincoln was inaugurated for his second term. Rather than gloating at the impending victory on the battlefield, Lincoln called for his fellow citizens to "bind up the nation's wounds." That same month, Congress created the Bureau of Refugees, Freedmen, and Abandoned Lands to ease the transition from slavery to freedom. Nine days later, the Confederate government, after hotly debating whether to recruit slaves to fight as soldiers if their owners agreed, finally decided to do so after Lee, desperate for men, supported the measure.

Abraham Lincoln. This picture of Lincoln, taken four days before his assassination, shows the toll four years of war had taken on the fifty-six-year-old president.

Appomattox and Assassination, April 1865

The Confederates' slave recruitment law did not have time to convert slaves to soldiers, for Grant soon began his final assault on Confederate troops in Virginia. Richmond fell on April 3. Lee hoped to lead his army to the train station at **Appomattox** Court House to resupply them, but on April 9, Grant intercepted Lee's men just short of their destination. Lee, with nowhere else to go and no other armies to come to his aid, surrendered. Though a number of Confederate armies had yet to surrender and Jefferson Davis remained at large, it was clear that the war had ended. Cities and towns across the North erupted in celebration and relief as crowds filled the streets. Southerners began to straggle home. Two days later, Lincoln addressed a Washington audience about what would come next for the freedmen. He admitted that Northerners differed "as to the mode, manner, and means of Reconstruction" and that the white South was "disorganized and discordant."

Lincoln did not live to take part in the planning, for he was assassinated on April 14 by **John Wilkes Booth,** a failed actor and Southern sympathizer. Booth attacked Lincoln while the president sat with Mrs. Lincoln at Ford's Theater in Washington, shooting him in the back of the head and then leaping to the stage. Lincoln died early the next morning. Americans hearing the news were shocked. Anti-Southern sentiment flared in the North, and one newspaper fumed that the conspirators "have stricken down the MAN who stood forth their best intercessor before the nation . . . their finest, most forgiving friend, he who pleaded with his people to temper justice with mercy." From a beleaguered president, Lincoln had become a heroic martyr.

Booth, John Wilkes (1838–1865)
An actor and Southern sympathizer who assassinated Abraham Lincoln on April 14, 1865.

The Costs and Consequences of the War

The North lost almost 365,000 men to death and disease in the Civil War, and the South lost 260,000 (see Figures 14.1 and 14.2). Another 277,000 Northerners were wounded, along with 195,000 Southerners. Black Americans lost 37,000 men in the Union army and at least another 10,000 men, women, and children in the contraband camps. Widows and orphans, black and white, Northern and Southern, faced decades of struggling without a male breadwinner. Many people found their

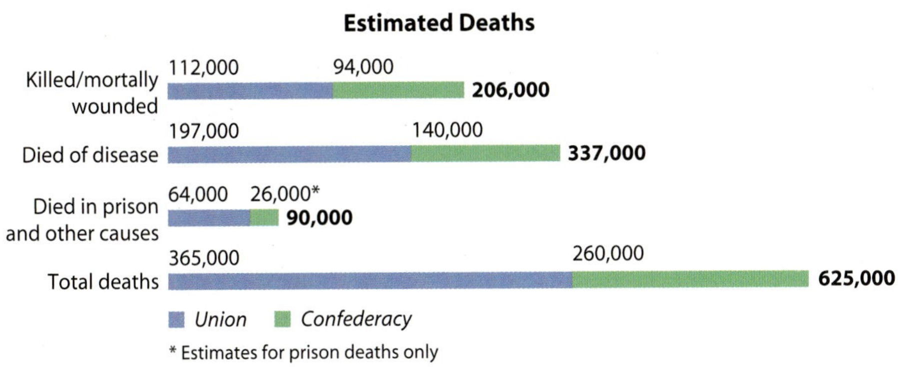

FIGURE 14.1
Estimated Deaths
Disease killed even more men than did the bullets of the enemy.

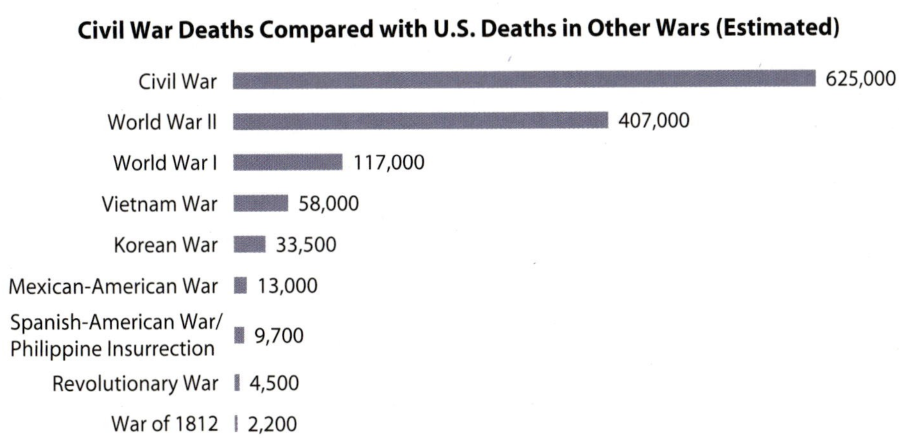

FIGURE 14.2
Civil War Deaths
The Civil War exacted a horrible cost, far outstripping every other conflict in which the United States has fought.

emotional lives shattered by the war. Alcohol, drug abuse, crime, and violence became widespread problems.

The Southern slave-based economy collapsed. Major Southern cities had been reduced to ash. Railroads had been destroyed; fields had turned to weeds and brush as farm values fell by half. Recovery was slow. In Georgia, for example, as late as 1870 the state recorded 1 million fewer pigs, 200,000 fewer cattle, and 3 million fewer acres under cultivation than in 1860. Just as damaging in the long run, lines of credit had been severed. Before emancipation, planters had used their slaves as collateral for loans. Now, with the destruction of that form of "collateral," few people outside the South were willing to loan money to planters or other investors to revive the economy.

The Civil War did not mark a sudden turn in the Northern economy, but it did accelerate processes already well under way. The nationalization of markets, the accumulation of wealth, and the consolidation of manufacturing firms became more marked after 1865. Greenbacks, bonds, and a national banking system regularized the flow of capital and spurred the growth of business. In 1862, the Republicans passed the Department of Agriculture Act, the Morrill College Land Grant Act, the Homestead Act, and the Union Pacific Railroad Act, all using the power of the federal government to encourage settlement of the West, strengthen public education, and spur economic development.

The Civil War changed the United States more deeply than perhaps any other event in American history. The conflict brought the deaths of more than 625,000 soldiers, a proportion of the population equivalent to 5 million people today. Men who had been seriously wounded would haunt the United States for generations to come, reminders of a horrific war. Children would grow up without fathers, and many young women would never find husbands. The war, despite the blessings of Union and freedom it brought, also brought a steep price in social disorder.

The Civil War also triggered a major expansion of the federal government. The demands of wartime created greenbacks, the draft, and government involvement in transportation and business. It brought a profound shift in the balance of power among the regions: after Appomattox, the South's political domination of the national agenda was broken. It would be half a century before another Southern-born man—Woodrow Wilson—was elected president.

Most important, the war brought what few Americans could have imagined at the end of 1860: the immediate emancipation of 4 million enslaved people. Nowhere else in the world had so many people become free so quickly. Yet freedom emerged from the war through a circuitous route. The war began as a war for union, but it became a war to end slavery. Many white Northerners supported emancipation because it seemed the best way to end the war, but the New York City draft riots and the close elections of 1863 demonstrated that others resisted the embrace of black freedom. Lincoln's assassination made an already confused situation far more so, ending slavery and restoring the Union without a blueprint and without leadership.

CHAPTER REVIEW, 1861–1865

SUMMARY

- The states of the Upper South divided, with Virginia, North Carolina, Tennessee, and Arkansas going to the Confederacy and Kentucky, Maryland, and Missouri staying in the Union.
- The United States and the Confederacy built vast armies and mobilized their entire societies to wage war.
- In the beginning, the United States won early victories on the rivers of Tennessee and Louisiana, while the Confederacy was successful in Virginia.
- African American soldiers began to enlist in great numbers.
- In 1863, the Union won decisive victories at Gettysburg and Vicksburg.
- Southerners rioted in Richmond; Northerners rioted in New York City.
- The Union drove to victory in the Shenandoah Valley, in Tennessee, in Georgia, and in the Carolinas, but struggled in Virginia until the spring of 1865.
- Robert E. Lee surrendered his troops in April 1865.
- Abraham Lincoln, reelected in the winter of 1864, was assassinated in the spring of 1865.
- The passage of the Thirteenth Amendment at the war's conclusion ended slavery.

IDENTIFICATIONS

Jefferson Davis
writ of habeas corpus
Anaconda Plan
Robert E. Lee
Thomas J. "Stonewall" Jackson
George B. McClellan
greenbacks
blockade runners
Trent affair
Ulysses S. Grant
Virginia and *Monitor*
battle of Vicksburg
battle of Antietam
contrabands
Port Royal
Copperheads
emancipation
"twenty negro law"
bread riots
Impressment Act
Conscription Act
African American soldiers
battle of Milliken's Bend
New York City draft riots
Fort Wagner
Gettysburg Address
Wade-Davis Bill
William T. Sherman
Andrew Johnson
Special Field Order 15
Thirteenth Amendment
Appomattox
John Wilkes Booth

MAKING CONNECTIONS: LOOKING AHEAD

Chapter 15 will show that the most profound change in American history, the end of slavery, came to a nation exhausted by war and a region unprepared for freedom.

1. As the war ended, what forms did it appear that Reconstruction might take? Who would control the fates of newly emancipated African Americans?
2. What did black Southerners most want and need from emancipation?

RECOMMENDED READINGS

Crofts, Daniel W. *Reluctant Confederates: Upper South Unionists in the Secession Crisis* (1989). Analyzes the crucial border states with keen insight.

Faust, Drew Gilpin. *Creation of Confederate Nationalism: Ideology and Identity in the Civil War South* (1988). Discusses the development of Confederate identity through religion, politics, the wartime economy, and slavery.

Faust, Drew Gilpin. *This Republic of Suffering: Death and the American Civil War* (2008). Examines the collective national impact and legacy of the war's colossal human losses.

Fellman, Michael. *Inside War: The Guerilla Conflict in Missouri During the American Civil War* (1989). Makes palpable the internal struggles in the border areas.

Gallagher, Gary W. *The Confederate War: How Popular Will, Nationalism, and Military Strategy Could Not Stave Off Defeat* (1997). Explores why the Confederacy could fight as long as it did.

Jones, Howard. *The Union in Peril: The Crisis over British Intervention in the Civil War* (1992). Provides a fresh interpretation of a critical episode.

Litwack, Leon. *Been in the Storm So Long: The Aftermath of Slavery* (1979). Beautifully evokes the conflicting emotions and motives surrounding freedom.

McPherson, James M. *Battle Cry of Freedom: The Civil War Era* (1988). The best one-volume account of the Civil War.

Rose, Willie Lee. *Rehearsal for Reconstruction: The Port Royal Experiment* (1964). A classic account of the first efforts to create Northern policy for freed people.

Rubin, Anne Sarah. *A Shattered Nation: The Rise and Fall of the Confederacy, 1861–1868* (2005). Examines the development of Confederate nationalism and its impact on the postwar period.

Silber, Nina. *Daughters of the Union: Northern Women Fight the Civil War* (2005). Gives a fine overview of women's changing roles in the wartime North.

Smith, John David. *Black Soldiers in Blue: African American Troops in the Civil War Era* (2002). A collection of essays examining African American military service in the Civil War.

Weber, Jennifer L. *Copperheads: The Rise and Fall of Lincoln's Opponents in the North* (2006). Traces the development of the peace wing of the Northern Democratic Party during the war.

CourseMate Go to the CourseMate website at www.cengagebrain.com for additional study tools and review materials for this chapter.

15

Reconstruction: Its Rise and Fall

1865–1877

MAKING CONNECTIONS

LOOKING BACK

Chapter 14 described the series of catastrophic events known as the Civil War. At every point, both Northerners and Southerners thought the conflict might end with one more key victory by their side. Instead, each battle seemed to bring another. Before starting Chapter 15, you should be able to answer the following questions:

1. What did the Confederacy need to accomplish in order to claim victory in the Civil War?
2. Did the Civil War have a turning point—a point beyond which it became clear that the United States would defeat the Confederacy? What would you identify as this point?
3. How did emancipation become the Union's central goal for the war?

With the death of Abraham Lincoln in April 1865, a new president sought to reunite the nation at the end of the Civil War. The presence of Andrew Johnson in the White House took the Republican Party and the newly freed slaves in directions that shaped the way the North made policy toward the defeated South. The process became known as Reconstruction, and it has remained one of the most controversial periods in all of American history.

Reconstruction set out to change the South and better the lives of the people, white and black, who lived there. But these important efforts left many aspects of the southern economy in no better, and sometimes worse, shape than before Reconstruction began. A depressed economy and increased debt made sharecropping the lot of many southern farmers of both races by 1880 (see Map 15.1). Still, former slaves played a decisive role in building institutions and carrying on campaigns to expand their political impact in the South. The opportunity to build a multiracial society after the Civil War was a fleeting one, but it represented an important chapter in the lives of those individuals who formerly had been in bondage.

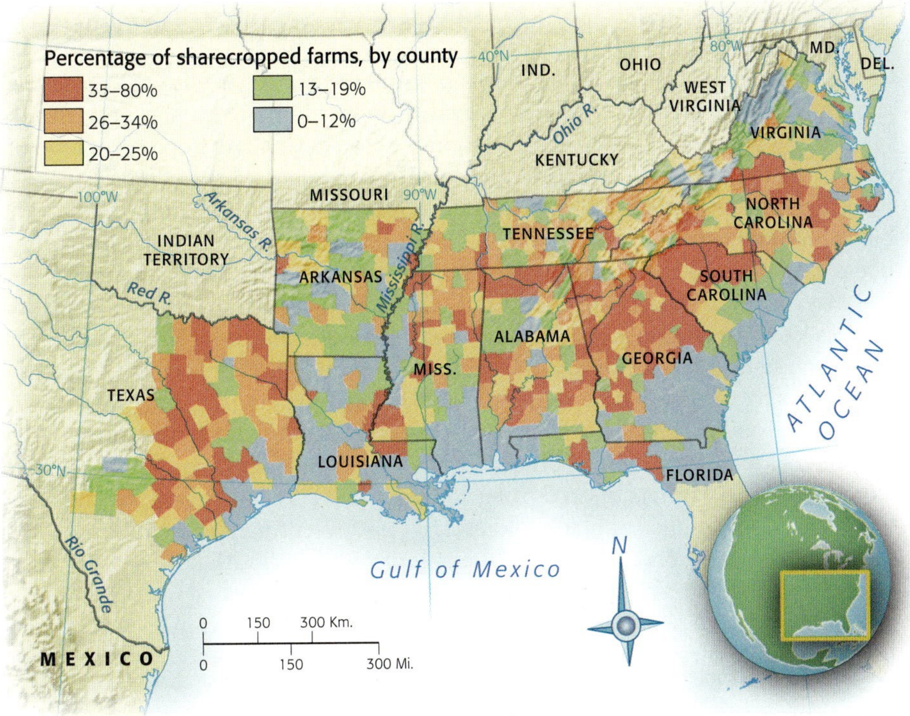

Source: U.S. Census Office, Tenth Census, 1889, *Report of the Production of Agriculture* (Washington, D.C. Government Printing Office, 1883), Table 5.

MAP 15.1
Sharecropping in the South by County, 1880
Just fifteen years after the start of Reconstruction, the economic system of sharecropping had taken over agriculture in the South. Hard times, racial discrimination, and an absence of capital forced many farmers into this difficult situation, raising the question of the extent to which Reconstruction really changed the South.

❖ Reconstruction Under Andrew Johnson, 1865–1867

In the wake of Lincoln's assassination, the nation looked to the new president for leadership. Andrew Johnson was an unknown element to most, but his promise to pursue Lincoln's policies seemed reassuring. As it turned out, Johnson had a firm idea of how he wanted to deal with the South, but his Reconstruction policies proved neither effective nor in tune with majority opinion in the North.

CHAPTER TIMELINE 1867 1869 1871 1873 1875 1877

POLITICS AND DIPLOMACY

- 1865–1868 Andrew Johnson presidency
- 1867 Reconstruction Act
- 1869–1877 Ulysses S. Grant presidency
- 1868 Johnson impeached/acquitted
- 1869 Fifteenth Amendment
- 1876 Sioux defeat Custer at Little Big Horn
- 1877 Compromise of 1877 ends Reconstruction

SOCIETY AND CULTURE

- 1869 Licensing of women lawyers begins
- 1869 Wyoming Territory adopts woman suffrage
- 1870 KKK terror raids in South
- 1874 Women's Christian Temperance Union founded
- 1876 Centennial Exposition in Philadelphia

ECONOMICS AND TECHNOLOGY

- 1869 Transcontinental Railroad completed
- 1871 Chicago fire
- 1873 Panic of 1873 starts economic depression

Wartime Reconstruction in the South

Toward the end of the Civil War, slaves became former slaves with the passage of the Thirteenth Amendment. Some seized their freedom at the first opportunity, taking their families to Union camps or joining the army. Many freed people set off on journeys in desperate efforts to find family members sold away in earlier years. For others, sheer survival was the highest priority. Freedom came in the late spring, barely in time to get crops in the ground. Some former slaves figured that their best bet was to stay where they were for the time being. They had heard rumors that the government would award them land. Between July and September 1865, however, those dreams died. Union officers had promised land to former slaves in Virginia, Louisiana, Mississippi, and South Carolina, but then Washington revoked the promises. The land would be returned to its former owners.

White southerners also responded in many different ways. Some former slave owners fled to Latin America; others whipped and chained workers to keep them from leaving. Still others offered to let former slaves stay in their cabins and work for wages. The presence of black soldiers triggered resentment and fear among former slave owners; one declared, "The people of the South are in very great danger. . . . I tell you most seriously that the whole south is resting upon a volcano."

Freedmen's Bureau Federal agency created in 1865 to supervise newly freed people. It oversaw relations between whites and blacks in the South, issued food rations, and supervised labor contracts.

Many African Americans had no choice but to compromise with white landowners. At first, in the spring of 1865, planters insisted that the former slaves work as they had worked before emancipation, in "gangs." In return for their work, they would receive a portion of the crop, shared among all the workers. Many black people chafed at this arrangement, preferring to work as individuals or families. In such places, landowners found that they had little choice but to permit black families to take primary responsibility for a portion of land. These former slaves, called "sharecroppers," provided the labor and received part of the crop in return. Planters realized they had few choices: they possessed little cash to pay wage workers and no alternative labor.

(Photographic History Collection, National Museum of American History, Smithsonian Institution)

African American Mother and Child. After slavery ended, African Americans pursued education with determination. Here a daughter was photographed as she taught her mother how to read.

The Bureau of Refugees, Freedmen, and Abandoned Lands—the **Freedmen's Bureau**—oversaw the transition from a slave economy to a wage economy. Its agents, approximately nine hundred for the entire South, dispensed medicine, food, and clothing from the vast stores of the federal government to displaced white and black southerners. It created courts to adjudicate conflicts and draw up labor contracts between landholders and laborers. It established schools and coordinated female volunteers who came from the North to teach in them. Although many white southerners resented and resisted the Freedmen's Bureau, it helped smooth the transition from slavery to freedom, from war to peace.

Throughout the South, former slaves and former free blacks gathered in mass meetings, Union Leagues, and conventions to announce their vision of the new order. They wanted, above all else, equality before the law and the opportunity to vote. Their spokesmen generally did not demand confiscation of land or speak extensively of economic concerns. Let us have our basic rights before the courts and at the ballot box, they said, and we will take care of ourselves. But without the leadership of Abraham Lincoln, black southerners rightly worried, the forces of reaction might overwhelm their freedom and economic opportunity. Southerners of both races watched to see what President Andrew Johnson might do.

Andrew Johnson

Johnson had been chosen for the vice presidency in 1864 because he was a Unionist southerner. As a result, both northerners and southerners distrusted him. The new president's well-known disdain for the wealthy planters of the South appealed to equally disdainful Republicans in Washington, and his public statements suggested a harsh peace for the Confederate leaders: "*Treason* is a crime, and crime must be punished." Unlike some Republicans, however, Johnson held little sympathy for black people or for expansion of the powers of the federal government. Johnson saw himself pursuing Lincoln's highest goal, reuniting the Union. Reunification should start by winning the support of white southerners.

Johnson enjoyed a brief period in which to enact his vision of how to return the South to the Union. Congress was not in session at the time of Lincoln's death and would not be for seven months, so Johnson used the opportunity to implement his plan of reunion. In "Presidential Reconstruction," Johnson offered amnesty to former Confederates who took an oath of loyalty to the Union, restoring their political and civil rights and immunizing them against the seizure of their property and prosecution for treason. By 1866, Johnson had granted more than seven thousand pardons to wealthy southerners and Confederate senior officers who applied individually for pardons.

Johnson's plans for political reunion left out any provision for black voting or participation in politics. Indeed, his plan would give the South even greater national power than it had held before because the entire African American population would now be considered individually when the number of representatives was calculated, not merely as three-fifths of a person as before the war. White southerners could hardly believe their good fortune. The members of the state conventions elected in 1865 flaunted their opinions of the North. Some refused to fly the American flag, some refused to ratify the Thirteenth Amendment, and some even refused to admit that secession had been illegal. Former Confederates filled important posts in state governments. Georgia elected Alexander H. Stevens, the former vice president of the aborted nation, to Congress. Even Johnson recognized that "there seems, in many of the elections something like defiance."

The North erupted in outrage when the new state governments enacted the so-called **black codes,** laws for controlling former slaves. The southern white legislatures granted the barest minimum of rights to black people: the right to marry, to hold property, to sue and be sued. Most of the laws decreed what African Americans could not do: move from one job to another, own or rent land, testify in court, practice certain occupations. When the members of Congress convened in December 1865, they reacted with fury. To northerners, the former Confederates seemed to deny all the war had decided with this blatant attempt to retain racially based laws. Many blamed Johnson for the turn of events.

black codes (colonial) Laws passed by colonial assemblies to define slavery and control the black population.

Johnson and the Radicals

Northern leaders who came to be known as the Radical Republicans were particularly incensed by presidential reconstruction. Senator Thaddeus Stevens called for land to be seized from wealthy planters and given to the former slaves; Senator Charles Sumner wanted immediate and universal suffrage for blacks. But other northerners simply resented the easy pass given to former Confederates. "As for Negro suffrage," wrote a Chicago newspaper editor, "the mass of Union men in the Northwest did not care a great deal. What scares them is the idea that the rebels are all to be let back . . . and made a power in the government again." Moderates tried to devise plans acceptable to both sides.

([LC-B8184-10690]/Library of Congress Prints and Photographs Division)

Andrew Johnson. Andrew Johnson attempted to forge a new alliance between white northerners and white southerners, callously abandoning black southerners in the process.

Though understaffed and underfunded, the Freedmen's Bureau offered some measure of hope for former slaves by mediating between whites and blacks. Its commissioner, General Oliver Howard, advocated education as the foundation for improving living conditions and prospects for blacks. By 1869, approximately three thousand schools, serving more than 150,000 students, reported to the bureau. The bureau also insisted on the innovation of formal contracts between laborer and landlord. Moderate reformers also pushed for a civil rights bill to define American citizenship for all those born in the United States, including blacks. Citizenship would bring with it equal protection under the law, though the bill said nothing about black voting. The bureau struggled against a public that, in the words of one Mississippi commissioner, failed to "conceive of the Negro having any rights at all."

Republicans supported the Freedmen's Bureau and civil rights bills as the starting point for rebuilding the nation. But Johnson vetoed both bills, claiming that they violated the rights of the states and of white southerners who had been excluded from the decision making. Republicans closed ranks to override Johnson's veto, the first major legislation ever enacted over a presidential veto.

To prevent any future erosion of black rights, the Republicans proposed the Fourteenth Amendment, which, as eventually ratified, guaranteed citizenship to all American-born people and equal protection under the law for those citizens. The amendment decreed that any state that abridged the voting rights of any male inhabitants who were over age twenty-one and citizens would suffer a proportionate reduction in its congressional representation. It was the first constitutional amendment to use the word *male*, angering feminist abolitionists, who challenged the denial of suffrage based on sex. On Johnson's advice, the southern states refused to ratify the amendment.

Throughout the second half of 1866, the North watched, appalled, as much that the Civil War had been fought for seemed to be brushed aside in the South. Not only did the southern men who met in the state conventions refuse to accept the relatively mild Fourteenth Amendment, but they fought back in every way they could against further attempts to remake the South. The spring of that year saw riots in Memphis and New Orleans in which policemen and other whites brutally assaulted and killed black people and burned their homes with little or no provocation. It was in 1866, too, that the **Ku Klux Klan** appeared. Founded by Nathan Bedford Forrest in Tennessee, the Ku Klux Klan dedicated itself to maintaining white supremacy. The Klan became, in effect, a military wing of the Democratic Party, intimidating and killing white and black men who dared to associate with Republicans or support black rights.

Ku Klux Klan Founded in 1866 as an organization to terrorize blacks in the South during Reconstruction. It was revived in 1915 as a means of enforcing, often through violence and intimidation, the cultural values of rural, prohibitionist America against minority groups including African Americans, Jews, and Catholics.

Johnson toured the country in the fall of 1866 to denounce Republicans and their policy, to no avail. Republicans won control of Congress as well as the governorship and legislature in every northern state. The Republicans felt they had a mandate to push harder than they had before, but they faced internal disagreements over the vote, land distribution, the courts, and education. Some wanted to put the South under military control for the indefinite future; others sought to return to civilian control as soon as possible. Finally, on March 2, 1867, as time was running out on the session, they passed the Reconstruction Act.

The Reconstruction Act of 1867

The Reconstruction Act placed the South under military rule. All of the southern states except Tennessee, which had been readmitted to the Union after it ratified the Fourteenth Amendment, were divided into five military districts. Once order had been instituted, the states could proceed to elect conventions to draw up new constitutions, but those constitutions had to accept the Fourteenth Amendment and provide universal manhood suffrage. Once a majority of the state's citizens and both houses of the national Congress had approved the new constitution, the state could be readmitted to the Union.

To ensure that Andrew Johnson did not undermine the plan, which soon became known as "Radical Reconstruction," Congress sought to curb the president's power. With no threat of his veto after the 1866 elections, the Republicans called Congress into special session and voted to limit the president's authority as commander-in-chief of the army. They also passed the Tenure of Office Act, which prevented the president from removing officials who had been confirmed by the Senate. Johnson, characteristically, did not accept such restrictions of his power. When he violated the Tenure of Office Act by removing Secretary of War Edwin Stanton in the summer of 1867, many in Congress decided that Johnson warranted **impeachment.** Proceedings dragged on throughout the fall, while the first elections under the Reconstruction Act took place in the South. Finally, on May 16, 1868, Johnson was acquitted in the Senate by one vote, as even his political foes came to realize that using impeachment for anything less than criminal offenses while in office would have been unwise. But the constitutional and political significance of Johnson's impeachment endured.

impeachment The act of charging a public official with misconduct in office, impeachment is the constitutional procedure for removing presidents who are found guilty of "treason, bribery, or other high crimes and misdemeanors" as interpreted by Congress. Presidents Andrew Johnson, Richard Nixon, and Bill Clinton have been the subject of impeachment proceedings.

After word of the Reconstruction Act circulated in the spring and summer, both black and white men claimed leadership roles within the Republican Party. Black northerners came to the South looking for appointive and elective office. Ambitious black southerners, many of whom had been free and relatively prosperous before the Civil War, put themselves forward as the natural leaders of the race. Such men became the backbone of the Republican Party in black-belt districts that had a predominantly African American population.

White southerners sneered at supporters of the Republican cause. They called white northerners who came South to support Radical Reconstruction "carpetbaggers." These men were supposedly so unsuccessful back home that they could throw everything they had into a carpetbag (a cheap suitcase) and head south as soon as they read of the opportunities Radical Reconstruction had created. But the majority of white northerners who became Republican leaders in the South had been well educated in the North before the war, and many held property in the South. Like white southerners, however, the northern-born Republicans found the postwar South a difficult place in which to prosper. Meanwhile, white southern Republicans were labeled "scalawags" by their enemies and considered traitors to their race and region. Few white Republicans emerged in the plantation districts because they endured ostracism, resistance, and violence. In the upcountry districts, however, former Whigs and Unionists asserted themselves against the planters and Confederates. The Republican Party became strong in the mountains of eastern Tennessee, western North Carolina, eastern Kentucky, northern Alabama, and northern Georgia. Blacks, largely propertyless, called for an activist government to raise taxes and provide

(Cheekwood Museum of Art)

African American Man Voting. African American men voted during Reconstruction in the South but they often put their lives on the line in doing so.

schools, orphanages, and hospitals. Many whites, who owned land, called mainly for lower taxes.

Throughout the South, most whites watched, livid, as local black leaders, ministers, and Republicans mobilized black voters in enormous numbers in fall 1867. Membership in Union Leagues swept the region, with local leagues assisting with labor contracts and school construction as well as political activity. An Alabama league demanded recognition of black citizenship: "We claim exactly the same rights, privileges and immunities as are enjoyed by white men—we seek nothing more and will be content with nothing less." While many white Democrats boycotted the elections, the Republicans swept into the constitutional delegate positions. Although many black men voted, African Americans made up only a relatively small part of the convention delegates. They held the majority in South Carolina and Louisiana, but much smaller proportions elsewhere. About half of the 265 African Americans elected as delegates to the state conventions had been free before the war, and most were ministers, artisans, farmers, and teachers. During the next two years, these delegates would meet to write new, much more democratic constitutions for their states.

Republicans in 1867 believed that they had taken important steps toward a newer and more just society. "We have cut loose from the whole dead past," said Timothy Howe of Wisconsin, "and have cast our anchor out a hundred years." But the struggle over black rights that had begun during the Civil War was far from over. Many white voters in the North thought that the Radicals had gone too far in their concern with black rights and wanted officeholders to devote their energies to problems closer to home. In the South, in the decade that followed the war, blacks pursued their dreams of political equality and economic opportunity, while many whites sought to preserve as many of the features of slavery as they could. Violence, brutality, election fraud, and raw economic intimidation ended the experiment in multiracial politics known as Reconstruction.

In the mid-1870s, a severe economic depression made African American rights seem a less urgent issue. For many in the North, the hum of industry, the spread of railroads, and the rise of cities seemed more in tune with national progress than preserving the rights of former slaves. With a western frontier to open and Native Americans to subdue, the nation retreated from the principles for which the Civil War had been fought. By the disputed presidential election of 1876, white Americans no longer wished to be involved with the fate of blacks in the South.

❖ From Johnson to Grant, 1867–1868

During the months of Johnson's impeachment and trial, Congress completed expansion on the North American continent with the purchase of Alaska from Russia. The Alaska purchase was a major strategic and geographic victory for the United States. Amid the controversy over the impeachment of Johnson and the upcoming presidential election, the acquisition of this northern territory did not attract great attention, however.

The Election of 1868

The issues of the Civil War defined the 1868 presidential race. The Republicans nominated the great hero of the conflict, Ulysses S. Grant, whose popularity transcended partisanship. Republicans believed that they had selected a candidate "so independent of party politics as to be a guarantee of peace and quiet." In his official letter of acceptance, Grant said, "Let us have peace," and that phrase became the theme of the Republican campaign. The Republicans were not campaigning on any promise to expand Reconstruction or to do more for the rights of black Americans.

The Democrats turned to the former governor of New York, Horatio Seymour. Along with his running mate, Frank Blair of Missouri, Seymour relied on racial bigotry and white supremacy as the keynotes of his appeal. To win, the Democrats agreed, they had to arouse "the aversion with which the masses contemplate the equality of the negro." Grant garnered 53 percent of the vote; Seymour totaled 47 percent. Although Grant carried the electoral college by a margin of 214 to 80, the signs were not good for a continuation of Reconstruction. Over time, white voters had become less willing to help African Americans; whatever goals African Americans sought, they would have to achieve them on their own. The high point of post–Civil War racial reform had passed.

The Fifteenth Amendment

After the 1868 election, Republicans pushed for the adoption of the Fifteenth Amendment to the Constitution to finish the political reforms that Reconstruction brought. Under its terms, the federal and state governments could not restrict the right to vote because of race, color, or previous condition of servitude. Congress approved the amendment in February 1869 over Democratic opposition. The purpose of the change was to limit the legal right of the southern states to exclude African Americans from the political process. Democrats assailed it as a step toward black equality and a social revolution. In fact, the new amendment did not ensure African Americans the right to hold office, and it left untouched the restrictions that northern states imposed on the right of males to vote. Nevertheless, state legislatures endorsed the amendment promptly, and it was added to the Constitution in 1870. The adoption of the three Civil War amendments had changed the nature of the government as the administration of President Grant got under way, but American politics responded slowly to the impact of these new additions to the nation's fundamental law.

❖ The First Grant Administration, 1869–1873

Ulysses S. Grant, who came to the White House without political experience, believed that he should administer the government rather than promote new programs. "I shall on all subjects have a policy to recommend," he said in his inaugural address, "but none to enforce against the will of the people." He promised, unlike Andrew Johnson, to carry out the laws that Congress passed. Those who hoped for a period of calm after the storms of Johnson's presidency were soon disappointed, however. Grant's passive view of the presidency and aversion to partisan battles allowed Congress to play a dominant role. Without a clear objective of a war before him in which victory was the goal, the president seemed confused, and he followed a shifting policy in selecting his cabinet and making appointments. His cabinet mixed some strong appointments, such as Secretary of State Hamilton Fish, with other individuals whose qualifications were questionable. As a result, the executive office itself lost some of the authority Lincoln had acquired for it.

A Troubled Administration

Hard choices confronted the new president, particularly in the South. Southern Republicans begged for help from Washington to fight off resurgent Democrats. Yet many party members in the North believed that support for black aspirations seemed an electoral loser. As a result, African Americans in the South had to rely more and more on their own resources and personal courage. They made valiant efforts to involve themselves in regional politics, often at the risk of their lives. For their part, Democrats played down their racism in public statements and argued that former Confederates should now be allowed to participate in public life. The strategy produced mixed results in 1869: Republicans did well in Mississippi and won a close race for governor in Texas, while Democrats triumphed in Virginia and Tennessee. Overall, the results suggested that Republican strength was eroding as the Democrats reentered politics.

Making matters worse were allegations of scandal against the new administration. In the summer of 1869, two speculators, Jay Gould and Jim Fisk, manipulated the gold market to achieve huge profits for themselves. The price of gold rose until financial turmoil erupted on September 24, 1869. Investors who had promised to sell gold at lower prices faced ruin. Then the government sold its own gold supplies, the price of gold broke, and the market returned to its normal level. In the resulting inquiries, the public learned that some members of Grant's family had helped Gould and Fisk carry out their plan. Doubts spread about the ethical standards of Grant's presidency.

To the odor of corruption was soon added White House disarray and incompetence. The administration talked of forcing Spain to give up Cuba and then backed away from the idea. The president wanted to annex the Dominican Republic (Santo Domingo). An agent of the president worked out a treaty of annexation with Santo Domingo's rulers, and the pact was sent to the Senate. Grant pushed hard for its approval, but the Senate, fearful of the influence of speculators and lobbyists, balked. As a result, the treaty was defeated and the president embarrassed.

Grant's administration had more success with American claims for maritime losses against Great Britain. The claims were related to the *Alabama*, one of several Confederate raiders constructed in British shipyards during the Civil War. The *Alabama* had sunk numerous Union vessels. Charles Sumner, chair of the Senate Foreign Relations Committee, wanted to use the claims as leverage in an effort to acquire Canada. In 1871, the State Department worked out an amicable settlement of the issue that left Canada alone.

Grant, Congress, and Republican Discord

The president deferred too much to Congress as congressional Republicans split on issues such as the protective tariff and the currency. The mainstream members of the party believed that a tariff policy to "protect" American industries against foreign competition helped business, workers, and the party itself. A minority of Republicans called the protective policy wrong economically and a potential source of corrupt influence from the affected industries. On the currency, eastern Republicans favored the gold standard and what was known as "hard money," where every dollar was backed by an equal amount of gold. Western Republicans advocated an expansion of the money supply through paper money, or "greenbacks," and, when necessary, even the issuance of dollars backed by silver as an alternative to gold. Civil service was another divisive issue. Since government was still small, who held coveted jobs became a question for public dispute. Some Republicans argued that the government should follow "civil service reform," a merit system of appointing its officials. Reformers maintained that competence and nonpartisanship were better ways to staff these positions.

Republicans who wanted to reduce the tariff, rely on the civil service, and treat the South with more leniency defected from the Grant administration. They formed **Liberal Republican** alliances with Democrats in such states as West Virginia and Missouri. In the 1870s, *liberal* meant someone who favored smaller government, lower tariffs, civil service, and, most important, an end to Reconstruction. If African Americans were the victims of southern violence, the liberal Republicans were willing to tolerate that result.

Liberal Republicans Organization formed in 1872 by Republicans who were not content with the political corruption and the policies of President Grant's first administration.

With his presidency under attack, Grant turned to Republican leaders in Congress who disliked the Liberal Republican program and its leaders. Grant knew that he could never satisfy the demands of the Liberals on Reconstruction or the civil service. Instead, he conciliated mainstream Republicans. He dismissed dissenting cabinet officers and aligned himself with party members willing to defend Congress and the White House. Officeholders who supported Liberal Republican candidates or Democrats were fired. Despite these actions, the 1870 elections went to Grant's opponents. Liberal Republicans won races in West Virginia and Missouri. The Democrats added forty-one seats to their total in the House and picked up another six seats in the Senate. The Republicans retained control of both houses, but their position was weakening. Grant's enemies even thought he might be defeated in 1872.

The Problem of the Ku Klux Klan

Mounting racial violence in the South added to the president's problems. By the summer of 1870, reports reached Washington of Klan violence against blacks and white Republicans across the South. The Klan and its offshoots, such as the Knights of the White Camelia, White Leagues, and the White Brotherhood, acted as the paramilitary arm of the Democratic Party to crush Republicanism through any means. In Tennessee a black Republican was beaten after he won an election for justice of the peace. His assailants told him "that they didn't dispute I was a very good fellow . . . but they did not intend any nigger to hold office in the United States." Four blacks died when the Klan attacked an election meeting in Alabama in October 1870. A "negro chase" in South Carolina left thirteen blacks dead. A wave of shootings and brutality undermined the chances of the Republican Party to survive and grow below the Mason-Dixon line.

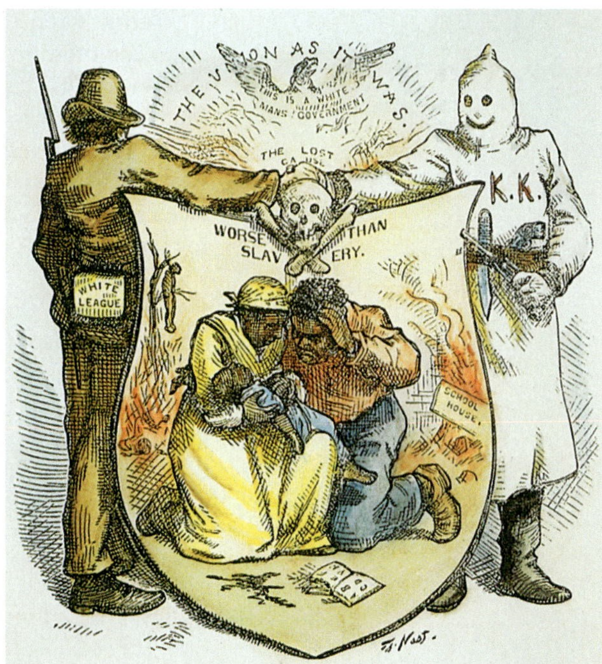

(The Granger Collection, New York)

In the 1870s, political cartoonist Thomas Nast brought attention to terror organizations like the Ku Klux Klan.

Viewing the wreckage of their southern parties after the 1870 elections, Republicans recognized that the Klan's terror tactics had worked to intimidate voters and demoralize their leaders. Yet the party was divided about the right answer to terror in the South. As 1871 began, the Republicans had less stomach for sending troops to the South to affect politics. As an Illinois newspaper observed, "the negro is now a voter and a citizen. Let him hereafter take his chances in the battle of life." Republican leaders asked themselves whether the cost of maintaining party organizations in the South in the face of such resolute Democratic opposition justified the effort.

Still, the violence of the Klan presented a challenge that could not be ignored. Congress passed the Ku Klux Klan Act of 1871, outlawing conspiracies to deprive voters of their civil rights, and banned efforts to bar any citizen from holding public office. The government also received broader powers to fight the Klan through the use of federal district attorneys to override state laws. As a last resort, military force could also be employed. The Justice Department, established in 1870, argued that the threat the Klan posed to democratic government amounted to war. Officials in Washington mobilized federal district attorneys and U.S. marshals to institute prosecutions against the Klan. The legal offensive in 1871 brought results; in state after state, Klan leaders were indicted. Federal troops assisted the work of the Justice Department in South Carolina. The Klan was discredited as a public presence in southern politics; its violence became more covert and less visible. Although the prosecutions of the Klan showed that effective federal action could compel southern states to comply with the rule of law, sentiment in the North for such stern measures began to recede.

Farmers and Railroads

The expansion of railroads posed new challenges for farmers in the South and West. Throughout the 1860s, two transcontinental railroads laid tracks across the country. The Union Pacific built westward while the Central Pacific started eastward from the West Coast. The two lines faced difficult obstacles of money and geography. The Central Pacific crossed the Sierra Nevada Mountains through rocky gorges and across treacherous rivers. Several thousand Chinese laborers did the most dangerous work: they tunneled into snowdrifts to reach their work sites and then toiled on sheer cliffs with picks and dynamite. On the Union Pacific side, more than ten thousand construction workers, many of them Irish immigrants, laid tracks across Nebraska and Wyoming. When the two lines met at Promontory, Utah, on May 10, 1869, railroad executives drove a golden spike into the ground with a silver sledgehammer: the transcontinental lines had become a reality.

Railroad construction accelerated. In 1869, railroad mileage stood at about 47,000 miles; four years later, the total had risen to 70,268 miles. The new railroad lines employed tens of thousands of workers and extended across a far larger geographical area than any previous manufacturing enterprise. American business was starting to become much larger than any previous endeavor in the nation; that development would have important consequences.

Farmers too enjoyed postwar prosperity with higher prices for wheat and other commodities. Beneath the surface, however, tensions between agrarians and the new industries grew. In late 1867, the Patrons of Husbandry, also known as the Grange, was formed to press the case for the farmers. The Grange complained about the high mortgages the farmers owed, the prices they paid to middlemen such as the operators of grain elevators, and the economic discrimination they faced in the form of higher charges at the hands of railroads in moving their goods to market. These grievances contributed to the turbulence of politics in the 1880s and 1890s.

To balance the power of the railroads, some states created railroad commissions. In Illinois, a new constitution in 1870 instructed the legislature to pass laws establishing maximum rates for the movement of passengers and freight. The legislature set up the Illinois Railroad Commission with wide powers. Neighboring states such as Iowa, Minnesota, and Wisconsin followed the Illinois example during the next several years. Railroad companies challenged some of these laws in court, but the U.S. Supreme Court upheld the authority of such commissions in *Munn v. Illinois* (1877) (see Chapter 16).

Indian Policies

The opening of the West to railroads and the spread of farmers onto the Great Plains meant that Native Americans had to once again, as in the 1830s and 1850s, resist an encroaching white presence. What had once been called the "Great American Desert" now beckoned as the home for countless farmers. The tribes that were living in the West and the Native Americans who had been displaced there in the 1830s and 1840s found their hunting grounds and tribal domains under siege.

Treatment of Native Americans after the Civil War mixed benevolence and cruelty. Grant brought more insight and respect to the issue of Native Americans than most previous presidents. His administration pursued what became known as the "peace policy." Although a majority of western settlers advocated the removal or outright extermination of the Indian tribes, advocates of the Indians convinced Grant that the hostile tribes should be located in Dakota Territory and the Indian Territory (now Oklahoma). The government would stop treating the entire West as a giant Indian reservation. Instead, specific areas would be set aside for the Native Americans. On these "reservations," the inhabitants would learn the cultural values of white society, be taught to grow crops, and be paid a small income until they could support themselves. (See Map 15.2.)

Grant appointed Ely Parker, a Seneca, as commissioner of Indian affairs. Congress appropriated $2 million for Indian problems and set up the Board of Indian Commissioners to distribute the funds. Indian agents would be chosen from nominees that Christian churches provided. The peace policy blended kindness and force. If the Indians accepted the presence of church officials on the reservations, the government would leave them alone. Resistance, however, would bring the army to see that Indians stayed on the reservations. To whites, the peace policy was humane. For Native Americans, it undermined their way of life.

MAP 15.2

Indian Reservations in the West

Following the end of the Civil War and the adoption of the peace policy of President Ulysses S. Grant, a network of Indian reservations spread across the West. This map shows how extensive the reservation system was.

The 1870s brought increasing tensions on the frontier. The 1870 census reported more than 2.7 million farms; ten years later, that number had risen to more than 4 million. Competition for space and resources intensified. With millions of acres under cultivation and the spread of cattle drives across Indian lands, the tribes found themselves squeezed from their traditional nomadic hunting grounds.

The systematic destruction of the buffalo herds beginning in the 1860s dealt Indians another devastating blow. In the societies of the Plains tribes, the meat of the bison supplied food, and the hides provided shelter and clothes. Removal of these resources hurt the Indians economically, but the cultural impact was even greater because buffalo represented the continuity of nature and the renewal of life cycles. As railroads penetrated the West, hunters could send buffalo hides and other products to customers with relative ease. More than 5 million buffalo were slaughtered during the early 1870s, and by the end of the century, only a few of these animals were alive. Conservation eventually saved the buffalo from the near extinction.

During the mid-1870s, Native Americans tried a last effort to block the social and economic tides overwhelming their way of life. By that time, Grant's peace policy had faltered as corruption and politics replaced the original desire to treat the Indians in a more humane manner. The tribes that continued to hunt and pursue their nomadic culture found unhappy whites and a hostile military in their way. The Red River War, led by Cheyenne, Kiowas, and Comanches, erupted on the southern Plain, but Indian resistance ultimately collapsed when food and supplies ran out.

The discovery of gold in the Black Hills of Dakota brought white settlers into an area where the Sioux had dominated. The Indians refused to leave, and the government sent troops to protect the gold seekers. The Indian leaders, **Crazy Horse** and **Sitting Bull,** rallied their followers to stop the army. Near what the Indians called the Greasy Grass (whites called it the Little Bighorn), Colonel **George Armstrong Custer** led a force of six hundred men in 1876. With a third of his detachment, he attacked more than two thousand Sioux warriors. Custer and his soldiers perished. The whites called it "Custer's Last Stand." The Indian victory, shocking to whites, was only a temporary success, however. The army pursued the Indians during the ensuing months. By the end of the Grant administration, the Sioux had been conquered. Only in the Southwest did the Apaches successfully resist the power of the military. Native Americans now faced cruelty, exploitation,

Crazy Horse (1842?–1877) Native American Sioux leader who defeated George Custer in battle.

Sitting Bull (c. 1831–1890) Lakota Sioux Chief, he defeated George Custer in the Battle of Little Big Horn (1876).

Custer, George Armstrong (1839–1876) Lieutenant colonel famous for his defeat at Little Big Horn by the Sioux Indians.

([LC-USZC4-5613]/Library of Congress Prints and Photographs Division)

Pima Indian Reservation School, 1870. The Peace Policy of the Grant administration moved Native Americans onto reservations like this one at Pima, Arizona.

and oppression that extended through the rest of the nineteenth century and beyond 1900.

❖ Women in the 1870s

White women during this time did not have anything that approached social or political equality with men. Amid the male-dominated public life, women struggled for some political rights, a foothold in the new industrial economy, and a way to make their voices heard about social issues. But they faced significant barriers to any kind of meaningful participation in public affairs, a condition that continued into the early twentieth century.

The debates over the adoption of the Fifteenth Amendment underscored this problem. Women had hoped that they might share in the expansion of political rights. In fact, several major advocates of woman **suffrage,** including **Susan B. Anthony,** opposed the amendment because it left women out. In Anthony's mind, black and Asian men should be barred from voting unless women had the right of suffrage as well. That put her at odds with champions of black suffrage such as Frederick Douglass. (See *Doing History: Women's Rights and Black Suffrage During Reconstruction.*)

suffrage The right to vote, extended to African American men by the Fifteenth Amendment (1870). See also woman suffrage.

Anthony, Susan B. (1820–1906) Advocate of woman's suffrage and leader in the woman's rights movement along with Elizabeth Cady Stanton.

At a meeting of the Equal Rights Association in May 1869, two distinct groups of suffragists emerged. The National Woman Suffrage Association reflected the views of Susan B. Anthony and Elizabeth Cady Stanton that the Fifteenth Amendment should be shunned until women were included. The American Woman Suffrage Association, led by Lucy Stone and Alice Stone Blackwell, endorsed the amendment and focused its work on gaining suffrage in the states. Amid this dissension, the new territory of Wyoming granted women the right of suffrage in 1869. Nonetheless, their action represented a small step forward while the major suffrage groups feuded.

For women the decade of the 1870s offered both some opportunities and more reminders of their status as second-class citizens. On the positive side, educational opportunities expanded. The number of women graduating from high school stood at nearly nine thousand in 1870, compared with seven thousand men. Aware of these statistics, state universities and private colleges opened their doors to female students in growing numbers. By 1872, nearly one hundred institutions of higher learning admitted women, including Cornell University in Ithaca, New York. One of its first woman graduates was M. Carey Thomas, who received her B.A. in 1877. Five years later, she earned a Ph.D. at a German university. By the 1890s, she had become the president of Bryn Mawr, a women's college outside Philadelphia.

Obtaining a degree was not a guarantee of access to professions that males controlled. Myra Bradwell tried to become a lawyer in Illinois, but the state bar association rejected her application. She sued in federal court, and in 1873 the U.S. Supreme Court decided that the law did not grant her the right to be admitted to the bar. One justice wrote that "the paramount destiny and mission of woman are to fulfill the noble and benign offices of wife and mother." Although licensing of lawyers began in 1869, a year later there were only five female lawyers in the nation.

The Supreme Court also rebuffed efforts to secure woman suffrage through the courts. Virginia Minor, president of the Woman Suffrage Association of Missouri, tried to vote during the 1872 election, but the registrar of voters turned her away. She sued on the grounds that the action denied her rights as a citizen. In the case of *Minor v. Happersett* (1875), the Supreme Court unanimously concluded that suffrage was not one of the rights of citizenship because "sex has never been made one of the elements of citizenship in the United States." To gain the right to vote, women would have to amend the Constitution or obtain the right of suffrage from the states.

Doing History Women's Rights and Black Suffrage During Reconstruction

One of the unexpected aspects of Reconstruction occurred during debates about the wisdom of extending the vote to black males but not to women in general. Out of these discussions would come the Fifteenth Amendment to the Constitution, which affirmed the right of citizens to vote without regard to their race, color, or status as former slaves. The amendment, however, said nothing about gender. Advocates of woman suffrage believed that women should be accorded the right to vote as well as men. The dispute divided African American men such as Frederick Douglass from champions of woman suffrage such as Elizabeth Cady Stanton. The divisions between Stanton and Douglass shed light on the interplay between race and gender that cut across American society in the nineteenth century.

The exchange of views between Stanton and Douglass that follows came at a meeting of the American Equal Rights Association in New York City during May 1867. George Downing was a black man who had asked Stanton about views on male suffrage for blacks and suffrage for all Americans.

Elizabeth Cady Stanton, 1867

WE DO NOT demand the right step for this hour in demanding suffrage for any class; as a matter of principle I claim it for all. But in a narrow view of the question as a feeling between classes, when Mr. Downing puts the question to me, are you willing to have the colored man enfranchised before the woman, I say no; I would not trust him with all my rights, degraded, oppressed himself, he would be more despotic with the governing power than even our Saxon rulers are.

Frederick Douglass, 1867

I champion the right of the Negro to vote. It is with us a matter of life and death, and therefore cannot be postponed. I have always championed woman's right to vote; but it will be seen that the present claim for the Negro is one of the most urgent necessity. The assertion of the right of women to vote meets nothing but ridicule; there is no deep seated malignity in the hearts of the people against her; but name the right of the Negro to vote, all hell is turned loose and the Ku-Klux and the Regulators hunt and slay the unoffending black man. The government of this country loves women. They are sisters, mothers, wives and daughters of our rulers; but the Negro is loathed.

Source: Both quotations are from Elizabeth Cady Stanton et al., *History of Woman Suffrage* (6 vols., New York: Flower and Wells, 1881–1922), 2: 214 (Stanton), 310–311 (Douglass), as cited in Rosalyn M. Terborg-Penn, "Afro Americans in the Struggle for Woman Suffrage" (Ph.D. dissertation, Howard University, 1977), 77 (Stanton), 79 (Douglass).

QUESTIONS for REFLECTION

1. What was Stanton's opinion of the capacity of black men to use the vote wisely?
2. How did Douglass see the issue as between black suffrage and votes for women?
3. In what ways did racial ideas and gender biases shape the debate about the Fifteenth Amendment?

The Rise of Voluntary Associations

Blocked off from politics, women carved out a public space through voluntary associations. Black churchwomen established missionary societies to work in both the United States and abroad. Clubs and literary societies sprang up among white women. In New York City, women created Sorosis, a club for women only, after the New York Press Club barred females from membership. In 1873, delegates from local Sorosis clubs formed the Association for the Advancement of Women. The New England's Women's Club, located in Boston, had local laws changed during the early 1870s to allow women to serve on the Boston School Committee. Later the club founded the Women's Education Association to expand opportunities in schools and colleges. During the two decades that followed, the women's club movement put down strong roots in all parts of the nation. Soon they also found ways to exert an influence on political and cultural issues.

Despite being turned away at the polls, women made their political presence felt, bringing energetic fervor to the **temperance movement** in particular. "The women are in desperate earnest," said a Missouri resident who witnessed a temperance campaign. In August 1874, a group of women active in the temperance cause met at Lake Chautauqua, New York, and set a national meeting that evolved into the Woman's Christian Temperance Union (WCTU). By the end of the 1870s, a thousand unions had been formed, with an estimated twenty-six thousand members. In 1879, Frances Willard became president of the WCTU, and she took the organization beyond its original goal of temperance and into broader areas of social reform such as woman suffrage and the treatment of children. As it had before the Civil War, the campaign against alcohol revealed some of the underlying social and cultural strains of society.

temperance movement Nineteenth century reform movement that encouraged the reduction or elimination of alcoholic beverage consumption.

Women at Work

The 1870s also brought greater economic opportunities for women in sales and clerical positions in the workplace. Sales of typewriters began in 1874. E. Remington and Sons, which produced the typewriter, said in 1875 that "no invention has opened for women so broad and easy an avenue to profitable and suitable employment as the 'Type-Writer.'" By 1880, women accounted for 40 percent of the stenographers and typists in the country.

The most typical experience of American women, however, remained toil in the fields and at home. Black women in the South labored in the open alongside their husbands who were tenant farmers or sharecroppers. In the expanding cities, women worked in textile factories or became domestic servants. Many urban women also took in boarders. Middle-class women with domestic servants had some assistance, but they still did a daunting amount of work. Preparing food, washing laundry by hand, keeping the house warm before electricity, and disposing of waste all demanded hard labor. In the daily rhythms of American society in this period, the often unpaid and unrecognized labor of women was indispensable to the nation's advancement.

American families faced challenges and changes during the postwar period. Divorce became an option in many states, and defenders of marriage moved to tighten the conditions under which marriages could be dissolved. Laws to limit the sale of birth control devices and restrict abortions reflected the same trend. The New York Society for the Suppression of Vice was formed in 1872 under the leadership of Anthony Comstock. It lobbied successfully for a national law barring information deemed obscene about birth control and abortion from being sent through the mails. Although women had made some gains after the Civil War, they remained second-class citizens within the masculine political order of the period. However, that brand of politics was also coming into question as voters prepared to decide whether President Grant deserved a second term.

❖ Political and Economic Turmoil

By 1872, many commentators and voters in the North were dismayed at the spectacle of national politics. "We are in danger of the way of all Republics," said one critic of the existing system. "First freedom, then glory; when that is past, wealth, vice and corruption." Restoring ethical standards was the goal of the Liberal Republicans who wanted to field a candidate against President Grant in 1872. These men, including Senator Carl Schurz, a Missouri Republican, and Charles Francis Adams, the son of former president John Quincy Adams, believed that only in that way could Reconstruction be ended and civil service reform achieved. They saw what happened in the South as an unwise experiment in racial democracy.

But Liberal Republicans did not have a good national candidate to run against Grant. Few party leaders were men with real stature. Schurz was a native of Germany and therefore ineligible to run. The race came down to Charles Francis Adams, Lyman Trumbull of Illinois, and **Horace Greeley**, editor of the *New York Tribune*. After six ballots, Greeley became the nominee. At the age of sixty-one, Greeley was an odd choice. He favored the protective tariff, unlike most reformers, and he was indifferent about the civil service. His main passion was ending Reconstruction. "That Grant is an Ass no man can deny," said one Liberal in private, "but better an Ass than a mischievous idiot."

Greeley, Horace (1811–1872) Grant's opponent in the 1872 election. Seen as a political oddball in the eyes of many Americans, the sixty-one-year-old editor favored the protective tariff and was indifferent to civil service reform. He was also passionate about vegetarianism and the use of human manure in farming.

The 1872 Election

Grant was renominated on a platform that stressed the need to preserve Reconstruction: voters in the North must safeguard what they had won during the Civil War. The Democrats were in a box: if they rejected Greeley, they had no chance to win; picking him, however, would alienate southern voters who remembered Greeley's passion against the Confederacy. In the end, the Democrats accepted Greeley as their only alternative. The Liberal Republican–Democratic nominee made a vigorous public campaign, while Grant observed the tradition that the incumbent did not take part in the race personally.

The Republicans made their appeal on the issues of the war. The black leader Frederick Douglass said of the impending contest: "If the Republican party goes down, freedom goes down with it." When the voters went to the polls, the outcome was a decisive victory for Grant and his party. There were still enough Republicans in the South to enable Grant to carry all but five of the southern states in one of the last honest elections the region would see for many years. The Democrats had reached a low point behind Greeley, who died in late November. The triumph was a mixed one for Grant: he remained in the White House, but scandals would soon plague his second term.

A Surge of Scandals

As the excitement of the 1872 election faded, allegations of corruption in Congress surfaced. The first controversy turned on the efforts of the Crédit Mobilier Company to purchase influence with lawmakers during the 1860s. The directors of the Union Pacific had established Crédit Mobilier to build the transcontinental line. Participants in the venture sold bonds that were marketed at a large profit to investors and insiders, but much of the money in effect came from the federal government through loans and guarantees. To avoid a congressional probe into the company, Crédit Mobilier's managers offered leading Republicans a chance to buy shares in the company at prices well below their market value. When the lawmakers sold their shares, they pocketed the difference, the equivalent of a bribe. A newspaper broke the story in late 1872, and an investigation ensued. The probe produced a few scapegoats but cleared most of the individuals involved. Nevertheless, the episode damaged the credibility of public officials.

Another embarrassing scandal occurred in February 1873. At the end of a congressional session, a last-minute deal gave senators and representatives a retroactive pay increase. The public denounced the action as the "Salary Grab." The *Chicago Tribune* said that it was "nothing more nor less than an act of robbery." When Congress reconvened in December 1873, repeal of the salary increase sailed through both houses as politicians backtracked. These two incidents produced widespread calls for reducing government expenditures and rooting out corruption.

Scandals persisted throughout Grant's presidency. Within the Treasury Department, the Whiskey Ring was exposed. Officials involved took kickbacks from liquor interests in return for not collecting federal excise taxes on whiskey. The administration also faced queries concerning the secretary of war, W. W. Belknap, whose wife had been receiving cash gifts from a man who sold supplies to the army. When these ties were revealed, a congressional committee sought to start impeachment proceedings, and Belknap resigned. Few doubted Grant's personal honesty, but his cabinet selections often seemed corrupt.

Humorist Mark Twain captured the spirit of the times in his novel *The Gilded Age*, published in 1873. The main character, Colonel Beriah Sellers, was an engaging confidence man who embodied the faith in progress and economic growth of the postwar years, along with a healthy amount of deceit that accompanied the rapid expansion of business. In time, the title of Twain's book came to be used for the entire era between the end of Reconstruction and the start of the twentieth century. During the Gilded Age, Americans grappled with issues of political corruption, social disorder, and economic inequities in ways that challenged older assumptions about the role of government in society.

Doing History Online

Grant and the Union Pacific Railroad

Go to the CourseMate website for this chapter and link to Primary Sources. After reading Edward Winslow Martin's account of the Crédit Mobilier scandal (Document 14), how do you think the scandals of the Grant era affected Reconstruction policy?

www.cengagebrain.com

The Panic of 1873 and Its Consequences

A sense of national crisis deepened in September 1873 when the banking house of Jay Cooke and Company failed. The bank, which had invested heavily in the Northern Pacific Railroad, could not pay its debts or return money to its depositors and had to close. As this important bank collapsed, others followed suit, businesses cut back on employment, and a downturn began. The problems rivaled similar panics that had occurred in 1819, 1837, and 1857; however, the panic of 1873 was the worst of them all. The panic of 1873 occurred because of a speculative post–Civil War boom in railroad building. When large railroads such as the Northern Pacific failed because of their overexpansion and inability to pay debts, the damage rippled through society. Economic activities that were dependent on the rail lines, such as car making, steel rail production, and passenger services, also fell off. Layoffs of employees and bankruptcies for businesses followed. More than ten thousand companies failed in 1878, the worst year of the depression.

The immediate effects of the problem lasted until 1879. Americans faced an economy in which falling prices placed the heaviest burdens on people who were in debt or who earned their living by selling their labor. An abundance of cheap unskilled labor proved a boon for capitalists who wanted to keep costs down. For the poor, however, it meant that they had little job security and could easily be replaced if they protested against harsh working conditions.

Americans out of work during the 1870s had no system of unemployment insurance to cushion the shock. In some cities, up to a quarter of the workforce looked for jobs without success. Laborers in the Northeast mounted a campaign called "Work for Bread" that produced large demonstrations in major cities. In January 1874, a demonstration at Tompkins Square in New York City pitted a crowd of seven thousand unemployed laborers against police. Many marchers were arrested; others were injured in the melee. Strikes marked 1874 and 1875.

In Pennsylvania the railroads used their control of police and strikebreakers to put down a protracted walkout of coal miners and their supporters. Conservatives feared that the nation was on the verge of revolution.

Discontent also flared in the farm belt. The price of wheat, which had stood at $1.16 a bushel in 1873, dropped to 95 cents a bushel a year later. The price of corn stood at 64 cents a bushel in 1874 but 42 cents in 1875. These changes meant substantial drops in farm income. As a result, farmers' land- and equipment-related debts posed an even greater burden. The Grange tried to use political pressure to press these issues, and its efforts reached Congress in 1873–1874, but little was accomplished for the next fifteen years.

The decline in consumer prices and the growing burden of debt on farmers and businessmen in the South and West created pressure for laws to put more money into circulation, which would make debts easier to pay. The Treasury Department's decision to end the coinage of silver aroused particular anger among southern and western advocates of inflation, who called it the "Crime of 1873." Proponents of the move argued that an overabundance of silver in the marketplace required the move to a gold standard. By coining silver into money at a price above its market levels, the government was subsidizing American silver production and cheapening the currency. Finally, an effort to inject a modest amount of inflation into the economy came in 1875. A currency bill cleared both houses of Congress, providing some $64 million in additional money for the financial system, but such intervention was controversial. President Grant ultimately decided to veto the bill in April 1875, and Congress sustained his action. The government would not intervene in the deepening economic crisis.

❖ The Failure of Reconstruction, 1875–1877

After the presidential election of 1872, the North's already weakened commitment to Reconstruction ebbed still more. The panic of 1873 distracted attention from the rights of black Americans. The Grant administration backed away from southern politics, and the Justice Department prosecuted fewer individuals for violations of the Ku Klux Klan Act and pardoned some of those who had earlier been convicted of terrorist activity. Liberal Republicans and northern Democrats spread racist propaganda to block the aspirations of southern blacks. The editor of *The Nation* said that black residents of South Carolina had an "average of intelligence but slightly above the level of animals." Northerners found it easier to believe that the South would be better off when whites were dominant.

A damaging setback to the economic hopes of African Americans came in 1874 with the failure of the Freedmen's Savings and Trust Company in Washington, D.C. Since its founding in 1865, the bank had managed the deposits of thousands of former slaves. It was supposed to provide lessons in thrift for its depositors. However, its manager sought larger returns by investing in speculative railroad projects. The panic of 1873 caused huge losses, and the bank failed a year later; most customers lost all of their money.

The Stigma of Corruption

Corruption among southern Republican governments became a favorite theme of critics of Reconstruction. There was no doubt that white governments that took over after Reconstruction also displayed lax political ethics; nevertheless, the corruption issue gave opponents of black political participation a perfect weapon. Of course, it would not have mattered if Reconstruction governments had lacked any moral flaws at all. Any government that represented a biracial community was unacceptable to white southerners.

Although participation of African Americans in southern politics increased dramatically during Reconstruction, their role in the region's public life never approached that of whites. Sixteen blacks served in Congress during the period, including two in the Senate, but it was not long before most were unseated by white opponents. Many more held offices in the state legislatures, but even there, their numbers were comparatively modest. In 1868, for example, the Georgia legislature had 216 members, of whom only 32 were black. In only one state, South Carolina, did blacks ever hold a majority in the legislature, and they did so in only one house. Six African Americans held the office of lieutenant governor in the states of Louisiana, Mississippi, and South Carolina. Thus, by the 1870s, blacks had made their presence felt in politics, but the decline of Reconstruction made that trend a short-lived one.

The Resurgence of the Democrats

Hard economic times arising from the panic of 1873 worked against the Republicans. Discontent farmers wanted the government to inflate the currency and raise prices on their crops. Factory workers clamored for more jobs to become available. In this setting, the fate of African Americans in the South became a secondary concern. In the 1874 congressional races, angry voters turned to the Democrats, who used the issue of Republican corruption to regain control of the House of Representatives for the first time in sixteen years. The Democrats added seventy-seven seats in the House and ten seats in the Senate, in what one happy party member called a "Tidal Wave."

In the South, the revitalized Democrats "redeemed," as they called it, several states from Republican dominance. They began with Texas in 1873, then won back Arkansas the next year, and elected most of the South's members in the U.S. House of Representatives. Louisiana saw the emergence of the White League, which was determined that "the niggers shall not rule over us." In September 1874, open fighting erupted in New Orleans between armed Republicans and more than three thousand White League partisans. President Grant sent in federal troops to restore calm, but this action angered northern Democrats and a growing number of northern Republicans. In Alabama, the Democrats also relied on violence and murder to oust the Republicans; seven blacks were killed and nearly seventy wounded. In view of the wide support for the Democratic Party among southern whites, honest elections would probably have produced similar results for that party at the polls; but intimidation and violence were key elements in the victories that the Democrats secured in the South in 1874.

The Democrats intended to use their control of the House of Representatives to roll back Reconstruction and prevent any further expansion of black rights. During the lame-duck congressional session of 1874–1875, Republicans, who were soon to lose power, enacted a path-breaking civil rights law that gave black citizens the right to sue in federal courts when they confronted discrimination in public accommodations such as a hotel or restaurant. However, it remained to be seen how federal courts would rule when black plaintiffs sued to enforce their rights. Without a national consensus behind civil rights and Reconstruction, the fate of black Americans lay in the hands of white southerners who were determined to keep African Americans in economic, political, and cultural subjugation. (See Map 15.3.)

The Centennial Year, 1876

As the nation's one hundredth birthday neared, the Centennial International Exhibition to be held in Philadelphia attracted public fascination. In May 1876, some 285 acres of fairgrounds held several hundred buildings crammed with

MAP 15.3

Reconstruction in the South

This map shows the times at which the states of the former Confederacy reentered the Union and then saw the Democrats regain political control. Note how quickly this process occurred for most of the southern states. The relative brevity of Reconstruction is one of the keys to why more sweeping racial change did not take place.

exhibits, specimens, and artifacts from thirty-seven nations. The doors opened on May 10 for two hundred thousand spectators, including both houses of Congress, who heard a welcoming address by President Grant. One of the most popular attractions was the huge Corliss steam engine, which stood 40 feet tall and weighed 700 tons. Equally alluring was the "harmonic telegraph" of Alexander Graham Bell, as the telephone was then called.

The complexity of American life in the 1870s was not depicted at the exhibit, however. African Americans had almost no representation. Native American cultures were displayed as "curiosities" consisting of totem poles, tepees, and trinkets. The Women's Pavilion stressed the joys of homemaking. That exhibit evoked a protest from Elizabeth Cady Stanton and Susan B. Anthony. On July 4, 1876, they read a "Women's Declaration of Independence" that contrasted their aspirations with the traditional attitudes toward women expressed at the fair. Their protest had little effect on public opinion, however.

Nearly 10 million Americans came to the fair during its run, which ended on November 10. The fair lost money, but nevertheless contributed to a growing sense of national pride and confidence. Those emotions would be tested during the bitter presidential election that dominated the second half of 1876.

The Race for the White House

A key test of the nation's institutions occurred during the disputed presidential election of 1876. As the election process commenced, the Democrats felt optimism about their chances to regain power for the first time since 1860. Difficult economic times in the East and Midwest made voters sympathetic to the Democrats. For its candidate, the party selected **Samuel J. Tilden,** the governor of New York. An opponent of corruption in his home state, he was also a corporate lawyer who believed in the gold standard, limited federal action, and restraints on spending. The Democratic platform spoke of a "revival of Jeffersonian democracy" and called for "high standards of official morality." Because Tilden was not in good

Tilden, Samuel J. (1814–1886) Governor of New York and Democratic candidate for president in 1876. He narrowly lost what has been considered the most controversial election in American history.

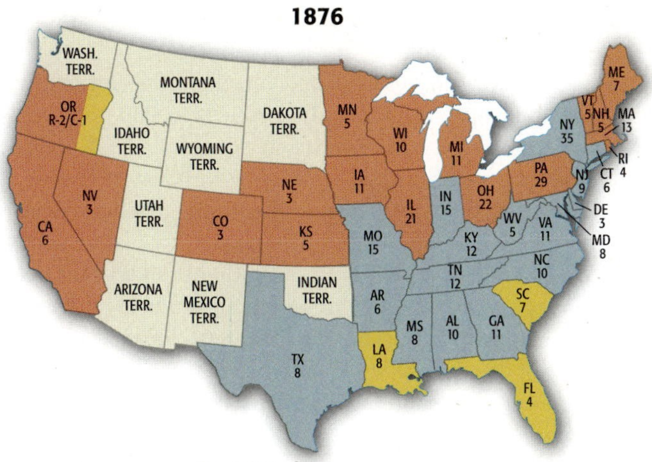

Candidate (Party)	Uncontested Electoral Vote	Electoral Vote		Popular Vote	
Hayes (Republican)	165	185	50%	4,034,311	48.0%
Tilden (Democrat)	184	184	50%	4,288,546	51.0%
Contested					
Territories					

MAP 15.4
The Election of 1876
The presidential election of 1876 between Samuel J. Tilden for the Democrats and Rutherford B. Hayes for the Republicans turned on the votes of Florida, Louisiana, and South Carolina to produce the narrow one-vote victory in the electoral college for Hayes.

health, the custom that presidential candidates did not campaign during that era worked to his advantage.

Among Republicans, the front-runner for the nomination was James G. Blaine, a former Speaker of the House of Representatives. With the nomination seemingly in his grasp, Blaine came under fire for financial dealings with an Arkansas railroad while he was in the House. His candidacy lost momentum at the national convention, where Republicans selected Governor **Rutherford B. Hayes** of Ohio. Hayes had the virtues of a good military record in the Civil War and a spotless record in public office. In the campaign, the Democrats stressed Republican corruption and Tilden's honesty. In response, the Republicans relied on Reconstruction and war memories, as they had in 1868 and 1872. This rhetoric became known as "waving the bloody shirt," in memory of a Republican speaker who had held up a bloodstained Union tunic and urged voters to remember the sacrifices of the Men in Blue.

Hayes, Rutherford B. (1822–1893) Nineteenth president of the United States (1877–1881), he won the most fiercely disputed election in American history.

When the election results rolled in, it seemed at first that Tilden had won. (See Map 15.4.) With most of the South in his column, the Democrat also carried New York, Connecticut, and New Jersey. The electoral vote totals indicated that Tilden had won 184 votes, one short of the 185 he needed to become president. Hayes had 165 electoral votes. Three southern states, Louisiana, Florida, and South Carolina, plus a disputed elector in Oregon, were still in doubt. If they all went for Hayes, he might prevail. Republican operatives moved to contest the outcome in the three undecided states. Telegrams to party members asked for evidence that African American voters had been intimidated. Honest returns from these states, Republicans argued, would show that Hayes had carried each one.

The Constitution did not specify how a contested presidential election was to be resolved. Each of the states in question was submitting two sets of election returns that claimed to be official and to reflect the will of the people. The House of Representatives had the responsibility for electing a president if no one won a majority in the electoral college. At the same time, the Senate had the constitutional duty to tabulate the electoral vote. With Republicans in control of the

Senate and with Democrats in control of the House, neither party could proceed without the support of the other.

To resolve the crisis, Congress created an electoral commission of fifteen members, ten from the Supreme Court. In a series of eight-to-seven votes along straight party lines, the electoral commission accepted the Republican returns from Louisiana, Florida, and South Carolina, and allocated the single disputed Oregon electoral vote to Hayes as well. The ruling declared that Hayes had received 185 electoral votes and Tilden 184. But who had really been elected president in 1876? Tilden had a margin of 250,000 popular votes over Hayes and had carried sixteen states. Hayes had won eighteen states in addition to the three contested southern states. In Louisiana, Florida, and South Carolina, Tilden had received a majority of the white vote, but black Republican voters had been intimidated and terrorized to such an extent that an honest count was in doubt. Essentially the election had ended in a tie.

Despite the decision of the electoral commission, the Democratic House still had to declare Hayes the winner. To prevent a crisis, complex negotiations began among leaders from both sides to put Hayes in the White House in return for Republican agreement to end Reconstruction. Democrats insisted that the South be freed from federal military intervention. After much discussion, an unwritten understanding, which later became known as the Compromise of 1877, along these lines led Congress to decide on March 2, 1877, that Republican Rutherford B. Hayes had been elected president of the United States.

Why Reconstruction Failed

The election of 1877 is often considered to have heralded the end of Reconstruction, but its failure is not so easily explained. Reconstruction failed to change American race relations because it challenged long-standing racist arrangements in both the North and South. The Civil War had called these traditions into question. In the years after the fighting ended, African Americans sought and to some degree succeeded in expanding their political role and taking charge of their collective destiny. Then the panic of 1873, the scandals of the Grant presidency, and waning interest in black rights led white Americans to back away from an expansion of racial justice.

To help the freed slaves overcome the effects of slavery and racial bias would have involved an expansion of national governmental power to an extent far beyond what Americans believed was justified during the nineteenth century. Better to keep government small, argued whites, than to improve the lot of the former slaves in the South. As a result, black Americans experienced segregation and deepening oppression. The political gains of the Reconstruction era, especially the Fourteenth and Fifteenth amendments, remained unfulfilled promises. That failure would be one of the most bitter legacies of this period of American history.

CHAPTER REVIEW, 1865–1877

SUMMARY

- The country embarked on an experiment in a multiracial democracy.
- African Americans in the South made a brave effort to participate in politics and economic life.
- Currents of racism and the opposition of white southerners doomed Reconstruction.
- Settlement of the West accelerated with the end of the Civil War and put pressure on Native American culture.
- Transcontinental railroads brought the nation together as a more cohesive economic unit.
- Although they were excluded from voting, women played a significant part in public life through voluntary associations.
- The panic of 1873 began a decade-long slump that brought protests from unhappy farmers and workers.
- By the nation's centennial in 1876, the disputed election between Hayes and Tilden marked the ebbing away of the issues of the Civil War and the eventual abandonment of Reconstruction.

IDENTIFICATIONS

Freedmen's Bureau
black codes
Ku Klux Klan
impeachment
Liberal Republicans
Crazy Horse
Sitting Bull
George Armstrong Custer
suffrage
Susan B. Anthony
temperance movement
Horace Greeley
Samuel J. Tilden
Rutherford B. Hayes

MAKING CONNECTIONS: LOOKING AHEAD

The next chapter takes up the process of industrialization and its effects on the economy and society. Elements in this chapter explain the rise of industrialism and set up the treatment of this issue in Chapter 16. Let's examine a few of them now.

1. What economic changes in the 1870s undercut Reconstruction and made industrialism seem more important?
2. How did the political system respond to the economic downturn of the 1870s, and how did these attitudes carry forward during the rest of the nineteenth century?
3. How did the political system then resemble modern alignments between Republicans and Democrats, and in what important ways were there differences?

RECOMMENDED READINGS

Edwards, Laura F. *Gendered Strife and Confusion: The Political Culture of Reconstruction* (1997). Looks at the role of women after the Civil War.

Fitzgerald, Michael W. *Splendid Failure: Postwar Reconstruction in the American South* (2007). A stimulating brief account of the successes and failures of Reconstruction.

Foner, Eric. *Reconstruction: America's Unfinished Revolution, 1863–1877* (1988). An excellent treatment of the whole period, especially the decline of Reconstruction.

Hahn, Steven. *A Nation Under Our Feet: Black Political Struggles in the Rural South from Slavery to the Great Migration* (2003). A prize-winning study of how African Americans built political institutions in the Reconstruction era.

Perman, Michael. *Emancipation and Reconstruction, 1862–1879*, 2nd ed. (2003). A good brief account of the issues and problems of Reconstruction.

Richardson, Heather Cox. *The Death of Reconstruction: Race, Labor, and Politics in the Post–Civil War North, 1865–1901* (2001). Considers how changing attitudes toward African Americans and labor undercut Reconstruction.

Simpson, Brooks D. *The Reconstruction Presidents* (1998). A treatment of Reconstruction from the perspective of the chief executives.

Smith, Jean Edward. *Grant* (2001). A full-scale, sympathetic biography of the general and president.

Wang, Xi. *The Trial of Democracy: Black Suffrage and Northern Republicans, 1860–1910* (1997). Discusses how voting issues shaped the adoption and then the abandonment of Reconstruction.

CourseMate Go to the CourseMate website at www.cengagebrain.com for additional study tools and review materials for this chapter.

APPENDIX

The Declaration of Independence

The Unanimous Declaration of the Thirteen United States of America

When in the Course of human events it becomes necessary for one people to dissolve the political bands which have connected them with another, and to assume among the Powers of the earth, the separate and equal station to which the Laws of Nature and of Nature's God entitle them, a decent respect to the opinions of mankind requires that they should declare the causes which impel them to the separation.

We hold these truths to be self-evident, that all men are created equal, that they are endowed by their Creator with certain unalienable Rights, that among these are Life, Liberty and the pursuit of Happiness. That to secure these rights, Governments are instituted among Men, deriving their just Powers from the consent of the governed. That whenever any Form of Government becomes destructive of these ends, it is the Right of the People to alter or to abolish it, and to institute new Government, laying its foundation on such principles and organizing its Powers in such form, as to them shall seem most likely to effect their Safety and Happiness. Prudence, indeed, will dictate that Governments long established should not be changed for light and transient causes; and accordingly all experience hath shewn, that mankind are more disposed to suffer, while evils are sufferable, than to right themselves by abolishing the forms to which they are accustomed. But when a long train of abuses and usurpations, pursuing invariably the same Object evinces a design to reduce them under absolute Despotism, it is their right, it is their duty, to throw off such Government, and to provide new Guards for their future security. Such has been the patient sufferance of these Colonies; and such is now the necessity which constrains them to alter their former Systems of Government. The history of the present King of Great Britain is a history of repeated injuries and usurpations, all having in direct object the establishment of an absolute Tyranny over these States. To prove this, let Facts be submitted to a candid world.

He has refused his Assent to Laws, the most wholesome and necessary for the public good.

He has forbidden his Governors to pass Laws of immediate and pressing importance, unless suspended in their operation till his Assent should be obtained; and when so suspended, he has utterly neglected to attend to them.

He has refused to pass other Laws for the accommodation of large districts of people, unless those people would relinquish the right of Representation in the Legislature, a right inestimable to them and formidable to tyrants only.

He has called together legislative bodies at places unusual, uncomfortable, and distant from the depository of their Public Records, for the sole Purpose of fatiguing them into compliance with his measures.

He has dissolved Representative Houses repeatedly, for opposing with manly firmness his invasions on the rights of the People.

He has refused for a long time, after such dissolutions, to cause others to be elected; whereby the Legislative Powers, incapable of Annihilation, have returned to the People at large for their exercise; the State remaining in the mean time exposed to all the dangers of invasion from without, and convulsions within.

He has endeavoured to prevent the Population of these States; for that purpose obstructing the Laws for Naturalization of Foreigners; refusing to pass others to encourage their migrations hither, and raising the conditions of new Appropriations of Lands.

He has obstructed the Administration of Justice, by refusing his Assent to Laws for establishing Judiciary Powers.

He has made Judges dependent on his Will alone, for the tenure of their offices, and the amount and payment of their salaries.

He has erected a multitude of New Offices, and sent hither swarms of Officers to harass our People, and eat out their substance.

He has kept among us, in times of peace, Standing Armies without the Consent of our legislatures.

He has affected to render the Military independent of and superior to the Civil Power.

He has combined with others to subject us to a jurisdiction foreign to our constitution, and unacknowledged by our laws; giving his Assent to their Acts of pretended Legislation:

For Quartering large bodies of armed troops among us:

For protecting them, by a mock Trial, from Punishment for any Murders which they should commit on the Inhabitants of these States:

For cutting off our Trade with all parts of the world:

For imposing Taxes on us without our Consent:

For depriving us in many cases, of the benefits of Trial by Jury:

For transporting us beyond Seas to be tried for pretended offences:

For abolishing the free System of English Laws in a neighbouring Province, establishing therein an Arbitrary government, and enlarging its Boundaries so as to render it at once an example and fit instrument for introducing the same absolute rule into these Colonies:

Text is reprinted from the facsimile of the engrossed copy in the National Archives. The original spelling, capitalization, and punctuation have been retained. Paragraphing has been added.

For taking away our Charters, abolishing our most valuable Laws, and altering fundamentally the Forms of our Governments:

For suspending our own Legislatures, and declaring themselves invested with Power to legislate for us in all cases whatsoever.

He has abdicated Government here, by declaring us out of his Protection, and waging War against us.

He has plundered our seas, ravaged our Coasts, burnt our towns, and destroyed the lives of our people.

He is at this time transporting large Armies of foreign Mercenaries to compleat the works of death, desolation and tyranny, already begun with circumstances of Cruelty and perfidy scarcely paralleled in the most barbarous ages, and totally unworthy the Head of a civilized nation.

He has constrained our fellow Citizens taken Captive on the high Seas to bear Arms against their Country, to become the executioners of their friends and Brethren, or to fall themselves by their Hands.

He has excited domestic insurrections amongst us, and has endeavoured to bring on the inhabitants of our frontiers, the merciless Indian Savages, whose known rule of warfare, is an undistinguished destruction of all ages, sexes and conditions.

In every stage of these Oppressions We have Petitioned for Redress in the most humble terms: Our repeated Petitions have been answered only by repeated injury. A Prince, whose character is thus marked by every act which may define a Tyrant, is unfit to be the ruler of a free People.

Nor have We been wanting in attentions to our British brethren. We have warned them from time to time of attempts by their legislature to extend an unwarrantable jurisdiction over us. We have reminded them of the circumstances of our emigration and settlement here. We have appealed to their native justice and magnanimity, and we have conjured them by the ties of our common kindred to disavow the usurpations, which, would inevitably interrupt our connections and correspondence. They too have been deaf to the voice of justice and of consanguinity. We must, therefore, acquiesce in the necessity, which denounces our Separation, and hold them, as we hold the rest of mankind, Enemies in War, in Peace Friends.

We, therefore, the Representatives of the United States of America, in General Congress, Assembled, appealing to the Supreme Judge of the world for the rectitude of our intentions, do, in the Name, and by Authority of the good People of these Colonies, solemnly publish and declare, That these United Colonies are, and of Right ought to be Free and Independent States; that they are Absolved from all Allegiance to the British Crown, and that all political connection between them and the State of Great Britain, is and ought to be totally dissolved; and that, as Free and Independent States, they have full Power to levy War, conclude Peace, contract Alliances, establish Commerce, and to do all other Acts and Things which Independent States may of right do. And for the support of this Declaration, with a firm reliance on the protection of divine Providence, we mutually pledge to each other our Lives, our Fortunes and our sacred Honor.

The Constitution of the United States of America

We the People of the United States, in Order to form a more perfect Union, establish Justice, insure domestic Tranquility, provide for the common defence, promote the general Welfare, and secure the Blessings of Liberty to ourselves and our Posterity, do ordain and establish this Constitution for the United States of America.

Article I

SECTION 1 All legislative Powers herein granted shall be vested in a Congress of the United States, which shall consist of a Senate and House of Representatives.

SECTION 2 The House of Representatives shall be composed of Members chosen every second Year by the People of the several States, and the Electors in each State shall have the Qualifications requisite for Electors of the most numerous Branch of the State Legislature.

No Person shall be a Representative who shall not have attained to the Age of twenty five Years, and been seven Years a Citizen of the United States, and who shall not, when elected, be an Inhabitant of that State in which he shall be chosen.

Representatives and direct Taxes[1] shall be apportioned among the several States which may be included within this Union, according to their respective Numbers, which shall be determined by adding to the whole Number of free Persons, including those bound to Service for a Term of Years, and excluding Indians not taxed, three fifths of all other Persons.[2] The actual Enumeration shall be made within three Years after the first Meeting of the Congress of the United States, and within every subsequent Term of ten Years, in such Manner as they shall by Law direct. The Number of Representatives shall not exceed one for every thirty Thousand, but each State shall have at Least one Representative; and until such enumeration shall be made, the State of New Hampshire shall be entitled to chuse three; Massachusetts eight; Rhode Island and Providence Plantations one; Connecticut five; New York six; New Jersey four; Pennsylvania eight; Delaware one; Maryland six; Virginia ten; North Carolina five; South Carolina five; and Georgia three.

When vacancies happen in the Representation from any State, the Executive Authority thereof shall issue Writs of Election to fill such Vacancies.

The House of Representatives shall chuse their Speaker and other Officers; and shall have the sole Power of Impeachment.

SECTION 3 The Senate of the United States shall be composed of two Senators from each State, chosen by the Legislature thereof, for six Years; and each Senator shall have one Vote.[3]

Immediately after they shall be assembled in Consequence of the first Election, they shall be divided as equally as may be into three Classes. The Seats of the Senators of the first Class shall be vacated at the Expiration of the second Year, of the second Class at the Expiration of the fourth Year, and of the third Class at the Expiration of the sixth Year, so that one third may be chosen every second Year; and if Vacancies happen by Resignation, or otherwise, during the Recess of the Legislature of any State, the Executive thereof may make temporary Appointments until the next Meeting of the Legislature, which shall then fill such Vacancies.[4]

No Person shall be a Senator who shall not have attained to the Age of thirty Years, and been nine Years a Citizen of the United States, and who shall not, when elected, be an Inhabitant of that State for which he shall be chosen.

The Vice President of the United States shall be President of the Senate, but shall have no Vote, unless they be equally divided.

The Senate shall chuse their other Officers, and also a President pro tempore, in the Absence of the Vice President, or when he shall exercise the Office of President of the United States.

The Senate shall have the sole Power to try all Impeachments. When sitting for that Purpose, they shall be on Oath or Affirmation. When the President of the United States is tried, the Chief Justice shall preside: And no Person shall be convicted without the Concurrence of two thirds of the Members present.

Judgment in Cases of Impeachment shall not extend further than to removal from Office, and disqualification to hold and enjoy any Office of honor, Trust or Profit under the United States: but the Party convicted shall nevertheless be liable and subject to Indictment, Trial, Judgment and Punishment, according to Law.

SECTION 4 The Times, Places and Manner of holding Elections for Senators and Representatives, shall be prescribed in each State by the Legislature thereof, but the Congress may at any time by Law make or alter such Regulation, except as to the Places of chusing Senators.

The Congress shall assemble at least once in every Year, and such Meeting shall be on the first Monday in December, unless they shall by Law appoint a different Day.[5]

SECTION 5 Each House shall be the Judge of the Elections, Returns and Qualifications of its own Members, and a Majority of each shall constitute a Quorum to do Business; but a smaller Number may adjourn from day to day, and

Text is from the engrossed copy in the National Archives. Original spelling, capitalization, and punctuation have been retained.

[1]Modified by the Sixteenth Amendment.

[2]Replaced by the Fourteenth Amendment.

[3]Superseded by the Seventeenth Amendment.

[4]Modified by the Seventeenth Amendment.

[5]Superseded by the Twentieth Amendment.

may be authorized to compel the Attendance of absent Members, in such Manner, and under such Penalties as each House may provide.

Each House may determine the Rules of its Proceedings, punish its Members for disorderly Behaviour, and, with the Concurrence of two thirds, expel a Member.

Each House shall keep a Journal of its Proceedings, and from time to time publish the same, excepting such Parts as may in their Judgment require Secrecy; and the Yeas and Nays of the Members of either House on any question shall, at the Desire of one fifth of those Present, be entered on the Journal.

Neither House, during the Session of Congress, shall, without the Consent of the other, adjourn for more than three days, nor to any other Place than that in which the two Houses shall be sitting.

SECTION 6 The Senators and Representatives shall receive a Compensation for their Services, to be ascertained by Law, and paid out of the Treasury of the United States. They shall in all Cases, except Treason, Felony and Breach of the Peace, be privileged from Arrest during their Attendance at the Session of their respective Houses, and in going to and returning from the same; and for any Speech or Debate in either House, they shall not be questioned in any other Place.

No Senator or Representative shall, during the Time for which he was elected, be appointed to any civil Office under the Authority of the United States, which shall have been created, or the Emoluments whereof shall have been encreased during such time; and no Person holding any Office under the United States, shall be a Member of either House during his Continuance in Office.

SECTION 7 All Bills for raising Revenue shall originate in the House of Representatives; but the Senate may propose or concur with Amendments as on other Bills.

Every Bill which shall have passed the House of Representatives and the Senate shall, before it become a Law, be presented to the President of the United States; If he approve he shall sign it, but if not he shall return it, with his Objections to that House in which it shall have originated, who shall enter the Objections at large on their Journal, and proceed to reconsider it. If after such Reconsideration two thirds of that House shall agree to pass the Bill, it shall be sent, together with the Objections, to the other House, by which it shall likewise be reconsidered, and if approved by two thirds of that House, it shall become a Law. But in all such Cases the Votes of both Houses shall be determined by yeas and Nays, and the Names of the Persons voting for and against the Bill shall be entered on the Journal of each House respectively. If any Bill shall not be returned by the President within ten Days (Sundays excepted) after it shall have been presented to him, the Same shall be a Law, in like Manner as if he had signed it, unless the Congress by their Adjournment prevent its Return, in which Case it shall not be a Law.

Every Order, Resolution, or Vote to which the Concurrence of the Senate and House of Representatives may be necessary (except on a question of Adjournment) shall be presented to the President of the United States; and before the Same shall take Effect, shall be approved by him, or being disapproved by him shall be repassed by two thirds of the Senate and House of Representatives, according to the Rules and Limitations prescribed in the Case of a Bill.

SECTION 8 The Congress shall have power To lay and collect Taxes, Duties, Imposts and Excises, to pay the Debts and provide for the common Defence and general Welfare of the United States; but all Duties, Imposts and Excises shall be uniform throughout the United States;

To borrow Money on the credit of the United States;

To regulate Commerce with foreign Nations, and among the several States, and with the Indian Tribes;

To establish an uniform Rule of Naturalization, and uniform Laws on the subject of Bankruptcies throughout the United States;

To coin Money, regulate the Value thereof, and of foreign Coin, and fix the Standard of Weights and Measures;

To provide for the Punishment of counterfeiting the Securities and current Coin of the United States;

To establish Post Offices and post Roads;

To promote the Progress of Science and useful Arts, by securing for limited Times to Authors and Inventors the exclusive Right to their respective Writings and Discoveries;

To constitute Tribunals inferior to the supreme Court;

To define and punish Piracies and Felonies committed on the high Seas, and Offences against the Law of Nations;

To declare War, grant Letters of Marque and Reprisal, and make Rules concerning Captures on Land and Water;

To raise and support Armies, but no Appropriation of Money to that Use shall be for a longer Term than two Years;

To provide and maintain a Navy;

To make Rules for the Government and Regulation of the land and naval Forces;

To provide for calling forth the Militia to execute the Laws of the Union, suppress Insurrections and repel Invasions;

To provide for organizing, arming, and disciplining, the Militia, and for governing such Part of them as may be employed in the Service of the United States, reserving to the States respectively, the Appointment of the Officers, and the Authority of training the Militia according to the discipline prescribed by Congress;

To exercise exclusive Legislation in all Cases whatsoever, over such District (not exceeding ten Miles square) as may, by Cession of particular States, and the Acceptance of Congress, become the Seat of the Government of the United States, and to exercise like Authority over all Places purchased by the Consent of the Legislature of the State in which the Same shall be, for the Erection of Forts, Magazines, Arsenals, dock-Yards, and other needful Buildings;—And

To make all Laws which shall be necessary and proper for carrying into Execution the foregoing Powers, and all other Powers vested by this Constitution in the Government of the United States, or in any Department or Officer thereof.

SECTION 9 The Migration or Importation of such Persons as any of the States now existing shall think proper to admit, shall not be prohibited by the Congress prior to the Year one thousand eight hundred and eight, but a Tax or duty may be imposed on such Importation, not exceeding ten dollars for each Person.

The Privilege of the Writ of Habeas Corpus shall not be suspended, unless when in Cases of Rebellion or Invasion the public Safety may require it.

No Bill of Attainder or ex post facto Law shall be passed.

No Capitation, or other direct, Tax shall be laid, unless in Proportion to the Census or Enumeration herein before directed to be taken.

No Tax or Duty shall be laid on Articles exported from any State.

No Preference shall be given by any Regulation of Commerce or Revenue to the Ports of one State over those of another: nor shall Vessels bound to, or from, one State, be obliged to enter, clear, or pay Duties in another.

No Money shall be drawn from the Treasury, but in Consequence of Appropriations made by Law, and a regular Statement and Account of the Receipts and Expenditures of all public Money shall be published from time to time.

No Title of Nobility shall be granted by the United States: And no Person holding any Office of Profit or Trust under them, shall, without the Consent of the Congress, accept of any present, Emolument, Office, or Title, of any kind whatever, from any King, Prince, or foreign State.

SECTION 10 No State shall enter into any Treaty, Alliance, or Confederation; grant Letters of Marque and Reprisal; coin Money; emit Bills of Credit; make any Thing but gold and silver Coin a Tender in Payment of Debts; pass any Bill of Attainder, ex post facto Law, or Law impairing the Obligation of Contracts, or grant any Title of Nobility.

No State shall, without the Consent of the Congress, lay any Imposts or Duties on Imports or Exports, except what may be absolutely necessary for executing its inspection Laws: and the net Produce of all Duties and Imposts, laid by any State on Imports or Exports, shall be for the Use of the Treasury of the United States; and all such Laws shall be subject to the Revision and Controul of the Congress.

No State shall, without the Consent of Congress, lay any Duty of Tonnage, keep Troops, or Ships of War in time of Peace, enter into any Agreement or Compact with another State, or with a foreign Power, or engage in War, unless actually invaded, or in such imminent Danger as will not admit of delay.

Article II

SECTION 1 The executive Power shall be vested in a President of the United States of America. He shall hold his Office during the Term of four Years, and, together with the Vice President, chosen for the same Term, be elected, as follows:

Each State shall appoint, in such Manner as the Legislature thereof may direct, a Number of Electors, equal to the whole Number of Senators and Representatives to which the State may be entitled in the Congress: but no Senator or Representative, or Person holding an Office of Trust or Profit under the United States, shall be appointed an Elector.

The Electors shall meet in their respective States, and vote by Ballot for two Persons, of whom one at least shall not be an Inhabitant of the same State with themselves. And they shall make a List of all the Persons voted for, and of the Number of Votes for each; which List they shall sign and certify, and transmit sealed to the Seat of the Government of the United States, directed to the President of the Senate. The President of the Senate shall, in the Presence of the Senate and House of Representatives, open all the Certificates, and the Votes shall then be counted. The Person having the greatest Number of Votes shall be the President, if such Number be a Majority of the whole Number of Electors appointed; and if there be more than one who have such Majority, and have an equal Number of Votes, then the House of Representatives shall immediately chuse by Ballot one of them for President; and if no Person have a Majority, then from the five highest on the List the said House shall in like Manner chuse the President. But in chusing the President, the Votes shall be taken by States, the Representation from each State having one Vote; A quorum for this Purpose shall consist of a Member or Members from two thirds of the States, and a Majority of all the States shall be necessary to a Choice. In every Case, after the Choice of the President, the Person having the greatest Number of Votes of the Electors shall be the Vice President. But if there should remain two or more who have equal Votes, the Senate shall chuse from them by Ballot the Vice President.[6]

The Congress may determine the Time of chusing the Electors, and the Day on which they shall give their Votes; which Day shall be the same throughout the United States.

No Person except a natural born Citizen, or a Citizen of the United States, at the time of the Adoption of this Constitution, shall be eligible to the Office of President, neither shall any Person be eligible to that Office who shall not have attained to the Age of thirty five Years, and been fourteen Years a Resident within the United States.

In Case of the Removal of the President from Office, or of his Death, Resignation, or Inability to discharge the Powers and Duties of the said Office, the Same shall devolve on the Vice President, and the Congress may by Law provide for the Case of Removal, Death, Resignation or Inability, both of the President and Vice President, declaring what Officer shall then act as President, and such Officer shall act accordingly, until the Disability be removed, or a President shall be elected.[7]

The President shall, at stated Times, receive for his Services, a Compensation, which shall neither be encreased nor diminished during the Period for which he shall have been elected, and he shall not receive within that Period any other Emolument from the United States, or any of them.

Before he enter on the Execution of his Office, he shall take the following Oath or Affirmation:—"I do solemnly swear (or affirm) that I will faithfully execute the Office of President of the United States, and will to the best of my Ability, preserve, protect and defend the Constitution of the United States."

---

[6]Superseded by the Twelfth Amendment.
[7]Modified by the Twenty-fifth Amendment.

SECTION 2 The President shall be Commander in Chief of the Army and Navy of the United States, and of the Militia of the several States, when called into the actual Service of the United States; he may require the Opinion, in writing, of the principal Officer in each of the executive Departments, upon any Subject relating to the Duties of their respective Offices, and he shall have Power to grant Reprieves and Pardons for Offences against the United States, except in Cases of Impeachment.

He shall have Power, by and with the Advice and Consent of the Senate, to make Treaties, provided two thirds of the Senators present concur; and he shall nominate, and by and with the Advice and Consent of the Senate, shall appoint Ambassadors, other public Ministers and Consuls, Judges of the supreme Court, and all other Officers of the United States, whose Appointments are not herein otherwise provided for, and which shall be established by Law; but the Congress may by Law vest the Appointment of such inferior Officers, as they think proper, in the President alone, in the Courts of Law, or in the Heads of Departments.

The President shall have Power to fill up all Vacancies that may happen during the Recess of the Senate, by granting Commissions which shall expire at the End of their next Session.

SECTION 3 He shall from time to time give the Congress Information of the State of the Union, and recommend to their Consideration such Measures as he shall judge necessary and expedient; he may, on extraordinary Occasions, convene both Houses, or either of them, and in Case of Disagreement between them, with Respect to the Time of Adjournment, he may adjourn them to such Time as he shall think proper; he shall receive Ambassadors and other public Ministers; he shall take Care that the Laws be faithfully executed, and shall Commission all the Officers of the United States.

SECTION 4 The President, Vice President and all civil Officers of the United States, shall be removed from Office on Impeachment for, and Conviction of, Treason, Bribery, or other high Crimes and Misdemeanors.

Article III

SECTION 1 The judicial Power of the United States, shall be vested in one supreme Court, and in such inferior Courts as the Congress may from time to time ordain and establish. The Judges, both of the supreme and inferior Courts, shall hold their Offices during good Behaviour, and shall, at stated Times, receive for their Services, a Compensation, which shall not be diminished during their Continuance in Office.

SECTION 2 The judicial Power shall extend to all Cases, in Law and Equity, arising under this Constitution, the Laws of the United States, and Treaties made, or which shall be made, under their Authority;—to all Cases affecting Ambassadors, other public Ministers and Consuls;—to all Cases of admiralty and maritime Jurisdiction;—to Controversies to which the United States shall be a Party;—to Controversies between two or more States;—between a State and Citizens of another State;[8]—between Citizens of different States,—between Citizens of the same State claiming Lands under Grants of different States, and between a State, or the Citizens thereof, and foreign States, Citizens or Subjects.

In all Cases affecting Ambassadors, other public Ministers and Consuls, and those in which a State shall be Party, the supreme Court shall have original Jurisdiction. In all the other Cases before mentioned, the supreme Court shall have appellate Jurisdiction, both as to Law and Fact, with such Exceptions, and under such Regulations as the Congress shall make.

The Trial of all Crimes, except in Cases of Impeachment, shall be by Jury; and such Trial shall be held in the State where the said Crimes shall have been committed; but when not committed within any State, the Trial shall be at such Place or Places as the Congress may by Law have directed.

SECTION 3 Treason against the United States, shall consist only in levying War against them, or in adhering to their Enemies, giving them Aid and Comfort. No Person shall be convicted of Treason unless on the Testimony of two Witnesses to the same overt Act, or on Confession in open Court.

The Congress shall have Power to declare the Punishment of Treason, but no Attainder of Treason shall work Corruption of Blood, or Forfeiture except during the Life of the Person attainted.

Article IV

SECTION 1 Full Faith and Credit shall be given in each State to the public Acts, Records, and judicial Proceedings of every other State. And the Congress may by general Laws prescribe the Manner in which such Acts, Records and Proceedings shall be proved, and the Effect thereof.

SECTION 2 The Citizens of each State shall be entitled to all Privileges and Immunities of Citizens in the several States.

A Person charged in any State with Treason, Felony, or other Crime, who shall flee from Justice, and be found in another State, shall on Demand of the executive Authority of the State from which he fled, be delivered up, to be removed to the State having Jurisdiction of the Crime.

No Person held to Service or Labour in one State, under the Laws thereof, escaping into another, shall, in Consequence of any Law or Regulation therein, be discharged from such Service or Labour, but shall be delivered up on Claim of the Party to whom such Service or Labour may be due.

SECTION 3 New States may be admitted by the Congress into this Union; but no new State shall be formed or erected within the Jurisdiction of any other State, nor any State be formed by the Junction of two or more States, or Parts of

[8]Modified by the Eleventh Amendment.

States, without the Consent of the Legislatures of the States concerned as well as of the Congress.

The Congress shall have Power to dispose of and make all needful Rules and Regulations respecting the Territory or other Property belonging to the United States; and nothing in this Constitution shall be so construed as to Prejudice any Claims of the United States, or of any particular State.

SECTION 4 The United States shall guarantee to every State in this Union a Republican Form of Government, and shall protect each of them against Invasion; and on Application of the Legislature, or of the Executive (when the Legislature cannot be convened) against domestic Violence.

Article V

The Congress, whenever two thirds of both Houses shall deem it necessary, shall propose Amendments to this Constitution, or, on the Application of the Legislatures of two thirds of the several States, shall call a Convention for proposing Amendments, which, in either Case, shall be valid to all Intents and Purposes, as Part of this Constitution, when ratified by the Legislatures of three fourths of the several States, or by Conventions in three fourths thereof, as the one or the other Mode of Ratification may be proposed by the Congress; Provided that no Amendment which may be made prior to the Year One thousand eight hundred and eight shall in any Manner affect the first and fourth Clauses in the Ninth Section of the first Article; and that no State, without its Consent, shall be deprived of its equal Suffrage in the Senate.

Article VI

All Debts contracted and Engagements entered into, before the Adoption of this Constitution, shall be as valid against the United States under this Constitution, as under the Confederation.

This Constitution, and the Laws of the United States which shall be made in Pursuance thereof; and all Treaties made, or which shall be made, under the Authority of the United States, shall be the supreme Law of the Land; and the Judges in every State shall be bound thereby, any Thing in the Constitution or Laws of any State to the Contrary notwithstanding.

The Senators and Representatives before mentioned, and the Members of the several State Legislatures, and all executive and judicial Officers, both of the United States and of the several States, shall be bound by Oath or Affirmation, to support this Constitution; but no religious Test shall ever be required as a Qualification to any Office or public Trust under the United States.

Article VII

The Ratification of the Conventions of nine States, shall be sufficient for the Establishment of this Constitution between the States so ratifying the Same.

Done in Convention by the Unanimous Consent of the States present the Seventeenth Day of September in the Year of our Lord one thousand seven hundred and Eighty seven and of the Independence of the United States of America the Twelfth. In witness whereof We have hereunto subscribed our Names,

Articles in Addition to, and Amendment of, the Constitution of the United States of America, Proposed by Congress, and Ratified by the Legislatures of the Several States, Pursuant to the Fifth Article of the Original Constitution.

Amendment I[9]

Congress shall make no law respecting an establishment of religion, or prohibiting the free exercise there-of; or abridging the freedom of speech, or of the press; or the right of the people peaceably to assemble, and to petition the Government for a redress of grievances.

Amendment II

A well regulated Militia, being necessary to the security of a free State, the right of the people to keep and bear Arms shall not be infringed.

Amendment III

No Soldier shall, in time of peace, be quartered in any house, without the consent of the Owner, nor in time of war, but in a manner to be prescribed by law.

Amendment IV

The right of the people to be secure in their persons, houses, papers, and effects, against unreasonable searches and seizures, shall not be violated, and no Warrants shall issue, but upon probable cause, supported by Oath or affirmation, and particularly describing the place to be searched, and the persons or things to be seized.

Amendment V

No person shall be held to answer for a capital or otherwise infamous crime, unless on a presentment or indictment of a Grand Jury, except in cases arising in the land or naval forces, or in the Militia, when in actual service in time of War or public danger; nor shall any person be subject for the same offence to be twice put in jeopardy of life or limb; nor shall be compelled in any criminal case to be a witness against himself, nor be deprived of life, liberty, or property, without due process of law; nor shall private property be taken for public use, without just compensation.

Amendment VI

In all criminal prosecutions, the accused shall enjoy the right to a speedy and public trial, by an impartial jury of the State and district wherein the crime shall have been committed, which district shall have been previously ascertained by law, and to be informed of the nature and cause of the accusation; to be confronted with the witnesses against

[9]The first ten amendments were passed by Congress September 25, 1789. They were ratified by three-fourths of the states December 15, 1791.

him; to have compulsory process for obtaining witnesses in his favor, and to have the Assistance of Counsel for his defence.

Amendment VII

In suits at common law, where the value in controversy shall exceed twenty dollars, the right of trial by jury shall be preserved, and no fact tried by a jury, shall be otherwise reexamined in any Court of the United States, than according to the rules of the common law.

Amendment VIII

Excessive bail shall not be required, nor excessive fines imposed, nor cruel and unusual punishments inflicted.

Amendment IX

The enumeration in the Constitution, of certain rights, shall not be construed to deny or disparage others retained by the people.

Amendment X

The powers not delegated to the United States by the Constitution; nor prohibited by it to the States, are reserved to the States respectively, or to the people.

Amendment XI[10]

The Judicial power of the United States shall not be construed to extend to any suit in law or equity, commenced or prosecuted against one of the United States by Citizens of another State, or by Citizens or Subjects of any Foreign State.

Amendment XII[11]

The Electors shall meet in their respective States and vote by ballot for President and Vice-President, one of whom, at least, shall not be an inhabitant of the same State with themselves; they shall name in their ballots the person voted for as President, and in distinct ballots the person voted for as Vice-President, and they shall make distinct lists of all persons voted for as President, and of all persons voted for as Vice-President, and of the number of votes for each, which lists they shall sign and certify, and transmit sealed to the seat of the government of the United States, directed to the President of the Senate;—The President of the Senate shall, in the presence of the Senate and House of Representatives, open all the certificates and the votes shall then be counted;—The person having the greatest number of votes for President, shall be the President, if such number be a majority of the whole number of Electors appointed; and if no person have such majority, then from the persons having the highest numbers not exceeding three on the list of those voted for as President, the House of Representatives shall choose immediately, by ballot, the President. But in choosing the President, the votes shall be taken by states, the representation from each state having one vote; a quorum for this purpose shall consist of a member or members from two-thirds of the states, and a majority of all the states shall be necessary to a choice. And if the House of Representatives shall not choose a President whenever the right of choice shall devolve upon them, before the fourth day of March next following, then the Vice-President shall act as President, as in the case of the death or other constitutional disability of the President.—The person having the greatest number of votes as Vice-President, shall be the Vice-President, if such number be a majority of the whole number of Electors appointed, and if no person have a majority, then from the two highest numbers on the list, the Senate shall choose the Vice-President; a quorum for the purpose shall consist of two-thirds of the whole number of Senators, and a majority of the whole number shall be necessary to a choice. But no person constitutionally ineligible to the office of President shall be eligible to that of Vice-President of the United States.

Amendment XIII[12]

SECTION 1 Neither slavery nor involuntary servitude, except as a punishment for crime whereof the party shall have been duly convicted, shall exist within the United States, or any place subject to their jurisdiction.

SECTION 2 Congress shall have power to enforce this article by appropriate legislation.

Amendment XIV[13]

SECTION 1 All persons born or naturalized in the United States, and subject to the jurisdiction thereof, are citizens of the United States and of the State wherein they reside. No State shall make or enforce any law which shall abridge the privileges or immunities of citizens of the United States; nor shall any State deprive any person of life, liberty, or property, without due process of law; nor deny to any person within its jurisdiction the equal protection of the laws.

SECTION 2 Representatives shall be apportioned among the several States according to their respective numbers, counting the whole number of persons in each State, excluding Indians not taxed. But when the right to vote at any election for the choice of electors for President and Vice-President of the United States, Representatives in Congress, the Executive and Judicial officers of a State, or the members of the Legislature thereof, is denied to any of the male inhabitants of such State, being twenty-one years of age, and citizens of the United States, or in any way abridged, except for participation in rebellion, or other crime, the basis of representation therein shall be reduced in the proportion which the number of such male citizens shall bear to the whole number of male citizens twenty-one years of age in such State.

[10]Passed March 4, 1794. Ratified January 23, 1795.

[11]Passed December 9, 1803. Ratified June 15, 1804.

[12]Passed January 31, 1865. Ratified December 6, 1865.

[13]Passed June 13, 1866. Ratified July 9, 1868.

SECTION 3 No person shall be a Senator or Representative in Congress, or elector of President and Vice-President, or hold any office, civil or military, under the United States, or under any State, who, having previously taken an oath, as a member of Congress, or as an officer of the United States, or as a member of any State legislature, or as an executive or judicial officer of any State, to support the Constitution of the United States, shall have engaged in insurrection or rebellion against the same, or given aid or comfort to the enemies thereof. But Congress may by a vote of two-thirds of each House, remove such disability.

SECTION 4 The validity of the public debt of the United States, authorized by law, including debts incurred for payment of pensions and bounties for services in suppressing insurrection or rebellion, shall not be questioned. But neither the United States nor any State shall assume or pay any debt or obligation incurred in aid of insurrection or rebellion against the United States, or any claim for the loss or emancipation of any slave; but all such debts, obligations, and claims shall be held illegal and void.

SECTION 5 The Congress shall have the power to enforce, by appropriate legislation, the provisions of this article.

Amendment XV[14]

SECTION 1 The right of citizens of the United States to vote shall not be denied or abridged by the United States or by any State on account of race, color, or previous conditions of servitude—

SECTION 2 The Congress shall have power to enforce this article by appropriate legislation.

Amendment XVI[15]

The Congress shall have power to lay and collect taxes on incomes, from whatever source derived, without apportionment among the several States, and without regard to any census or enumeration.

Amendment XVII[16]

The Senate of the United States shall be composed of two Senators from each State, elected by the people thereof, for six years; and each Senator shall have one vote. The electors in each State shall have the qualifications requisite for electors of the most numerous branch of the State legislatures.

When vacancies happen in the representation of any State in the Senate, the executive authority of such State shall issue writs of election to fill such vacancies: *Provided*, That the legislature of any State may empower the executive thereof to make temporary appointments until the people fill the vacancies by election as the legislature may direct.

This amendment shall not be so construed as to affect the election or term of any Senator chosen before it becomes valid as part of the Constitution.

Amendment XVIII[17]

SECTION 1 After one year from the ratification of this article the manufacture, sale, or transportation of intoxicating liquors within, the importation thereof into, or the exportation thereof from the United States and all territory subject to the jurisdiction thereof for beverage purposes is hereby prohibited.

SECTION 2 The Congress and the several States shall have concurrent power to enforce this article by appropriate legislation.

SECTION 3 This article shall be inoperative unless it shall have been ratified as an amendment to the Constitution by the legislatures of the several States, as provided in the Constitution, within seven years from the date of the submission hereof to the States by the Congress.

Amendment XIX[18]

SECTION 1 The right of citizens of the United States to vote shall not be denied or abridged by the United States or by any State on account of sex.

Congress shall have power to enforce this article by appropriate legislation.

Amendment XX[19]

SECTION 1 The terms of the President and Vice-President shall end at noon on the 20th day of January, and the terms of Senators and Representatives at noon on the 3rd day of January, of the years in which such terms would have ended if this article had not been ratified; and the terms of their successors shall then begin.

SECTION 2 The Congress shall assemble at least once in every year, and such meeting shall begin at noon on the 3rd day of January, unless they shall by law appoint a different day.

SECTION 3 If, at the time fixed for the beginning of the term of the President, the President elect shall have died, the Vice-President elect shall become President. If a President shall not have been chosen before the time fixed for the beginning of his term, or if the President elect shall have failed to qualify, then the Vice-President elect shall act as President until a President shall have qualified; and the Congress may by law provide for the case wherein neither a President elect nor a Vice-President elect shall have qualified, declaring who shall then act as President, or the manner in which one who is to act shall be selected,

[14] Passed February 26, 1869. Ratified February 2, 1870.
[15] Passed July 12, 1909. Ratified February 3, 1913.
[16] Passed May 13, 1912. Ratified April 8, 1913.
[17] Passed December 18, 1917. Ratified January 16, 1919.
[18] Passed June 4, 1919. Ratified August 18, 1920.
[19] Passed March 2, 1932. Ratified January 23, 1933.

and such person shall act accordingly until a President or Vice-President shall have qualified.

SECTION 4 The Congress may by law provide for the case of the death of any of the persons from whom the House of Representatives may choose a President whenever the right of choice shall have devolved upon them, and for the case of the death of any of the persons from whom the Senate may choose a Vice-President whenever the right of choice shall have devolved upon them.

SECTION 5 Sections 1 and 2 shall take effect on the 15th day of October following the ratification of this article.

SECTION 6 This article shall be inoperative unless it shall have been ratified as an amendment to the Constitution by the legislatures of three-fourths of the several States within seven years from the date of its submission.

Amendment XXI[20]

SECTION 1 The eighteenth article of amendment to the Constitution of the United States is hereby repealed.

SECTION 2 The transportation or importation into any State, Territory, or possession of the United States for delivery or use therein of intoxicating liquors, in violation of the laws thereof, is hereby prohibited.

SECTION 3 This article shall be inoperative unless it shall have been ratified as an amendment to the Constitution by conventions in the several States, as provided in the Constitution, within seven years from the date of the submission hereof to the States by the Congress.

Amendment XXII[21]

No person shall be elected to the office of the President more than twice, and no person who has held the office of President, or acted as President, for more than two years of a term to which some other person was elected President shall be elected to the office of the President more than once.

But this Article shall not apply to any person holding the office of President when this Article was proposed by the Congress, and shall not prevent any person who may be holding the office of President, or acting as President, during the term within which this Article becomes operative from holding the office of President or acting as President during the remainder of such term.

Amendment XXIII[22]

SECTION 1 The District constituting the seat of Government of the United States shall appoint in such manner as the Congress may direct:

A number of electors of President and Vice President equal to the whole number of Senators and Representatives in Congress to which the District would be entitled if it were a State, but in no event more than the least populous State; they shall be in addition to those appointed by the States, but they shall be considered, for the purposes of the election of President and Vice President, to be electors appointed by the State; and they shall meet in the District and perform such duties as provided by the twelfth article of amendment.

SECTION 2 The Congress shall have power to enforce this article by appropriate legislation.

Amendment XXIV[23]

SECTION 1 The right of citizens of the United States to vote in any primary or other election for President or Vice President, or for Senator or Representative in Congress, shall not be denied or abridged by the United States or any State by reason of failure to pay any poll tax or other tax.

SECTION 2 The Congress shall have power to enforce this article by appropriate legislation.

Amendment XXV[24]

SECTION 1 In case of the removal of the President from office or of his death or resignation, the Vice President shall become President.

SECTION 2 Whenever there is a vacancy in the office of the Vice President, the President shall nominate a Vice President who shall take office upon confirmation by a majority vote of both Houses of Congress.

SECTION 3 Whenever the President transmits to the President pro tempore of the Senate and the Speaker of the House of Representatives his written declaration that he is unable to discharge the powers and duties of his office, and until he transmits them a written declaration to the contrary, such powers and duties shall be discharged by the Vice President as Acting President.

SECTION 4 Whenever the Vice President and a majority of either the principal officers of the executive department or of such other body as Congress may by law provide, transmit to the President pro tempore of the Senate and the Speaker of the House of Representatives their written declaration that the President is unable to discharge the powers and duties of his office, the Vice President shall immediately assume the powers and duties of the office of Acting President.

Thereafter, when the President transmits to the President pro tempore of the Senate and the Speaker of the House of Representatives his written declaration that no inability exists, he shall resume the powers and duties of his office unless the Vice President and a majority of either the principal officers of the executive department or of

[20]Passed February 20, 1933. Ratified Decembet 5, 1933.

[21]Passed March 12, 1947. Ratified March 1, 1951.

[22]Passed June 16, 1960. Ratified April 3, 1961.

[23]Passed August 27, 1962. Ratified January 23, 1964.

[24]Passed July 6, 1965. Ratified February 11, 1967.

such other body as Congress may by law provide, transmit within four days to the President pro tempore of the Senate and the Speaker of the House of Representatives their written declaration that the President is unable to discharge the powers and duties of his office. Thereupon Congress shall decide the issue, assembling within forty-eight hours for that purpose if not in session. If the Congress, within twenty-one days after receipt of the latter written declaration, or, if Congress is not in session, within twenty-one days after Congress is required to assemble, determines by two-thirds vote of both Houses that the President is unable to discharge the powers and duties of his office, the Vice-President shall continue to discharge the same as Acting President; otherwise, the President shall resume the powers and duties of his office.

AMENDMENT XXVI[25]

SECTION 1 The right of citizens of the United States, who are eighteen years of age or older, to vote shall not be denied or abridged by the United States or by any State on account of age.

SECTION 2 The Congress shall have power to enforce this article by appropriate legislation.

AMENDMENT XXVII[26]

No law, varying the compensation for the service of the Senators and Representatives, shall take effect, until an election of Representatives shall have intervened.

[25]Passed March 23, 1971. Ratified July 5, 1971.
[26]Passed September 25, 1789. Ratified May 7, 1992.

GLOSSARY

Ácoma Town located in New Mexico on a mesa west of the Rio Grande. When the Pueblos defended Ácoma in 1598, the Spanish killed many people, took the survivors prisoner, and destroyed the town.

Adams, John (1735–1826) First vice president (1789–1797) and second president (1797–1801) of the United States. He was a major figure during the American Revolution: he helped draft the Declaration of Independence and served on the commission to negotiate the Treaty of Paris (1783).

Adams-Onís Treaty (1819) Negotiated by John Quincy Adams, this treaty gave the United States control of Spanish Florida and the Oregon Territory, and recognized Spanish authority over southwestern territories from Texas to California.

African American soldiers Finally allowed to enlist in May 1863, African American soldiers accounted for more than one hundred eighty thousand troops and played a major role in the Union victory.

Agricultural Adjustment Act (AAA) (1933) Created under Roosevelt's New Deal program to help farmers, its purpose was to reduce production of staple crops, thereby raising farm prices and encouraging more diversified farming.

Albany Plan of Union (1754) Plan proposed to the Albany Congress of 1754 by Benjamin Franklin to unite the colonies for common defense. The Congress approved the design for an intercolonial government empowered to tax, pass laws, and supervise military defense, but the colonies and British government rejected it.

Allen, Richard (1760–1831) Reverend Allen was a former slave who founded the African Methodist Episcopal church and was a leader of the Philadelphia black community.

American Colonization Society Founded in 1816 to colonize freed slaves on land purchased in Africa and called "Liberia." Members included white slaveholders and opponents of slavery, as well as free African Americans.

American System Political program developed by Henry Clay and John C. Calhoun to strengthen the federal government and promote commerce and industry through a national bank, a strong navy, federally sponsored internal improvement projects, and protective tariffs.

Amistad Cuban slave ship on which forty-nine Africans rebelled in 1839 off the Cuban coast. The ship sailed to Long Island Sound where Spanish authorities demanded they be turned over for punishment. A group of American abolitionists, led by former President John Quincy Adams, won their freedom in 1841. The thirty-five who survived returned to Africa.

Amos 'n' Andy The most popular radio program of the Depression years, it portrayed the lives of two African American men in Harlem as interpreted by two white entertainers, Freeman Gosden and Charles Correll.

Anaconda Plan Term given to the strategy employed by the North during the Civil War in which the Confederacy would be slowly strangled by a blockade.

Anderson, Marian (1897–1993) Opera singer and human rights advocate, she performed on the steps of the Lincoln Memorial before a crowd of seventy-five thousand after being denied the use of Constitution Hall by the Daughters of the American Revolution. She helped focus national attention on the racial prejudice faced by African Americans in all facets of national life.

Andros, Sir Edmund (1637–1714) English colonial administrator in America whose attempt to unify the New England colonies under his governorship (1686–1689) was met by revolt.

annexation of Texas (1845) Incorporation of Texas into the United States as the twenty-eighth state. The Republic of Texas invited U.S. annexation following the Texas Revolution but annexation was delayed by disputes with Mexico. Annexation was hotly debated among supporters and opponents of slavery's expansion.

Anthony, Susan B. (1820–1906) Advocate of woman's suffrage and leader in the woman's rights movement along with Elizabeth Cady Stanton.

Antietam, battle of (1862) Civil War battle near Sharpsburg, Maryland, in September 1862 in which the Union Army stopped the Confederacy's drive into the North. With twenty-five thousand casualties, it was the bloodiest single-day battle of the Civil War.

Appomattox Small Virginia town where Confederate forces under Robert E. Lee surrendered to Ulysses S. Grant on April 9, 1865, generally recognized as bringing the Civil War to an end.

Armstrong, Louis (1901–1971) A trumpeter and a major innovator of jazz.

Articles of Confederation (1781) First Constitution of the United States. Adopted by the original thirteen states in 1781, it remained the supreme law until 1789.

Atlanta Compromise (1895) Speech by Booker T. Washington outlining a program for African American self-help, industrial education, and acceptance of white supremacy.

Atlantic Charter (1941) Composed during a meeting between President Franklin Roosevelt and British Prime Minister Winston Churchill, it listed eight principles for a better world, such as freedom from fear and want, self-determination for all people, and the disarming of aggressor nations. Many see the Atlantic Charter as a guiding force behind the establishment of the United Nations following World War II.

Atlantic slave trade In the 1440s Portugal initiated the trans-Atlantic trade that lasted four centuries. During that time, other European nations participated in a commerce that took more than 10 million people from Africa.

Austin, Stephen F. (1793–1836) Virginian who led efforts to settle U.S. citizens in Texas, negotiated with the Mexican and U.S. governments, commanded Texas forces in the early period of the Texas Revolution, and served as secretary of state for the Republic of Texas.

Aztecs Inhabitants of the Valley of Mexico who founded their capital, Tenochtitlán, in the early fourteenth century. Prior to the arrival of the Spanish, the Aztecs built a large empire in which they dominated many neighboring peoples. Their civilization included engineering, mathematics, art, and music.

baby boom (1946–1964) Increased numbers of births in the years after World War II.

Bacon's Rebellion (1676) Colonial revolt led by Nathaniel Bacon, in which landless freemen attacked neighboring Indians and burned Jamestown in an attempt to gain land and greater participation in the Virginia government.

Bank of North America (1781) The first bank in the United States, modeled on the Bank of England, helped to solve the wartime fiscal crisis. Instead of issuing paper currency through a land office, as farmers wanted, the bank issued money in the form of short-term loans backed by gold and silver plate.

Bank of the United States (1791–1811) National bank established as part of the system proposed by Alexander Hamilton to hold the federal government's funds and regulate state banks. Its chief purpose was to expand the money supply, thus encouraging commercial growth.

Bank War (1832–1834) Attacks by President Andrew Jackson on the Second Bank of the United States. By vetoing the renewal of the bank's charter and removing federal funds to state banks, he effectively destroyed the central bank.

Bataan Peninsula U.S. and Filipino World War II troops surrendered this peninsula in western Luzon, Philippines, to the Japanese in April 1942 after an extended siege; U.S. forces recaptured the peninsula in February 1945.

Bay of Pigs (1961) Place where fifteen hundred Cuban exiles, supported by the CIA, landed on April 17, 1961, in an unsuccessful attempt to overthrow the new Communist government of Fidel Castro.

Bell, Alexander Graham (1847–1922) His invention of the telephone in 1876 changed the nature of life in the United States.

Bell, John (1797–1869) Tennessee-born slaveholder who became the presidential candidate of the Constitutional Union Party, which was founded as a compromise party in 1860.

Bellamy, Edward (1850–1898) Reporter and novelist, the author of the popular utopian novel *Looking Backward* (1888).

Bethune, Mary McLeod (1875–1955) An educator who sought improved racial relations and educational opportunities for black Americans, she was part of the U.S. delegation to the first United Nations meeting (1945).

Bill of Rights (1791) The first ten amendments to the Constitution. These contain basic protection of the rights of individuals from abuses by the federal government, including freedom of speech, press, religion, and assembly.

bin Laden, Osama (1957–) Saudi-born Islamic radical who masterminded the September 11, 2001, terrorist attacks on the United States.

***Birth of a Nation, The* (1915)** Racist movie portrayal of the Reconstruction period in the South that depicted African Americans as ignorant and that glamorized the Ku Klux Klan.

black codes (colonial) Laws passed by colonial assemblies to define slavery and control the black population.

Black Power A movement for black racial pride in the 1960s that advocated all-black institutions, not racially integrated ones, as the best vehicles for advancing African American objectives.

Black Thursday October 29, 1929; the day the spectacular New York stock market crash began.

Bleeding Kansas Nickname given to the Kansas Territory in the wake of a number of clashes between proslavery and antislavery supporters in 1856.

blockade runners During the Civil War, ships that smuggled war supplies and imported goods into the Confederacy during the Union blockade of its coastline.

bloggers Commentators who post their views on the Internet; derived from the word *weblog*. They became influential in the political process because of the speed with which they could respond to breaking events in politics and international affairs.

Blount, William (1749–1800) Governor of the Tennessee Territory and a land speculator the Indians called "dirt king" who, after the Treaty of 1791, ignored President George Washington's guarantee to the Cherokees that they could retain their remaining lands.

Board of Trade and Plantations English government body established in 1696 to gather information and give advice about the colonies.

Bonus Army Thousands of veterans, determined to collect promised cash bonuses early, came to Washington during the summer of 1932 to listen to Congress debate the bonus proposal.

Booth, John Wilkes (1838–1865) An actor and Southern sympathizer who assassinated Abraham Lincoln on April 14, 1865.

bootleggers Enterprising individuals who moved alcohol across the border into the United States from Canada and the Caribbean during Prohibition. Their wares were sold at illegal saloons or "speakeasies" where city dwellers congregated in the evenings.

border ruffians Missouri settlers who crossed into Kansas to lend support for proslavery issues (1855).

Boss Politics Urban "political machines" that relied for their existence on the votes of the large inner-city population. The flow of money through the machine was often based on corruption.

Boston Massacre (1770) Pre-Revolutionary incident growing out of the resentment against the British troops sent to Boston to maintain order and to enforce the Townshend Act.

brain trust Group of prominent academics recruited as a source of ideas for the Franklin Roosevelt presidential campaign.

bread riots (1863) Riots in Richmond and other Southern cities, that occurred when poor women attacked the shops of merchants accused of hoarding food in order to profit from wartime inflation.

Breckinridge, John C. (1821–1875) Born in Kentucky, vice president under James Buchanan (1857–1861), and presidential candidate of the Southern wing of the Democratic Party in 1860.

***Brown v. Board of Education of Topeka* (1954)** Unanimous Supreme Court decision ruling that segregated facilities in public education were "inherently unequal" and violated the Fourteenth Amendment's guarantee of equal protection under the law. This decision overruled the long-standing "separate but equal" doctrine of *Plessy v. Ferguson*.

Brown, John (1800–1859) American abolitionist who, in 1859 with twenty-one followers, captured the U.S. arsenal at Harpers Ferry as part of an effort to liberate Southern slaves. His group was defeated, and Brown was hanged after a trial in which he won sympathy as an abolitionist martyr.

Bryan, William Jennings (1860–1925) Democratic presidential candidate in 1896, 1900, and 1908. Named secretary of state by President Wilson, he pursued world peace through arbitration treaties.

Buchanan, James (1791–1868) Fifteenth president of the United States (1857–1861). He tried to maintain a balance between proslavery and antislavery factions, but his views angered radicals in both the North and South.

Bush, George H. W. (1924–) Forty-first president of the United States (1989–1993), he was in office when the Soviet Union collapsed.

Bush, George W. (1946–) Forty-third president of the United States (2001–2009).

Calhoun, John C. (1782–1850) Vice president of the United States (1825–1832) under John Quincy Adams and Andrew Jackson. In his political philosophy he maintained that the states had the right to nullify federal legislation that they deemed unconstitutional.

Calvin, John (1509–1564) French-born Swiss Protestant theologian who broke with the Roman Catholic Church (1533) and set forth the tenets of his theology, the Reformed tradition including Puritans, Huguenots, Presbyterians, and Dutch Reformed, in *Institutes of the Christian Religion* (1536).

Camp David Accords (1978) Treaty between Egypt and Israel, brokered by President Carter at Camp David, that returned the Sinai Peninsula to Egypt in return for Egypt's recognition of the state of Israel.

Capone, Alphonse "Al" (1899–1947) Chicago gangster; devoted to gaining control of gambling, prostitution, and bootlegging.

Carnegie, Andrew (1835–1919) Scottish-born industrialist and philanthropist, he played a major role in the evolution of the U.S. steel industry.

Carter, James Earl (Jimmy) (1924–) Thirty-ninth president of the United States (1977–1981), his successes in office, including the Camp David Accords, were overshadowed by domestic worries and the seizure of American hostages at the U.S. Embassy in Iran. He was defeated by Ronald Reagan in 1980.

Castro, Fidel (1927–) Cuban revolutionary leader who overthrew dictator Fulgencio Batista in 1959 and soon after established a Communist state. Prime minister of Cuba from 1959 to 1976, he served as president of the government and First Secretary of the Communist Party from 1976 to 2008.

Catt, Carrie Chapman (1859–1947) Woman suffrage leader; president of the National American Woman Suffrage Association (1900–1906).

Census of 1790, U.S. To fulfill the constitutional requirement for a decennial census, Congress ordered a population count to provide an accurate enumeration for apportioning delegates to the House of Representatives and electoral college.

Champlain, Samuel de (1567–1635) Founder of New France (now Canada), with a temporary base at Port Royal on the Bay of Fundy in 1605 and the main settlement at Quebec on the St. Lawrence River in 1608.

***Charles River Bridge* case (1837)** Supreme Court decision that state charters for internal improvements such as bridges did not imply monopolies; marked a shift toward the definition of economic development as a public good.

Chavez, Cesar (1927–1993) Labor organizer who founded the National Farm Workers Association in 1962.

Chickamaugas Militant Cherokees who allied with Creeks and Shawnees against settlers along the frontier from Kentucky to Georgia during the 1780s and early 1790s.

Churchill, Sir Winston (1874–1965) British politician and writer. As prime minister (1940–1945 and 1951–1955) he led Great Britain through World War II. He published several books, including *The Second World War* (1948–1953), and won the 1953 Nobel Prize for literature.

Civil Works Administration (CWA) The agency tasked with creating jobs and restoring self-respect by handing out pay envelopes instead of relief checks. In reality, workers sometimes performed worthless tasks, known as "boondoggles," but much of the $1 billion budget was spent on projects of lasting value including airports and roads.

Civilian Conservation Corps (CCC) One of the New Deal's most popular programs, it took unemployed young men from the cities and put them to work on conservation projects in the country.

Clay, Henry (1777–1852) American statesman and a founder of the Whig party. He pushed the Missouri Compromise through the U.S. House of Representatives (1820) in an effort to reconcile free and slave states and served as secretary of state under John Quincy Adams (1825–1829).

Cleveland, Grover (1837–1908) Twenty-second and twenty-fourth president of the United States (1885–1889 and 1893–1897), he was the first Democrat elected to the presidency after the Civil War.

climate change Term used by scientists to describe the result of the global warming caused by human activity, especially the burning of fossil fuels.

Clinton, William Jefferson ("Bill") (1946–) Forty-second president of the United States (1993–2001). He secured passage of the North American Free Trade Agreement (NAFTA) in 1993 and welfare reform in 1996. Impeached for perjury and obstruction of justice in 1998, he was acquitted by the Senate in 1999.

Coercive Acts (1774) Passed by the British Parliament in 1774 in response to the Boston Tea Party, the acts closed the port of Boston, limited the power of town meetings, expanded the governor's control over the courts, and permitted quartering of British troops in private buildings.

Cold War State of intense geopolitical rivalry, such as existed between the United States and the Soviet Union following World War II, that stopped short of full-scale military conflict.

Columbus, Christopher (1451–1506) Italian mariner who sailed for Spain in 1492 in search of a western route to Asia. He located San Salvador in the West Indies, opening the Americas to European exploration and colonization.

***Common Sense* (1776)** Published by Thomas Paine in January 1776, Common Sense convinced the American public of the need for independence.

Compromise of 1850 Congressional compromise intended to balance demands among slave and free states. It admitted California as a free state but left the question of slavery open in other new territories; abolished the slave trade in Washington, D.C., but kept slavery legal there; declared that Congress had no power to regulate the interstate slave trade; and created a stronger fugitive slave law.

Conscription Act (1863) Union act instituting military draft; service could be avoided by hiring a substitute or paying a fee.

Constitutional Convention (1787) Fifty-five delegates met in

Philadelphia in May 1787 to reform the U.S. government. They chose to draft a new constitution rather than revise the Articles of Confederation.

containment U.S. national security doctrine during the Cold War. Attributed to State Department officer George Kennan, containment came to define America's political-military strategy for confronting Soviet expansion.

contrabands During the Civil War, term for slaves who made their way to Union lines. By defining the refugees as "contrabands of war," a term used to describe property that could be used in a war effort and was thus subject to confiscation, Union leaders justified the decision not to return escaped slaves to their masters.

Contras Nicaraguan military force trained and financed by the United States that opposed the socialist Nicaraguan government led by the Sandinista party.

Convention of 1800 Negotiated with France by a three-man commission appointed by President John Adams, the convention echoed provisions of the 1778 commercial treaty but voided the defensive alliance, thus eliminating the French claim to U.S. support against Great Britain.

Copperheads Derogatory term used by some Republicans to refer to Peace Democrats, implying that they were traitors to the Union. Peace Democrats thought that the war was a failure and should be abandoned.

Cortés, Hernán (1485–1547) Spanish explorer who conquered the Aztecs initially in 1519, retreated when they rebelled, then defeated them again, aided by a smallpox epidemic, in 1521.

Cotton South Southeastern United States; became a major cotton-producing region following the invention of the cotton gin in 1793 and the eviction of Native Americans from their lands in the decades after 1815. The spread of cotton cultivation led to the development of a vast interstate slave trade.

Crane, Stephen (1871–1900) American naturalist writer, author of *Maggie: A Girl of the Streets* (1893) and *The Red Badge of Courage* (1895).

Crazy Horse (1842?–1877) Native American Sioux leader who defeated George Custer in battle.

Creole Slaving ship sailing from Virginia to New Orleans in 1841 when it was seized by captives and sailed to the Bahamas, a British colony. Britain, which had recently emancipated its own slaves, gave sanctuary to the slaves.

Custer, George Armstrong (1839–1876) Lieutenant colonel famous for his defeat at Little Big Horn by the Sioux Indians.

Dale's Laws (1611) Governor Thomas Dale of Jamestown in 1611 established his "Laws Divine, Morall and Martiall" to bring the colony under control. The harsh punishments became a scandal in England and discouraged emigration.

Davis, Jefferson (1808–1889) United States senator, secretary of war, and then president of the Confederacy (1861–1865). He was captured by Union soldiers in 1865 and imprisoned for two years. Although he was indicted for treason (1866), he was never prosecuted.

Dawes Severalty Act (1887) Congressional legislation that distributed land to the Indians so that it could eventually be sold to whites.

Declaration of Independence (1776) The document, drafted primarily by Thomas Jefferson, that declared the independence of the thirteen mainland colonies from Great Britain and enumerated their reasons for separating.

détente An easing of tensions among countries, which usually leads to increased economic, diplomatic, and other types of contacts between former rivals.

Dix, Dorothea (1802–1887) American philanthropist, reformer, and educator who took charge of nurses for the United States during the Civil War.

dollar diplomacy Term for Secretary of State Philander C. Knox's foreign policy under President Taft, which focused on expanding American investments abroad, especially in Latin America and China.

Dominion of New England In an effort to centralize the colonies and create consistent laws and political structures, James II combined Massachusetts, New Hampshire, Maine, Plymouth, Rhode Island, Connecticut, New York, and New Jersey into the Dominion of New England.

domino theory A theory that if one nation comes under Communist control, neighboring nations will soon follow.

Douglas, Stephen A. (1813–1861) American politician who served as U.S. representative (1843–1847) and senator (1847–1861) from Illinois. He proposed legislation that allowed individual territories to determine whether they would allow slavery (1854), and in the senatorial campaign of 1858 he engaged Abraham Lincoln in a famous series of debates.

Douglass, Frederick (1817–1895) American abolitionist and journalist who escaped from slavery (1838) and became an influential lecturer in the North and abroad. He wrote *Narrative of the Life of Frederick Douglass* (1845) and cofounded and edited the *North Star* (1847–1860), an abolitionist newspaper.

Drake, Sir Francis (1540–1596) English naval hero and explorer who was the first Englishman to circumnavigate the world (1577–1580) and was vice admiral of the fleet that destroyed the Spanish Armada (1588).

***Dred Scott* case (1857)** An enslaved man sued for his freedom in 1847, leading to a crucial Supreme Court decision in 1857 in which the Court ruled that African Americans held no rights as citizens and that the Missouri Compromise of 1820 was unconstitutional. The decision was widely denounced in the North and strengthened the new Republican party.

Du Bois, W. E. B. (1868–1963) Initially a supporter of Booker T. Washington's education policy, he later criticized Washington's methods as having "practically accepted the alleged inferiority of the Negro."

Dust Bowl The name given to areas of the prairie states that suffered ecological devastation in the 1930s and then again to a lesser extent in the mid-1950s.

Dutch West India Company Chartered in 1621 by the Dutch government to establish commerce and colonies in America. It received broad powers, including the rights to make war and sign treaties.

Eaton, Peggy (1799–1879) Wife of John Eaton and the central figure in a controversy that divided President Jackson's cabinet into pro- and anti-Eaton factions.

Edison, Thomas Alva (1847–1931) The inventor of the phonograph, electric lights, and countless other products.

Eighteenth Amendment (1919) Constitutional amendment that barred the production and sale of alcoholic beverages. Its adoption represented the national high point of the prohibition movement.

Eisenhower, Dwight D. (1890–1969) U.S. general and thirty-fourth president of the United States (1953–1961). As supreme commander of the Allied Expeditionary Force in World War II, he launched the invasion of Normandy (June 6, 1944) and oversaw the defeat of Germany in 1945.

election of 1840 Whig innovations in campaign slogans, large rallies, and efforts to involve women supporters in this election marked a new style of political campaigning. The election, between Democrat Martin Van Buren and the Whig party's William Henry Harrison, was won by Harrison.

electoral college The group that elects the president. Each state received as many electors as it had congressmen and senators combined.

Elizabeth I (1533–1603) Queen of England (1558–1603), she succeeded the Catholic Mary I and reestablished Protestantism in England. Her reign was marked by several plots to overthrow her, the execution of Mary, Queen of Scots (1587), the defeat of the Spanish Armada (1588), and domestic prosperity and literary achievement.

Ellis Island Immigration station in New York Harbor, opened in 1892, where new arrivals were given a medical examination and questioned about their economic prospects.

emancipation The ending of slavery, initiated in the Emancipation Proclamation of 1863 but not accomplished in many places until the Confederate surrender in 1865.

Embargo Act (1807) Passed by Congress in response to British restrictions on U.S. trade and impressment of American sailors, the act prohibited exportation to all other countries. The policy had serious economic repercussions and was widely violated.

Emerson, Ralph Waldo (1803–1882) American writer, philosopher, and central figure of American transcendentalism. His poems, orations, and especially his essays, such as *Nature* (1836), are regarded as landmarks in the development of American thought and literary expression.

enclosure movement Economic process in which English landlords ended leases for tenant farmers living on their lands, confiscating common fields that peasant communities had shared for grazing their livestock and raising crops.

Enlightenment Philosophical movement of the eighteenth century that emphasized the use of reason to scrutinize previously accepted doctrines and traditions and that brought about many humanitarian reforms.

Enola Gay The B-29 bomber, named after the mother of pilot Colonel Paul W. Tibbets, that dropped the first atomic bomb on the Japanese city of Hiroshima on August 6, 1945, killing more than one hundred thousand people.

Equal Rights Amendment (ERA) Congress overwhelmingly passed the Equal Rights Amendment in 1972, but by the mid-1970s conservative groups had managed to stall its confirmation by the states.

Era of Good Feelings Period in U.S. history (1817–1823) when, the Federalist party having declined, there was little open party feeling.

Erie Canal First major American canal, stretching two hundred fifty miles from Lake Erie across the state of New York to Albany, where boats then traveled down the Hudson River to New York City. Begun in 1818, it was completed in 1825.

Evans, Oliver (1755–1819) American inventor who developed the first application of steam power in an industrial setting. He also developed a method of automating flour mills that had become standard in U.S. mills a generation later.

Farmers' Alliance First started as local groups of angry farmers in Texas during the 1880s, these alliances spread across the South and West and eventually formed into the Farmers' Alliance and Industrial Union in 1889. The Alliance was a forerunner of Populism.

Faubus, Orval (1910–1994) Governor of Arkansas in 1957 who triggered a confrontation between national authority and states' rights by defying a federal court order to integrate the all-white Little Rock Central High School.

Federalist, The Alexander Hamilton, James Madison, and John Jay wrote a series of eighty-five essays in support of the Constitution. First published in newspapers, they appeared in book form as *The Federalist* in the spring of 1788.

Federalists Name assumed by the supporters of the U.S. Constitution of 1787 during the contest for ratification. Also the group supporting policies of Alexander Hamilton that evolved into a political party during the 1790s.

Fillmore, Millard (1800–1874) Thirteenth president of the United States (1850–1853), who succeeded to office after the death of Zachary Taylor. He struggled to keep the nation unified but lost the support of his Whig party.

Finney, Charles Grandison (1792–1875) American evangelist, theologian, and educator. Licensed to the Presbyterian ministry in 1824, he had phenomenal success as a revivalist in the Northeast, converting many who later became noted abolitionists.

fire-eaters Before the Civil War, Southerners who enthusiastically supported Southern rights and, later, secession.

Fitzgerald, F. Scott (1896–1940) Jazz Age novelist; author of *The Great Gatsby* (1925). He and his wife Zelda embodied the free spirit of the Jazz Age.

Ford, Gerald R. (1913–) Thirty-eighth president of the United States (1974–1977), he was appointed vice president when Spiro Agnew resigned and became president when Richard Nixon resigned over the Watergate scandal. As president, Ford granted a full pardon to Nixon in 1974.

Fort Sumter Fort in the harbor of Charleston, South Carolina, that was fired on by the Confederacy on April 12, 1861, triggering the Civil War.

Fort Wagner Fort guarding the approach to Charleston Harbor, South Carolina. In the Union assault on July 18, 1863, nearly half of the 54th Massachusetts Volunteers leading the attack were killed, but their courage helped convince the North to continue recruiting African American soldiers.

forty-niners Prospectors and others, mostly men, lured to California by the gold rush of 1849.

forty-ninth parallel Line of latitude established as the border between the United States and Canada by the Treaty of 1818; extended to the Pacific by President Polk's secret negotiation of the Oregon Treaty in 1846.

Franciscan priests Members of the Roman Catholic order of Saint Francis of Assisi; they served as missionaries in colonial Spanish America.

Franklin, Benjamin (1706–1790) American public official, writer, scientist, and printer. He proposed a plan for union at the Albany Congress (1754) and played a major part in the American

Revolution. Franklin helped secure French support for the colonists, negotiated the Treaty of Paris (1783), and helped draft the Constitution (1787). His numerous scientific and practical innovations include the lightning rod, bifocal spectacles, and a stove.

Franz Ferdinand (1863–1914) Austrian archduke murdered along with his wife in Sarajevo, Bosnia. Austria's ultimatum to Serbia led to the outbreak of World War I.

Freed, Alan (1921–1965) The self-proclaimed father of rock 'n' roll, he was the first DJ to play black rhythm and blues artists on the radio.

Freedmen's Bureau Federal agency created in 1865 to supervise newly freed people. It oversaw relations between whites and blacks in the South, issued food rations, and supervised labor contracts.

freedom riders Interracial groups who rode buses in the South so that a series of federal court decisions declaring segregation on buses and in waiting rooms unconstitutional would not be ignored by white officials.

Free-Soil Party U.S. political party formed in 1848 to oppose the extension of slavery into the territories; merged with the Liberty Party in 1848.

Frémont, John C. (1813–1890) Republican presidential candidate in 1856; western explorer who had supported the Bear Flag Revolt in California during the Mexican-American War.

Friedan, Betty (1921–) Feminist who wrote *The Feminist Mystique* (1963) and founded the National Organization for Women in 1966.

Fugitive Slave Act (1850) Part of the Compromise of 1850, the federal law that provided for the return of escaped black slaves to their owners in the South.

fugitive slave clause (1787) Provision of the U.S. Constitution that prevented free states from emancipating slaves who had escaped from masters in other states.

Gadsden Purchase (1854) A piece of land, 29,670 square miles, purchased from Mexico in 1853 to provide a southern route for a transcontinental railroad; final extension of the southern U.S. border.

gag rule Congressional practice, starting in 1836, to ban consideration of antislavery petitions.

Garner, John Nance "Cactus Jack" (1868–1967) Speaker of the House in 1931 whose answer to the growing budget deficit was to offer a national sales tax. He ran against Roosevelt for the Democratic nomination for president but released his delegates and was in turn rewarded with the vice presidential nomination.

Garrison, William Lloyd (1805–1879) American abolitionist leader who founded the antislavery journal *The Liberator* (1831–1865).

Garvey, Marcus (1887–1940) Jamaican immigrant who promised to "organize the 400 million Negroes of the World into a vast organization to plant the banner of freedom in the great continent of Africa."

Genêt, Edmond (1763–1834) French ambassador who enlisted American mercenaries to assist the French against the British. Genêt's move threatened relations between the United States and Britain.

Geronimo (1829–1909) Apache leader who resisted white incursions until his capture in 1886.

Gettysburg Address (1863) Brief speech given by President Lincoln at the dedication of the Gettysburg Cemetery in November 1863 that declared that the Civil War was dedicated to freedom.

***Gibbons v. Ogden* (1824)** Supreme Court case that overturned a steamboat monopoly granted to Robert Fulton and Robert Livingston by New York State. The decision established federal authority over interstate navigation, as an extension of the federal power to regulate interstate commerce.

Gilman, Charlotte Perkins (1860–1935) Feminist who advocated that women should seek economic independence; author of *Women and Economics* (1898).

Glenn, John (1921–) Astronaut, U.S. Senator (1974–1998). On February 20, 1962, aboard the *Friendship 7*, he was the first American to orbit the earth; in 1998 he was the oldest person to participate in a space flight mission as a member of the space shuttle *Discovery*.

globalization The process by which the world's economies are becoming more integrated and interdependent. Those affected by such changes have often protested against the political and economic dislocation that accompanies this trend.

Glorious Revolution (1688) English Revolution against the authoritarian policies and Catholicism of James II. The revolution secured the dominance of Parliament over royal power.

good neighbor policy A new Latin American policy wherein Hoover withdrew the Marines from Nicaragua and Haiti, and in 1930 the State Department renounced the Roosevelt Corollary of 1904.

Gorbachev, Mikhail (1931–) General secretary of the Soviet Communist party (1985–1990) and president of the USSR (1990–1991), he ushered in an era of glasnost (openness) and perestroika (restructuring), and won the Nobel Peace Prize in 1990.

Grant, Ulysses S. (1822–1885) U.S. general and eighteenth president of the United States (1869–1877). He commanded the Union Army during the Civil War.

***Grapes of Wrath, The* (1939)** Novel by John Steinbeck depicting the struggle of ordinary Americans in the Great Depression, following the plight of the Joad family as it migrated west from Oklahoma to California.

Great Awakening Immense religious revival during the 1720s to the 1760s that swept across the Protestant world.

Great Compromise (1787) At the Constitutional Convention, plan proposed by the Connecticut delegation for a bicameral Congress with a House of Representatives, with representations based on a state's population, and the Senate, in which each state would be represented equally. Also known as the Connecticut Compromise.

Great Migration A massive movement of blacks leaving the South for cities in the North that began slowly in 1910 and accelerated between 1914 and 1920. During this time, more than six hundred thousand African Americans left the South.

Greeley, Horace (1811–1872) Grant's opponent in the 1872 election. Seen as a political oddball in the eyes of many Americans, the sixty-one-year-old editor favored the protective tariff and was indifferent to civil service reform. He was also passionate about vegetarianism and the use of human manure in farming.

greenbacks Paper currency issued by the Union under the Legal Tender Act of 1862, replacing the notes of individual banks with a unified national currency.

Grimké, Angelina (1805–1879) and Sarah (1792–1873) The first female abolitionist speakers; they were prominent figures in the antislavery movement of the late 1830s.

Gulf of Tonkin Resolution (1964) Following reports of a confrontation with North Vietnamese in the Tonkin Gulf in 1964, President Johnson requested, and received, congressional authority to "take all necessary measures" to repel "further aggression" in Vietnam, giving the president formal authority to escalate the war.

Gullah Creole tongue that evolved in the Lower South from English and various languages from southern Nigeria, the Gold Coast, Angola, and Senegambia.

Halfway Covenant The Puritan practice whereby parents who had been baptized but had not yet experienced conversion could bring their children before the church and have them baptized.

Hamer, Fannie Lou (1917–1977) Daughter of illiterate Mississippi sharecroppers, she helped lead the civil rights struggle in Mississippi, focusing on voting rights for African Americans and representation in the national Democratic party.

Hamilton, Alexander (1755–1804) First U.S. secretary of the treasury (1789–1795), he established the national bank and public credit system. In 1804 he was mortally wounded in a duel with his political rival Aaron Burr.

Handsome Lake (1735–1815) Seneca spiritual and political leader. He advocated peace, the U.S. acculturation policy, abstinence from drinking alcohol and practicing witchcraft, and return to ancestral rituals.

Harpers Ferry Virginia town that was the site of John Brown's raid in 1859, a failed attempt to lead a slave insurrection. It ignited public opinion in both the North and the South.

Harrison, Benjamin (1833–1901) Twenty-third president of the United States (1889–1893), he lost the popular vote but won a majority of the electoral college.

Harrison, William Henry (1773–1841) While governor of the Indiana Territory, he attacked and burned the nativist village of Prophetstown in 1811. The ninth president of the United States (1841), he died of pneumonia after one month in office.

Hartford Convention (1814) Gathering of Federalists in 1814 that called for significant amendments to the Constitution and attempted to damage the Republican party. The Treaty of Ghent and Andrew Jackson's victory at New Orleans annulled any recommendation of the convention.

Hawthorne, Nathaniel (1804–1864) Massachusetts writer whose novels were mostly set in colonial New England, including *The Scarlet Letter* (1850) and *The House of Seven Gables* (1851).

Hayes, Rutherford B. (1822–1893) Nineteenth president of the United States (1877–1881), he won the most fiercely disputed election in American history.

Haymarket Riot On May 4, 1886, workmen in Chicago gathered to protest police conduct during a strike at a factory of the McCormick Company.

Hearst, William Randolph (1863–1951) The most celebrated publisher of yellow journalism.

Henry, Patrick (1736–1799) Elected to the Virginia House of Burgesses at age twenty-nine, Henry introduced fourteen resolves against the Stamp Act. He was a brilliant speaker and served as governor of Virginia during the Revolution.

Hill, Anita (1956–) Government lawyer and law professor who brought charges of sexual misconduct against Clarence Thomas during his confirmation hearings as Supreme Court justice in 1991.

Hiss, Alger (1904–1996) State Department official accused of espionage at the height of the Cold War, he was convicted of perjury in 1950 in a controversial case.

Ho Chi Minh (1890–1969) Vietnamese leader and first president of North Vietnam. His army was victorious in the French Indochina War, and he later led North Vietnam's struggle to defeat the U.S.-supported government of South Vietnam. He died before the reunification of Vietnam.

Homeland Security U.S. cabinet department established in 2002 to coordinate defense of the American nation.

Homestead strike (1892) Labor uprising of workers at a steel plant in Homestead, Pennsylvania, that was put down by military force.

Hoovervilles Makeshift "villages" usually at the edge of a city with "homes" made of cardboard, scrap metal, or whatever was cheap and available and named for President Hoover who was despised by the poor for his apparent refusal to help them.

Hopkins, Harry (1890–1946) Roosevelt's choice to run the Federal Emergency Relief Administration. He eventually became Roosevelt's closest adviser.

horizontal integration A procedure wherein a company takes over competitors to achieve control within an industry.

House Un-American Activities Committee (HUAC) Formed in the 1930s as a watchdog against Nazi propaganda, HUAC was revived after World War II as a watchdog against Communist propaganda.

Hudson River School Group of mid-nineteenth-century landscape painters, including Thomas Cole, Asher Durand, and Frederic Edwin Church, whose work was influenced by Romanticism and known for its stirring depictions of American landscapes.

Huerta, Victoriano (1854–1916) Mexican general and president (1913–1914). The United States did not recognize Huerta's government, and President Wilson ordered U.S. military intervention in support of his rival, Venustiano Carranza.

Hughes, Charles Evans (1862–1948) Governor of New York (1907–1910), Supreme Court justice (1910–1916), and Republican candidate for president in 1916, when he was defeated by Woodrow Wilson. He served as secretary of state under Presidents Harding and Coolidge (1921–1925) and returned to the Supreme Court as Chief Justice in 1930.

Hull House Settlement house founded in Chicago in 1889 by Jane Addams and Ellen Gates Starr to help solve the troubling problems of city life.

Hurston, Zora Neale (1901–1960) African American novelist who embodied the creative and artistic aspirations of the Harlem Renaissance in the 1920s.

Hutchinson, Anne (1591–1643) English-born American colonist and religious leader who was banished from Boston (1637) for her religious beliefs, which included an emphasis on an individual's direct communication with God.

impeachment The act of charging a public official with misconduct in office, impeachment is the constitutional procedure for removing presidents who are found guilty of "treason, bribery, or other high crimes and misdemeanors" as interpreted by Congress. Presidents Andrew Johnson, Richard Nixon, and Bill Clinton have been the subject of impeachment proceedings.

Impressment Act (1863) Confederate legislation that authorized the seizure of produce and slaves for military purposes, and provided the means for Confederate farmers to appeal unfair prices paid for property seized.

Indian Removal Act (1830) Congressional legislation that set aside land in the Oklahoma Territory for American Indians who were to be removed from the eastern United States. During the next eight years, tens of thousands of Choctaw, Chickasaw, and Cherokee people were transported from their homes on what the Cherokees called the "Trail of Tears."

inoculation Medical procedure tested in 1721 by a Boston doctor, Zabdiel Boylston, to prevent smallpox epidemics. The procedure involved introducing the smallpox virus into an individual's body, thereby giving the person what was usually (but not always) a mild case of the disease.

Interstate Commerce Act (1887) Congressional legislation that set up the Interstate Commerce Commission (ICC) to supervise and regulate the nation's railroads.

Interstate Commerce Commission First federal regulatory agency, established by the Interstate Commerce Act (1887). It had the power to investigate complaints of railroad misconduct and file suit against the companies. The Hepburn Act (1906) gave the commission the authority to establish maximum rates and to review the accounts and records of the railroads.

Iran-Contra scandal A major scandal of the second Reagan term that involved shipping arms to Iran and diverting money from the sale of these weapons to the Contra rebels in Nicaragua.

Iron Curtain Military, political, and ideological barrier established between the Soviet bloc and Western Europe from 1945 to 1989.

Jackson, Andrew (1767–1845) U.S. general and seventh president of the United States (1829–1837). In the War of 1812, he defeated the Red Sticks at Horseshoe Bend (1814) and the British at New Orleans (1815). As president he denied the right of individual states to nullify federal laws and increased presidential powers.

Jackson, Jesse (1941–) Baptist minister and civil rights leader, he directed national antidiscrimination efforts in the mid-1960s and 1970s.

Jackson, Thomas J. "Stonewall" (1824–1863) Confederate general who commanded troops at both battles of Bull Run (1861 and 1862) and directed the Shenandoah Valley campaign (1862). He was accidentally killed by his own troops at Chancellorsville (1863).

Jamestown First permanent English settlement in America (1607), it was located on the James River in Virginia.

Jay, John (1745–1829) American diplomat and jurist who served in the Continental Congress and helped negotiate the Treaty of Paris (1783). He was the first chief justice of the U.S. Supreme Court (1789–1795) and negotiated the agreement with Great Britain that became known as the Jay Treaty.

Jay Treaty (1794) Treaty between the United States and Great Britain negotiated by John Jay. It settled difficulties arising from violations of the Treaty of Paris of 1783 and regulated commerce and navigation.

***Jazz Singer, The* (1927)** One of the first motion pictures with sound, it starred Al Jolson who specialized in rendering popular tunes in blackface.

Jefferson, Thomas (1743–1826) Third president of the United States (1801–1809). As a member of the second Continental Congress, he drafted the Declaration of Independence (1776). His presidency was marked by the purchase of the Louisiana Territory (1803) and the Embargo of 1807.

Johnson, "Jack" (1878–1946) First African American heavyweight boxing champion, taking the title in 1908.

Johnson, Andrew (1808–1875) Seventeenth president of the United States (1865–1869); he succeeded the assassinated Abraham Lincoln.

Johnson, Lyndon Baines (1908–1973) Thirty-sixth president of the United States (1963–1968), he succeeded after the assassination of President Kennedy and was elected in a landslide the following year. He piloted a number of important initiatives through Congress, including the Civil Rights Act of 1964 and the Voting Rights Act of 1965.

joint-stock companies Formed to explore trade routes and establish new markets, the companies obtained capital by selling shares of stock.

Judiciary Act of 1789 Congressional legislation that established the U.S. Supreme Court of six justices and a system of federal inferior courts, which were restricted primarily to consideration of federal crimes. State courts retained original jurisdiction in most civil and criminal cases, with the U.S. Supreme Court taking appeals from the highest state courts.

Kansas-Nebraska Bill (1854) Congressional legislation drafted by Stephen A. Douglas that provided that people of new territories could decide for themselves whether or not their states would permit slavery.

Kennedy, Robert F. (1925–1968) Attorney general during the presidency of his brother John F. Kennedy. Elected to the Senate in 1964, he was assassinated in Los Angeles while campaigning for the presidency.

Kent State University National Guardsmen were sent to this Ohio campus to restore order following a series of antiwar protests in May 1970. They fired into a crowd of students, killing four and wounding nine others.

Khrushchev, Nikita (1894–1971) Soviet politician and Stalin loyalist in the 1930s, he was appointed first secretary of the Communist party in 1953. As Soviet premier, he denounced Stalin, thwarted the Hungarian Revolution of 1956, and improved his country's image abroad. He was deposed in 1964 for failing to establish missiles in Cuba or improve the Soviet economy.

King, Martin Luther, Jr. (1929–1968) African American clergyman whose eloquence and commitment to nonviolence formed the foundation of the civil rights movement of the 1950s and 1960s. He led the 1963 march on Washington at which he delivered his now famous "I Have a Dream" speech. He was awarded the Nobel Peace Prize in 1964 and was assassinated four years later in Memphis, Tennessee.

Kissinger, Henry (1912–) German-born American political scientist, national security advisor (1969–1974), and secretary of state (1973–1977). He shared the 1973 Nobel Peace Prize for helping to negotiate the Vietnam cease-fire.

Knights of Labor Nineteenth-century labor organization that combined fraternal ritual, the language of Christianity, and a belief in the social equality of all citizens.

Know-Nothings Popular name for the American party, an anti-immigration party of the mid-1850s, derived from members' response to any question about their activities: "I know nothing."

Ku Klux Klan Founded in 1866 as an organization to terrorize blacks in the South during Reconstruction. It was revived in 1915 as a means of enforcing, often through violence and intimidation, the cultural values of rural, prohibitionist America against minority groups including African Americans, Jews, and Catholics.

L'Enfant, Pierre Charles (1754–1825) French-born American architect, who designed Washington, D.C., and its major buildings. His grandiose street plan and Greek and Roman architecture expressed an exalted vision of the republic.

La Follette, Robert M. (1855–1925) Progressive governor (1900–1906) and senator (1906–1925) from Wisconsin; Progressive Party candidate for president in 1924.

La Raza Unida Formed in 1969 by Mexican American activists, this group reflected the growing demand for political and cultural recognition of "Chicano" causes, especially in the Southwest.

La Salle, Sieur de (1643–1687) French explorer in North America who claimed Louisiana for France (1682).

Las Casas, Bartolomé de (1474–1566) Spanish missionary who condemned Spanish colonial policies toward Native Americans. He described atrocities in his book, *A Short Account of the Destruction of the Indies* (1542).

Lee, Ann (1736–1784) Founder of the Shakers in the United States. The sect believed in salvation by confession of sin, equality regardless of sex or race, opposition to slavery and war, sexual abstinence, and assistance to the poor.

Lee, Robert E. (1807–1870) U.S. and Confederate general. He led the Army of Northern Virginia in the American Civil War.

Leisler, Jacob (1640?–1691) German-born merchant and militia captain in New York who in 1689 led a rebellion of merchants and artisans who had been denied economic privileges to trade and mill flour under James II's government. Leisler was executed for treason when the new governor appointed by William and Mary arrived in 1691.

Lend-Lease (1941) Passed in 1941, this act forged the way for the United States to transfer military supplies to the Allies, primarily Great Britain and the Soviet Union.

Levittown An unincorporated community of 53,286 people in southeast New York on western Long Island, which was founded in 1947 as a low-cost housing development for World War II veterans.

Lewis and Clark Expedition From 1804 to 1806 Meriwether Lewis and William Clark led the Corps of Discovery from St. Louis to the Pacific coast and back. They informed Native Americans that the United States had acquired the territory from France and recorded geographic and scientific data.

Lewis, John L. (1880–1969) U.S. labor leader; president of the United Mine Workers of America (1920–1960) and the Congress of Industrial Organizations (1935–1940).

Liberal Republicans Organization formed in 1872 by Republicans who were not content with the political corruption and the policies of President Grant's first administration.

Liberty Bonds Thirty-year government bonds sold to individuals with an annual interest rate of 3.5 percent. They were offered in five issues between 1917 and 1920, and their purchase was equated with patriotic duty.

Liberty Party U.S. political party formed in 1839 to oppose the practice of slavery; it merged with the Free-Soil party in 1848.

Lincoln, Abraham (1809–1865) Sixteenth president (1861–1865), his election triggered Southern secession. He led the United States throughout the Civil War, strengthened the power of the presidency, and signed into law the Emancipation Proclamation. He was assassinated two days after Lee's surrender.

Lincoln, Benjamin (1733–1810) Revolutionary War general who in 1786–1787 successfully led the army funded by Boston merchants against the Shaysites in western Massachusetts.

Lindbergh, Charles A. (1902–1974) His solo flight across the Atlantic Ocean in 1927 made him an international hero.

Little Richard (Richard Wayne Penniman, 1932–) American rock 'n' roll singer noted for his flamboyant style, he influenced many artists including Elvis Presley and the Beatles.

Locke, Alain (1885–1954) African American poet and an important member of the Harlem Renaissance.

Locke, John (1632–1704) English philosopher and author of *An Essay Concerning Human Understanding* (1690), which challenged the notion of innate knowledge, and *Two Treatises on Civil Government* (1690), which discussed the social contract.

Long, Huey P. (1893–1935) Populist but dictatorial governor of Louisiana (1928–1932), he instituted major public works legislation; as a U.S. senator (1932–1935), he proposed a national "Share the Wealth" program.

Louisiana Purchase (1803) The acquisition of the Louisiana Territory west of the Mississippi River and New Orleans by the United States from France for $15 million.

Lovejoy, Elijah P. (1802–1837) Abolitionist editor, killed by proslavery advocates in an attack on his printing press in Alton, Illinois.

loyalists Residents of the British colonies who remained loyal to Great Britain during the American Revolution. Also called Tories after the pro-monarchy faction in England.

Lusitania British liner sunk by a German torpedo in May 1915. Among the nearly 1,200 passengers who died were 128 Americans.

Luther, Martin (1483–1546) German theologian and leader of the Reformation. His opposition to the wealth and corruption of the papacy and his belief that salvation would be granted on the basis of faith alone rather than by works caused his excommunication from the Catholic Church (1521). Luther confirmed the Augsburg Confession in 1530, effectively establishing the Lutheran Church.

MacArthur, Douglas (1880–1964) U.S. general. He served as chief of staff (1930–1935) and commanded the Allied forces in the South Pacific during World War II. Initially losing the Philippines to the Japanese in 1942, he regained the islands and accepted the surrender of Japan in 1945. He commanded the UN forces in Korea (1950–1951) until a conflict in strategies led to his dismissal by President Truman.

Madison, James (1751–1836) Fourth president of the United States (1809–1817). Member of the Continental Congress (1780–1783) and the Constitutional Convention (1787), he strongly supported ratification of the Constitution and was a contributor to *The Federalist*.

Malcolm X (Malcolm Little, 1925–1965) Black Muslim leader who advocated nationalism, self-defense, and racial separation. He split with the Black Muslim movement and formed the Organization of Afro-American Unity, which attracted thousands of young, urban blacks with its message of pride and self-help. He was assassinated by a Black Muslim at a New York rally in 1965.

manifest destiny Idea proposed by newspaper editor John L. O'Sullivan in 1845 that the United States was destined to grow from the Atlantic to the Pacific and from the Arctic to the tropics. Providence supposedly intended for Americans to have this area for a great experiment in liberty.

Mann, Horace (1796–1859) Educational reformer and promoter of public school education; first secretary of the Massachusetts Board of Education.

***Marbury* v. *Madison* (1803)** The first decision by the Supreme Court to declare unconstitutional and void an act passed by Congress that the Court considered in violation of the Constitution. The decision established the doctrine of judicial review, the authority of courts to declare statutes unconstitutional.

Marshall, George C. (1880–1959) U.S. general and statesman. As secretary of state (1947–1949), he organized the European Recovery Plan, often called the Marshall Plan, for which he received the 1953 Nobel Peace Prize.

Marshall, John (1755–1835) American politician and jurist. As chief justice of the United States (1801–1835), he helped establish the doctrine of judicial review.

Marshall Plan Post–World War II U.S. economic aid program, also known as the European Recovery Plan. The plan, costing about $13 billion, helped restore economic confidence throughout Western Europe, raise living standards, curb the influence of local Communist parties, and increase U.S. trade and investment on the European continent.

Maya Inhabitants of the Yucatan Peninsula whose civilization was at its height from 300 to 900 A.D. Their civilization included a unique system of writing, mathematics, architecture, sculpture, and astronomy.

Mayflower Compact (1620) When the *Mayflower* reached Cape Cod and the colonists decided to settle there, they lacked the legal basis to establish a government. Thus, the adult males of the colony signed a mutual agreement for ordering their society, later referred to as the Mayflower Compact.

McCarthy, Joseph R. (1908–1957) U.S. senator from Wisconsin (1947–1957), he presided over the permanent subcommittee on investigations and held public hearings in which he accused army officials, members of the media, and public figures of being Communists. These charges were never proved, and he was censured by the Senate in 1954.

McClellan, George B. (1826–1885) Major general of the United States Army who led forces in Virginia in 1861 and 1862. He was widely blamed for not taking advantage of his numerical superiority to defeat the Confederates around Richmond. McClellan ran against Abraham Lincoln for president in 1864 on the Democratic ticket.

***McCulloch* v. *Maryland* (1819)** Supreme Court case striking down Maryland's efforts to tax notes issued by the Bank of the United States. The decision established the constitutionality of the bank, the supremacy of federal over state laws, and the principle that the federal government possessed powers implied by but not enumerated in the Constitution.

McGillivray, Alexander (1759?–1793) Son of a Scottish trader and a French-Creek woman, McGillivray served as a Creek leader and allied with Spain to prevent white settlement on Creek lands during the 1780s.

McGovern, George (1922–) U.S. senator from South Dakota (1963–1981), he opposed the Vietnam War and was defeated as the 1972 Democratic candidate for president.

McKinley, William (1843–1901) Twenty-fifth president of the United States (1897–1901), he won by the largest majority of popular votes since 1872.

Melville, Herman (1819–1891) Author of *Moby-Dick* (1851), often considered the greatest American novel of the nineteenth century.

mercantilism Economic policy of the sixteenth to eighteenth centuries. European nations claimed the monopoly to trade with their colonies, which were to serve as markets for goods from the home country and provide raw materials, gold, and silver to increase its wealth.

Metacom (c. 1639–1676) Wampanoag leader who waged King Philip's War (1675–1676) with New England colonists who had encroached on Native American territory.

middle passage Transport of slaves across the Atlantic from Africa to the Americas.

midnight appointments Federal judicial officials appointed to office in the closing period of a presidential administration. The Republicans accused Adams of staying awake until midnight in order to sign the commissions for Federalist officeholders.

Midway Island Location of 1942 decisive World War II naval battle, in which land and carrier-based U.S. planes defeated a Japanese fleet.

midwives Women who traditionally attended at childbirth, treated the ill, and prescribed herbal remedies. They learned their skills through informal apprenticeships and from witnessing the childbirths of neighbors and relatives, and received payment for their services.

Milliken's Bend, battle of (1863) Battle on June 7, 1863, that turned to hand-to-hand combat between African American Union troops and Confederate soldiers during Grant's Vicksburg Campaign. The battle won Union recognition of African American soldiers' fighting abilities.

Missouri Compromise (1820–1821) Congressional legislation that ended the first of a series of crises concerning the extension of slavery.

Mondale, Walter (1928–) Vice president of the United States under Jimmy Carter (1977–1981), he earlier served as a U.S. senator from Minnesota (1965–1977) and was the unsuccessful 1984 Democratic nominee for president.

Monroe Doctrine (1823) U.S. foreign policy statement presented to Congress by James Monroe, declaring U.S. opposition to European interference in the Americas.

Monroe, James (1758–1831) Fifth president of the United States (1817–1825), whose administration was marked by the acquisition of Florida

(1819), the Missouri Compromise (1820), and the Monroe Doctrine (1823).

Montgomery bus boycott Begun in December 1955 as a result of an act of protest by Rosa Parks against the segregated transportation facilities and humiliating treatment facing African Americans in the capital city of Alabama, the boycott soon became an international event.

Moral Majority Political action group founded in 1979 and composed of conservative, fundamentalist Christians. Led by evangelist Rev. Jerry Falwell, the group played a significant role in the 1980 elections through its strong support of conservative candidates.

Morgan, J. P. (Pierpont) (1837–1913) U.S. financier. He purchased Carnegie Steel Company in 1901 for $480 million from Andrew Carnegie, creating United States Steel, which controlled 60 percent of the steel industry's productive capacity.

Morris, "Bill" (d. 1901) Black man burned at the stake in Balltown, Louisiana, for allegedly robbing and raping a white woman; no trial was held.

Morris, Robert (1734–1806) American Revolutionary politician and financier. A signer of the Declaration of Independence, he raised money for the Continental Army, attended the Constitutional Convention (1787), and was financially ruined by land speculation.

Morse, Samuel F. B. (1791–1872) American painter and inventor. He refined and patented the telegraph and developed the telegraphic code that bears his name.

muckrakers The name given to investigative reporters in the early 1900s.

***Muller v. Oregon* (1908)** Case in which the Supreme Court upheld limits on working hours for women.

multiculturalism The effort, particularly in academic life, to embrace the diversity of minority cultures. The movement was especially strong during the 1980s and 1990s.

National American Woman Suffrage Association (NAWSA) This association was formed in 1890 through the efforts of Lucy Stone Blackwell, and its first president was Elizabeth Cady Stanton.

National Association for the Advancement of Colored People (NAACP) Civil rights organization founded in 1909 to fight racial injustice.

National Industrial Recovery Act (NIRA) Enacted on June 16, 1933, this emergency measure was designed to encourage industrial recovery and help combat widespread unemployment.

National Road Federally sponsored road running from the Potomac River at Cumberland, Maryland, to the Ohio River at Wheeling, [West] Virginia, by 1818; extended to Vandalia, Illinois, by 1839.

National Woman's Party Created by Alice Paul, this organization pushed for the Equal Rights Amendment during the 1920s.

National Women's Trade Union League (1903–1950) Labor organization founded by women. It campaigned for better working conditions, protective labor laws, minimum wage regulation, and a ban on child labor.

natural philosophy The study of astronomy, physics, and chemistry, which was introduced into American college curricula under the influence of the Scottish Enlightenment.

Neolin Delaware prophet who preached in the 1760s that Indians must reject Christianity and European goods, particularly rum, and revitalize their ancient culture.

New Deal Term for the domestic programs and reforms instituted by President Franklin D. Roosevelt and his administration in response to the Great Depression of the 1930s.

New Jersey Plan Proposal for the U.S. Constitution drafted by William Paterson, it provided for a one-house (unicameral) Congress in which states had equal representation.

New Nationalism Theodore Roosevelt's far-reaching program that called for a strong federal government to stabilize the economy, protect the weak, and restore social harmony.

"New Negro" A term associated with the Harlem Renaissance of the 1920s that involved a proud assertion of the value of African American culture.

New York City draft riots (1863) Riots, July 13–16, 1863, among working people of New York, many of them recent immigrants, following news of heavy losses at Gettysburg and efforts to replace troop losses through the draft lottery.

Newton, Sir Isaac (1642–1727) English scientist who discovered universal laws that predictably govern the motion of planets, moons, and comets; the motion of falling bodies on earth (gravity); and the ebb and flow of tides.

Nisei A person born in the United States of parents who emigrated from Japan.

Nixon, Richard M. (1913–1994) Thirty-seventh president of the United States (1969–1974). Known early in his career as a hard-line anti-Communist, he was the first U.S. president to visit Communist China. He also worked skillfully to ease tensions with the Soviet Union. He became the first president to resign from office, due to his involvement in the Watergate scandal.

North Atlantic Treaty Organization (NATO) Military alliance, founded in 1949, between the United States and eleven other nations to protect Western Europe from invasion. It was a leading force in the Cold War struggle to contain Soviet aggression, expanding to include new nations over the years.

North, Oliver (1943–) Member of President Reagan's National Security Council staff and a Marine colonel, he was a central figure in the Iran-Contra scandal.

Northwest Ordinance (1787) Adopted by the Congress to establish stricter control over the government of the Northwest Territory ceded to the United States by the states. The ordinance was the most significant achievement of Congress under the Articles of Confederation.

nullification (1828–1833) Argument between leaders in South Carolina and in Washington, D.C., especially President Andrew Jackson, over the relationship between federal and state power. Theorists of nullification, especially John C. Calhoun, argued that a state had the authority to "nullify" a federal law within its own boundaries. The precipitating issue was a tariff, but the debate—eventually settled by compromise over the tariff and a threat of force by the federal government over the issue of authority—was seen as a trial case regarding slavery.

O'Connor, Sandra Day (1930–) Appointed by President Ronald Reagan, she was the first woman justice on the Supreme Court.

Oglethorpe, James (1696–1785) Along with John Viscount Percival, Oglethorpe sought a charter to colonize Georgia, the last of the British mainland colonies. Upon royal approval, he founded the colony with the intention of establishing a society of small farmers, without slavery or hard liquor.

Oklahoma City bombing (1995) Militant right-wing U.S. terrorists bombed the Alfred P. Murrah Federal Building in Oklahoma City in April 1995, causing the deaths of 168 people.

Oñate, Juan de (1549?–1624?) Spanish explorer and conquistador who claimed New Mexico for Spain in 1598 and served as its governor until he was removed on charges of cruelty in 1607.

Oneida Association Utopian community established in 1848 in upstate New York by John Humphrey Noyes (1811–1886) and his followers; practiced "complex marriage," economic cooperation, and gender equality of labor; also known for the community's steel manufacturing.

Opechancanough (1545?–1644?) Brother of Powhatan. In the 1620s Opechancanough organized a military offensive against English settlers.

Operation OVERLORD (1944) Code name for the Allied invasion of Normandy launched on D-Day, June 6, 1944.

Osceola (1800?–1838) Seminole chief who led opposition to Indian removal in the Second Seminole War.

Oswald, Lee Harvey (1939–1963) Alleged assassin of President John F. Kennedy, he was shot two days later while under arrest.

Panic of 1837 Financial crisis that began a major depression that lasted six years.

Panic of 1857 Financial crisis resulting from decreased European demand for American produce and decreased European investment following the Crimean War. The panic led to a wave of bank suspensions, individual bankruptcies, and a two-year depression.

paper currency After the Revolution, Americans hotly debated the issue of paper currency because it had resulted in inflation during the war, when the government used it to pay for goods and services. Many farmers favored issuing paper currency through a land office, which would provide capital based on the value of their land.

Parks, Rosa (1913–2005) Her refusal to give up her seat on a bus to a white man in Montgomery, Alabama, resulted in a citywide boycott of the bus company and stirred the civil rights movement across the nation.

Paul, Alice (1885–1977) A main figure in the radical wing of the woman suffrage movement in the early twentieth century.

Pearl Harbor Site of a U.S. naval base on the southern coast of Oahu, Hawaii, which the Japanese attacked on Sunday, December 7, 1941; the United States entered World War II the following day.

Pemberton, John (1831–1888) Atlanta druggist who in 1886 developed a syrup from an extract of the cola nut that he mixed with carbonated water and called "Coca Cola."

Penn, William (1644–1718) English Quaker leader who obtained a charter for Pennsylvania from Charles II in exchange for a debt owed to Penn's father. Penn intended to establish a model society based on religious freedom and peaceful relations with Native Americans, in addition to benefiting financially from the sale of the land.

Pennsylvania Abolition Society Organization founded in Philadelphia during the revolutionary period that advocated expansion of the state's 1780 act for gradual abolition and provided legal counsel to African Americans to defend their liberty.

Philadelphia Capital of colonial Pennsylvania and Delaware River port founded by William Penn.

piecework Early manufacturing system in which clothing, hats, and portions of shoes were sewn by women, generally working in their own homes, then sent to merchants in nearby cities for assembly and sale.

Pitt, Sir William (1708–1778) British political leader and orator who directed his country's military effort during the Seven Years' War.

***Plessy v. Ferguson* (1896)** Supreme Court decision that approved racial segregation.

Plessy, Homer A. (1863–1925) In a test of an 1890 law specifying that blacks must ride in separate railroad cars, this one-eighth-black man boarded a train and sat in the car reserved for whites. When the conductor instructed him to move, he refused and was arrested.

Plymouth Colony established by the English Pilgrims, or Separatists, in 1620. The Separatists were Puritans who abandoned hope that the Anglican church could be reformed. Plymouth became part of Massachusetts in 1691.

Popé Leader of the successful 1680 Pueblo rebellion against Spanish colonists and priests in New Mexico.

popular sovereignty The concept that settlers of each territory would decide for themselves whether to allow slavery.

Populist Party Also known as the People's Party, the Populists held their first national convention on July 4, 1892. The party platform took a stern view of the state of the nation, with planks endorsing the subtreasury, free coinage of silver, and other reforms.

Port Royal South Carolina port; abandoned by Confederate slaveholders early in the war, this became the site of a well-publicized experiment in the shift from slave to free labor.

Powell, Colin (1937–) U.S. general, national security adviser (1987–1989), chairman of the Joint Chiefs of Staff (1989–1993), and secretary of state (2001–2005). He was influential in planning U.S. strategy during the Persian Gulf War.

Powers, Francis Gary (1929–1977) Pilot of a U.S. U-2 high-altitude reconnaissance aircraft shot down over the Soviet Union on May 1, 1960.

Powhatan (1550–1618) Algonquian leader who founded the Powhatan confederacy and maintained peaceful relations with English colonists after the marriage of his daughter Pocahontas to John Rolfe (1614).

praying towns Established by John Eliot, praying towns were villages in which the Indians were supposed to adopt English customs and learn the fundamentals of Puritan religion.

predestination A theory that states that God has decreed who will be saved and who will be damned.

presidios Forts in colonial Spanish America built in an effort to defend the colonists and missions from Native American opponents.

Prince Henry of Portugal (1394–1460) Henry "the Navigator" established a school for navigators and geographers. He sought to increase the power of Portugal by promoting exploration of trade routes to the East by way of Africa.

Proclamation of 1763 In an attempt to keep white settlers out of the Ohio Valley, the Proclamation of 1763 drew a line along the crest of the Appalachian Mountains from Maine to Georgia and required all colonists to move east of the line.

progressivism Reform movement from 1890 to 1920 that sought to make state and national politics more democratic and government more efficient. The administrations of Theodore Roosevelt and Woodrow Wilson carried out many progressive reforms.

Protestant Reformation Religious rebellion against the Roman Catholic Church that began in 1517 when Martin Luther posted his ninety-five theses on a church door in Wittenberg, Germany.

Pullman, George (1831–1897) Developer of the railroad sleeping car and creator of a model town outside Chicago for his employees.

Pullman strike (1894) Strike by railway workers that led to nationwide unrest.

Puritanism Radical strain of English Protestantism that demanded purification of the Anglican church, including elimination of rituals, vestments, statues, and bishops.

Quakers (Society of Friends) Protestant sect originating in the English Civil War that challenged the authority of the Church of England and New England Puritans.

ratification Process by which the Constitution of 1787 and subsequent amendments must be approved. The original document required ratification by nine state conventions; states that refused to ratify could remain independent or unite under another frame of government.

Reagan, Ronald (1911–2004) Fortieth president of the United States (1981–1989), he represented the ascendancy of conservatism during the 1980s.

Regulators Name used in the late 1760s by the North Carolina Regulator movement and the South Carolina Regulators. Both groups demanded fair representation in the state legislatures but otherwise had distinct goals and membership.

Report on Public Credit (1790) Alexander Hamilton's plan for funding all Revolutionary War debts, including those of the states, by paying the interest with an import duty and excise tax on whiskey.

Republican Party (1790s) Led by Thomas Jefferson and James Madison, the party favored a strict interpretation of the Constitution and opposed Alexander Hamilton's vision of a strong central government and federal privileges for manufacturing and commerce.

Roanoke Island England's first attempt to establish a colony in North America was at Roanoke Island in 1585.

robber barons Railroad industry leaders such as Cornelius Vanderbilt and Jay Gould who became renowned for their ruthless methods against competitors.

Robinson, Jackie (1919–1972) First African American player in the Major Leagues in the twentieth century, he was a second baseman for the Brooklyn Dodgers, had a lifetime batting average of .311, and was inducted into the Baseball Hall of Fame in 1962.

Rockefeller, John D. (1839–1937) Key figure in the development of the oil industry and the growth of large corporations.

***Roe v. Wade* (1973)** Supreme Court decision that, along with *Doe v. Bolton*, legalized abortion in the first trimester.

Roosevelt Corollary (1904) Theodore Roosevelt's extension of the Monroe Doctrine to Latin American states and the right to supervise their behavior.

Roosevelt, Eleanor (1884–1962) Diplomat, writer, and First Lady of the United States (1933–1945) as the wife of President Franklin D. Roosevelt. A delegate to the United Nations (1945–1953 and 1961–1962), she was an outspoken advocate for human rights. Her written works include *This I Remember* (1949).

Roosevelt, Franklin D. (1882–1945) Thirty-second president of the United States (1933–1945), he assumed the presidency at the depth of the Great Depression and helped the American people regain faith in themselves. He brought hope with his inaugural address in which he promised prompt, vigorous action and asserted that "the only thing we have to fear is fear itself."

Rosie the Riveter Symbol of the new breed of working women during World War II.

Ross, John (1790–1866) Cherokee chief who challenged Indian removals in *Cherokee Nation v. Georgia* (1831).

Royal African Company English trading company granted the monopoly from 1672 to 1698 to supply enslaved people from Africa to labor in the English colonies.

royal fifth A tax on silver and gold of which one-fifth of its value went to the king of Spain.

Ruth, George Herman ("Babe") (1895–1948) Boston Red Sox pitcher who was sold to the New York Yankees in 1918 for $400,000. He belted out fifty-four home runs during the 1920 season, and fans flocked to see him play.

Sacagawea (1787?–1812?) Shoshone guide and interpreter who accompanied the Lewis and Clark expedition (1805–1806).

Sacco, Ferdinando Nicola (1891–1927), and **Vanzetti, Bartolomeo (1888–1927)** Italian immigrants tried for murder in Massachusetts in 1921. The trial attracted worldwide attention because of allegations of bias due to their anarchist beliefs. After exhausting their appeals, they were executed in 1927.

Sanger, Margaret (1883–1966) Social reformer and birth control pioneer. As a public health nurse in New York, she saw women suffering from disease and poverty because of the large number of children they bore. In 1914 she coined the term *birth control* and in 1915 she opened a clinic in Brooklyn. In 1921 she founded the American Birth Control League, which became Planned Parenthood in 1942.

Santa Anna, Antonio López de (1794–1876) Mexican general and politician. Leader of Mexico at the time of the battle at the Alamo. Taken prisoner at San Jacinto, he signed the Treaties of Velasco, which granted Texas its independence and recognized the Rio Grande as the boundary.

Scopes trial (1925) Trial of biology teacher John Thomas Scopes in Dayton, Tennessee, for teaching evolution. The jury found him guilty and assessed a small fine.

Scots-Irish Ulster Scot Presbyterians who settled in New York, Pennsylvania, Delaware, western Maryland, and the southern backcountry.

Scottsboro boys Nine black youths convicted by an all-white jury in 1931 on charges of raping two white women in Alabama. The case became a source of controversy and the focus of civil rights activism in the early 1930s.

Second Bank of the United States (1816–1836) New national bank created to stabilize the economy and distribute scarce money across the country. President Jackson believed the bank had too much power, and he vetoed the rechartering of the bank in 1836.

Second Great Awakening Protestant religious revivals that began in 1797 and lasted into the 1830s.

Seguín, Juan (1806–1890) Tejano cavalry commander who played a key role in defeating Mexican troops at the Battle of San Jacinto, which secured the independence of Texas.

Seminoles Native American people made up of various primarily Creek groups who moved into northern Florida during the eighteenth and nineteenth centuries, later inhabiting the Everglades region as well.

Seneca Falls Convention (1848) First major gathering of women's rights advocates, held in Seneca Falls, New York.

Serra, Junípero (1713–1784) Franciscan missionary who in 1769 established Spanish missions along the Pacific coast from San Diego to San Francisco.

sharecropping Labor system in the South after the Civil War. Tenants worked the land in return for a share of the crops produced, instead of paying cash rent. A shortage of currency in the South made this a common form of land tenure, and African Americans endured it because it eliminated the labor gangs of the slavery period.

Sherman Antitrust Act (1890) Federal legislation designed to curb the growth of large monopolistic corporations.

Sherman, William T. (1820–1891) Union general under Ulysses S. Grant who took Atlanta and led the "March to the Sea."

Shippen, Dr. William, Jr. (1712–1801) Trained in medicine in England and Scotland, Shippen initiated his practice of obstetrics in 1762, giving lectures in anatomy to Philadelphia midwives and doctors. Soon he accepted only male students.

Simms, William Gilmore (1806–1870) Prominent southern essayist, novelist, poet, and proslavery advocate.

Sinclair, Upton (1878–1968) Progressive era writer whose novel *The Jungle* exposed abuses in the meat-packing industry.

Sitting Bull (c. 1831–1890) Lakota Sioux Chief, he defeated George Custer in the Battle of Little Big Horn (1876).

Sixteenth Amendment (1913) Constitutional amendment that made a federal income tax constitutional.

Slater, Samuel (1768–1835) British-born textile pioneer in America. He oversaw construction of the nation's first successful water-powered cotton mill (1790–1793).

Slave Power Before the Civil War, term referring to the disproportionate power that Northerners believed wealthy slaveholding politicians wielded over their constituents and, as a result, over national political decisions.

Smith, John (1580–1631) English colonist, explorer, and writer. His maps and accounts of his explorations in Virginia and New England were invaluable to later explorers and colonists.

Smith, Joseph (1805–1844) American religious leader who founded the Church of Jesus Christ of Latter-Day Saints (1830). He led his congregation from New York State to western Illinois, where he was murdered by an anti-Mormon mob.

Social Darwinism Nineteenth-century philosophy that argued that the social history of humans closely resembled Darwin's principle of "survival of the fittest." According to this theory, human social history could be understood as a struggle among races, with the strongest and the fittest invariably triumphing.

Songhai Dominant West African state in the fifteenth and sixteenth centuries. Askia Mohammed (ruled 1493–1528) expanded the empire; reformed government, banking, and education; and adopted Islamic law.

Sons of Liberty Groups of small merchants, shopkeepers, and craftsmen who successfully opposed the Stamp Act in 1765–1766 by establishing networks to organize boycotts of British goods.

sovereignty Supreme political power. In Spanish and English colonial America, sovereignty rested in the monarch. Under the U.S. Constitution, sovereignty rests in the people (voters).

Special Field Order 15 Issued by William T. Sherman in January 1865, this order reserved land in coastal South Carolina, Georgia, and Florida for former slaves. Those who settled on the land would receive forty-acre plots.

spoils system Initiated by President Andrew Jackson, civil service system by which the victorious political party rewarded its supporters with government jobs.

Sputnik I First artificial space satellite, launched by the Soviet Union in October 1957. News of its success provoked both anger and anxiety among the American people who had always taken their country's technological superiority for granted.

Squanto (d. 1622) Patuxet Indian who helped the Plymouth colonists develop agricultural techniques and served as an interpreter between the colonists and the Wampanoags.

Square Deal Theodore Roosevelt's policy of treating capital and labor on an equal basis.

St. Domingue French West Indies colony in which blacks led by Toussaint L'Ouverture, a former slave, defeated local whites and invading European armies. Napoleon failed to regain control of the island and, in 1804, the victorious rebels established Haiti as an independent nation.

Stamp Act (1765) British law requiring colonists to purchase a stamp for official documents and published papers, including wills, newspapers, and pamphlets.

standing army After the American Revolution, the issue of a standing, or peacetime, army pitted revolutionary ideology against the need for defense.

Stanton, Elizabeth Cady (1815–1902) American feminist and social reformer who helped organize the first woman's rights convention, held in Seneca Falls, New York (1848), for which she wrote a Declaration of Rights and Sentiments calling for the reform of discriminatory practices that perpetuated the subordination of women.

statute for religious freedom (1786) Virginia legislation written by Thomas Jefferson and passed in 1786 that disestablished the Episcopal (Anglican) Church in Virginia.

stock market crash of 1929 The collapse of stock prices that ended the speculative boom of the 1920s and is associated with the onset of the Great Depression.

Stono uprising (1739) Revolt of enslaved Africans against their owners near the Stono River in South Carolina.

Stowe, Harriet Beecher (1811–1896) Author of *Uncle Tom's Cabin* (1852), the most important abolitionist novel.

Strategic Defense Initiative (SDI) Proposed by President Reagan in 1983, a Defense Department program to develop a space-based system to defend against strategic ballistic missiles.

Students for a Democratic Society (SDS) Formed in Port Huron, Michigan, in 1962, this group became one of the leading New Left antiwar organizations of the 1960s, exemplifying both the idealism and the excesses of radical student groups in the Vietnam era.

suffrage The right to vote, extended to African American men by the Fifteenth Amendment (1870). See also woman suffrage.

Sugar Act (1764) British law that initiated the policy of charging duties primarily for revenue rather than for regulating trade. The act reduced the duty on foreign molasses; added timber, iron, and hides to the list of enumerated goods; and increased the powers of vice-admiralty courts.

Sullivan, John L. (1858–1918) Irish American boxing champion of the late nineteenth century.

Sumner, Charles (1811–1874) U.S. senator from Massachusetts (1851–1874), he was a noted orator with an uncompromising opposition to slavery.

Taft, William Howard (1857–1930) Twenty-seventh president of the United States (1909–1913), who split with Theodore Roosevelt once in office. He served as Chief Justice of the United States Supreme Court (1921–1930).

Taney, Roger B. (1777–1864) Chief Justice of the United States (1836–1864). In the *Dred Scott* decision (1857) he ruled that slaves and their descendants could not become citizens of the United States.

Tarbell, Ida (1857–1944) Preeminent crusading journalist, she exposed the abuses of the oil trust in *A History of the Standard Oil Company* (1904).

Taylor, Zachary (1784–1850) U.S. general and twelfth president (1849–1850), he defeated Mexico in the Mexican-American War. As Whig president, he tried to avoid entanglements of both party and region.

Tecumseh (1768?–1813) Shawnee leader who attempted to establish a confederacy to unify Native Americans against white encroachment. He sided with the British in the War of 1812 and was killed in the Battle of the Thames.

Tejanos Mexicans in Texas who supported the revolt for independence from Mexico.

temperance movement Nineteenth century reform movement that encouraged the reduction or elimination of alcoholic beverage consumption.

Tennessee Valley Authority (TVA) Created in 1933 during the New Deal's first hundred days, it was a massive experiment in regional planning that focused on providing electricity, flood control, and soil conservation to one of the nation's poorest regions, covering seven states in the Tennessee Valley.

Tenskwatawa (1768–1834) Called the Shawnee Prophet, he became prominent among the people of the Great Lakes and Ohio Valley. With his brother, Tecumseh, he inspired a nativist movement to resist the U.S. government's acculturation policy and land seizure.

Tet offensive (1968) Major military operation in South Vietnam launched by the North Vietnamese and Vietcong. Though beaten back, there were tremendous casualties, and coordinated attacks undermined President Johnson's claim that steady progress was being made in Vietnam.

Thirteenth Amendment (1865) Constitutional amendment abolishing slavery.

Thomas, Clarence (1948–) Supreme Court justice appointed by George H. W. Bush in 1991, whose confirmation became controversial due to allegations of sexual misconduct made against him.

Tiananmen Square Adjacent to the Forbidden City in Beijing, China, this large public square was the site of many festivals, rallies, and demonstrations. During a student demonstration in 1989, Chinese troops fired on the demonstrators, killing an estimated two thousand or more.

Tilden, Samuel J. (1814–1886) Governor of New York and Democratic candidate for president in 1876. He narrowly lost what has been considered the most controversial election in American history.

Townshend Revenue Act (1767) Conceived by Charles Townshend, the British chancellor of the exchequer, the act placed duties on tea, glass, paper, lead, and paint to help pay British colonial administrative and military costs in North America.

Trail of Tears Forced migration of Indians from southeastern states to what is now Oklahoma, in accordance with the Indian Removal Act (1830). Thousands died on the march known as the Trail of Tears.

transcendentalists Members of an intellectual and social movement of the 1830s and 1840s that emphasized the active role the mind plays in constructing what we think of as reality. A loose grouping of intellectuals in Massachusetts sought to "transcend" the limits of thought in conventional America, whether religious or philosophical.

Treaty of Paris (1783) Signed on September 3, 1783, the Treaty of Paris established the independence of the United States from Great Britain. It set specific land boundaries and called for the evacuation of British troops.

Treaty of Tordesillas (1494) Treaty between Spain and Portugal that located the Line of Demarcation 370 leagues (about 1,000 miles) west of the Azores. It expanded the principle of "spheres of influence."

Treaty of Utrecht (1713) Ending Queen Anne's War between Great Britain and France, the Treaty of Utrecht ceded control of Nova Scotia, Newfoundland, and the Hudson Bay territory to the British.

***Trent* affair (1861)** Diplomatic incident growing out of the Union seizure of two Confederate envoys aboard a British ship, which highlighted the question of whether European countries would recognize Confederate nationhood.

Triangle Shirtwaist Fire (1911) Fire at the Triangle Shirtwaist Company in New York that killed 146 female workers and spurred reform legislation regulating factories and protecting workers.

Triple Alliance Pre–World War I alliance between Germany, Austria-Hungary, and Italy, established in 1882.

Truman Doctrine (1947) Reflecting a tougher approach to the Soviet Union following World War II, President Truman went before Congress in 1947 to request $400 million in military aid for Greece and Turkey, claiming the appropriation was vital to the containment of communism and to the future of freedom everywhere.

Truman, Harry S (1884–1972) Thirty-third president of the United States (1945–1953), he took office following the death of Franklin D. Roosevelt. Reelected in 1948 in a stunning political upset, Truman's controversial and historic decisions included the use of atomic weapons against Japan, desegregation of the U.S. military, and dismissal of General MacArthur as commander of U.S. forces during the Korean War.

trustbuster Term applied to Theodore Roosevelt's efforts to enforce the Sherman Act.

Truth, Sojourner (1797–1883) Former slave who became an advocate for abolitionism and for woman's rights.

Tubman, Harriet (c. 1820–1913) Escaped slave who returned to the South and led hundreds of enslaved people to freedom in the North. Active throughout the 1850s, Tubman became famous as the most active member of the Underground Railroad.

Turner, Nat (1800–1831) American slave leader who organized about seventy followers and led a rebellion in Virginia, during which approximately fifty whites were killed (1831). He was then captured and executed.

Twelfth Amendment (1804) Constitutional amendment requiring electors to draw up distinct lists for president and vice president, thus avoiding the deadlock of 1800 in which Thomas Jefferson and Aaron Burr tied for the presidency.

Twentieth Amendment (1933) Constitutional amendment that moved the presidential inauguration date from four months after the election to January 20.

"twenty negro law" Confederate law exempting from military service one white man for every twenty slaves he supervised.

U-2 U.S. spy plane. One piloted by Francis Gary Powers was shot down over the Soviet Union in 1960, which led to the angry breakup of a summit meeting in Paris between President Eisenhower and Soviet Premier Nikita Khrushchev.

Ulloa, Antonio de (1716–1795) First Spanish governor of Louisiana, who arrived in 1766 and tried to govern jointly with the last French governor.

Universalists Protestant denomination established in 1779 by an Englishman, John Murray. Its message of universal salvation had wide influence, though the Universalist church itself remained small.

vacuum domicilium English legal doctrine meaning that lands not occupied could be taken. It served as a basis for taking Native American territory.

Van Buren, Martin (1782–1862) Eighth president of the United States (1837–1841). A powerful Democrat from New York, he served in the U.S. Senate (1821–1828), as secretary of state (1829–1831), and as vice president (1833–1837) under Andrew Jackson before being elected president in 1836. He unsuccessfully sought reelection in 1840 and 1848.

vertical integration A procedure wherein a company gains control of all phases of production related to its product.

Vesey, Denmark (1767?–1822) American insurrectionist. A freed slave in South Carolina, he was implicated in the planning of a large uprising of slaves and was hanged. The event led to more stringent slave codes in many southern states.

viceroy Governor of a country, province, or colony who rules as the representative of the sovereign.

Vicksburg, battle of (1863) Mississippi battle site under siege by Grant's army for six weeks. Before falling it became the symbol of Confederate doggedness and Union frustration.

Vietnamization President Nixon's policy whereby the South Vietnamese were to assume more of the military burdens of the war. This transfer of responsibility was expected to eventually allow the United States to withdraw.

Virginia and Monitor Two ironclad vessels that fought in the harbor at Hampton Roads on March 9, 1862, in the first American battle between ironclads. Though neither won, the encounter established the importance of ironclads for the remainder of the war.

Virginia Company In 1606 King James I chartered the Virginia Company; one group was centered in London and founded Jamestown, a second group from Plymouth in western England founded the Plymouth colony.

Virginia Plan Constitutional proposal written by James Madison, the Virginia Plan proposed a powerful central government dominated by a National Legislature of two houses (bicameral). It also favored a system of greater representation based on a state's population.

Virginia slave debates (1831–1832) Debates in the Virginia state legislature following Nat Turner's Revolt over proposals to end slavery in Virginia. Although the legislature decided against abolition, the debates revealed white fears and divisions.

Wade-Davis Bill (1864) Congressional legislation for reconstructing the South. The Radical Republicans proposed stringent conditions for states that had seceded to reenter the Union. The bill provided that a majority of citizens in the states sign oaths swearing that they had never supported secession. The bill passed in the Senate and House but was pocket-vetoed by President Lincoln, who favored a more lenient approach.

Walker, David (1785–1830) African American abolitionist and author of *Walker's Appeal... To the Coloured Citizens of the World* (1829), an early and powerful call for black self-awareness and opposition to slavery.

Wallace, George (1919–1998) Governor of Alabama (1963–1967, 1971–1979, 1983–1987), he first came to national attention as an outspoken segregationist. Wallace ran unsuccessfully for the presidency in 1968 and 1972.

Washington, Booker T. (1856–1914) Educator, founder of Tuskegee Institute. He argued that African Americans should emphasize hard work and personal development rather than agitating for social reform.

Washingtonian temperance movement Nineteenth century reform movement that encouraged the reduction or elimination of alcoholic beverage consumption.

Watergate Nixon administration scandal touched off when the Democratic National Headquarters at the Watergate complex in Washington, D.C., was burglarized in 1972. Several top government officials were convicted of crimes and President Nixon was forced to resign in 1974.

Watts riot (1965) Among the most violent urban disturbances in U.S. history, it erupted in an African American neighborhood in Los Angeles following the arrest of a black motorist. By the time it ended, five days later, thirty-four people were dead, a thousand were injured, property damage topped $200 million, and National Guardsmen had to be called in to restore order.

Wells-Barnett, Ida B. (1862–1931) African American journalist and leader of an anti-lynching campaign.

Westmoreland, William (1914–2005) U.S. general; senior commander of U.S. troops in Vietnam from 1964 to 1968.

Whigs (Revolutionary era) Residents of the British colonies who opposed Great

Britain during the American Revolution. Also called patriots, they took the name Whigs from the English party that had opposed the Crown.

Whiskey Rebellion In the early 1790s western Pennsylvania farmers resisted the whiskey tax: they held protest meetings, tarred and feathered collaborators, and destroyed property. In 1794 the Washington administration sent thirteen thousand troops to restore order, but the revolt was over by the time they arrived.

Whitefield, George (1714–1770) Anglican minister who arrived from England in 1739. Called the Grand Itinerant, he promoted the Great Awakening by touring and encouraging New Lights throughout the colonies.

Whitman, Walt (1819–1892) Visionary poet who wrote *Leaves of Grass* (1855), inventing a new American idiom.

Whitney, Eli (1765–1825) American inventor and manufacturer whose invention of the cotton gin (1793) revolutionized the cotton industry. He also established the first factory to assemble muskets with interchangeable parts.

Williams, Roger (1603–1683) English cleric in America who was expelled from Massachusetts for his criticism of Puritan policies. He founded Providence Plantation (1636), a community based on religious freedom, and obtained a charter for Rhode Island in 1644.

Willkie, Wendell (1892–1944) Wall Street lawyer who ran against Franklin D. Roosevelt in his bid for a third consecutive term, which Roosevelt won.

Wilson, Woodrow (1856–1924) Twenty-eighth president of the United States (1913–1921), he was an advocate for the New Freedom and the League of Nations.

Witchcraft hysteria (1691–1692) The prosecution of almost two hundred people in Salem, Massachusetts, and its environs on charges of practicing witchcraft.

Wolfe, James (1727–1759) British general during the Seven Years' War. He defeated the French at Quebec (1759) but was mortally wounded in the battle.

woman suffrage The right of women to vote, which they achieved in 1919–1920 after an intense struggle in congress.

Women of the Army Name given by General George Washington to the approximately twenty thousand women who served in the Continental Army as nurses, cooks, laundresses, and water carriers. They drew rations and were subject to military discipline.

Woodstock A musical festival that was a fusion of rock music, hard drugs, free love, and an antiwar protest. It drew four hundred thousand people to a farm in upstate New York in the summer of 1969.

Wounded Knee, Battle of (1890) The last major chapter in the Indian wars, it was fought on the Pine Ridge Reservation in South Dakota.

writ of habeas corpus Constitutional provision allowing prisoners to petition against unlawful detention. The writ was suspended by Lincoln as a wartime measure to prevent the release of prisoners accused of aiding the Confederacy.

writs of assistance General search warrants; a writ of assistance authorized customs officials to search for smuggled goods.

XYZ Affair (1797–1798) Diplomatic incident in which the French government demanded, through three agents known to the American public as X, Y, and Z, that the U.S. government pay a bribe and apologize for criticizing France.

Yalta Conference (1945) World War II conference where Franklin Roosevelt, Winston Churchill, and Joseph Stalin attempted to establish the political future of a liberated Europe. Though Stalin agreed that Soviet forces would enter the war against Japan within three months of Germany's surrender, his determination to dominate Eastern Europe effectively ended the so-called Grand Alliance.

Yamassees Native Americans who traded with South Carolina merchants but, after enduring fraud and other unfair practices, in 1715 with help from the Creeks waged an unsuccessful war against the colony.

yellow journalism A type of journalism that stressed lurid and sensational news to boost circulation.

Young, Brigham (1801–1877) Mormon leader after the death of Joseph Smith; he led his followers to the Great Salt Lake.

Zimmermann telegram (1917) Secret German diplomatic telegram to the German ambassador in Mexico that was intercepted and decoded by the British. It dangled the return to Mexico of Arizona, New Mexico, and Texas as bait to entice the Mexicans to enter the war on the side of Germany.

INDEX